California

Political
Almanac

1 9 9 5 - 1 9 9 6
Fourth Edition

California Journal Press

Political Almanac

1 9 9 5 - 1 9 9 6
F o u r t h   E d i t i o n

Stephen Green, Editor

With
Amy Chance • James Richardson
Rick Rodriguez • Kathie Smith

Introduction by Dan Walters

John L. Hughes, Production Editor
Lori Korleski Richardson, Graphics
Mary E. Hughes, Indexer

California Journal Press

ISBN: 0-930302-29-X

Preface

Election Year 1994 was extraordinary for its nastiness, levels of spending, unreliable polls and lack of voter interest.

This "Year of the Smear" saw the defeat of 11 congressional and legislative incumbents — the most in any election year since 1966 — and sent several score politicians back to Washington or Sacramento with the lowest pluralities of their careers. The change was especially dramatic in the Assembly, where 28 of the 80 members were freshmen.

Pundits would say that an angry electorate sent California's political leadership a resounding message to shape up. Yet when one looks at the demographics of those who actually voted, it becomes obvious that the preponderance of those venting their frustrations at the polls were the older, white and more affluent Californians. The result was a dramatic recasting of California's congressional and legislative membership.

This fourth edition of the California Political Almanac provides a comprehensive overview of the '94 elections, their implications and historical context. The extraordinary battle for the Assembly speakership has been dissected. We've updated all chapters while sharpening the focus on California's continuing fiscal woes, the crisis in county and local government, and the fallout from the unfolding Orange County bankruptcy.

Officeholders and appointees have been profiled. New data on the economy and social change in the Golden State have been analyzed along with the continuing impacts of reapportionment. Throughout, the reader will find more and better graphics, and an expanded index. Some of the more revealing passages also delve into the drama, intrigue and occasional lunacy of California political life.

This effort had its beginnings in 1989 when a team of writers and editors at The Sacramento Bee was assembled by longtime political columnist Dan Walters. Our goal was to produce a book that would give California what The Almanac of American Politics provides on the national scene — a reliable and comprehensive source book on the issues, the players and the political process. The result was the first California Political Almanac, published the following winter. In the years since, it's been immensely gratifying to see our efforts gain acceptance as the standard reference on California politics.

The writing and editing team, meanwhile, has changed slightly with each edition. But it still includes some of the most knowledgeable political journalists in the state. They account for more than 150 years of combined experience covering government at all levels, from local cemetery districts to the halls of Congress.

We are indebted to the editors, librarians and managers of The Sacramento Bee and McClatchy News Service, who have given us moral support and generously allowed us to use their computer systems. We received excellent counsel from the staff of California Journal magazine, a subsidiary of our publisher. Many readers also sent us thoughtful comments and suggestions for updating the work. And finally, we wish to thank our spouses, families and significant others, who tolerated the long nights and weekends that were spent away from them while we completed this project.

Stephen Green
Sacramento

Contents

Charts

Maps

1

California–a state of change

An overview by Dan Walters

California is the planet's most diverse society. At no time in mankind's history have so many people of so many ethnic and national groups, practicing so many different religions, speaking so many different languages and engaged in so many different kinds of economic activities gathered in one place. It would follow, therefore, that California's politics would be equally complex. And they are, but not exactly in ways one might think.

Rather than reflecting the incredible socioeconomic and demographic diversity, the state's politics have been, at least through the 1980s and into the early 1990s, the almost exclusive province of California's relatively affluent and middle-aged Anglo population. And except for the 1992 elections, that has meant a steady rightward movement in the state's political climate.

The Democrats won big in California in 1992. But just two years later, the state's voting pattern was more Republican than even the 1980s as the GOP not only re-elected a governor but captured several of the statewide constitutional offices, made gains in the state Senate and congressional delegation and won a majority of the state Assembly seats for the first time in more than a quarter-century — although subsequent parliamentary maneuvering returned Democrat Willie Brown to the speakership, at least temporarily.

The state's political evolution, meanwhile, both reflects and contrasts with its rapid socioeconomic evolution. As it functions as a social laboratory, so does California test the ability of the traditional American system of government to cope with change beyond the wildest imagination of the system's creators. A major question for the 1990s and beyond is whether features of government developed in the 18th and 19th centuries — the two-party system, separately elected legislative and executive branches of government, counties and cities formed along traditional

1

lines — can function within such a wide range of social and cultural values.

There has been renewed interest in academic and some political circles for broader restructuring of the California political system in order to attune it to social reality. A unicameral Legislature, perhaps expanded to several hundred members, the encouragement of multiple parties, experimentation with the parliamentary system and reformation of counties into regional governments are among the structural changes now being studied. California voters have signaled they want change through the adoption of legislative and congressional term limits, and some new legislators, coming into the Capitol under those same limits, are demanding change as well.

To understand the political currents flowing through California in the late 20th century, one must first understand its social and economic currents. And if one accepts the wave theory of social development — each wave consisting of economic change, followed by social change, followed by political change — California is in the third, or political phase, of its third wave.

The first wave lasted for roughly a century, from the early days of white settlement in the 1840s to the onset of World War II. The gold rush aside, California in that century was a relatively unimportant place in the larger scheme of things. Its economy was resource-based — mining, agriculture, timber — and it had a decidedly rural ambience. Los Angeles, with its orange groves, vegetable fields and low buildings, resembled an overgrown Midwestern farm city, the presence of a few movie studios after World War I and the Pacific Ocean notwithstanding. San Francisco had a more cosmopolitan reputation, along with its cable cars and Chinatown, but it was the exception. California was white, Republican and quiet. It was largely ignored by the rest of America, whose population was centered in the East and had, if anything, a European outlook.

WAR BRINGS ECONOMIC AND SOCIAL CHANGE

All of that changed, on Dec. 7, 1941, when the Japanese bombed Pearl Harbor and plunged the United States into world war. Suddenly, America was forced to consider Asia as a factor in its future, and the window through which the nation viewed the war in the Pacific was California. Overnight, seemingly, the state was transformed into an industrial giant to serve the war effort, sprouting countless dozens of aircraft assembly lines, shipyards, steel mills and all of the other trappings needed to fight modern war. And it became a staging point for the war, a training ground for soldiers, sailors and airmen.

It was war, but it also was a sudden economic change for the state. California was jerked into the industrial 20th century. And that economic transformation had an equally rapid social impact: hundreds of thousands and then millions of Americans were drawn or sent to the state to participate in the war effort.

While there had always been a steady flow of domestic emigrants to the state (some of whom, like the ill-fated Donner Party, regretted the decision to move), it was nothing compared to what happened during World War II and continued almost unabated after the war. "Gone to California" became a terse explanation for the sudden absence of families in hundreds of Midwestern, Southern and Eastern communities. It was one of history's great migrations, and one that actually began a few years before the war, when refugees from the Dust Bowl, as chronicled in John Steinbeck's *Grapes of Wrath*, came to California in a desperate search for work and formed the nucleus of life and politics in agricultural areas of the state.

As the expanding industrialism of California created jobs, it drew emigrants and they, in turn, formed a new industrial middle class. These new residents had vast ambitions for themselves and their families. They wanted schools, highways, parks and homes. And they provided, during the postwar years, the core backing for politicians who promised to fulfill those desires.

California's prewar Republicanism was of a particular variety. Rooted in the abolitionism of the Civil War era and the prairie populism of William Jennings Bryan and Robert La Follette, California's Republicans were reformist and progressive. The state's great Republican reformer, Hiram Johnson, set the tone for the 20th century when he led efforts to break the stranglehold that Southern Pacific Railroad and other entrenched economic interests had on the Legislature. Small farmers had battled for decades with the railroad over freight rates, the clashes being both political and, in one instance, violent. With Johnson — governor and later a U.S. senator — marshaling public opinion, California enacted a series of pioneering political reforms that included the initiative, referendum and recall, all processes designed to increase popular control of politicians. Decades later, the initiative was to become a tool of special interests, rather than a barrier, but that was after social and political developments beyond Johnson's ability to foresee.

Johnson set a tone of high-minded Republicanism that survived for decades. Democrats were weak, able to elect only a single, one-term governor, Culbert Olson, in 1938, despite the dramatic rise of the Democratic Party nationally after Franklin Roosevelt became president.

Olson's Republican successor, Earl Warren, was out of the Johnson mold, and he became the only governor ever elected three times, going on to even greater fame as chief justice of the U.S. Supreme Court from 1953 to 1969. Warren was governor during and immediately after World War II, while the state was undergoing its big economic and social evolution. He responded to California's growth with far-reaching investments in public infrastructure — schools, highways, parks and other facilities — that not only served the state's fast-growing population but laid the foundation for even greater public works in the future.

It was during this period that California began developing a national reputation for political unpredictability, as it became a battleground for the ideological wars sweeping through America. Postwar California politics revolved mainly around Cold War issues, typified by the 1950 U.S. Senate contest between a young Republican congressman named Richard Nixon and a liberal political activist named Helen Gahagan Douglas, the wife of actor Melvyn Douglas. Nixon won after a brutal, bigoted campaign in which he implied that Douglas was sympathetic to communism. It was a polarizing political battle that launched Nixon on his way toward political immortality — and some would say, immorality. And it marked a turn away from centrist politics by both parties.

Democrats began veering to the left through such organizations as the California Democratic Council, which was established by Alan Cranston and other liberals to strengthen party identification in a state where cross-filing allowed candidates to obtain the nominations of both parties. The CDC also battled the more conservative elements then in control of the party. Republicans took a turn to starboard, with conservatives such as U.S. Sen. William Knowland, an Oakland newspaper publisher, assuming a larger role in the party as moderates of the Earl Warren-Goodwin Knight faction fell from grace in the absolutist atmosphere of the day.

At the time, in the mid- and late-1950s, social change favored the Democrats. Immigrants who had come to California to take jobs in the expanding industrial economy, their ranks swollen by returning veterans, put down roots and became politically active, often as members of industrial unions. They expanded the Democratic Party's base — especially since the Republicans' right turn had alienated voters who had supported Warren's moderates.

THE NEW BREED

Jesse Unruh was archetypal of the postwar breed of lawmakers. Unruh came to California from Texas during the war, remaining to attend the University of Southern California, where he became active in campus politics as leader of a band of liberal veterans. Within a few years after graduating from USC, Unruh was heavily involved in politics on a larger scale and won a seat in the state Assembly. It was the perfect territory for the consummate political animal, and his arrival coincided with the general rise of Democratic fortunes in the 1950s.

The 1958 election was the pivotal event in the postwar rise of the Democratic Party, a direct result of the social and economic changes brought about by World War II. Sen. Knowland, who had led the right-wing Republican contingent in the Senate during the early- and mid-1950s, was openly hostile to President Dwight Eisenhower's modern Republicanism, which included Warren's appointment to the Supreme Court. Knowland saw Eisenhower, Warren, Thomas Dewey and other Republican leaders from the East as leading the party, and the nation, astray, refusing to confront expansionist communism around the globe and temporizing on such domestic issues as labor union rights and welfare spending.

Knowland wanted to take the party back to the right and hoped to run for president in 1960, when Eisenhower's second term would end. But he thought the California governor's office would be a more powerful platform for a presidential campaign than a Senate seat. Knowland's major impediment was the moderate Republican governor of the time, Goodwin Knight, who didn't want to give up the governorship. Knight had been Warren's lieutenant governor, had inherited the top spot when Warren was appointed to the Supreme Court and had then won a term on his own in 1954. He wanted to run for re-election in 1958.

Knowland solved his problem simply by ordering Knight to step aside. With the rightists firmly in control of the party machinery, Knight was forced to obey, reluctantly agreeing to run for Knowland's Senate seat. But Knowland, in his preoccupation with Eisenhower, Communist expansionism and other weighty matters, didn't bother to consider whether his forced switch with Knight would sit well with California voters. With an arrogance that bordered on stupidity, he assumed voters would do whatever he wanted them to do. He was wrong. Democrat Edmund G. "Pat" Brown Sr., the liberal attorney general, was elected governor and Democratic Rep. Clair Engle was elected to the U.S. Senate. Knight might have been re-elected governor and Knowland given another term in the Senate, but instead voters retired both.

DEMOCRATS TAKE OVER

It was a banner year for Democrats. They also took firm control of the Legislature and over the next eight years the most ambitious policy agenda in California history became reality. With Unruh as Assembly speaker, the early Brown years saw a torrent of liberal, activist legislation ranging from an ambitious water development scheme to pioneering civil rights and consumer protection measures.

While Unruh sharpened the ideological focus of the Assembly, taking it to the

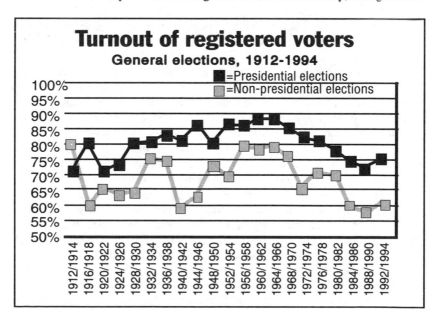

left, the state Senate remained a bastion of rural conservatism. For a century, the Senate's 40 seats had been distributed on the basis of geography, rather than population, in a rough approximation of the U.S. Senate's two-to-a-state system. No senator represented more than two counties and giant Los Angeles County, with a third of the state's population, had just one senator. With most of California's 58 counties being small and rural, it gave the Senate a decidedly rural flavor. Conservative Democrats and Republicans formed a solid majority. Even so, Pat Brown guided much of his progressive agenda through the upper house, using his unmatched skills of personal persuasion on Democratic senators.

In 1966, as Brown was winding up his second term, the U.S. Supreme Court, still under the leadership of Earl Warren, handed down its far-reaching one-man, one-vote decision, which required state legislative seats to be apportioned by population. As the Senate's districts were redrawn in response to the ruling, there was a huge shift of power from rural to urban counties, strengthening not only Democrats generally but liberals within the party. But that didn't take effect until after another man had assumed the governorship, the result of another clash between two big-name politicians.

THE RISE OF RONALD REAGAN

Brown wanted to run for a third term in 1966 but Jesse Unruh thought — or so he said later — that Brown had promised to step aside in his favor. Whatever the truth of the matter, there was a big rupture between the two most powerful California politicians of the day, and in the long run, both would suffer from it. Brown ran for his third term, but his break with Unruh, some public fumbles, a rising level of social unrest and the appearance of an ex-movie actor named Ronald Reagan spelled disaster for those ambitions.

Reagan, a moderately successful B-movie leading man and television actor, was enticed to run against Brown by a consortium of wealthy Southern California businessmen. At the time, television had become a new and powerful factor in political campaigning. Televised debates had doomed Richard Nixon's bid for the presidency in 1960, which was followed by a hopelessly desperate run against Brown for the governorship in 1962. In 1964, Reagan made a powerful television speech for Barry Goldwater, the Republican presidential candidate. Reagan was, the businessmen decided, just the man to take on non-telegenic Pat Brown in 1966.

The GOP kingmakers were right. Even though the Democratic phase of the postwar political era was not yet concluded, and even though a large majority of California voters were Democrats, Reagan buried Pat Brown and his bid for a third term by emphasizing Brown's shortcomings and stressing a conservative, get-tough attitude toward civic and campus unrest. The strength of Reagan's win swept several other Republicans into statewide offices.

Two years earlier, Reagan's old chum from Hollywood, song-and-dance-man George Murphy, had defeated Pierre Salinger for a California Senate seat. Salinger, who had been John Kennedy's press secretary, was appointed to the Senate by Pat Brown after Clair Engle died during his first term.

With Murphy in the U.S. Senate (he was defeated in his second-term bid by John Tunney in 1970), Reagan in the governor's office and Republicans holding other statewide offices, the GOP appeared once again to be on the ascendancy. But it all proved to be a short spurt. It would take another socioeconomic cycle for the Republicans to begin a real, long-term rise in influence among voters.

The GOP won control of the Assembly (for two years) in 1968, but for most of Reagan's eight years as governor, he had to deal with a Democratic-controlled Legislature. Unruh was gone after losing his own bid for the governorship in 1970, but another Southern California liberal, Bob Moretti, took his place. There were occasional compromises between the conservative governor and liberal legislators, most notably on welfare reform, but it was a period remarkable for its dearth of serious policy direction from Sacramento. The Pat Brown-Jesse Unruh legacy was not undone, Reagan's rhetoric notwithstanding. But neither could liberals advance their agenda. It was a time of stalemate.

DE-INDUSTRIALIZING CALIFORNIA

Even as Reagan and Moretti battled in Sacramento, another economic-social-political cycle, largely unnoticed at the time, was beginning to manifest itself.

The period of intense industrialization in California began to wind down in the 1960s. Asia, principally Japan, had risen from the devastation of the war to become a new industrial power. Californians began buying funny-looking cars stamped Made in Japan and domestic automakers began shutting down their plants in California. The steel for those cars was made not in Fontana but Japan or Korea. Even tire production began to shift overseas. One factory at a time, California began to de-industrialize.

California was not the only state to experience damaging foreign competition in basic industrial production in the 1960s and 1970s, but what happened here was unusual. The state underwent a massive economic transformation, from a dependence on basic industry to an economy rooted in trade (much of it with the nations of Asia), services and certain kinds of highly specialized manufacturing, especially of the high-tech variety centered in the Silicon Valley south of San Francisco. Computers and associated devices and services — including a huge aerospace industry tied to Pentagon contracts — became the new backbone of the California economy, one that exploded with growth until a corrosive recession struck the state in 1990. But before both the boom and the bust, there was a lull.

Rapid population growth that California had experienced during the postwar years slowed markedly in the 1970s as industrial job opportunities stagnated. California was still growing, even growing a bit faster than the nation as a whole, but the pace was much less dramatic. And California began to experience another phenomenon: an outflow of residents to other states.

In retrospect, that lull in growth may have been politically misleading. It persuaded the state's leaders, first Reagan and then his successor, Democrat Edmund G. "Jerry" Brown, that the infrastructure of services and facilities that had been built after World War II was adequate, that it was time to retrench, to tighten budgets and to cut back on public works, whether they be state buildings in Sacramento or Los Angeles freeways. It was a collective and indirect policy decision that was to have serious and adverse consequences in later years.

A DIFFERENT KIND OF POLITICIAN

Jerry Brown, son of the man Reagan defeated for governor in 1966, burst into state politics in 1970 by getting elected secretary of state, a mostly ministerial office with few powers or opportunities for publicity. But Brown, a young former seminarian who was the personal antithesis of his back-slapping father, seized the moment.

The Watergate scandal had erupted in 1972 and destroyed Richard Nixon's presidency two years later, focusing public attention on political corruption. Brown

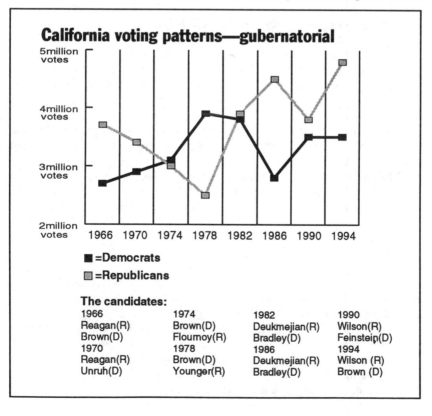

California voting patterns—gubernatorial

■ =Democrats
▨ =Republicans

The candidates:

1966	1974	1982	1990
Reagan(R)	Brown(D)	Deukmejian(R)	Wilson(R)
Brown(D)	Flournoy(R)	Bradley(D)	Feinstein(D)
1970	1978	1986	1994
Reagan(R)	Brown(D)	Deukmejian(R)	Wilson (R)
Unruh(D)	Younger(R)	Bradley(D)	Brown (D)

grabbed the issue by proposing a political reform initiative and shamelessly pandering to the media, especially television. He bested a field of relatively dull Democratic rivals, including Bob Moretti, to win the party's nomination for governor and then took on Houston Flournoy, the colorless Republican state controller, who was a throwback to the earlier era of Republican moderation.

Even so, it was whisker-close. Ultimately, Brown was elected not so much on his political acumen, but because of his name and the post-Watergate political climate, which had raised Democratic voter strength to near-record levels. At the height of Democratic potency in California in 1976, 59 percent of California voters identified themselves as Democrats in an annual party preference poll while just over 30 percent said they were Republicans. Democrats ran up huge majorities in the Legislature; at one point, after the 1976 elections, Republicans fell to just 23 seats in the 80-member Assembly. Even Orange County, the seemingly impregnable GOP bastion, had a Democratic registration plurality.

There was a spurt of legislative activity — much of it involving issues such as farm labor and bread-and-butter labor benefit bills — that had been stalled during

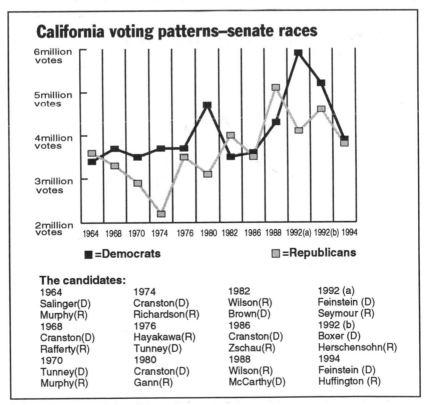

California voting patterns–senate races

■ =Democrats   ▨ =Republicans

The candidates:

1964	1974	1982	1992 (a)
Salinger(D)	Cranston(D)	Wilson(R)	Feinstein (D)
Murphy(R)	Richardson(R)	Brown(D)	Seymour (R)
1968	1976	1986	1992 (b)
Cranston(D)	Hayakawa(R)	Cranston(D)	Boxer (D)
Rafferty(R)	Tunney(D)	Zschau(R)	Herschensohn(R)
1970	1980	1988	1994
Tunney(D)	Cranston(D)	Wilson(R)	Feinstein (D)
Murphy(R)	Gann(R)	McCarthy(D)	Huffington (R)

the Reagan years. Brown preached a homegrown political philosophy that defied easy categorization. It was liberal on civil rights, labor rights and environmental protection, but conservative on taxes and spending. Brown defined the philosophy in a series of slogan-loaded speeches in which he talked of teachers being content with psychic income rather than salary increases and of California facing an era of limits. It contrasted directly with the expansionist policies of his father and most other postwar governors.

THE PROPERTY TAX REVOLT

At first, Brown was a hit. The words and a rather odd personal lifestyle drew attention from national political reporters starved for glamour in the post-John F. Kennedy world of Jerry Ford and Jimmy Carter. Soon, there was a steady stream of pundits to Sacramento and a flurry of effusively praiseful articles. Brown was a star, it seemed, a Democratic Reagan. Brown believed it. And scarcely more than a year after becoming governor, he was running for president. As Brown turned his political attention eastward — or skyward, according to some critics — Brown neglected California politics. And they were changing again.

While the state's economy roared out of a mid-1970s recession, property values soared. As they rose, so did property tax bills. It was an issue too prosaic for Jerry Brown, whose sights by then were firmly fixed on the White House. But it was just the ticket for two aging political gadflies, Howard Jarvis and Paul Gann.

Raising the specter of Californians being driven out of their homes by skyrocketing property taxes, Jarvis and Gann placed on the ballot a radical measure to slash property taxes and hold them down forever. Republican candidates, seeking an issue to restore their political power, seized upon Proposition 13, as the measure was numbered on the June 1978 ballot. Belatedly, Brown and legislative leaders devised a milder alternative for the same ballot.

Proposition 13 was enacted overwhelmingly and Brown, then running for re-election against the state's terminally dull attorney general, Evelle Younger, did a 180-degree turn. Sensing that the tax revolt could be his political downfall, Brown proclaimed himself to be "a born-again tax cutter" and pushed a state tax cut as a companion to Proposition 13. Younger failed to exploit the opening in the fall campaign and Brown breezed to an easy re-election victory in November. Almost immediately, Brown began plotting another run for the White House in 1980, this time as an advocate of balanced budgets, spending limits and tax cuts. Brown was nothing if not ambitious and opportunistic, qualities that were to be his political undoing.

Brown's re-election aside, the 1978 elections marked the beginning of a long slide for the Democratic Party after two decades of dominance. Democrats suffered major losses in legislative races that year and a flock of conservative Republicans, dubbing themselves "Proposition 13" babies, came to Sacramento — out of caves, liberals said — to conduct ideological war.

In ensuing years, Republicans both gained and lost legislative seats, with a net increase even in the face of a Democratic reapportionment plan in 1982 that was designed specifically to keep Democrats in power. Throughout the 1980s Democrats suffered a massive hemorrhage of voter strength. Their lead in party identification eroded year by year until it reached parity at about at about 45 percent each in the late 1980s. There was a corresponding shrinkage in the voter registration gap as well. In the mid-1970s, voter registration favored Democrats by, at most, a 57 percent to 34 percent margin. By the late 1980s, the Democrats had dipped to below 50 percent for the first time in a half-century while Republican registration climbed to nearly 40 percent. Democrats even lost a fraction of a point in 1988, when they committed $4 million to a huge voter registration drive in support of Michael Dukakis' presidential campaign, and the slide continued in 1990, contributing to Democrat Dianne Feinstein's narrow loss to Republican Pete Wilson in their duel for the governorship.

The unofficial voter registration numbers were even worse for the Democrats. It's estimated that at least 1 million, and perhaps as many as 2 million, of California's 14-plus million registered voters don't exist. The official euphemism for those phantom names is deadwood, and it exists because California's voter registration laws make it relatively difficult to drop people from the rolls when they die or move. Some mobile Californians may be counted two or three times as registered voters in different jurisdictions. And because Democrats are more likely to change addresses than Republicans, an adjustment for the deadwood tends to reduce Democratic ranks more.

It's generally acknowledged that stripping the voter rolls of duplicate or missing names would reduce official Democratic registration to 47 percent or 48 percent and raise Republican registration above 40 percent. That's why Democratic legislators have resisted efforts to purge the rolls. Adjustment to a true figure would bring registration closer to the 45 percent to 45 percent identification margin scene in polls. The state's leading pollster, Mervin Field, adjusts the voter registration split to 48 percent to 42 percent in his polling, saying the number is based on surveys of actual registration.

Whatever the real number, the Democratic side declined and the Republican side gained. And some Democratic officials, most notably Secretary of State March Fong Eu, were warning that the party was in danger of slipping into minority status.

The roots of the trend may be found in the socioeconomic currents evident in California during the late 1970s and 1980s. As the state's postindustrial economy shifted into high gear in the late 1970s, it created millions of jobs and, like the postwar period of industrialization, began attracting new waves of immigrants to fill them. But these immigrants didn't come from Indiana, Tennessee and Texas. They came from Mexico, Taiwan, Korea and the Philippines.

By the late 1980s, California's population was growing by some 2,000 people a day and half of them were immigrants, mostly from other Pacific Rim nations with whom California was establishing ever-stronger economic ties. California was developing, in short, into the new American melting pot.

As newcomers poured into central cities, especially Los Angeles, San Francisco and San Jose, there was an outpouring of Anglo families into the suburbs. And as those suburbs filled and home prices soared, there was an even more dramatic movement into the new suburbs in former farm towns such as Modesto and Stockton in Northern California and Riverside and Redlands in Southern California. These new suburbanites — white and middle-class — shifted their political allegiance to the Republicans and their promises of limited government and taxes. Areas that had once been dependably Democratic, such as Riverside and San Bernardino counties, evolved into Republican registration majorities as they suburbanized. Prosperity encouraged the conversion, as did the popularity of Ronald Reagan in the White House.

A 1988 California Poll found Anglo voters favored Republicans by a 50 percent to 41 percent margin. And that was critical because non-Anglos, while identifying with the Democratic Party by substantial margins, were not voting in numbers

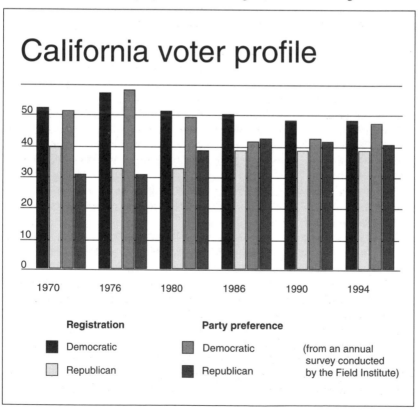

California voter profile

anywhere close to their proportions of the population. Exit polls in elections during the 1980s revealed that more than 80 percent of California's voters were Anglos, even though they had dipped to under 60 percent of the population.

At the other extreme, Asians doubled their numbers in California between the late 1970s and the late 1980s, surpassing African Americans to become almost 10 percent of the population. Yet Asians accounted for just 2 percent to 4 percent of voters. The fast-growing Latino population was approaching one-fourth of the total by the late 1980s, but were only 6 percent or 7 percent of the voters until the 1992 election, when their numbers spiked upward a bit. Among non-Anglo minorities, only African Americans voted in proportion to their numbers—roughly 8 percent of both population and the electorate. But they are also the slowest growing minority.

Thus, the 1980s saw a widening gap between the ethnic characteristics of California and those of voters, who not only were white but better educated, more affluent and — perhaps most important — markedly older than the non-voters. By 1986, half of California's voters were over 50 years old, a reflection of the rapid aging of the Anglo population, and the aging process continued as the state entered the 1990s and the baby boomers edged into middle age.

THE CHARACTERISTIC GAP

In brief, while California's population was moving in one direction — toward a multiracial, relatively young profile — the electorate was moving in another. And this characteristic gap was driving California politics to the right, toward a dominant mood of self-protection and reaction. Republicans scored well among older voters with appeals on crime, taxes and, in 1994, illegal immigration. Democrats, hammered on these and other hot-button issues, scrambled to find some response and were mostly unsuccessful, despite a sharp but, as it turned out, fleeting change in 1992.

The characteristic gap made itself evident on a wide variety of specific issues and contests, but was most noticeable when it came to issues of taxation and spending. The Proposition 13 property tax revolt in 1978 and the subsequent passage of Proposition 4, a public spending limit promoted by Proposition 13 co-author Paul Gann in 1979, were the first signs that the climate had changed. Republican George Deukmejian's 1982 election to the governorship on a no-new-taxes, tough-on-spending platform (along with tough-on-crime) was another indication. Deukmejian, a dull-as-dishwater former legislator and attorney general, represented a 180-degree change of style from the unpredictable Jerry Brown.

Demands for more spending were coming from and for a growing, relatively young non-Anglo population, while the political power was being held by a relatively old, Anglo bloc of voters. By the late 1980s, a majority of California's school children were non-Anglo, while less than a quarter of California's voters had children in school — one example of how the characteristic gap affected political decision-making. A 1987 poll conducted for the California Teachers Association revealed that older voters would kill any effort to raise state taxes for education. A CTA consultant told the group that even arguments about grandchildren and overall societal need don't work. And if education was losing its basic political constituency — voters with children in public schools — other major spending programs, such as health and welfare services for the poor, had even less support.

Deukmejian resisted new taxes, vetoed Democratic spending bills, trimmed the budget and saw his popularity soar. He was re-elected by a landslide in 1986, defeating for the second time Los Angeles Mayor Tom Bradley. Even Deukmejian, who gloried in the "Iron Duke image," relented in 1989 as the Gann spending limit enacted by voters 10 years earlier gripped the state budget. He was under pressure from business interests to spend more to relieve traffic congestion. Finally, the governor and legislative leaders reached agreement on a complex package that put a measure to loosen the Gann limit and to increase the gasoline tax before voters in 1990. It passed, but other tax measures on the 1990 ballot were summarily rejected, indicating that only something as universally used and popular as transportation could overcome the continuing voter resistance to higher taxes.

THE ESSENTIAL QUESTION

As California entered the 1990s, therefore, the essential public policy question was whether an aging Anglo population would continue to dominate the political agenda, even in the face of pressure from business executives for more spending on infrastructure to maintain the business climate.

Democrats, watching an erosion of support among white, middle-class Californians, pinned their hopes at the start of the decade on a strategy of registering and organizing the millions of non-Anglo voters. Ex-Gov. Jerry Brown, who went into political exile after losing a U.S. Senate bid in 1982, returned to the stage in 1989 by running for and winning the state Democratic Party chairmanship on a promise to bring more minorities and economically displaced whites into the party. Unfaithful, Republican-voting Democrats would, in effect, be banished from the party as it took a couple of steps to the left.

But as simple as that sounds, it has proven to be a very complex task. There are barriers of citizenship, language and a tendency among refugees from authoritarian regimes to be apolitical. That's a tendency most evident among Asians, whose cultural traditions discourage direct connections to government and politics.

There are problems for Democrats, too, in creating a party image that is attractive to minorities who may be social and political conservatives. Republicans regularly garner 40-plus percent of the Hispanic vote, for instance, and some Democratic Party positions, such as being pro-choice on abortion, are hard-sells among them. GOP candidates often do even better among Asian voters.

There also are internal barriers, such as the traditionally powerful role that African Americans have played within the Democratic Party. Rhetoric about a

Rainbow Coalition notwithstanding, minority groups do not automatically cooperate on matters political and there is, in fact, some friction.

While Brown raised millions of dollars during the first two years of his party chairmanship, he also spent millions on staff and infrastructure, and when Democrats narrowly lost the governorship in 1990, many supporters of Democratic candidate Dianne Feinstein blamed Brown. Feinstein had consciously attempted to woo middle-class white voters back from the Republicans and her failure touched off another round in the Democrats' perennial debate over ideological positioning and tactics.

The issue was resolved when Brown was replaced as state party chairman by Phil Angelides, a one-time legislative staffer who had become a prominent and wealthy land developer in Sacramento. Brown quit to run for the U.S. Senate but then, for reasons that remained unclear, switched courses again and made a run for the presidency that became one of the oddest footnotes to the 1992 campaign.

Angelides, who had played a prominent role in Dukakis' presidential campaign in 1988, also favored the strategy of trying to bring back middle-class voters and that coincided nicely with the ascendancy of Bill Clinton as the party's presidential candidate in 1992. With Angelides' organizational and fund-raising ability on conspicuous display, Democrats got their act together in California in 1992, signing up hundreds of thousands of new voters, especially in middle-class suburbs where reapportionment threatened the party's grip on the Legislature and the congressional delegation. For the first time in more than a decade, Democratic voter strength, both in registration and party identification polls, increased, albeit not dramatically.

The Democrats' new-found organizational strength was accompanied by a virtual disintegration of the Republican Party structure in the state because of deep divisions between moderates, led by Gov. Wilson, and a strong religious-right coalition. The GOP split, ironically, occurred just as the party won a hard-fought battle over reapportionment.

After the 1980 census, Democrats maintained their hold on the Legislature and expanded their control of the state's congressional delegation with a highly partisan reapportionment plan. In effect, they preserved their power in the face of real-world trends. The plans were approved by then-Gov. Brown and a state Supreme Court dominated by liberal Brown appointees. Conditions for the Democrats were not as favorable for the post-1990 census reapportionment and the stakes were much higher.

The relative lull in California population growth during the 1970s meant that the state was awarded only two new congressional seats after the 1980 census, its delegation increasing from 43 to 45. Prior to the 1980s reapportionment, the 43-member delegation had been divided 22-21 in favor of Democrats. It was a fair division of the seats in terms of both overall party identification and congressional vote in the state, both of which were evenly divided between parties. But after the late Rep. Phil Burton completed a gerrymandered plan he called "my contribution to modern art," the delegation was 28-17 in favor of Democrats. And it was so well done that Republicans were able to gain only two seats in subsequent elections, leaving the delegation at 26-19.

California's population growth was much higher in the 1980s. The state gained 6 million people between 1980 and 1990 or roughly a quarter of total U.S. population growth. The state was awarded seven new congressional seats, giving it not only the largest congressional delegation in the nation but the largest of any state in history.

Republicans wanted redress. They believed they should have roughly half of the California seats, which would mean receiving all of the new ones. And it would have been very difficult for the Democrats to pull a repeat of 1982, not only in congressional reapportionment, but in the redrawing of legislative districts.

After Deukmejian's decision not to run for a third term in 1990 — which meant he wouldn't be available to veto any gerrymander drawn by majority Democrats in the Legislature — GOP leaders, stretching as high as the White House, engineered a strategic coup. They persuaded Wilson, the one-time San Diego mayor who had defeated Jerry Brown for a U.S. Senate seat in 1982 and won a second term handily in 1988, to run for governor in 1990.

Selection of a Democratic candidate didn't go as easily. Attorney General John Van de Kamp, a liberal with strong environmental and consumer protection credentials, was the early favorite. His only declared rival, ex-San Francisco Mayor Dianne Feinstein, refused to drop out, however, even when her campaign manager quit with a blast at her commitment to the race.

Feinstein fashioned a decidedly more centrist image, arguing that a liberal such as Van de Kamp was headed for certain defeat at Wilson's hands. Among other things, she supported the death penalty, a litmus test issue for many Democrats.

Feinstein won the nomination and engaged in an expensive shootout with Wilson, her one-time political ally when she was mayor of San Francisco and he was a U.S. senator. Wilson won a narrow victory and became California's 36th governor, thus putting himself into position to protect Republican interests on reapportionment — as well as to confront the many problems of a fast-growing and diverse state, including a worsening budget crisis. Although Wilson and Feinstein spent more than $40 million in 1990, it was a less-than-overwhelming Republican victory since Wilson won less than 50 percent of the total vote.

A final factor in reapportionment was that minority groups, especially those representing Hispanics, believed they, too, were damaged by the 1982 reapportionment. So they pressured Democrats for new representation in both congressional and legislative seats. Initially, Democrats — led by Assembly Speaker Willie Brown — tried to negotiate their way out of their dilemma, offering Republicans guaranteed gains in both the Legislature and Congress in return for equally strong guarantees that Democrats would retain control. There was a substantial sentiment among Republican politicians toward such a settlement, primarily because the alternative, throwing the issue to the courts, was less certain.

Brown tried to capitalize on the Republican divisions, openly courting conservative Assembly members who were at ideological odds with Wilson, promising them locked-in congressional seats if they would abandon the governor. Ultimately, however, Brown and a few right-wing plotters could not put together a veto-proof deal and Democrats simply passed their plans and allowed Wilson to veto them, thus moving the reapportionment debate to the state Supreme Court.

The court hired the same consultants it had used two decades earlier to draw reapportionment maps after a similar stalemate between the Democratic Legislature and Republican Gov. Ronald Reagan. Within weeks, the court's consultants had created 172 legislative and congressional districts that closely followed demographic trends — shifting more power from the cities to the suburbs, which enhanced Republican prospects, and creating more minority seats, especially Latino seats, within urban areas. The federal Voting Rights Act largely dictated the latter.

SNATCHING DEFEAT FROM JAWS OF VICTORY

Wilson and Republican leaders were jubilant. They saw an unprecedented opportunity to seize control of the Capitol for the first time in decades — a prospect

Social and political demographics

	1970	1980	1990	1994	1994 voters*
Population	20M	23.8M	29.8M	32.1M	8.9M
Anglo	15.6M 78%	15.8M 66/4%	17M 57%	17.6M 55%	78%
Hispanic	2.4M 12%	4.6M 19.3%	7.6M 26%	8.7M 27%	10%
Asian	.6M 3.2%	1.6M 6.6%	2.6M 9%	3.3M 10.3%	3%
African American	1.4M 6.9%	1.8M 7.5%	2M 7%	2.3M 7%	6%
*Exit polls of voters, November 1994 election					

enhanced by passage the 1991 of Proposition 140, the term limits initiative, which eventually would force entrenched Democratic incumbents to surrender their seats.

What looked good for Republicans on paper, however, needed first to overcome their own divisiveness.

The postwar history of the California Republican Party has been one of recurrent conflict between moderates and conservatives. In 1982, with the election of Deukmejian to the governorship (after he had defeated the right-wing candidate, Mike Curb, in the primary) and Pete Wilson to the U.S. Senate, the centrists regained the influence they had lost during the Ronald Reagan and early post-Proposition 13 years.

With patronage from the governor's office and the Senate, Republican moderates enjoyed a rebirth of influence within the party and right-wingers complained about being ignored. Their only bastion was the Assembly Republican caucus, which continued to be dominated by the "Proposition 13 babies."

Conservatives stopped short of open revolt. They didn't balk, for instance, about having Wilson as their candidate for governor in 1990 because they wanted a winner who would protect the party on reapportionment. But issues such as abortion divide the party bitterly as it seeks some new common theme in the post-Cold War, post-Reagan era.

Wilson had scarcely been inaugurated when sniping began. Conservatives were irritated by Wilson's selection of moderate state Sen. John Seymour — a former conservative who had flip-flopped on abortion — as his successor in the U.S. Senate and were put off by Wilson's advocacy of new taxes during his first year in office to balance the state budget. The moderate-conservative split flared sharply late in the 1991 session of the Legislature, when moderates, encouraged if not abetted by Wilson, seized control of the Assembly GOP caucus. And it raged throughout 1992.

The right captured much of the party apparatus and fielded numerous candidates for legislative and congressional seats while Wilson and the moderates belatedly challenged them in the June primaries. Conservatives won most of the head-to-head battles but several found themselves unelectable in swing districts that more moderate Republican candidates could have won.

After more than a dozen years of electoral gains, Republicans were hurt in 1992, too, by the state's rapidly deteriorating economy; by the unpopularity of Republican President George Bush, who virtually abandoned a state that the GOP had won in the previous five presidential elections; by resurgent political activism of women over abortion; and, finally, by the fact that California Democrats finally had gotten their act together under state party chairman Angelides.

Thus, what had appeared to be a golden opportunity for Republicans to make legislative gains turned into a virtual wash while Democrats swept the major races for president and two U.S. Senate seats. It was, in brief, a Republican debacle that left open the question of whether Wilson could win re-election in 1994.

Democrats emerged from the 1992 elections with high hopes for ousting Wilson, and state Treasurer Kathleen Brown, daughter of one former governor and sister of another, was the presumptive Democratic candidate. Brown made up her mind to run in late 1992, as Wilson's popularity plummeted to record lows. One respected poll had her leading Wilson by a 23-point margin and the Eastern media flocked to California to anoint her as the new political star. Brown easily bested a couple of Democratic foes in the primary.

Something, or many things, went terribly wrong for Brown. Her campaign changed managers, slogans and themes so many times that even the most dedicated watchers lost count. She raised immense amounts of money but couldn't buy ads on the last weekend of the campaign. And Wilson, starting early in 1994, began demonstrating the highly focused, if highly graceless, campaign style that had previously vanquished a couple of other Democratic stars, Jerry Brown and Dianne Feinstein.

Wilson focused on illegal immigration and crime as his issues while Kathleen Brown tried, and failed, to develop alternative themes that were attractive to voters. The more she campaigned, first in the primary season and later against Wilson, the worse she did in the polls. By June 1994, Wilson was dead-even in the polls and by the November election he had trounced her by 14 percentage points, the most impressive comeback in California's recent history.

The massive nature of Wilson's win, coupled with his penchant for bashing President Clinton, propelled the governor into unofficial contention for the 1996 Republican presidential nomination. Wilson's presidential prospects are enhanced by the state's long-overdue decision to move its presidential primary election from June to March and by the GOP's selection of San Diego, where Wilson was mayor, for the 1996 convention. But Wilson's White House ambitions, if any, are undercut by his almost painfully bland campaign style and the fact that were he to become president or vice president, he would have to turn the governorship over to a Democrat, Lt. Gov. Gray Davis, a former top aide to Jerry Brown. Wilson insists he's not interested in national office.

In the last dozen years, reapportionment, as partisanly slanted as it may have been, was one of the Legislature's few decisive actions. Increasingly, the Legislature drew within itself, preoccupied with such games of inside baseball as campaign strategy, fund-raising and partisan and factional power struggles. It seemed unable, or unwilling, to cope with the huge policy issues raised by the dynamics of the real world outside the Capitol: population growth, ethnic diversification, transportation congestion, educational stagnation, environmental pollution.

The Legislature, which Jesse Unruh recast as a full-time professional body in the 1960s, once was rated as the finest in the nation. The 1980s saw not only policy gridlock but a rising level of popular disgust with its antics, fueled by several official investigations into corruption.

California's political demography is at least partially responsible for the Legislature's lethargy. Legislators are torn between the demands and aspirations of

California's new immigrant-dominated population and the limits set by white, middle-class voters. But the very professionalism that was Unruh's proudest achievement also has contributed to the malaise. Full-time legislators, many of them graduates of the Legislature's staff, are preoccupied with their personal political careers. Thus legislative duties that conflict with those careers are shunted aside.

Throughout the 1980s, reformers proposed institutional changes to restore the Legislature's luster, such as imposing limits on campaign spending and fund raising (which have increased geometrically) and providing public funds to campaigns. Voters endorsed a comprehensive reform initiative in 1988, but they also approved a more limited version placed on the ballot by some legislators and special-interest groups. The first provided public funds for campaigns while the second specifically barred such spending, and the second gained more votes. The result was that most of the first initiative was negated, but nearly all of the second was invalidated by the courts.

As a years-long federal investigation of Capitol corruption spawned indictments in 1989, the Legislature began drafting reforms designed to raise its standing with an increasingly cynical public. These reforms — a tightening of conflict-of-interest rules, including a ban on receiving speaking fees from outside groups—were approved by voters in 1990. But voters also approved an initiative that imposed tough term limits on lawmakers, eliminated their pensions and sharply reduced the Legislature's spending on operations.

Term limits and reapportionment produced bumper crops of new legislators in 1992 and 1994. As the 1995 legislative session began, scarcely 20 of the Assembly's 80 members had more than two years' experience and in 1996, the remaining older members will have to give up their seats.

There is endless speculation as to the effects of term limits beyond bringing a huge turnover. A full evaluation cannot be made until later in the decade, but it's clear that the new legislators are bringing to the Capitol a more diverse group, with many newcomers emerging from local government rather than the legislative staff. That is changing the dynamics of lobbying by making grass-roots organization more important and one-on-one relationships less important. Power also is shifting from the constantly changing Assembly to the more settled and experienced Senate.

The 1994 elections also produced a partisan shift. Republicans won a bare majority of the 80-member Assembly by picking up eight new seats, although the defection of one Republican left a historic 40-40 tie over the all-powerful Assembly speakership as the session began.

The deadlock lasted for seven weeks. Ostensibly, leaders of the two partisan factions, longtime Speaker Willie Brown and GOP leader Jim Brulte, were engaged in negotiations aimed at a bipartisan agreement on sharing power. But while negotiations came close to success, they faltered on the all-important issue of time. Democrats wanted an agreement for two years while Republicans insisted that if they regained a 41-seat majority, they wanted the ability to take control.

The impasse was resolved, after a fashion, when Democrats seized power through parliamentary maneuvers. Brown was presiding by dint of his seniority and he issued a series of procedural rulings that allowed Democrats to vote to oust Republican Assemblyman Richard Mountjoy, alleging that he had ceded his claim on the seat because he had been elected to the Senate in a special election.

Brown and the Democrats then adopted new rules that provided at least the appearance of power-sharing with the Republicans, who vowed to recall Republican-turned-independent Paul Horcher, elect a successor to Mountjoy and to claim control of the house. If nothing else, the dramatic events illustrated the close partisan makeup of the Legislature — itself a product of term limits and reapportionment — and indicated that a months- and perhaps years-long legislative power struggle would mark the final decade of the century.

The chronic impotence of the Legislature manifested itself in an explosion of initiative campaigns that took issues directly to voters, bypassing the Capitol altogether. Initiatives became so popular that lawmakers and even candidates for governor began sponsoring them as vehicles to make policy or gain favorable publicity. In 1990, gubernatorial candidate Wilson trumpeted an initiative to deal with crime, and in 1994, as he sought re-election, Wilson backed Proposition 187, a highly controversial measure that would, if validated by the courts, cut off public education and social benefits to illegal immigrants.

Despite the controversy in 1994 over illegal immigration, it did not substantially change the dominant profile of California voters, who remain overwhelmingly Anglo (non-Latino white), middle- to upper-middle-class and middle-aged. That is unlikely to change dramatically in the near future. While half of California's current voters are over 50, the mean could reach 60 percent by the turn of the century.

The state, meanwhile, is heading toward a non-Anglo majority by the late 1990s and the largest unsettled question about California politics is not whether Republicans or Democrats control, but whether the surging Latino and Asian populations will claim political power commensurate with their numbers. There are some signs of that occurring, mostly at the local level, but neither community has developed charismatic leaders who could move their latent political power in one direction or another.

Thus, the real story of California's 21st century political development will be the extent to which today's newcomers become tomorrow's voters and how their cultural values change the political landscape.

2

An election-year budget

On July 8, 1994 — eight days after the constitutional deadline for a budget to be signed — Gov. Pete Wilson put his pen to the final budget documents for the new fiscal year and proclaimed: "No one is going to be pleased with this budget."

Truer words on the budget wouldn't be spoken again until after the November election. The $57.1 billion budget was out of balance by $4.5 billion, and everyone involved in the process knew it. Wilson needed a "no-new-taxes" budget to get him past the election. Republicans demanded it. Democrats acquiesced. And most of the politicos then left town for the more serious business of getting re-elected.

Of all the pixie dust that went into compiling the 500-plus-page budget, the silliest assumption was that the federal government would come through with $3.6 billion to reimburse California for immigrant-related state costs.

Long gone were the days when former Gov. George Deukmejian kept a $1 billion reserve for shortfalls, emergencies and natural disasters. The new budget had no reserve. It depended upon many itemized savings — a Rand Corp. study called them "potential time bombs" — in departments and programs which turned out to be overly optimistic due to court challenges, implementation delays, estimating errors and plain old bureaucratic inertia.

By law, the budget must be balanced. But this one demanded $7 billion in short-term borrowing at higher-than-normal interest rates. With the state's bond rating sliding and the reliance on a fictitious federal bail out, lenders required a repayment guarantee from a syndicate of banks before they would accept $4 billion of the state's paper. That guarantee alone cost $31 million.

The new budget may have had no general tax increase, but it boosted fees for state university students by 10 percent — the fifth consecutive year of double-digit fee hikes. Benefits for welfare families were reduced for the fourth year in a row.

Grants for aged, blind and disabled people were cut for the third consecutive year. Health and welfare programs were cut 3.3 percent. And the $114-per-month increase for care of a new child born to a welfare recipient was abolished altogether. Spending for K-12 students was frozen. And a host of new responsibilities were shoved onto city and county government without full funding to pay for them.

Wilson promised more efficient government. But among his budget vetoes was a demand for an independent study of how the Department of Motor Vehicles had spent seven years and $49 million on a computer system that couldn't be made to work.

There was a winner in the budget, though. The youth and adult corrections budget went up 9.4 percent, reflecting, in part, the longer sentences criminals will be serving in response to a spate of new sentence enhancement laws. Since 1980, corrections spending as a share of the state budget had tripled from 3 percent to 9 percent.

The best that could be said for the new budget was that it was less painful to compile than its counterpart for the 1992-93 fiscal year. That year, California was without a budget for a record 64 days while Wilson and legislators carped at each other. And that budget was still out of balance when Wilson signed it.

The 1994-'95 budget attempted to project spending for two years rather than just one as in previous years. And it contained a so-called "trigger mechanism" intended to ensure that it stayed on track. The trigger required automatic spending cuts to be implemented — absent corrective action by the Legislature and the governor — if the state's cash position failed to meet projections. The revenue picture did brighten somewhat by the end of 1994, thanks to higher tax collections and welfare caseloads and public school enrollments that were lower-than-expected. But given the built-in time bombs and a scheduled state worker pay increase on Jan. 1, 1995, the trigger pulling in the 1995-96 fiscal year could resemble a machine-gun burst.

Many taxpayers express bewilderment at California's fiscal morass. After all, Deukmejian left office in 1991 claiming he'd taken the state from IOU to A-OK. But the source of the problem was simple enough: As the economy weakened, state revenues dropped and gobbled up the outgoing governor's reserve funds — and then some.

State finances suffer quickly in a recession; fewer paychecks and less spending prompt a slump in sales and income taxes, and state costs increase as more people call upon welfare, unemployment and other safety-net programs. In 1991, California's big economic engine could still be counted on to generate more revenue than had been available in the previous year, but nowhere near enough to keep pace with the state's rising Medi-Cal, welfare, school and prison populations.

Early evidence suggested Deukmejian's administration would leave the state foundering in more than $800 million of red ink by the end of the 1990-91 fiscal year — and that was before the Persian Gulf War began. Nothing in the state's 140-year history compared to the financial disarray incoming Gov. Wilson confronted as he took the podium in the state Assembly on Jan. 9, 1991, to deliver his State of the State message as California's 36th governor.

"Now more than ever, to lead is to choose," Wilson said. "And our choice must be to give increasing attention and resources to the conditions that shape children's lives. The emphasis must be more preventative than remedial — a vision of government that is truly as uncomplicated as the old adage that an ounce of prevention is worth a pound of cure."

Wilson's message represented a sharp shift from Deukmejian's approach to California's problems. But where Deukmejian had fought to close a $3.6 billion gap between anticipated revenues and spending demands for the 1990-91 budget, Wilson would face a recession-driven shortfall of monster proportions. By the end of March 1991, Wilson was declaring a budget emergency, projecting a $12.6 billion shortfall.

Wilson faced most of the same problems as Deukmejian in shaping a state budget to fit his priorities. State finances have been in a turmoil ever since 1978, when Proposition 13, the famous property tax limitation initiative, gutted local government finances and prompted a redistribution of state revenues. More tax measures followed, among them one indexing the income tax to inflation to protect Californians against bracket creep — the automatic tax hikes that occurred as inflation pushed taxpayers into higher tax brackets. Inheritance and gift taxes were repealed, the business inventory tax was wiped out and new tax credits were invented and spread around.

The loss to state government between 1978 and the 1988-89 fiscal year exceeded $190 billion, according to a study by Legislative Analyst Elizabeth Hill. Most notably, voters approved Proposition 4 in 1979, writing a state and local spending limit into the Constitution. The cap became known as the Gann limit after its main sponsor, the late Paul Gann, who hated taxes so much he went through personal bankruptcy twice to keep from paying them. Spending was tied to population growth and inflation. Excess revenue was to be returned to taxpayers.

The Gann limit meant little until the 1986-87 fiscal year, when California's once powerful economy produced an unexpected surge in revenue. After nearly a decade of Proposition 13 austerity, the state's public schools and universities needed the money, but the spending cap dictated otherwise. Just over $1 billion was returned to the state's taxpayers during the Christmas season of 1987-88.

Those were the years of federal tax reform, state tax conformity, deficit spending on the federal level and unpredictable peaks and troughs for California's revenues. Shortage followed surplus. Teachers, school administrators, parents and other educators, with the exception of those representing the state's two university systems, launched an initiative campaign designed to protect themselves from gubernatorial vetoes and wavering finances.

In June 1988, they failed at the polls. But in November, 50.7 percent of the voters

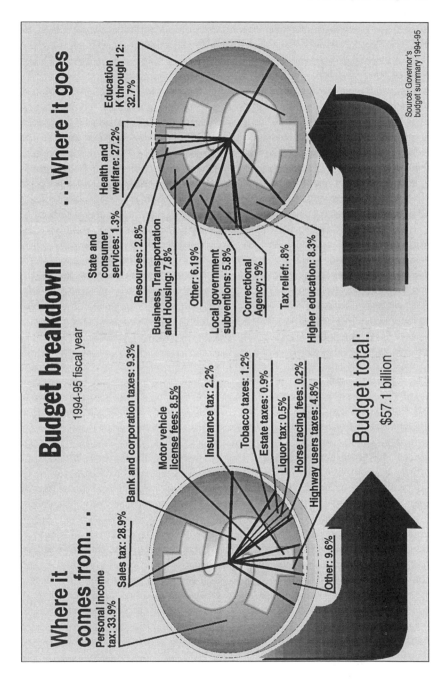

Budget breakdown

1994-95 fiscal year

Where it comes from. . .

Personal income tax: 33.9%

Sales tax: 28.9%

Bank and corporation taxes: 9.3%

Motor vehicle license fees: 8.5%

Insurance tax: 2.2%

Tobacco taxes: 1.2%

Estate taxes: 0.9%

Liquor tax: 0.5%

Horse racing fees: 0.2%

Highway users taxes: 4.8%

Other: 9.6%

. . .Where it goes

Education K through 12: 32.7%

Health and welfare: 27.2%

State and consumer services: 1.3%

Resources: 2.8%

Business, Transportation and Housing: 7.8%

Other: 6.19%

Local government subventions: 5.8%

Correctional Agency: 9%

Tax relief: .8%

Higher education: 8.3%

Budget total:

$57.1 billion

Source: Governor's budget summary 1994-95

— the barest of majorities — approved Proposition 98, under which public schools and community colleges were henceforth guaranteed some 40 percent of the state's general fund budget and, in the event of a Gann limit surplus, half of the money that would have gone back to taxpayers.

To Wilson in his first days in office, the state's finances must have resembled a windshield just after an encounter with a cantaloupe-sized bug — some cleaning up would be necessary before he could even see where he wanted to go. On all sides were problems that confronted the state, and he mentioned many: overstuffed schools, more homeless people, workers without health insurance, growing welfare and Medi-Cal caseloads, swollen prisons, overwhelming crime, child abuse and neglect, and failing county governments.

Where were the solutions? By 1991, there were some answers, and they helped a little. A trigger was in place to automatically trim welfare grants and other cost-of-living increases when state revenues lagged. The trigger was a victory for the Assembly Republicans, who won it the previous year as part of the settlement that ended what was then the longest budget stalemate in state history. The savings for Wilson's budget amounted to $800 million, of which almost $150 million would come from the Aid to Families with Dependent Children program.

Proposition 98 also was amended under provisions of Proposition 111, the omnibus budget reform and transit tax measure approved in June 1990, which requires a cut in school spending in proportion with other budget cuts when state revenues lag. The savings here totaled $500 million in the 1990-91 fiscal year, giving a boost to Wilson's upcoming spending proposals.

In addition, the voters, by approving Proposition 111, had agreed to double state motor vehicle fuel taxes, part of an $18.5 billion, 10-year transportation plan that would at least keep the Caltrans budget from contributing to the fiscal mess. The Caltrans budget sprang to life, and so did the state's highway and mass transit programs. But the building euphoria didn't last. A succession of killer earthquakes crumbled highway bridges and exposed the fact that hundreds of bridges were at risk in California. Caltrans eventually developed plans for fixing or replacing them. But by 1995, the work was hopelessly behind schedule and hundreds of projects intended to relieve congestion were on the shelf indefinitely.

In his first budget as governor, Wilson eventually agreed to some $7 billion in new taxes and fees along with a series of internal reforms. Not only did the $7 billion fail to stave off a deficit at the end of Wilson's first full fiscal budget year, but conservative Republicans, never warm to moderate Wilson, erupted in outrage. Wilson had signed the biggest tax increases in California history, they screamed. He'd out-taxed and out-spent even the most liberal of Democratic governors.

No doubt that strengthened Wilson's resolve to come out of the next round of budget talks in better political shape. He vowed to hold the line on taxes and spurn smoke-and-mirrors fixes offered by Democratic leaders. They'd do it his way, or not at all. In the end, Wilson didn't give much. Nonetheless, the next two budget cycles came and went with much less acrimony. As of this writing, illegal, roll-over deficit budgeting had become an accepted way of life in California government.

THE BUDGET PROCESS

Politicians love to declare that government should be run like a business. They are fond of insisting the state should live within its means. They insist state finances can be managed like a frugal family bank account. Statements like those may pave the high road in fiscal debates for elective office, but against the reality of California's annual budget bill they are about as valid as assertions that groundhogs can predict the weather.

The California economy is the sixth or seventh largest in the world. The state's budget is by far the largest in the nation. The business of collecting and spending more than $57.1 billion a year on schools, welfare, health, prisons, parks, highways and a myriad of other governmental functions is complex, tedious, politically intricate and a task that requires the expertise of hundreds of people.

The money flows in from taxes, fees, tideland oil royalties, multinational corporations and even the poor, who make co-payments for Medi-Cal and other services. Much of it goes exclusively into one or another of nearly 1,000 special funds earmarked for specific needs. Sales taxes, personal income taxes and bank and corporation taxes flow into the biggest pot of all, the $43.9 billion general fund.

All of that complexity is compressed into a single legislative vehicle, the annual budget bill, which is introduced by the governor within the first 10 days of each calendar year. By January, the budget has been months in the making. Department heads, agency heads and the governor's Department of Finance have been shaping it since the previous April to balance it with anticipated revenue. Reams of calculations have been completed. Programs are trimmed or expanded to conform to the governor's priorities. There will be winners and losers. If there is any fight left in the losers, and there always is, they will take their case to the Legislature.

In practice, the budget is introduced separately in both the Senate and the Assembly. The governor may be Republican, Democrat, independent or Martian, but his budget bills are officially authored by the chairmen of the Senate and Assembly fiscal committees, both of whom are members of the majority party. They reshape the governor's proposals, following guidance from their colleagues. They are in effective command of the most important bill of any legislative session, a two-volume document that lists appropriations for virtually every function of state government.

Much has to be done, of course, before the budget bills even begin to take shape for consideration by the full Legislature. In late February, the nonpartisan legislative analyst reports on the governor's budget proposal. The study commonly exceeds 1,400 pages of detail distilled from the work of dozens of specialists drawing upon the expertise throughout the government and the state as a whole. The budget subcommittees start on the smaller budgets first, particularly those that depend on special funds and have the money they need to confront the problems they manage. Programs that rely on the general fund come later. The final revenue estimates arrive in May, once the April tax bills are opened and the money is counted.

Eventually, the Assembly and Senate bills must pass by a two-thirds majority in each house (a constitutional requirement that gives the minority party, or minority coalitions, the power to block the budget). Differences are worked out in a six-member conference committee. In the end, a unified product must be approved, again by a two-thirds majority.

The constitutional deadline for final legislative action is June 15. The governor is supposed to sign the bill by the beginning of the new fiscal year, July 1. He can use his line-item veto authority to reduce appropriations set by the Legislature, but he cannot restore any spending the lawmakers cut. Usually the governor is able to sign the budget on time, but major budget delays occurred in 1978, 1979, 1980, 1983, 1990 and 1992. Eight of the last 10 budgets have been late.

3

The constitutional officers

To be governor of California in recent decades is to stand in the wings of the national political stage. Ronald Reagan proved most adept at moving into the spotlight, and George Deukmejian did his best to avoid it. But the state's chief executive automatically commands attention, owing largely to the 54 electoral votes that make California enormously important in any presidential election.

In the wake of a 1994 Republican tidal wave that saw voters decisively re-elect GOP Gov. Pete Wilson and just as commandingly approve the initiative he endorsed barring services to illegal immigrants, it was Wilson's turn in the national spotlight.

Speculation began immediately that he would seek the presidency. Wilson had said flatly during the campaign that he would not run in 1996, and close observers took him at his word. But he clearly enjoyed the national courting and the leverage he holds as governor of a state President Bill Clinton must win to survive for a second term.

Forgotten for the moment was Wilson's dismal debate performance during the 1994 campaign, in which he had rambled and squeaked his way through his answers against a more articulate Kathleen Brown. Wilson had once again proven that his political stamina — admirers refer to his "iron butt" — and an astute understanding of California politics were enough to carry him farther than his uninspiring public demeanor would suggest.

Wilson had earned the enmity of those who saw his crusade against illegal immigration as the worst sort of pandering to voters' racial fears. Yet even those who believed Wilson had elevated political scapegoating to an art form had to admit that his tenacity and tactics had worked. By the close of the campaign, owing in part to an astoundingly inept effort by his Democratic challenger, Wilson seemed to have run — and won — as much against Clinton as he had Brown.

California governors have flirted with the national limelight before. Earl Warren, elected three times as governor, sought the Republican presidential nomination twice before going on to preside for 16 years as chief justice of the U.S. Supreme Court. Edmund G. "Jerry" Brown Jr. shone in a string of 1976 primaries as he made a characteristically tardy bid to seize the Democratic presidential nomination from Jimmy Carter, then tried to unseat Carter in 1980.

Brown's father, Edmund G. "Pat" Brown Sr., had been governor for two years when he first toyed with the possibility of a vice presidential nomination. The former state attorney general, who defeated Republican William Knowland for the governor's job in 1958, was eventually frustrated in his hopes for higher office. The elder Brown turned his energies to a vision of California's future. Three decades later, his accomplishments — a bond issue to increase water supplies to Southern

SALARIES	
Governor	$120,000
Lt. Governor	$90,000
Attorney General	$102,000
Secretary of State	$90,000
Controller	$90,000
Treasurer	$90,000
Supt. of Public Instruction	$102,000
Insurance Commissioner	$95,052
Member, Board of Equalization	$95,052
Speaker of the Assembly	$86,400
Senate President Pro Tem	$86,400
Assembly/Senate Floor Leaders	$79,200
Legislator	$72,000
Chief Justice, Supreme Court	$133,459
Associate Justice	$127,267
Appellate Court Judge	$119,314
Superior Court Judge	$104,262
Municipal Court Judge	$95,214
President, University of California	$243,500
UC chancellors	$165,000-240,000
Chancellor, California State University system	$175,000
CSU presidents	$121,753-140,343

Many elected officials opted to take a 5 percent pay cut beginning in 1991 as California struggled through a recession. Legislators receive other direct compensation, including per diem pay of $109 a day for attending legislative sessions ($21,210 a year tax free) and their $4,800 car allowance. They also receive health, dental and vision benefits.

California, more investment in the university system, faster freeway construction for a rapidly growing state — are remembered fondly by elected officials facing a new crush of growth.

Pat Brown's governorship was memorable for its contribution to capital punishment history in a state where voters have demanded that political leaders be willing to put violent criminals to death. An opponent of capital punishment who nevertheless believed it was his job as governor to carry out state law, Brown described the agony of his clemency decisions in death penalty cases in a book published in 1989. "It was an awesome, ultimate power over the lives of others that no person or government should have, or crave," he wrote. "Each decision took something out of me that nothing — not family or work or hope for the future — has ever been able to replace."

The issue that had plagued Pat Brown and his son, Jerry, when he was governor, haunted Kathleen Brown as she sought in 1994 to become the third member of her family and the first woman to serve as California governor. But her cautious campaign also failed to define her for voters in any meaningful way, and eventually it dawned on disappointed Democrats that growing up as Pat Brown's daughter did not automatically make Kathleen Brown a mature politician. In the end, she blamed her defeat in 1994 on the baggage she carried as a Democrat, a woman and a Brown.

Despite their status as members of California's preeminent political family, the Browns had known serious defeat before. Pat Brown, whose defeat of Republican gubernatorial candidate Richard Nixon in 1962 prompted Nixon's infamous "You won't have Nixon to kick around anymore" press conference, looked forward in 1966 to running against a political neophyte named Ronald Reagan. But the mediagenic actor, railing against disorder on college campuses and appealing to an electorate unnerved by the Watts riots, denied Brown a chance to join Warren as a three-term governor.

Reagan continued while governor to fine-tune the conservative message that would propel him to the presidency, but he was largely unsuccessful in matching his fiscal actions with his anti-government rhetoric. In 1967, the former Democrat who bashed the bureaucracy and welfare state in his public appearances, signed what was then the largest tax increase in state history in order to shore up the sagging budget he inherited from Pat Brown.

Reagan was replaced by Jerry Brown, a self-proclaimed spokesman for a younger generation demanding change and imagination in government. If Jerry Brown followed his father's footsteps to the governor's office, he seemed determined to create his own path once he got there. The father was a consummate political mingler; the son standoffish. Pat was a spender; Jerry a relative tightwad. Pat laid pavement; Jerry discouraged freeway construction in favor of car pooling and mass transit. Similarly, the younger Brown's contributions as governor were less concrete. More than anything else, he is remembered for his personal idiosyncrasies: his refusal to live in the governor's mansion, the mattress on the floor of his

ELECTIONS 1902-1994

1902		
George C. Pardee (R)	48.06%	
Franklin K. Lane (D)	47.22%	
1906		
James Gillett (R)	40.4%	
Theodore Bell (D)	37.7%	
1910		
Hiram Johnson (R)	45.9%	
Theodore Bell (D)	40.1%	
1914		
Hiram Johnson (Pg)	49.7%	
John Fredericks (R)	29.3%	
J.B. Curtin (D)	12.5%	
1918		
William Stephens (R)	56.3%	
Theodore Bell (I)	36.5%	
1922		
Friend Richardson (R)	59.7%	
Thomas Woolwine (D)	36%	
1926		
C.C. Young (R)	71.2%	
Justus Wardell (D)	24.7%	
1930		
James Rolph Jr. (R)	72.1%	
Milton Young (D)	24.1%	
1934		
Frank Merriam (R)	48.9%	
Upton Sinclair (D)	37.7%	
Raymond Haight (C)	13.4%	
1938		
Culbert Olson (D)	52.5%	
Frank Merriam (R)	44.2%	
1942		
Earl Warren (R)	57%	
Culbert Olson (D)	41.7%	
1946		
Earl Warren (R & D)	91.6%	
Henry Schmidt (Pr)	7.1%	

1950		
Earl Warren (R)	64.8%	
James Roosevelt (D)	35.2%	
1954		
Goodwin Knight (R)	56.8%	
Richard Graves (D)	43.2%	
1958		
Pat Brown (D)	59.8%	
William Knowland (R)	40.2%	
1962		
Pat Brown (D)	51.9%	
Richard Nixon (R)	46.8%	
1966		
Ronald Reagan (R)	56.6%	
Pat Brown (D)	41.6%	
1970		
Ronald Reagan (R)	52.8%	
Jesse Unruh (D)	45.1%	
1974		
Jerry Brown (D)	50.2%	
Houston Flournoy (R)	47.3%	
1978		
Jerry Brown (D)	56%	
Evelle Younger (R)	36.5%	
1982		
George Deukmejian (R)	49.3%	
Tom Bradley (D)	48.1%	
1986		
George Deukmejian (R)	60.54%	
Tom Bradley (D)	37.37%	
1990		
Pete Wilson (R)	49.25%	
Dianne Feinstein (D)	45.79%	
1994		
Pete Wilson (R)	55.18%	
Kathleen Brown (D)	40.63%	

C:	Commonwealth	Pg:	Progressive
I:	Independent	Pr:	Prohibition

austere apartment, his 1979 trip to Africa with singer Linda Ronstadt.

Brown used his appointment power to fill state jobs with a more diverse group of people, but some appointments became enormous liabilities with voters. Supreme Court Chief Justice Rose Bird, ultimately ousted by voters in 1986, came to symbolize a criminal justice system seen as too sympathetic to criminals.

But it also was Brown's slapdash style and nearly perpetual campaign for president — a quest he continued unsuccessfully in 1992 — that voters turned away from in 1982, when they elected Courken George Deukmejian Jr. Deukmejian decided from the beginning to stick to the basics. He didn't bombard Californians with many new ideas. He said he was convinced voters wanted a competent manager, and he did little to deviate from that mission. He did his best to avoid revenue-raising measures that might be labeled tax increases, built prisons and appointed judges whom he said took a common-sense approach to fighting crime.

Republicans — Deukmejian being the chief example — prospered during the 1980s by aligning themselves with the Proposition 13-inspired mood of limited taxation and government spending. Democrats, who ordinarily favor a more activist government, were left befuddled by the onset of tax-cut fever.

Republican Pete Wilson won election as governor by finding a middle ground, denouncing his opponent, Democrat Dianne Feinstein, as a tax-and-spend liberal while refusing to rule out tax increases himself. Within weeks of Wilson's inauguration, it was clear that he had been wise to avoid an anti-tax pledge. As California's recession deepened, his first term was marked by the largest package of tax increases in California history. He also was responsible for sweeping cuts in state services, including a first-ever series of welfare cuts that even Reagan or Deukmejian had never dared attempt.

PETE WILSON RESURRECTED

As Pete Wilson debated in 1989 whether to run for governor, political consultant Stu Spencer warned him that California might very well be ungovernable. Wilson considered, then ignored the advice. Yet two years into Wilson's first term, it became apparent that Spencer had perhaps been right.

A string of man-made, natural, economic and political disasters seemed to follow Wilson like a cloud. He faced fires, floods, earthquakes, drought and California's first execution in 25 years. He signed the largest tax increase in state history to cope with California's worst financial mess since the Great Depression, and presided for 64 days in 1992 over a budget deadlock that forced state government to issue IOUs for the first time since the 1930s. His longtime political aide and press liaison, Otto Bos, died in June 1991 of a heart attack at age 47 while playing soccer in a weekend league.

As the bad news multiplied, Wilson's job rating hit a record low. His scores in early 1992 were worse than the worst marks voters had given California's four previous governors. "Stick a fork in him — he's done," crowed Democratic political

CALIFORNIA GOVERNORS

Governor	Party	Inauguration
Peter H. Burnett	Independent	December 1849
John McDougal	Independent	January 1851
John Bigler	Democrat	Jan. 1852, Jan.1854
J. Neeley Johnson	American	January 1856
John B. Weller	Democrat	January 1858
Milton S. Latham	Lecompton Democrat	January 1860
John G. Downey	Lecompton Democrat	January 1860
Leland Stanford	Republican	January 1862
Frederick F. Low	Union	December 1863
Henry H. Haight	Democrat	December 1867
Newton Booth	Republican	December 1871
Romualdo Pacheco	Republican	February 1875
William Irwin	Democrat	December 1875
George C. Perkins	Republican	January 1880
George Stoneman	Democrat	January 1883
Washington Bartlett	Democrat	January 1887
Robert W. Waterman	Republican	September 1887
Henry H. Markham	Republican	January 1891
James H. Budd	Democrat	January 1895
Henry T. Gage	Republican	January 1899
George C. Pardee	Republican	January 1903
James N. Gillett	Republican	January 1907
Hiram W. Johnson	Republican	January 1911
Hiram W. Johnson	Progressive	January 1915
William D. Stephens	Republican	March 1917, Jan. 1919
Friend Wm. Richardson	Republican	January 1923
C.C. Young	Republican	January 1927
James Rolph Jr.	Republican	January 1931
Frank F. Merriam	Republican	June 1934, Jan. 1935
Culbert L. Olson	Democrat	January 1939
Earl Warren	Republican*	Jan. 1943, Jan. 1947, Jan. 1951
Goodwin J. Knight	Republican	Oct. 1953, Jan. 1955
Edmund G. "Pat" Brown	Democrat	Jan. 1959, Jan. 1963
Ronald Reagan	Republican	Jan. 1967, Jan. 1971
Edmund G. "Jerry" Brown Jr.	Democrat	Jan. 1975, Jan. 1979
George Deukmejian	Republican	Jan. 1983, Jan. 1987
Pete Wilson	Republican	Jan. 1991, Jan. 1995

* Earl Warren won both the Republican and Democratic primaries in 1946.

consultant Kerman Maddox, summarizing the conventional wisdom at the time. Few would have envisioned the outcome of the 1994 campaign, one in which Wilson dispatched Democratic nominee Kathleen Brown with relative ease.

Even as a weakened Wilson in 1993 dealt with a third recessionary budget year and a state unemployment rate topping 10 percent, he began to set the stage for his comeback. Seizing on public demand for a crackdown on crime in the wake of the murder of Petaluma 12-year-old Polly Klaas, he signed "three strikes" legislation that critics warned would decimate higher education funding for decades to come. He blamed California's budget problems in large part on what he called President Bill Clinton's failure to reimburse

Pete Wilson

California for its costs for delivering education and health services to illegal immigrants.

Building his campaign on the twin pillars of illegal immigration (specifically, Proposition 187) and crime, Wilson deflected attention from education, management of state government and other issues on which voters saw him as less credible. To Democrats, it seemed at times as if he had also constructed a tougher-than-Teflon political shield. Advertising for Kathleen Brown reminded the electorate that California was experiencing the worst recession since the Great Depression. But it also helped make Wilson's point: The Republican governor had led California during some unusually tough times.

In the end, voters seemed to sympathize and agree with Wilson enough to give him a second chance. Given the string of economic and natural disasters he had confronted — and the lack of a legitimate alternative in Kathleen Brown — a majority concluded Wilson had done the best he could. Yet term limits made him a lame duck from the outset of his second term. The question is how will Wilson complete the job Spencer had warned was impossible.

Wilson campaigned for governor in 1990 as a "compassionate" conservative. But that label saw little play four years later, as he argued determinedly against education and health care for illegal immigrant children. In language that made even some supporters cringe, he said California "cannot educate every child from here to Tierra del Fuego," and that eliminating the services would convince their parents to "self deport." Once again, the pragmatic ex-Marine had proven he is a politician who defies ideological characterization.

In his first year in office Wilson had won approval for his tax hikes by threatening Republicans privately that they would make themselves "fucking irrelevant" if they refused to compromise with Democrats on a budget-balancing deal. But he spent much of the next year sounding like a reincarnation of anti-tax crusader Howard Jarvis, refusing to consider any tax increases to balance the budget. When pressed about the inconsistency, he offered a revisionist view of his willingness to raise taxes the year before, saying he had argued at the time that raising taxes was a mistake.

Wilson also sent mixed signals on gay rights. One year after vetoing a 1991 bill banning job discrimination against homosexuals, Wilson signed a narrower measure that he said would protect gay rights without exposing California employers to costly lawsuits.

Democrats, who gave Wilson an extended honeymoon his first year, were confused by his new-found anti-tax zeal and his wavering position on gay rights. Was he the compassionate conservative who proposed preventive programs to keep children healthy, in school and out of prison? Or was he the heartless budget-cutter who would sacrifice his moderate social positions in an instant to mollify the religious right?

The cooperative spirit in the Capitol was severely tested by the political pressures that came with the once-a-decade redistricting of legislative and congressional districts and by budget constraints brought on by a severe recession. In the 1992 budget fight, Wilson vowed to allow chaos to reign for as long as it took to convince Democratic legislators to do things his way. But he underestimated the degree of pain it would take to force their capitulation. The stalemate damaged both California's national reputation and its bond rating without finding a long-term solution to the budget mess. In the end, Wilson and lawmakers faced another multibillion dollar shortfall in 1993.

Wilson also irritated Democrats by proposing a 1992 ballot initiative (Proposition 165) to expand the governor's budgetary powers. Legislators began to charge the governor with abandoning democracy in favor of one-man rule. By the time a budget was signed in 1992, critics had variously called him a pip-squeak, a terrorist and a petulant child. In November, voters defeated Proposition 165 after a campaign featuring heavy spending by Democrats and state employees, whom Wilson also had thoroughly antagonized. That raised speculation that voters might also be in no mood to grant Wilson a second term.

Peter Barton Wilson, however, is nothing if not persistent. He failed the bar exam twice before passing on his third try. He practiced law only briefly, however, devoting much of his time after law school to a series of political jobs. He was an advance man for Richard Nixon's gubernatorial campaign in 1962, a paid staff member for a local Republican club and executive director of the San Diego Republican Party Central Committee in 1964. He finally grabbed an Assembly seat in 1966.

As Wilson contemplated leaving his Assembly seat to run for mayor of San Diego, his administrative assistant sketched out the pros and cons on a yellow legal pad. There were big problems in San Diego, a city racked by government scandal and rampant growth. The Navy town, tucked away near the Mexican border, was hardly noticed by most Californians. The job was probably a political cul-de-sac.

On the other hand, managing a city might demonstrate executive ability, experience that Wilson could point to if he someday ran for governor. "I knew he wanted to be governor, and I wanted him to be governor," said Bob White, who has been Wilson's top aide ever since. Wilson pulled up his Sacramento stakes and went south to take charge of San Diego.

Wilson's plan to catapult from San Diego into statewide office failed in 1978, when he finished fourth in a bid for the GOP gubernatorial nomination. Four years later he considered another try, but settled for a successful U.S. Senate race against outgoing Gov. Jerry Brown.

Wilson continues to come across as someone who wears starched shirts on Saturdays. When he does relax, he smokes a cigar, turns on some Broadway show tunes and knocks back a couple of scotches. Wilson's father, James, a hard-charging advertising executive whom Wilson describes as one of his heroes, never wanted his son in politics. Ironically, it was at the dinner table, when his dad would deliver minilectures on one's obligation to society, that Wilson said his interest in public service began.

When speaking publicly, Wilson's self-confident attitude can border on smugness. A long line of aides has tried unsuccessfully to convince him to punch up a speaking style that at times sounds unintelligible. Wilson also has long stuck with a style that makes it difficult to classify his political views. He has courted the environmental vote with consistent stands on coastal protection, limits on offshore oil drilling, expansion of transit systems and planned growth. But he took a rightward turn on environmental questions during California's recession, disappointing those who had been won over by his earlier positions. On other matters, Wilson, as a U.S. senator, generally supported Reagan administration policies and was an early backer of George Bush's candidacy. He worked for California industry, particularly agriculture, aerospace and computer electronics.

Efforts on behalf of agricultural interests came back to haunt him in 1994, as Democrats labeled him a hypocrite for his efforts as a U.S. senator to let Mexican citizens enter the country legally to do farm work. In its final form, Democrats argued, the federal program contributed to an upswing in the illegal immigration that Wilson so vigorously fought as governor. Wilson had never supported illegal immigration, and responded accurately that Democrats had altered the tougher plan he originally proposed. But it was also true that Wilson's political career has reflected California's historical love-hate relationship with immigrant labor.

Probably the most memorable moment of Wilson's Senate years came in May 1985, when he was recovering from an emergency appendectomy. The Senate was considering a complex budget measure, which included a freeze on cost-of-living increases for Social Security recipients, and it appeared that Vice President Bush would be needed to break a tie. At the critical moment, a pajama-clad Wilson was wheeled onto the Senate floor to cast the deciding vote in favor. Senate Republican leader Bob Dole joked at the time that Wilson "does better under sedation."

Wilson has never been a favorite of many state Republicans; he endorsed Gerald Ford over Reagan in the 1976 presidential campaign. At the 1985 Republican state convention, conservatives almost booed him off the stage. In November 1988, however, Wilson did something that none of his predecessors had been able to do for 36 years: He held onto his U.S. Senate seat for a second term. His opponent, Lt. Gov. Leo McCarthy, had gotten nowhere with his campaign charge that Wilson left no footprints in Washington, and it appeared that the jinxed seat from California finally had an occupant who would make a career of the Senate.

Then came Deukmejian's announcement that he wouldn't seek a third term. GOP leaders, desperate to have a Republican in the governor's chair when the state was reapportioned after the 1990 census, cast about for someone electable. With no other Republicans holding statewide office, most agreed that only Wilson fit the bill. He was quick to hit the campaign trail again. "I see it very likely as a career capper — and a damn good one," he said.

Wilson hit a low point in the 1992 elections, as Republican candidates he backed took a beating and his budget and welfare initiative, Proposition 165, was soundly defeated. The state campaign for President Bush that he led never got off the ground, and the national campaign eventually opted to write off California. His appointee to the U.S. Senate, John Seymour, lost his seat to Democrat Dianne Feinstein. Wilson, who had hoped to capture a majority in the 80-seat Assembly and oust Democratic Assembly Speaker Willie Brown, settled for an embarrassing 32 GOP seats.

The election also opened wide rifts within the state Republican Party, divisions expressed early in primary fights in legislative races between Wilson and conservative Christians. The difficulty of the balancing act facing Wilson was evident. He angered conservatives by backing challengers against them in primary fights. Yet he disappointed moderates by wholeheartedly supporting Christian-right candidates who won primaries, and by making it clear after the election that he would not lead an intra-party effort to oust the religious right.

Tables turned dramatically in 1994, as Wilson's decision to unite with social conservatives helped Republicans take a majority of seats in the state Assembly. Wilson also emerged with a national image leaning decidedly to the right.

His support of Proposition 187's curbs on education and health services for illegal immigrants won him plaudits from Pat Buchanan, the man Wilson had accused in 1992 of making "downright racist" remarks. It earned him public criticism from GOP moderates Jack Kemp and former Education Secretary William Bennett, who argued that the measure would foster a "nativist, anti-immigration climate" — and hurt the GOP's standing among Latino and Asian voters.

Wilson, having helped launch the court fight over services for illegal immigrants, mounted a public relations offensive to reassure critics that his target was illegal — not legal — immigration. As he had predicted, court action blocking implementation of the measure spared him from carrying it out. By the time the U.S. Supreme Court decides the matter, he noted during the campaign, "I will have completed the four years of my second term."

PERSONAL: elected 1990; born Aug. 23, 1933, in Lake Forest, Ill.; home, San Diego; education, B.A. Yale University 1955, J.D. UC Berkeley 1962; wife, Gayle; Protestant.

CAREER: U.S. Marine Corps, 1955-58; attorney, 1963-66; Assembly, 1966-71; San Diego mayor, 1971-83; U.S. Senator, 1983-91.

OFFICES: Sacramento (916) 445-2841; Los Angeles (213) 897-0322; San Diego (619) 525-4641; San Francisco (415) 703-2218; Fresno (209) 445-5295.

GRAY DAVIS: DEMOCRATIC SURVIVOR

In an election year when Republicans dominated California's constitutional offices, Democratic veteran Gray Davis successfully dodged the GOP bullets to move from the controller's office to become lieutenant governor. Davis' fundraising ability and well-known name had frightened off potential Democratic competitors. He then drew as an opponent state Sen. Cathie Wright, the weakest of the Republicans competing for statewide office in 1994. Davis' marginally upward career move, coupled with election losses that cut the legs off California's Democratic bench, made him a top — if shopworn — contender for the party's gubernatorial nomination in 1998. But even before he took office he was the victim of public humiliation at the hands of Gov. Pete Wilson, who evicted the lieutenant governor's offices from the Capitol.

His 1994 victory was another chapter in a saga of political survival for Davis, who embarrassed himself with a sleazy campaign ad in his 1992 primary campaign for the U.S. Senate. The television ad likened Democratic opponent Dianne Feinstein to Leona Helmsley, the New York hotelier convicted of tax evasion. "Helmsley is in jail; Feinstein wants to be a senator," the ad said, attempting to equate Helmsley's legal problems with a civil suit filed against Feinstein by the Fair Political Practices Commission.

Davis' attack had little effect on Feinstein, who went on to win the U.S. Senate seat and hold it against a self-financed challenge by Rep. Michael Huffington in 1994. Instead, Davis sabotaged his own standing in political circles with a campaign remembered as sexist and unfair.

Slim, smooth and soft-spoken in public, Davis also has a temperamental side. Former staffers remember him as a boss with a scathing tongue. Born Joseph Graham Davis Jr. in New York, Davis moved to California with his family at age 11. A graduate of Stanford University and Columbia University law school, he served two years in the U.S. Army in Vietnam. In 1974, with a stint as finance director for Tom Bradley's successful mayoral race under his belt, Davis made his first run at statewide office. He filed for the Democratic nomination for state treasurer,

Gray Davis

then learned to his dismay that former Assembly Speaker Jesse Unruh had decided to enter the race. "It was no contest," Davis later recalled. "I was the doormat Jess stepped on in his road back to political prominence."

Davis then went to work as chief of staff for Jerry Brown, who became governor that year. Putting aside his own ambitions, Davis helped forge Brown's thrifty image and ran interference with the Legislature, surviving a continual power struggle among the young governor's top aides. By 1981, however, Davis was restless and ready to run for the state Assembly. Elected to the 43rd District representing West Los Angeles in 1982, he won re-election two years later.

Those years laid the groundwork for Davis' second statewide run. When veteran state Controller Kenneth Cory announced his retirement just days before the filing deadline in 1986, Davis was sitting on a $1 million campaign fund that enabled him to dash in and win. He also was helped politically by publicity he had generated for himself with his 1985 effort to encourage companies to picture missing children on milk cartons, grocery bags and billboards. The program featured prominently in his campaign ads.

Although controversial Supreme Court Chief Justice Rose Bird presided at Davis' 1983 wedding, he sidestepped the issue in his race for controller, saying he did not want to prejudice cases involving the controller's office that someday could come before the court. He emerged largely unscathed by the Bird-bashing and Brown-battering leveled at Democratic candidates that year. He later narrowly escaped prosecution for using state staff and equipment in his 1986 campaign for controller. Attorney General John Van de Kamp, another Democrat, concluded that taxpayer funds had been used in the campaign, but found insufficient evidence to accuse Davis of any criminal intent. Davis used the office as a platform to fight offshore oil drilling, defend the state's family planning program, hunt for people to whom the state owed money and, on two occasions, press corporations to donate wetlands to the public.

Replacing retiring three-term Lt. Gov. Leo McCarthy, Davis now serves as a regent for the University of California and a trustee for the state university system. He is also in a position to move into the governor's chair if the state's chief executive vacates the office. That makes Davis a serious stumbling block for Gov. Pete Wilson if the Republican governor were to hold any national political aspirations for 1996.

PERSONAL: elected 1986; born Dec. 26, 1942, in New York; home, Los Angeles; education, B.A. Stanford University, J.D. Columbia University Law School; wife, Sharon Ryer Davis.

CAREER: chief of staff to Gov. Jerry Brown 1974-1981; Assembly 1983-1986; state controller 1987-1995.

OFFICES: Sacramento (916) 445-8994; San Francisco (415) 557-2662; Los Angeles (310) 412-6118.

LIEUTENANT GOVERNORS SINCE 1950		
Goodwin J. Knight	Republican	elected 1950
Harold J. Powers	Republican	appointed 1953
Harold J. Powers	Republican	elected 1954
Glenn M. Anderson	Democrat	elected 1958, '62
Robert Finch	Republican	elected 1966
Ed Reinecke	Republican	appointed 1969
Ed Reinecke	Republican	elected 1970
Mervyn Dymally	Democrat	elected 1974
Mike Curb	Republican	elected 1978
Leo T. McCarthy	Democrat	elected 1982, '86, '90
Gray Davis	Democrat	elected 1994

DANIEL LUNGREN: VICTORY WITHOUT COURAGE

Dan Lungren, long considered a Republican rising star, easily won re-election as attorney general in 1994 — but not before setting what may be a new standard for political indecision and cowardice. Lungren waited until after 4 p.m. on the day before the election to take a position on the most high-profile political issue of the year, the ballot measure denying education and health services to illegal immigrants.

Dan Lungren

He said he would vote for Proposition 187, though he believed it was an "imperfect answer" to the problem. Two days later, after the measure passed in a landslide, he was on "Larry King Live" to defend it in language that would have left most viewers surprised to learn he hadn't backed it solidly from the start.

His apparent reluctance to alienate moderate voters was perhaps further evidence that Lungren has his sights set on the governor's office down the line. He had previously ducked issues that might contribute to his hard-right reputation, keeping a low profile on fights over school prayer and welfare reform while pursuing less controversial topics — violence in high school football and video games.

Few familiar with Lungren's tough brand of conservatism, however, would feel comfortable classifying him as a centrist. Lungren began his first term as state attorney general remaking the office in his conservative image. He insisted that lawyers hired for the office's criminal division handle death penalty appeals regardless of their personal views on the issue and vigorously pursued California's first execution in 25 years, that of double-murderer Robert Alton Harris. He generated controversy as he demoted civil rights lawyer Marian Johnston and folded prosecution units specializing in fraud and white-collar crime into the department's criminal division. He also quit handling lawsuits involving most state personnel matters, which had been a major responsibility of the office. Lungren blamed the cuts on budget troubles, as a national recession coincided with a flood of federal death penalty appeals.

Lungren also cited budget constraints for his failure to implement a state-of-the-art computer system for tracking criminals, an issue that came back to haunt him in his 1994 re-election campaign. His Democratic opponent, Tom Umberg, ran an ad in which the grandfather of Petaluma murder victim Polly Klaas said Lungren bore some responsibility for her death. Standing at the site where the 12-year-old's body was found, Joe Klaas wore a T-shirt reading "Remember Polly. Dump Lungren." While the charge was unfounded — police officers never checked the computer system in that case — it was true that Lungren had cut funding for computerized databases that local police agencies and prosecutors use to keep track of criminals. The system is still plagued by a backlog that prevents law enforcement officers from receiving up-to-date information.

Democrats hoped to block Lungren's political ascension in 1988, when the state senate refused to confirm his nomination as state treasurer by then-Gov. George Deukmejian. But Republicans had the last laugh in 1990, when Lungren was elected in his own right as attorney general, an even more prominent constitutional office. Lungren, who spent 10 years in Congress as a law-and-order conservative, abandoned an exploratory candidacy for the U.S. Senate in 1986 because he was unable to raise enough money. When his hopes of becoming state treasurer were dashed, he returned to private practice in a Sacramento law firm and began to plan his campaign for attorney general instead.

Lungren, who at 6 years of age began walking precincts for a GOP congressional candidate, isn't the only member of his family with political ties. His father, John, was Richard Nixon's personal physician, and his younger brother, Brian, is a political consultant who managed his first campaign for attorney general. Lungren served as an assistant to Republican U.S. Sens. George Murphy of California and Bill Brock of Tennessee, and was a special assistant to the Republican National Committee. He was practicing law in Long Beach when he was elected to Congress. Watchdog groups consistently classified his congressional votes as conservative, and he earned the wrath of Japanese-American groups for voting against reparations for World War II internees.

Lungren is a dynamic public speaker, and his competitive nature and intense personality make him a candidate to be reckoned with should he decide to run for governor. Given the prospect of another contentious primary fight for governor on the Democratic side in 1998 — John Garamendi makes no secret about his desire to run again — Lungren is well-positioned for that race.

PERSONAL: elected 1990; born Sept. 22, 1946, in Long Beach; home, Roseville; education, B.A. University of Notre Dame 1964, J.D. Georgetown University Law School 1971; wife, Barbara "Bobbi" Lungren; children, Jeffrey, Kelly and Kathleen.

CAREER: U.S. Senate aide, 1969-70; Republican National Committee staff, 1971-72; private law practice in Long Beach, 1973-78, and in Sacramento 1989-1991; U.S. House of Representatives 1979-1989.

OFFICES: Sacramento (916) 322-3360; San Francisco (415) 703-1985; Los Angeles (213) 897-2000; San Diego (619) 645-2001.

ATTORNEYS GENERAL SINCE 1950

Edmund G. "Pat" Brown	Democrat	elected 1950, '54
Stanley Mosk	Democrat	elected 1958, '62
Thomas C. Lynch	Democrat	appointed 1964
Thomas C. Lynch	Democrat	elected 1966
Evelle J. Younger	Republican	elected 1970, '74
George Deukmejian	Republican	elected 1978
John Van de Kamp	Democrat	elected 1982, '86
Dan Lungren	Republican	elected 1990, '94

KATHLEEN CONNELL: BRIGHT LIGHT FOR DEMOS

The political collapse of Kathleen Brown in 1994 made Kathleen Connell the Democratic woman to watch. More politically mainstream than the liberal newly elected state schools chief, Delaine Eastin, Connell won election to the controller's office on the strength of her business-like appearance in television ads financed with a sizable chunk of her own money.

The first woman to hold the office of state controller, Connell brings impressive credentials to the post. She was the owner and president of Connell & Associates, an investment banking firm, where she held six licenses from the Securities & Exchange Commission. In her Ph.D dissertation at UCLA she examined the performance of municipalities in timing bond sales to

Kathleen Connell

secure lower-cost financing. Connell had another advantage — personal wealth. To win her first elective office as state controller, she loaned her campaign a cool $1.8 million. Married to a Los Angeles real estate developer, she's the adoptive mother of two preschoolers. It might all seem a little too perfect if she didn't wear a Mickey Mouse watch.

In her campaign against anti-tax crusader Tom McClintock, Connell called, among other things, for a series of audits of state government to identify billions of dollars in savings. Like Kathleen Brown, however, she offered superficial political proposals, not details, for government waste-cutting. Connell pointed to Texas, where she claimed fiscal reviews saved state government $6 billion. But California already had implemented many of the Texas ideas, and much of that savings was the result of fee increases — not the spending cuts Connell's campaign implied.

Connell got her start in government with former Los Angeles Mayor Tom Bradley, who was impressed enough by a presentation she made on urban transportation in 1975 to hire her as a special assistant. She later dodged some adverse publicity as city housing director after some critical audits by the U.S. Department of Housing and Urban Development. She ultimately left for a job with Chemical Bank in New York before returning to California to start her own business.

The controller's office gives Connell wide-ranging responsibilities, from paying state lottery winners to administering the state's payroll. It also gives her a seat on 63 boards, committees and commissions, including the State Lands Commission and the Board of Equalization. She serves as chair of the Franchise Tax Board, which oversees collection of personal and corporate income taxes. She also has a voice in managing some $130 billion in state employee and teacher pension funds.

PERSONAL: elected 1994; born June 30, 1947, in Denver, Colo.; home, Los Angeles; education B.A. Hastings College in Nebraska; attended American University in Washington, D.C.; M.P.A. University of Pittsburgh; Ph.D. University of California, Los Angeles; husband, Robert Levenstein; two sons, Adam and Garrett.

CAREER: special assistant to the Los Angeles mayor, 1975-1977; Los Angeles city housing director, 1977-1983; director of financial services, Chemical Bank in

CONTROLLERS SINCE 1950

Thomas H. Kuchel	Republican	elected 1950
Robert C. Kirkwood	Republican	appointed 1952
Robert C. Kirkwood	Republican	elected 1954
Alan Cranston	Democrat	elected 1958, '62
Houston I. Flournoy	Republican	elected 1966, '70
Kenneth Cory	Democrat	elected 1974, '78, '82
Gray Davis	Democrat	elected 1986, '90
Kathleen Connell	Democrat	elected 1994

New York, 1983-1985; president, Connell & Associates, financial consulting firm based in Culver City, 1985-1994.
OFFICES: Sacramento (916) 445-3028; Los Angeles (310) 446-8846.

MATT FONG: REPUBLICAN RISING STAR

Gov. Pete Wilson, seeking to build bridges with the state's Asian American community in 1990, encouraged Matthew K. Fong to run for state controller. The son of longtime Democratic Secretary of State March Fong Eu, the young and inexperienced Fong launched his political career with the Republican Party. After the all too predictable loss, Wilson kept Fong's political career alive by naming him to the state Board of Equalization.

Matthew K. Fong

Four years later, with the political dry run under his belt and a Republican wind behind him, Fong won a tough race for state treasurer to become a rising GOP star in his own right. In winning election as state treasurer, Fong outmaneuvered former state Democratic Party Chairman Phil Angelides, who had angered insider Democrats by waging a particularly nasty primary campaign against former state Senate President Pro Tem David Roberti.

Wilson had named Fong to the equalization post to replace Paul Carpenter, who was convicted on corruption charges. Despite a negligible background in tax issues, Fong immediately became an activist on the board and earned respect for working to master complex subjects. His 1994 campaign for treasurer capitalized on those strengths, but also emphasized a proposed "taxpayer protection plan" to cut $2 billion that his position as treasurer gives him little power to enact.

Fong's grandfather, who had a pharmacy in San Francisco's Chinatown, was the first Chinese-American to work for the Board of Equalization. Fong says his grandfather was recruited to explain its laws to the Chinese community and to collect their sales taxes. Fong himself is the second Asian-American, after his mother, to hold a statewide office in California. But an ugly episode in the course of his latest campaign — a saboteur replaced the phone message on his campaign's 800 number with racist remarks referring to Eu and Fong — made it clear that Fong is still pioneering.

The treasurer's job has been a political incubator for higher offices. But Fong will have to prove his ability to cope with topics more controversial than bond and investment plans. In 1990, for example, Fong ducked a question on abortion at the press conference announcing his controller's campaign and has continued to dodge the issue ever since.

PERSONAL: elected 1994; born Nov. 20, 1953, in Oakland; home, Hacienda Heights; education, B.S. U.S. Air Force Academy, M.B.A. Pepperdine University, J.D. Southwestern Law School; wife, Paula; two children, Matthew and Jade.

CAREER: U.S. Air Force, 1971-80; Air Force reserves, 1980-present (currently a major); lawyer, Sheppard, Mullin, Richter & Hampton in Los Angeles, 1985-90; member, state Board of Equalization; 1990-1995.

OFFICES: Sacramento (916) 653-2995; Los Angeles (213) 620-4467.

TREASURERS SINCE 1950		
Charles G. Johnson	Progressive	elected 1950, '54
Ronald Button	Republican	appointed 1956
Bert A. Betts	Democrat	elected 1958, '62
Ivy Baker Priest	Republican	elected 1966, '70
Jesse M. Unruh	Democrat	elected 1974, '78, '82, '86*
Thomas Hayes	Republican	appointed 1987
Kathleen Brown	Democrat	elected 1990
Matthew K. Fong	Republican	elected 1994

*Elizabeth Whitney served as acting treasurer following Unruh's death, August 1987-January 1989.

BILL JONES: GOP BOY SCOUT

If there were a merit badge for loyalty offered by the state Republican Party, Secretary of State Bill Jones would have earned it. An obedient lieutenant in California's GOP power structure, he is an officeholder who plays by the rules and responds when duty calls. As an Assembly member, Jones performed for a short time in the thankless job of caucus leader, straddling the group's conservative-moderate split on behalf of Gov. Pete Wilson. He was a reserved, careful and honest — if boring — legislator who now has the chance to apply both his passion for fair play and his strong GOP ties to the office that oversees California's elections.

Jones blocked acting Secretary of State Tony Miller's bid to become the state's first openly gay constitutional officer, winning the right to replace longtime

Secretary of State March Fong Eu, who resigned to become ambassador to Micronesia. Jones' victory margin was close enough — fewer than 33,000 votes — that he may owe his election to the state's fledgling Green Party. Although the Green Party endorsed "none of the above" in the race for governor in a concerted effort to prevent a Green candidate from siphoning off the votes that would allow the Democratic candidate to defeat the Republican, the Greens ran their own candidate, Margaret Garcia, for secretary of state. The 314,144 votes Garcia received were more than enough to account for the difference between Miller and Jones.

Bill Jones

A Fresno businessman, row-crop farmer and cattle rancher, Jones served in the Assembly as a lawmaker for farm interests. A pilot, he also flew himself back and forth from his district to Sacramento. He campaigned for the seat in 1982 amid some adverse publicity over a handgun incident in which he dropped a gun and accidentally shot himself in both legs. Locals laughed that he was a politician who shot himself in the foot, but he easily won election to the seat. His brief tenure as GOP leader ended in 1992, when Republicans actually lost an Assembly seat after bragging that redistricting that year would allow them to capture a majority in the house. In 1994, Jones carried California's "three strikes" legislation on behalf of Mike Reynolds, the Fresno father who sought the measure in the wake of his daughter Kimber's murder. Jones admitted that the measure had flaws, but refused to correct them, saying the courts could do that. He also failed to deal with the financial consequences of locking up thousands of more prisoners. But the measure figured prominently in his secretary of state campaign, although the office has nothing to do with controlling violent crime.

Jones also focused on voter fraud in his 1994 campaign, calling for tightening security in "bounty hunter" voter registration programs and purging voter rolls of deadwood. Promising to make sure "illegal aliens don't vote," he proposed requiring a photo identification for registration and voting, as well as requiring a Social Security or naturalization number on registration affidavits. His position puts him at the head of Wilson's efforts to block implementation of federal "motor voter" legislation in California, where Republicans fear registering voters as they apply for drivers' licenses will boost Democratic participation. An opponent of public campaign financing, calling it "welfare for politicians," he instead called for limits on contributions.

PERSONAL: elected 1994; born Dec. 20, 1949, in Coalinga, Calif.; home, Fresno; education, B.S. CSU Fresno; wife, Maurine; two children, Wendy and Andrea.

CAREER: family partner in a 3,000-acre ranch and investments firm; chairman of the board of California Data Marketing Inc., a computer service and direct mail firm; assemblyman 1982-1994.

OFFICES: Sacramento (916) 445-6371; San Francisco (415) 703-2601; Los Angeles (213) 897-3131; San Diego (619) 525-4113.

SECRETARIES OF STATE SINCE 1950

Frank M. Jordan	Republican	elected 1950, '54, '58, '62, '66
Pat Sullivan	Republican	appointed 1970
Edmund G. "Jerry" Brown Jr.	Democrat	elected 1970
March Fong Eu	Democrat	elected 1974, '78, '82, '86, '90
Bill Jones	Republican	elected 1994

EASTIN IN UNFRIENDLY TERRITORY

If the good news in 1994 for Delaine Eastin was her election in a political free-for-all for state schools chief, the bad was that she found herself surrounded by a political power structure at odds with her liberal views. Republican Gov. Pete Wilson's re-election meant that Eastin's opponent in the election, Maureen DiMarco, retained her position as Wilson's secretary of child development and education. Eastin must also work with a conservative state Board of Education emboldened after a successful court struggle with former state schools chief Bill Honig that increased the board's power over education policy.

Eastin's response immediately after the election was to call for a political truce. But no one familiar with her feisty and outspoken reputation expects her to serve quietly. This is the legislator, after all, who called Wilson a "knucklehead" — then quickly apologized — in a speech shortly after his election as governor. More recently, Eastin in her campaign denounced Wilson's veto of legislation reforming CLAS, the California Learning Assessment System, as "a crass campaign move . . . to appease the radical right at the expense of California's children."

Eastin also assumed an office that had atrophied following Honig's conflict-of-interest conviction in 1993. Without the intense and determined Honig at the helm, education seemed to slide off the list of issues capturing Sacramento's attention. Wilson sought to appoint former state Sen. Marian Bergeson to fill the job and was blocked by the Democratic-controlled Legislature. Among those spearheading the effort was Eastin, who soon thereafter began running for the office.

In the absence of political leadership, the state Department of Education in 1994 was the focal point for controversy over CLAS, a statewide test intended to measure critical thinking skills that some parents viewed as too touchy-feely and intrusive. Initial insistence by then-acting schools chief Dave Dawson that allowing parents to see the test would violate confidentiality requirements only added fuel to the flap. The department then re-

Delaine Eastin

versed course and put copies of some tests on display. Following Wilson's veto of legislation intended to address concerns, Eastin took office without a uniform statewide testing mechanism in place.

A former Union City councilwoman, Eastin was a tenacious and outspoken legislator who served as chair of the Assembly Education Committee and was seen as the darling of the California Teachers Association and other school unions. She could use the office, as Honig did, as a bully pulpit to press Wilson for education spending. But those who opposed her election said her strident style and leftward politics would further polarize California's already divided and unaccountable system of governing public education.

PERSONAL: elected 1994; born Aug. 20, 1947, in San Diego; home, Fremont; education, B.A. UC Davis, M.A. UC Santa Barbara; husband Jack Saunders.

CAREER: corporate planner, Pacific Bell, 1979-86; political science professor, De Anza and Cañada Community colleges, 1972-79; member, Union City City Council, 1980-1986; assemblywoman, 1986-1994.

OFFICES: Sacramento (916) 657-2451.

SUPERINTENDENTS OF PUBLIC INSTRUCTION SINCE 1950	
Roy Simpson	elected 1950, '54, '58
Max Rafferty	elected 1962, '66
Wilson Riles	elected 1970, '74, '78
Bill Honig	elected 1982, '86, '90
Delaine Eastin	elected 1994

INSURERS PICK QUACKENBUSH

Charles Quackenbush is the insurance commissioner packaged and elected by the industry he is supposed to regulate. His predecessor, John Garamendi, made much of his refusal to take campaign contributions directly from insurers, but voters chose a very different course when they made Quackenbush the state's second elected commissioner. The industry contributed the bulk of the money Quackenbush spent to win the Republican nomination and then defeat Democrat Art Torres. Insurance agents staffed phone banks and wrote letters on his behalf to their customers. At one point, Allstate Insurance Co. agents who made campaign phone calls misrepresented themselves as police officers, an embarrassing turn of events that led Quackenbush to apologize.

Charles Quackenbush

Garamendi delighted in telling audiences that insurers were used to regulators who "snuggle in bed" with them. "I'll be damned if I'm their lover," he'd say. Insurers responded in kind, saying Garamendi had gone overboard in his pro-consumer zeal, treating insurance companies like "criminals . . . like pigs at a trough." It was Garamendi's clumsy handling of the office, they argued, that prompted them to work so hard for a commissioner who would not drive them out of business.

Quackenbush insisted he would remain independent, denying charges that he would become the insurers' lackey while unapologetically taking their money. But barring any legal constraints against unlimited contributions to the commissioner from the industry he regulates, the elected position created in November 1988 by voters with Proposition 103 remains as vulnerable to influence as the previous appointed post.

Quackenbush pointed to his actions as a legislator as proof that he could act against the interests of his contributors. In 1989, he was one of only two Assembly Republicans to support an assault-weapons ban despite the fact that he had taken National Rifle Association contributions. A moderate, youthful-looking Republican, Quackenbush also voted against the GOP caucus position on such issues as abortion. He joined the Assembly in 1986 and, following Gov. Pete Wilson's election in 1990, quickly became a favorite in the governor's office. Quackenbush now has the opportunity to team up with Wilson to push proposals for no-fault automobile insurance and tort reform.

But he also heads a 1,000-employee agency whose growing pains are not over. Still ahead are major issues: implementation of Proposition 103, major rate increase requests from insurers and a homeowners' insurance crisis in the wake of a series of natural disasters that has left many insurers reluctant to issue policies in the state. Quackenbush now has a chance to prove that he truly can balance the interests of consumers and insurers. Many California consumers are waiting to see if he is up to the job. But his early utterances didn't provide much assurance. Just before taking office he told the trade magazine Insurance Journal that "after the last four years, my administration is going to seem like heaven to [the industry]."

PERSONAL: elected 1994; born April 20, 1954, in Tacoma, Wash.; home, Sacramento; Army 1976-1981; education, B.A. Notre Dame University; wife Chris, three children, Carrey, Joseph and Chucky.

CAREER: owner, Q-Tech, an electronics industry employment service, 1979-1989; assemblyman 1986-1994; business investor.

OFFICES: San Francisco (415) 557-1126; Los Angeles (213) 736-2572; Sacramento (916) 322-3555.

BOARD OF EQUALIZATION

The 1849 California Constitution advanced the notion that taxation shall be equal and uniform throughout the state, and by 1879 the people made the Board of Equalization a constitutional agency to see to it. Today, the board boasts of its powers to affect virtually every aspect of commerce and government in California, including taxes paid by more than 1 million businesses, 300 private utilities and 4.5 million homeowners.

Operating quasi-judicially, the board hears tax appeals and sets assessments on pipelines, flumes, canals, ditches, aqueducts, telephone lines and electrical systems — in a word, utilities. It acts in a quasi-legislative fashion to adopt rules, regulations and guidance for county tax assessors, and as an administrative body that determines capitalization rates, classifies properties, sets the electrical energy surcharge rate and administers taxes on sales, fuel, alcoholic beverages, cigarettes, insurance, timber, hazardous waste, telephone services and city, county and transit district sales and use taxes. The board collects about $26.5 billion in taxes each year for state and local governments.

But the board frequently is called an anachronism, outmoded, outdated and outpaced by events it governs. Proposals have been advanced to consolidate it with the Franchise Tax Board and create one tax agency. But the only such measure ever to get to a governor's desk was vetoed in 1994 by Pete Wilson.

The board consists of state Controller Kathleen Connell and four members elected to four-year terms. Each member represents one quarter of the state, or roughly 8 million people.

In the past, board membership had been a political backwater, albeit a well-paid one, where members could expect to win re-election and serve comfortably until retirement. But in the 1980s, some board members began to demonstrate a bent toward using the job as a rung on the ladder to higher office. Some accepted political contributions from public utilities and other donors who later won favorable board consideration on tax appeals. Three of the board's five seats gained new occupants in the 1994 elections, with member Matt Fong moving to become state treasurer. One new Democrat, Johan Klehs, and one new Republican, Dean Andal, won election to the board in 1994. With Democrat Kathleen Connell occupying the ex officio seat held by California's controller, Democrats comprise a majority of the board.

Dean Andal
2nd District

Dean Andal, a former Assembly member from Stockton, defeated Democratic state Sen. Robert Presley in 1994 to win a Board of Equalization seat that is, as Andal put it, at "the bottom of the political food chain." His election, however, didn't mean he had abandoned his interest in legislative politics.

Elected to the Legislature as an anti-tax crusader, Andal had been at the center of controversy in the Assembly shortly after defeating Democrat Patti Garamendi to win that seat in a 1991 special election. In 1993, he was thwarted in his bid to become vice chairman of the Assembly Ways and Means Committee when Republican Paul Horcher accepted an ap-

Dean Andal

Board of Equalization districts

Percent of Democrats and Republicans in each district

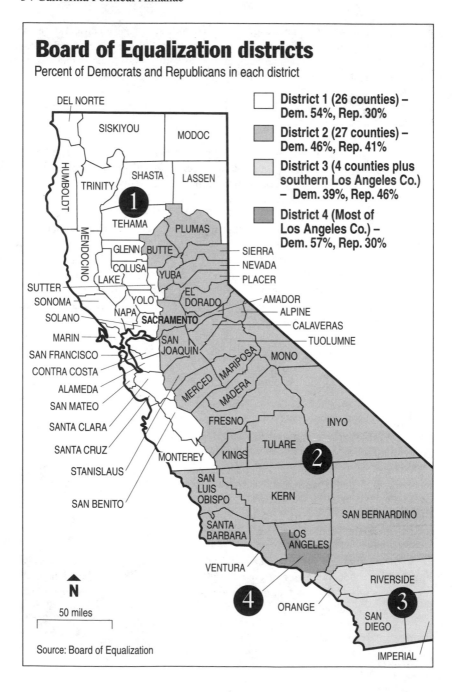

District 1 (26 counties) –
Dem. 54%, Rep. 30%

District 2 (27 counties) –
Dem. 46%, Rep. 41%

District 3 (4 counties plus
southern Los Angeles Co.)
– Dem. 39%, Rep. 46%

District 4 (Most of
Los Angeles Co.) –
Dem. 57%, Rep. 30%

DEL NORTE
SISKIYOU
MODOC
HUMBOLDT
TRINITY
SHASTA
LASSEN
TEHAMA
PLUMAS
GLENN BUTTE
SIERRA
COLUSA
NEVADA
LAKE
YUBA
PLACER
MENDOCINO
SUTTER
YOLO
EL DORADO
AMADOR
SONOMA
SOLANO
NAPA
SACRAMENTO
ALPINE
CALAVERAS
MARIN
SAN JOAQUIN
TUOLUMNE
SAN FRANCISCO
MARIPOSA
MONO
CONTRA COSTA
ALAMEDA
MERCED
MADERA
SAN MATEO
SANTA CLARA
FRESNO
INYO
SANTA CRUZ
TULARE
MONTEREY
KINGS
STANISLAUS
SAN LUIS OBISPO
KERN
SAN BENITO
SAN BERNARDINO
SANTA BARBARA
LOS ANGELES
VENTURA
RIVERSIDE
ORANGE
SAN DIEGO
IMPERIAL

N
50 miles

Source: Board of Equalization

pointment to the post from Assembly Speaker Willie Brown. Following Horcher's decision after the 1994 elections to leave the GOP and to support Brown's re-election as speaker, Andal leapt into the Assembly leadership fray by leading a recall effort against Mike Machado, the Democrat who won Andal's seat in the Legislature. Andal was rumored as a potential candidate to replace Machado should Republicans need the vote to gain control in the Assembly.

The board district Andal won consists of these counties: Alpine, Amador, Butte, Calaveras, El Dorado, Fresno, Inyo, Kern, Kings, the northern portion of Los Angeles, Madera, Mariposa, Merced, Mono, Nevada, Placer, Plumas, Sacramento, San Bernardino, San Joaquin, San Luis Obispo, Santa Barbara, Sierra, Stanislaus, Tulare, Tuolumne, Ventura and Yuba.

PERSONAL: elected 1991; born October 3, 1959, in Salem, Ore; home, Stockton; education, A.A. Delta College, B.A. UC San Diego; wife, Karie, son Patrick.

CAREER: owner of a communications company; San Joaquin County Board of Education; California assemblyman, 1991-1994.

OFFICES: 450 N St., Sacramento 95814, (916) 445-4664; Suite D, 7540 Shoreline Dr., Stockton 95219, (209) 473-6579.

Kathleen Connell
Member-at-Large

State Controller Kathleen Connell is an ex officio voting member of the board. Her biographical information appears earlier in this chapter.

Ernest J. Dronenburg Jr.
3rd District

Ernest J. Dronenburg Jr., the longest serving member of the board, is a staunch defender of the system it represents, arguing that citizens prefer elected rather than appointed tax officials. He was the chief architect of the Taxpayers' Bill of Rights, which the Legislature enacted in 1989 to give taxpayers better standing when appealing assessments before the board. It has been called the most significant reform in board operations in this century.

When he was elected in 1978, Dronenburg became the first Republican to sit on the board in 24 years. Previously, he had worked as an auditor and field audit supervisor in the board's business taxes department. In off-hours, he and two friends started a

Ernest Dronenburg Jr.

racquetball equipment manufacturing and distribution firm in San Diego. He served as president of the manufacturing company and vice president of the distribution company until he resigned after his election to the board.

In the mid-1980s, Dronenburg became a director of Seapointe Savings & Loan, which became one of the nation's fastest and most spectacular S&L failures. When state and federal regulators seized it in May 1986, the S&L had been in business for only 13 months. It had never hired a loan officer and had lost $24 million gambling investors' money on bond futures. Dronenburg, nonetheless, has never suffered politically for the bank failure.

Active in Republican politics, Dronenburg also has been president of the Federation of Tax Administrators and an executive board member of the National Tax Association. He has been active in issues involving women, disabled people and his Christian faith. His wife, Kathy, is an appointed member of the state Board of Education. Under term limits, Dronenburg is now in his final term on the board, representing these counties: Imperial, Orange, Riverside, San Diego and a southern piece of Los Angeles County.

PERSONAL: elected 1978; born Aug. 9, 1943, in Washington, D.C.; home, East San Diego County; B.S. San Diego State University; wife, Kathy; three daughters.

CAREER: auditor and field audit supervisor, state Board of Equalization, 1971-1978; small business owner.

OFFICES: 450 N St., Sacramento 95814, (916) 445-5713; Suite 1709, 110 W. C St., San Diego 92101, (619) 237-7844.

Johan Klehs
1st District

With a push from the passage of term limits, Johan Klehs abandoned his 12-year Assembly career in 1994 for a seat on the Board of Equalization. Generally a liberal legislator, he had proposed a constitutional amendment to give tax credits to individuals and corporations who contribute toward research for an AIDS vaccine, and proposed closing corporate tax loopholes to fund anti-drug programs. He also carried legislation in 1994 to abolish the Franchise Tax Board and transfer its powers and duties to the board on which he now serves as chairman. It had bipartisan support, but was vetoed by Gov. Pete Wilson.

Johan Klehs

In the Legislature, Klehs quickly put to work the knowledge gained as a former aide to then-Assemblyman Bill Lockyer, moving into positions of political power. As head of the Assembly Revenue and Taxation Committee, he dealt with some of the same state tax issues that will come his way on the board. The first district seat remained vacant for nearly 28 months after

Democrat William Bennett resigned, as Gov. Pete Wilson struggled without success to find a Republican who could win confirmation from legislative Democrats. The district's new boundaries encompass the northern top of the state and the Bay Area. The district consists of the following counties: Alameda, Colusa, Contra Costa, Del Norte, Glenn, Humboldt, Lake, Lassen, Marin, Mendocino, Modoc, Monterey, Napa, San Benito, San Francisco, San Mateo, Santa Clara, Santa Cruz, Shasta, Siskiyou, Solano, Sonoma, Sutter, Tehama, Trinity and Yolo.

PERSONAL: elected 1994; born June 27, 1952 in Alameda, Calif.; home, Castro Valley; education, B.A. and M.A., CSU Hayward; attended Harvard University John F. Kennedy School of Government; single.

CAREER: account executive for a direct-mail advertising firm; San Leandro City Council 1978-1982; legislative assistant to Assemblyman Bill Lockyer 1973-1976; California assemblyman 1982-1994.

OFFICES: 450 N St., Sacramento 95814, (916) 445-4081; 22320 Foothills Blvd., Hayward 94541 (510) 247-2125.

Brad Sherman
4th District

Brad Sherman is a tax lawyer and certified public accountant with a Harvard law degree who accurately refers to himself as a bit on the nerdish side. He won the Democratic nomination for the job in 1990 with an upset over former Assemblyman Lou Papan.

Sherman, now in his last term on the board, had hoped to maneuver his way into running for controller in 1994, but he ran into trouble as other Democrats began to position themselves for various races. At one point, to protect himself as redistricting threw him into the same board district as Matt Fong, Sherman may have set a dubious record by filing "intent-to run" papers for four offices at once. Ultimately, he settled for another four years on the board.

Brad Sherman

Sherman ran for the board as a political reformer, saying he wanted to give people more confidence in the board and in the property-tax process. But he isn't as apolitical as his self-effacing manner and campaign rhetoric would suggest. One of his first actions as a board member was to put three of his campaign workers and a campaign aide to Democratic gubernatorial candidate Dianne Feinstein on the state payroll as his transition team.

Sherman, who served as a board member of California Common Cause during 1986-1989, is a party activist who estimates he has walked precincts, registered voters, stuffed envelopes and worked in other capacities in more than 40 campaigns in 20 years. He also worked as an intern for Secretary of State Jerry Brown in 1973.

Sherman, who was replaced by Johan Klehs as board chairman in 1995, was one of the board's most active chairmen, working hard on all the board's arcane tax issues and establishing a record for fairness.

His district includes the southern and central sections of Los Angeles County.

PERSONAL: elected 1990; born Oct. 24, 1954; education, B.A. UCLA, J.D. Harvard University; single.

CAREER: private practice in tax, business and estate law; certified public accountant.

OFFICES: 450 N St., Sacramento 95814, (916) 445-4154; Suite 210, 901 Wilshire Blvd., Santa Monica 90401, (310) 451-5777.

4

The California judiciary

In 1986, a California electorate, enraged by the state Supreme Court's failure to affirm death sentences, ousted three sitting justices. Today, with a conservative majority appointed by Republican Govs. George Deukmejian and Pete Wilson securely in control and regularly upholding verdicts in capital cases, the court has entered a period notable for its lack of controversy.

Chief Justice Malcolm Lucas did weather a storm in November 1993 over his personal travel and excessive absences from the court after the San Francisco Chronicle reported that he had accepted trips to Thailand, Austria and Hawaii from a Lloyds of London subsidiary and lawyers representing insurance companies. A review of Supreme Court files showed that the groups had filed eight petitions with the court since 1987. The trips totaled more than $11,000 in travel expenses and legal experts raised questions of possible ethical violations.

The California Code of Judicial Conduct allows judges to receive compensation and travel reimbursement "if the source of such payments does not give the appearance of influencing the judge's performance of judicial duties." Lucas was cleared in early 1994 of any misconduct by the state Commission on Judicial Performance, which said the funding did not influence his decisions or interfere with his performance on the court.

Nonetheless, Lucas' actions led to new legislation to strengthen ethical standards for judges by setting $250 limits on travel and gifts. The commission's report also drew criticism from one court scholar. "The commission habitually seems more interested in defending judges than in policing their conduct," said Stephen Barnett of the University of California's Boalt Hall School of Law.

But for the most part the court has settled into a low-profile role following the ouster of Chief Justice Rose Elizabeth Bird and Associate Justices Cruz Reynoso and Joseph Grodin. All had been appointed by former Democratic Gov. Jerry Brown, and all were targets of demands by crime victims groups for swift executions.

"We need the death penalty. We don't need Rose Bird," Deukmejian told audiences as he campaigned for re-election in 1986. Voters agreed, handing him the opportunity to replace the three liberal jurists with conservatives.

By the time Deukmejian left office in 1991 he had secured the sweeping impact on the state's judiciary that he had sought to exert when he became governor. As a state senator in 1978 Deukmejian had authored the law reinstating the death penalty. Later as attorney general he cited the governor's ability to appoint judges as his principal reason for wanting the job. Deukmejian had appointed a majority of the Supreme Court justices and about two-thirds of the roughly 1,500 sitting judges in lower courts by the end of his second four-year term in office. Most of his appointees were white males from prosecutorial backgrounds.

To fill the Supreme Court vacancies created by the 1986 election Deukmejian selected three Court of Appeal justices — John Arguelles, David Eagleson and Marcus Kaufman. The governor elevated Associate Justice Malcolm Lucas, his former Long Beach law partner, to chief justice. All three of Deukmejian's new associate justices stayed scarcely long enough to fatten their pensions with the salary base provided by the state's top court. They were replaced by Associate Justices Joyce Kennard, Marvin Baxter and Armand Arabian.

The ousted justices did not go quietly. In the emotional campaign to remove Bird and the others, crime victims groups argued that the justices were allowing their personal views against capital punishment to influence their interpretations of the law. Bird, the subject of controversy since her 1977 appointment as the first woman on the court, televised campaign ads, something previously unheard of in a Supreme Court election. She attacked Deukmejian for using the politics of death to advance his career.

Lucas, however, described the circumstances that led to Bird's departure and his elevation as "some very unusual times" and said the court would not preside over a "rush to death." The Lucas court has given more latitude to trial courts and has been less likely to reverse cases for what prosecutors had argued for years were inconsequential errors.

Although the death penalty was reinstated in 1978, legal challenges prevented anyone from being executed until convicted double murderer Robert Alton Harris died in San Quentin's gas chamber on April 21, 1992. Sentenced to death for the 1978 murders of two San Diego teenagers, Harris was the first person executed by the state in 25 years. The last had been police killer Aaron Mitchell in 1967. In 1993, multiple killer David Edwin Mason was executed after saying he was willing to be put to death to pay for a life of crime. There were no executions in 1994.

In 1993, the court issued an opinion with widespread implications for California's political process, refusing to revive a voter-approved initiative intended to reform the financing of legislative campaigns. Lucas wrote the lead opinion that buried Proposition 68, arguing that a rival measure, Proposition 73, remained the law despite the fact that the courts had struck down the contribution limits it sought to establish. The court's dissenters — Justices Arabian, Kennard and Stanley Mosk — argued that the action killed "the only real chance at reforming the link between money and politics that the voters of California have had in a generation."

The decision, which both the state Republican and Democratic parties had urged, was a factor cited by state Sen. Tom Hayden in his decision to mount a surprise primary campaign for governor in 1994. "The failure of our party to take a strong stand in favor of fundamental campaign finance and lobbying reform," Hayden charged, "is a serious moral and political failure."

The court weighed in on another political issue in 1992, siding with Wilson in the state's redistricting fight. A six-member majority led by Lucas established legislative and congressional district lines that at the time seemed certain to level the political playing field for Republicans and undercut the Democrats' decade-long dominance. The new lines provided little immediate benefit for the GOP, as Democrats capitalized on Republican divisiveness and Bill Clinton's coattails to make an unexpectedly good showing in state races in 1992. But it helped the GOP capture a majority of seats in the state Assembly two years later. The chief justice earns $133,459 a year. The salary for associate justices is $127,267.

State Supreme Court Justices

303 Second Street, South Tower, San Francisco 94107; (415) 396-9400.

Chief Justice Ronald George 5-96 See next page

~~Malcolm Millar Lucas~~

Lucas, the 26th chief justice of the court, was Gov. George Deukmejian's first appointee to the state Supreme Court in 1984. A longtime resident of Long Beach, Lucas practiced law there with Deukmejian from 1962 to 1967. He was then appointed by Gov. Ronald Reagan to the Los Angeles County Superior Court and was named by President Richard Nixon to the U.S. District Court in Los Angeles in 1971.

The Berkeley native earned both his undergraduate and law degrees from the University of Southern California. His great-grandfather was a two-term governor of Ohio and later the first territorial governor of Iowa.

Malcolm M. Lucas

PERSONAL: born April 19, 1927, in Berkeley; wife Joan Fisher; children Gregory and Lisa.

CAREER: appointed by Deukmejian 1987; associate justice, state Supreme Court 1984-1987; U.S. District Court, Central District of California 1971-1984; Superior Court judge, Los Angeles County 1967-1971; private law practice 1954-1967.

Stanley Mosk

Stanley Mosk

Mosk, who was state attorney general when Gov. Edmund G. "Pat" Brown named him to the court in 1964, was widely considered the front-runner to move up when Chief Justice Donald Wright retired in 1977. But Pat Brown's son, Gov. Jerry Brown, instead chose Rose Bird, a close friend and political ally with no prior judicial experience. The philosophically liberal Mosk had been one of four state Supreme Court justices originally targeted for defeat by conservative organizations. But crime victims groups ultimately opted not to pursue Mosk, and he is now the court's senior member and the only Democratic appointee.

Mosk earned his bachelor's and doctorate of law degrees at the University of Chicago. Before his election as state attorney general he served as a Los Angeles County Superior Court judge.

PERSONAL: born Sept. 4, 1912, in San Antonio, Texas; wife Edna Mitchell; son Richard Mitchell.

CAREER: appointed by Gov. Pat Brown 1964; state attorney general 1959-1964; Superior Court judge, Los Angeles County 1943-1959; executive secretary to Gov. Culbert Olson 1939-1943; private law practice 1935-1939.

Ronald George Chief Justice

Ronald George

George, a conservative law-and-order judge who played a pivotal role in the celebrated Hillside Strangler case, was Gov. Pete Wilson's first appointee to the court. The seat became vacant when Justice Allen Broussard announced in early 1991 that he intended to retire, leaving court observers to speculate that he had grown lonely as the court's only African American and the only remaining appointee of Gov. Jerry Brown. Wilson's choice left the court without either an African American or Hispanic for the first time since 1977. Citing George's top rating from the State Bar commission that evaluates judicial nominees,

Wilson said it would have been dishonest and unfair to ignore that evidence and appoint a minority to the post.

Educated at Princeton University and Stanford University Law School, George was seen in Los Angeles legal circles as a brilliant and ambitious judge who had long coveted a seat on the state's highest court. As a Superior Court judge in 1981 he rejected a motion by then-Los Angeles County District Attorney John Van de Kamp to drop murder charges against Hillside Strangler suspect Angelo Buono. Van de Kamp later conceded his decision not to prosecute Buono for the murders of 10 women was a mistake; Buono ultimately was convicted on nine of 10 murder counts with George presiding at the trial.

PERSONAL: born March 11, 1940, in Los Angeles; wife Barbara; sons Eric, Andrew and Christopher.

CAREER: appointed by Gov. Pete Wilson 1991; associate justice 2nd District Court of Appeal 1987-1991; Superior Court judge, Los Angeles County 1977-1987; Municipal Court judge, Los Angeles 1972-1977; deputy state attorney general 1965-1972.

Kathryn Mickle Werdegar

Werdegar was nominated in 1994 by longtime friend Gov. Pete Wilson to replace retired Supreme Court Justice Edward Panelli, for whom she had served as senior staff attorney before accepting an appointment to the 1st District Court of Appeal in 1991. Werdegar had been Wilson's law school classmate at the U.C. Berkeley's Boalt Hall, and although she did not formally tutor him there the future governor said he was the beneficiary when the two studied together.

The first woman editor of the University of California Law Review, she later transferred to George

Kathryn M. Werdegar

Washington University Law School, where she graduated first in her class. The author of a criminal procedure bench book for trial court judges, Werdegar came to be known as a legal scholar whose judicial leanings ranged from conservative to moderate.

Her career began in the U.S. Department of Justice's civil rights division under Robert Kennedy, where she wrote appellate briefs, drafted civil-rights related legislation and worked to release Martin Luther King Jr. from prison.

PERSONAL: born April 5, 1936, in San Francisco; husband Dr. David Werdegar; children Maurice and Matthew.

CAREER: appointed by Gov. Wilson 1994; associate justice, 1st District Court of Appeal 1991-1994; senior staff attorney to California Supreme Court Justice Edward Panelli 1985-1991; senior staff attorney, 1st District Court of Appeal 1981-

1985; associate dean for Academic and Student Affairs and associate professor, University of San Francisco School of Law 1978-1981; attorney, California Continuing Education of the Bar 1971-1978; consultant and author California College of Trial Justices 1968-1971; special consultant, state Department of Mental Hygiene 1967-1968; associate, U.C. Berkeley Center for Study of Law and Society 1965-1967; consultant, California State Study Commission on Mental Retardation 1963-1964; legal assistant, U.S. Department of Justice civil rights division 1962-1963.

Joyce Luther Kennard

Kennard, an immigrant of Chinese-Indonesian, Dutch, Belgian and German descent, is the first Asian-born justice in the court's history. The second woman nominated for the court (the first was Bird), Kennard was the lone woman serving until Werdegar's appointment in 1994. Kennard grew up in the Japanese-occupied Dutch East Indies, where her father died in a Japanese internment camp. She faced further adversity at age 16, when she lost her leg to amputation as she attended high school in Holland.

Joyce L. Kennard

At age 20, Kennard immigrated alone to the United States and worked as a secretary for several years before her mother's death left her with enough money to pursue her education. She became a naturalized citizen in 1967 in Los Angeles, where Kennard — who had never used a telephone or seen a television set until she was a teenager — earned bachelor's and master's degrees in public administration and her law degree from the University of Southern California. As a trial judge with a reputation as a tough sentencer, Kennard was appointed to the state Supreme Court by Gov. George Deukmejian. She succeeded Associate Justice John A. Arguelles, who retired.

PERSONAL: born May 6, 1941, in West Java, Indonesia; husband Robert Kennard.

CAREER: appointed by Gov. Deukmejian 1989; Superior Court judge, Los Angeles County 1987-1989; Municipal Court judge, Los Angeles Judicial District 1986-1987; senior attorney for former Associate Justice Edwin F. Beach, 2nd District Court of Appeal 1979-1986; deputy attorney general, California Department of Justice, Los Angeles 1975-1979.

Armand Arabian

Arabian, a longtime friend of Gov. George Deukmejian, was the first Armenian American to be named to the court. Appointed to replace Associate Justice Marcus M. Kaufman, a Deukmejian appointee who served just three years, Arabian has pledged to remain in his job for at least eight years. An outspoken and conservative jurist who is a recreational parachutist in his leisure time, Arabian has won a reputation as a judicial maverick. As a trial judge in a rape case he once refused to give the jury the instruction, required at the time, that testimony of rape victims should bc viewed skeptically. When the case reached the state Supreme Court the justices chided Arabian for failing to comply with precedent. But they then ordered the instruction be barred in all future cases. His action in that case, coupled with his extensive writings on rape law reform, won Arabian the strong backing of women attorneys at his confirmation hearing for the state's highest court.

Armand Arabian

He has law degrees from both the Southern California Law School and Boston University in addition to a bachelor's degree from BU.

PERSONAL: born December 12, 1934, in New York City; wife Nancy Megurian; children Allison and Robert.

CAREER: appointed by Gov. Deukmejian 1990; associate justice, 2nd District Court of Appeal, Division Three, 1983-1990; Superior Court judge, Los Angeles County 1973-1983; Municipal Court judge, Los Angeles Judicial District 1972-1973; private law practice, 1963-1972; deputy district attorney, Los Angeles County 1962-1963.

Marvin Ray Baxter

As appointments secretary to Gov. George Deukmejian, one of Baxter's chicf responsibilities was recommending judges. As Deukmejian's second term drew to a close, Baxter became a nominee himself, accepting an appointment to the 5th District Court of Appeal in Fresno. In 1990, he became the second Armenian American appointed to the state Supreme Court, replacing retiring Justice David Eagleson.

Baxter, who was co-chairman of Deukmejian's 1982 campaign for governor, grew up in a farming community outside Fresno. He has a bachelor's degree from Fresno State College and a law degree from Hastings College of Law.

Marvin Ray Baxter

PERSONAL: born January 9, 1940, in Fowler, Calif.; wife Jane Pippert; children Laura and Brent.

CAREER: appointed by Gov. Deukmejian 1990; associate justice, 5th District

Court of Appeal 1988-1990; governor's appointments secretary, 1983-1988; private law practice 1969-1983; deputy district attorney, Fresno County 1967-1969.

California Appellate Court Justices

Court of Appeal, 1st Appellate District, Division One, 303 Second Street, South Tower, San Francisco 94107; (415) 396-9666.

Presiding Justice Gary E. Strankman; Associate Justices Robert L. Dossee, William A. Newsom and William D. Stein.

Court of Appeal, 1st Appellate District, Division Two, 303 Second Street, South Tower, San Francisco 94107; (415) 396-9666.

Presiding Justice J. Anthony Kline; Associate Justices John E. Benson, Michael J. Phelan and Jerome A. Smith.

Court of Appeal, 1st Appellate District, Division Three, 303 Second Street, South Tower, San Francisco 94107; (415) 396-9666.

Presiding Justice Clinton W. White; Associate Justices Ming W. Chin, Robert W. Merrill and Carol A. Corrigan.

Court of Appeal, 1st Appellate District, Division Four, 303 Second Street, South Tower, San Francisco 94107; (415) 396-9666.

Presiding Justice Carl West Anderson; Associate Justices James F. Perley, Marcel Poche and Timothy A. Reardon.

Court of Appeal, 1st Appellate District, Division Five, 303 Second Street, South Tower, San Francisco 94107; (415) 396-9666.

Presiding Justice J. Clinton Peterson; Associate Justices Zerne P. Haning III and Donald B. King.

Court of Appeal, 2nd Appellate District, Division One, 300 South Spring St., Los Angeles 90013; (213) 897-2307.

Presiding Justice Vaino H. Spencer; Associate Justices William A. Masterson, Reuben A. Ortega and Miriam A. Vogel.

Court of Appeal, 2nd Appellate District, Division Two, 300 South Spring St., Los Angeles 90013; (213) 897-2307.

Presiding Justice Roger W. Boren; Associate Justices Morio L. Fukuto, Donald N. Gates and Michael G. Nott.

Court of Appeal, 2nd Appellate District, Division Three, 300 South Spring St., Los Angeles 90013; (213) 897-2307.

Presiding Justice Joan Dempsey Klein; Associate Justices H. Walter Croskey, Edward A. Hinz Jr. and Patti S. Kitching.

Court of Appeal, 2nd Appellate District, Division Four, 300 South Spring St., Los Angeles 90013; (213) 897-2307.

Presiding Justice Arleigh Woods; Associate Justices Norman L. Epstein, J. Gary Hastings and Charles S. Vogel.

Court of Appeal, 2nd Appellate District, Division Five, 300 South Spring St., Los Angeles 90013; (213) 897-2307.

Presiding Justice Paul A. Turner; Associate Justices Orville A. Armstrong, Margaret M. Grignon and Ramona Godoy Perez.

Court of Appeal, 2nd Appellate District, Division Six, 1280 South Victoria, Room 201, Ventura 93003; (805) 654-4502.

Presiding Justice Steven J. Stone; Associate Justices Arthur Gilbert and Kenneth R. Yegan.

Court of Appeal, 2nd Appellate District, Division Seven, 300 South Spring St., Los Angeles 90013; (213) 897-2307.

Presiding Justice Mildred L. Lillie; Associate Justices Earl Johnson Jr. and Fred Woods.

Court of Appeal, 3rd Appellate District, 914 Capitol Mall, Sacramento 95814; (916) 653-0310.

Presiding Justice Robert K. Puglia; Associate Justices Coleman A. Blease, Rodney Davis, Fred Morrison, George Nicholson, Vance W. Raye, Arthur G. Scotland, Richard M. Sims III, Keith F. Sparks and Janice Rogers Brown.

Court of Appeal, 4th Appellate District, Division One, 750 B Street, Suite 500, San Diego 92101; (619) 237-6558.

Presiding Justice Daniel J. Kremer; Associate Justices Patricia D. Benke, Charles W. Froehlich Jr., Richard D. Huffman, Gilbert Nares, William L. Todd Jr., Howard B. Wiener and Don R. Work.

Court of Appeal, 4th Appellate District, Division Two, 303 West Fifth Street, San Bernardino 92401; (714) 383-4442.

Presiding Justice Manuel A. Ramirez; Associate Justices Howard M. Dabney, Thomas E. Hollenhorst, Art W. McKinster and Robert J. Timlin.

Court of Appeal, 4th Appellate District, Division Three, P.O. Box 1378, Santa Ana 92701; (714) 558-6779.

Presiding Justice David G. Sills; Associate Justices Thomas F. Crosby Jr., Henry J. Moore Jr., Sheila Prell Sonenshine and Edward J. Wallin.

Court of Appeal, 5th Appellate District, P.O. Box 45013, Fresno 93718; (209) 445-5491.

Presiding Justice Hollis G. Best; Associate Justices James A. Ardaiz, Tim S. Buckley, Nikolas J. Dibiaso, Thomas A. Harris, Robert L. Martin, William A. Stone, James F. Thaxter and Steven M. Vartabedian.

Court of Appeal, 6th Appellate District, 333 West Santa Clara Street, San Jose 95113; (408) 277-1004.

Presiding Justice Christopher C. Cottle; Associate Justices P. Bamattre-Manoukian, Franklin D. Elia, Nathan D. Mihara, Eugene M. Premo and William M. Wunderlich.

5

The big bad bureaucracy

With 268,548 employees, the state bureaucracy that carries out the decrees of the governor and the Legislature still represents less than 1 percent of California's population. There are, of course, another 250,000 county employees, hefty school district and special district payrolls and a substantial sprinkling of federal workers toiling at the countless chores aimed at keeping the state's people educated and healthy, its streets and workplaces safe and its commerce bustling. And behind all of them stands a virtual army of nonprofit and profit-making entrepreneurs hired to undertake the state's pursuits — clinics, emergency rooms, hospitals, janitorial services, security specialists, mental health programs, drug treatment centers and a host of councils, commissions, think tanks and task forces.

Yet taken together, they hardly represent the threat to freedom or the drain on resources that some politicians like to portray. While bureaucrats may be wrapped in red tape and devoted to the evenhanded distribution of blame for their failings, their numbers are not overwhelming.

Nonetheless, the first task of any governor is to tame the previous administration's bureaucracy and to put those countless workers to his or her own use. The civil service system is designed to protect taxpayers against political exploitation of the work force, but a carefully tailored system of civil service exemptions and gubernatorial appointments gives the chief executive the authority to take the reins of government in hand.

When Gov. Pete Wilson took office in 1991, for instance, he had approximately 550 exempt positions to fill in his executive offices and another 100 or so on state boards and commissions, roughly the same as his predecessor, George Deukmejian. In addition, governors can generally reshape the state's judiciary according to their views as appointments become available — in all a significant pool of patronage that becomes theirs to dispense.

Wilson, like most governors before him, has used his patronage power to find jobs for political supporters and former Republican officeholders who lost elections or decided not to seek re-election. Within days of his Nov. 6, 1991, victory, for example, Wilson named defeated Republican state Treasurer Thomas Hayes, a respected Capitol veteran, his director of finance. The appointment of Hayes, who eventually left government service for the private sector, didn't raise many eyebrows, but others have.

After Wilson's hand-picked successor in the U.S. Senate, Republican John Seymour, lost to former San Francisco Mayor Dianne Feinstein in November, 1992, Wilson appointed Seymour, a former state senator and a Realtor by trade, to a $98,076-a-year job as executive director of the state Housing Finance Agency, a small state office that provides loans to low- and moderate-income home buyers. Seymour left the agency in January 1995. About the same time as Seymour's appointment, Wilson named former Republican state Sen. Ed Davis, who did not seek re-election to his Valencia-area Senate seat, to a part-time $25,500-a-year job on the Alcoholic Beverage Control Appeals Board. And he picked former GOP Rep. John Rousselot, who lost his attempt in November 1992 to return to Congress, for a $76,872-a-year job on the state Board of Prison Terms. In 1993, Wilson named a

	THE STATE WORK FORCE		
Year	Governor	Employees	Employees per 1,000 population
1976-77	Brown	213,795	9.7
1977-78	Brown	221,251	9.9
1978-79	Brown	218,530	9.6
1979-80	Brown	220,193	9.5
1980-81	Brown	225,567	9.5
1981-82	Brown	228,813	9.4
1982-83	Transition	228,489	9.2
1983-84	Deukmejian	226,695	9.0
1984-85	Deukmejian	229,845	8.9
1985-86	Deukmejian	229,641	8.7
1986-87	Deukmejian	232,927	8.6
1987-88	Deukmejian	237,761	8.6
1988-89	Deukmejian	248,173	8.8
1989-90	Deukmejian	254,589	8.8
1990-91	Transition	260,622	8.7
1991-92	Wilson	261,713	8.5
1992-93	Wilson	268,419	8.6
1993-94	Wilson	268,727	8.4
1994-95	Wilson	268,548	8.3

former Cabinet member, Carl Covitz, to the California Commission on Government Organization and Economy. More commonly known as the Little Hoover Commission, the panel is charged with investigating government operations and recommending cost savings. Covitz, a millionaire developer and longtime Republican fund-raiser, had resigned his job as Wilson's secretary of business, transportation and housing after allegations that he treated state employees as servants and used California Highway Patrol officers as personal chauffers.

Wilson also came under fire for hiring two political consultants onto his gubernatorial staff despite the state's weakened fiscal condition. First, he hired veteran Republican political consultant Joe Shumate, who was given the title of deputy chief of staff and a $95,052-a-year salary. His job was primarily to figure out ways to elect more Republicans to the Legislature in 1992, an objective met by failure. Even so, a little more than a month after Election Day in 1992, Wilson hired Joe Rodota, then a 32-year-old Sacramento political consultant whose specialty is researching dirt on Democrats. Rodota was given the title of Cabinet secretary and a $94,813-a-year salary. Both Shumate and Rodota left their government posts in 1994 in order to work on Wilson's re-election campaign. Rodota returned to the governor's Cabinet after the election while Shumate has remained in the political consulting business.

Leaders of the state Senate and Assembly also have considerable patronage to dispense. All employees who work for the Legislature technically work for the Rules Committees in each house, which are controlled by the majority party. In addition, the Assembly speaker and Senate president pro tem also make appointments to a number of boards and commissions, some of which pay handsomely. The Senate appointments are made through the Rules Committee, which is chaired by the Senate president pro tem. In December 1994, that committee made headlines around the state when it voted 4-0, with one abstention, to name former Senate President David Roberti, D-Van Nuys, to a four-year seat on the Unemployment Insurance Appeals Board. Roberti, who had been forced out of the Senate by term limits and then defeated in a bid for the Democratic Party nomination for state treasurer in June 1994, will be paid $97,088 a year in his new job. The post Roberti filled was previously held by Debra Berg, wife of Roberti's chief staff person in the Senate, Cliff Berg.

WHITTLING AT THE BUREAUCRACY

The actual size of the state government work force is measured in personnel-years, which represent the number of full-time positions or their equivalent. For example, a position that was filled only half of the year would represent 0.5 personnel-years, while three half-time jobs that were filled would represent 1.5 personnel-years. The concept sounds simple enough, but the politicians have been able to find ingenious ways to manipulate the numbers to their advantage.

In 1983, for example, the state work force stood at 228,489 personnel-years —

a slight reduction from the year before. Although growth in the work force had been lagging behind the state's population growth for years — a product of the post-Proposition 13 budget crunch — and even behind the growth in state operating expenses, incoming Gov. George Deukmejian was determined to pare back the bureaucracy even more. His budget called for a reduction of 1,016 personnel-years, a half-percent cut. He wanted to achieve the cut while increasing the state's prison and juvenile corrections work force by 1,078 personnel-years. Critics argued that the staff cutbacks represented reductions in service to the state's neediest people, the poor and unemployed. The administration insisted it was trimming fat, not muscle, and that services remained intact or even improved. In the succeeding years, Deukmejian proposed cutback after cutback in state personnel, all the while

BARGAINING AGENTS AND BARGAINING UNITS

Union	Employees Represented
California State Employees' Association	
Administrative, financial and staff services	34,372
Education and library	2,394
Office and allied	34,456
Professional scientific	2,287
Printing trades	729
Custodial and services	4,459
Registered nurses	2,928
Medical and social services support	2,036
Misc. educational, maritime, library, consultants	566
Association of California State Attorneys	
(attorneys and hearing officers)	2,698
California Association of Highway Patrolmen	5,028
California Correctional Peace Officers Assn.	21,273
California Union of Safety Employees	6,082
California Department of Forestry Employees	
Association (firefighters)	3,996
Professional Engineers in California Government	7,879
California Association of Professional Scientists	2,287
International Union of Operating Engineers	
(stationary engineers)	737
(craft and maintenance)	10,639
Union of American Physicians and Dentists	1,317
California Association of Psychiatric Technicians	6,882
American Federation of State, County and Municipal Employees	
(health and social services, professional)	3,499

balancing the reductions with increases for the growing correctional system. As the state's population continued to balloon, the work force as measured as a ratio of employees per 1,000 residents declined.

Wilson has continued efforts to cut that ratio. While total state employment in 1993-94 was up by 52,800 from 10 years ago, the ratio of employees per 1,000 residents declined from 9.2 to 8.6 over the same time. In his budget proposal for the 1993-94 fiscal year, Wilson proposed chopping the ratio to 8.4 employees per 1,000 residents. A similar ratio is estimated for 1994-95. In fact, Wilson has proposed eliminating several agencies — the Franchise Tax Board, State Allocation Board, the Office of Savings and Loan, the California Energy Commission, the State Lands Commission, the Agricultural Labor Relations Board, the Commission on State Finance and district agricultural associations. Wilson has also pushed major consolidations and has shed advisory boards and commissions that were largely inactive or outdated. One panel that Wilson cut, along with its nine-member working staff, was the Commission on State Finance, which forecast economic trends and provided analyses of the governor's budget proposals. Eliminated in early 1994, it was chaired by the Democrat who later challenged Wilson's re-election bid, state Treasurer Kathleen Brown. She complained that her panel's demise was politically motivated, but Wilson said its function was performed by other state agencies and that its closure would save taxpayers $800,000 a year.

In the midst of the state's budget woes in 1991, it was the governor's appointment power that allowed Wilson to strongly suggest to his top appointees that they voluntarily take a 5 percent pay cut. Wilson also took the voluntary cut. But the days have long since passed when state employees depended upon the largess of the governor and the Legislature to increase their pay or improve benefits. Under the Ralph C. Dills Act of 1977, the administration now negotiates memorandums of understanding on working conditions and wages with 21 recognized bargaining units, represented by 12 employee associations. The MOUs are legal contracts that may remain in force for as long as three years.

MAJOR AGENCIES AND DEPARTMENTS

California's bureaucracy includes everything from the Abrasive Blasting Advisory Committee to the Yuba-Sutter Fair Board. There are commissions on the status of women, government efficiency, water and heritage preservation, councils on the arts and job training, and offices for small business, tourism and community relations. The most significant offices, however, fall under the 11 umbrella agencies and departments whose leaders comprise the governor's Cabinet.

BUSINESS, TRANSPORTATION, HOUSING AGENCY

This superagency oversees 11 departments dealing with housing, business and regulatory functions and transportation, including the California Highway Patrol, the state Department of Transportation (Caltrans) and the Department of Motor

Vehicles. The agency employs more than 40,000 workers and has a total budget of nearly $6 billion.

For most of Gov. Wilson's first years in office, the agency's secretary was his old friend, Carl D. Covitz. A developer before his appointment, he resigned in December 1992 while under investigation for misusing government equipment and staff. In early January 1993, Wilson named Covitz's successor, Thomas Sayles, a low-profile member of the administration who had served as commissioner of the state Department of Corporations since 1991. Sayles has also headed the state's revitalization task force in Los Angeles since June 1992. But Sayles didn't last long in his Cabinet post. He resigned just

Dean Dunphy

11 months after his appointment to become vice president of public affairs for the Southern California Gas Co.

The agency is now headed by Dean Richard Dunphy, a San Diego businessman who served on the California Transportation Commission since 1991. Dunphy also served as a member of the Commission of the Californias for 10 years ending in 1977, and was a founding vice president of the U.S./Mexico Border Cities Conference during the 1970s. Salary: $115,083; Office: 801 K St., Suite 1918, Sacramento 95814, (916) 323-5400; Employees: 42,167; Fiscal '94-'95 budget: $6.4 billion (including federal funds mostly for transportation).

Department of Alcoholic Beverage Control

Licenses and regulates the manufacture, sale, purchase, possession and transportation of alcoholic beverages within the state. Director: Jay R. Stroh; Salary: $107,939; Office: 3810 Rosin Ct., Suite 150, Sacramento 95834, (916) 263-6898; Employees: 405; '94-'95 budget: $27,023,000.

Department of State Banking

Protects the public against financial loss from the failure of state-chartered banks and trust companies, including foreign banking corporations, money order or traveler's check issuers and business and industrial development corporations. Superintendent: vacant; Salary: $107,939; Office: 111 Pine St., Suite 110, San Francisco 94111, (415) 447-3535; Employees: 226; '94-'95 budget: $16,717,000.

Department of Corporations

Regulates the sale of securities, licenses brokers and agents, and oversees franchises, various financial institutions and health plans. Also controls the solicitation, marketing and sale of securities, oversees companies that lend money or receive funds from the public, and deters unscrupulous or unfair promotional schemes. Commissioner: Gary S. Mendoza; Salary: $107,939; Office: 1107 Ninth

St., Room 800, Sacramento 95814, (916) 445-6351; Employees: 417; '94-'95 budget: $33,665,000.

Department of Housing and Community Development

Guides and supports public- and private-sector efforts to provide decent homes for every Californian, administers low-income housing programs, administers standards for manufactured homes and manages the state's Proposition 77 and Proposition 84 bonded earthquake safety and homeless housing programs. Director: Tim Coyle; Salary: $107,939; Office: 1800 Third St., Suite 450, Sacramento 95814, (916) 445-4782; Employees: 632; '94-'95 budget: $142,118,000.

Department of Real Estate

Licenses real estate agents and developers, protects the public in offerings of subdivided property and investigates complaints. Commissioner: vacant; Salary: $107,939; Office: 2201 Broadway, P.O. Box 187000, Sacramento 95818, (916) 227-0782; Employees: 385; '94-'95 budget: $27,509,000.

Office of Savings and Loan

Protects the $96 billion in funds deposited in savings accounts held in state associations to ensure the saving and borrowing public is properly and legally served and to prevent conditions or practices that would threaten the safety or solvency of the institutions or be detrimental to the public. Acting Commissioner: Keith P. Bishop; Salary: $107,939; Office: 300 S. Spring St., Suite 16502, Los Angeles 90013-1204, (213) 897-8208; Employees: 3; '94-'95 budget: $464,000.

Office of Real Estate Appraisers

Regulates and licenses residential and commercial real estate appraisers. Established in accordance with federal law in 1991. Director: Robert J. West; Salary: $88,860; Office: 1225 R St., Sacramento 95814, (916) 322-2500; Employees: 33; '94-'95 budget: $3,422,000.

California Department of Transportation (Caltrans)

Builds, maintains and rehabilitates roads and bridges in accord with the State Transportation Improvement Program, manages airport and heliport safety and access, helps small- and medium-sized communities obtain and maintain air service, regulates airport noise, helps local governments provide public transportation and analyzes transportation questions. Director: James W. van Loben Sels; Salary: $107,939; Office: 1120 N St., Sacramento 95814, (916) 654-2852; Employees: 18,910; '94-'95 budget: $4.6 billion.

California Highway Patrol

Patrols state highways to ensure the safe, convenient and efficient transportation of people and goods, monitors school bus and farm labor transportation safety and oversees the transportation of hazardous wastes. Commissioner: M.J. Hannigan; Salary: $115,083; Office: 2555 First Ave., P.O. Box 942898, Sacramento 94818, (916) 657-7235; Employees: 9,134; '94-'95 budget: $721,620,000.

Department of Motor Vehicles

Registers vehicles and vessels, issues and regulates driver's licenses and oversees the manufacture, delivery and disposal of vehicles. In 1994, the department scrapped a new $49 million computer system after it was determined that it could never be made to work. Director: Frank Zolin; Salary: $107,939; Office: 2415 First Ave., Sacramento 95818, (916) 657-7016; Employees: 8,551; '94-'95 budget: $501,559,000.

Housing Finance Agency

Provides assistance to low- and moderate-income home buyers through the sale of tax-exempt bonds. Director: Maureen Higgins; Salary: $111,650; Office: 1121 L St., 7th floor, Sacramento 95814, (916) 322-3991; Employees: 147; '94-'95 budget: $12,386,000.

X TRADE AND COMMERCE AGENCY

Julie Meier Wright

This agency, whose director is a Cabinet-level appointee, was created in 1992. The new agency took over and expanded duties of the former Department of Commerce. It is the primary agency that promotes business development and job creation and retention in the state. The agency also leads state efforts to promote California exports. The World Trade Commission and international trade offices fall under its jurisdiction. Agency Secretary Julie Meier Wright served in Wilson's 1990 gubernatorial campaign as statewide chairwoman of Pro-Wilson '90, a women's coalition supporting his candidacy against now U.S. Sen. Dianne Feinstein. Prior to being appointed director of commerce in 1991, Wright worked for TRW Inc. in Redondo Beach as director of public relations for the company's space and defense sector. In an effort to help businesses, Wright has promoted what she calls a Red Team approach to bring the government and private sectors together to try to encourage business expansion. Salary: $115,083; Office: 801 K St., 17th floor, Sacramento 95814, (916) 322-1394; Employees: 229; '92-'93 budget: $46,177,000.

DEPARTMENT OF FOOD AND AGRICULTURE

This is one of three superdepartments whose directors (food, finance and industrial relations) are in the governor's Cabinet. This department is responsible for regulating — some would say protecting — California's food industry, governing everything from pest eradications to raw milk inspections. Other duties include weights and measures enforcement, protecting farm workers, keeping foreign insects and weeds out of the state or eradicating them, maintaining plant inspection stations, checking the safety of meat and poultry, predatory animal control, animal health programs and livestock drug controls, and marketing, statistical and laboratory services for agriculture.

Director Henry Voss was appointed in May 1989 after serving seven years as the chairman of the California Farm Bureau Federation. Wilson kept Voss on, but to appease critics gave responsibility for monitoring and regulating pesticides to a new California Environmental Protection Agency. That transfer put an end to the conflict of interest in which the Department of Food and Agriculture was responsible both for promoting agribusiness and regulating key elements of its safety.

Henry Voss

A farmer's son born in San Jose, Voss was forced by urbanization to move to Stanislaus County, where the Voss family currently owns 500 acres of peaches, prunes, walnuts and almonds near Ceres. Voss is a specialist in agricultural marketing and has led trade missions on behalf of California agriculture to Europe, Japan, Southeast Asia and Israel. He is a member of Sunsweet Growers, Blue Diamond Almond Growers and Tri-Valley Growers, three of the state's leading agricultural cooperatives, and is a past president of the Apricot Producers of California and past chairman of the California Apricot Advisory Board. Salary: $115,083; Office: 1220 N St., Sacramento 95814, (916) 654-0466; Employees: 1,654; '94-'95 budget: $187,351,000.

DEPARTMENT OF FINANCE

The Department of Finance serves as the governor's chief fiscal policy agency, preparing the governor's January budget proposal and his annual May budget revision, reviewing all state spending practices and proposals and administering the state budget after it has been adopted by the Legislature and signed by the governor. The department also monitors all legislation that has fiscal implications for the state and recommends which bills and budget provisions should be adopted or vetoed. The department also conducts research, produces revenue estimates, analyzes tax policy and tracks population changes. In 1994, it came under intense bipartisan criticism for failing in its role to oversee mammoth computer acquisitions by state agencies. Wilson was expected to place computer procurement and development in a separate department in 1995.

Russell Gould

The finance director, Russell Gould, was appointed Aug. 2, 1993, after the resignation of Thomas Hayes, formerly an appointed state treasurer. Gov. Wilson had tapped Hayes to become head of the Finance Department after he narrowly lost to Democrat Kathleen Brown in a bid to be elected treasurer in 1990. At the time of Hayes' appointment, Gould was one of the agency's chief deputies, but Wilson subsequently named him health and welfare secretary, a Cabinet post the governor had trouble filling after people turned down the job.

As finance director, Gould develops and manages the state's $57.1 billion budget and serves on more than 60 authorities, boards and commissions. Salary: $115,083; Office: State Capitol, Room 1145, Sacramento 95814, (916) 445-3878; Employees: 323; '94-'95 budget: $21,031,000.

DEPARTMENT OF INDUSTRIAL RELATIONS

The Department of Industrial Relations is responsible for enforcing California's occupational safety and health laws, administering the compulsory workers' compensation insurance law, adjudicating workers' compensation claims, negotiating in threatened strikes, enforcing laws and promulgating rules on wages, hours and conditions of employment, and analyzing and disseminating statistics on labor conditions. Director: Lloyd Aubry; Salary: $115,083; Office: 1121 L St., Suite 300, Sacramento 95814, (916) 324-4163 or San Francisco office (415) 703-4590; Employees: 2,796; '94-'95 budget: $197,994,000.

HEALTH AND WELFARE AGENCY

This superagency, which covers 13 state departments, administers the state's health, welfare, employment and rehabilitation programs serving people who are poor, mentally ill, developmentally disabled, elderly, unemployed or who have alcohol and drug addiction problems. The agency also administers Proposition 65, the Safe Drinking Water and Toxics Enforcement Act of 1986; is the state's lead agency in administering the Immigration Reform and Control Act of 1986; and manages the state's emergency medical services program. Five departments within the agency oversee long-term care services in residential and institutional settings for the aging, disabled, mentally ill and other needy citizens.

Sandra Smoley

In October 1993, Wilson named former Sacramento County Supervisor Sandra Smoley as the department's director. Smoley had joined the governor's Cabinet just 10 months earlier as the new head of the State and Consumer Services Agency, a post she assumed after her term as a Sacramento County supervisor ended Jan. 4, 1993. Smoley was an unsuccessful candidate for

Congress in 1978 and 1992, losing the last campaign in the GOP primary. In 1986, she also lost a state Senate race to Sen. Leroy Greene, D-Carmichael. Salary: $115,083; Office: 1600 Ninth St. Room 460, Sacramento 95814, (916) 654-3454; Employees: 40,471; '94-'95 budget: $38 billion (including both state and federal funds and local assistance).

Office of Statewide Health Planning and Development

Responsible for developing a statewide plan for health facilities, ensuring construction plans for health facilities conform to state building codes, maintaining a uniform system of accounting and disclosure for health facility costs and ensuring available federal and state assistance is provided to develop needed facilities. Director: Dr. David Werdegar; Salary: $107,939; Office: 1600 Ninth St., Sacramento 95814, (916) 654-1499; Employees: 360; '94-'95 budget: $31,887,000

Department of Aging

State focal point for federal, state and local agencies that serve more than 4 million elderly Californians, working through 33 Area Agencies on Aging. The agencies manage programs that provide meals, social services and health-insurance counseling and act as advocates for senior citizen issues. The department also manages the state's adult day health care centers, the Alzheimer's Day Care Resource Centers and the multipurpose senior services program, an experimental effort to keep the frail elderly from being unnecessarily admitted to skilled nursing homes or intermediate care facilities. Director: Robert P. Martinez; Salary: $95,239; Office: 1600 K St., 4th floor, Sacramento 95814, (916) 322-3887; Employees: 140; '94-'95 budget: $127,590,000.

Department of Alcohol and Drug Programs

Coordinates planning and development of a statewide alcohol and drug-abuse prevention, intervention, detoxification, recovery and treatment system, serving 300,000 Californians largely through programs operated by counties. The department is responsible for licensing the state's methadone treatment programs, multiple-offender drinking driver programs and alcoholism recovery facilities. In addition, the department manages programs aimed at alcohol and drug-abuse prevention, particularly among youth, women, the disabled, ethnic minorities and the elderly. The department expects to receive an increase of $22.5 million from the federal Alcohol, Drug Abuse and Mental Health Administration. Director: Andrew Mecca; Salary: $107,939; Office: 1700 K St., 5th floor, Sacramento 95814, (916) 445-0834; Employees: 294; '94-'95 budget: $285,070,000.

Department of Health Services

Manages health programs including the state's $17 billion Medi-Cal program (serving about 5.5 million people monthly), the Office of AIDS and the Family

Planning program. The department is in charge of preventive medical services, public water supplies, environmental health, epidemiological studies, rural and community health, radiologic health, maternal and child health and the early detection of genetic disease and birth defects in newborns. The Food and Drug Program seeks to protect consumers from adulterated, misbranded or falsely advertised foods, drugs, medical devices, hazardous household products and cosmetics and to control botulism in canned products. A licensing office regulates care in some 6,000 public and private health facilities, clinics and agencies. Director: S. Kimberly Belshé; Salary: $107,939; Office: 744 P St., Sacramento 95814 or P.O. Box 942732, Sacramento 94234, (916) 445-4171; Employees: 4,679; '94-'95 budget: $17.1 billion (including federal funds).

Department of Developmental Services

Coordinates services under the Lanterman Developmental Disabilities Services Act of 1977 for people with developmental disabilities, such as mental retardation, autism or cerebral palsy, to meet their needs at each stage of their lives through individual plans for treatment within their home communities where possible. The department provides 24-hour care for more than 6,000 severely disabled clients through seven state developmental hospitals (Agnews, Camarillo, Fairview, Lanterman, Porterville, Sonoma and Stockton) and indirect care for clients through a statewide network of private, nonprofit regional centers. Director: Dennis Amundson; Salary: $107,939; Office: 1600 Ninth St., 240, Sacramento 95814, (916) 654-1690; Employees: 10,131; '94-'95 budget: $641,512,000.

Department of Mental Health

Administers the Lanterman-Petris-Short Act, the Bronzan-McCorquodale Act and other federal and state statutes governing services to the mentally ill through county and community nonprofit agencies and through the direct operation of the Atascadero, Metropolitan, Napa and Patton state hospitals and treatment programs for 600 clients at the Department of Developmental Services' Camarillo State Hospital. Services also include community education and consultation, crisis evaluation and emergency care, 24-hour acute care, 24-hour residential treatment, day-care treatment, outpatient care, case management and socialization. The department manages special programs for the homeless mentally ill, for mental illness associated with AIDS and other special categories. Director: Stephen W. Mayberg; Salary: $107,939; Office: 1600 Ninth St., 151, Sacramento 95814, (916) 654-3665; Employees: 6,338; '94-'95 budget: $282,068,000.

Employment Development Department

Assists employers in finding workers and workers in finding jobs through a statewide database, manages the unemployment insurance program, collects payroll taxes that support worker benefit programs, provides economic and labor market data and administers the Job Training Partnership Act. Under federal guidance, the department manages field offices that provide job placement, employment counseling, vocational testing, workshops and referral services, targeted at groups such as veterans, older workers, the disabled, youth, minorities, welfare families and migrant and seasonal farm workers. Director: Thomas Nagle; Salary: $107,939; Office: 800 Capitol Mall, Sacramento 95814, (916) 653-0707; Employees: 11,897; '94-'95 budget: $4.5 billion.

Department of Rehabilitation

Helps rehabilitate and find employment for people with mental and physical handicaps. Director: Brenda J. Premo; Salary: $107,939; Office: 830 K St., 322, Sacramento 95814, (916) 445-3973; Employees: 1,990; '94-'95 budget: $330,201,000

Department of Social Services

Administers the state's $11.5 billion welfare program for poor children, disabled and elderly residents; provides or manages social services, community-care licensing and inspections, disability evaluations, refugee assistance and adoption services; manages the federal food stamp program; regulates group homes, nurseries, preschools, foster homes, halfway houses and day-care centers; administers programs designed to protect children, the disabled and the elderly from abuse or neglect and manages the state's Greater Avenues for Independence (GAIN) workfare program. Director: Eloise Anderson; Salary: $107,939; Office: 744 P St., 1740, Sacramento 95814, (916) 657-3661; Employees: 4,049; '94-'95 budget: $12.1 billion.

CALIFORNIA ENVIRONMENTAL PROTECTION AGENCY

Gov. Wilson said he wanted to take charge of California's environment in the 1990s. To that end, Wilson called James Strock, a veteran from the U.S. Environmental Protection Agency, to his team in California. Strock, an environmental lawyer, is California's third secretary for the environment.

James Strock

Strock has received mixed reviews from competing interests and was on leave during 1992 working on President George Bush's unsuccessful re-election campaign. Strock has overseen the transfer of the regulation of pesticides from the Department of Food and Agriculture as Wilson had pledged, but farm worker and environmental advocates say he has been slow to force chemical manufacturers to comply with disclosure laws. Strock's toxic waste cleanup program has been a continuing scandal and he supported successful legislation in 1994 to reduce cleanup standards at major hazardous waste sites.

As secretary, Strock oversees the operations of the Air Resources Board, California Integrated Waste Management Board, Department of Pesticide Regulation, State Water Resources Control Board, Department of Toxic Substances Control and the Office of Environmental Health Hazard Assessment. Salary: $115,083. Office: 555 Capitol Mall, Suite 235, Sacramento 95814, (916) 445-3846; Employees: 4,264; '94-'95 budget: $642,431,000.

Air Resources Board

Holds the primary responsibility for California air quality, including the establishment of clean air standards, research into air pollution, emissions enforcement and smog limitations on automobiles and industries. Chair: John Dunlap; Salary: $103,175; Members: Joseph C. Calhoun; Petaluma Mayor Patricia Hilligoss; Jack Parnell; Fresno County Supervisor Doug Vagim; Eugene Boston, M.D.; Lynne T. Edgerton; John S. Lagarias; San Bernardino County Supervisor Barbara Riordan; former Orange County Supervisor Harriett Wieder. Members' compensation: $29,354; Office: 2020 L St., Sacramento 95814, (916) 322-5594; Employees: 939; '94-'95 budget: $104,244,000.

State Water Resources Control Board

Regulatory agency with responsibility for administering and granting water rights, maintaining state water quality through monitoring and waste discharge permits, managing toxic cleanups and administering grants for waste treatment facilities. Chairman: John Caffery; Salary: $103,178; Members: James M. Stubchaer, Marc Del Peiro, Mary Jane Forster, John W. Brown. Salaries: $72,465; Office 901 P St. 4th floor, Sacramento 95814, (916) 657-0941; Employees: 1,283; budget '94-'95: $642,431,000.

California Integrated Waste Management Board

Responsible for promoting waste reduction, recycling and composting, including environmentally safe transformation of wastes into harmless or useful products or land disposal. Manages landfills through local agencies and administers the California Tire Recycling Act of 1989 to reduce the number of used tires in landfills. Chairman: Vacant; Members: Wesley Chesbro, Sam Egigian, Janet Gotch, Edward G. Heidig and Paul Relis; Salaries: $103,178; Office: 8800 Cal Center Dr., Sacramento 95826, (916) 255-2200; Employees: 412; '94-'95 budget: $82,462,000.

Department of Pesticide Regulation

Duties of this relatively new department previously were in the state Department of Food and Agriculture. For years, the old arrangement had prompted charges that the agriculture department was too cozy with agribusiness to monitor the use of pesticides. All pesticide regulation, from registration and use, to enforcement of pesticide laws, falls under the jurisdiction of this department. Director: James Wells; Salary: $107,939; Office: 1020 N St., Room 100, Sacramento 95814, (916) 445-4000; Employees: 395; '94-'95 budget: $46,123,000.

YOUTH AND ADULT CORRECTIONAL AGENCY

Joe Sandoval

This superagency oversees the Department of Corrections and the Youth Authority, which are responsible for the control, care and treatment of convicted felons and civilly committed addicts, and the confinement and rehabilitation of juvenile delin quents. The agency employs some 42,000 workers and has an annual budget of $3.7 billion. The agency has managed the biggest prison and prison camp construction program in the world in recent years, although the inmate population continues to grow more quickly than prisons can be built. In 1994, the state prison system housed 123,000 inmates and the Youth Authority had more than 8,500 wards. The agency also manages state parole programs, which are being severely cut back, and oversees the state Board of Corrections, the Youthful Offender Parole Board and the Board of Prison Terms.

Secretary Joe Sandoval was appointed on Oct. 12, 1988, having been Gov. Deukmejian's chief of the California State Police, and was reappointed Feb. 25, 1991, by Gov. Wilson. Sandoval is a veteran of 26 years with the Los Angeles Police Department. Salary: $115,083; Office: 1100 11th St., 400, Sacramento 95814, (916) 323-6115.

Department of Corrections

Manages 30 correctional facilities, including eight reception centers. The department also manages parole programs, prison camps and a community correctional program designed to reintegrate released offenders to society. Director: James H. Gomez; Salary: $107,939; Office: 1515 S St., 351, Sacramento 95814, (916) 327-5075; Employees: 35,900; '94-'95 budget: $3.1 billion.

Youth Authority

Provides programs in institutions and the community to reduce delinquent behavior, help local agencies fight juvenile crime and encourage delinquency prevention programs. The department operates reception centers and clinics as well as 18 conservation camps and institutions for young men and women. Director: vacant; Salary: $107,939; Office: 4241 Williamsbourgh Dr., Sacramento 95823,

(916) 262-1480; Employees: 5,187; '94-'95 budget: $388,189,000.

RESOURCES AGENCY

Douglas Wheeler

This superagency is responsible for departments and programs that manage the state's air, water and land resources and wildlife. The main departments are Forestry and Fire Protection, Parks and Recreation, Conservation, Fish and Game, Boating and Waterways, the Conservation Corps and the Department of Water Resources, which among its many duties includes the state's Drought Center (and, on occasion, its Flood Center). The agency also oversees or provides backup for the Tahoe Regional Planning Agency, the Wildlife Conservation Board, the Santa Monica Mountains Conservancy, the state Coastal Conservancy, the San Francisco Bay Conservation and Development Commission, the Colorado River Board of California and the environmental license plate fund. It has some 14,000 employees and an annual budget of nearly $1.8 billion.

Keeping his pledge to bring an environmental ethic to state government, Gov. Wilson chose Douglas P. Wheeler, vice-president of the World Wildlife Fund and Conservation Foundation, to be his secretary for resources. Wheeler has held positions in the U.S. Department of Interior, the American Farmland Trust, the National Trust for Historic Preservation and the Sierra Club, where he was executive director in 1985-86. (He left the Sierra Club position amicably, deciding he was not the activist that the organization seemed to want.)

Wheeler inherited a troubled agency, and after four years under his direction it's still troubled. Fish and Game, and Parks and Recreation have suffered some of the most intense budget difficulties of any state agency. Fish and Game has been beset by management scandals. The Coastal Commission, after years of Deukmejian budget cuts, has been under attack for not protecting the coastline. In response, environmentalists have been turning to the initiative, with varying success, to protect state forests and wildlife and to launch aggressive mass transit programs. Salary: $115,083; Office: 1416 Ninth St., Room 1311, Sacramento 95814, (916) 653-3006.

California Conservation Corps

A work force of some 2,000 young men and women performs nearly 3 million hours of conservation work each year, including flood patrol, fire restoration, tree planting, stream clearance, trail building, park maintenance, landscaping, home weatherization and wildlife habitat restoration. Director: Al Aramburu; Salary: $95,233; Office: 5851-A Alder Ave., Sacramento 95828, (916) 387-2582; Employees: 396; '94-'95 budget: $35,461,000.

Department of Conservation

Promotes the development and management of the state's land, energy, mineral and farmland resources, and disseminates information on geology, seismology, mineral, geothermal and petroleum resources, agricultural and open-space land, and container recycling and litter reduction. Director: Michael Francis Byrne; Salary: $95,239; Office: 801 K St., 24th floor, Sacramento 95814, (916) 322-7683; Employees: 579; '95-'95 budget: $398,820,000.

Department of Forestry and Fire Protection

Provides fire protection and watershed management services for private and state-owned watershed lands. Responsibilities include fire prevention, controlling wildlife damage and improving the land and vegetative cover for economic and social benefits. Director: Richard A. Wilson; Salary: $107,939; Office: 1416 Ninth St., 1505, Sacramento 95814, (916) 653-5121; Employees: 4,456; '94-'95 budget: $297,051,000.

Department of Fish and Game

Responsible for maintaining all species of wildlife; providing varied recreational use of wild species, including hunting and fishing; providing for the scientific and educational use of wildlife; and protecting the economic benefits of natural species, including commercial harvesting of wildlife resources. The department also has charge of the newly enacted oil-spill prevention and cleanup program. Director: Boyd H. Gibbons; Salary: $107,939; Office: 1416 Ninth St., 12th Floor, Sacramento 95814, (916) 653-7667; Employees: 2,053; '94-'95 budget: $156,954,000.

Department of Boating and Waterways

Responsible for public boating facilities, water safety, water hyacinth control, beach erosion, small-craft harbor development (through loans and grants) and yacht and ship broker's licensing. Director: John R. Banuelos; Salary: $87,305; Office: 1629 S St., Sacramento 95814, (916) 445-2616; Employees: 64; '94-'95 budget: $28,100,000.

Department of Parks and Recreation

Acquires, designs, develops, operates, maintains and protects the state park system; helps local park agencies through loans and grants; and interprets the natural, archaeological and historical resources of the state. State parks, recreation areas and historic monuments are designed to provide recreation, improve the environment and preserve the state's history and natural landscapes. The department is involved in underwater parks, a statewide trail network, state beaches and piers, coastal and Sierra redwood parks, an off-highway vehicle system, management of the Hearst San Simeon Castle and the Anza-Borrego Desert State Park. Director: Donald W. Murphy; Salary: $107,939; Office: 1416 Ninth St., 1405, Sacramento 95814, (916) 653-6995; Employees: 2,794; '94-'95 budget: $196,571,000.

Department of Water Resources

Responsible for managing, developing and conserving the state's water, from flood control to drought responses and drinking water safety, under the provisions of the California Water Plan. The department operates Oroville Reservoir, the California Aqueduct and related facilities, and manages the key Delta water supply in conjunction with the U.S. Bureau of Reclamation. Director: David Kennedy; Salary: $107,939; Office: 901 P St., P.O. Box 100, Sacramento 95812, (916) 657-2390; Employees: 2,863; '94-'95 budget: $273,821,000.

STATE AND CONSUMER SERVICES AGENCY

This superagency covers an array of departments and programs that include the departments of Consumer Affairs, Fair Employment and Housing, General Services and the Fair Employment and Housing Commission, Building Standards Commission, State Personnel Board, State Fire Marshal, Franchise Tax Board, Museum of Science and Industry, the Public Employees Retirement System and the State Teachers' Retirement System.

Joanne C. Kozberg

The agency's secretary, Joanne Corday Kozberg, is a longtime member of Gov. Wilson's cadre of devoted staff employees. From 1984 to 1988, Kozberg acted as senior policy adviser to then U.S. Sen. Wilson. She specialized in entertainment, transportation and arts issues. She has also held executive posts with the NAACP Legal Defense and Education Fund and the Coro Foundation, a nonpartisan public affairs training institute in Los Angeles. In 1991, Wilson tapped Kozberg to become executive director of the California Arts Council, before naming her consumer services secretary in December 1993. Salary: $115,083; Office: 915 Capitol Mall, Suite 200, Sacramento 95814, (916) 653-2636; Employees: 14,539; '94-'95 budget: $789,820,000.

Department of Consumer Affairs

Oversees the Bureau of Automotive Repair, the Contractors' State License Board and the California Medical Board, the Division of Consumer Services and two dozen more small boards, bureaus and commissions that for the most part license and regulate professional services. A number of the semiautonomous boards have had severe staff reductions and have been accused of protecting people in professions they regulate. The boards are Accountancy, Architectural Examiners, Barber Examiners, Barbering and Cosmetology, Behavioral Science Examiners, Dental Examiners, Funeral Directors and Embalmers, Geologists and Geophysicists, Guide Dogs for the Blind, Landscape Architects, Examiners of Nursing Home

Administrators, Optometry, Pharmacy, Polygraph Examiners, Professional Engineers, Registered Nursing, Certified Shorthand Reporters, Structural Pest Control, Examiners in Veterinary Medicine, Vocational Nurse and Psychiatric Technician Examiners and the Cemetery Board; the bureaus of Collection and Investigative Services, Electronic and Appliance Repair, Personnel Services and Home Furnishings; the Tax Preparers Program; and the Athletic Commission. Director: Marjorie M. Berte; Salary: $107,939; Office: 400 R St., 3000, Sacramento 95814, (916) 445-1254; Employees: 1,153; '94-'95 budget: $231,896,000.

Department of Fair Employment and Housing

Enforces the state civil rights laws that prohibit discrimination in employment, housing and public services and endeavors to eliminate discrimination based on race, religion, creed, national origin, sex, marital status, physical handicap, medical condition or age (over 40). Complaints are pursued before the Fair Employment and Housing Commission, but staff cutbacks have severely blunted the department's effectiveness. Director: Nancy Gutierrez; Salary: $95,239; Office: 2016 T St., Suite 210, Sacramento 95814, (916) 227-2873; Employees: 199; '94-'95 budget: $12,308,000.

Office of the State Fire Marshal

Coordinates state fire services, adopts and enforces minimum statewide fire and panic safety regulations, controls hazardous materials and helps the film industry with special effects. State fire marshal: Ronny J. Coleman; Salary: $95,239; Office: 7171 Bowling Drive, Suite 800, Sacramento 95823, (916) 262-1870; Employees: 126; '94-'95 budget: $8,098,000.

Franchise Tax Board

Administers the personal income tax, the bank and corporation tax laws, the homeowners and renters assistance program, and performs field assessments and audits of campaign expenditure reports and lobbyist reports under the Political Reform Act of 1974. The members are state Controller Kathleen Connell; Board of Equalization Chairman Brad Sherman; and state Finance Director Russell Gould. Executive officer: Gerald Goldberg; Salary: $107,939; Office: P.O. Box 2229, Sacramento 95812, (916) 369-4543; Employees: 4,745; '94-'95 budget: $284,234,000.

Department of General Services

Manages and maintains state property, allocates office space, monitors contracts, insurance and risks, administers the state school building law and helps small and minority businesses obtain state contracts. It also has jurisdiction over the state architect, the offices of telecommunications, local assistance, procurement, energy assessments, buildings and grounds and the state police. The department has been beset by a series of contracting and procurement scandals. Director: John Lockwood; Salary: $107,939; Office: 1325 J St., 1910, Sacramento 95814, (916) 322-9902; Employees: 4,241; '94-'95 budget: $175,305,000.

State Personnel Board

Manages the state civil service system, hears appeals from disciplined employees and runs the Career Opportunities Development Program. Members: President Richard Carpenter, Alice Stoner, Lorrie Ward, Florence Bos and one vacancy. Members' compensation: $29,354; Executive officer: Gloria Harmon; Salary: $98,388; Office: 801 Capitol Mall, 5th floor, Sacramento 95814, (916) 653-1028; Employees: 183; '94-'95 budget: $6,937,000.

Public Employees' Retirement System

Administers pension, disability, health, Social Security and death benefits for more than 1 million past and present public employees, and is the nation's largest pension plan. Participants include state constitutional officers, legislators, judges, state employees, most volunteer firefighters, school employees (except teachers) and employees of many local governments. Executive officer: James Burton; Salary: $110,004; Office: 400 P St., Ste. 3340, Sacramento 95814, (916) 635-3829; Employees: 959; '94-'95 budget: $164,154,000; investment portfolio: $73.9 billion (as of October 1994).

State Teachers' Retirement System

Administers the largest teacher retirement system in the United States with 340,700 members and 123,900 receiving benefits. Chief executive officer: James Mosman; Salary: $110,004 ; Office: 7667 Folsom Blvd., Sacramento 95826, (916) 387-3700. Employees: 440; '94-'95 budget: $86.6 million; investment portfolio: $49.7 billion (as of August 1994).

DEPARTMENT OF VETERANS AFFAIRS

In July 1994, Gov. Wilson signed a bill making the Department of Veterans Affairs an independent state agency that can be managed only by a military veteran. Wilson also indicated at that time that he would elevate the department to Cabinet-level status. Previously, the department fell under the jurisdiction of the State and Consumer Services Agency. The department administers the Cal-Vet farm and home loan program, helps veterans obtain benefits and rights to which they are entitled and supports the Veterans Home of California, a retirement home with nursing care and hospitalization. The program is expanding rapidly in response to a 1992 court ruling that all California residents who are veterans are eligible for loan programs, not just those who entered the service from California. Director: Ret. Col. Jay Vargas, USMC; Salary: $107,939; Office: 1227 O St., Sacramento 94295, (916) 653-2158; Employees: 1,129; '94-'95 budget: $836,160,000.

SECRETARY OF CHILD DEVELOPMENT, EDUCATION

Maureen DiMarco

Declaring children to be the state's most precious resource, Gov. Wilson pledged to give them a healthy start in life and in school. To this end he expanded his Cabinet to include a new position, secretary for child development and education, a post for which he chose Maureen DiMarco, a Democrat who had endorsed his gubernatorial campaign.

Wilson gave DiMarco the task of restructuring the state's delivery of social, health and mental health services to children in a period of severe budget constraints. She also chairs a new Inter-Agency Council for Child Development. Wilson said his approach would be preventive rather than corrective for the state's educational and children's needs. He considered such expenses to be investments in the future rather than costs.

DiMarco, of Cyprus, was immediate past president of the California School Boards Association and outgoing president of the board of the Garden Grove Unified School District in Orange County. She had worked as a consultant for former state schools chief Bill Honig, and was frequently critical of former Gov. George Deukmejian's education policies. In 1994, DiMarco tried to succeed Honig, who was forced to leave office after his conviction on felony conflict-of-interest charges. Dimarco emerged from a crowded field of primary election contenders as one of the top two vote-getters vying for the nonpartisan state superintendent of public instruction post. But in the November run off, DiMarco was no match for former Democratic Assemblywoman Delaine Eastin, who went on to become the state's first female schools chief. Salary: $115,093. Office: Building, 1121 L St., 600, Sacramento 95814, (916) 323-0611; Employees: 23; '94-'95 budget: $3,176,000.

BOARD OF EDUCATION

Establishes policy and adopts rules and regulations for kindergarten through 12th grade, where authorized by the Education Code. Major duties include selecting textbooks for grades kindergarten through eight, developing curriculum frameworks, approving district waivers from regulations and regulating the state testing program, teacher credentialing and school district reorganizations. In the past, the board was seen as a subsidiary to the state superintendent of public instruction, who is an elected constitutional officer. In recent years, however, the board frequently clashed over the budget and educational reforms with former Superintendent Bill Honig. Board members also filed a lawsuit that successfully wrested more power away from the superintendent's office.

In 1994, the previously obscure state board gained national notoriety for its role in a controversy that ended in the demise of the California Learning Assessment

System, a new exam developed by Department of Education officials that was supposed to help teachers and parents determine how well students were learning.

Members: President Marion McDowell, Gerti B. Thomas, Kathryn Dronenburg, Jerry Hume, Yvonne W. Larsen, Dorothy Jue Lee, S. William Malkasian, Sanford Sigoloff, Gary L. Weston (student member). Office: 721 Capitol Mall, Room 532, Sacramento, 95814, (916) 657-5478.

DEPARTMENT OF EDUCATION

Administers the state's kindergarten through high school education system for 5.1 million pupils by coordinating and directing the state's local elementary and high school districts. The primary goal is to provide education policy to local districts, approve instructional materials and offer curriculum leadership. Superintendent: Delaine Eastin; Salary: $102,000; Office: 721 Capitol Mall, Sacramento 95814, (916) 657-2451; Employees: 2,275; '94-'95 budget: $18.5 billion.

UC BOARD OF REGENTS

Governs the nine campuses of the University of California, five teaching hospitals and three major laboratories operated under contracts with the U.S. Department of Energy. The 18 members have been appointed to 12-year terms since 1974, when terms were reduced from 16 years. The same amendment reduced the number of ex-officio members from eight to seven. The long-term appointment of a regent is considered to be among the most prestigious civic positions in California, much prized by the wealthy and politically well-connected. As the UC system has struggled with budget cuts, regents have been forced to give up some lavish perks.

Ex-officio members of the Board of Regents are Gov. Wilson, president; Lt. Gov. Gray Davis; the speaker of the Assembly; Superintendent of Schools Delaine Eastin; UC President Jack Peltason; David Flinn, president of the UC Alumni Association; Peter Preuss, vice president of the Alumni Association; The regents (and the end of their terms) are: Howard H. Leach, chairman, (2001); William Bagley (2002); Roy Brophy (1998); Clair W. Burgener (2000); Glenn Campbell (1996); Frank Clark Jr. (2000); Ward Connerly (2005); John G. Davies (2004); Tirso del Junco (1997); Alice Gonzales (1998); S. Sue Johnson (2002); Meredith Khachigian, (2001); Leo Kolligian (1997); David S. Lee (2006); Velma Montoya (2005); Stephen Nakashima (2004); Tom Sayles (2006); Dean Watkins (1996); Terrence Wooten (student regent, 1995). President Peltason's salary: $243,500 plus $36,500 in deferred compensation; Office of the President: 300 Lakeside Dr., Oakland 94612, (510) 987-0700. The university system's overall budget, including federal funds and research labs, is about $9 billion. The system has an enrollment of 163,100 students.

University of California Chancellors

Jack Peltason, UC president; Chang-Lin Tian, Berkeley; Larry N. Vanderhoef, Davis; Laurel L. Wilkening, Irvine; Charles Young, Los Angeles; Raymond L.

Orbach, Riverside; Richard Atkinson, San Diego; Joseph B. Martin, M.D., San Francisco; Henry T. Yang, Santa Barbara; Karl S. Pister, Santa Cruz; Charles Shank, director, Lawrence Berkeley Laboratory; C. Bruce Tarter, director, Lawrence Livermore National Laboratory; and Siegfried Hecker, director, Los Alamos National Laboratory.

TRUSTEES OF THE STATE UNIVERSITIES

Sets policy and governs collective bargaining; personnel matters, including appointment of the system president and university chancellors; and budget decisions and capital outlays. Members are appointed by the governor for eight-year terms. The trustees (and the end of their terms) are: Gov. Wilson; Lt. Gov. Gray Davis; the speaker of the Assembly; Superintendent of Schools Delaine Eastin; Barry Munitz, chancellor; Jim Considine, chairman, (1996); Roland Arnall (1998); Marian Bagdasarian (1996); William Campbell (1995); Ronald Cedillos (1999); Martha C. Fallgatter (1995); Bernard Goldstein (faculty, 1995); James Gray (1998); William Hauck (2001); Christopher A. Lowe (1995); Joan Otomo-Corgel (2000); Ralph R. Pesqueria (1996); Ted J. Saenger (1997); J. Gary Shansby (1999); Michael D. Stennis (2000); Anthony M. Vitti (1997); Stanley T. Wang (2002). Chancellor's salary: $175,000; Office: 400 Golden Shore, Long Beach, 90802, (310) 985-2800. Enrollment: 319,000. System budget '94-'95: $2.1 billion.

California State University Presidents

Barry Munitz, CSU chancellor; Tomas Arciniega, Bakersfield; Manuel A. Esteban, Chico; Robert Detweiler, Dominguez Hills; John Welty, Fresno; Milton Gordon, Fullerton; Norma Rees, Hayward; Alistair McCrone, Humboldt; Robert C. Maxson, Long Beach; James Rosser, Los Angeles; Peter W. Smith, Monterey Bay; Blenda Wilson, Northridge; Bob Suzuki, California Polytechnic State University, Pomona; Donald Gerth, Sacramento; Anthony Evans, San Bernardino; Thomas Day, San Diego; Robert Corrigan, San Francisco; J. Handel Evans, San Jose; Warren Baker, California Polytechnic State University, San Luis Obispo; Bill Stacy, San Marcos; Ruben Arminana, Sonoma; Lee R. Kerschner, Stanislaus.

GOVERNORS, CALIFORNIA COMMUNITY COLLEGES

California's 71 community college districts comprise the largest postsecondary education system in the nation, with 107 campuses statewide serving approximately 1.4 million students. Each district is managed by a locally elected governing board, but a statewide Board of Governors and chancellor provide leadership, a presence before the Legislature and policy guidance.

Board members are President Larry Toy of Orinda; Robert Alleborn of Newport Beach; Phillip Bardos of Channel Islands; Philip E. del Campo of San Diego; Joe Dolphin of San Diego; Timothy Haidinger of San Diego; Paul Kim of Los Angeles; Vishwas More of Orinda; Alice S. Petrossian of Glendale; Paul Priolo of San

Francisco; Shirley Ralston of Orange; John W. Rice of Palo Alto; Wilbert L. Smith of Pasadena; Julia Li Wu of Los Angeles.

Chancellor: David Mertes; Salary: $101,340; Office: 1107 Ninth St., Sacramento 95814, (916) 445-8752; '94-'95 budget (all campuses): $2.7 billion.

FAIR POLITICAL PRACTICES COMMISSION

Established by the voter-approved Political Reform Act of 1974, the commission enforces campaign expenditure reporting, conflict-of-interest statements, other disclosure rules and campaign restrictions. Propositions 73 and 68, rival initiatives that were both approved in 1988, fell largely under the commission's jurisdiction but were gutted by court decisions in 1990. Proposition 68 was sponsored by Common Cause and Proposition 73 was sponsored by the unlikely alliance of Assembly Republican leader Ross Johnson of La Habra, Independent Sen. Quentin Kopp of San Francisco and Democratic Sen. Joseph Montoya of Whittier. (Montoya later was sentenced to prison on political corruption charges.)

In the first of the court decisions, U.S. District Court Judge Lawrence Karlton ruled in September 1990 that Proposition 73's contribution limits and its ban on fund transfers among candidates unfairly limited political speech. Two months later, the state Supreme Court ruled that no provisions of Proposition 68 could take effect because Proposition 73 had won more votes and provided a comprehensive regulatory scheme related to the same subject.

The decisions meant that California no longer had any restrictions on how much money individuals or organizational political action committees could contribute to political candidates, and fund transfers between candidates for the Legislature, once banned, were permissible, according to one analysis. The decisions also meant Proposition 73's restrictions against public campaign financing were thrown out, too, but so far no one has stepped up to enact such a provision.

Meanwhile, the Legislature passed an ethics package that included restrictions on travel, health-related expenses, gift and other purchases with campaign proceeds and reimbursements of unused campaign funds. A significant part of the package became Proposition 112, approved in the June 1990 primary election, further restricting gifts and honorariums for lawmakers and personal use of campaign funds while establishing an independent Citizens Compensation Commission to set the pay for legislators and constitutional officers.

Within this framework, the FPPC adopts regulations governing disclosure of conflicts of interest, campaign finances and lobbyist activities and is empowered to fine public officials and candidates. Other elements of campaign enforcement are the responsibility of the secretary of state and the attorney general. Chairman: Ravinder Mehta; Salary: $103,178; Members: James Rushford, Deborah Seiler and Raquelle de la Rocha, one vacancy; Office: 428 J St., Suite 800, Sacramento 95814, (916) 322-5901; Employees: 61; '94-'95 budget: $4,526,000.

✗ TRANSPORTATION COMMISSION

Administers state highway planning and construction and other state transportation programs, including mass transit and rail transportation services. Chairman: Jerry Epstein; Members: Octavia Diener, Daniel Fessler, Kenneth F. Kevorkian, Joseph A. Duffel, Robert H. Shelton (vice chairman), Robert A. Wolf, Mary F. Berglund; Executive director: Robert I. Remen; Commissioners receive $100 a day plus expenses, but they have voted not to take the pay. Office: 1120 N St., Room 2233., Sacramento 95814, (916) 654-4245; Employees: 16; '94-'95 budget: $368,311,000.

CALIFORNIA ENERGY RESOURCES CONSERVATION AND DEVELOPMENT COMMISSION

Responsible for siting major power plants, forecasting energy supplies and demands, developing energy conservation measures and conducting research into questions of energy supply, consumption, conservation and power plant technology. Chairman: Charles Imbrecht; Salary: $95,403; Members: Richard A. Bilas, W. Doug Noteware, Sally A. Rakow, Jananne Sharpless; Salaries: $103,178; Office: 1516 Ninth St., Sacramento 95814, (916) 647-4287; Employees: 464; '94-'95 budget: $49,077,000.

PUBLIC UTILITIES COMMISSION

Responsible for providing the public with the lowest reasonable rates for utilities and transportation services, and assures that utilities and transportation companies render adequate and safe services. President: Daniel Fessler; Salary $100,173; Commissioners: Patricia Eckert, Norman Shumway, P. Gregory Conlon, Jessie J. Knight; Salaries: $92,465; Office: 505 Van Ness Ave., San Francisco 94102-3298, (415) 703-1282; Employees: 1,075; '94-'95 budget: $79,081,000.

⊥ SEISMIC SAFETY COMMISSION

Responsible for improving earthquake safety in California; inventories hazardous buildings, sponsors legislation, pursues programs to strengthen state-owned buildings. Executive director: L. Thomas Tobin; Salary: $84,656; Office: 1900 K St., Suite 100, Sacramento, 95814, (916) 322-4917; Employees: 10; '94-'95 budget: $1,436,000.

STATE LANDS COMMISSION

Administers state interest in more than 4 million acres of navigable waterways, swamp and overflow lands, vacant school sites and granted lands and tidelands within 3 miles of the mean high-tide line (one of the few state agencies not controlled by the governor). Members: State Finance Director Russell Gould, Lt. Gov. Gray Davis, and Controller Kathleen Connell. Executive Officer: Robert C. Hight; Salary: $98,659; Office: 1807 13th St., Sacramento 95814, (916) 322-7777; Employees: 222; '94-'95 budget: $17,207,000.

CALIFORNIA COASTAL COMMISSION
Charged with the state management of coastal resources, an area extending generally about 1,000 yards inland (but as much as 5 miles inland in some areas) and 3 miles seaward for the 1,100-mile length of the California coast, excluding San Francisco Bay. The commission was established in 1976 to succeed the California Coastal Zone Commission, a temporary agency created by the voters in 1972. The 15-member commission certifies local governments to manage the coastal zone in accordance with state-approved plans. Gov. Deukmejian promised to abolish the agency in the early years of his administration and when that failed, he cut the commission's budgets sharply. Executive director: Peter Douglas; Salary: $88,860; Office: 45 Fremont St., Suite 2000, San Francisco 94105, (415) 904-5200; Employees: 112; '94-'95 budget: $8,813,000.

MAJOR RISK MEDICAL INSURANCE BOARD
A program designed to provide health insurance for residents who are unable to find insurance in the open market by supplementing the cost of premiums with $30 million from tobacco taxes. Chairman: Clifford Allenby; Members: Thomas Topuzes, S. Kimberly Belshé, Rita Gordon, Emery Dowell; Office: 818 K St., Room 200, Sacramento 95814, (916) 324-4695; Employees: 15; '94-'95 budget: $103,138,000.

6

California Legislature–slipping and sliding

"I look forward, when all of the votes are counted, to leading a 41- or 42-member-strong Republican majority in the California state Assembly. It is our turn, and I promise you Republicans will use this opportunity wisely."
—Assembly Republican leader Jim Brulte, predicting his imminent rise to the speakership, Nov. 10, 1994.

"There is no termination date on this speakership. Any time that I leave, it will be self-imposed."
—Assembly Speaker Willie Brown, hours after winning the speakership for a record eighth term, Jan. 24, 1995.

Even by standards of the California Legislature — with its late-night floor votes, backroom maneuvers and months-long budget stalemates — the drama that unfolded in the halls of the Assembly at the beginning of the 1995-96 session was extraordinary.

Out of power for nearly a quarter of a century, Republicans found themselves after the November 1994 election on the brink of seizing control of the lower house — a house that had been dominated for 14 years by the will of its Democratic speaker, Willie Lewis Brown Jr. But political power is a slippery thing, and the Republican revolution that Jim Brulte so confidently predicted in November had been thwarted by Brown and the Democrats by late January. It was a drama shaped by guile, threat, bluff, calculation, miscalculation and, according to the outmaneuvered GOP caucus, sheer treachery. When the parliamentary theatrics were over, Brown was left in the speaker's elegant second-floor suite of offices, but presiding with substantially reduced powers over a dramatically changed house. Republicans were left barking at the door, vowing recalls, revenge and, once again, a GOP takeover of the house at some later date.

The unlikely chain of events was born in the 1994 general election, which produced a Republican sweep nationwide. In California, Democrats managed to hold on to a thin majority of seats in the 40-member state Senate, which quickly organized under the leadership of President Pro Tem Bill Lockyer of Hayward and Republican leader Ken Maddy of Fresno and began conducting its business. But in the 80-seat Assembly, where a slew of members facing term limits had bailed out to seek higher office, the Democrats' previous 47-33 advantage evaporated. The election produced a mix of 41 Republicans and 39 Democrats, and Brulte — a young lawmaker from San Bernardino County who had served as Republican leader for two years — quickly staked his claim to the speakership. Democratic staffers started updating their resumés while their GOP counterparts prowled the halls scouting for the best office space.

But few observers familiar with Brown's 30-year history in the Assembly were willing to count him out — in part because of the shaky status of two Republicans who had been re-elected to the house. One, Richard Mountjoy of Arcadia, had also been elected to the state Senate in a special election that coincided with the general election. He said he intended to move to the upper house as soon as he had helped elect Brulte as speaker. The other, Paul Horcher of Whittier, had been an outcast in the GOP caucus ever since Brown appointed him vice chairman of the Ways and Means Committee and he accepted, ignoring the wishes of the caucus. Horcher also had been critical of the party's right wing and had challenged Mountjoy for the open Senate seat. His commitment to a Brulte speakership was openly questioned.

When the house convened in December 1994 to elect a speaker, fireworks began. Democrats were ready with a strategy to deprive the Republicans of their 41-vote majority by ousting Mountjoy, whom they believed could not hang on to his Assembly seat since he had been elected to the upper house as well. "He clearly has earned the right to be on a milk carton by now in the state Senate," Brown opined. Ironically, the presiding officer of the house — Chief Clerk E. Dotson Wilson, a Brown protégé and former Brown aide — made a series of procedural rulings that blocked the Democrats. But when the roll was called on the speakership vote, Horcher — who that day switched his party affiliation to independent — slammed his fist on his desk and yelled out, "Brown!" The day ended with a historic 40-40 tie between Brulte and Brown for the speakership, outraging Republicans.

The next day, the chief clerk called in sick — he had been admitted to a hospital the previous evening suffering from exhaustion and stress — paving the way for Brown, as the Assembly's senior member, to take the dais and presumably make whatever rulings he wanted on the Mountjoy question. Republicans fled the Capitol, denying Brown a quorum.

The house adjourned for the rest of December, and what followed was a seven-week stalemate. Without a speaker, committees could not be formed and offices could not be reassigned, but both caucuses argued that December and January were traditionally months of little or no legislative activity anyway. The two sides issued a series of letters back and forth, requesting meetings, offering compromises, making accusations of obstructionism and the like. Republicans — though Brulte said his caucus wasn't involved — started recall drives against Horcher and several Democrats in swing districts who had voted for Brown. And when the Assembly returned in early January, Republicans were betting that Brown would not have the votes to oust Mountjoy. He was a duly elected and sworn-in member of the Assembly, they argued, and besides, they had legal opinions saying Brown would need 41 or 54 votes to force Mountjoy out — not the 40 he would have at most.

At first, that thinking appeared to be on target. Brown, instead of making a power play, announced the two caucuses were beginning negotiations to split the powers of the house — dividing resources, committee assignments and leadership positions. But sticking points quickly became apparent. Republicans wanted a power-sharing arrangement that could be negated as soon as the recall elections provided them a new majority later in the year; Democrats wanted a secure two-year deal. The composition of committees and the titles of house leaders also divided the parties, and the discussions stagnated. Democrats convinced Republican Assemblyman Bernie Richter of Chico to offer himself as a compromise candidate for speaker, but Richter could secure no votes in his own caucus.

It was, typically, a late-night maneuver that ended the impasse. With Californians distracted by the beginning of the O.J. Simpson murder trial and the approach of a Super Bowl featuring two California teams, Brown convened the house on the evening of Jan. 23, 1995. Chief Clerk Wilson had stepped aside, allowing Brown to preside. Brown quickly issued rulings that disqualified Mountjoy from voting on his own ouster and then brought the question to a vote. Brown's caucus held together, and on a 40-39 vote, Mountjoy was sent packing to the Senate. With a 79-member house left, Brown was quickly elected speaker with 40 votes and was sworn in just before 1 a.m. Jan. 24.

THE NEW HOUSE

The stunning move was denounced by the outflanked Republicans as the equivalent of a coup d'etat. But Brown's capture of the speakership was accompanied by the adoption of new house operating rules that gave the GOP more power than it had enjoyed in years. Many of the speaker's powers over committee assignments, resource distribution and the like were transferred elsewhere. The Rules Committee, comprised of equal numbers of Republicans and Democrats, would divide up the legislative budget and confirm the speaker's appointments to boards and commissions. Committee memberships would be evenly divided between parties, and chairmanships would be split evenly as well.

The new arrangement had a number of far-reaching implications, only some of which had begun to emerge by the end of January 1995. For one, the stability of the

Speakers of the Assembly

Name	P*	Year(s)	Name	P*	Year(s)
Thomas J. White	–	1849	John C. Lynch	R	1895
John Bigler	D	1849,51	Frank L. Coombs	R	1897
Richard P. Hammond	D	1852	Howard E. Wright	R	1899
Isaac B. Wall	D	1853	Alden Anderson	R	1899
Charles S. Fairfax	D	1854	Cornelius W. Pendleton	R	1901
William W. Stow	W	1855	Arthur G. Fisk	R	1903
James T. Farley	A	1856	Frank C. Prescott	R	1905
Elwood T. Beatty	D	1857	R.L. Beardslee	R	1907
N.E. Whiteside	D	1858	P.S. Stanton	R	1909
William C. Stratton	D	1859	A.H. Hewitt	R	1911
Phillip Moore	D	1860	C.C. Young	R-P	1913-17
R.N. Burnell	DD	1861	Henry W. Wright	R	1919,21
George Barstow	R	1862	Frank Merriam	R	1923,25
Tim Machin	U	1863	Edgar C. Levey	R	1927-31
William H. Sears	U	1864	Walter J. Little	R	1933
John Yule	U	1866	F.C. Clowdsley	R	1934
Caisas T. Ryland	D	1868	Edward Craig	R	1935
George H. Rogers	D	1870	William Moseley Jones	D	1937
Thomas B. Shannon	R	1872	Paul Peek	D	1939
Morris M. Estee	I	1874	Gordon H. Garland	D	1940,41
G.J. Carpenter	D	1876	Charles W. Lyon	R	1943,45
Campbell P. Berry	D	1878	Sam L. Collins	R	1947-52
Jabez F. Cowdery	R	1880	James W. Silliman	R	1953-54
William H. Parks	R	1881	Luther H. Lincoln	R	1955-58
Hugh M. Larue	D	1883	Ralph M. Brown	D	1959-61
William H. Parks	R	1885	Jesse M. Unruh	D	1961-68
William H. Jordan	R	1887	Robert T. Monagan	R	1969-70
Robert Howe	D	1889	Bob Moretti	D	1971-74
Frank L. Coombs	R	1891	Leo T. McCarthy	D	1974-80
F.H. Gould	D	1893	Willie Brown Jr.	D	1980-

Key to parties: A=American, D=Democrat, DD=Douglas Democrat, I=Independent, P=Progressive, R=Republican, U=Union; – denotes no party.

new arrangement was uncertain; Republicans continued to pursue recall efforts and suggested that things could change later in the year. In addition, the even division of duties had the potential to spell gridlock on some of the controversial issues facing the Legislature, particularly the state budget, which still requires 54 votes for passage. Brown himself hinted that the dynamics of the budget battle had been altered by the speakership impasse. Because Gov. Pete Wilson had intervened in house affairs, supporting the recall effort against Horcher, Brown said he no longer felt a need to round up votes for the governor's budget, as he had done every year for both Wilson and former Gov. George Deukmejian.

Those proposing a power-sharing arrangement throughout the impasse argued that a new organizational structure was necessary for the term-limits era, when members would enter and leave the house more frequently and partisan control, when it existed, would be based on much narrower margins than in the past. In fact, the advent of term limits is one of the most important changes to hit both houses of the Legislature in decades.

Voters approved term limits in 1990 by passing Proposition 140, the brainchild of retiring Los Angeles County Supervisor Pete Schabarum. The initiative limited constitutional officers — except for the insurance commissioner — and state senators to two four-year terms and members of the Assembly to three two-year terms. (The measure also shut down the Legislature's retirement system and reduced its operating budget by 38 percent, resulting in sharp staffing cuts and a loss of policy experts.) All limits were imposed for life, meaning legislators and constitutional officers could not sit out a term and then run for their old office again.

But they could seek a new office, and they have begun doing so. Term limits don't officially start kicking out a large number of lawmakers until 1996 — the year Brown and Brulte both must exit — but in 1994 many legislators opted out of the Assembly early to launch campaigns for Senate seats or constitutional offices that wouldn't come up again for another four years.

In all, the Assembly got 28 new members in the 1994 election — no small factor in the leadership shake-up. At the beginning of the 1995-96 session, 51 of the Assembly's 80 members had served in the house just two years or less. The emergence of a younger, less experienced house inherently transfers some amount of power to other institutions — the state Senate, the executive branch, the lobbying corps. Speaker Brown began appointing more first-term members to power positions in the Assembly beginning in 1993 in order to begin the transfer of power to the new generation of members. That trend will only accelerate in coming years. Several freshmen were named to chair Assembly committees at the start of the 1995-96 session.

Term limits was also the justification given for a substantial pay hike state lawmakers were granted at the start of the 1995-96 session. Members of the California Citizens Compensation Commission, established by the passage of Proposition 112 in 1990, voted in May 1994 to give lawmakers their first salary increase in four years — a 37 percent jump to $72,000 a year, the highest in the nation. The commission argued that the loss of pension benefits and the establishment of term limits meant the Legislature would no longer be a career job and that some enticement was needed to convince qualified — and not necessarily rich — people to take time out from their careers for public service in Sacramento. Under the new salary structure, the Assembly speaker and Senate president pro tem earn $86,400 a year, and floor leaders in each house make $79,200. Lawmakers also receive a "per diem" payment of $109 a day — an average $22,890 a year — for living expenses in Sacramento, along with perks that include health benefits, access

Presidents pro tempore of the Senate

Name	P*	Year(s)	Name	P*	Year(s)
E. Kirby Chamberlain	-	1849	Benjamin Knight Jr.	D	1885
Elcan Haydenfeldt	W	1851	Stephen M. Whitte	D	1887, 1889
Benjamin F. Keene	D	1852-1854	Thomas Fraser	R	1891
Roy T. Sprague	D	1855	R.B. Carpenter	R	1893
Delos R. Ashley	A	1856	Thomas Flint Jr.	R	1895-1903
Samuel H. Dosh	D	1857	Edward I. Wolfe	R	1905-1909
Samuel A. Merritt	D	1858	A.E. Boyton	R	1911, 1913
W.B. Dickenson	D	1859	N.W. Thompson	R	1915
Isaac N. Quinn	D	1860	Arthur H. Breed	R	1917-1933
Richard Irwin	DD	1861	William P. Rich	R	1935, 1937
James Safter	R	1862	Jerrold L. Seawell	R	1939
A.M. Crane	U	1863	William P. Rich	R	1941
R. Burnell	U	1864	Jerrold L. Seawell	R	1943, 1945
S.P. Wright	U	1866	Harold J. Powers	R	1947-1953
Lansing B. Misner	U	1868	Clarence C. Ward	R	1954-1955
Edward J. Lewis	D	1870	Ben Hulse	R	1955-1956
James T. Farley	D	1872	Hugh M. Burns	D	1957-1969
William Irwin	D	1874	Howard Way	R	1969-1970
Benjamin F. Tuttle	D	1876	Jack Schrade	R	1970
Edward J. Lewis	D	1878	James R. Mills	D	1971-1980
George F. Baker	R	1880	David Roberti	D	1980-1994
William Johnston	R	1881	William Lockyer	D	1994-
R.F. Del Valle	D	1883			

* Key to parties: A=American, D=Democrat, DD=Douglas Democrat,
I=Independent, P=Progressive, R=Republican, U=Union; - denotes no party.

to state cars and use of state credit cards for gasoline and telephone calls.

THE CONSTANT CAMPAIGN

While in office, legislators live their lives on a constant campaign, much like their congressional counterparts in Washington. It is the nearest thing to Congress outside Washington, D.C., says political scientist Alan Rosenthal of Rutgers University in New Jersey, an authority on state legislatures. California is way out there beyond where any other legislatures are in terms of political partisanship, full-time campaigning and the cost of campaigns. California is almost another nation.

When the Legislature is in session — generally eight-to-nine months each year minus vacation recesses — lawmakers usually arrive Monday morning and are gone by midafternoon Thursday. By day, legislators juggle committee assignments, floor sessions and their own bills. By night, many partake of the fund-raiser circuit at Sacramento watering holes frequented by lobbyists and staffers. On weekends, lawmakers spend their time toiling in their districts doing constituent work, which is not very different from campaigning. Those from Southern California spend much of their life getting to and from airports.

In the 1990s, it cost an average of $700,000 to win a seat in the state Senate, more than twice as much as it did to win a seat in Congress. That number continues to climb as races become more competitive and term limits lure wealthy candidates who have the luxury of taking time off to spend a few years in the Legislature. Legislators without personal wealth, and even those who have their own economic resources, spend considerable time and energy courting those who can write checks to fill campaign coffers.

Federal probes, term limits and budget stalemates have done nothing to change that fact of Capitol life. Campaign spending studies, however, consistently show that legislators spend comparatively little money on actual electioneering. Mostly, they spend money being a politician — junkets, meals to schmooze donors and power-brokers, tickets to sports events, gifts for supporters, charitable contributions to make a favorable impression in the community and donations to other politicians. A computer analysis by The Sacramento Bee showed legislative incumbents with safe seats spent an average of 40 percent of their campaign funds on such activities.

For a brief time, it appeared voters might have done something to stem the campaign fund-raising binge by approving Proposition 73 in 1988. Although the measure had serious flaws, it put limits on campaign contributions. But in a lawsuit engineered by then-state Democratic Party Chairman Jerry Brown, the contribution limits were thrown out by a federal judge in 1990. The free-for-all campaign spending resumed in California for the 1992 election just in time for Jerry Brown to run for president as a born-again believer in contribution limits.

Federal agents had been investigating members of the California Legislature almost continually since the early 1980s. Those efforts bore fruit in the 1990s. Four senators, Democrats Paul Carpenter, Joseph Montoya and Alan Robbins, and

Republican Frank Hill were convicted of a slew of federal corruption charges for taking bribes while in office. Former Assembly GOP leader Pat Nolan went to jail on similar charges.

The first of the investigations began in the early 1980s after the Legislature passed a bill that would have overturned local ordinances banning fireworks (it was vetoed by then-Gov. Jerry Brown). The probe of the activities of former fireworks mogul W. Patrick Moriarty yielded convictions of several Southern California officials, but only one legislator — Democratic Assemblyman Bruce Young of Norwalk. His conviction was later overturned.

Legislators had no sooner caught their breath from the Moriarty affair when the FBI lifted the lid in August 1988 on an even bigger investigation, officially code-named "Brispec" for Bribery Special Interest. Beginning in 1985, undercover agents had posed as Southern businessmen in search of a bill to benefit their sham companies in return for campaign contributions. They spread more than $50,000 among Capitol figures.

Agents gathered enough evidence in their sting to obtain search warrants for the offices of Nolan, the Assembly's Republican leader at the time; his close associate, then-Assemblyman Frank Hill, R-Whittier; Assemblywoman Gwen Moore, D-Los Angeles; and Sen. Joseph Montoya, D-Whittier. Montoya eventually was convicted and sentenced to federal prison on bribery and money-laundering charges. Former Sen. Paul Carpenter, by then a member of the state Board of Equalization, was convicted on similar charges soon thereafter and eventually was sentenced to the longest prison term in the six-year string of Capitol corruption prosecutions — seven years and three months for conspiracy, money-laundering and mail fraud in connection with the bribery of a fellow senator. U.S. District Judge Edward J. Garcia lengthened Carpenter's sentence because of the former lawmaker's flight to Costa Rica after his December 1993 conviction, and for abuse of his position as a legislator. The judge also fined Carpenter $50,000. Moore eventually was cleared.

Robbins, D-Encino, also was convicted, under a plea bargain, with evidence that flowed in after the sting. Prosecutors discovered an unexpected benefit of their sting when witnesses were emboldened to come forward with new tales of corruption under the dome. Sending chills through the lobbying corps, it was soon revealed that Robbins had been wearing a hidden microphone for the FBI. Not long after, the biggest of the big-time lobbyists, Clayton Jackson, whose lobbying firm had been consistently the most lucrative in Sacramento, was raided by federal authorities with search warrants. Jackson eventually was sentenced to 61/2 years in prison for bribing Robbins.

In connection with the Jackson probe came yet another. A Sacramento-based federal grand jury indicted Mark Nathanson, a Beverly Hills real estate tycoon whom Speaker Brown had appointed to the Coastal Commission. Federal prosecutors threw the book at Nathanson for allegedly taking a bribe. Nathanson eventually was sentenced to four years, nine months in prison and ordered to pay $200,000 in fines and restitution for using his office as a racketeering enterprise and for avoiding taxes. Nathanson acknowledged trying to extort hundreds of thousands of dollars from coastal property owners.

Hill was eventually sentenced to 46 months in prison and fined $2,500 for corruption in office.

Shaken by all this federal activity, the Legislature tightened its ethical standards by placing Proposition 112 on the June 1990 ballot. Once approved, the measure subjected legislators for the first time to enforceable conflict-of-interest laws, banned honorariums and restricted gifts to $250 a year from any single source.

INITIATIVES ABOUND

The Legislature's biggest achievements were usually accomplished under the threat of a more Draconian initiative from the outside. A number of organizations found it easier and cheaper than lobbying the Legislature to draft their own law, gather enough signatures and take their measure directly to voters. The result was a bewildering array of ballot proposals, some by outsiders, many by individual lawmakers and others by the Legislature itself.

However, voters administered a dose of tonic in November 1990, when they rejected all but six of 28 ballot measures. That election may have signaled that the high-water mark for initiatives has passed. On the June 1992 primary ballot, there were no initiatives; the November general election ballot had a manageable 13 propositions and eight were rejected, including the governor's welfare-cutting proposal. In the November 1994 general election there were 10 initiatives on the ballot — six passed and four failed.

California became the 10th state in the nation to enact the initiative and referendum by special election on Oct. 10, 1911, during the term of reformist Gov. Hiram Johnson. Petitions designed to enact or reform statutes can be placed on the ballot with the valid signatures of 5 percent of the total number of votes cast for governor in the most recent gubernatorial election. Constitutional amendments can be placed before the voters with the backing of 8 percent of the total vote. In theory, initiatives are restricted to making one change at a time in the Constitution, not wholesale revisions. There were signs that the courts were beginning to enforce that single-subject rule. An appellate court struck down Proposition 105, the consumer's right-to-know act, on grounds that it was too broad. However, the state Supreme Court dashed hopes of legislators by refusing to strike down term limits based on the single-subject rule.

BIOGRAPHICAL SKETCHES

Biographical sketches for each legislator follow this introduction. Legislators are listed in alphabetical order. Following the sketches are election results for the previous two campaigns, where applicable, and the amount of money raised for the campaign, where available. The 1992 figures are for contributions raised during an

18- month period. The 1994 figures represent one year of fund-raising. Voter registration figures listed are those as of the Nov. 8, 1994, general election.

RATINGS

Ratings are listed from a spectrum of six ideological and trade groups. The score represents the percentage of time the officeholder voted in agreement on bills of interest to that organization. Where NR is listed, the legislator was not rated by that organization, usually because the legislator did not cast enough votes for a fair rating or because the legislator was elected too late in the session.

Rating methodologies used by organizations vary. For a complete list and analysis of how each organization compiled its ratings, the reader should contact the organization. Ratings of the California Public Interest Research Group and the California Teachers' Association, included in previous editions, were not completed in time for publication.

AFL-CIO — The California American Federation of Labor-Congress of Industrial Organizations, the largest labor federation in the nation, based its ratings on how lawmakers in both the Senate and the Assembly voted on 26 bills in 1993. The issues included immigration, housing, health care and consumer protection. (916) 444-3676; (415) 986-3585.

CLCV — The California League of Conservation Voters, largest and oldest state political action committee, is a political arm for more than 100 environmental organizations. Ratings are based on 1994 votes on 22 bills in the Assembly and 20 in the Senate. Issues included air quality, coastal protection, land use, toxics regulation and wildlife management. (415) 896-5550; (310) 441-4162.

NOW — California National Organization for Women, a women's rights group affiliated with the national organization, based its ratings for members of both houses on 21 bills in 1994. The issues included domestic violence, poverty, gay rights, child support and women's health. (916) 442-3414.

CofC — The California Chamber of Commerce, a statewide business group, based its 1994 ratings on 17 bills for senators and 22 bills for Assembly members. Bills included proposals on limited-liability companies, tort reform, property rights, employee relations and toxic cleanup. (916) 444-6670.

CalFarm — California Farm Bureau, representing agricultural interests, based its 1994 ratings on five bills for senators, nine bills for Assembly members. Issues included legislation on the lawful killing of endangered species, opposition to restrictions on bobcat trapping and support for speedy registration of pesticides. (916) 446-4647.

GO — Gun Owners of California, which lobbies against firearm restrictions in the state, rated lawmakers with a letter grade based on legislative votes. For incumbent senators in odd-numbered districts, who were not required to seek re-election in 1994, the gun owners' 1992 rating is given. (916) 361-3109.

COMMON ABBREVIATIONS

AB — Assembly Bill
ACA — Assembly Constitutional Amendment
AI — American Independent Party
Assn. — Association
CSU — California State University
J.D. — Juris doctor (modern law degree)
L — Libertarian party
M.P.A. — Masters, Public Administration
NR — Not Rated
P&F — Peace and Freedom party
SB — Senate Bill
SCA — Senate Constitutional Amendment
UC — University of California
USC — University of Southern California

Senators and district numbers

1 LESLIE, Tim, R-Carnelian Bay
2 THOMPSON, Mike, D-St. Helena
3 MARKS, Milton, D-San Francisco
4 JOHANNESSEN, Maurice,
   R-Redding
5 JOHNSTON, Patrick, D-Stockton
6 GREENE, Leroy, D-Carmichael
7 BOATWRIGHT, Daniel,
   D-Concord
8 KOPP, Quentin, I-San Francisco
9 PETRIS, Nicholas, D-Oakland
10 LOCKYER, Bill, D-Hayward
11 CAMPBELL, Tom, R-Stanford
12 MONTEITH, Dick, R-Modesto
13 ALQUIST, Alfred, D-San Jose
14 MADDY, Ken, R-Fresno
15 MELLO, Henry, D-Santa Cruz
16 COSTA, Jim, D-Hanford
17 ROGERS, Don, R-Tehachapi
18 O'CONNELL, Jack,
   D-Carpinteria
19 WRIGHT, Cathie, R-Simi Valley
20 ROSENTHAL, Herschel,
   D-Van Nuys

21 RUSSELL, Newton, R-Glendale
22 POLANCO, Richard,
   D-Los Angeles
23 HAYDEN, Tom, D-Santa Monica
24 SOLIS, Hilda, D-El Monte
25 HUGHES, Teresa, D-Inglewood
26 WATSON, Diane, D-Los Angeles
27 BEVERLY, Robert,
   R-Redondo Beach
28 DILLS, Ralph, D-Gardena
29 MOUNTJOY, Richard, R-Arcadia
30 CALDERON, Charles, D-Whittier
31 LEONARD, William, R-Upland
32 AYALA, Ruben, D-Chino
33 LEWIS, John, R-Orange
34 HURTT, Rob, R-Garden Grove
35 VACANT (Bergeson)
36 HAYNES, Ray, R-Murrieta
37 KELLEY, David, R-Hemet
38 CRAVEN, William, R-Oceanside
39 KILLEA, Lucy, I-San Diego
40 PEACE, Steve, D-Chula Vista

California Senate districts

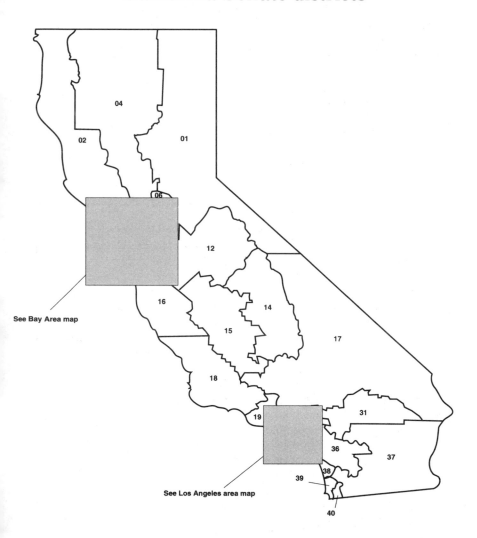

Bay Area Senate districts

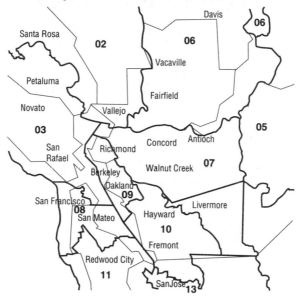

Los Angeles Senate districts

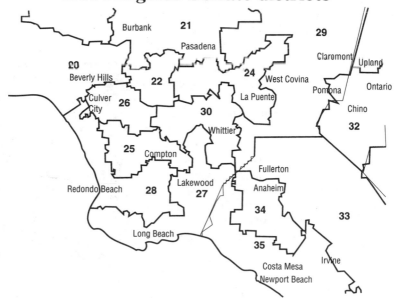

SENATE
Vacant
35th Senate District

With redistricting, the 35th Senate District lost its sprawling, gerrymandered outer edges while retaining the northern Orange County coast, including three cities with beach in their names — Huntington, Newport and Laguna — and it was perfect for then Republican Sen. Marian Bergeson, whose home is in Newport Beach. Bergeson easily won re-election to a third term in 1992. Given the overwhelming Republican registration of the district, approaching 60 percent, the Democrats never even considered a challenge.

In 1993, Bergeson was nominated by Gov. Wilson to serve as state school superintendent, but her nomination was rejected by the Assembly on a vote that closely followed party lines. One of the charges against her was that her Mormon beliefs conflicted with scientific evidence of human evolution.

Halfway through her four-year term, in January 1995, Bergeson resigned her Senate seat to take a seat she won in June 1994 on the Orange County Board of Supervisors. Among the potential candidates vying to replace her were former Republican Assemblyman Gil Ferguson of Newport Beach and Assembly members Doris Allen of Cypress and Ross Johnson of Fullerton. Ferguson, a conservative Republican, gave up his Assembly seat to run for the Senate seat.

REGISTRATION: 32.38% D, 53.39% R

Alfred Alquist (D)
13th Senate District

Lying in the core of Santa Clara County, the 13th Senate District takes in the heart of San Jose and portions of Santa Clara, Sunnyvale and Mountain View. The area has mirrored the transformation and growth of California in the last 30 years. Where once there were orchards and canneries, now there are housing tracts, high-tech industries, traffic and smog. Following the 1992 reapportionment, the district is almost one-third Latino and 18 percent Asian.

Democrat Alfred Alquist, the oldest member of the Legislature, has served long enough to have seen all of those changes. Elected to the part-time Assembly in 1962, Alquist was among the first class of full-time legislators elected to the Senate in 1966. Alquist

Alfred Alquist

has had a generally successful career, though one with plenty of ups and downs. His landmark legislation created the Energy Commission, the Seismic Safety Commission and established earthquake construction standards for hospitals. Alquist has had his stamp on every major piece of earthquake preparedness legislation of the last three decades. He could take grim satisfaction in knowing that many of the laws he authored doubtlessly saved thousands of lives in the Oct. 17, 1989, Loma Prieta quake and the Jan. 17, 1994, Northridge quake.

Alquist, iron-faced, publicly devoid of humor (although wryly funny in private), well past his prime, is still a force not to be crossed lightly. At his peak, Alquist was chairman of the all-powerful Appropriations Committee. But in 1986, he agreed to relinquish his post to mollify critics of then-Senate President Pro Tem David Roberti within his own party. Roberti split Alquist's committee in two. Alquist kept his imprint on the immensely complicated state spending plan as chairman of a new Budget and Fiscal Review Committee, a panel chiefly responsible for the Senate version of the state budget each year, but lost power over the daily workings of legislation, which go before the reduced Appropriations Committee.

Each year, Alquist and Assembly Ways and Means Chairman John Vasconcellos take turns chairing the budget conference committee, where the final budget legislation is shaped. In 1992, during the longest budget stalemate for any state in American history, it was Alquist's turn to chair the budget conference committee. But it was clear that Alquist was tired and Vasconcellos, for all intents and purposes, ran meetings.

In 1994, Alquist charged that the election-year budget was "balanced on the backs of the poorest and most defenseless people in our society." Alquist complained that a provision to continue an income tax surcharge on wealthy Californians was stripped out in final negotiations.

Alquist is known for a stormy temper, much in evidence in 1985, when he had a fabled shouting match with *enfant terrible* then-Assemblyman Steve Peace over an Alquist bill to establish a nuclear waste disposal compact with other states. Exactly what was said is still disputed; some witnesses (including Sen. Ken Maddy) claim Peace called Alquist a senile old pedophile while thrusting his right index finger toward him. Peace claims that he (only) called the elder senator a pitiful little creature. Whoever was right was unimportant; an outraged Senate responded by killing all of Peace's remaining bills for the year.

Alquist's first wife, Mai, died in 1989. Outspoken, and a character in her own right in the Legislature, she was her husband's political confidant for years. Many thought that he would retire at the end of 1992, but he chose to seek one more term and won easily.

PERSONAL: elected 1966; born Aug. 2, 1908, in Memphis, Tenn.; home, Santa Clara; Army (WWII); education, attended Southwestern University; wife, Elaine; one child; Protestant.

CAREER: railroad yardmaster; transportation supervisor; Assembly 1962-1966.

COMMITTEES: Budget and Fiscal Review (chair); Appropriations; Constitutional Amendments; Energy, Utilities and Communications; Governmental Organization; Revenue and Taxation.

OFFICES: Capitol, (916) 445-9740, FAX (916) 323-8386; district, 100 Paseo de San Antonio, 209, San Jose 95113, (408) 286-8318, FAX (408) 286-2338.

TERM LIMIT: 1996

REGISTRATION: 53.52% D, 29.72% R

1992 CAMPAIGN:	Alquist D	60.5%	$732,237
	Michael Iddings R	31.2%	Not Available
	John Webster L	8.3%	Not Available
1988 CAMPAIGN:	Alquist D	64.8%	$592,405
	Daniel Bertolet R	31.4%	$66,314

RATINGS:	AFL-CIO	CLCV	NOW	CofC	CalFarm	GO
	88	33	B+	41	80	F

Ruben Ayala (D)
32nd Senate District

Ruben Ayala

This largely Latino district includes the communities of Pomona, the dairy farms and prisons of Chino, and boom towns along the Interstate 10 corridor: Fontana, Upland, Ontario and part of western San Bernardino with concentrations of minorities. Fontana, in particular, has undergone a remarkable turnabout. Facing economic collapse when Kaiser Steel closed its World War II-vintage mill, the working-class town has come back from the dead with housing tracts and new businesses.

Ruben Ayala, who was squeezed out of the district in the 1992 reapportionment, chose to bail out of the new 34th District and to run in a March 1993 special election for the redrawn 32nd District seat, since it contained his home in Chino and territory he has represented for two decades. More than anything else, Ayala is and remains a San Bernardino County politician.

Ayala is an energetic legislator, jealously guarding the parochial interests of San Bernardino County. He has kept a state building in San Bernardino by warding off the encroachments of Riverside's legislators to the south, and sought new escape-proofing measures for the cluster of prisons in Chino at the behest of middle-class homeowners terrified by the bloody massacre of a family by an escapee in 1984.

Ayala is the former chairman of the principal committee on water issues and has labored to expand and modernize the state's water system with little success. To be sure, the task might defy even the most diplomatic and clever of lawmakers, but the bullheaded Ayala's efforts took on the trappings of a personal war. In 1987-88, backed by Gov. George Deukmejian, Ayala worked out a limited proposal to upgrade levees in the Sacramento River Delta. The plan also included rehabilitation projects at the Salton Sea and elsewhere in the southern end of the water system. But the proposal met unexpected opposition from Northern California Republican Sen. Jim Nielsen, and that was just too much for Ayala. Giving up in a burst of fury on the Senate floor, Ayala lashed out at all who had differences with him on the details, and the state entered its worst drought in decades with few significant improvements to its water system.

At the start of the 1993-94 session, Ayala won a coveted seat on the five-member Senate Rules Committee, which runs the Senate, replacing Democrat Henry Mello. But Ayala had to give up his chairmanship of the agriculture and water committee. In one of those strangely choreographed legislative dances, Ayala ended up being named vice chairman of the committee, allowing him to keep a heavy hand in water issues.

In 1994, Ayala was one of several members of the Senate who co-authored a controversial bill that called for the paddling of juveniles caught painting graffiti. It was first corporal punishment proposed as state law in California in more than 100 years. The California Civil Liberties Union and the California PTA labeled the legislation "barbaric."

In one of the few memorable moments in the 1994 campaign, Ayala's Republican opponent Earl DeVries, staged a "Tax Freedom Day" rally at Ruben S. Ayala Park.

PERSONAL: elected 1974 (special election); born March 6, 1922, in Chino; home, Chino; USMC (WWII); education, attended junior college and UCLA Extension, graduated electronics school; wife, Irene; three children; Roman Catholic.

CAREER: insurance; Chino School Board 1955-1962; Chino City Council 1962-1964; mayor 1964-1965; San Bernardino County Board of Supervisors 1965-1973.

COMMITTEES: Agriculture & Water Resources (vice chair); Local Government (vice chair); Veterans Affairs (vice chair); Business & Professions; Legislative Ethics; Rules; Transportation.

OFFICES: Capitol, (916) 445-6868, FAX (916) 445-0128; district, 9620 Center Ave., 100, Rancho Cucamonga 91730, (909) 466-6882, FAX (909) 941-7219.

TERM LIMIT: 1998

REGISTRATION: 52.17% D, 37.36% R

1994 CAMPAIGN:	Ayala D	60.74%	$225,589
	Earl deVries R	39.62%	$8,355
1990 CAMPAIGN:	Ayala D	51.8%	$1,032,997
	Charles Bader R	48.2%	$761,778

RATINGS: AFL-CIO   CLCV   NOW   CofC   CalFarm   GO
          83   32   B-   47   40   D

Robert G. Beverly (R)
27th Senate District

Bob Beverly is the visual embodiment of a distinguished politician with his snow-white hair and courtly manners. And until 1992, he never had much trouble getting himself elected to the Legislature from districts along Los Angeles County's southern coast, first as an assemblyman for 10 years and since 1976 as a member of the Senate. But reapportionment maps drawn up by the state Supreme Court did Republican Beverly no favors. His old 29th District was split and his home in Manhattan Beach (where he had been city attorney, city councilman and mayor before his election to the Legislature) was placed in a district with a Democratic tilt. To run for re-election in 1992, Beverly had to move his residence to Redondo

Robert Beverly

Beach, part of the reconfigured and renumbered 27th District, which had a much-better GOP registration profile.

It also meant that Beverly had to campaign in some communities, such as Bellflower, Lakewood and Hawaiian Gardens, that were not only new to him but had strong Democratic leanings, while retaining more familiar and more Republican territory in Long Beach (the district includes two-thirds of that city). The district also has an overseas component: Catalina Island and its 3,000 strongly Republican residents 26 miles off the coast.

The upshot was that Beverly found himself in a surprisingly desperate battle against Democrat Brian Finander and only the infusion of help from friends in the Legislature and in the lobbying corps in Sacramento saved Beverly from an ignominious end to his long legislative career. He wound up winning re-election by just over 5,000 votes — and may have been saved by the strong showing (9,000 votes) of a Peace and Freedom Party candidate. Beverly thus has one last term in the Senate before term limits end his 30-year legislative career.

The book on Beverly is that he isn't the most productive person to serve in the Legislature, but by no means is he the worst. He's an insider who never participates in the Capitol's ideological wars and only rarely in the power struggles. He's also a close personal friend of the Senate's Republican leader, Ken Maddy, and someone who takes care of the minimal legislative needs of his district while voting as a loyal Republican. The badge of his insider status is his seat on the Senate Rules Committee, the panel that exercises bipartisan control over the business of the house.

He gets along well with Democrats in the Senate, and was a key swing vote for former Senate President Pro Tem David Roberti's bill banning semiautomatic assault weapons. Labeling Beverly, however, does not do justice to the role he plays in the Senate. He shows himself motivated to a great extent not by ideology but personal relationships. Beverly often presides over the Senate; his quick rulings and even temper at the rostrum are richly valued by his colleagues. Beverly may be in the minority but he is certainly in the club that runs the Legislature. When Sen. Bill Lockyer, who moved on to become pro tem, crashed a meeting in David Roberti's office in the spring of 1989 to complain about secret budget deals, he found Beverly among those inside. When Assembly Speaker Willie Brown went to Lloyd's of London in 1986 as part of an insurance industry sponsored fact-finding trip, among those he took with him was Beverly.

The jovial Beverly carries water for a lot of people. He authored the 1987 bill for Gov. George Deukmejian that rebated $1.1 billion to taxpayers. A 1987 Beverly bill restored $86.6 million in aid to the state's urban school districts previously cut by Deukmejian. Other, lesser bills by Beverly are worthy of note. In the waning days of the 1989 session, he pushed a measure allowing members of the Signal Hill City Council to circumvent conflict-of-interest laws so they could vote on a proposed development that stood a chance of boosting their property values. He has pushed hard on a measure to exempt certain over-the-counter stock transactions from state regulation. One of the most hotly contested measures behind the scenes was a Beverly bill to exempt employees of mortgage banking firms from having to hold a real estate license.

PERSONAL: elected 1976; born July 1, 1925, in Belmont, Mass.; home, Redondo Beach; USMC (1943-1946); education, attended UCLA 1946-1948, J.D. Loyola University; wife Bettelu, three children; Protestant.

CAREER: city attorney; Manhattan Beach City Council, mayor 1958-1967; Assembly 1967-1976 (Assembly Republican Leader).

COMMITTEES: Rules (vice chair); Elections and Reapportionment; Finance, Investment, and International Trade; Governmental Organization; Criminal Procedure.

OFFICES: Capitol, (916) 445-6447; district, 1611 S. Pacific Coast Highway, 102, Redondo Beach 90277, (310) 540-1611, FAX (310) 540-2192.

TERM LIMIT: 1996

REGISTRATION: 46.8% D, 40.7% R

1992 CAMPAIGN:	Beverly R	47.3%	$481,381
	Brian Finander D	45.4%	$123,483
1988 CAMPAIGN:	Beverly R	67.2%	$248,232
	Jack Hachmeister D	29.5% $0	

RATINGS:	AFL-CIO	CLCV	NOW	CofC	CalFarm	GO
	53	21	B-	71	40	C

Daniel E. Boatwright (D)

7th Senate District

As the San Francisco Bay Area has grown into the fourth-largest metropolitan region in the United States, development has oozed out through the Caldecott tunnel in the Berkeley Hills into Contra Costa County. The Diablo Valley, once a sleepy string of towns connected by two-lane roads, is now crisscrossed with freeways and covered with concrete-and-glass towers. Walnut Creek even has a skyline.

Daniel Boatwright

In the 1930s, it was a long train ride to Oakland for basic services such as medical care for the oil refinery workers in Avon, and not much in-between. Now the massive Bishop Ranch industrial park houses high-tech industry and housing tracts cover the hillsides and valleys. The headquarters of Chevron is here, and its executives live nearby in places such as the exclusive walled community of Blackhawk with its nearby classic car museum and a supermarket with brass carts and a pianist.

Combative Democrat Dan Boatwright has been a central figure in Contra Costa politics for three decades, first in local offices, then eight years in the Assembly and, since 1980, the Senate. He has survived tough elections, a 1980s Internal Revenue Service investigation that sought $112,000 in back taxes for 1976 and a 1984 civil trial in which he was acquitted of taking money for official favors. Newspapers have written about the $10,000 Boatwright received from a law firm, one of whose clients was seeking an $8.7 million tax break through a Boatwright bill. His girlfriend was a featured witness in his civil trial.

In the Capitol, Boatwright has been one of the Legislature's biggest bullies. In 1986, when he chaired the Appropriations Committee, he arbitrarily killed without a hearing dozens of Assembly bills in a single day, setting off howls of protests from offended lawmakers. Then Senate Pro Tem David Roberti stuck up for his demagogic chairman, but was repaid a year later when Boatwright tried to line up enough votes to depose Roberti as Senate leader. Roberti swiftly sacked Boatwright as Appropriations chair, setting off a vintage Boatwright outburst: "If he wants to sit up in his little ivory tower and be besieged every day for the rest of his term, he's come to the right guy," Boatwright said of Roberti. "I was a combat infantryman in Korea, had my ass shot off, and I know how to fight a war. If he wants war, he's got war . . . I'll throw hand grenades, go get a big bazooka. I mean, I know how to fight a war."

But no amount of public invective got Boatwright his job back (and he was not wounded in Korea). Roberti reached a detente with Boatwright in 1988, when he poured in thousands of dollars and drafted innumerable Senate staffers to help Boatwright meet a tough challenge from popular Contra Costa Supervisor Sunne McPeak. Roberti bolstered Boatwright's status by giving him a new job, chairmanship of the new Bonded Indebtedness Committee. After the conviction of Sen. Joseph Montoya on federal corruption charges, Boatwright moved into one of the Senate's best assignments, chairman of the Business and Professions Committee, with authority over regulatory legislation.

In Oct. 1994, Boatwright, who was chairing a hearing of the Select Committee on State Procurement and Expenditure, stopped the proceeding and asked the sergeant-at-arms to remove Insurance Commissioner John Garamendi from the witness table. Garamendi and Sen. Quentin Kopp, I-San Francisco, had been sparring over Garamendi's explanation for spending more than $50 million from failed insurance company assets on outside law firms instead of using lawyers from the attorney general's office at $90 an hour. Boatwright, Kopp and Garamendi had exchanged several sharp questions and answers, repeatedly talking over and through each other. Finally Boatwright had had it. "We've heard enough," he snapped. "You're through; that's it." The Concord Democrat then motioned Garamendi away from the witness table, telling him, "Take your seat back there." When Garamendi hesitated, Boatwright stopped the hearing and asked the sergeant-at-arms to escort him.

Despite the minidrama with Garamendi, some of Boatwright's old bluster has mellowed. His new demeanor may reflect the fact that his Senate district also has changed, from one that solidly favored Democrats to one that most likely will elect a Republican whenever Boatwright departs. Following the 1992 reapportionment, the district kept its number seven but lost loyal Democratic voters in the largely African American city of Richmond and was pushed farther into wealthier, Republican-voting communities of southern Contra Costa County and eastern Alameda County, including much of the Livermore Valley. Those changes dropped Democratic registration 7 percentage points. It had little effect on Boatwright's 1992 re-election over Republican Gil Marguth, a former state assemblyman who made a token and ill-financed effort.

PERSONAL: elected 1980; born, Jan. 29, 1930, in Harrison, Ark.; home, Concord; Army 1948-1952 (Korea); education, B.A. and J.D. UC Berkeley; wife Teresa, three children; Protestant.

CAREER: lawyer; Contra Costa deputy district attorney 1960-1963; Concord City Council 1966-1972; mayor 1966-1968; Assembly 1972-1980.

COMMITTEES: Business & Professions (chair); Budget & Fiscal Review; Elections & Reapportionment; Revenue & Taxation; Transportation; Criminal Procedure.

OFFICES: Capitol, (916) 445-6083, FAX (916) 446-7367; district, 1001 Galaxy Way, 210, Concord 94520, (510) 689-1973, FAX (510) 689-0618.

TERM LIMIT: 1996

REGISTRATION: 45.43% D, 40.19% R

1992 CAMPAIGN:	Boatwright D	58.0%	$1,023,657
	Gilbert Marguth Jr. R	41.9 %	$183,193
1988 CAMPAIGN:	Boatwright D	63%	$1,215,545
	William Pollacek R	37%	$243,386

RATINGS:	AFL-CIO	CLCV	NOW	CofC	CalFarm	GO
	85	67	B-	35	0	B+

Charles M. Calderon (D)
30th Senate District

Charles Calderon

The reapportionment plan that the state Supreme Court adopted in 1992 after a partisan stalemate in the Capitol contained an ethnic bias — one dictated largely by federal law. The federal Voting Rights Act requires that maximum effort be made to enhance political opportunities for underrepresented minorities. That meant the creation of legislative and congressional districts specifically for Latinos. The San Gabriel Valley east of downtown Los Angeles met the criteria for special treatment and thus the area's one Latino state senator, Charles Calderon, found his district divided into two, each with a very large Latino population base.

He could have chosen either the 24th or the 30th for the final half of his term and he chose the latter with its 75 percent Latino population and extremely strong Democratic registration. Having established his district office in the 30th, Calderon ran for re-election there in 1994.

The 30th District runs from Huntington Park on the west to Whittier on the east and from Montebello on the north to Norwalk — the largest city in the district — on the south. In addition to Latinos, the district is the home to a significant number of Asians, although the largest Asian communities of the San Gabriel Valley were concentrated in the 24th District.

Calderon's predecessor, Joe Montoya, held this seat for 12 years and probably would have been re-elected indefinitely. But Montoya, one of the Capitol's biggest juice players, was convicted on federal bribery and racketeering charges in 1990, the first legislator imprisoned in the FBI's Brispec undercover investigation. During Montoya's travails, Calderon moved from Monterey Park to Whittier and in so doing perfectly positioned himself to grab off Montoya's seat. Calderon had little trouble winning the seat in an April 1990 special election. His only formidable potential opponent, then-Assemblywoman Sally Tanner, decided not to run.

Calderon, a former prosecutor, couldn't have left the Assembly at a better time.

He had fallen in with four other youngish Assembly members who hung out at Paragary's restaurant in midtown Sacramento. The group eventually plotted the overthrow of Speaker Willie Brown and became known as the "Gang of Five." At the start of the 1989 session, the rebels formed a brief alliance with Republican Assembly leader Ross Johnson that had Republicans voting for Calderon for speaker. The effort failed. Calderon had no trouble winning a full Senate term in November 1990. Less than a year into his new job, in January 1992, he ran for the Los Angeles County Board of Supervisors, but did not make the run-off.

Aside from involvement in the endless petty intrigues of the Capitol, Calderon is generally a competent legislator. His chief legislative accomplishment has been in shepherding interstate banking legislation through to Gov. George Deukmejian's signature, despite the best efforts of then-Sen Alan Robbins to kill it. Calderon's bill opened California to out-of-state banks over a phased-in period.

Robbins, meanwhile, joined Montoya in federal prison as he, too, fell victim to the federal investigation. Calderon did not inherit the chairmanship of the Senate Business and Professions Committee from Montoya, but the Senate leadership did make him chairman of the Toxics and Public Safety Management Committee — a significant position for a politician from the heavily polluted San Gabriel Valley.

In 1994, Calderon won enactment of a bill that many environmentalists considered to be the worst of the session. The legally dubious SB 923 allows the state to pick 30 sites that would be restored to levels that are safe for future use, rather than to their former natural conditions. The industry-written bill represented a major retreat from the concept of holding polluters responsible for their own messes. Calderon claimed the bill would end endless litigation and speed cleanup of toxic sites.

The same year, Calderson agreed to pay the state a $15,000 fine for using $931 in campaign funds for personal purposes during 1990 and 1991. The state Fair Political Practices Commission said Calderon illegally spent the money on modeling photos for his then-wife, entertainment for his son's birthday party and a tennis outfit he wore for a celebrity tournament.

PERSONAL: elected 1990 (special election); born March 12, 1950, in Montebello; home, Whittier; education, B.A. CSU Los Angeles, J.D. UC Davis; divorced, two children; unaffiliated Christian.

CAREER: lawyer; city attorney's prosecutor; school board member 1979-1982; legislative aide to Assembly members Richard Alatorre and Jack Fenton; special consultant to Secretary of State March Fong Eu; Assembly 1982-1990.

COMMITTEES: Agriculture & Water Resources; Finance, Investment & International Trade; Judiciary (chair); Appropriations; Local Government.

OFFICES: Capitol, (916) 327-8315; district, 400 N. Montebello Blvd. 101, Montebello 90640, (213) 724-6175, FAX (213) 724-6566.

TERM LIMIT: 1998

REGISTRATION: 65.21% D, 23.97% R

1994 CAMPAIGN:	Calderon D		67.90%	$300,950
	Ken Gow R		32.10%	Not Available
1990 CAMPAIGN:	Calderon D		62.8%	$106,931
	Joe Urquidi R		32%	$1,190

| **RATINGS:** | AFL-CIO | CLCV | NOW | CofC | CalFarm | GO |
| | 90 | 71 | B+ | 29 | 60 | D |

Tom Campbell (R)

11th Senate District

Sen. Rebecca Morgan, R-Los Altos, had hoped to be appointed state superintendent of schools after Bill Honig was convicted of using his office to assist his wife's educational company. But when Gov. Pete Wilson showed no inclination to appoint her, Morgan assessed her limited political future and left the Senate to run an industry trade group in Silicon Valley.

Tom Campbell

That created an opening for Tom Campbell, who served two terms in the U.S. House of Representatives before losing the 1992 GOP U.S. Senate primary to Bruce Herschensohn. Herschensohn then lost to Barbara Boxer.

This is a seat that Democrats should have been able to take. But the most electable candidate, Assemblyman Byron Sher, D-Palo Alto, backed out after Campbell entered the race. Campbell seems well suited to the district's constituency, which is anchored in academic and computer electronics fields. While in the House, he had the most liberal voting record of any member of the GOP delegation from California, including a 100 percent rating from the League of Conservation Voters. He has worked in the White House, the U.S. Justice Department, the Federal Trade Commission and was a Stanford law professor. In addition to trade and tax expertise, he is a prodigious fund-raiser.

New state senators often wind up taking a back seat to more senior members, a tradition that is only slowly fading as term limits force the political elders to quit. But Campbell has something to say about nearly every issue that comes before the Senate. Campbell's other unusual habit is a courteousness that is seldom seen these days — inside or outside public office.

In an interview after winning the seat he said: "I could have run for (state) treasurer. I could have run for lieutenant governor.... I chose this, and I am delighted with this choice. There is so much substance to this job as compared with those others." He added that he didn't intend to slight anyone running for those offices.

Since entering the Senate, Campbell has continued to solidify his image as a fiscal conservative with moderate-to-liberal leanings on social issues. Campbell shows indications of being anti-affirmative action, a subject that is sure to gain much attention in 1995 and 1996. But Campbell also carried a bill that would have required that all state armories be made available to shelter homeless people, except when the facilities are needed for military or emergency purposes. The bill was vetoed by Gov. Pete Wilson.

The 11th District begins at Half Moon Bay and loops over the San Andreas fault to the wealthy bedroom communities of the mid-San Francisco Peninsula, including Redwood City, Palo Alto and Menlo Park. Then it curves around to the equally affluent western suburbs of San Jose, Campbell and Los Gatos. Downsizing in the computer-electronics industry has led to high unemployment in the area, but it continues to be one of the foremost research and development centers in the United States.

PERSONAL: elected 1993; born Aug. 14, 1952, in Chicago, Ill.; home, Palo Alto; education, B.A. and M.A. University of Chicago 1973, J.D. Harvard University 1976, Ph.D. University of Chicago 1980; wife Susanne; no religious affiliation.

CAREER: attorney 1978-80; White House and U.S. Justice Department positions, 1980-81; Federal Trade Commission, 1981-83; Stanford law professor, 1983-88.

COMMITTEES: Housing and Land Use (chair); Revenue and Taxation (vice chair); Budget and Fiscal Review; Criminal Procedure; Education; Judiciary.

OFFICES: Capitol, (916) 445-6747, FAX (916) 3234529; district, 373 First St., 100, Los Altos, 94022, (415)-949-5401, FAX 415-949-5495

TERM LIMIT: 2000

REGISTRATION: 46% D, 38.3 R

1993 CAMPAIGN:	Campbell R		59.5%	Not Available
	Hal Plotkin D		11%	Not Available

RATINGS:	AFL-CIO	CLCV	NOW	CofC	CalFarm	GO
	NA	32	B	82	60	NA

Jim Costa (D)
16th Senate District

Most of the valley floor of the southern San Joaquin Valley lies in this district, an area where agriculture and oil coexist with relative harmony. Severe overdrafting of groundwater and the buildup of salts and wastes from irrigation threaten the agricultural future of this area, as does the steady erosion of air quality caused by the oil industry and suburban sprawl. But this is not an area where environmental awareness has much of a following. Political leadership springs from business interests with 19th century attitudes. And no one ever got far here taking on agribusiness or big oil.

Reapportionment lines were carefully drawn to create a mostly Hispanic district

(51 percent). It begins south of Chowchilla, skirts around Madera and follows a contorted path south to include poorer areas of Fresno and the Highway 99 cities stretching to Bakersfield. If Latinos would vote, this would be a safe place for one of their own. But the power structure remains in the hands of white growers and small-town business people. There also are a number of new prisons in the district whose employees tend to be conservative.

Jim Costa

Republican Sen. Don Rogers of Bakersfield had represented large portions of this district. But the new Democratic numbers gave him incentive to move south to Tehachapi in 1992 and to run in an area more suited to Republicans. Once elected he resigned the 16th District, spurring a special election in March 1993 between Assemblyman Jim Costa, D-Fresno, and former Assemblyman Phil Wyman, R-Tehachapi. But they had to run within the old 16th District boundaries since the new district lines didn't become effective until the 1994 election. That made the turf more friendly to Wyman. After a malodorous campaign, Wyman squeaked by.

The rematch in 1994, however, put Costa in the catbird seat with registration numbers on his side. Following his election in 1993, Wyman had moved to Hanford in the center of his new district and immediately started campaigning non-stop. But Costa defeated him in 1994 after an expensive, bruising and bitter campaign in which each candidate attempted to paint the other as a radical.

Costa is a tenacious and skillful politician who worked hard for his Assembly district. But he is also weighed down by political baggage.

During his more than 10 years in the Assembly, Costa had became an ace legislative technician and one of Assembly Speaker Willie Brown's lieutenants. In 1990, he was chosen by his fellow Assembly Democrats as caucus leader, the No. 4 party position in the lower house.

On the upside of Costa's career, he's carried several major bond issues, including one that voters approved in 1990 that will result in the expenditure of $1 billion on upgrading rail transportation. On the downside, Costa has become one of the Capitol's big juice players, carrying legislation for special-interest groups and accepting large campaign contributions, gifts and speaking fees. He unsuccessfully pushed several anti-rent-control bills for landlords, as well as a measure for beer wholesalers that would have guaranteed them territorial monopolies. That measure was eventually vetoed by Gov. George Deukmejian.

But it was Costa's arrest on the last night of the 1986 legislative session that brought him his greatest notoriety. Just weeks before he was to face voters for re-election, and while traveling in a state-leased car with a known prostitute at his side, Costa offered $50 to an undercover woman police officer to join them in a three-way sex act, Sacramento police said. Nearly a week later, with his mother nearby, Costa admitted during a press conference in his home district that he had made an error in judgment. Later that month, he was fined $1 and given three years' probation. The episode would have spelled the end of a political career for anyone from a district with a different makeup of voters. But Republicans failed to capitalize on the incident and Costa easily won re-election.

PERSONAL: elected 1994; born April 13, 1952, in Fresno; home, Fresno; education, B.S. CSU Fresno; single; Roman Catholic.

CAREER: aide to Rep. B.F. Sisk 1974-1975 and Rep. John Krebs 1975-1976; assistant to Assemblyman Richard Lehman 1976-1978; Assembly 1978-94, caucus chair 1991-1992.

COMMITTEES: Agriculture and Water Resources (chair); Housing and Land Use; Budget and Fiscal Review; Public Employment and Retirement; Finance, Investment and International Trade.

OFFICES: Capitol, (916) 445-7558, FAX (916) 323-1097; district, 1111 Fulton Mall, 914, Fresno 93721, (209) 264-3078, FAX (209) 445-6506; 512 N. Irwin, Hanford 92320, (209) 582-2869.

TERM LIMIT: 2002

REGISTRATION: 57.81% D, 32.19% R,

1994 CAMPAIGN:	Costa D	51.57%	$1,095,221
	Phil Wyman R	48.43%	$799,212

RATINGS:	AFL-CIO	CLCV	NOW	CofC	CalFarm	GO *
	84	45	B	50	77.7	C

* Based on Assembly service.

William A. Craven (R)
38th Senate District

Sliced out of upscale beach communities of North County (the northern part of San Diego County), the safely Republican 38th District stretches along Interstate 5 from the horse track of Del Mar to the Marine Corps base at Camp Pendleton. Much of San Diego County's growth over the last decade has been here and North County politics tend to focus on growth control. It is a land of checkerboard development, strawberry farms and quick-buck artists. It is one of the most livable corners of the state, where life is easy and a home is expensive. The Supreme Court's 1992 reapportionment gave the district a chunk of Southern Orange County, including San Juan Capistrano and San Clemente, where Richard Nixon once had his Western White House. If anything, it is a safer GOP district than ever.

Republican Bill Craven has long been a figure in North County's civic and political life. An ex-Marine major, he epitomizes the Californians who have found their paradise in northern San Diego County. Craven came from Philadelphia, settled in North County and served on the Oceanside Planning Commission. He won a seat on the San Diego County Board of Supervisors in 1970. Five years later, he was in the Assembly, and moved to the Senate three years later.

During David Roberti's tenure as Senate president pro tem, Craven was often called Roberti's favorite Republican. Democrat Roberti often looked to Craven for advice. The two built a cordial, trusting friendship verging on a cross-party alliance. Craven was one of the barons of the five-member Rules Committee that runs the Senate. The chain-smoking Craven retained the committee appointment when

William Craven

Democrat Bill Lockyer took over the senate leadership after Roberti's departure. But in late 1994, in a move by Senate conservatives to exert their power, Craven was dumped from the committee and replaced by the more conservative John Lewis.

Ironically, Craven was outraged in 1986 at the behavior of Lewis, who was charged with forgery as an assemblyman for faking Ronald Reagan's name on campaign literature. Although the charges were thrown out, Craven moved to close loopholes in the law that helped Lewis.

Craven has served as a bridge between the ideological poles of an increasingly fractured Senate. He helps the house function. In 1992, poor health caused him to be absent for much of the session and many thought his absence made it harder to end the 64-day budget stalemate.

In the emotion-charged atmosphere that surrounded the 1994 campaign for Proposition 187 — the "Save Our State" measure to bar undocumented immigrants from receiving tax-supported services — the San Diego Union-Tribune reported that Craven said the Legislature should study requiring all Latinos to carry ID cards to verify that they are in the United States legally. Craven said the newspaper had jumbled his words. All Americans — not just Latinos — should carry a tamper-proof ID card to verify they can legally work in the U.S., he said.

Craven's legislative accomplishments are solid, though hardly flashy. In 1990, he successfully authored SB 2475, which restricts advertisements for adult videos to sections of stores reserved for adults only. After years of labor, he also won approval of a state university campus for his district in San Marcos. The administration building was named for Craven. Although Craven was back at his desk at the start of the 1993-94 session, friends and colleagues continued to worry about his health.

In the wake of Orange County's fiscal disaster in 1994, Craven was named chairman of the Senate Special Committee on Local Government Investment Practices.

PERSONAL: elected 1978; born June 30, 1921, in Philadelphia; home, Oceanside; USMC 1942-1946, 1950-1953; education, B.S. economics Villanova University; wife Mimi, three children; Roman Catholic.

CAREER: actor, salesman, county information officer and analyst; San Marcos city manager; San Diego County supervisor; Assembly 1973-78.

COMMITTEES: Local Government (chair); Legislative Ethics (chair); Elections & Reapportionment (vice chair); Agriculture & Water Resources; Business & Professions

OFFICES: Capitol, (916) 445-3731; district, 916-446-7382; 2121 Palomar Airport Road, 100, Carlsbad 92009, (619) 438-3814, FAX (619) 931-5745.

TERM LIMIT: 1998

REGISTRATION: 31.11% D, 52.12% R

1994 CAMPAIGN:	Craven R	65.52%	$122,961
	Thomas Berry D	25.60%	$3,477
1990 CAMPAIGN:	Craven R	66.7%	$442,621
	Jane Evans P&F	18.2%	$0
	Scott Olmsted L	15.1%	Not Available

RATINGS:	AFL-CIO	CLCV	NOW	CofC	CalFarm	GO
	54	27	C+	59	20	C

Ralph C. Dills (D)
28th Senate District

When the state Supreme Court redrew legislative district lines after the 1990 census, it divided the state into 80 Assembly districts and then designated pairs to create 40 Senate districts, a process called "nesting." One of the weirder results of this process is the 28th Senate District, which encompasses the white, Republican-leaning 53rd Assembly District and its central Los Angeles County coastal communities of Redondo Beach and Manhattan Beach, and the overwhelmingly minority, heavily Democratic 55th Assembly District, which includes Carson and portions of Long Beach.

Ralph Dills

Reapportionment left veteran Sen. Ralph Dills without a natural home and he eventually opted to move into the 28th, although it meant giving up his home base in Gardena, which had been attached to another district. It also meant two tough campaigns in 1994 for Dills, who had been used to winning re-election every four years without lifting a finger.

Dills survived a bloody and expensive primary battle against Torrance City

Councilman George Nakano only to face a stiffer challenge from Republican David Cohen, who had one of the most unusual ethnic backgrounds (Jewish and Samoan) ever seen in a California politician and who called on a network of Asian and Pacific Islander supporters. Cohen described Dills as being too old — often mentioning that his mother was born the same year (1938) that Dills was first elected to the Legislature — but Dills turned it around by buying billboards saying he was "too old to quit" and eventually bested the underfinanced Cohen by 8 percentage points.

It's hard to think of the Legislature without Dills, who arrived in the Assembly during the second term of Franklin D. Roosevelt in the days when the Legislature was controlled by corrupt lobbyist Artie Samish. Dills was known then mostly as one of the Dills Brothers. His brother, Clayton, was an assemblyman until his death. Another brother was a Capitol elevator operator. Although Dills has been there a very long time, he is not the oldest legislator; that distinction goes to Al Alquist of San Jose.

Dills has had several careers, nearly all of them lengthy. In the 1930s, he was a saxophone player working jazz clubs and then a teacher. An organizer in Democratic New Deal worker leagues, he won an Assembly seat in 1938. In his first 10 years in the Assembly, Dills authored the legislation creating California State University, Long Beach. He quit to accept a judgeship in 1949, then returned to Sacramento as a senator in 1967 in the first class of full-time lawmakers.

Dills became chairman of the powerful Governmental Organization Committee in 1970, a panel with an ironclad grip on liquor, horse racing, labor unions, oil leases and gambling legislation. Dills has long been known as the liquor industry's best friend in Sacramento. He has pushed legislation to give beer and wine distributors regional monopolies — bills vetoed with a vengeance by Gov. George Deukmejian as reeking with special-interest odor. But his connections helped him with the money he needed to turn back challengers in 1994.

Dills has not fared much better with Gov. Pete Wilson. In 1992, the governor vetoed Dills' bill to require the state to grant any employee a paid leave of absence in order for the employee to serve as a union official. The governor said operational needs of the state should not be subordinated to union needs. Dills also has helped bury anti-smog bills, incurring the wrath of environmentalists, who are left wondering why the bills went to his committee in the first place.

At the start of the 1991-92 session, Dills was given a seat on the Revenue and Taxation Committee, where he became a proponent of tax loopholes for various interests, including the snack food, newspaper and candy industries.

As the most senior senator, Dills is entitled by protocol to preside over the floor sessions of the Senate, a largely ceremonial post but with power to gum up the works. His parliamentary calls and flowery mannerisms have irritated some of his younger colleagues, who have persuaded him to preside less often. He has also toned down his garish clothing style.

PERSONAL: elected 1966; born Feb. 10, 1910, Rosston, Tex.; home, Gardena;

education, attended Compton College, B.A. UCLA; M.A. USC; J.D. Loyola University; wife Elizabeth Bette Lee, three children.

CAREER: saxophone player; teacher; lawyer; Assembly 1938-1949; municipal judge 1949-1966.

COMMITTEES: Governmental Organization (chair); Education; Veterans Affairs.

OFFICES: Capitol, (916) 445-5953, FAX (916) 323-6056; district, 16921 S. Western Ave., 201, Gardena 90247, (310) 324-4969, FAX (310) 329-5244.

TERM LIMIT: 1998

REGISTRATION: 65.1% D, 24.7% R

1994 CAMPAIGN:	Dills D	50.48%	$1,122,336
	David Cohen R	42.8%	$123,167
1990 CAMPAIGN:	Dills D	68.3%	$615,454
	Timothy Poling R	31.7	% $0

RATINGS:	AFL-CIO	CLCV	NOW	CofC	CalFarm	GO
	92	88	A-	29	20	D

Leroy F. Greene (D)
6th Senate District

The Capitol is not only where Leroy Greene spends most of his working hours, it is also in the heart of his district, which encompasses nearly all of the city of Sacramento and much of the unincorporated urban area that spreads east of the city.

The district was originally tailored to Greene's political specifications by Democratic leaders after the stunning 1980 defeat of the Democratic dean of the Senate, Al Rodda, by conservative Republican upstart John Doolittle. During the post-census reapportionment, Democrats reconfigured Rodda's old district to lop off the most Republican suburbs and to concentrate strength in Democratic city precincts. And a clever change of district numbers forced

Leroy Greene

Doolittle to stand for re-election in 1982, just two years into his first term. Doolittle faced Greene, who had spent 20 years in the Assembly representing a mid-Sacramento district. Greene won, but another change of district lines after the election created another new district in which Doolittle successfully ran in 1984.

Greene represents a quickly maturing city that teeters on the verge — local boosters think it is already there — of big-city status. The area's traditional dependence on government payrolls has lessened in the last decade with the arrival and expansion of financial and high-tech industries, many of them relocating from the Bay Area. That change, coupled with continuing suburbanization, has produced a shift to the right in Sacramento-area politics. The central city remains solidly Democratic, however, and while reapportionment after the 1990 census changed the 6th District's boundaries a bit, the district remains comfortably Democratic.

A civil engineer who practiced in Sacramento for years, Greene has developed a reputation as a colorful and independent-minded legislator unafraid of voicing unpopular or slightly off-the-wall views. He was highly active in the Assembly, where he chaired the Assembly Education Committee and carried numerous bills to finance school construction and operations. In the Senate, Greene faded into the background, seemingly content to support the Democratic Party line and to carry local-interest bills.

His appointment in 1993 as chairman of the Senate Revenue and Taxation Committee raised his profile somewhat, and Greene gained attention in the 1993-94 session on other scores. He used his post as chairman of the Senate Legislative Ethics Committee to call for the expulsion of Sen. Frank Hill, who was convicted in the FBI corruption sting — a sentiment that was not universally popular. He stood out again when he called the "three strikes and you're out" crime bill a "turkey" and said he supported releasing nonviolent offenders in pink jumpsuits with electronic bracelets instead of sending them to jail.

Greene, who survived a stiff 1986 election challenge from Republican Sandra Smoley, then a Sacramento County supervisor, drew only token opposition in 1990 before attracting a serious competitor again in 1994. This time it was Republican Sacramento County Supervisor Dave Cox, who attacked Greene as soft on crime and anti-business. The entertaining campaign included Cox's charge that Greene's accidents in state cars had cost the state $90,000 in auto repairs and personal-injury settlements. But Greene, backed strongly by Democratic leaders worried about their razor-thin majority in the Senate, flooded the district with mailers questioning Cox's financial background, tax problems and votes on contributors' land deals. "Throw Dave a bone and he'll roll over," Greene's campaign literature said. In the end, Greene won comfortably; his appointment as chairman of the Senate Education Committee returns him to familiar policy ground as he carries out his final term.

PERSONAL: elected 1982; born Jan. 31, 1918, in Newark, N.J.; home, Carmichael; Army (WWII); education, B.S. Purdue University; widower, one child; no religious affiliation.

CAREER: civil engineer 1951-1978, owned firm; Assembly 1962-1982; newspaper columnist; radio talk show host.

COMMITTEES: Education (chair); Legislative Ethics (vice chair); Appropriations; Business and Professions; Governmental Organization

OFFICES: Capitol, (916) 445-7807, FAX (916) 324-4937; district, State Capitol 2082; P.O. Box 254646, Sacramento 95825.

TERM LIMIT: 1998

REGISTRATION: 53.83% D, 34.68% R

1994 CAMPAIGN:	Greene D			53.71%		$777,114
	Cox R			46.29%		$436,033
1990 CAMPAIGN:	Greene D			53.7%		$507,849
	Joe Sullivan R			40.4%		$8,745
RATINGS:	AFL-CIO	CLCV	NOW	CofC	CalFarm	GO
	89	53	B	18	60	F

Thomas E. Hayden (D)
23rd Senate District

Tom Hayden

This Los Angeles County coastal district includes comfortable Pacific Palisades, the beach houses and canyons of Malibu, portions of liberal West Los Angeles and the left-of-center environs of Santa Monica. The district extends into Beverly Hills and over the ridges into the San Fernando Valley to include part of Woodland Hills. The Democrat who represents this district happens to be one of the nation's most controversial figures, Tom Hayden. How he got there in 1992 proved to be one of the most expensive high-profile shoot-outs among Democrats in years.

Hayden was first reapportioned out of his Assembly district by Willie Brown, who was anxious to be rid of Hayden, and then by the state Supreme Court. Hayden's legislative career appeared to be at an end. But Hayden instead challenged longtime Senate Democrat Herschel Rosenthal for the 23rd District seat. Rosenthal, who wasn't facing re-election for another two years in the 22nd District, decided to try for the seat because it looked safer than his own.

What followed was a blitz of mailers in a three-way Democratic primary between Hayden, Rosenthal and Democratic activist Catherine O'Neill of Pacific Palisades. Hayden, who spent more than $750,000 on the primary — mostly his own money — ended up winning the Democratic nomination by less than 600 votes. Winning in November was largely pro forma given the heavy Democratic registration.

Never one to follow convention, Hayden caught his fellow Democrats off-guard in February 1994 when he announced his candidacy for the Democratic gubernatorial nomination, joining Insurance Commissioner John Garamendi and Treasurer Kathleen Brown. At the time, Hayden said he had "no illusions" about winning. Instead, he said he had joined the race to force the other candidates to address the issues of campaign and government reform. By the end of the race, Garamendi and Brown had embraced campaign reform in concept if not in detail.

The weekend before the June 1994 primary, Hayden delivered a final message to voters in the form of a documentary-style television ad dubbed "Bucks, Lies and Videotape." The 15-minute commercial reminded voters that Hayden performed well in recent campaign debates, poked fun at the political handlers of his rivals and asked Democratic voters to "trust their idealistic instinct" by voting for Hayden. "Can I do it? I don't know. Miracles have happened," Hayden said, in footage shot by hand-held video cameras in his living room. No miracle happened. Brown won easily. And yet Hayden emerged from the campaign with increased stature. Pundits who had been poking fun at him for years had to acknowledge that Hayden not only raised the level of the debate but offered clear and thoughtful policy initiatives — a welcome break from the opportunistic sound-bite campaigns.

Hayden is probably the best known member of the California Legislature. He is a subject in scores of books, magazine and newspaper articles spanning three decades. He is certainly the only legislator whose comings and goings are charted by People magazine.

As a founder of Students for a Democratic Society, and as one of the authors of The Port Huron Statement, the New Left's manifesto in the 1960s, Hayden's place in postwar American history is assured. He was put on trial as one of the Chicago Eight, accused of fomenting the riot at the 1968 Democratic Convention and sentenced to five years in prison. Back then, Hayden was urged to go underground because friends feared he would be murdered in prison. Those were the days when Hayden vented speeches calling for revolutionizing youth through a series of sharp and dangerous conflicts.

But Hayden drew back from the revolutionary life. His Chicago conviction was overturned in 1972. His marriage to actress Jane Fonda won him star status and something the New Left had lacked: a sizable bank account. With Fonda's money, Hayden rejoined the mainstream by running for the U.S. Senate in 1976 against Democratic incumbent John Tunney. Hayden lost and incurred the wrath of many Democratic leaders, who accused him of weakening Tunney, leaving him vulnerable to defeat by Republican S.I. Hayakawa.

In the wake of his U.S. Senate campaign, Hayden created the Campaign for Economic Democracy (which evolved into Campaign California.) Hayden's groups have won success at the ballot box, most notably the Proposition 65 water purity measure, and in helping to close Sacramento's troubled Rancho Seco nuclear power plant. But his organizations also have suffered notable setbacks. Hayden was one of the major backers of the Big Green environmental initiative in 1990 that would have created a new elected statewide position of environmental advocate. Some thought the position tailor-made for Hayden. He and his organizations poured money into the initiative. But it went down in flames after multimillion dollar spending by industrial and agribusiness opponents.

Hayden's fame and success have come with a heavy price. There are those who will always consider him a traitor for having supported the Communist side during the Vietnam War and believe he should have been put on trial for treason. Some of Hayden's colleagues when he was in the Assembly, particularly Gil Ferguson, routinely refused to vote for a Hayden bill regardless of its merits because his name was on it. And legislative life appears to have contributed to the breakup of his marriage with Fonda.

Hayden often is alone in the Senate in opposing gubernatorial appointments whom he claims will be tools of special interests. More often than not, he's been right.

PERSONAL: elected 1992; born Dec. 11, 1939, in Detroit; home, Santa Monica; education, B.A. University of Michigan; wife Barbara Williams, one child and one stepchild; Roman Catholic.

CAREER: founder, Students for a Democratic Society; founder, Campaign for Economic Democracy, Campaign California; author; teacher; Assembly 1982-1992.

COMMITTEES: Natural Resources & Wildlife (chair); Education; Insurance; Toxics & Public Safety Management; Transportation; Energy, Utilities and Communications.

OFFICES: Capitol, (916) 445-1353, FAX (916) 324-4823; district, 10951 W. Pico Blvd., 202, Los Angeles 90064, (310) 441-9684, FAX (310) 441-0724.

TERM LIMIT: 2000
REGISTRATION: 55.32% D, 30.44% R

1992 CAMPAIGN:					
Hayden D			55.9%		$1,018,084
Leonard McRoskey R			33.1%		$35,495

RATINGS:	AFL-CIO	CLCV	NOW	CofC	CalFarm	GO
	97	89	A-	24	40	F

Ray Haynes (R)
36th Senate District

The heart of the populated west end of Riverside County is in this district, a slice of mountainous northern San Diego County, including Palomar and Fallbrook. This district is much compacted in size from when it stretched out through ritzy desert communities and pockets of rural poverty to the Colorado River in Blythe. The center of gravity is Riverside, the earth-toned stucco housing tracts of Moreno Valley, the horse country of Norco and the chicken ranches near Corona.

When Robert Presley won this seat in 1974, there were considerably fewer people living in that vast expanse. In the years since, it has become the fastest-

Ray Haynes

growing region of the state — and increasingly conservative. Presley would have been the victim of term limits in 1998, had he been re-elected in 1994. Instead, Presley ran unsuccessfully for a seat on the state Board of Equalization.

This seat was a perfect target for Ray Haynes, a conservative Republican with ties to the Christian right, who had won a seven-way primary battle for the Assembly in 1992 after Republican incumbent Dave Kelley chose to run for the senate. Haynes served one undistinguished term in the Assembly.

In 1990, Haynes had run for the Senate against Presley and received 46.4 percent of the vote. During his second attempt in 1994, Haynes reportedly told supporters that God had told him to run. In the middle of his 1994 campaign against longtime Riverside County Supervisor Kay Ceniceros, Haynes, speaking at a church meeting, called Democratic congressional candidate Mark Takano "a homosexual, liberal Democrat." When questioned about the remark, Haynes told the Riverside Press Enterprise, "I said quite clearly I personally don't want a homosexual representing me in Congress." Some observers thought that Haynes had hurt his own chances by interjecting himself in another contest. In addition, it was brought out that Haynes took $12,150 in political contributions from manufacturers of unvented fireplaces who would benefit from a bill Haynes carried in 1994. But, in the end, Ceniceros was no match for the overwhelmingly Republican registration.

A rabid opponent of unfunded mandates, within a month of reaching the Senate Haynes apparently had another message from above and reintroduced a bill that would mandate high school students to learn and be tested on the Declaration of Independence, the U.S. Constitution, and The Federalist Papers. No funding provision was attached to the bill.

PERSONAL: elected 1994; born Aug. 26, 1954, in Merced; home, Murrieta; B.A. California Lutheran University, M.A. and J.D. USC; wife Pamela, two children; Protestant.

CAREER: lawyer; Moreno Valley Planning Commission; founding member and treasurer, Moreno Valley Committee for No New Taxes; free counsel for Western Center of Law and Religious Freedom, Riverside Citizens for Responsible Behavior; Assembly, 1992-1994.

COMMITTEES: Health and Human Services (vice chair); Budget and Fiscal Review; Education; Governmental Organization.

OFFICES: Capitol, (916) 445-9781, FAX (916) 447-4457; district, 29377 Rancho California, 102, Temecula 92591, (909) 699-1113, FAX (909) 694-4457.

TERM LIMIT: 2002

REGISTRATION: 49.76% R, 38.30% D

1994 CAMPAIGN:

Haynes R		55%	Not Available
Kay Ceniceros D		41.54%	$833,048

RATINGS:

AFL-CIO	CLCV	NOW	CofC	CalFarm	GO *
4	6	C-	82	55.5	A

* Based on Assembly service.

Teresa P. Hughes (D)

25th Senate District

When Teresa Hughes moved from the Assembly to the Senate in 1992, she continued a linear political succession dating back three decades. Mervyn Dymally began the sequence in 1962, when he was elected to the state Assembly. He moved up to the Senate in 1966 and his aide, Bill Greene, succeeded him in the Assembly. When Dymally was elected as California's first African American lieutenant governor in 1974, Greene took his place in the Senate and another Dymally aide — Hughes — took Greene's place in the Assembly. Dymally, meanwhile, was defeated for re-election in 1978 and shifted to Congress two years later. He retired from politics in 1992 as did Greene, who had been plagued by ill health.

Teresa Hughes

That opened the door for Hughes to capture the Senate seat that Dymally and Greene had held, and she did so with no serious challenge.

As reconstituted and renumbered by the state Supreme Court's 1992 reapportionment plan, the 25th District is a compact chunk of impoverished South-Central Los Angeles that exemplifies the social and political trends on the poorer side of the Santa Monica Freeway. Inglewood, home of the Los Angeles Lakers and the Hollywood Park horse racing track, anchors the northwestern corner of the district.

While the district is more than 40 percent Latino, fewer than 10 percent of its registered voters are Latino, and African American politicians remain dominant, despite a shrinking African American population that's already less than 40 percent. And that's not likely to change until sometime in the 21st century. There's also a growing Asian population in the district, including the heavily Asian city of Gardena.

Hughes, a former social worker, teacher, school administrator and college professor, was most visible in the Legislature as chairwoman of the Assembly Education Committee. But at the start of the 1991-92 session, she was summarily booted off the committee by Speaker Willie Brown and replaced with Delaine Eastin of Union City, a suburb south of Oakland. The move marked a major power shift on the education panel away from the gorilla-sized Los Angeles Unified School District and toward suburban schools. The speaker never publicly explained why he canned Hughes, but privately those close to Brown said he thought Hughes was plodding and ineffective. Brown also was under pressure from more aggressive and intellectually supple liberals in the Democratic caucus, who wanted a crack at forging education policy. And Hughes was already planning to leave the Assembly to run for the Senate.

Hughes has pushed several AIDS-related bills, including a 1987 measure signed into law that allows doctors to disclose AIDS test results to spouses of people who have been tested. She also has backed legislation to require condom standards to make sure that the prophylactics block the AIDS virus. If Hughes was alienated from Speaker Brown in the Assembly, the Senate's Democratic leaders gave her a warm welcome by appointing her to chair the Public Employment and Retirement Committee, a politically important position that solidified her close connections to public employee unions.

PERSONAL: elected 1992; born Oct. 3, 1932, in New York City; home, Los Angeles; education, B.A. Hunter College, M.A. New York University, Ph.D. Claremont College; husband Frank Staggers, two children; Roman Catholic.

CAREER: teacher, school administrator; professor of education, CSU Los Angeles; aide to Sen. Mervyn Dymally 1973; Assembly 1975-1992.

COMMITTEES: Public Employment & Retirement (chair); Education; Energy, Utilities and Communications; Governmental Organization; Insurance; Health and Human Services.

OFFICES: Capitol, (916) 445-2104, FAX (916) 445-3712; district, 1 Manchester Blvd., Inglewood 90301, (310) 412-0393, FAX (310) 412-0996.

TERM LIMIT: 2000

REGISTRATION: 75.2% D, 15.0% R

1992 CAMPAIGN:					
Hughes D		76.8%		$513,681	
Cliff McClain R		18.8%		$0	

RATINGS:	AFL-CIO	CLCV	NOW	CofC	CalFarm	GO
	96	73	A-	24	80	F

Rob Hurtt (R)
34th Senate District

After a decade of sitting in the California Senate and saying little, Edward Royce moved on to Congress after the 1992 election. Garden Grove businessman Rob Hurtt, who had been bankrolling conservative candidates for other offices, couldn't recruit a suitable candidate for the special election, so he ran himself, loaned his campaign $200,000 and won it in the primary.

Hurtt immediately established himself as a powerhouse in the Senate. When Hurtt didn't have the votes to dump moderate Republican Senate leader Ken Maddy, R-Fresno, and take over himself, he joined Maddy in an uneasy power-sharing alliance, with Hurtt serving as head of fund raising and elec-

Rob Hurtt

toral strategy. Hurtt continued to play a strong role in the string of special elections held during 1993, helping to recruit conservatives to oppose the more moderate candidates Maddy was backing. It was the same pattern in 1994, when the GOP gained more Senate seats. As the 1995 session opened, Maddy was still the GOP leader, but his grip on the job was tenuous.

Hurtt inherited his father's food container business in Garden Grove and has been plowing money into conservative causes for years. In 1992, Hurtt and three other wealthy Southern Californians formed the Allied Business Political Action Committee to boost business-oriented candidates from the Christian right. In 1992 alone, their PAC was the fourth-largest contributor to legislative races, spending $915,745. Hurtt spent an additional $165,865 on other GOP efforts. He also has been a force behind the Capitol Resource Institute, a private lobby group for family policy in the Capitol.

Senate Pro Tem Bill Lockyer saw Hurtt's threat and responded in the 1994 campaign year by using Hurtt as a Republican bogeyman, bringing huge, multicolored charts to Democratic fund-raisers to show which senators were most threatened with defeat, the money available to each party and the top political action committees in the state, including Allied Business PAC, Hurtt's group. It gave $1.2 million in 1991-92 to legislative races, second only to the California Medical Association, and ahead of the correctional officers, teachers, trial lawyers and other powerful groups.

Lockyer described how Hurtt, savings and loan heir Howard Ahmanson and two other wealthy donors — Lockyer called them "four theocratic right-wing families" — gave nearly $3 million in 1992-93 to legislative candidates, the state GOP, the school voucher campaign and other conservative, Christian and anti-abortion rights causes.

Hurtt is justifiably proud of what he's accomplished for the conservatives and predicts his wing of the party will dominate in both legislative houses before the decade is over. He's also credited with helping push Gov. Pete Wilson more to the right politically.

Hurtt easily won re-election in 1994 even though the district is slightly less friendly to Republicans thanks to reapportionment. The new district cuts off Fullerton, but adds Santa Ana. Other communities include Stanton, La Habra, Garden Grove, Anaheim, Orange and Tustin.

PERSONAL: elected 1993 (special election); born May 19, 1944, in Santa Monica; home, Garden Grove; education, B.A. Claremont McKenna College; wife, Nancy; four children; United Presbyterian.

CAREER: family can manufacturing business.

COMMITTEES: Industrial Relations (vice chair); Budget and Fiscal Review; Finance, Investment and International Trade; Revenue and Taxation.

OFFICES: Capitol, (916) 445-5831; district, 11642 Knott St., Suite 8, Garden Grove 92641, (714) 898-8353, FAX (714) 898-8033.

TERM LIMIT: 2002
REGISTRATION: 46.64% D, 41.91% R

| **1994 CAMPAIGN**: | Hurtt R | 57.31% | $844,124 |
| | Donna Chessen D | 36.58% | $265,337 |

1993 CAMPAIGN: Hurtt R   75.9%

| **RATINGS**: | AFL-CIO | CLCV | NOW | CofC | CalFarm | GO |
| | 9 | 0 | D+ | 94 | 40 | A+ |

Maurice Johannessen (R)
4th Senate District

Maurice Johannessen

The 4th Senate District is so huge that some of its residents commute to jobs in San Francisco while others commute to Oregon. It runs from Fairfield to the Oregon border, taking in the college town of Davis and the flat farmlands of the northern Central Valley. It includes Redding, the largest California city north of Sacramento, and spectacular river country, including the wild McCloud. Also in the district are Mount Shasta and the headwaters of the Sacramento River.

The region is friendly to Republicans and elected Jim Nielsen in 1978. But after some personal scandals and bigoted pronouncements, Nielsen was ousted by Democrat Mike Thompson in 1990. Two years later, reapportionment carved Thompson's hometown of St. Helena out of the district. Democratic numbers looked better in the adjacent 2nd District. When it became open with the resignation of Sen. Barry Keene in 1992, Thompson ran for that seat and won.

The race to replace Thompson in the 4th District turned out to be one of the most closely watched in the state. For all intents, it was over in the GOP primary, when Shasta County Supervisor Maurice Johannessen beat former Assemblywoman Bev Hansen. It was a mudfest of a campaign. Hansen was backed by Senate Minority Leader Ken Maddy and fellow moderates. Johannessen was the candidate of Sen. Rob Hurtt and the Christian-right faction in the GOP caucus.

For the runoff, Johannessen drew an obscure Democratic attorney from Arbuckle who advocated legalizing pot. The Democratic money men sat this one out. Johannessen, who spent much of the campaign bashing illegal immigrants, was embarrassed late in the campaign when it was revealed that he was once an illegal immigrant. But it's not clear whether that cost him any votes.

Johannessen was re-elected in 1994 following another bruising battle, this time with Democrat Michael McGowan, a former mayor of West Sacramento, who offered himself as a moderate alternative to the ultraconservative Johannessen. Democratic leaders of the Senate boasted that the changing demographics of the district, especially its being weighted toward the commuter suburbs of Solano County by reapportionment, would allow them to knock off Johannessen, who had won his seat in the prereapportionment boundaries. Johannessen was too conservative, Democrats said, for a district that had a 10-point Democratic registration edge.

Johannessen's platform included cutting off public services for undocumented immigrants, cracking down on juvenile crime and cutting back government. The campaign was among the grungiest in one the dirtiest campaign years on record with the slime thrown from both sides. Johannessen linked McGowan to Patrick Purdy, who killed five children in a 1989 Stockton schoolyard massacre. Johannessen alleged in radio ads and a mailer that McGowan, working on contract as a public defender for Yolo County in 1984, represented Purdy in an attempted purse-snatching case. McGowan condemned Johannessen's claims as "unconscionable" and "fundamentally wrong."

Purdy's felony charge was reduced to a misdemeanor, Johannessen says, allowing Purdy to later buy the weapons he used in the 1989 attack. McGowan campaign consultant Craig Reynolds said if McGowan did represent Purdy, he simply did his job as a public defender and that Johannessen was "trying to exploit the death of these children to protect his job."

McGowan retaliated, putting out his own mailer claiming that in 1972 Johannessen was arrested for battery and brandishing a weapon when he accompanied a woman to her ex-husband's Redding home and the ex-husband confronted them. A fight ensued in which Johannessen removed his gun from its holster, according to court documents provided by McGowan's campaign. Johannessen later pleaded no contest to a charge of criminal trespass, and other charges were dropped. But McGowan's mailer linked the incident to a bill Johannessen authored in 1994 that, according to McGowan, would make it easier to get a concealed weapon permit.

In addition, Johannessen almost single-handedly killed a carefully negotiated revision of the California Endangered Species Act between the Farm Bureau, the Audubon Society, developers, environmental groups and agencies when he quibbled over a single word in the new document.

The Democratic effort went for naught, however, when Johannessen, who had virtually unlimited funds from his own personal fortune and Sen. Hurtt, scored a 9-percentage point victory.

PERSONAL: elected 1993 (special election); born July 16, 1934, in Oslo, Norway; home, Redding; Army 1953-56; education, attended Stockton and Citrus Junior Colleges and Los Angeles State College; wife, Marianne; four children; Protestant.

CAREER: merchant seaman, machinist, Realtor, property manager, owner of a roller rink; Redding City Council and mayor 1986-90; Shasta County Board of Supervisors 1990-93.

COMMITTEES: Business and Professions (vice chair); Veterans Affairs; Agriculture and Water Resources; Finance, Investment and International Trade; Natural Resources and Wildlife.

OFFICES: Capitol, (916)445-3353, 1-800-887-3007; district, 410 Hemsed Drive, 200, Redding, 96002, (916) 224-4706, FAX (916) 224-4794.

TERM LIMIT: 2002

REGISTRATION: 48% D, 38% R

1994 CAMPAIGN:	Johannessen R	54.3%	$834,643
	Michael McGowan D	45.6%	$1,081,796.
1993 CAMPAIGN:	Johannessen R	55%	Not Available
	Montana Podva D	39.6%	Not Available

RATINGS:	AFL-CIO	CLCV	NOW	CofC	CalFarm	GO
	NA	10	C-	100	40	A

Patrick W. Johnston (D)
5th Senate District

Patrick Johnston

The 5th Senate District includes all but the rural southwest corner of San Joaquin County and the southern portion of Sacramento County, including portions of east Sacramento, Campus Commons, Arden-Arcade, Rancho Cordova, part of Carmichael, Laguna, Elk Grove, Galt and others. San Joaquin County cities in the district include Stockton, Lodi, Manteca, Lathrop and Tracy.

In the mid-1970s, some newcomers burst onto the political scene in Stockton and surrounding areas. A young rancher named John Garamendi won an Assembly seat and then quickly moved into the state Senate. He hired another young man, Patrick Johnston, as his aide. Johnston won election to the Assembly in his own right in 1980 and by 1990 he found himself opposing not only Garamendi, who was on his way to becoming the first elected state insurance commissioner, but Garamendi's wife, Patti, who was eager to replace her husband in the Senate.

Garamendi quit his seat early — more than two months before the November election for insurance commissioner — in an attempt to give his wife an edge over Johnston. The plan was to have the special election for his seat consolidated with the general election. Since Johnston could not have his name removed as a candidate for re-election to the Assembly, it was hoped that he would look overly ambitious as he technically ran for two offices. But the maneuver backfired. The Garamendis were accused of trying to manipulate the process. Johnston beat Patti Garamendi and nine others in the first round of the special election and then easily won the run-off, defeating the top Republican vote-getter, Philip Wallace.

It wasn't Johnston's first tough election. In 1980, he challenged a Democratic incumbent, Assemblyman Carmen Perino, in the June primary. It was a nasty battle made worse by a power struggle for the speakership of the Assembly that year and by the personal nature of local Stockton politics. Johnston defeated Perino, but his struggle was just beginning. His November tussle with Republican Adrian Fondse was one of the sleaziest in California history, complete with anti-Johnston mailings appealing to racial prejudices and other dirty tricks. The initial vote count showed Fondse winning, but a recount, certified by Johnston's fellow Democrats in the Assembly, unseated Fondse and declared Johnston the victor by 35 votes out of 84,000 cast.

Johnston, a former journalist who once aspired to the Roman Catholic priest-hood, has achieved a reputation as a liberal reformer and as one of the state's brighter legislators. He proved his adaptability while chairing the Assembly's Finance and Insurance Committee, a major juice committee with jurisdiction over banks and insurance companies. Members of the committee are routinely showered with attention from industry lobbyists. Johnston has not been shy about accepting campaign contributions, trips and other goodies from special interests, but he earned kudos from affected industries and consumers alike for his honesty and evenhanded operation of the committee.

Johnston put himself in the thick of the battles over auto insurance and was a critic of both the industry and its self-appointed reformers in what seemed to be a politically dangerous move during California's wild, five-way insurance initiative war in 1988. Since then, he has continued to avoid the populist road paved by Proposition 103, the winner of that initiative war, and instead has joined with consumer groups in pushing a no-fault system that he has said holds out the best chance to control insurance rates and service.

Johnston took a front seat in the controversial battle over workers' compensation reform when he accepted the chairmanship of the Senate Industrial Relations Committee for the 1993-94 legislative session.

In 1992, Johnston crafted the Delta Protection Act, which was signed into law by Gov. Pete Wilson. The act established a 19-member commission with the task of developing a resource management plan for the Delta to protect it from overdevelopment. The bill met with resistance from developers and some local officials, who feared the loss of local autonomy, but Johnston persevered, conducting local hearings and inviting input from citizens. Ultimately, the plan received the blessings of the California Farm Bureau, the Audubon Society, the boating and fishing industries and a number of local governments. In 1994, Senate President Pro Tem Bill Lockyer named Johnston chairman of the Senate Appropriations Committee, one of the most power positions in the Legislature. Johnston promised to take a conservative approach to his new job with a tough look at all spending legislation in light of the state's continuing financial woes. That same year, the California Journal rated Johnston best senator overall and the member with the most potential.

PERSONAL: elected 1991 (special election); born Sept. 3, 1946, in San Francisco; home, Stockton; education, B.A. St. Patrick's College, Menlo Park; wife Margaret Mary, two children; Roman Catholic.

CAREER: Reporter for a Catholic newspaper; probation officer, Calaveras County; chief of staff to Sen. John Garamendi 1975-1980; Assembly 1980-1991.

COMMITTEES: Appropriations (chair); Constitutional Amendments; Local Government; Insurance; Natural Resources & Wildlife; Transportation.

OFFICES: Capitol, (916) 445-2407, FAX (916) 327-4213; district, 31 E. Channel St., 440, Stockton 95202, (209) 948-7930, FAX (209) 948-7993.

TERM LIMIT: 2000

REGISTRATION: 49.08% D, 40.56% R

1992 CAMPAIGN:	Johnston D		57.5%	$585,609
	Ron Stauffer R		37.3%	$30,144
1991 CAMPAIGN:	Johnston D		56.8%	$565,424
	Philip Wallace R		38.2%	$58,234

RATINGS:	AFL-CIO	CLCV	NOW	CofC	CalFarm	GO
	91	67	B+	41	60	F

David G. Kelley (R)
37th Senate District

Whether the state Supreme Court intended it or not, its creation of this district in the 1992 reapportionment was tailor-made for Republican David Kelley. It takes in rural and desert portions of Riverside County, the agriculturally rich Imperial County and rural eastern San Diego County along the U.S.-Mexico border. Upscale communities including Palm Springs and Rancho Mirage are within the district. So, too, are intensely poor communities such as Calexico and El Centro. The district has a large Latino population — 28 percent — which is politically muted (only 12 percent of the registered voters are Latino).

David Kelley

Citrus farmer David Kelley did not have to work hard to get elected in this district in 1992. In his 14 years in the Assembly, Kelley had coasted through legislative life, heard from occasionally with outbursts against farm-worker unions and the leaders of the GOP Assembly caucus, whom he can now safely ignore. He carried little legislation beyond his pet gold-coin collector bills. He did not even do much in the way of district bills, leaving that to Riverside

County Democrats. Kelley's quarrels with various Assembly Republican leaders won him a number of enemies. Finally, Kelley backed a winner for Assembly Republican leader — fellow farmer Bill Jones of Fresno. But Jones did not put Kelley on his leadership team during his brief and unproductive reign.

Kelley came to the Legislature relatively late in life after becoming wealthy from his acres of productive trees in the Hemet-San Jacinto Valley. He was instrumental in helping George Deukmejian gain the trust of agricultural interests in the 1982 GOP gubernatorial primary, but Kelley got little in return.

In 1990, Kelley persuaded the state Department of Fish and Game to propose a 2,800-acre wildlife area next to his ranch in an unsuccessful attempt to protect his irrigation supply. Although the agency staff drew up a proposal to buy the $4.1 million property, the Kelley-backed proposal died when a review board found nothing environmentally sensitive about the land — and a huge housing development went there instead. The developer accused Kelley of a conflict of interest because he was the ranking Republican on the Assembly Water, Parks and Wildlife Committee, which oversees the Fish and Game Department. "Well, it wasn't necessarily in my interest," Kelley responded to an interviewer. "It's an interest of a lot of growers out there, too, because they don't want to lose the water that they have for their farming operations."

During the tense 1993 budget battles Kelley was notable by his absence. Kelley, who had gone fishing in Alaska, was the only legislator who failed to vote on the main budget bill. But after missing out on the Senate's all-night debate and early-morning vote on Tuesday, Kelley was back Wednesday at the Capitol to vote on the "trailer bills" needed to implement the budget. Senate Republican leader Ken Maddy, R-Fresno, said he told Kelley's staff that the senator should return.

PERSONAL: elected 1992; born Oct. 11, 1928, in Riverside; home, Hemet; education, B.S. agriculture, Calif. State Polytechnic University, Pomona; USAF 1949-1953; wife Brigitte, four children; Lutheran.

CAREER: citrus farmer; Assembly 1978-1992.

COMMITTEES: Constitutional Amendments (chair); Agriculture & Water Resources; Appropriations; Business & Professions; Transportation; Energy, Utilities and Communications.

OFFICES: Capitol, (916) 445-5581, FAX (916) 327-2187; district, 11440 West Bernardo Ct., 104, San Diego 92127, (619) 675-8211, FAX (619) 675-8262.

TERM LIMIT: 2000

REGISTRATION: 38.71% D, 46.72% R

1992 CAMPAIGN:			
Kelley R		52.5%	$480,375
Jim Rickard D		37.7%	$14,837

RATINGS:	AFL-CIO	CLCV	NOW	CofC	CalFarm	GO
	13	11	C-	100	60	A

Lucy L. Killea (independent)
39th Senate District

Starting on Coronado Island, the 39th District heads east, taking in the heart of San Diego's feature-less bedroom neighborhoods on the bluffs overlooking San Diego's sports stadium. The district includes Democratic pockets in Hillcrest and Mission Hills, but is otherwise strongly Republican and has the smallest minority population of any San Diego County district.

Lucy Killea

Upon the retirement of Republican Jim Ellis, another Republican, Larry Stirling, had little trouble getting elected to this seat in 1988. But to the total surprise of Capitol insiders, he quit after less than a year to take a judgeship in the San Diego Municipal Court. Stirling's 1989 resignation set off one of the strangest political events in modern state history: a special election that became a national referendum on abortion rights and the bounds of the Catholic Church's involvement in politics.

At first glance, it looked as if Democratic Assemblywoman Lucy Killea stood no chance of winning. But Killea, a Catholic, was solidly pro-choice on abortion and her rival, Assemblywoman Carol Bentley — then in her first term — was anti-abortion. Polls showed that while the region was conservative, more than two-thirds of adults were pro-choice. And polls also showed Killea was better known.

The special election snoozed along as a local affair until Roman Catholic Bishop Leo T. Maher, now deceased, faxed Killea a letter informing her that she could no longer receive communion at her parish. He leaked the letter to a television station — and everything backfired on him. Killea's campaign became an overnight national media event. She took a quick trip to New York to appear on the Phil Donahue show with Geraldine Ferraro. (Bentley declined Donahue's invitation.) Killea was the subject of stories in USA Today, the Washington Post and the New York Times. Her election-night headquarters in an El Cajon union hall was covered not just by local media but by national networks, including live CNN broadcasts. It was more than Bentley could overcome and Killea was elected.

With her new-won notoriety, Killea was not long in the Senate before she signaled she was not content to slip back into legislative obscurity. She soon complained that while every other Democrat chaired a committee, she had none. Senate President Pro Tem David Roberti reshuffled committee assignments and gave her the chair of the Senate Bonded Indebtedness Committee. That, however, was not good enough. In truth, Killea, the improbable winner of a special election, looked at the numbers for the district in 1992 and did not like what she saw. No matter how reapportionment shook out, Killea would have a tough time holding the seat. Compounding the equation, Republican Ellis said he would come out of retirement to take it back for the Republicans.

So, Killea took a big gamble. She dropped out of the Democratic Party and ran as an independent. Her move cost her friends and admirers — including many who had worked in her special election. But in November 1992, she not only held the seat, she demolished the conservative Ellis. Democrats can still grumble about her traitorous behavior, but Killea votes like a Democrat and is still pro-choice on abortion.

Killea's route to the Legislature was a bit unusual. She was an Army intelligence officer in World War II and was then detailed to the State Department as an aide to Eleanor Roosevelt during the first general assembly of the United Nations. She went on to serve nine years in the CIA in the 1950s. Killea later lectured in history, and is an expert on Mexican border affairs, having served as executive director of Fronteras de las Californias. Although a Democrat at the time, she was appointed by Republican Mayor Pete Wilson to the San Diego City Council to fill a vacancy in 1978. She has remained cordial with Wilson and his chief of staff, Bob White.

As a legislator, Killea has authored numerous bills on hazardous waste and was among the many parents of the 1985 legislative effort that brought forth the state's workfare program. She has also concentrated on international trade incentives and Mexican border issues, both of major interest to the San Diego area. Killea has been pushing for a state constitutional convention to reform the California Legislature into a unicameral body — an idea that does not win her many friends among her colleagues. Her bill, SB 16, created the California Constitutional Revision Commission, which began meetings in late 1994. Killea, a member of the commission, said she hopes the commission's recommendations will inspire the governor and Legislature to be bold, although she admitted that there is likely to be disappointment in the end because the commission cannot possibly solve all of California's complex problems.

PERSONAL: elected 1989 (special election); born July 31, 1922, in San Antonio, Tex.; home, San Diego; Army 1943-1948 WWII; education, B.A. Incarnate World College, Tex.; M.A. University of San Diego; Ph.D. UC San Diego; husband John, two children; Roman Catholic.

CAREER: State Department personal secretary and administrative assistant to Eleanor Roosevelt (delegate to United Nations 1946); Central Intelligence Agency 1948-1957; U.S. Information Agency 1957-1960; vice president Fronteras de las Californias; university lecturer; research and teaching assistant; San Diego City Council 1978-1982; Assembly 1982-1989.

COMMITTEES: Investment and International Trade (chair); Finance; Appropriations; Business & Professions; Natural Resources and Wildlife; Insurance.

OFFICES: Capitol, (916) 445-3952, FAX (916) 327-2188; district, 2550 5th Ave., 152, San Diego 92103-6691, (619) 696-6955, FAX (619) 696-8930.

TERM LIMIT: 1996
REGISTRATION: 40.52% D, 41.98% R

| **1992 CAMPAIGN**: | Killea I | 60.4% | $587,412 |
| | Jim Ellis R | 33.0% | $395,234 |

DEC. 5, 1989 SPECIAL ELECTION:

| | Killea D | 51% | $474,703 |
| | Carol Bentley R | 48.9% | $195,689 |

RATINGS:	AFL-CIO	CLCV	NOW	CofC	CalFarm	GO
	91	87	B+	18	80	F

Quentin L. Kopp (independent)
8th Senate District

Starting on the western tip of San Francisco, this district takes in many of the city's older neighborhoods, including the Sunset district, and then stretches to the fog-shrouded suburb of Pacifica. Moving south, the district includes upscale Burlingame and Hillsborough and the middle-class communities of South San Francisco, Milbrae, Daly City and part of San Mateo. Heavily Democratic, this district has remained as sure a bet for Democrats as there can be in politics — which is to say strange things can happen.

Quentin Kopp

The Assembly's "Lead-foot Lou" Papan (so named for his speeding tickets while commuting between the Bay Area and Sacramento) thought he was a shoo-in to replace retiring Sen. John Foran in 1986. But Republicans, mortified at the prospect of having the highly partisan Papan in the Senate, deserted their own candidate and threw money behind San Francisco Supervisor Quentin Kopp, who ran as an independent. Kopp was elected as the Legislature's first independent in decades. The district, which after the 1992 reapportionment is half white and 28 percent Asian, is still safe for Kopp.

Kopp remains more interested in San Francisco politics than in the Capitol. His scraps with Dianne Feinstein when she was mayor are legendary (Kopp actually had a date with Feinstein in their younger days). In fact, his scraps with nearly every San Francisco political figure from Willie Brown on down are legendary. In March 1987, Kopp hinted that he might (again) run for mayor with typical Kopp elocution: "Many people are importuning me to make the race." Instead, one of his aides managed the mayoral campaign of San Francisco Examiner columnist Warren Hinkel. Kopp toyed with running in 1991 but again bowed out.

In the Capitol, Kopp has shown plenty of shrewdness. He votes with Democrats on leadership issues, although he has increasingly gone his own way on budget and tax matters. His sharp elbows earned him a powerful post — and the wrath of Gov. George Deukmejian. A day before the 1988 confirmation vote on Deukmejian's hand-picked nominee for state treasurer, Dan Lungren, Kopp said he was behind Lungren all the way. On the day of the vote, Kopp switched, earning the gratitude of then Senate President Pro Tem David Roberti. Democrat Wadie Deddeh, who voted for Lungren, found himself stripped of the powerful chairmanship of the Transportation Committee. Kopp got Deddeh's job.

As a senator, Kopp pushed for an early presidential primary date. He also has sponsored bills to strengthen public records and open meetings laws. He successfully authored a bill that tightened the conflict-of-interest rules for members of the state Board of Equalization. In recent sessions, Kopp has promoted consolidation of the Board of Equalization with the state Franchise Tax Board — an idea Gov. Pete Wilson swiped to use in his January 1993 budget proposal but vetoed when the measure got to his desk.

In 1988, Kopp joined forces with Republican Assemblyman Ross Johnson and Democratic Sen. Joe Montoya to write Proposition 73, a measure that limited the size of campaign contributions while banning public financing for campaigns. That initiative was approved by the voters in June, but was ruled unconstitutional by a federal judge in 1990. Montoya eventually went to federal prison on corruption convictions, but Kopp has remained his friend, even helping him draft appeals.

In the wake of the huge amount of pretrial publicity in the murder trial of former football player O.J. Simpson, lawmakers expressed concerns about whether Simpson could get a fair trial. Kopp authored two of three bills signed by Wilson that set rules about how and when jurors and witnesses can sell their stories and ordered the California Bar Association to draw up rules of professional conduct on trial publicity as a way of limiting out-of-court statements by attorneys.

PERSONAL: elected 1986; born Aug. 11, 1928, in Syracuse, N.Y.; home, San Francisco; USAF 1952-1954; education, B.A. Dartmouth College, J.D. Harvard University; wife Mara, three children; Jewish.

CAREER: lawyer; San Francisco Board of Supervisors 1972-1986.

COMMITTEES: Transportation (chair); Agriculture & Water Resources; Budget & Fiscal Review; Local Government; Revenue & Taxation; Criminal Procedure; Housing and Land Use.

OFFICES: Capitol, (916) 445-0503, FAX (916) 327-2186; district, 363 El Camino Real, 205, South San Francisco 94080, (415) 952-5666, FAX (415) 589-5953.

TERM LIMIT: 1998

REGISTRATION: 58.2% D, 24.4% R

1994 CAMPAIGN:	Kopp I	63.53%	$423,353
	Patrick Fitzgerald D	19.96%	Not Available
	Tom Spinosa R	14.40%	Not Available

1990 CAMPAIGN: Kopp I   72.7% $1,227,499
                 Patrick Fitzgerald D   18% $0
                 Robert Silvestri R   9.3% $0
RATINGS: AFL-CIO   CLCV   NOW   CofC   CalFarm   GO
              60   58   B-   65   80   D

William R. Leonard Jr. (R)
31st Senate District

William Leonard

The heir to archconservative, gun-toting Bill Richardson's Senate district was Assemblyman Bill Leonard. And the district he got was mostly desert and rock, spanning a territory from San Bernardino north hundreds of miles across the Mojave Desert to Bishop, deep in the Owens Valley. The district is so immense that it abutts a district represented by a senator from Stockton. Leonard said he did not mind the district — but he wore out a lot of tires covering it.

So when the 1992 reapportionment maps were approved, Leonard was delighted with his new district. Still unbeatable for a Republican, Leonard got suburban portions of Riverside and San Bernardino counties, including upscale Redlands, Upland, Yucaipa and the boom-town bedroom communities of Moreno Valley. Other friendly territories include the retirement communities of Hemet and San Jacinto. He still has southern San Bernardino County desert land, including the Twenty-Nine Palms Marine base. Ninety percent of the registered voters in this district are white.

Leonard, who is both smoother and much more intellectual than Richardson, has a conservatism that is just as rigid — with some innovations. The San Bernardino native son won the seat after serving 10 years in the Assembly. He originally came to Sacramento as one of the Proposition 13 babies, elected the same year the property tax limitation initiative passed. After his Senate election, Leonard successfully passed off his Assembly seat to former aide Paul Woodruff.

Leonard has moved swiftly through the ranks of Senate Republicans. He was elevated to the second ranking position as Republican Caucus chairman soon after John Doolittle vacated the post to run for Congress in 1990. In 1992, Leonard took the lead for Senate Republicans on workers' compensation issues, a cornerstone of Gov. Pete Wilson's agenda. Leonard proved himself a tenacious but pragmatic fighter for the governor's program.

On other issues, Leonard is unwavering in his opposition to gun control and is intensely anti-abortion. He has opposed anything that looks like a tax increase. But he is not anti-government. While in the Assembly, Leonard introduced legislation to ban the internal combustion engine. He honed the idea into a serious bill that won Assembly approval in 1987. That measure would have phased in clean-burning methanol vehicles in the 1990s. The bill was supported by major auto manufacturers. But after opposition from oil companies, the bill was buried in the Senate by Democratic Sen. Ralph Dills of Gardena, who was then chairman of the Governmental Organization Committee.

In 1990, Leonard succeeded in moving SCA 1, which would have allowed local school districts to approve bonds with a majority vote instead of two-thirds. The constitutional amendment was defeated largely by Republicans in the Assembly, who pulled the measure down on a 43-28 vote. Some months later, Leonard's idea was enthusiastically embraced by Wilson, who prominently mentioned it in his first State of the State address.

Leonard considered running for one of the new congressional seats that opened up in 1992, but decided instead to remain in the state Senate — for the time being. In 1994, Gov. Wilson appointed Leonard to the state Constitutional Revision Commission.

PERSONAL: elected 1988; born Oct. 29, 1947, in San Bernardino; home, Big Bear; education, B.A. UC Irvine, graduate work CSU Sacramento; wife Sherry Boldizsar, three children; Presbyterian.

CAREER: Real estate management; director San Bernardino Valley Municipal Water District 1974-1978; Assembly 1978-1988; Republican Caucus Chairman 1990-present.

COMMITTEES: Industrial Relations; Appropriations; Toxics and Public Safety Management; Energy, Utilities and Communications.

OFFICES: Capitol, (916) 445-3688, FAX (916) 327-2272; district, 400 N. Mountain Ave., 109, Upland 91786, (909) 946-4889, FAX (909) 982-1197.

TERM LIMIT: 1996
REGISTRATION: 40.11% D, 47.83% R

1992 CAMPAIGN:	Leonard R		99.9%		$498,399
1988 CAMPAIGN:	Leonard R		66%		$402,887
	Sandra Hester D		34%		$70,153

RATINGS:	AFL-CIO	CLCV	NOW	CofC	CalFarm	GO
	19	6	D+	94	20	A

Robert Timothy Leslie (R)
1st Senate District

This district begins in Modoc County in the northeastern corner of the state and runs south through mountains, Lake Tahoe and into the Sierra foothills. It ends in the desert of Mono County on the eastern side of the Sierra and Calaveras County on the west. At one point, the district protrudes onto the Sacramento Valley floor, taking in Butte and Yuba counties. It is a heavily forested and lightly populated district throughout most of its expanse. Pockets of population include Susanville, with its prisons, the overbuilt Tahoe basin and the valley cities of Chico, Oroville and Marysville. Western Placer County, which is rapidly filling up with Sacramento suburbanites, is one of the fastest-growing areas of the state. The 1992 reapportionment strengthened the 1st District as a Republican stronghold.

The district's state senator, Tim Leslie, a former lobbyist and legislative aide of minimal distinction, has been in the right places at the right times. After several tries for public office, Republican Leslie was

Tim Leslie

elected to the Assembly in 1986, the improbable winner over a Democratic candidate hand-picked by Assembly Speaker Willie Brown. Leslie's opponent, Jack Dugan, went down in flames after it was discovered he had never voted in a statewide election.

In the Assembly, Leslie did little of note. His district was decidedly suburban, upscale and conservative. He got in a minor flap over sponsoring a tax-break bill for a local company in Loomis, one of the more affluent communities near Sacramento. Mostly, Leslie did the bidding of Republican governors and legislative leaders, voting their way and keeping his mouth more or less shut.

When John Doolittle won a seat in Congress in 1990, the politically reliable Leslie became the pick of Gov. Pete Wilson to succeed Doolittle in the state Senate. The only problem was that Leslie did not live in the district. So he rented a home in Auburn in order to run in the special election. Despite a spirited challenge from Republican Bob Dorr, an El Dorado County supervisor, Leslie won the GOP primary in March 1991. In the May runoff, he beat Democrat Patti Mattingly, a Siskiyou County supervisor.

In late 1994, Leslie, Doolittle, four Republican operatives and the California Republican Party agreed to pay an $8,000 fine for trying to shift money surreptitiously to Leslie's 1991 Senate campaign. In stipulated agreements with the Fair Political Practices Commission, all defendants acknowledged breaking the law and waived rights to further appeals. Leslie also has agreed to pay a separate $12,000 fine for missing or late campaign disclosure reports for in-kind contributions of $94,675 from the Republican Party for items such as mailers, postage and consulting services. Leslie also failed to meet deadlines to disclose $57,280 in expenditures and the transfer of $48,000 between two committees he controlled.

In the sedate Senate, Leslie has shown moderate signs of life. He carried the governor's 1991 Sierra Accord timber bill that would have preserved some old-growth stands and protected trees along rivers and streams. But the bill ran into heavy flak from environmentalists, who called it a sell-out, and business interests, who thought it went too far. Leslie was not a skilled enough technician to get the bill approved by his former Assembly colleagues in February 1992. He also has worked on crime and budget issues, and is a steady vote for the Christian Coalition agenda.

PERSONAL: elected 1991; born Feb. 4, 1942, in Ashland, Ore.; home, Carnelian Bay; education, B.S. CSU Long Beach; M.A. USC; wife Clydene, two children; Presbyterian.

CAREER: real estate; Assembly Ways & Means Committee consultant 1969-1971; lobbyist for County Supervisors' Association of California 1971-1980; Assembly 1986-1991.

COMMITTEES: Appropriations (vice chair); Judiciary (vice chair); Health & Human Services; Natural Resources & Wildlife.

OFFICES: Capitol, (916) 445-5788; district, 1200 Melody Lane, 110, Roseville 95678, (916) 969-8232.

TERM LIMIT: 1996

REGISTRATION: 40.94% D, 45.28% R

1992 CAMPAIGN:	Leslie R		54.7%		$404,667
	Thomas Romero D		35.8%		$10,379
1991 CAMPAIGN:	Leslie R		54.6%		$729,227
	Patti Mattingly D		43.1%		$450,368

RATINGS:	AFL-CIO	CLCV	NOW	CofC	CalFarm	GO
	11	0	D+	88	20	B

John Lewis (R)
33rd Senate District

Senatorial representation for mid-Orange County underwent two traumatic changes in 1991. First, Sen. John Seymour resigned to accept an appointment to the U.S. Senate from his old friend, newly elected Gov. Pete Wilson. (Seymour was defeated by Democrat Dianne Feinstein in 1992.) Second, the state Supreme Court sharply altered legislative districts after taking over reapportionment from a deadlocked Capitol.

Seymour's departure touched off a battle among Republicans — Democrats weren't a factor because of the district's overwhelming GOP registration — with three Republican members of the Assembly in a field of seven candidates fighting in the March 1991

John Lewis

special election. The winner was the most conservative and controversial of the three, John Lewis, and he easily won re-election in 1992 in the reconfigured district.

Seymour's old 35th District underwent slenderization and a change of numbers, to 33, during reapportionment as Orange County was awarded a new Senate district, the 34th. As reconstituted, the 33rd stretches from Fullerton in the northern end of the county to Mission Viejo in the south and includes pieces of the two largest cities, Santa Ana (the county seat) and Anaheim, the home of the county's most famous feature, Disneyland.

Lewis, an heir to a dog food fortune, had represented much of the district as an assemblyman for 11 years before the 1991 special election. It was anything but a high-profile legislative career since Lewis, perhaps the most conservative member of the Legislature, almost never made a floor speech and only rarely even carried a bill. He devoted himself, instead, to behind-the-scenes plotting on behalf of other conservatives running for legislative office. In the Assembly, he was considered the tactical brains behind the so-called "cavemen," a conservative faction that dominated Assembly GOP politics for much of the 1980s. That led to Lewis' role in a bizarre incident stemming from the 1986 campaigns, when Republican leader Pat Nolan, head of the cavemen faction, made a strenuous effort to expand GOP ranks in the Assembly.

In 1989, Lewis was indicted by a Sacramento County grand jury and accused of forgery for sending out letters bearing the faked signature of President Ronald Reagan during the '86 campaign. Going to households in several hotly contested races, the letters accused Democratic incumbents of favoring drug dealers. Lewis contended that the indictment was political, arguing that Democratic state Attorney General John Van de Kamp ignored campaign dirty tricks committed by Democratic legislative candidates in seeking charges against him.

The state Court of Appeal in Sacramento threw out the indictment on the grounds that a faked signature on campaign literature did not constitute legal forgery. Although Lewis beat the rap, Sen. Bill Craven, a fellow Republican, said Lewis' behavior was reprehensible and pushed legislation to fill the loophole.

As a senator, Lewis has pretty much followed his pattern as an assemblyman: saying and doing little publicly while confining his political effort to the back rooms of the Capitol. He votes against many bills, especially those that cost money, but seems to pursue no overall legislative goals. In 1991, the FBI made an undercover recording of a conversation between insurance Lobbyist Clay Jackson and then-Sen. Alan Robbins. Both have since been convicted for racketeering. During that conversation, Jackson described Lewis as "one of our main robots. It's unfortunate that he's very conservative because he's not terribly programmable. He just naturally falls into every place you want him to go." When the tape became public in 1993, Lewis responded: "I see that as a compliment about somebody who is very independent."

In 1994, Lewis launched a successful effort to win one of two seats on the powerful Senate Rules Committee long held by more moderate Republicans.

PERSONAL: elected 1991; born Nov. 2, 1954, in Los Angeles; home, Orange; education, B.A. USC; wife Suzanne Henry; Protestant.

CAREER: aide to Assemblyman Dennis Brown; investment manager; Assembly 1980-1991.

COMMITTEES: Insurance (vice chair); Governmental Organization; Rules; Appropriations.

OFFICES: Capitol, (916) 445-4264, FAX (916) 324-2896; district, 1940 W. Orangewood Ave., 106, Orange 92668, (714) 939-0730.

TERM LIMIT: 1996

REGISTRATION: 56.70% R, 30.62% D

1992 CAMPAIGN:	Lewis R	64.1%	$417,086
	Samuel Eidt D	39.0%	$0
MAY 14, 1991, SPECIAL ELECTION:			
	Lewis R	67.7%	$222,789
	Frank Hoffman D	26.7%	

RATINGS:	AFL-CIO	CLCV	NOW	CofC	CalFarm	GO
	4	5	C-	94	40	A

William Lockyer (D)
10th Senate District

Bill Lockyer is something of a throwback — a state legislator who was bred into the system, so to speak, by working as an aide to a lawmaker before running for the state Assembly and then moving up to the Senate. Lockyer also possesses one of the more mercurial personalities in the Capitol, one that can be all smiles and charm one moment and an eruption of red-faced invective the next. And to top it off, Lockyer is the Senate's president pro tem — in effect its leader — which gives him power over policy and politics he has long coveted.

Locker achieved the Senate's top position in early 1994 after spending months courting other Democrats, many of whom were openly skeptical that he

William Lockyer

could keep his temper under control when confronted by the pressures of leadership. The position opened when the Senate's longtime president pro tem, David Roberti, was forced out by term limits.

Lockyer promised Democratic colleagues that he not only had matured but could protect their majority in the Senate during the critical 1994 elections, when retirements and reapportionment put a number of seats in jeopardy. As it turned out, 1994 was an extraordinarily strong Republican year, making Lockyer's job even more difficult. But he delivered, losing just two Democratic seats to the Republicans but gaining one from the GOP for a net loss of one. The elections left Lockyer with a paper-thin majority, just 21 Democratic seats in a 40-member house, plus two independents who normally vote with Democrats. He'll have to perform again in 1996, when retirements, term limits and reapportionment create a solid opportunity for Republicans to take control.

During his first year as pro tem, Lockyer kept his temper under control — most of the time — and proved to be an effective leader, helping deliver a state budget on time and facilitating other legislation. But he also demonstrated a more partisan bent than Roberti, trashing some appointees of Republican Gov. Pete Wilson and engaging in a running feud with the hierarchy of the University of California. At year's end, Lockyer moved to place his own stamp on the Senate superstructure by shaking up the long-entrenched staff he inherited from Roberti, rearranging committees and appointing his own loyalists to key positions.

In a postelection interview, the Hayward lawyer said: "I don't view my role as being the Horatio-at-the-bridge figure. . . . Most of the work of the Senate is nonpartisan and I don't expect that to change." At the same time, Lockyer conceded that "some philosophical differences" would exist between the Senate and the Assembly if the Republicans ever manage to wrest control from the Democrats.

Lockyer's temperament remains the stuff of Capitol legends. During a particularly tedious committee hearing in 1985, Lockyer cut short fellow Democrat Diane Watson of Los Angeles, leaving her sputtering, "Can I finish my thought?" Lockyer retorted, "Well, if you had a thought it would be great" and added that he was fed up with her "mindless blather." Lockyer later apologized, but Watson has barely spoken to him since, and she was "present but not voting" when he was re-elected pro tem at the start of the 1995-96 session.

His temper also got the best of him during the last week of the 1990 legislative session. In a hallway outside the Senate chambers, Lockyer began baiting trial lawyer/lobbyist Bob Wilson, a former senator who was one of Lockyer's predecessors as chairman of the Judiciary Committee. Wilson lost his cool and the two got into a shoving match. Lockyer later said Wilson threw a "girlie punch" at him.

In June 1989, Lockyer barged into a private meeting between Roberti and a handful of other senators working out which big-ticket bills would move out of the Appropriations Committee. To their wonderment, Lockyer protested that he wanted a chance to make a pitch for his bills. Lockyer has blamed his erratic tendencies — which have included incidents outside the Capitol as well — on a fondness for junk food and once told the Oakland Tribune, "I would like people to know that I am a lovable eccentric and not a dysfunctional, strange one."

One of the Democrats' wins in 1994 was Lockyer's own re-election to a fourth — and last — term in the Senate. Term limits will compel Lockyer to step down in 1998, allowing someone else to represent the district he's held since 1982.

Taking in San Francisco Bay's eastern shoreline south of Oakland, the Alameda

County district includes the middle-class cities of San Leandro, Fremont and Hayward before extending over the hills into a portion of the Livermore Valley. Although it is a Democratic district, it has a conservative bent and was changed little in either economic or political orientation by the court-ordered reapportionment that followed the 1990 census.

PERSONAL: elected 1982; born May 8, 1941, in Oakland; home, Hayward; education, B.A. UC Berkeley, teaching credential CSU Hayward, J.D. McGeorge; divorced, one child; Episcopalian.

CAREER: teacher; school board member; legislative assistant to Assemblyman Bob Crown 1968-1973; Assembly 1973-1982.

COMMITTEES: Rules (chair) Legislative Ethics; Judiciary.

OFFICES: Capitol, (916) 445-6671; district, 22634 Second Street, 104, Hayward 94541, (510) 582-8800, FAX (510) 582-0822.

TERM LIMIT: 1998

REGISTRATION: 55.25% D, 29.44% R

1994 CAMPAIGN:	Lockyer D		62.97%	$1,903,233
	Anthony Smith R		37.03%	Not Available
1990 CAMPAIGN:	Lockyer D		60.6%	$1,037,242
	Howard Hertz R		39.4%	$528

RATINGS:	AFL-CIO	CLCV	NOW	CofC	CalFarm	GO
	95	78	B+	29	60	F

Kenneth L. Maddy (R)
14th Senate District

This sprawling district takes in a big chunk of the farm-dominated San Joaquin Valley as well as some of the most scenic areas in the Sierra Nevada. Prior to the 1992 reapportionment, this district had stretched from Yosemite to the outskirts of Santa Barbara. Now the 14th District is focused in Fresno. The population is three-fourths white and safely Republican.

Whatever the district boundaries, Republican Ken Maddy has had no trouble getting re-elected. A political moderate who is popular with colleagues in both parties, Maddy has parlayed his agricultural roots, concerns about health care and lifelong love for horses and horse racing into legislative successes.

Ken Maddy

As Republican leader, Maddy enjoyed a good working relationship with former

Democratic leader and Senate President Pro Tem David Roberti. Maddy and Roberti protected each other in the house to mutual advantage. The arrangement gave Maddy more power in the Senate than Republican strength would otherwise have dictated. Maddy, for all intents and purposes, named the Republican members of committees and vice chairs. In return, Roberti could count on Maddy's cooperation in running the Senate and did not have to endure the disruptive and counterproductive antics that are the rule in the Assembly. Maddy has a less cordial history with Roberti's successor, Senate President Pro Tem Bill Lockyer. But in 1994, Maddy gave Lockyer a backhanded compliment, saying that Lockyer came in sounding more partisan than Roberti, but he eventually saw that it was easier to get things done cooperatively.

During Maddy's early career, he endured tough campaigns and a couple of political and personal setbacks. In 1978, while still an assemblyman, he made a bid for governor with a campaign that got him nearly a half-million votes despite being unknown outside Fresno County. Having given up his Assembly seat to run for governor, Maddy was out of politics for a few months. But the resignation of Sen. George Zenovich quickly created a new opening, and Maddy won a hard-fought special election to fill the seat.

Maddy's first marriage foundered after he won his Senate seat, and he later married the wealthy heiress to the Foster Farms chicken fortune, Norma Foster. That gave him resources to pursue his passion for thoroughbred horse racing. The Maddys have become A-list socialites, not only in Sacramento and the San Joaquin Valley, but in the playgrounds of the wealthy along Orange County's gold coast, where they maintain a weekend residence.

Maddy saw his star rise quickly in the Senate. While he has toyed with seeking statewide office again, he has never taken the plunge, except to apply for a gubernatorial appointment as state treasurer.

In 1992, conservative Garden Grove businessman Rob Hurtt won a special election to the Senate. Hurtt immediately tried to dump Maddy as minority leader. Although he was unsuccessful, Hurtt established himself as a powerhouse and Maddy reluctantly agreed to a power-sharing arrangement, with Hurtt serving as head of fund-raising and electoral strategy. That move gave Hurtt the ability to recruit candidates who were more conservative than the moderate Maddy.

Maddy retained the leadership role in 1994 but will undoubtedly step aside sometime before 1998, when he will be forced out of office by term limits. There's also the distinct possibility that Hurtt will make another run at him.

PERSONAL: elected 1979 (special election); born May 22, 1934, in Santa Monica; home, Fresno and ranch east of Modesto; USAF 1957-60; education, B.S. CSU Fresno, J.D. UCLA; wife Norma Foster; three children and six stepchildren; Protestant.

CAREER: lawyer; horse breeder; Assembly 1970-1979; Senate Minority Leader 1987- present.

COMMITTEES: Governmental Organization (vice chair); Health and Human Services; Constitutional Amendments; Revenue & Taxation; Legislative Ethics.

OFFICES: Capitol, (916) 445-9600, FAX (916) 327-3523; district, 2503 W. Shaw Ave., 101, Fresno 93711, (209) 445-5567, FAX (209) 445-6009; 841 Mohawk St., Bakersfield 93309, (805) 324-6188 FAX (805) 324-4456.

TERM LIMIT: 1998

REGISTRATION: 43.5% D, 45.7% R

1994 CAMPAIGN:	Maddy R			70.62%		$737,556
	Tony Hagopian D			29.38%		Not Available
1990 CAMPAIGN:	Maddy R			100%		$815,745

RATINGS:	AFL-CIO	CLCV	NOW	CofC	CalFarm	GO
	5	15	C	100	40	C

Milton Marks (D)
3rd Senate District

This district, which includes Marin County, part of Sonoma County and northeastern San Francisco, is tailor-made for a Democrat — or a Milton Marks.

He has represented the area for more than three decades, including the first 19 years as a moderate-to-liberal Republican. Throughout his career, which began in the Assembly in 1958, Marks has been a maverick.

Marks took a brief respite from the Legislature in 1966, when Democratic Gov. Pat Brown appointed him a San Francisco Municipal Court judge. But he returned to politics the following year, when California's new Republican governor, Ronald Reagan, supported Marks' successful effort to fill a

Milton Marks

vacant state Senate seat in a special election. In the subsequent years, Marks steered an independent course in the Senate, often voting with Democrats on environmental, civil liberties and social issues, much to the consternation of GOP colleagues. In 1989, he was one of the few legislators who voted against a resolution urging that flag burning be made a crime.

His credentials as a Republican got a brief boost in 1982, when, at the coaxing of the Reagan White House, he unsuccessfully ran against powerful Democratic Rep. Phil Burton, who died shortly after his re-election victory. Democrats, infuriated at Marks' challenge of Burton, targeted him in 1984, supporting Lia Belli, then wife of prominent San Francisco attorney Melvin Belli. But Marks won easily. As Assembly Speaker Willie Brown once said: "The streets of San Francisco are paved with Democrats who've tried to beat Milton Marks."

But Marks' became a Democrat in January 1986, when he cut a deal with then Senate President Pro Tem David Roberti. In exchange for his switch in affiliations, Marks was immediately made caucus chairman, the No. 3 position among Senate Democrats. Some Republicans weren't bothered by Marks' defection. "We'll miss him like a case of hemorrhoids," quipped ultraconservative Sen. H.L. Richardson, who once punched Marks when both were Republicans in the Senate.

Marks was chairman of the Elections and Reapportionment Committee during the 1992 reapportionment. He and his able staff worked hard to draft a plan, but in the end, they had no real impact on redistricting since it was eventually done by the state Supreme Court.

Marks has carried many substantive bills, including measures to purge voter rolls of nonvoters in combination with programs aimed at increasing registration. He has proposed making it a crime to raise veal calves in small enclosures and to give tax advantages to artists, a measure vetoed by Gov. George Deukmejian. In 1994, Marks chaired the Judiciary subcommittee on the rights of the disabled. He proposed unsuccessful legislation requiring government buildings to create "fragrance-free" entrances and to post the date of the most recent pesticide application.

Many thought Marks would retire at the end of his 1992 term. But Marks, who is known far and wide in San Francisco for attending every bar mitzvah, birthday and funeral, had no intention of going anywhere except back to Sacramento. Marks has slowed his pace as of this writing and often seems preoccupied during floor sessions and hearings. It's as though he's waiting for term limits to retire him in 1996.

PERSONAL: elected 1967 (special election); born July 22, 1920, in San Francisco; home, San Francisco; Army WWII (Philippines); education, B.A. Stanford University, J.D. San Francisco Law School; wife Carolene Wachenheimer, three children; Jewish.

CAREER: lawyer; Assembly 1958-1966; municipal court judge 1966.

COMMITTEES: Criminal Procedure (chair); Revenue and Taxation; Industrial Relations; Housing & Land Use; Judiciary.

OFFICES: Capitol, (916) 445-1412, FAX (916) 327-7229; district, 711 Van Ness Ave., 310, San Francisco 94102, (415) 474-0308, FAX (415) 346-4009.

TERM LIMIT: 1996

REGISTRATION: 59.73% D, 21.95% R

1992 CAMPAIGN:	Marks D	66.4%	$742,627
	Bill Boerum R	25.1%	$13,117
1988 CAMPAIGN:	Marks D	66.4%	$578,897
	Carol Marshall R	30%	$155,500

RATINGS:	AFL-CIO	CLCV	NOW	CofC	CalFarm	GO
	91	95	C	35	80	F

Henry Mello (D)
15th Senate District

Henry Mello

This is one of the most diverse Senate districts, not only geographically but politically and demographically. It contains some of the state's most beautiful beach communities — Carmel, Monterey, Pacific Grove, Santa Cruz — and some of the state's most productive farmland, including the Salinas Valley, the setting for John Steinbeck's novels. The political spectrum ranges from the liberal Santa Cruz to the conservative farm-area politics of Hollister. Residents include the wealthy and movie stars — Clint Eastwood was briefly mayor of Carmel — as well as burgeoning Latino populations in cities such as Salinas, Soledad and Watsonville. While court-ordered reapportionment changed the district's number (from 17) and its boundaries somewhat, it remains largely what it has been for decades.

Henry Mello, a farmer, businessman and hulking Capitol presence, has attempted to walk a political tightrope in response to his diverse constituency. He is a moderate Democrat and a nervous one. On some controversial issues, he tries to give a little to each side. In 1989, for example, he voted in favor of a virtual ban of semiautomatic military-style assault weapons despite heavy pressure in his district from members of the National Rifle Association. Later in the year, when a key vote came up to require purchasers of rifles to wait 15 days between the time they buy rifles and they can be picked up, Mello, again under pressure from the NRA, called the waiting period outrageous and voted against it.

The switcheroo on gun control is typical of Mello's situational approach to politics, which eschews consistency of any kind. For years, that made him the swing vote on the powerful five-member Rules Committee, which routes legislation to committees and can block confirmation of gubernatorial appointees. Mello held the balance of power, which made him a frequent target of lobbyists for and against bills and nominees. Most of the time, there was no telling how Mello would vote. Often, his position seemed to depend on who talked to him last or whether he had taken a personal interest in the outcome.

Mello gave up his seat on Rules as the 1993 legislative session began and became the Senate's majority floor leader, the No. 2 Democrat, succeeding Barry Keene, who resigned his seat. Mello was tapped for the position by then-Senate President Pro Tem David Roberti to head off a political fight between two other senators, Bill Lockyer and Art Torres, who wanted the majority leader's position as a stepping stone to Roberti's job when he was forced out by term limits in 1994.

By bringing Mello into the leadership position, however, Roberti elevated a politician who is, by common consent, one of the least popular in the Capitol for his inconsistent, tit-for-tat approach to politics and his often-bullying demeanor. On occasion, Mello has generated controversy in his district by carrying bills to help local developers and other businesses in ways that some believe might have adverse environmental effects or benefit big contributors. In 1990, for example, a timber company controlled by Orange County developer Donald Koll, a large contributor to legislative and statewide campaigns, couldn't get a harvesting permit and subsequently couldn't find a buyer for some land. Mello carried a bill to have the state purchase the 1,500 acres of forest in the Santa Cruz mountains for $6 million, claiming the move would save a grove of redwoods. But the purchase, inserted in a statewide park bond, was voted down in November 1990.

In 1991, when the state was facing an unprecedented budget deficit requiring cuts in many vital programs, Mello was criticized for proposing a $3.5 million allocation for the state to participate in the 1992 World's Fair in Spain. He also played hardball with the Walt Disney Co. in 1991 and its bill to waive some environmental regulations so that it could build a new theme park in Long Beach Harbor. After months of trying to meet the ever-increasing price of Mello's support, Disney gave up under the thin cover that it was turning its attention to expansion of Disneyland in Anaheim.

When he isn't involved in heavy-handed politics, Mello seems to have a genuine interest in services to senior citizens. He carried a bill to create the Senior Legislature, an annual gathering of California senior citizens at which they set their legislative priorities. Mello has frequently carried Senior Legislature proposals, measures ranging from housing and day care to lunch programs and nursing homes. He has also taken a special interest in victims of Alzheimer's.

Given the relatively weak Democratic registration in his district and the enmity he generates among environmentalists and others on the Democratic left, Mello should be vulnerable to a serious Republican challenge. But none has been forthcoming through four elections, although local Republicans have fantasized about recruiting actor Clint Eastwood as their candidate. Mello faced a semiserious Democratic primary challenge in 1992 from a candidate who made much of Mello's cozy relations with developers and other special interests, but Mello breezed to an easy re-election.

PERSONAL: elected 1980; born March 27, 1924, in Watsonville; home, Watsonville; education, attended Hartnell Junior College; wife Helen, four children.

CAREER: farmer; Santa Cruz Board of Supervisors 1967-1974; Assembly 1976-1980; Senate Majority Leader 1992-present.

COMMITTEES: Appropriations; Housing and Land Use; Governmental Organization; Health & Human Services; Elections and Reapportionment; Natural Resources & Wildlife.

OFFICES: Capitol, (916) 445-5843, FAX (916) 448-0175; district, 92 Fifth St., Gilroy, 95020, (408) 848-1437, FAX (408) 848-6311.
TERM LIMIT: 1996
REGISTRATION: 52.25% D, 31.72% R

1992 CAMPAIGN:	Mello D	58.4%	$961,060
	Edward Laverone R	34.1%	$31,773
1988 CAMPAIGN:	Mello D	71%	$603,760
	Harry Damkar R	29%	$115,863

RATINGS:	AFL-CIO	CLCV	NOW	CofC	CalFarm	GO
	88	75	B+	35	80	C

Richard Monteith (R)
12th Senate District

This San Joaquin Valley district includes the foothill counties of Stanislaus, Merced, Tuolumne and Mariposa and all but the southeast corner of Madera county. It ends in Fresno County at the northwest suburbs of the city of Fresno.

In the 1992 reapportionment, the district lost urban Santa Clara County, where Democratic Sen. Dan McCorquodale was once a county supervisor. The result was a much more rural constituency. Although the valley is rapidly urbanizing, it retains its strong rural and conservative roots, which are not fully apparent in its predominately Democratic registration.

Richard Monteith

In anticipation of redistricting, McCorquodale bought a small house on the outskirts of Modesto in the mid-1980s. Following reapportionment, he and his wife moved to Stanislaus County. At the same time, he lobbied for and won a choice assignment as chair of the Senate Agriculture and Water Resources Committee, which oversees key legislation on water issues. All of that was designed to give McCorquodale a leg up in establishing himself as an expert on issues of importance to the economic welfare of his agriculture-based district.

Despite his best efforts, McCorquodale could not fend off the Republican surge of 1994 or the well-financed and highly choreographed campaign by Sen. Rob Hurtt to unseat McCorquodale and replace him with his hand-picked candidate, Dick Monteith.

Monteith narrowly defeated McCorquodale by 2 percentage points in a nasty campaign of competing press releases. Many political observers felt that the McCorquodale camp was not prepared for the onslaught. But others attributed the defeat to the mood of the electorate and the inherently conservative makeup of the district. McCorquodale became the first incumbent Democratic senator to lose re-election since 1982.

A retired Stanislaus County businessman, Monteith started a second career running snow cone shacks such as those found at carnivals and street fairs. His single biggest qualification for the Senate job apparently was his heartfelt belief in right-wing political causes, having no experience in public office and a virtually nonexistent record of community involvement.

When Monteith's name first cropped up as a perfect, hometown candidate with deep valley roots, longtime valley resident and Republican Senate Minority Leader Ken Maddy of Fresno said he had never heard of Monteith. Eventually, Maddy jumped on the Monteith bandwagon and even hosted a fund-raiser for the candidate.

When the Senate Rules Committee announced committee assignments Monteith immediately responded with a wordy press release citing his plans to take on "radical environmentalists, outrageous vehicle inspection programs" and the bureaucrats who have "turned saving salmon and smelt into a regulated drought for agriculture." Even many moderate Republicans, who were often at odds with the liberal McCorquodale, were wondering what the 12th District election had wrought.

PERSONAL: elected 1994; born, Feb. 7 1932, in Los Banos; home, Modesto; education, A.A. Menlo College; B.A. Stanford University; wife, Jeanine Foster; two children, three stepchildren; United Methodist.

CAREER: family farm implement business; agribusiness manager; snow cone outlet manager.

COMMITTEES: Housing and Land Use (vice chair); Natural Resources and Wildlife; Transportation; Agriculture and Water Resources.

OFFICES: Capitol, (916) 445-1392, FAX (916) 445-0773; district, 1620 N. Carpenter Rd., A-4, Modesto 95358, (209) 577-6592, FAX (209) 577-4963.

TERM LIMIT: 2002

REGISTRATION: 49.94 D, 38.92 R

1994 CAMPAIGN:

Monteith R		49.44%	$444,634
Dan McCorquodale D		47.32%	$768,939

RATINGS: Newly elected.

Richard L. Mountjoy (R)
29th Senate District

Bobbing and weaving through the San Gabriel Valley, the 29th Senate District covers the eastern-most part of Los Angeles County. It takes in the old neighborhoods of Claremont and Pomona and the conservative think tanks nearby, as well as the instant housing developments of Diamond Bar and West Covina. The district also crosses the Whittier Hills and includes a piece of Whittier. It is carved around pockets of Latinos and is therefore safe for Republicans.

Frank Hill had little trouble getting re-elected in his new district in 1992, facing the same Democratic opponent, Sandy Hester, he had faced in a 1990 special election in the prereapportionment 31st District. Hester attempted to make something of press reports that Hill was under scrutiny by federal investigators who were delving into vote-peddling in the Capitol, but given the district's strong Republican registration and the lack of both a smoking gun and serious campaign money, Hester's drive fell well short.

Richard Mountjoy

Two years later, however, Hill was in federal prison, serving a term for corruption after being convicted by a federal jury. The evidence against Hill included videotapes of Hill conducting business with federal agents posing as Georgia businessmen. Hill's departure from the Senate — he initially refused to resign after being convicted and had to be forced out by Senate leaders — left a vacancy that attracted the 29th Senate District's two Republican assemblymen, Paul Horcher and Richard Mountjoy.

Mountjoy, one of the "Proposition 13 babies" elected to the Assembly in 1978 and a strident political warrior, bested Horcher, who had alienated many Republicans by accepting a key committee appointment from Assembly Speaker Willie Brown that Horcher's fellow Republicans wanted to go to another GOP lawmaker.

It was an incident that was to have major repercussions because Horcher, deeply in debt from the special Senate election campaign and kicked around by other Republicans, defected to Brown after the November 1994 election. He renounced his Republican Party membership and declared himself to be an independent. He then voted for Brown's re-election as speaker, which created a 40-40 tie between Democrats and Republicans.

Mountjoy, who had been re-elected to the Assembly at the same time he was being elected to fill the remainder of Hill's term in the Senate, chose to delay his resignation from the Assembly while Brown and Republicans tried to negotiate a power-sharing agreement. While Mountjoy vowed to renounce his Senate seat and stay in the Assembly as long as Brulte needed his vote, it was clear that he was only biding his time until he could move. He showed up at the first Senate GOP caucus meeting of the session and cast a vote, and he told his staff to prepare to relocate.

To keep Brown from removing Mountjoy, the Assembly Republicans retreated to the Hyatt Hotel across the street. They feared that if any GOP member showed up in the Capitol, Brown could have them brought to the floor to constitute a quorum. Fellow Republicans were furious when Mountjoy casually wandered onto the floor the day after his caucus retreated to the Hyatt. "He wanted to get hijacked, thrown out of the Assembly and made a hero," one bitter Republican said afterward. "He was driving us on to war (in the caucus) but unwilling to risk anything himself."

Mountjoy had been talking tough about a holy war with the Democrats in the

GOP caucus, but Assemblyman Bernie Richter, who made an abortive attempt to become the compromise choice for speaker, claimed Mountjoy also was talking to him. "Mountjoy came into my office and was disdainful of his own leadership," Richter recalled. "He expressed real concern about their character, about their veracity . . . and used a lot of swear words to express it. But he never expressed those views in the caucus. In fact, he supported them."

Negotiations and maneuvering between Brown and Brulte continued for seven weeks. Finally, on Jan. 24, 1995, Brown, who was presiding over the Assembly as the house's senior member, ruled that Mountjoy could not vote on the question of his own ouster. Mountjoy's ouster then passed on a 40-39 vote, with Horcher joining the Democrats. Brown was re-elected just hours later by the same margin.

Once booted from the Assembly, Mountjoy quickly arranged to be sworn in as a senator the following day. In the upper house, Mountjoy strengthens the GOP's conservative bloc and gives it a man known for his love of political combat, whether the issue is reapportionment, gun control, workers' compensation or immigration. In 1990, Mountjoy single-handedly campaigned against Proposition 112, the Legislature's ethics reform package. Mountjoy and Ruth Holton, a lobbyist for Common Cause, faced-off on countless radio talk shows on the issue. Mountjoy maintained that while the ethical standards were desirable, the measure had a catch: a commission that, he said, almost certainly would give lawmakers a pay raise. He was right. The measure passed, and lawmakers got a raise. By some accounts, Mountjoy's constant drum-beating on illegal immigration was the inspiration for Proposition 187, which voters approved in November 1994.

When Mountjoy isn't politicking, he operates a construction company. He often flies his own plane between Southern California and Sacramento, once surviving a crash-landing at Sacramento's Executive Airport.

PERSONAL: elected 1994 (special election); born Jan. 13, 1932, in Monrovia; home, Monrovia; Navy 1951-1955 (Korea); wife Earline; three children; Protestant.

CAREER: general contractor; commercial pilot; Monrovia City Council and mayor 1968-1976.

COMMITTEES: Unassigned at time of publication.

OFFICES: Capitol, (916) 445-2824, FAX (916) 442-8429; district, 208 N. First Ave., Arcadia 91006, (818) 446-3134, FAX (818) 445-3591.

TERM LIMIT: 2002

REGISTRATION: 41.4% D, 45.6% R

1994 CAMPAIGN:

Mountjoy R			65.2%		$227,299
Sandra Hester D			34.7%		$24,960

RATINGS:

AFL-CIO	CLCV	NOW	CofC	CalFarm	GO
7	0	C-	100	66.6	A*

* Based on Assembly votes.

Jack O'Connell (D)

18th Senate District

On a coastal corridor from San Luis Obispo to Ventura, the 18th Senate District includes growth-controlled Santa Barbara, Oxnard and the laid-back communities surrounding UC Santa Barbara. The district, running along the spine of the low but rugged Santa Ynez Mountains, has an environmentalist ethic but is decidedly upscale, with a small Democratic plurality in registration, making it an increasingly volatile battleground.

Jack O'Connell

Democrat Gary Hart balanced the sometimes conflicting political tendencies of this district for a dozen years, repeatedly winning re-election easily. But reapportionment extended its boundaries northward into San Luis Obispo County, adding more Republicans, and Hart, who seemed bored in the Senate, decided to retire from the Legislature in 1994 rather than campaign in the redrawn district.

Democrats put up a Hart clone, Jack O'Connell. Tall and lanky like Hart, a former teacher like Hart, an affable and effective campaigner like Hart, O'Connell took over Hart's old seat in the Assembly when the latter moved up to the Senate in 1982. O'Connell became something of a Capitol legend for his prodigious ability and willingness to walk precincts and otherwise maintain a strong grass-roots campaign organization in an era of media and money.

O'Connell's political abilities made him a favorite of Assembly Speaker Willie Brown, and he was eventually promoted into the inner leadership circle as speaker pro tem, the person who presides over the body's floor sessions most of the time. As the presider, O'Connell proved to be unflappably cool and pleasant — if highly partisan when the need arose.

Most of O'Connell's legislative output has dealt with education issues, including repeated attempts to make it easier for school districts to levy parcel taxes by reducing the voter approval margin from two-thirds to a simple majority. Gov. Pete Wilson repeatedly vetoed the bill, however. With term limits looming, O'Connell quickly seized the chance to run for Hart's seat in 1994.

Republicans went with Steve MacElvaine, a rancher and San Luis Obispo County supervisor who, it was thought, would have particular appeal in the new territory added to the 18th District by the 1992 reapportionment. O'Connell didn't miss a beat. He took his shoe-leather campaign northward and ran up huge margins in private polls, which discouraged GOP leaders from giving MacElvaine more than token financial support. The result was a 3-2 victory for O'Connell, which meant that tens of thousands of Republicans had voted for him.

PERSONAL: elected 1994; born Oct. 8, 1951, in Glen Cove, N.Y.; home, Carpinteria; education, B.A. CSU Fullerton, teaching credential CSU Long Beach; wife Doree Caputo, one child; Roman Catholic.

CAREER: high school teacher; aide to Sen. Omer Rains; Assembly, 1982-94, speaker pro tem 1991-94.

COMMITTEES: Toxic and Public Safety (chair); Judiciary; Natural Resources and Wildlife; Education; Business and Professions; Budget and Fiscal Review.

OFFICES: Capitol, (916) 445-5405, FAX (916) 322-3304; district, 228 W. Carrillo St., Ste. F, Santa Barbara 93101, (805) 966-2296, FAX (805)966-3707.

TERM LIMIT: 2002

REGISTRATION: 44.9% D, 40.5% R

1994 CAMPAIGN: O'Connell D   59.04% $1,333,928
                Steve MacElvaine R   40.96% $462,211

RATINGS: AFL-CIO CLCV   NOW   CofC   CalFarm   GO*
            97   75   A-   18   44.4   F

*Based on Assembly service.

Steve Peace (D)
40th Senate District

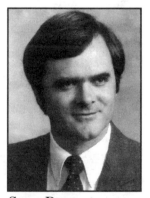

Steve Peace

Sen. Wadie Deddeh, D-Chula Vista, ended 27 undistinguished years in the Legislature in mid-1993, when he resigned to return to community college teaching. Deddeh's departure set the stage for a special election on Dec. 28 that pitted Democratic Assemblyman Steve Peace, once an aide to Deddeh, against Republican Joe Ghougassian, former U.S. ambassador to Qatar. Peace won, with a campaign war chest of $1,152,722 in the race, placing him third among the top-10 legislative fund-raisers of 1993.

Peace was once known for two things: He was the producer of the cult film, "Attack of the Killer Tomatoes," and he was Speaker Willie Brown's man to see in San Diego. Socially chummy with the speaker, Peace was considered a genius at political strategy — and that may be why Brown tolerated Peace so long. Many of Peace's colleagues consider him immature and obnoxious. His floor speeches are sometimes nothing more than rants. His fabled fight with Sen, Al Alquist (when witnesses heard Peace call Alquist a "senile old pedophile") earned him undying hatred in a body where he now sits as a member.

In 1987, Peace and four of Assembly colleagues turned on Brown, dubbing themselves the "Gang of Five." They pulled parliamentary maneuvers for a year, tying the Assembly up in petty intrigues. They eventually reconciled in 1989. As a legislator, Peace has paid attention to the border issues that so plague his district, working on getting a sewage treatment plant for the area. He has labored for years over a low-level nuclear waste compact with other states (which got him in trouble with Alquist), and he has kept proposed nuclear waste dumps out of Democratic districts. He also has been a key player in crafting workers' compensation reform legislation.

In 1994, Ghougassian challenged Peace in a rematch for the Senate, but Peace retained the seat.

Among legislation Peace has carried since coming to the Senate was SB 22x, restricting inmates' access to weight training equipment. Gov. Wilson signed that bill as well as a law-and-order measure by Peace that permits 14- and 15-year-olds accused of violent crimes to face trial as adults.

Peace joined the majority of his Senate colleagues in 1994 when he sided with the tobacco industry and opposed a bill that would have eliminated state tax deductions for tobacco advertising and promotions. The bill, SB 1271, failed on a 16-20 vote, with 21 votes needed to pass. Peace questioned whether the Legislature would consider taking the same action against fast food advertisers. "People are killed every day . . . by virtue of overconsumption of potato chips and other unhealthy foods," said Peace, who noted that he doesn't smoke.

The 40th Senate District remains Democratic despite better GOP numbers after the 1992 reapportionment. The district covers inland poor and middle-class areas of San Diego County, including parts of the city of San Diego, El Cajon, La Mesa, National City, Chula Vista and San Ysidro.

PERSONAL: elected 1993 (special election); born March 30, 1953, in San Diego; home, Rancho San Diego; education, B.A. UC San Diego; wife Cheryl, three children; Methodist.

CAREER: partner, Four Square Productions of National City, a film production firm; aide to Assemblymen Wadie Deddeh 1976-1980 and Larry Kapiloff 1980-1981; Assembly 1982-1993.

COMMITTEES: Energy, Utilities and Communications; Education; Insurance; Toxics and Public Safety Management; Budget and Fiscal Review.

OFFICES: Capitol (916) 445-6767, FAX (916) 327-3522, district, 430 Davidson St., Suite B, Chula Vista 91910, (619) 427-7080, FAX (619) 426-7369

TERM LIMIT: 2002

REGISTRATION: 49.03% D, 37.17 % R

1994 CAMPAIGN: Peace D   48.04% $542,205

Joe Ghougassian R   45.05% $217,756

1993 CAMPAIGN: Peace D   52.1%

Joe Ghougassian R   47.9%

RATINGS:	AFL-CIO	CLCV	NOW	CofC	CalFarm	GO
	86	47	B	47	40	C

Nicholas C. Petris (D)

9th Senate District

Lining San Francisco Bay's eastern shoreline, the 9th Senate District takes in a polyglot that includes the affluent, white Piedmont hills, the intensely poor African American neighborhoods of Oakland and the leftist environs of Berkeley and its University of California campus. Reapportionment removed a piece of conservative Contra Costa County and added Richmond, which made it more safely Democratic. The district is 32 percent African American, 13 percent Latino and 14 percent Asian.

Democrat Nicholas Petris, one of the last unbending liberals in the Capitol, is the only senator this district — in all its incarnations — has known since the inception of the full-time Legislature in 1966. For

Nicholas Petris

years, the silver-haired, courtly Petris has railed against growers for their treatment of farm workers; pushed, with limited success, bills requiring warning signs in fields where pesticides have been sprayed; and championed the rights of criminal defendants, mental patients, the poor and the elderly. And he is a vocal champion of the state's influential trial lawyers, standing against all efforts to tighten the state's "deep pockets" tort liability laws, efforts he sees as victimizing consumers.

But the last decade of Republican rule in the governor's office has not been kind to Petris. It has been two decades since he authored landmark legislation such as the Lanterman-Petris-Short Act, which brought major changes to the mental-health system, and the post-Proposition 13 world has not been receptive to his pleas for more funding for health care and education.

The cantankerous, right-wing Sen. H.L. Richardson, now retired, once claimed that Petris pulled the strings of former Senate President Pro Tem David Roberti. Although that's a vast overstatement, Petris' influence in keeping the Senate Democrats left of center should not be underestimated. He has used his position on the Judiciary Committee as a bully pulpit, and he also sits on the all-powerful Rules Committee. But, clearly, he is slowing down.

Beyond policy matters, one of Petris' major interests is Greece. He quotes from the Greek classics during his floor speeches and serves as the unofficial leader of the equally unofficial caucus of Greek American legislators, often authoring resolutions that support that nation in its squabbles with Turkey. The high-point for that group came in 1988, when Michael Dukakis ran for president.

Petris' home in the Oakland Hills burned during the tragic fire in October 1991. Lost in the inferno was his collection of more than 10,000 books, painstakingly collected over a lifetime, including an extensive collection of Greek works and a volume written by Harry Truman that the president had signed, along with a framed picture of Petris and Truman while Truman was signing the book. At a ceremony on the Senate floor, fellow senators presented Petris with volumes from their own collections. Some gave him one or two; others, such as Ruben Ayala, gave him a box of books. "It was very moving thing. It reduced me to tears," Petris said.

PERSONAL: elected 1966; born Feb. 25, 1923, in Oakland; home, Oakland; Army 1943-1946 (WWII); education, B.A. UC Berkeley, J.D. Stanford University; wife Anna S. Vlahos; no children; Greek Orthodox.

CAREER: lawyer, Assembly 1958-1966.

COMMITTEES: Rules; Toxics and Public Safety Management; Constitutional Amendments; Budget and Fiscal Review; Industrial Relations; Judiciary; Legislative Ethics; Revenue and Taxation.

OFFICES: Capitol, (916) 445-6577, FAX (916) 327-1997; district, 1970 Broadway 1030, Oakland 94612, (510) 286-1333, FAX (510) 286-3885.

TERM LIMIT: 1996

REGISTRATION: 70.25% D, 13.39% R

1992 CAMPAIGN:	Petris D	84.6%	$376,727
	David Campbell P&F	15.4%	Not Available
1988 CAMPAIGN:	Petris D	74.7%	$342,680
	Greg Henson R	21.4%	$0

RATINGS:	AFL-CIO	CLCV	NOW	CofC	CalFarm	GO
	93	90	B+	29	80	F

Donald A. Rogers (R)
17th Senate District

This cactus-and-sagebrush district takes in most of the Mojave Desert, the San Gabriel Mountains and the southern end of the San Joaquin Valley in oil-rich Kern County. The northern two-thirds of San Bernardino County, including the gas-stop towns of Barstow and Victorville, are also included as well as all of sparsely populated Inyo County. Geographically, the district is centered in Death Valley. But 70 percent of its people live in a chunk of northern Los Angeles County. The district is heavily Republican and has an active Ku Klux Klan klavern.

When Republican Sen. Don Rogers, who had represented the Bakersfield area in the Legislature since 1978, was reapportioned into a heavily Democratic district, he decided to set up political shop in the 17th District. The move,

Don Rogers

however, meant he had to run for election in 1992 even though he had won re-election to the Senate only two years earlier in the old 16th District. After winning in the 17th, Rogers resigned from the 16th District, forcing a special election for that seat.

Rogers has always had an appeal in the southern San Joaquin Valley. Bakersfield voters, many of them conservative descendants of the Dust Bowl migration, seem to identify with the Louisiana-born man who built his first career as an oil geologist. It didn't seem to bother them when Rogers filed Chapter 13 bankruptcy protection in 1992 to keep the Internal Revenue Service from selling his assets to pay back taxes, interest and penalties. The IRS succeeding in seizing Rogers private plane, at one point, but most of his other assets were safely squirreled away in trusts.

As a legislator, Rogers has marked himself as perhaps the Senate's strongest opponent of environmental legislation, particularly anything affecting the oil industry. His knee-jerk opposition is so strong it is taken for granted by colleagues, thus diluting whatever persuasive powers he might have. In 1990, he was the lone no vote in the Senate against a bill to set up a $100 million fund for oil-spill cleanups (in the Assembly, the single "no" vote was cast by fellow Bakersfield legislator Trice Harvey). Rogers' floor speech against the bill on Aug. 31, 1990, left many in the chamber gasping.

"Sure, we're probably going to have more oil spills," he began. "But let's state fact. The ones that have occurred — the one that occurred in Santa Barbara, it was too bad. That was a blow out. However, the effect did not last very long. It wasn't but a few months until all effects, all evidence of the spill, had disappeared due to the work of Mother Nature and the work of the response people. . . . Even up in Alaska, you go there now and you have to look pretty hard to find any evidence of the spill up in Prince William Sound."

Rogers was a vocal opponent of a ban on semiautomatic assault weapons. He didn't endear himself to his Democratic colleagues when he mailed a fund-raising appeal billing himself as the commanding officer and founder of the Republican Air Force. The plea went on: "The RAF has remained high above the quagmire of socialism and has effectively stayed the evils constantly trying to invade the California Legislature."

Rogers draws fire from other legislators occasionally for his penchant for speaking before groups identified as having racist and anti-Semitic agendas. But Rogers insists he is not racist and sees no reason to apologize. When he first went to the Senate, someone with a sense of humor gave Rogers a desk on the Senate floor next to the only African American in the house, Sen. Diane Watson, D-Los Angeles. Within days, he moved to a different desk.

At the start of the 1993-94 session, Rogers got one of the few chairmanships handed to a Republican, albeit a minor one — chair of the Senate Veterans Affairs Committee. The move allowed Senate leaders to finesse Rogers off the more important Budget and Fiscal Review Committee — a panel that has enough trouble passing a budget without having ideologues running amok.

PERSONAL: elected 1986; born April 22, 1928, in Natchitoches, La.; home, Tehachapi; USMC 1946-1948; education, B.S. Louisiana State University; wife Marilyn L. Miller, three children; Mormon.

CAREER: oil geologist; owner of a geological consulting firm and partner in a petroleum firm; Bakersfield City Council 1973-1978; Assembly 1978-1986.

COMMITTEES: Veterans Affairs (chair); Public Employment & Retirement (vice chair); Agriculture & Water Resources; Insurance, Natural Resources & Wildlife.

OFFICE: Capitol, (916) 445-6637, FAX (916) 443-4015; district, 1326 H St., Bakersfield 93301, (805) 323-0442.

TERM LIMIT: 1996

REGISTRATION: 36.48% D, 49.35% R

1992 CAMPAIGN:	Rogers R	52.2%	$296,985
	William Olenick D	38.9%	$9,872
1990 CAMPAIGN: (in 16th District):			
	Rogers R	52%	$492,674
	Ray Gonzales D	44%	$120,072

RATINGS:	AFL-CIO	CLCV	NOW	CofC	CalFarm	GO
	11	0	D+	94	40	A

Richard Polanco (D)

22nd Senate District

Even with reapportionment, Richard Polanco didn't have to worry about winning another term in the Assembly in 1992. So he spent most of that year dabbling in other districts, representing one of the two major Latino political factions that have emerged in Los Angeles during the last decade.

Polanco is a partner in the alliance that includes former state Sen. Art Torres and Los Angles City Councilman Richard Alatorre. The group is locked in a perpetual power struggle with a faction headed by Los Angeles County Supervisor Gloria Molina and Rep. Lucille Roybal-Allard. At stake is the question of who will be in control as Los Angeles' huge Latino population becomes politically active and, someday,

Richard Polanco

dominates. Polanco acts as the Sacramento agent for his group after replacing Alatorre in the Assembly in 1985. His own special election was one of the many contests between the rival factions.

As a legislator, Polanco has rarely risen above the pedestrian, although in 1990 he won some plaudits in his district for carrying a bill — albeit unsuccessfully —

to ban the aerial spraying of malathion to combat the Mediterranean fruit fly in urban areas. His major pieces of legislation have been tainted by special-interest sponsorship, such as a tobacco industry-sponsored bill that would have created a law to regulate free promotional distribution of tobacco products statewide. He dropped the bill after health and local government groups argued that the statewide standards would prevent tougher local ordinances.

In 1994, Polanco saw his chance to move on to the Senate when Democrat Herschel Rosenthal gave up the 22nd Senate District to run for the 20th District seat formerly held by Senate President Pro Tem David Roberti, who was the Legislature's first casualty of term limits. The election took on racial overtones when some Latino politicians became upset because Polanco interjected himself into the 45th Assembly District race by endorsing his former chief of staff, Bill Mabie, who is white, against Antonio Villaraigosa. The seat had been held by Latinos since 1972. Polanco, who sent out a last-minute mailer urging the district's Latino voters to support Mabie, responded that he was merely backing the candidate he viewed as best suited for the job. During the primary, Villaraigosa accused Mabie and Polanco of maliciously spreading rumors that he was arrested in 1977 for a felony assault. Mabie and Polanco denied that they sought to taint Villaraigosa's campaign. Villaraigosa was initially arrested on a felony charge in the case, but he was tried on a misdemeanor assault charge and was not convicted.

In his Senate race, Polanco had to overcome a strong challenge by former legislative aide Yolanda Gonzalez in the Democratic primary. She eventually captured 40.6 percent of the vote to Polanco's 59.4 percent. Polanco had raised $172,949 to Gonzalez's $20,000. Polanco had no trouble defeating his Republican opponent, Los Angeles physician Yong Tai Lee in the general election.

Much of the area includes Polanco's former Assembly district, which he had represented since 1986. The district stretches from Highland Park through Echo Park and Silver Lake to South-Central, including parts of the Eastside, Mid-City and Hollywood.

PERSONAL: elected 1994; born March 4, 1951, in Los Angeles: home, Los Angeles; education, attended Universidad Nacional de Mexico and University of Redlands, A.A. East Los Angeles Community College; wife Olivia, three children; Methodist.

CAREER: special assistant, Gov. Jerry Brown 1980-1982; chief of staff Assemblyman Richard Alatorre 1983-1985; Assembly, 1985-1994.

COMMITTEES: Elections and Reapportionment (chair); Appropriations; Criminal Procedure; Transportation; Finance, Investment, and International Trade; Health and Human Services.

OFFICES: Capitol, (916) 445-3456, FAX (916) 324-4657; district, 110 North Ave., 56, Los Angeles 90042, (213) 255-7111, FAX (213) 620-4411.

TERM LIMIT: 2002

REGISTRATION: 64.77% D, 20.07% R

1994 CAMPAIGN:	Polanco D	68%	$485,295
	Yong Tai Lee, R	23.13%	Not Available
1992 CAMPAIGN:	Polanco D	64.6%	$426,039
	Kitty Hedrick R	26.1%	$0

RATINGS:	AFL-CIO	CLCV	NOW	CofC	CalFarm	GO*
	98	60	B+	36	22.2	F

*Based on Assembly service.

Herschel Rosenthal (D)

20th Senate District

This compact district was drawn to hold the heavily Latino population of East Los Angeles. Two-thirds of the population is Spanish-speaking and Asian Americans comprise 16 percent. Democratic registration is overwhelming; Republican candidates need not apply. It is a cinch that a non-white Democrat will win this seat — eventually.

Herschel Rosenthal

At the moment, however, the 20th District is represented by Herschel Rosenthal, an old-fashioned liberal who is a product of the political organization led by Reps. Henry Waxman and Howard Berman. Before the state Supreme Court started carving up the district, Rosenthal's 22nd Senate District was the heart of the liberal west side of Los Angeles. Reap-portionment stuck that territory into the new 23rd Senate District, so Rosenthal decided to move with his turf and sought the new 23rd District seat in 1992, even though he had been re-elected to the old 22nd two years earlier.

The election for the 23rd District should have been a cinch for Rosenthal, except that he was up against none other than Assemblyman Tom Hayden, who was fighting for his political life. After a bruising and expensive Democratic primary in June 1992 between Hayden, Rosenthal and Catherine O'Neill, Hayden emerged the winner by less than 600 votes. It marked a major loss for the Berman-Waxman machine and left Rosenthal's political future up in the air.

In 1994, Rosenthal won election in the 20th District, the seat previously held by Senate President Pro Tem David Roberti. Roberti was the first member of the Legislature forced out by term limits. Roberti lost the 1994 Democratic primary for state treasurer after fending off a recall campaign from gun control opponents. Rosenthal's opponent for the Senate seat in November was Dolores White, an activist in the Roberti recall campaign.

Rosenthal has made his legislative mark primarily in utilities law. He was the

Senate Democrats' negotiator in breaking a tricky two-year stalemate over how to spend $154 million that California received from a national $2.1 billion judgment against several oil companies for overcharging during the 1974 oil crisis. The agreement reached in the spring of 1989 earmarked $60 million to start replacing about one-third of the state's unsafe school buses, and the rest was used to help poor people meet their utility bills and other energy and traffic projects.

Rosenthal's yearly financial disclosure statements have been among the more entertaining for their restaurant and travel listings. He is among the more traveled lawmakers, enjoying a steady stream of junkets courtesy of corporations, most of which have business pending before the public utilities committee he chairs. On the side, Rosenthal is a horse racing fanatic who owns all or part of several horses. He even dresses like a race-track tout in mismatched slacks and plaid jackets that look as though a horse once wore them.

Rosenthal, who was among the Democrats underwhelmed with his party's crop of candidates for governor in 1990, won notoriety in an otherwise boring summer of 1989 by trying to get actor James Garner to run for governor. Garner declined, reportedly telling Rosenthal it would mean giving up his $6 million a year income. In recent years, Rosenthal has been showing his age. His speech is halting, at times, and occasionally he loses his train of thought.

PERSONAL: elected 1982; born March 13, 1918, in St. Louis, Mo.; home, Los Angeles; Navy; education, attended UCLA; wife Patricia Staman, two children; Jewish.

CAREER: partner ADTYPE Service Co. Inc.; Assembly 1974-1982.

COMMITTEES: Insurance (chair); Energy, Utilities and Communications; Local Government; Business & Professions; Governmental Organization; Industrial Relations.

OFFICES: Capitol, (916) 445-7928; district, 6150 Van Nuys Blvd, 400, Van Nuys 91401, (818) 901-5588, FAX (818)901-5562

TERM LIMIT: 1998

REGISTRATION: 63.3% D, 21.2% R

1994 CAMPAIGN:	Rosenthal D	58.46%	$338,500
	Dolores Bender White R	41.54%	Not Available
1990 CAMPAIGN:	Rosenthal D	64.6%	$875,866
	Michael Schrager R	30.9%	$4,671

RATINGS:	AFL-CIO	CLCV	NOW	CofC	CalFarm	GO
	97	100	B+	24	60	F

Newton R. Russell (R)
21st Senate District

Democrats needn't apply in this Los Angeles County district that includes territory north of downtown Los Angeles, picking up pieces of wealthy suburbs in the San Fernando and San Gabriel valleys. The district includes the posh — and very white — suburbs of San Marino and Pasadena, La Canada, Sunland-Tujunga and Burbank. Latinos compromise 22 percent of the population, but a considerably smaller proportion of the registered voters.

Newton Russell has been in the Legislature since 1964. After 10 years in the Assembly, he moved to the Senate in 1974. The senator is a hard-working, consummate conservative, rarely breaking from the Republican caucus line. In fact, it was something of a mild surprise when Russell reversed himself in 1989 and supported a bill that would have heavily fined insurers who illegally canceled automobile policies following the passage of Proposition 103.

Newton Russell

In recent years, Russell has been most visible for his involvement in bills dealing with sex education at schools. In 1988, he successfully pushed a bill, signed into law by Gov. George Deukmejian, that requires schools to encourage students to abstain from intercourse until they are ready for marriage and to teach respect for monogamous, heterosexual marriage. Russell said the measure was not intended to preach morals. It was intended to give teens useful, factual tips. The following year, he introduced a bill to require written parental consent for children to receive sex education, and another to prohibit schools from providing counseling to students, other than career, academic or vocational, without written parental consent.

His legislation for the 1993-94 session had a law-and-order tilt, perhaps reflecting the post-Los Angeles riot fear of his constituents. His bills include one to increase penalties for suspects fleeing police.

Russell also is one of the Senate's resident parliamentarians, frequently rising to object to breaches of rules. His protests led to a series of procedural reforms in the Senate designed to prevent legislation from slipping into law without notice and full airing.

PERSONAL: elected 1974 (special election); born June 25, 1927, in Los Angeles; home, Glendale; Navy WWII; education, B.S. USC, attended UCLA and Georgetown University; wife Diane Henderson; three children; Protestant.

CAREER: insurance agent; Assembly 1964-1974.

COMMITTEES: Finance, Investment, and International Trade; Energy & Public Utilities (vice chair); Insurance; Local Government; Transportation; Legislative Ethics; Public Employment and Retirement.

OFFICES: Capitol, (916) 445-5976, FAX (916) 324-7543; district, 401 N. Brand Blvd., 424, Glendale 91203-2364, (818) 247-7021, FAX (818) 240-5672.

TERM LIMIT: 1996

REGISTRATION: 45.26% D, 41.73% R

1992 CAMPAIGN:	Russell R		50%	$460,284
	Rachel Dewey D		43.7%	$14,241
1988 CAMPAIGN:	Russell R		68.4%	$284,413
	Louise Gelber D		28.3%	$121,146

RATINGS:	AFL-CIO	CLCV	NOW	CofC	CalFarm	GO
	21	5	C-	100	40	A

Hilda L. Solis (D)

24th Senate District

This district includes much of the San Gabriel Valley and is a Latino majority district. Many of its cities are havens for new immigrants, such as Azusa, Baldwin Park, El Monte, Monterey Park, Alhambra, San Gabriel, Irwindale, Rosemead, El Monte and La Puente. More than 60 percent of the residents are Latino, and the district also has a huge Chinese immigrant population.

Hilda L. Solis

When the state Supreme Court consciously created a number of legislative and congressional districts with Latino voter concentrations as required by provisions of the federal Voting Rights Act, it touched off a renewal of the rivalry between two groups of Hispanic politicians in Los Angeles County. The factions — one headed by Los Angeles County Supervisor Gloria Molina and the other by Los Angeles City Councilman Richard Alatorre and then-Sen. Art Torres — chose their 1992 election candidates to go head-to-head in districts throughout Southern California.

The Alatorre-Torres bloc won most contests, but lost one in the 57th Assembly District, previously represented by retiring Assemblywoman Sally Tanner. The Molina group achieved the breakthrough with Hilda Solis, a Rio Hondo college trustee. She bested a field of Democratic candidates in the primary, then had little difficulty overcoming token Republican opposition in November to claim the Assembly seat.

Soon thereafter, Solis saw an opportunity to move to the Senate in 1994, when Torres did not seek re-election, choosing instead to wage an unsuccessful campaign for state insurance commissioner. During her short time in the Assembly, Solis was not a prominent player. She introduced one fairly innovative piece of legislation that requires the Los Angeles Sanitation District to turn over the Puente Hills Landfill to the Los Angeles Department of Parks and Recreation for conversion to a public park.

At age 37, she became the youngest sitting state senator in 1994 and was given the chair of the Industrial Relations Committee.

PERSONAL: elected 1992; born Oct. 20, 1957, in Los Angeles; home, La Puente; education, B.A. Cal Poly Pomona, M.A. USC; husband Sam; Catholic.

CAREER: management analyst, U.S. Office of Budget and Management; director of access program, Whittier Union High School District; trustee, Rio Hondo Community College District.

COMMITTEES: Industrial Relations (chair); Judiciary; Finance, Investment, and International Trade; Health and Human Services; Natural Resources and Wildlife; Public Employment and Retirement.

OFFICES: Capitol, (916) 445-1418, FAX (916) 445-0485; district, 4401 Santa Anita Ave., 2nd Floor, El Monte 91731, (818) 448-1271, FAX (818) 448-8062.

TERM LIMIT: 2002

REGISTRATION: 58.96% D, 27.64% R

1994 CAMPAIGN:	Solis D	63.13%	$299,627
	Dave Boyer R	32.65%	$45,988
1992 CAMPAIGN:	Solis D	60.9%	$205,467
	Gary Woods R	34.3%	$3,959

| **RATINGS**: | AFL-CIO | CLCV | NOW | CofC | CalFarm | GO* |
| | 100 | 95 | A- | 14 | 22.2 | F |

* Based on Assembly Service

Michael Thompson (D)
2nd Senate District

Michael Thompson

The craggy North Coast with its dwindling stands of old-growth forest remains outside the economic mainstream of the state. Quaint bed-and-breakfast inns dot the Mendocino and Humboldt County coastlines. The district has a national park — Redwoods — although residents nearby have always resented it as a symbol of a lost timber industry. The new Pelican Bay state prison in Crescent City has brought a new economic base for some, but the unlikely spot for a prison is awkward for transporting prisoners, and it has brought urban problems with it.

The district was reconfigured in the 1992 reapportionment and now takes in the premier wine-growing regions of Lake, Napa and Sonoma counties. Grapes have now supplanted marijuana as the district's chief cash crop.

A generation ago, California's scantly populated north coast voted Republican most of the time, even though it had a majority of nominally Democratic voters. But the area's politics began to change in the late 1960s, when the decline of the timber industry was accompanied by an influx of counterculture urban refugees. As loggers became fewer and the newcomers more numerous, the political pendulum made a slow but steady swing to the left, with environmental and lifestyle issues becoming dominant in local politics.

By the late 1980s, the region was voting solidly Democratic. The harbinger of that change occurred in 1972, when a young Democratic attorney from Santa Rosa, Barry Keene, was elected to a vacant state Assembly seat. Keene spent six years in the Assembly before moving into the region's state Senate district, where he stayed until he resigned in 1992.

Sen. Mike Thompson, D-St. Helena, gave up his seat in the adjoining 4th District to run for the Keene's seat after reapportionment moved Thompson's home, along with much of the Democratic-voting area around it, into the 2nd District. Nevertheless, the absentee votes had to be counted before Thompson was declared the winner over construction company owner Margie Handley of Willits in the special election.

The ice-cool Thompson worked for seven years as an aide to Assemblywoman Jacqueline Speier, D-South San Francisco, and Assemblyman Lou Papan, D-Millbrae, both liberals. He also has been a political science lecturer at state universities.

In his first year in the Senate, Thompson was clearly the low Democrat on the totem pole. Time and again, Democratic leader David Roberti shambled over to his desk to ask for a hard vote — and got it. At the start of the 1993 session, he was rewarded with chairmanship of the Natural Resources and Wildlife Committee.

In 1994, Thompson carried legislation calling for spending $8 million to beef up the inadequate criminal tracking computer system that failed to notify officers of Richard Allen Davis' criminal background on the night he allegedly kidnapped 12-year-old Polly Klaas from her Petaluma home and then killed her. The money allows the state Department of Justice to improve computer systems that warehouse and match fingerprints, track sex offenders and violent felons and distribute information on missing adults and children.

PERSONAL: elected 1990; born Jan. 24, 1951, in St. Helena; home, St. Helena; Army, Vietnam; education, B.A. and graduate work CSU Chico; wife Jan, two children.

CAREER: chief of staff, Assemblyman Louis Papan 1984-1987; chief of staff, Assemblywoman Jacqueline Speier 1987-1990.

COMMITTEES: Natural Resources & Wildlife (vice chair); Revenue and Taxation (chair); Toxics and Public Safety Management; Agriculture & Water Resources; Budget & Fiscal Review; Governmental Organization; Health & Human Services; Veterans Affairs.

OFFICES: Capitol, (916) 445-3375, FAX (916) 323-6958; district, 1040 Main St., 101, Napa 94559, (707) 224-1990.

TERM LIMIT: 1998

REGISTRATION: 54.48% D, 31.44% R

1994 CAMPAIGN:	Thompson D	60.3%	$464,480
	Frank McMichael R	35.6%	$18,630
1993 CAMPAIGN:	Thompson D	47.5%	Not Available
	Margie Handley R	46.9%	Not Available

RATINGS:	AFL-CIO	CLCV	NOW	CofC	CalFarm	GO
	92	88	B+	24	80	D

Diane Watson (D)

26th Senate District

When the 1993-94 session of the Legislature convened, Diane Watson returned to Sacramento with an attitude — maybe more of an attitude would be more accurate. Watson has long been considered one of the Legislature's most contentious and demanding members, someone who appeared to be in a perpetual state of anger. But her dudgeon reached new heights in 1992, when she lost a very close election for a powerful seat on the Los Angeles County Board of Supervisors to former Rep. Yvonne Brathwaite Burke amid charges and countercharges of election dirty tricks.

In 1994, Watson ran for re-election from a district whose boundaries were much altered by the state

Diane Watson

Supreme Court's 1992 reapportionment plan, but whose despair never seems to change. The Supreme Court dropped the more upscale oceanside portions of Watson's 26th District (Watson's old district was the 28th) and it is now concentrated in the poorest portions of South-Central Los Angeles, plus Culver City. It's the area that was most directly and disastrously affected by the April-May 1992 riots that erupted after a jury acquitted white policemen of beating African American motorist Rodney King — the worst riots in American history.

Fewer than half of the 26th District's residents are African American, thanks to fast-growing populations of poor immigrants from Latin America and Asia, but the district's voters are overwhelmingly African American and Democratic. Their majority among voters will likely remain unchallenged for years.

Watson spent three short years on the Los Angeles school board as one of its most vocal (and most televised) members in the 1970s, during a period of high racial tensions involving the district's forced busing plan. She made a splash when she first came to Sacramento in 1975. She was the first African American woman elected to the Senate, a club heretofore comprised primarily of old white men set in their ways (symbolized by the high leather chairs in the back of their chambers). In those years, she seemed to specialize in crashing the party and opening the windows.

But Sacramento has gotten used to her. Most of the old boys have retired or died, and many of the newcomers are better at grandstanding than Watson. Though she can cause havoc, Watson doesn't generate much warmth from her colleagues and has increasingly found herself isolated. She has crossed swords with her colleagues on numerous issues, ranging from welfare revision to setting ethical standards — and lost. Her snits with Democratic Sen. Bill Lockyer are legendary, with the two trading insults across the dais in the Judiciary Committee back before Lockyer was elected Senate president pro tem. She is also known as one of the most difficult bosses in the Capitol, treating legislative staffers with disdain.

Watson, however, showed her loyalty to former Senate President Pro Tem David Roberti during leadership tussles, and he returned the loyalty, even to the point of paying off her delinquent credit cards.

As chairwoman of the Health and Human Services Committee, Watson oversees the welfare system in the state, enabling her to position herself as one of the chief critics of Republican social program slashing. In 1985, she attempted to filibuster a bipartisan legislative package for major welfare reforms (dubbed GAIN) that set up a workfare program for 190,000 recipients, most of them single mothers. Watson called it a forced labor program, and held a lengthy committee hearing in the waning hours of that year's session, but the bill passed over her objections.

When Republican Pete Wilson became governor and proposed cuts in welfare grants to balance the state budget, Watson quickly emerged as a leading opponent — although summitry did eventually produce welfare reductions. "We had a wonderful two or three days with him. The honeymoon is over," she huffed not long after his inaugural.

Her dogma notwithstanding, Watson has looked for new solutions to some of the more vexing problems of her urban district. At the start of the 1991-92 session she introduced SB 224, which would enact procedures for the establishment of graffiti abatement districts with taxing powers to attack vandalism. And she has fought hard to protect family planning funds and expand health care and educational programs.

Watson's career has been marked by brushes with scandal. The circumstances surrounding her Ph.D. in education administration were called into question in 1989, when the Sacramento County District Attorney's Office investigated allegations that she had used state staff and equipment to prepare her dissertation. District Attorney Steve White concluded that legislative record-keeping was so shoddy that the allegations could not be proved or disproved.

She has not escaped scrutiny from the Fair Political Practices Commission. In December 1989, Watson agreed to pay a penalty of $21,075 for using campaign funds to pay for such expenses as a family reunion, credit-card charges, airline tickets and a party. Watson takes numerous junkets worldwide from trade associations and others with business in the Legislature. She routinely uses her campaign fund for a wide range of expenses not traditionally associated with campaigning, such as buying flowers for friends. She voted against the 1989 ethics reform package that ultimately tightened the rules for such spending, telling colleagues that it went too far. During an ethics workshop for senators in January 1991, Watson made clear her standards. "We're not ordinary people," she said.

PERSONAL: elected 1978; born Nov. 12, 1933, in Los Angeles; home, Los Angeles; education, A.A. Los Angeles City College, B.A. UCLA, M.S. CSU Los Angeles, Ph.D. Claremont Graduate School; single; Roman Catholic.

CAREER: teacher; school administrator; textbook author; Los Angeles Unified School District board 1975-1978.

COMMITTEES: Health & Human Services (chair); Budget & Fiscal Review; Education; Housing and Land Use; Criminal Procedure.

OFFICES: Capitol, (916) 445-5215, FAX (916) 327-2599; district, 4401 Crenshaw Blvd., 300, Los Angeles 90043, (213) 295-6655, FAX (213) 295-0910.

TERM LIMIT: 1998

REGISTRATION: 52.1% D, 33.5% R

1994 CAMPAIGN:	Watson D		82.93%		$92,907
	Joe Piechowski R		13.62%		Not Available
1990 CAMPAIGN:	Watson D		85.2%		$291,369

RATINGS:	AFL-CIO	CLCV	NOW	CofC	CalFarm	GO
	96	83	A-	18	40	F

Cathie Wright (R)
19th Senate District

The canyons and badlands of the northwestern San Fernando Valley hold amusement parks, old citrus groves and Highway 101. The 19th Senate District sprawls over pieces of two counties — Los Angeles and Ventura — and its new suburbs and old money translate into solidly Republican territory, one with a GOP registration that approaches 50 percent and far outweighs the Democratic strength.

Ed Davis, the colorful former Los Angeles police chief, represented the 19th District for 12 years. When he decided to retire, it touched off a battle royal between two factions of Republicans who had been feuding for years, one headed by Davis and the other by Assemblywoman Cathie Wright. Their squab-

Cathie Wright

bling dated back to 1986, when Davis ran for the U.S. Senate and charged that another Republican candidate, Rep. Bobbi Fiedler, had tried to bribe him to quit the race. The resulting investigation and prosecution of Fiedler fatally injured both senatorial campaigns.

In 1992, Wright plunged into the primary race to replace Davis while the Davis faction backed a former assemblywoman, Marion LaFollette, who had been an integral part of the factional feud. Wright emerged as the winner, which, given the overwhelming Republican registration of the district, made her election to the Senate a certainty. The depth of the enmity between Davis and Wright was displayed when a reporter asked Davis whether he could ever support Wright as his successor. "Maybe," he replied, "if she was running against a mass murderer. But it would depend on how many people he had killed."

Wright hasn't played a big role in shaping legislation since her first election to the Assembly in 1980, but her extracurricular activities have made headlines at home and in Sacramento. In 1989, a series of published reports said Wright had interceded with state motor vehicle and judicial authorities in early 1988 to prevent her daughter, Victoria, from losing her driver's license for a string of traffic tickets. Wright denied doing any wrong, but a report from the Ventura County District Attorney's Office concluded that she had tried to fix Victoria's tickets on several occasions and had even solicited help in contacting judicial officials from the Assembly's top Democrat, Speaker Willie Brown.

Her links to Brown also caused friction in her own party. In December 1988, Wright refused to go along with Republican efforts to deny Brown re-election as speaker, and for that, there were demands among Republicans that Wright be stripped of her seat on the Assembly Rules Committee. The GOP caucus voted to drop Wright from the committee, but Brown, invoking another rule, protected her from being dumped. In 1991, Wright was appointed by Brown as vice chair of the Assembly Ways and Means Committee, the single most powerful committee slot for a minority party member. That made her the lead Republican during the protracted budget battle, during which she often infuriated colleagues of both parties with obtuse positions. Republicans were more furious than Democrats because she undercut their efforts to eliminate boards and commissions. Some obscure commission would no sooner be on the chopping block, with Republicans and Democrats in agreement, when Wright would ride to its rescue.

Ideologically, Wright has ranged from alliances with the far right to more moderate positions. While she maintained a working relationship with Brown, she was one of four Republicans to vote in August 1990 for a resolution by Gil Ferguson that sought to justify internment of Japanese Americans during World War II as a military necessity.

In 1994, Wright won the Republican nomination for lieutenant governor and ran against Democrat Gray Davis. Wright trailed Davis badly in opinion polls throughout the campaign and Davis easily won the election with 52.4 percent of the vote to 40.3 percent for Wright.

PERSONAL: elected 1992; born May 18, 1929, in Old Forge, Pa.; home, Simi Valley; education, A.A. Scranton Community College; widow; one child; Roman Catholic.

CAREER: insurance underwriter; school board; City Council and mayor Simi Valley 1978-1980; Assembly 1980-1992.

COMMITTEES: Budget & Fiscal Review (vice chair); Agriculture and Water Resources; Judiciary; Legislative Ethics; Toxics and Public Safety Management.

OFFICES: Capitol, (916) 445-8873, FAX (916) 324-7544; district, 2345 Erringer Rd., 212, Simi Valley 93065, (805) 522-2920, FAX (805) 522-1194.

TERM LIMIT: 2000

REGISTRATION: 40.47% D, 45.32% R

1992 CAMPAIGN:	Wright R		53.2%		$593,975
	Henry Starr D		38.8%		$83,605

RATINGS:	AFL-CIO	CLCV	NOW	CofC	CalFarm	GO
	12	10	C-	88	40	A

Assembly districts

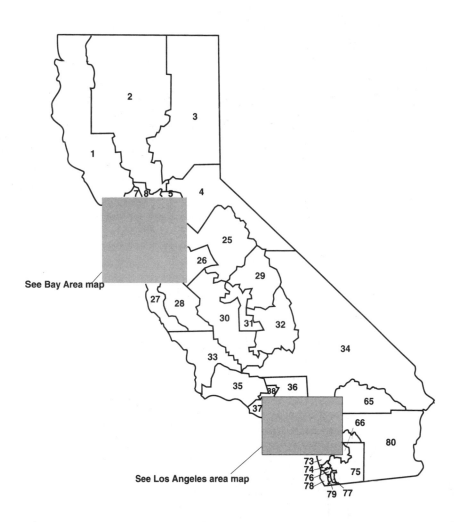

See Bay Area map

See Los Angeles area map

Bay Area districts

Los Angeles districts

Assembly members and district numbers

1 HAUSER, Dan, D-Arcata
2 WOODS, Tom, R-Shasta
3 RICHTER, Bernie, R-Chico
4 KNOWLES, David, R-Cameron Park
5 ALBY, Barbara, R-Fair Oaks
6 MAZZONI, Kerry, D-Novato
7 BROWN, Valerie, D-Sonoma
8 HANNIGAN, Tom, D-Fairfield
9 ISENBERG, Phillip, D-Sacramento
10 BOWLER, Larry, R-Elk Grove
11 CAMPBELL, Robert, D-Martinez
12 BURTON, John, D-San Francisco
13 BROWN, Willie, D-San Francisco
14 BATES, Tom, D-Berkeley
15 RAINEY, Richard, R-Walnut Creek
16 LEE, Barbara, D-Oakland
17 MACHADO, Mike, D-Linden
18 SWEENEY, Michael, D-Hayward
19 SPEIER, Jackie, D-Burlingame
20 FIGUEROA, Liz, D-Fremont
21 SHER, Byron, D-Palo Alto
22 VASCONCELLOS, John,
      D-Santa Clara
23 CORTESE, Dominic, D-San Jose
24 CUNNEEN, Jim, R-Cupertino
25 HOUSE, George, R-Hughson
26 CANNELLA, Sal, D-Ceres
27 MCPHERSON, Bruce, R-Santa Cruz
28 FRUSETTA, Peter, R-Tres Pinos
29 POOCHIGIAN, Charles, R-Fresno
30 SETENCICH, Brian, R-Fresno
31 BUSTAMANTE, Cruz, D-Fresno
32 HARVEY, Trice, R-Bakersfield
33 BORDONARO, Tom,
      R-Paso Robles
34 OLBERG, Keith, R-Victorville
35 FIRESTONE, Brooks, R-Los Olivos
36 KNIGHT, William 'Pete,'
      R-Palmdale
37 TAKASUGI, Nao, R-Oxnard
38 BOLAND, Paula, R-Granada Hills
39 KATZ, Richard, D-Panorama City
40 FRIEDMAN, Barbara,
      D-North Hollywood
41 KUEHL, Sheila, D-Santa Monica

42 KNOX, Wally, D-Los Angeles
43 ROGAN, James, R-Glendale
44 HOGE, Bill, R-Pasadena
45 VILLARAIGOSA, Antonio,
      D-Los Angeles
46 CALDERA, Louis, D-Los Angeles
47 MURRAY, Kevin, D-Los Angeles
48 ARCHIE-HUDSON, Marguerite,
      D-Los Angeles
49 MARTINEZ, Diane, D-Rosemead
50 ESCUTIA, Martha,
      D-Huntington Park
51 TUCKER, Curtis Jr., D-Inglewood
52 MURRAY, Willard, D-Paramount
53 BOWEN, Debra, D-Marina Del Rey
54 KUYKENDALL, Steven,
      R-Rancho Palos Verdes
55 MCDONALD, Juanita, D-Carson
56 HAWKINS, Phil, R-Bellflower
57 GALLEGOS, Martin, D-El Monte
58 NAPOLITANO, Grace, D-Norwalk
59 VACANT (Mountjoy), R-Arcadia
60 HORCHER, Paul, I-Whittier
61 AGUIAR, Fred, R-Ontario
62 BACA, Joe, D-San Bernardino
63 BRULTE, Jim,
      R-Rancho Cucamonga
64 WEGGELAND, Ted, R-Riverside
65 GRANLUND, Brett, R-Yucaipa
66 THOMPSON, Bruce, R-Fallbrook
67 ALLEN, Doris, R-Cypress
68 PRINGLE, Curt, R-Garden Grove
69 MORRISSEY, Jim, R-Santa Ana
70 BREWER, Marilyn, R-Irvine
71 CONROY, Mickey, R-Orange
72 JOHNSON, Ross, R-Fullerton
73 MORROW, Bill, R-Oceanside
74 KALOOGIAN, Howard, R-Carlsbad
75 GOLDSMITH, Jan, R-Poway
76 DAVIS, Susan, D-San Diego
77 BALDWIN, Steve, R-El Cajon
78 ALPERT, Deirdre, D-Coronado
79 DUCHENY, Denise Moreno,
      D-San Diego
80 BATTIN, Jim, R-Palm Desert

ASSEMBLY

Vacant
59th Assembly District

While the floor of the San Gabriel Valley is a center of Latino population and political power, the residential uplands overlooking the valley are white and Republican. The 59th Assembly District is the heart of the region, encompassing communities such as Monrovia and Arcadia. The district had been represented since 1978 by Richard Mountjoy and he fit his district perfectly: a middle-aged, white Republican businessman who joined the Legislature as one of the self-proclaimed "Proposition 13 babies."

Mountjoy's district and the adjacent 60th district held by Assemblyman Paul Horcher, R-Whittier, both fit within the 29th Senate District, which was held by Frank Hill, also a Whittier Republican. When Hill was sent to federal prison following his conviction on corruption charges evolving out of an FBI sting operation in the Capitol, both Mountjoy and Horcher ran for the seat. It was an ugly race that Mountjoy won with heavy backing from other members of the Assembly caucus. At the start of the 1995-96 session, Mountjoy tried to maintain both his Assembly seat and his new Senate seat long enough to support GOP leader Jim Brulte in the speakership fight. But Democrats — with the aid of a vote from Horcher — eventually kicked him out and the Assembly seat was declared vacant. A special election will be held and, given the conservative bent of the district, Mountjoy's replacement undoubtedly will be a Republican.

REGISTRATION: 38.6% D, 46.5% R

Fred Aguiar (R)
61st Assembly District

The 61st Assembly District includes Chino, Chino Hills, Ontario, Rancho Cucamonga and Pomona's Latino neighborhoods. In the 1992 redistricting, the Supreme Court designed the 61st as a minority district. As a result, more than half the district's residents are minorities, including the 41.7 percent who are Latino. But Latinos account for only 20 percent of the registered voters. And while Democrats have a slight voter registration edge, 45.2 percent compared to 43.2 percent for Republicans, the district's electorate tends to favor GOP candidates.

Republican Fred Aguiar has now twice been the beneficiary of that voting trend. In 1994, the former

Fred Aguiar

Chino mayor easily defeated his Democratic opponent, Larry Silva, a residential youth counselor. Two years earlier, Aguiar captured the seat with a win against Democratic fireman Larry Simcoe. While Simcoe won the district's Los Angeles precincts in that election, Aguiar swept larger Republican portions of San Bernardino County. A veteran of local politics and a former Democrat, Aguiar was first elected to the Chino City Council in 1978 and was re-elected in 1982. In 1986, he was elected to the first of his two terms as mayor. He became a Republican in 1989.

PERSONAL: elected 1992; born Dec. 3, 1948, in Artesia; home, Chino; attended Mt. Sac Junior College and Cal Poly Pomona; wife Patti, one child; Roman Catholic.

CAREER: businessman/developer; Chino City Council, 1978-1986; mayor, 1986-1992.

COMMITTEES: Appropriations; Health; Insurance; Rules; Transportation.

OFFICES: Capitol, (916) 445-1670, FAX (916) 445-0385; district, 304 West F St., Ontario 91762; (909) 984-7741, FAX (909) 984-6695.

TERM LIMIT: 1998

REGISTRATION: 45.2% D, 43.2% R

1994 CAMPAIGN:	Aguiar R	64%	$214,942
	Larry Silva D	35.9%	Not Available
1992 CAMPAIGN:	Aguiar R	58.4%	$375,163
	Larry Simcoe D	36.3%	$135,920

RATINGS:	AFL-CIO	CLCV	NOW	CofC	CalFarm	GO
	8	5	C	100	77.7	A

Barbara Alby (R)
5th Assembly District

This increasingly conservative district, covering Sacramento's northern and northeastern suburbs, got a new Assembly member in 1993 after popular Assemblyman B.T. Collins died following a heart attack. The outrageous and outspoken Collins, a former chief of staff to Gov. Jerry Brown and director of the California Youth Authority and California Conservation Corps, was legendary for his Irish wit and attention-getting stunts — including one in which he downed a malathion-laced drink in 1981 to prove the pesticide was safe.

Collins was elected to the Assembly after Tim Leslie vacated this seat in 1991 to move to the state Senate. Collins squared off against Barbara Alby in a

Barbara Alby

shrill special election campaign. Alby denounced Collins' atheism and abortion-rights stance, while Collins went after Alby's anti-abortion position and her ties to the religious right. As head of Sacramento's conservative Women's Lobby, Alby had been outspokenly pro-gun and a supporter of school vouchers and prayer in public schools. She also had been no friend of Gov. Pete Wilson, calling him "as bad as any tax-and-spend liberal" and announcing triumphantly that she refused to vote for him when he ran for governor in 1990. Collins won the seat and re-election the next year after defeating Alby again in the 1992 GOP primary.

From the moment of Collins' death, the 5th District was Alby's to lose. She bested a pack of Republicans in the special election and won the seat in a runoff with Joan Barry, an underfinanced Democrat. Alby again faced Barry in 1994 and again defeated her.

In both her races against Barry, Alby cooled her rhetoric and ran on a pro-business, pro-law enforcement, anti-tax platform. As she told an interviewer: "We have to learn to speak . . . just as a missionary does. A missionary doesn't go over to India and pound the Hindus over the head with spiritual laws, even though that is the agenda." Her pitch is well-suited to a district that covers Sacramento's whitest suburbs, both poor and affluent, and has been a favored homestead for newcomers escaping the Bay Area and other regions of the state.

In the Legislature, Alby has been a quiet vote against social programs and gun control. Her main accomplishment in her first full term was passage of a bill setting up a 900 telephone number in the state Department of Justice allowing the public to find out if someone is a registered sex offender. Alby also made news when she denounced a Sacramento County plan to declare a local medical emergency and implement a needle exchange program to prevent the spread of AIDS among drug addicts. Alby called the move an "end run around the law" and asked for an attorney general's opinion about its legality.

More than most newcomers, Alby seems to thrive on the socializing and camaraderie in the Legislature. She will race to be first on the floor to announce the results of the legislative bowling tournament, and she pens doggerel poking fun at colleagues, which she then faxes around the Capitol at public expense. When Republicans passed out committee leadership assignments in 1995, Alby was passed over in favor of less senior members.

PERSONAL: elected 1993 (special election); born Aug. 9, 1946, in Chicago, Ill.; home, Fair Oaks; education, attended University of Wisconsin; husband Dennis, five children; Assembly of God.

CAREER: family construction business, conservative activist.

COMMITTEES: Budget; Environmental Safety & Toxic Materials; Judiciary; Rules; Utilities & Commerce.

OFFICES: Capitol, (916) 445-4445, FAX (916) 323-9411; district, 4811 Chippendale Drive, 501, Sacramento 95841, (916) 349-1995, FAX (916) 349-1999.

TERM LIMIT: 1998

REGISTRATION: 44.1% D, 44.0% R

1994 CAMPAIGN:	Alby R			60.3%		$146,284
	Joan Barry D			39.7%		$18,951
1993 CAMPAIGN:	Alby R			48.3%		Not Available
	Joan Barry D			39.3%		Not Available
RATINGS:	AFL-CIO	CLCV	NOW	CofC	CalFarm	GO
	0	10	D+	95	78	A

Doris J. Allen (R)
67th Assembly District

Democrats enjoyed a brief period of dominance in Orange County politics in the 1970s, but one by one, Democratic legislators fell to Republican challenges beginning in 1978. The 71st Assembly District, in the central portion of the county, was one of the Democratic bastions. In 1982, incumbent Chester Wray was beaten by Doris Allen, who had gained local prominence as a school district trustee and leader of an anti-busing campaign.

Doris Allen

As a woman and a Republican, Allen has not been part of the Assembly's ruling circles. She feuded publicly with one of the more influential Republican leaders, Gerald Felando, who was defeated in his 1992 re-election bid. The issue that divided Allen and Felando is the one that became her legislative preoccupation: mismanagement of the state Fish and Game Department (another male-dominated bastion) and, in particular, its regulation of commercial fishing. She saw Felando, who represented San Pedro, as pushing interests of commercial fishermen over sport fishermen. Allen embarrassed Gov. George Deukmejian's administration by exposing several management scandals in the department. But few in her caucus have shown any interest in supporting attempts to make the agency more accountable.

On a shoestring budget, Allen successfully promoted Proposition 132 on the November 1990 ballot, which banned use of gill nets in coastal waters. Commercial fisherman opposed the measure. Her proposition was the only one of six environmental measures to pass.

Early in 1991, Allen was one of three Assembly members who ran for a state Senate seat vacated by John Seymour, who had been appointed to Gov. Pete Wilson's former U.S. Senate post. But she lost in the primary to John Lewis. In 1992, Allen opposed a legislative proposal to raise cigarette taxes by 2 cents a pack to fund breast cancer research and prevention programs. Allen argued that the lawmakers were looking in the wrong place for research funds. Both she and her sister have suffered from breast cancer, Allen told her hushed colleagues as she spoke on the floor of the Assembly, but neither of the women smoked. A better source of funding, she said, would be to tax birth control pills and fertility drugs. The measure failed that time, but was resurrected a year later. The second time, Allen supported the measure, and it eventually won legislative passage and Wilson's signature.

Reapportionment put Allen in the same district with two Republican incumbents, Tom Mays of Huntington Beach and Nolan Frizelle of Fountain Valley. Assembly colleagues made no secret of their support of either of the men over Allen. But she squeaked by the primary and easily won the runoff against an underfunded Democrat. Allen's battles with her GOP brethren continued into 1994. She had to overcome a primary challenge from Tony Nottke, a onetime aide to former Republican Assemblyman Gil Ferguson of Newport Beach before claiming a landslide victory in the general election. Allen could face Ferguson in her next race. Both politicians, and Republican Assemblyman Ross Johnson of Fullerton, are expected to run for the Senate seat left vacant by the GOP's Marian Bergeson, who left the Legislature to serve on the Orange County Board of Supervisors.

PERSONAL: elected 1982; born May 26, 1936, in Kansas City, Mo.; home, Cypress; education, attended University of Wyoming, Golden West College, IBM School in Kansas City, Long Beach Community College and Hallmark Business School; divorced, two children; Protestant.

CAREER: co-owner, lighting business; trustee, Huntington Beach Union School District.

COMMITTEES: Education; Health (chair); Housing & Community Development; Water, Parks & Wildlife.

OFFICES: Capitol, (916) 445-6233, FAX (916) 445-2751; district, 16052 Beach Blvd., Ste. 160, Huntington Beach 92647; (714) 843-9855.

TERM LIMIT: 1996

REGISTRATION: 34.9% D, 51.3% R

1994 CAMPAIGN:	Allen R	73.4%	$98,917
	Jonathan Woolf-Willis D	26.6%	Not Available
1992 CAMPAIGN:	Allen R	59.2%	$335,951
	Ken LeBlanc D	33%	$54,413

RATINGS:	AFL-CIO	CLCV	NOW	CofC	CalFarm	GO
	15	5	C	91	44.4	C-

Deirdre W. Alpert (D)
78th Assembly District

This elongated district runs down the south San Diego County coast from La Jolla to Imperial Beach. It includes Coronado, Mission Bay and Balboa Park. Voters here tend to be moderate and independent — almost half of them voted for Dianne Feinstein in the 1990 gubernatorial race despite a strong Republican registration edge.

In 1988, Republican Sunny Mojonnier breezed to an easy, third-term re-election as the district's Assembly member. But in the succeeding two years, Mojonnier ran into a world of trouble. She was fined $13,000 by the state Fair Political Practices Commission for double billing the state and her campaign fund for personal expenses. She used campaign funds to send staffers to a fashion consultant. She used Assembly sergeants-at-arms to do personal chores such as picking up her son at school. And she skipped out of Sacramento in July 1990 to take a vacation in Hawaii during the bitter summer budget impasse.

Deirdre Alpert

There should have been no way for Deirdre "Dede" Alpert to win this seat under the old district configurations. Voter registration favored Republicans by 20 percentage points. But Mojonnier's well-publicized gaffes caught up with her and she barely won her GOP primary. The weakened Mojonnier could not hang on in the general election.

Alpert, a travel agent and a member of the Solana Beach School District Board, skillfully capitalized on Mojonnier's flakiness. Alpert's patrician manners also helped in this middle- to upper-middle class district. Soon after the election, Alpert's husband, Michael, half-joked that he hoped his wife would become a Republican because he figured that was the only way she could hold the seat.

But hold on to it she did, against a well-known moderate Republican, former Assemblyman Jeff Marston. Marston had lost his re-election bid in 1990 to Democrat Mike Gotch in the old 78th District, but he seemed ready and able to take on Alpert. Instead, Marston's campaign faltered from the beginning and Alpert defeated him easily with 54 percent of the vote. In 1994, the GOP candidate Bruce Henderson's effort to unseat Alpert also fell far short. However, the Assembly's Republican leadership initiated a recall campaign against Alpert in early 1995 as part of its effort to wrest control of the Assembly from Democrat Willie Brown.

PERSONAL: elected 1990; born Oct. 6, 1945, in New York City; home, Coronado; education, Pomona College; husband Michael, three children.

CAREER: Pacific Bell 1966-1969; travel agent 1985-1989; Solana Beach School Board 1983-1990, president 1990.

COMMITTEES: Education (chair); Public Employees, Retirement & Social Security; Utilities & Commerce.

OFFICES: Capitol, (916) 445-2112, FAX (916) 445-4001; district, 1350 Front St., Ste. 6013, San Diego 92101; (619) 234-7878, FAX (619) 233-0078

TERM LIMIT: 1996

REGISTRATION: 39.3% D, 42.8% R

1994 CAMPAIGN:	Alpert D	52.5%	$520,094
	Bruce Henderson R	44.6%	$103,425

1992 CAMPAIGN: Alpert D   53.4% $726,083
               Jeff Marston R   41.3% $649,400

RATINGS:	AFL-CIO	CLCV	NOW	CofC	CalFarm	GO
	94	75	A-	27	44.4	D

Marguerite Archie-Hudson (D)
48th Assembly District

In relative terms, the African American population of Los Angeles is shrinking as Latinos and Asians become more numerous. But politically, the city's African American community remains strong because of its high tendency to vote as illustrated by the 48th Assembly District. When the state Supreme Court created this district in 1992 in the heart of South-Central Los Angeles, African Americans were outnumbered by Latinos. But despite the fact that the 48th is more than 50 percent Hispanic, only 6 percent of its voters have that ethic designation so it remains a bastion of African American and Democratic political cal power. It is, in fact, the most Democratic Assembly district in the state at nearly 90 percent, leaving Republicans (there are only about 6,000 of them registered in the district) an endangered species.

Marguerite Archie-Hudson

For 14 years, the district was represented by Maxine Waters, an aggressive protégé of Assembly Speaker Willie Brown. But she was elected to Congress in 1990. The race to replace Waters ended in the June primary when Marguerite Archie-Hudson, a former administrator at the University of California, Los Angeles, defeated Los Angeles City Councilman Robert Farrell. The Republican candidate in the November general election got only 15 percent of the vote. In 1992, Archie-Hudson cruised to an easy re-election as the district shrank, becoming even more Democratic as it lost its coastal arms. Republicans didn't even bother putting up a candidate in 1994.

Archie-Hudson's 1990 campaign wasn't easy. A onetime aide to Assembly Speaker Brown, she had to battle charges that she didn't live in the district and was illegally allowed to use the offices of Waters, who endorsed her. At the start of the Democratic primary campaign, Archie-Hudson downplayed the importance of endorsements. Endorsements already had haunted her once. After spending nine years on the Los Angeles Community College District board of trustees, she lost re-election in 1987, largely on the strength of teachers' union opposition. But in her race for the Assembly, she eventually got strong support from labor and other key officials.

Archie-Hudson pledged to end busing of students, opting to keep them in neighborhood schools. She promised to offer tax incentives to attract business to South-Central Los Angeles and proposed to establish a community plan that would integrate services from government agencies, schools and churches — promises that rang hollow when the area was wracked by riots in 1992.

PERSONAL: elected 1990; born Nov. 18, 1937, on Younges Island, S.C.; home, Los Angeles; education, B.A. psychology Talladega College, Ala., Ph.D. education UCLA; husband, G. Bud Hudson.

CAREER: program director, UCLA; program director, Occidental College; associate dean and director for educational opportunity for CSUS; district chief of staff, Rep. Yvonne Brathwaite Burke; Southern California chief of staff for Assembly Speaker Willie Brown; Board of Trustees, Los Angeles Community College District.

COMMITTEES: Higher Education (chair); Insurance; Judiciary; Utilities & Commerce.

OFFICES: Capitol, (916) 445-2363, FAX (916) 323-9640; district, 700 State Dr., 103, Los Angeles 90037, (213) 745-6656, FAX (213) 745-6722.

TERM LIMIT: 1996

REGISTRATION: 87.7% D, 4.9% R

1994 CAMPAIGN:	Archie-Hudson D	100%	Not Available
1992 CAMPAIGN:	Archie-Hudson D	93.1%	$162,376
	Jonathan Leonard II R	6.9%	$1,240

RATINGS:	AFL-CIO	CLCV	NOW	CofC	CalFarm	GO
	99	63	A-	27	33.3	F

Joe Baca (D)
62nd Assembly District

The Supreme Court carved out the 62nd Assembly District in San Bernardino County as a minority district. The district was crafted to draw in the minority neighborhoods of San Bernardino plus the cities of Rialto, Colton and Fontana. The population of Latinos, African Americans and Asians tops 56 percent. Latino registration is 22 percent.

In his first month on the job, Joe Baca became embroiled in a battle of legislative egos when he insisted on a piece of legislation to attract a Defense Department accounting center to Norton Air Force Base in San Bernardino County. The base closed in March 1994, and it was estimated that the center would employ 750 people and bring a payroll of

Joe Baca

$22.5 million to the region, which was hit hard by the recession. Baca authored a bill to appropriate $10 million from special state funds for job training and to establish the base as an enterprise zone, which would help avoid zoning delays. The bill passed the Assembly 73-0 and was sent to the Senate. But veteran Sens. Ruben Ayala, D-Chino, and William Leonard, R-Redlands, already had worked out an agreement with Gov. Pete Wilson's administration to carry Norton legislation and Ayala reportedly wasn't pleased with upstart Baca's interference. "I'm very angry with you," Ayala reportedly shot at Baca during one of many off-the-floor meetings on the issue. "I'll just give you both bills. You'll be the big shot."

Leonard characterized it as a dispute over authorship and worried aloud that it could jeopardize the accounting center bid. Eventually, Baca carried a bill to appropriate $1.5 million to upgrade facilities at Norton and provide economic incentives. And Ayala carried legislation to appropriate $10 million for worker training. In May 1994, the Defense Department announced that Norton would be one of four California bases where the centers would be located.

Baca, a community college trustee, won his Assembly seat following two earlier failed primary bids against Democratic incumbent Gerry Eaves. When Eaves decided to run for San Bernardino County supervisor, Baca saw his opportunity. He defeated Rialto Mayor John Longville and Lois Carson, another community college trustee, in the primary. In the general election, Baca handily defeated Republican firefighter Steve Hall. In 1994, Baca's bid for re-election was a cakewalk. Without a primary opponent, he bested the GOP's Tom Hibbard by winning 60 percent of the vote.

At the start of the 1995-96 session, Baca was elected president pro tempore of the Assembly. That put him in Speaker Willie Brown's inner circle. The job, which requires that Baca preside over floor sessions when the speaker is not present, is chiefly ceremonial, but the fact he was selected infers significant trust and the possibility he will be Brown's successor when term limits end the speakers' reign in 1996. It also was something of a rub for GOP Leader Jim Brulte, who represents an adjoining district. Brulte and Baca have a testy relationship. With Baca presiding most of the time, Brulte will be forced to deal with Baca on most procedural matters.

PERSONAL: elected 1992; born Jan. 23, 1947, in Belin, New Mexico; home, Rialto; education, A.A. Barstow Community College, B.A. CSU Los Angeles; wife Barbara, four children; Roman Catholic.

CAREER: travel agency owner; community college trustee.

COMMITTEES: Education; Governmental Organization; Higher Education; Utilities & Commerce.

OFFICES: Capitol, (916) 445-7454, FAX (916) 324-6980; district, 201 North E Street, Ste. 102, San Bernardino, Ste. 92401, (909) 885-2222, FAX (909) 888-5959.

TERM LIMIT: 1998

REGISTRATION: 58.4% D, 31.7% R

1994 CAMPAIGN:	Baca D			59.6%	$260,121
	Tom Hibbard R			40.4%	$10,898
1992 CAMPAIGN:	Baca D			58.6%	$281,318
	Steve Hall R			35.1%	$46,824
RATINGS:	AFL-CIO	CLCV	NOW	CofC	CalFarm	GO
	100	60	A-	36	44.4	A

Steve Baldwin (R)
77th Assembly District

Steve Baldwin

This San Diego County district includes the communities of Chula Vista, La Mesa, El Cajon and Lemon Grove as well as a portion of the city of San Diego east of National City. The district was clearly seen by Republicans as one of their havens after the Supreme Court's 1992 reapportionment, due to its GOP registration advantage — 44 percent to the Democrats' 41 percent.

It was, however, also one of the battlegrounds for a squabble between the religious right and moderate Republicans in 1992. Conservative Steve Baldwin won the primary, but Democrat Tom Connolly came out of nowhere to win the November runoff, thanks to a last-minute infusion of Democratic money that financed mailers portraying Baldwin as a right-wing Christian fanatic. That image was further enhanced by a 1991 speech in which Baldwin claimed that the U.S. Air Force had an official witch.

Since the campaign had focused on Baldwin, voters were given little information about Connolly, but once in the Assembly he proved to be something of a loose cannon, often mocking his leaders and saying and doing unpredictable things. And then the bomb hit. The San Diego Union-Tribune published a series of articles that detailed a background of drug abuse, missed child-support payments and other peccadilloes. The November election was a replay of 1992, with Baldwin returning as the GOP candidate. But this time the issue was clearly Connolly, and the Republican scored an 11-percentage-point win.

Baldwin was once a leader of the National College Republican organization in Washington, D.C., and an aide to House Speaker Newt Gingrich before settling in San Diego as a commercial real estate agent.

PERSONAL: elected 1994; born June 16, 1956, in Santa Monica; home, El Cajon; education, B.A. Pepperdine University; wife Patti Jo, three children; Baptist.

CAREER: Owner, property management company.

COMMITTEES: Education (vice chair); Consumer Protection, Governmental

Efficiency & Economic Development; Health; Revenue & Taxation.
OFFICES: Capitol, (916) 445-3266, FAX (916) 323-8470; district, 9584 Murray Drive, La Mesa 91942, (619) 465-7723, FAX (619) 465-7765.
TERM LIMIT: 2000
REGISTRATION: 40.6% D, 44.1% R

1994 CAMPAIGN:			
	Baldwin R	55.8%	$598,998
	Tom Connolly (incumbent) D	44.2%	$451,058

RATINGS: Newly elected

Tom H. Bates (D)
14th Assembly District

Tom Bates

It took the Republicans and the state Supreme Court to give Tom Bates what he could never get from fellow Democrats: a compact district that didn't include tracts of disgruntled Republicans. Bates' old 12th District was composed of pieces of Alameda and Contra Costa counties left over after Democratic leaders of the Assembly had drawn districts to the specifications of others. The 14th, however, is a solidly Democratic chunk of the East Bay shoreline, including Richmond, Berkeley and Oakland. Court-ordered reapportionment in 1992 actually improved Bates' registration margin by a few points, giving him a district in which Democrats outnumber Republicans more than 5-1.

After his re-election in 1992, Bates was boasting to colleagues that he would be the Legislature's all-time vote-getter, in part because Republicans didn't even try to run someone against him. He won overwhelmingly again in 1994, securing a 10th and final term, even with a GOP opponent. Bates is perhaps the Assembly's most consistently liberal member, and his credentials were solidified when he married Loni Hancock, then mayor of Berkeley, the spiritual home of the American political left.

Although Bates ranks among the highest in seniority in the Assembly, he has never wielded front-rank power, a reflection of his own rather quiet personality and the extremity of his politics. Bates, previously an Alameda County supervisor, has concentrated on liberal issues such as health care and only in recent years achieved a modicum of authority by becoming vice chairman of the Human Services Committee, which deals with welfare-related legislation. He remains a voice of dissent on many of the popular proposals in the current political climate, from paddling graffiti vandals to papering over budget deficits.

Bates' departure from the Assembly in 1996 represents one part of the Bay

Area's substantial loss of clout in the lower house due to term limits; other lawmakers in the region who will be leaving include Willie Brown, John Burton, John Vasconcellos, Byron Sher and Jackie Speier. Bates could move up to the Senate, where incumbent Nicholas Petris faces a term limit the same year, but Assemblywoman Barbara Lee of Oakland may want that seat as well.

PERSONAL: elected 1976; born Feb. 9, 1938, in San Diego; home, Berkeley; education, B.A. UC Berkeley; wife Loni Hancock, two children; no religious affiliation.

CAREER: real estate; Alameda County Board of Supervisors 1972-1976.

COMMITTEES: Human Services (vice chair); Budget; Consumer Protection, Governmental Efficiency & Economic Development; Natural Resources.

OFFICES: Capitol, (916) 445-7554, FAX (916) 445-6434; district, 3923 Grand Ave., Oakland 94610-1005; (510) 428-1423, FAX (510) 428-1599.

TERM LIMIT: 1996
REGISTRATION: 70.8% D, 11.8% R

1994 CAMPAIGN:	Bates D		78.5%	$32,868
	David Anderson R		15.3%	Not available
1992 CAMPAIGN:	Bates D		82.1%	$158,796
	Marsha Feinland P&F		17.9%	Not Available

RATINGS:	AFL-CIO	CLCV	NOW	CofC	CalFarm	GO
	96	100	A-	14	22	F

Jim Battin (R)
80th Assembly District

Of all the Assembly seats that Republicans swiped from Democrats in 1994 — a net exchange of eight — perhaps no victory was sweeter than Jim Battin's. Not only did the television executive claim territory that is marginally Democratic, but in doing so, he sent packing from the Legislature the person who was on track to be Willie Brown's successor as Assembly speaker, Julie Bornstein. Though a freshman, Bornstein was elected chair of the Democratic caucus, the No. 3 Democratic leadership post. Bornstein could have become California's first female speaker in 1996, when term limits will force out Brown and Assemblyman Tom Hannigan, the No. 2 Democrat.

Jim Battin

But Bornstein's quick rise to power also proved to be her undoing. In 1992, she won election by narrowly defeating Republican Assemblywoman Tricia Hunter, who had moved from her old district into the newly reapportioned 80th Assembly District. The area includes all of Imperial County and the desert communities of Riverside County. Hunter came into the general election badly damaged after her GOP opponent complained she was a carpetbagging incumbent. Bornstein had no incumbency baggage and a legitimate claim of residency in the district. Two years later, Republicans would use the incumbency tag against her, citing as evidence her rise within the Democratic leadership and the "Rookie of the Year" title bestowed upon her by the California Journal. Given the voters' preference for Republicans and nonincumbents in 1994, the strategy worked wonders for Battin, who won by 12 percentage points.

Born and reared in Montana, Battin is a 10-year resident of his district, where he was an account executive at television station KMIR, a local NBC affiliate. He's been involved with local Republican politics and charities, serving on the directors' board of Martha's Kitchen, a food program for the needy people in the Coachella Valley.

PERSONAL: elected 1994; born, July 28, 1962, in Billings, Mont.; home, La Quinta; education, B.S. University of Oregon; wife, Mary; three children; Presbyterian.

CAREER: account executive, KMIR-TV; small business owner.

COMMITTEES: Agriculture; Health; Judiciary; Televising the Assembly & Information Technology; Water, Parks & Wildlife.

OFFICES: Capitol, (916) 445-5416, FAX (916)323-5190; district, 73-7110 Fred Waring Dr., Suite 112, Palm Desert 92260, (619) 568-0408.

TERM LIMIT: 2000

REGISTRATION: 48.1% D, 39.8% R

1994 CAMPAIGN:

Battin R		56.3%	$545,314
Julie Bornstein (incumbent) D		43.6%	$677,364

RATINGS: Newly elected.

Paula L. Boland (R)
38th Assembly District

The further north and west one goes in the San Fernando Valley, the more Republican the territory becomes. The 38th Assembly District lies at the western extremity of the valley and laps over the hills into Simi Valley. Among the other communities of note are Fillmore, Chatsworth and Northridge. Simi Valley, home of the Ronald Reagan presidential library, was the focus of nationwide attention in 1992 when an all-white jury in that community acquitted four police officers in the beating of African American motorist Rodney King. The acquittals sparked several days of riots in Los Angeles.

When Marian LaFollette, who had represented the district since 1980, decided not to seek re-election in 1990, there was a scramble on the Republican side to fill the seat. The winner was conservative Paula Boland, a real estate broker and former Granada Hills Chamber of Commerce president. Boland got a tougher-than-expected challenge in the general election, however, from Democrat Irene Allert, who hammered away at Boland's anti-abortion views. Boland prevailed in that race and in another tough battle in 1992 against Democrat Howard Cohen. In 1994, the challenger she drew was Josh Arce, an 18-year-old student at UCLA who recruited his best friend to be his campaign manager and then built enough support to outpoll an older rival for the Democratic nomination. Boland still won by 40 percentage points.

Paula Boland

Among the bills Boland has gotten passed and signed are ones providing an exemption to the statute of limitations for adults filing criminal charges against someone who sexually abused them as children, guaranteeing that victims of sexual assault can receive their attackers' HIV test results, and requiring school officials to expel or send to an alternative school any student found with a firearm or knife at school.

Boland's house was damaged in the Northridge earthquake that hit in January 1994, and Boland slept in her car for the night. Parts of her district suffered heavily as well. But Boland, conservative to the core, told a reporter soon after the quake that she saw no need for additional state taxes to help pay for quake repairs in the region. But federal help? That was another matter. "The federal government owes us because of all the defense cutbacks," she said.

PERSONAL: elected 1990; born Jan. 17, 1940, in Oyster Bay, N.Y.; home, Granada Hills; education, San Fernando Valley High School; husband Lloyd, three children; Roman Catholic.

CAREER: owner of a real estate brokerage firm.

COMMITTEES: Public Safety (chair); Education; Housing & Community Development; Natural Resources.

OFFICES: Capitol, (916) 445-8366, FAX (916) 322-2005; district, 10727 White Oak, 124, Granada Hills, 91344, (818) 368-3838, FAX (818) 885-3307.

TERM LIMIT: 1996

REGISTRATION: 40.5% D, 46.0% R

1994 CAMPAIGN:	Boland R	67.1%	$132,505
	Josh Arce D	25.9%	$15,337
1992 CAMPAIGN:	Boland R	53.7%	$384,751
	Howard Cohen D	40.7%	$15,745

RATINGS:	AFL-CIO	CLCV	NOW	CofC	CalFarm	GO
	6	0	C-	100	56	A

Tom J. Bordonaro Jr. (R)

33rd Assembly District

This scenic Central Coast district includes all of San Luis Obispo County and part of Santa Barbara County. It has farm-based communities such as Santa Maria and the sleepy coastal towns of Pismo Beach and Morro Bay. Several state and federal prison facilities lie within the district, as does Vandenberg Air Force Base, which has severely cut back its employment.

Eric Seastrand held this seat from 1982 until he died of cancer in 1990. His wife, Andrea, was heavily involved in his career and after his death, she easily won election to the seat and was re-elected in 1992. Andrea Seastrand backed a strongly conservative agenda and in 1994 moved on to win a congressional

Tom Bordonaro Jr.

seat representing the area. In the race to replace her, Paso Robles farmer and small businessman Tom Bordonaro defeated six opponents in the Republican primary by a healthy margin, then faced San Luis Obispo urban planner John Ashbaugh in the general election. Ashbaugh, unopposed in the primary, did not make an all-out effort for the seat in this Republican district — but he did benefit from voter registration efforts by Jack O'Connell, the Democratic assemblyman from a neighboring district who won a state Senate seat in 1994.

Bordonaro easily overcame the narrowed GOP registration advantage and defeated Ashbaugh by more than 20 points. Bordonaro's win virtually assures a Republican hold on this seat for several years. He also, incidentally, became the Legislature's only member who uses a wheelchair.

PERSONAL: elected 1994; born March 22, 1959, in Fullerton; home, Paso Robles; education, B.S. Cal Poly San Luis Obispo, M.S. UC Davis; wife Kerstin; Roman Catholic.

CAREER: Managing partner of ranch, general manager of construction firm, general partner in bookkeeping service.

COMMITTEES: Agriculture; Governmental Organization; Higher Education; Human Services.

OFFICES: Capitol, (916) 445-7795, FAX (916) 324-5510; district, 1060 Palm St., San Luis Obispo 93401, (805) 549-3381, FAX (805) 549-3400.

TERM LIMIT: 2000

REGISTRATION: 42.8% D, 43.9% R

1994 CAMPAIGN:			
Bordonaro R		58.4%	$315,698
John Ashbaugh D		37.9%	$124,171

RATINGS: Newly elected

Debra Bowen (D)

53rd Assembly District

The 53rd Assembly District embraces upscale coastal residential areas of Los Angeles County that voted Republican for decades. But conventional political wisdom went out the window in 1992, when a number of factors converged to give the district to a Democrat. For one, the district—including Redondo Beach, Torrance, Manhattan Beach and Marina Del Rey — is closely tied to the aerospace industry, which suffered heavy blows in the post-Cold War economy. In addition, Republicans nominated the most conservative of the GOP candidates who ran in the primary. And the Democrats hustled, turning voter registration around from a slight Republican plurality to a slight Democratic advantage.

Debra Bowen

As it turned out, Democrat Debra Bowen, well known in the area as an environmental activist and attorney, won fairly easy with more than 54 percent of the vote over Republican Brad Parton, the mayor of Redondo Beach. In 1994, Bowen faced an underfinanced GOP challenger, businessman Julian Sirull, who was unable to respond to Bowen's mailers painting him as a candidate of the far right. Still, Bowen won with just 51 percent of the vote, probably due in part to the electorate's more conservative impulses in 1994.

A moderate with an independent streak, Bowen proved one of the rising Democratic stars of the 1992 freshman class. She got a bill passed and signed establishing an on-line computer database of legislative information and other state records. She also chaired a special committee on computer technology. Bowen pushed several election-related bills, including a bipartisan effort at campaign finance reform that got wide public attention but died in committee. Another widely noticed bill of Bowen's, to punish ticket brokers who fail to deliver tickets to sports fans at contracted prices, addressed a complaint of fans at the 1994 Rose Bowl game. The bill, however, drew a gubernatorial veto.

One of the new breed of legislators who pledged to break political gridlock when they came to Sacramento, Bowen had the opportunity to do just that in the 1993 budget battle. She provided the decisive 54th vote in the Assembly — at 4:52 in the morning — for a budget compromise that squeezed local governments and that many Democrats had to be cajoled to support. "I felt like I was being given the choice between ax-murdering my mother or torturing the rest of my family," Bowen said. She also became an important player in the internal politics of the Assembly, serving as one of the behind-the-scenes negotiators during the speakership impasse at the start of the 1995-96 session.

PERSONAL: elected 1992; born Oct. 27, 1955, in Rockford, Ill.; home, Marina Del Rey; education, B.A. Michigan State University, J.D. University of Virginia, studied at International Christian University in Tokyo; husband, Brian Gindoff; no stated religious affiliation.

CAREER: lawyer specializing in environmental issues.

COMMITTEES: Banking & Finance (vice chair); Televising the Assembly & Information Technology (vice chair); Environmental Safety & Toxic Materials; Natural Resources.

OFFICES: Capitol, (916) 445-8528, FAX (916) 327-2201; district, 18411 Crenshaw Blvd., 280, Torrance 90504, (310) 523-4831, FAX (310) 523-4972.

TERM LIMIT: 1998

REGISTRATION: 43.4% D, 40.9% R

1994 CAMPAIGN:	Bowen D	51.2%	$335,719
	Julian Sirull R	44.0%	$30,535
1992 CAMPAIGN:	Bowen D	54.1%	$488,315
	W. Brad Parton R	41.2%	$799,822

RATINGS:	AFL-CIO	CLCV	NOW	CofC	CalFarm	GO
	90	85	A-	27	44	F

Larry Bowler (R)
10th Assembly District

This geographically diverse district covers southern Sacramento and northern San Joaquin counties. It reaches into the suburbs of Sacramento and the outskirts of Stockton. In between, it traverses a largely rural area that has seen explosive growth with the construction of a number of housing developments and planned communities, particularly in the Elk Grove and Laguna area of southern Sacramento County. The district has a conservative orientation, though the party registration numbers are fairly even.

Larry Bowler

Larry Bowler, a retired Sacramento County sheriff's lieutenant, first won the seat in 1992 with a campaign that focused heavily on his distaste for Assembly Speaker Willie Brown. But the freshman, who had sworn never to cast a vote for Brown as speaker, quickly learned that he would have to pay a price for his strategy. He was immediately assigned the Capitol's smallest office, a room without windows that is often used for storage and is affectionately known as "the closet." Brown followed up by refusing to grant Bowler's request for an assignment to the Assembly's Public Safety Committee. Bowler, instead, drew committees on education, public employees and utilities.

That helps explain why Bowler was so gleeful after Republicans won 41 seats in the 1994 election. But when GOP plans to take over the speakership began to unravel the following January, Bowler seemed to unravel as well — stalking the halls, button-holing people and making shrill denunciations of Brown. "The man is an enemy," Bowler fumed. "He is evil! He is dangerous!"

Bowler readily confessed to being the person who snipped wires to the microphones in the Assembly Rules Committee hearing room, where the Republican Caucus had been meeting, because he was afraid that private caucus conversations were being bugged by Democrats. "I should be given a medal," he said. Sacramento Bee columnist John Jacobs opined that it was that kind of paranoid thinking in the GOP caucus — members "with penchants for thinking with their glands instead of their brains, [that] made it virtually impossible for Brown to hammer out any kind of negotiated agreement with the GOP" on sharing power in the Assembly.

In his first campaign, Bowler defeated Democrat Kay Albiani, who ran with a risky strategy by backing Ross Perot's independent candidacy for president. Bowler survived disclosures that he was heavily financed by the religious right and had been accused of sexual harassment in 1990 for telling a woman subordinate that she looked as though she had been "rode hard and put away wet." In 1994, he drew Democratic challenger Kathleen Wishnick, who showed some initial promise and was backed financially by the California Teachers Association. But her emphasis on education as a policy issue didn't fit the "get tough" tenor of the campaign year, and Bowler won handily.

Bowler consistently votes the conservative GOP line. In his first term, he worked on legislation aiding the conversion of two area military bases, allowing law enforcement agencies to share more information about juvenile criminals and tightening disclosure laws on last-minute political contributions. But Bowler conceded that much of his effort during the session went into trying to block legislation pushed by liberals.

PERSONAL: elected 1992; born July 30, 1939, in Sacramento; home, Elk Grove; Navy; education, B.A. University of San Francisco; wife Melva, three children; Nazarene.

CAREER: retired lieutenant, Sacramento County Sheriffs' Department.

COMMITTEES: Transportation (vice chair); Banking & Finance; Education; Public Safety.

OFFICES: Capitol, (916) 445-7402; FAX (916) 324-0013; district, 10370 Old Placerville Rd., 106, Sacramento 95827, (916) 362-4161, FAX 362-4164.

TERM LIMIT: 1998

REGISTRATION: 45.7% D, 43.3% R

1994 CAMPAIGN:	Bowler R	58.7%	$158,936
	T. Kathleen Wishnick D	37.7%	$50,544
1992 CAMPAIGN:	Bowler R	53.1%	$613,827
	Kay Albiani D	42.0%	$307,332

RATINGS: AFL-CIO CLCV   NOW   CofC   CalFarm   GO
          4   9   C-   100   67   A

Marilyn C. Brewer (R)
70th Assembly District

Imbedded on the tony beachfront of Orange
County, this district includes Newport Beach, Costa
Mesa and Laguna Beach — towns that are the epitome
of upscale California suburbanization. Condos, hotels and estates are jammed along the bluffs above the
beach. Development here is one of the major reasons
voters statewide approved the Coastal Protection Act
in 1972, setting up the Coastal Commission and a
system for shoreline growth control.

Marilyn Brewer

Not surprisingly, this stronghold of BMWs and
cellular phones had been the most Republican district
in the state during the 1980s. But there are pockets of
Democratic voters, particularly in Laguna Beach,
which has a politically active gay community. For 10
years, this Republican safe haven was represented in the Assembly by Gil Ferguson,
a shoot-from-the-hip conservative infamous for lashing out at all things liberal.
When Ferguson stepped down to prepare for a Senate run in a 1995 special election,
three Republicans lined up to take his place. Odds were that another conservative
of Ferguson's ilk would emerge, but moderate Marilyn Brewer came away as the
GOP primary winner. The two other Republican candidates — Tom Reinecke, who
was backed by Ferguson, and Irvine City Councilman Barry Hammond, who had
support from Sen. Rob Hurtt's Allied Business PAC — split the conservative vote.
Brewer's general-election race against Democrat Jim Toledano was more or less a
formality.

For eight years, Brewer worked for Orange County Supervisor Thomas F. Riley,
advising him on matters related to criminal justice, including county jail and
juvenile detention facilities. She also worked on gang awareness and prevention
programs and served on the county grand jury in the mid-1980's. She founded and
co-owns a 23-year-old manufacturing company in Anaheim that employs about 100
people.

PERSONAL: elected 1994; born May 26, 1937, in Moneffen, Pa.; home, Irvine;
A.A. Fullerton College; husband, Charles Brewer; four children; no religious
preference.

CAREER: small-business owner; aide to Orange County Supervisor Thomas F.
Riley, 1986-1994; .

COMMITTEES: Appropriations; Insurance; Local Government; Transportation.

OFFICES: Capitol, (916) 445-7222, FAX (916) 324-3657; district, 18952 MacArthur Blvd, Suite 220, Irvine, 92714, (714) 863-7070.

TERM LIMIT: 2000

REGISTRATION: 29.3% D, 55.5% R

1994 CAMPAIGN:	Brewer R	71.7%	$465,687
	Jim Toledano D	28.3%	$66,157

RATINGS: Newly elected.

Valerie Brown (D)
7th Assembly District

The 7th Assembly District was one of the few in the state altered in the 1992 redistricting process to make it less hospitable for Republican candidates, and it is now decidedly more Democratic than it used to be. It embraces all of Napa County and the most heavily populated parts of Sonoma and Solano counties, including Santa Rosa and Vallejo. Within that area is the heart of the wine country, Mare Island Naval Shipyard, the California Maritime Academy and a growing high-tech industry.

Valerie Brown

When former Republican Bev Hansen decided to quit the Assembly in 1992, the race for the open seat pitted Sonoma Vice Mayor Valerie Brown against Janet Nicholas, a former Sonoma County supervisor who was appointed to the state Board of Prison Terms by Gov. Pete Wilson. Brown, an educator and former marriage and family counselor, won the seat with a campaign that capitalized on Wilson's unpopularity. She also was the beneficiary of a significant Democratic voter registration drive, one that was repeated in many districts across the state as a fractured Republican Party was unable to unify its moderate and conservative forces to perform the nuts-and-bolts work of the 1992 election.

Brown was considered one of the brighter lights of the 1992 freshman class. Speaker Willie Brown (no relation) quickly picked her out for leadership training by appointing her to the Ways and Means Committee. But she also got an eye-opening introduction to the ways of the Capitol when she introduced a controversial measure to cut state public information officers and cap the salaries of political appointees to state boards and commissions. Opposed by both the speaker and the governor, the bill drew considerable attention as it was batted around the halls of the Legislature, finally passing out of the Assembly but losing in the Senate. She did get legislation signed setting out penalties for habitual child molesters.

Valeric Brown cruised through her 1994 re-election campaign, defeating Sonoma businessman Roger Williams by nearly 20 percentage points.

PERSONAL: elected 1992; born Oct. 30, 1945, in Kansas City, Missouri; home, Sonoma; education, B.S. University of Missouri, M.A. Lindenwood College; divorced, one child; Presbyterian.

CAREER: former marriage, family and child counselor; mayor and vice mayor, Sonoma; owner and operator of the Sonoma Valley Education Center; .

COMMITTEES: Appropriations (vice chair); Agriculture; Consumer Protection, Governmental Efficiency & Economic Development; Health.

OFFICES: Capitol, (916) 445-8492, FAX (916) 322-0674; district, 50 D St., 301, Santa Rosa 95404, (707) 546-4500, FAX (707) 546-9031.

TERM LIMIT: 1998

REGISTRATION: 56.1% D, 31.6% R

1994 CAMPAIGN:	Brown D	58.5%	$151,365
	Roger Williams R	39.0%	$30,111
1992 CAMPAIGN:	Brown D	60.2%	$524,935
	Janet Nicholas R	35.9%	$422,065

RATINGS:	AFL-CIO	CLCV	NOW	CofC	CalFarm	GO
	100	95	B+	23	78	D

Willie L. Brown Jr. (D)

13th Assembly District

Willie Lewis Brown Jr. engineered what may be remembered as the coup of his legislative career at the start of his 16th and final term in the California Assembly, overcoming long odds — and, some argue, abusing his powers and tarnishing the institution — to win re-election as speaker. It was a display alternately described as dazzling in its exhibition of parliamentary mastery and dastardly in its use of raw political force. In either case, the unprecedented eighth term as speaker that Brown won in the early-morning hours of Jan. 24, 1995, added another entertaining chapter to his extraordinary personal biography. What remains to be seen is what the audacious move means for his legacy — a subject of more than

Willie L. Brown Jr.

passing interest to Brown himself — as he heads toward a 1996 term limit in the lower house.

Brown remains the ranking state legislator in seniority. For years, he has been the most powerful Assembly member, and certainly he continues to be the most interesting — someone who engenders strong loyalty, fear and loathing in equal proportions. Rising from the humblest of origins, Brown has held center court in the California state Capitol for most of his career and for more than 14 years as "Mr. Speaker," breaking all records for longevity and functioning as one of the nation's most influential African American political figures. A fiery orator and a brilliant strategist, Brown has an explosive temper and an equally sharp, urbane wit.

But he has left many, even those who admire him, wondering if he has any core beliefs other than holding power and enjoying to the hilt all that comes with it. Brown, despite his insistence during the 1995 speakership battle that "the institution" was first in his mind, has often behaved as if all that counted was Willie Brown. His district has almost been an afterthought in his political career, although the Supreme Court's reapportionment of his district changed his personal constituency dramatically for the 1992 elections.

Brown once represented the more affluent western and northern sections of San Francisco, but reapportionment divided the city into western and eastern districts and Brown opted for the eastern one, a much poorer area that also includes many of the city's African American and Latino residents. It made no difference in terms of Brown's own re-election in 1992 or 1994. The entire city is so overwhelmingly Democratic that all Brown has needed to do is file his re-election papers every two years. And his influence goes far beyond routine ballot-box matches. Former San Francisco Supervisor Terry Francois put it this way a few years ago: "He [Brown] engenders fear like you wouldn't believe. I have just become enthralled at the way he wields power. I don't know a politician in San Francisco that dares take him on."

Brown is a star, and not just in San Francisco and the tight little world of Sacramento politics. He was, for example, the Rev. Jesse Jackson's national campaign chairman in 1988. In 1994, Brown took a trial run at expanding his stardom in another direction: into the world of broadcasting. He hosted a half-hour daily talk show on a Sacramento TV station. The show pulled disappointing ratings and ended after a 13-week run, but the genre remains an option for him.

Brown's roots are modest. An African American youth who had shined shoes in Mineola, Texas, he left the Lone Star State to follow a colorful uncle to San Francisco and never looked back. He went to college at San Francisco State and earned a law degree at Hastings. Brown was a man who seemed destined for big things from the moment he walked onto the Assembly floor as a freshman legislator in 1965. He was a flamboyant, left-leaning, angry-talking young street lawyer who had formed a homegrown liberal political organization with the Burton brothers (Philip and John) and George Moscone, the son of a local fisherman. Brown had an opinion on everything and would voice it to anyone who would listen.

One of his first votes was against the re-election of the legendary Jesse Unruh as speaker. But Unruh tolerated Brown, perhaps because both were raised dirt poor in Texas, both emigrated to California after World War II and both began their political careers as rabble-rousers. "It's a good thing you aren't white," Unruh remarked to

Brown one day after the latter had made an especially effective floor speech early in his career. "Why's that?" Brown asked. "Because if you were, you'd own the place," Unruh replied.

Civil rights was the early focus of Brown's legislative career, and no matter what the event, he was ready with a quote. When African American athletes Tommy Smith and John Carlos raised their fists in a "black power" salute at the 1968 Olympics, Brown said, "They will be known forever as two niggers who upset the Olympic Games. I'd rather have them known for that than as two niggers who won two medals." Despite statements of that sort, Brown was developing a reputation among Capitol insiders for smart political work. In 1970, he took his first big step up the ladder when his friend, Bob Moretti, became speaker and he elevated Brown to chairmanship of the powerful Ways and Means Committee. Brown became a master of arcane matters of state finance and recruited a staff of young advisers who today form the nucleus of his Assembly senior staff.

California's political establishment was beginning to respect, if not like, the young politician. He led the George McGovern faction from California to the Democratic National Convention in 1972 and during a complex and bitter credentials fight delivered his famous "Give me back my delegation" speech that thrust him into the national spotlight.

Moretti was planning to step down in 1974 to run for governor and wanted to lateral the speakership to Brown, but Brown made the worst tactical error of his career in taking for granted the support of Latino and African American members. Secretly, San Francisco's other assemblyman, Leo McCarthy, had courted the minority lawmakers, promising them committee chairmanships and other goodies. When the vote came, they stood with McCarthy, who snatched the speakership from under Brown's nose.

That was the beginning of an in-house exile for Brown, one that became even more intense when he and some supporters plotted an unsuccessful coup against McCarthy. At one point, Brown was given an office so small that he had to place his filing cabinets outside in the hall. The exile lasted for two years, during which, Brown said later, he underwent intense self-examination and concluded he had been too arrogant in dealings with colleagues — such as calling one member a "500-pound tub of Jell-O" in public.

McCarthy resurrected Brown's legislative career in 1976 by naming him chairman of the Revenue and Taxation Committee, a fairly substantial job. That gesture paid off in 1979, when another bloc of Democratic Assembly members, led by Howard Berman of Los Angeles, tried to oust McCarthy from the speakership. Brown declared loyalty to his old rival and maintained it during a year of bitter infighting.

At the conclusion of the 1980 elections, Berman had seemingly won enough contested seats to claim the speakership, but the desperate McCarthy backers cut a deal with Republicans to name Willie Brown speaker. Republicans, who openly feared a Berman speakership, were promised some extra consideration by the new regime. Although they later were to claim that Brown reneged, he has always maintained that he stuck to the letter of the agreement.

Brown's speakership has been nothing if not controversial. His Democratic flock has both expanded and contracted during his tenure. But until the Supreme Court decreed a reapportionment plan in 1992 after Brown and Republican Gov. Pete Wilson reached a stalemate, Democratic control of the house was never in doubt. The court-drawn maps gave Republicans a theoretical opportunity to turn out Brown and the Democrats. But internal GOP strife, coupled with strong organizational work by the Democrats, staved that off in 1992. Although Brown had privately conceded Republicans would pick up at least three or four seats that year, the GOP actually lost one and Brown quickly claimed a major victory.

Republicans regrouped in 1994 and, thanks to a nationwide GOP sweep coupled with a last-minute infusion of money from the caucus to targeted GOP candidates, the GOP came out of the 1994 elections with a 41-39 majority. But as the overconfident Republicans were counting their chickens after the election, Brown stole one egg and grabbed for another.

Assemblyman Paul Horcher, who had been at odds with the Assembly GOP leadership, abandoned the Republican Party in December 1994 and became an independent. He voted for Brown for speaker, which left the house divided 40-40 and unable to elect a speaker. Brown was initially thwarted from breaking the tie when the Assembly's chief clerk, E. Dotson Wilson, a Brown protégé, ruled against efforts by Democrats to unseat Richard Mountjoy, who had been elected to the Senate in a special November election held at the same time Mountjoy was being re-elected to the Assembly. Seven weeks of negotiations over a power-sharing agreement between Demorcats and Republicans ensued. During that time, Brown offered a variety of proposals and repeatedly said that he would not necessarily have to hold the title of speaker. "At some point your personal ambitions go on hold, and you begin to think institutionally," he said.

But Brown eventually gave up on reaching a compromise and instead crushed the Republican's 40th egg. Presiding as the senior member of the Assembly, Brown ruled that Mountjoy could not vote on the issue of whether he could keep his Assembly seat. With Mountjoy unable to vote, the Democrats and Horcher then voted to declare Mountjoy's seat vacant and followed that with a 40-39 vote to return Brown to the speaker's chair. Immediately, Democrats instituted new house rules transferring many of the speaker's powers to the Rules Committee and dividing power on policy committees evenly between the parties. Brown said these changes constituted a substantial step toward creating a more stable house in the uncertain era of term limits. But the Republicans were unmollified. They screamed that Brown's antics were a "blatant and corrupt abuse of power," and in early 1995, they launched recall efforts against Horcher and several vulnerable Democrats who had voted for Brown. The Democrat's 40-39 majority was tenuous at best.

Whether Brown is remembered for the power play or for the creation of a more fairly structured house remains to be seen. Even before the divisive 1995 speakership battle, Brown's critics argued that he has rarely exercised his talents on behalf of substantive policy issues and has, instead, presided over a decline both in the performance and the moral atmosphere of the Legislature. He has been accused of shaking down special interests for millions of dollars in campaign funds, of presiding over a blatantly partisan reapportionment of legislative districts in 1981 and of being too consumed with the inside game. After first winning the speakership, Brown took the vast inherent powers of the office and shaped them into a personal tool, controlling the activity of the house with his authority over committee assignments and resource allocation. But Brown argues that he has made life easier for lawmakers of both parties, and he takes credit for rounding up votes for the budgets of Republican governors — budgets ultimately passed with more Democratic support than Republican.

Outside the confines of the Capitol, Brown is a controversial figure. Republicans routinely use Brown as a tool to stir up supporters and to raise money, a fact he acknowledged during the 1995 speakership fight. "All your lives you've been running to get elected to public office on the theory that you would somehow vanquish Willie Brown — the hated speaker, the demon speaker," he said in a floor speech aimed at Republicans. "No matter how you desperately attempt to rewrite history, for 14 years I have carried the title of speaker of this house, and in many cases I have distinguished this house by virtue of it."

Given his complete immersion in the aura and power of the speakership, it was not surprising that Brown took it very personally when the voters in November 1990 passed Proposition 140, imposing term limits on legislators and forcing them to cut their staffs. Voter antipathy toward the Legislature was aimed, in part, at Brown — and he knew it. In the wake of Proposition 140, Brown bitterly lashed out at the press, calling reporters despicable and moving their desks from the side of Assembly chambers to the rear. Brown viewed passage of term limits as an image problem and not as the result of a more deeply seated institutional malaise.

At least some of the controversy stems from Brown's high-flying personal lifestyle. The $1,500 Italian suits, the low-slung sports cars and the flashy parties that he throws for personal and political reasons all contribute to the image, as do his liaisons with a string of attractive women (he's long separated from his wife, Blanche, a reclusive dance teacher).

But it is what Brown does to support that lifestyle that has raised the most eyebrows over the years. He has represented, as an attorney and quasi-lobbyist, a number of well-heeled corporations. His blue-chip client list has included one of the largest landowners in California, the Santa Fe-Southern Pacific Realty (renamed Catellus Inc.). Developers such as the East Bay's Ron Cowan and bond adviser Calvin Grigsby also have put the speaker on retainer.

Until the 1995-96 session, the greatest threat to Brown's hold on the speakership had come in 1987, when five Democratic members, all of whom had enjoyed close relations with the speaker, declared their independence. The "Gang of Five," as the group was immediately dubbed, demanded procedural changes they said were reforms to lessen the power of the speaker. Before long, they were demanding that Brown step down as speaker. They could have formed a new majority with Republicans, but the GOP leader at the time, Pat Nolan, also had established a close relationship with Brown and protected the speaker's right flank. Brown stripped the five of their best committee assignments and the war of nerves went on for a year. Eventually, Republicans agreed to form a coalition with the gang. But Brown bolstered his loyalists with enough victories at the polls in 1988 to eke out a paper-thin re-election as speaker.

In recent years, Brown has appeared to take a heightened interest in his own legacy and the condition in which he leaves the house as term limits force his departure. He began appointing more first-termers to powerful positions in an attempt to pass on institutional experience to the new generation of leaders; his efforts to pass budgets on time in 1993 and 1994 after the long stalemate of 1992 also were viewed as attempts to improve the image of the institution. The 1995 speakership battle adds an interesting new twist to this discussion.

Whatever the ultimate outcome of that battle, Brown has the potential to continue adding chapters to his legislative autobiography for years to come. The most talked about next step for him: election to the state Senate in 1996, when the seat held by Milton Marks of San Francisco opens up.

PERSONAL: elected 1964; born March 20, 1934, in Mineola, Texas; home, San Francisco; National Guard Reserves 1955-1958; education, B.A. San Francisco State University, J.D. Hastings College of Law; wife Blanche Vitero, three children; Methodist.

CAREER: lawyer, maintains a law practice while in office; Assembly speaker 1980 to present.

COMMITTEES: The speaker is technically a non-voting member of all Assembly committees.

OFFICES: Capitol, (916) 445-8077, FAX (916) 445-4189; district, 455 Golden Gate Ave., 2220, San Francisco 94102, (415) 557-0784, FAX (415) 557-8936; 300 S. Spring St., 16505, Los Angeles 90013, (213) 620-4356.

TERM LIMIT: 1996

REGISTRATION: 65.1% D, 14.3% R

1994 CAMPAIGN:	Brown D	73.0%	$3,087,363
	Marc Wolin R	19.6%	$31,912
1992 CAMPAIGN:	Brown D	69.5%	$4,826,842
	John Sidline R	18.9%	$4,739

RATINGS:	AFL-CIO	CLCV	NOW	CofC	CalFarm	GO
	95	81	A-	18	22	F

James L. Brulte (R)

63rd Assembly District

Assemblyman Ross Johnson, who tended to view the 1994-95 speakership fight in Biblical terms, once compared fellow conservative and GOP leader Jim Brulte to Moses. Brulte appeared to have produced a miracle out of the 1994 November elections. With the tactical wit of a political pro and a last-minute loan of $1 million, he managed to get 41 Republicans elected to the Assembly. It was the first time in more than two decades that the GOP owned a majority of the seats in the 80-member lower house, and Brulte was hailed as the leader who had delivered his party from 14 years of house rule under Democratic Speaker Willie Brown.

Jim Brulte

But, just as Moses' journey ended at the River Jordan, Brulte was unable to cross over into a political land of milk and honey. On the December day he was to be elected speaker, one of his flock — Assemblyman Paul Horcher — betrayed him. Horcher, who had been on the outs with his fellow Republicans for years, declared himself an independent and voted for Brown. It was an embarrassing turn of events for Brulte, who boasted for weeks before the speakership vote that he had the 41 ballots necessary to become the new speaker. Instead, the Assembly was deadlocked in a 40-40 a tie, and Brulte was forced to enter negotiations with Brown over a power-sharing deal even as Republicans mounted recall campaigns against Horcher and other vulnerable Democrats in an effort to win back a majority of Assembly seats.

Capitol insiders marveled at how the wily Brown, whose political wizardry is legendary, managed once again to foil Republicans. They questioned how Brulte — who by then was being compared to Fatty Arbuckle — could have failed to secure Horcher's fealty. Was it stupidity or just arrogance?

An imposing man of 6-foot-4 and 260 pounds, Brulte's rise to political power would come as no surprise to anyone familiar with his background. He worked his way into the Legislature, not through service to the community but by service to other politicians. His resumé is stuffed with political jobs, having been active in political campaigns since he was 10. He was an aide to S.I. Hayakawa and an advance man for George Bush. He currently represents a GOP-dominated district in San Bernardino County that was once the domain of another Republican, Charles Bader, whom Brulte served as chief of staff.

Brulte won the top job as the Assembly Republican caucus' leader at the start of the 1993 session when he replaced Fresno's Bill Jones, who stepped down after the Republicans failed to live up to expectations at the polls in 1992. (Jones was elected secretary of state in 1994.) Almost immediately after assuming his new post, Brulte crashed head-on into the considerable political force of Speaker Brown.

First, Brown created a logistical nightmare for Republican whips with a seating assignment that separated GOP freshmen from the rest of the caucus on the Assembly floor. Then, in a move that later played into to the Brown-Brulte speakership fight, the speaker refused to name then-GOP Assemblyman Dean Andal of Stockton to the Assembly Ways and Means Committee, even though he was the Republicans' pick. Brown instead named Horcher as vice chair of Ways and Means. Brulte, for his own political reasons, chose not to clash openly with Brown so early in the legislative year. Instead, he ignored Horcher's Ways and Means assignment and announced that Assemblyman Pat Nolan of Glendale, would be the Republicans' lead person on the committee and that Andal would be the caucus' budget watchdog.

The day of Horcher's defection, Brown announced to the world that he had the means of securing the speakership by expelling Republican Assemblyman Richard Mountjoy, who — by a fluke of election laws — won seats in both the Assembly and the Senate on Nov. 8, 1994. But Brulte still didn't get it. He continued for a while to claim his intent to take the speakership, mounting recall elections while claiming he had nothing to do with the recalls. All that did was solidify Brown's support within his own caucus.

Brulte began serious negotiations with Brown over a power-sharing agreement, but it soon became clear that Brulte's control of his caucus was nominal. The real power was in the hands of Johnson and other archconservatives, none of whom would have any part of a power-sharing agreement with Brown and the Democrats. Brulte also had to try to quell a rebellion by GOP Assemblyman Bernie Richter, who came within a hair of being elected speaker with Democratic backing. By late January, with the house still dysfunctional and Republicans threatening to hole up in the Hyatt Hotel across the street until recalls gave them a clear majority, Brown exercised the "Mountjoy option." Mountjoy was excluded on a party-line vote, giving the House 39 Republicans, 39 Democrats and one independent (Horcher). With Horcher's vote, Brown was then elected speaker. "The Republicans blew it at every step of the way," Brown said. "They made mistake after mistake after mistake."

Brulte brayed that Brown had won the speakership with "brutal and corrupt" procedural moves. But in the next breath, he admitted that the GOP had no grounds to mount a legal challenge.

As seats shuffle due to vacancies and possible recalls in 1995, it seems likely that Republicans will eventually win control of the House. But it's an open question as to whether Brulte will be the next speaker given the deep divisions in his caucus. Brulte is answerable not only to them but to influential contributors to GOP campaigns who also were dismayed at the turn of events.

PERSONAL: elected 1990; born April 13, 1956, in Glen Cove, N.Y.; home,

Ontario; Air National Guard Reserve 1974-present; education, B.A. Cal Poly Pomona; single.

CAREER: Staff, U.S. Sen. S.I. Hayakawa in Washington D.C; staff, Republican National Committee; staff, Assistant Secretary of Defense for Reserve Affairs; advance staff, Vice President George Bush; executive director, San Bernardino County Republican Party; chief of staff, Assemblyman Charles Bader 1987-1990; owns a management consulting firm.

COMMITTEES: As Assembly Republican Leader, Brulte does not serve on any standing committees. He is a member of the Joint Rules Committee.

OFFICES: Capitol, (916) 445-8490, FAX (916) 323-8544; district, 10681 Foothill Blvd., 325, Rancho Cucamonga 91730, (714) 466-9096, FAX (909) 466-9892.

TERM LIMIT: 1996
REGISTRATION: 39.8% D, 48.6% R

1994 CAMPAIGN:	Brulte R	67.5%	$949,750
	Richard Edwards D	32.5%	$4,653
1992 CAMPAIGN:	Brulte R	56.1%	$506,548
	Larry Westwood D	31.3%	Not Available
	Joseph Desist Green L	12.7%	Not Available

RATINGS:	AFL-CIO	CLCV	NOW	CofC	CalFarm	GO
	5	5	C-	95	77.7	A

John L. Burton (D)
12th Assembly District

Traditionally, San Francisco has been divided into two Assembly districts. When John Burton returned to the Assembly in 1988, he inherited the district that had been held by Art Agnos, who had been elected the city's mayor. Assembly Speaker Willie Brown represented the other district. Court-ordered reapportionment in 1992 created a new division of the city into western and eastern districts. Brown, who had represented the more affluent western and northern sections of San Francisco, opted to take the new eastern district, which is much poorer and includes many of the city's African American and Latino residents. Burton wound up with the more affluent western half, renumbered as the 12th District. Both districts are

John Burton

overwhelmingly Democratic, and Burton, one of the most liberal members of the Assembly, breezed to ridiculously easy re-elections in 1992 and 1994.

Burton is one of the Capitol's genuine characters: loud, profane, combative and the building's only self-acknowledged former drug abuser. Burton, his late brother Philip, Brown and George Moscone, who became mayor of San Francisco and was assassinated in 1978, were the founders of a political organization that dominated San Francisco's major-league politics for more than a generation. John Burton and Willie Brown began in politics together as idealistic young men and close friends. In 1964, they went to the Assembly, where Brown flourished. Burton moved on to Congress in 1974.

The organization's greatest triumph came in the 1981 reapportionment in which brother Philip made his self-proclaimed contribution to modern art by carving up congressional districts in such a manner that lopsided majorities for the Democrats were preserved throughout the 1980s. One of the more bizarrely shaped districts was created for John Burton.

But then the Burton machine faltered. John Burton suddenly quit his seat in Congress, admitting publicly that he had a cocaine and alcohol problem. In 1983, Philip Burton died. His wife, Sala, took over his congressional seat, but she died in 1987. The organization was brought back to life in 1987 to move then-Assembly-man Art Agnos into the mayor's office, which in turn opened the door for John Burton to run for the Assembly again. The 1988 special election for Agnos' Assembly seat pitted Burton, who had undergone extensive therapy for his substance abuse, against Roberta Achtenberg, an activist for lesbian and gay rights who was bidding to become the state's first openly lesbian legislator. Burton's name, his heavier spending and the organization's professional-class efforts won out, and he returned to Sacramento.

Brown gave Burton a series of important committee assignments, including chairmanship of the Public Safety Committee, where Burton gleefully killed Republican lock-'em-up anti-crime bills. Brown removed Burton from the panel in 1994, the year of "three strikes and you're out" and a wave of other anti-crime legislation. But he continued as chairman of the Rules Committee, the body that acts as the Assembly's internal housekeeper with power over staff, office perks and the like. Burton also functions as a member of Brown's inner circle; the two have represented a potent political force on behalf of San Francisco's parochial issues.

Burton's impact on the Assembly is more often theatrical than legislative. His interruptions of proceedings to make acerbic observations have livened up many a dull floor session. But he could point to several substantive accomplishments in the 1993-94 session, among them successful bills strengthening open-meeting laws and providing for notification of victims when a convicted stalker is released from prison. Burton also brokered a bipartisan compromise reinstating California's asset forfeiture laws and placing new restraints on police efforts to seize property.

PERSONAL: elected 1988 (special election); born Dec. 15, 1932, in Cincinnati; home, San Francisco; Army 1954-1956; education, B.A. San Francisco State University, J.D. University of San Francisco Law School; divorced, one child.

CAREER: lawyer; Assembly 1964-'74; House of Representatives 1974-'82.

COMMITTEES: Rules (chair); Appropriations; Health; Public Safety.
OFFICES: Capitol, (916) 445-8253, FAX (916) 324-4899; district, 455 Golden Gate Ave., 2202, San Francisco 94102, (415) 557-2253, FAX (415) 557-2592.
TERM LIMIT: 1996
REGISTRATION: 61.2% D, 19.0% R

1994 CAMPAIGN:	Burton D			70.8%		$330,683
	Philip Wing R			24.3%		$1,551
1992 CAMPAIGN:	Burton D			65.1%		$534,129
	Storm Jenkins R			26.1%		$40,741

RATINGS:	AFL-CIO	CLCV	NOW	CofC	CalFarm	GO
	98	91	B+	9	33	D

Cruz M. Bustamante (D)
31st Assembly District

This San Joaquin Valley district includes parts of two counties: Fresno, including the southern part of the city of Fresno, and western Tulare County. The district divides the cities of Fresno, Visalia and Tulare in order to maximize the Latino presence, which is now about 52 percent. The overall minority population is almost 69 percent.

Cruz Bustamante

Just days before the November 1992 election in which incumbent Democrat Bruce Bronzan was running unopposed, news articles disclosed that Bronzan had told his staff he would quit the Legislature the following January to accept a job with the University of California, San Francisco, medical school. Almost simultaneously, Bronzan endorsed his field director, Cruz Bustamante, for the job. In this heavily Democratic district, that was as good as a done deal. The handoff to Bustamante was ratified by the voters on April 27, 1993, despite a spirited campaign by his GOP rival, Fresno County Supervisor Doug Vagim. In 1994, Bustamante withstood a substantial challenge from Tulare County sheriff's deputy Glen Peterson to win re-election.

Bustamante, the son of a Dinuba barber, is the first Latino elected to the Legislature from the San Joaquin Valley. He joins many other Assembly members who spent most of their working lives on political staffs before winning an office themselves. As a student intern, Bustamante worked for former U.S. Rep. B.F. Sisk. He later worked for former U.S. Rep. Richard Lehman. He spent five years on Bronzan's staff while also serving in numerous local community service posts.

Bustamante came to the Legislature with a solid knowledge of the district's immigration and agricultural issues. Among the bills he carried were ones increasing the amount of information required for a request to list a species as threatened or endangered and authorizing a state program for care of young migrant children. Bustamante also authored the successful Proposition 189, which allows judges to deny bail for people accused of committing felony sexual assault.

PERSONAL: elected 1993 (special election); born Jan. 4, 1953, in Dinuba; home, Fresno; education, A.A. Fresno City College, attended Fresno State University; wife, Arcelia; three children; Roman Catholic.

CAREER: Fresno Employment and Training Commission, 1977-83; field director for U.S. Rep. Richard Lehman, 1983-88; field director for Assemblyman Bruce Bronzan, 1988-93.

COMMITTEES: Agriculture; Appropriations; Elections, Reapportionment & Constitutional Amendments; Governmental Organization.

OFFICES: Capitol, (916) 445-8514, FAX (916) 324-7129; district, 2550 Mariposa Mall, 5006, Fresno 93721, (209) 445-5532, FAX (209) 445-6006.

TERM LIMIT: 1998

REGISTRATION: 60.9% D, 29.4% R

1994 CAMPAIGN:	Bustamante D	58.4%	$171,206
	Glen Peterson R	41.6%	Not available
1993 CAMPAIGN:	Bustamante D	57.6%	Not Available
	Doug Vagim R	42.4%	Not Available

| **RATINGS**: | AFL-CIO | CLCV | NOW | CofC | CalFarm | GO |
| | 91 | 50 | B+ | 36 | 56 | C |

Louis Caldera (D)
46th Assembly District

When Assemblywoman Lucille Roybal-Allard decided to follow her father's footsteps to Congress, it left a hole in the 46th Assembly District and set up another battle between two Latino political factions feuding for control of politics on the heavily Hispanic east side of Los Angeles. Roybal-Allard and Los Angeles County Supervisor Gloria Molina backed Berta Saavedra, who was Roybal-Allard's assistant. The other faction, headed by City Councilman Richard Alatorre, state Sen. Art Torres and Assemblyman Richard Polanco, chose Louis Caldera, a deputy county counsel who had been educated at West Point and Harvard and was a military police officer. Caldera won the primary with 52 percent of the vote and coasted to election in this heavily Democratic district.

Louis Caldera

Among Capitol insiders, Caldera is being hailed as a comer because of his attractive attributes, someone who can carry Latino politics into a new dimension as term limits bring him and other newcomers into relatively high seniority later in the decade.

In 1993, Caldera penned one of the year's most hotly contested bills — a measure requiring California children under the age of 18 to wear helmets while riding bicycles or face a $25 fine. Opponents such as former GOP Assemblyman Dean Andal of Stockton, who called the measure the "ultimate nanny bill," attacked the proposal as government intrusion into families' daily lives. But Caldera persuaded a bare majority of his legislative colleagues to back the bill, arguing that safety helmets could save lives. Gov. Pete Wilson agreed and signed it into law.

PERSONAL: elected 1992; born April 1, 1956, in El Paso, Texas; home, Los Angeles; education, B.S. U.S. Military Academy; law degree and MBA, Harvard University; wife Eva; Catholic.

CAREER: lawyer, Los Angeles deputy county counsel, 1991-92.

COMMITTEES: Banking and Finance; Budget; Higher Education; Revenue and Taxation.

OFFICES: Capitol, (916) 445-4843, FAX (916) 443-6812; district, 304 S. Broadway, 580, Los Angeles 90013, (213) 680-4646, FAX (213) 680-1851.

TERM LIMIT: 1998

REGISTRATION: 67.2% D, 18.3% R

1994 CAMPAIGN:	Caldera D	72.6%	$115,881
	Yongchul Yang R	21.3%	Not Available
1992 CAMPAIGN:	Caldera D	71.8%	$175,610
	David Osborne R	21.3%	$0

RATINGS:	AFL-CIO	CLCV	NOW	CofC	CalFarm	GO
	100	95	A-	18	44.4	F

Robert J. Campbell (D)
11th Assembly District

This district stretches across northern Contra Costa County from San Pablo Bay in the west to the edge of the Sacramento-San Joaquin Delta in the east; included are Hercules, Martinez, Concord, Pittsburg and Antioch. Reapportionment after the 1990 census moved the district out of Richmond, the traditional home base of Assemblyman Robert Campbell, and further into the East Bay suburbs. The switch halved the district's once-immense Democratic registration margin, but the blue-collar workers and minority residents of the new district still provided Campbell with a more than 20-point edge that has discouraged Republicans from mounting a challenge to him. Campbell was elected to a seventh and final term in 1994 with more than four-fifths of the vote against a candidate of the Peace and Freedom party.

Campbell, a former insurance broker and Richmond city councilman, is one of the most consistently liberal members of the Assembly. One of his key interests is education funding; as chairman during the Democratic majority years of the Assembly budget subcommittee dealing with education, he had significant influence on where education dollars were spent. He has fought to restore funding cuts for community colleges and state universities as well as to limit increases in fees.

Campbell's liberal leanings also have been evident on environmental legislation, civil liberties issues and measures to help minorities and recently arrived immigrants. And he was one of only a few legislators who had an announced policy of refusing to take fees for speeches before the practice was outlawed.

Robert Campbell

But the mild-mannered Campbell has not been much of an inside player. Several legislators with less seniority have more clout, and with term limits bringing his Assembly career to an end in 1996, Campbell seems destined to remain a mostly marginal player. A move to the state Senate is possible, since Democratic Sen. Daniel Boatwright's seat will be opening up as Campbell's term expires, but Republican Assemblyman Richard Rainey could also make a run for the seat in a Senate district that has taken on a more conservative bent.

PERSONAL: elected 1980; born Dec. 20, 1937, in Los Angeles; home, Martinez; Army, National Guard Reserves 1961-1972; education, B.A. San Francisco State University, postgraduate studies UC Berkeley; divorced, two children; Roman Catholic.

CAREER: insurance broker; Richmond City Council 1975-1982.

COMMITTEES: Housing & Community Development; Public Employees, Retirement & Social Security; Transportation; Water, Parks & Wildlife.

OFFICES: Capitol, (916) 445-7890, FAX (916) 327-2999; district, 815 Estudillo St., Martinez 94553, (510) 372-7990, FAX (510) 372-0934.

TERM LIMIT: 1996

REGISTRATION: 54.0% D, 31.2% R

1994 CAMPAIGN:	Campbell D	82.7%	$77,898
	Amanda Coughlan P&F	17.3%	Not available
1992 CAMPAIGN:	Campbell D	98.1%	$153,927

RATINGS:	AFL-CIO	CLCV	NOW	CofC	CalFarm	GO
	98	90	B+	18	22	D

Salvatorre Cannella (D)
26th Assembly District

When the state Supreme Court's reapportionment experts decided the fast-growing Modesto area should have an additional state Assembly seat, it meant a substantial change for one-term Assemblyman Sal Cannella, but one for the better, since Cannella is a Democrat.

Cannella was first elected in 1990 after a fierce partisan battle in the old 27th District, which included all of Stanislaus County and the Atwater-Snelling region of the northern tip of Merced County. Once a solidly Democratic district, albeit one with a conservative tone, the 27th was undergoing rapid change as the Modesto area became a suburban extension of the San Francisco Bay Area. Suburbanizing areas traditionally move toward the Republican Party, and the GOP saw the district as a future growth possibility.

Sal Cannella

Cannella won the seat twice in 1990, once in a special election after Gary Condit was elected to Congress and the second time in the general election. For Cannella, one-time tool-and-die maker, it was deja vu because he had succeeded Condit as mayor of Ceres and later as a Stanislaus County supervisor.

The Supreme Court's reapportionment plan changed the district dramatically when it created a new Modesto-area district prior to the 1992 elections. Most of the Republican areas were placed in the adjacent 25th District, and Cannella wound up with a strong Democratic registration margin. Cannella had an easy re-election win.

Cannella has been a go-along, get-along regular for Assembly Speaker Willie Brown. He got points for dedication when he left a hospital bed in 1990 to cast a crucial vote in favor of a compromise ending a 28-day stalemate between Gov. George Deukmejian and the Legislature on the budget. In early 1993, Cannella was given an opportunity to expand his political horizons, when Brown elevated him to the chairmanship of the Public Employees, Retirement and Social Security Committee — a plum for someone with strong union connections.

In the 1995-96 leadership debacle, Cannella voted for Democrat Willie Brown for speaker and was immediately threatened with a recall election by anti-Brown forces. Cannella stood firm, though, saying that the Republican's pick for speaker, Assemblyman Jim Brulte of Rancho Cucamonga, was not a friend of Central Valley interests. The recall threat against Cannella never materialized.

PERSONAL: elected 1990 (special election); born Sept. 23, 1942, in Newark, N.J.; home, Ceres; National Guard 1960-1966; education, Modesto Community College; wife Donna, three children; Roman Catholic.

CAREER: tool-and-die maker.

COMMITTEES: Public Employees, Retirement & Social Security (vice chair); Agriculture; Local Government; Water, Parks & Wildlife.

OFFICES: Capitol, (916) 445-8570, FAX (916) 445-8849; district, 384 E. Olive, 2, Turlock, 95380, (209) 669-6115, FAX (209) 669-0349.

TERM LIMIT: 1996
REGISTRATION: 53.3% D, 35.1% R

1994 CAMPAIGN:	Cannella D	53.6%	$157,389
	Greg Thomas R	41.7%	$21,160
1992 CAMPAIGN:	Cannella D	56.8%	$304,957
	Scott Weimer R	35.2%	$10,695

| **RATINGS**: | AFL-CIO | CLCV | NOW | CofC | CalFarm | GO |
| | 94 | 57 | B+ | 36 | 55.5 | B+ |

Mickey Conroy (R)
71st Assembly District

Mickey Conroy

Republicans have this Orange County district wrapped up so tightly that Democrats represent little more than a blip on the registration rolls. It includes Orange, Villa Park, Mission Viejo and a slice of San Clemente.

Conservative Republican Mickey Conroy won a 1991 special election following a game of musical chairs that saw the former assemblyman for the district, John Lewis, elected to the state Senate to replace John Seymour, who had been appointed to the U.S. Senate by Gov. Pete Wilson. Conroy, a retired Marine Corps pilot, defeated Orange City Councilman William Stener, a moderate backed by the governor, to take the GOP nomination in the special election and then easily won the runoff. In his 1992 re-election bid, Conroy outdistanced his Democratic opponent by a wide margin and triumphed again in 1994, despite charges of sexual harassment by a fired office aide who claimed in a lawsuit against Conroy and his chief of staff that she routinely had to kiss the legislator and give him back rubs. Conroy and his top aide denied any wrongdoing.

One of Conroy's first actions upon arriving in Sacramento was to revive old arguments that former anti-Vietnam War activist Tom Hayden should be thrown out of the Legislature. Conroy, a Vietnam veteran, asked the Senate to refuse Hayden the 23rd Senate District seat he won in the 1992 election because Hayden's anti-war activities allegedly violated the state constitution.

Hayden, a Santa Monica Democrat who had served in the Assembly since 1982, countered in a letter to lawmakers that Conroy was recycling false and slanderous charges and was attempting to have the Senate override the will of voters. Hayden survived similar moves to oust him from the Assembly and weathered the Conroy attack as well.

Yet the controversy was small potatoes compared to the smorgasbord of media coverage Conroy cooked up in 1994, when he capitalized on the country's fascination with the plight of Michael Fay, the American teenager who was caned in Singapore for alleged acts of graffiti vandalism. Conroy introduced a bill calling for the court-supervised paddling of youthful graffiti artists in California that touched off a blizzard of media attention. He was quoted in national news magazines and appeared on television shows such as "Good Morning America" and CNN. "This state is a mess from a bunch of self-absorbed punks who get their kicks at the expense of others," Conroy would say. "It's costing beaucoup bucks to clean this stuff up. It's time for some discipline." The bill, however, was killed in a legislative committee and never came to a vote on the Assembly floor.

PERSONAL: elected 1991 (special election); born Nov. 1, 1927, in Footedale, Pa.; home, Orange; USMC retired; education, attended University of Maryland and University of Virginia; wife Ann, two children; Roman Catholic.

CAREER: 21 years in the USMC; businessman.

COMMITTEES: Higher Education; Housing & Community Development; Insurance; Utilities and Commerce (chair)

OFFICES: Capitol, (916) 445-2778, FAX (916) 324-6872; district, 1940 N. Tustin St., 102, Orange, 92665, (714) 998-0980, FAX (714) 998-7102.

TERM LIMIT: 1996

REGISTRATION: 28.9% D, 57.8% R

1994 CAMPAIGN:	Conroy R		71.8%	$150,135
	Jeanne Costales D		28.2%	$17,279
1992 CAMPAIGN:	Conroy R		61.8%	$195,735
	Bea Foster D		38.2%	$2,450

RATINGS:	AFL-CIO	CLCV	NOW	CofC	CalFarm	GO
	8	10	C-	86	55.5	A

Dominic L. Cortese (D)
23rd Assembly District

Dominic Cortese spent 12 years on the Santa Clara County Board of Supervisors before he was elected to the Assembly in 1980. It prepared him well for what has become his primary role in the lower house: an advocate for local government.

For years, Cortese was chairman of the Assembly Committee on Local Government, figuring out ways for local governments to operate in the wake of property tax-cutting Proposition 13. One of his proposals was to permit, with voter approval, creation of county service areas that would have allowed assessments on residents for increased police protection. It was vetoed. Cortese also authored several major — though obscure — laws regulating land development.

In 1990, Cortese moved on to a more daunting challenge: He became chairman of the Water, Parks and Wildlife Committee. As such, he emerged as a major player on water issues. More than once, he introduced a bill that sent shivers up the backs of developers: It would have required them to identify a long-term, reliable supply of water before permits could be issued for a project. And at the behest of the wine industry, he proposed a modest increase in the liquor tax in a constitutional amendment (Proposition 126) designed to head off a steeper tax (Proposition 134) also on the November 1990 ballot. Both efforts failed.

Cortese, a political moderate, comes from a third-generation San Jose-area farm family and is independently wealthy through his family grocery. His political ascent faced a challenge in 1990, when he was charged by the Sacramento County district attorney with illegally receiving a gift exceeding $10 from a lobbyist. Cortese allegedly contacted Carl Burg, a lobbyist for the Painting and Decorating Contractors of California, about bids for a house-painting job when Cortese was sponsoring a bill of interest to painters and decorators. Burg contacted a contractor who bid $3,740 and painted the house. Prosecutors said the contractor wasn't paid, and Cortese later listed it as a gift. He denied any wrongdoing but eventually pleaded no contest; he was fined $7,050 and ordered to do community service.

Dominic Cortese

Republicans, curiously, did not attempt to exploit Cortese's troubles in the 1990 election, and there were reports that Speaker Willie Brown had made a clandestine deal with GOP leaders. They would lay off Cortese, and in return, so it was said, the Democrats would not attempt to unseat Glendale Assemblyman Pat Nolan, who was then under investigation and was later convicted in the FBI probe of Capitol corruption.

Whatever the case, Cortese faced more substantial trouble in 1992, when reapportionment radically altered districts in the San Jose area. But colleague John Vasconcellos gave Cortese the more Democratic of the new districts, which allowed him to win re-election; Cortese easily won an eighth and final Assembly term in 1994. Cortese and Vasconcellos are both out of the Assembly in 1996, as is the state senator in their area — longtime lawmaker Al Alquist.

Cortese quickly made news at the start of the 1995-96 session. He was one of several Democrats whom Republicans were hoping to win over in the initial speakership vote in December 1994, and he was wavering until a last-minute meeting with Brown. The longtime speaker brought along Republican Paul Horcher, who was about to declare his independent status and vote for Brown. That tip secured Cortese's vote for Brown and produced the historic 40-40 tie between Brown and Republican leader Jim Brulte.

PERSONAL: elected 1980; born Sept. 27, 1932, in San Jose; home, San Jose;

Army 1954-1956; education, B.S. University of Santa Clara; wife Suzanne, five children; Roman Catholic.

CAREER: businessman and farmer, part-owner of Cortese Bros. grocery chain; Santa Clara County Board of Supervisors, 1968-1980.

COMMITTEES: Water, Parks and Wildlife (chair); Governmental Organization; Public Employees, Retirement & Social Security; Transportation.

OFFICES: Capitol, (916) 445-8243, FAX (916) 323-8898; district, 100 Paseo de San Antonio, 300, San Jose 95113, (408) 269-6500, FAX (408) 277-1036.

TERM LIMIT: 1996

REGISTRATION: 60.1% D, 24.1% R

1994 CAMPAIGN:	Cortese D	64.3%	$64,802
	Frank Jewett R	27.5%	Not available
1992 CAMPAIGN:	Cortese D	65.9%	$177,654
	Monica Valladares R	34.1%	$1,065

RATINGS:	AFL-CIO	CLCV	NOW	CofC	CalFarm	GO
	95	65	A-	32	56	D+

Jim Cunneen (R)
24th Assembly District

This district to the west of San Jose covers the affluent South Bay suburbs of Los Altos, Cupertino, Los Gatos, Campbell and Saratoga — home of the Silicon Valley and its burgeoning computer industry. Republican Charles Quackenbush held the seat for eight years before making a successful run for state insurance commissioner in 1994.

Jim Cunneen

The battle to replace Quackenbush was hard-fought in a district with a very narrow Democratic registration edge but a generally Republican outlook. The race pitted Republican Jim Cunneen, corporate affairs manager for a high-tech firm in the Silicon Valley, against Democrat Ed Foglia, former president of the California Teachers Association. Cunneen had the support of three of his former bosses, all popular with folks in the South Bay: state Sen. Tom Campbell, former state Sen. Becky Morgan and former U.S. Rep. Ed Zschau. Foglia had better name recognition and the deep pockets of the CTA behind him.

Foglia argued that Cunneen didn't know the district well enough and suggested he was too close to corporate interests. But Cunneen pointed out Foglia's ties to labor unions and questioned whether the Democrat represented the voters' interests. Helped in part by the strong Republican tide, Cunneen prevailed by a narrow margin. He jumped straight into his legislative work, appearing at a press confer- ence on the first day of the session — even before the speakership vote was taken — to announce co-authorship of a bill reforming the state budget process.

PERSONAL: elected 1994; born May 24, 1961, in Palo Alto; home, Cupertino; education, B.A. UCLA; wife Jennifer; Roman Catholic.

CAREER: corporate affairs manager for Applied Materials, a Silicon Valley high-tech company; former aide to Rep. Tom Campbell, state Sen. Becky Morgan and Rep. Ed Zschau.

COMMITTEES: Banking & Finance; Budget; Insurance; Revenue & Taxa- tion.

OFFICES: Capitol, (916) 445-8305, FAX (916) 323-9989; district, 901 Campisi Way, 300, Campbell 95008, (408) 369-8170, FAX (408) 369-7174.

TERM LIMIT: 2000

REGISTRATION: 43.6% D, 41.0% R

1994 CAMPAIGN:	Cunneen R	51.2%	$515,341
	Ed Foglia D	48.9%	$317,424

RATINGS: Newly elected

Susan A. Davis (D)
76th Assembly District

This compact district lies completely within the city boundaries of San Diego from Rancho Bernardo in the north to Mission Valley in the south. It touches the beach at only one spot, north of La Jolla near Del Mar. With 216,036 registered voters, it is one of the most vote-rich districts in the state.

It also is a district highly coveted by Republicans, who have been unable to take hold of the seat despite registration figures that favor GOP candidates. For seven years, the district was represented by Democrat Lucy Killea, until she won a seat in the state Senate in a special election. After Killea left and later be- came an independent, a special election to fill her seat was held on the same day as the June 1990 primary.

Susan Davis

Republican Jeff Marston won the seat, nosing out former San Diego City Council- man Mike Gotch, a Democrat and an ally of Killea's. In the same June election, however, Marston and Gotch won their respective party primaries, so they again faced off in November. This time, Gotch won. Thus the hapless Marston was an assemblyman for all of six months.

When Gotch left the Legislature in 1994, Susan Davis became the newest Democrat to win the district's Assembly seat. Though Republicans targeted the district for victory, Davis, a San Diego school board member, defeated GOP businessman Bob Trettin, a frequent candidate in local races. Davis comes to the Assembly with an extensive background in education, health and social issues. She once chaired the state superintendent of public instruction's school board advisory committee and was an appointee to a legislative advisory committee on school restructuring. Davis was among those legislators swept up in the December 1994 power struggle. The Republican leadership threatened to mount a recall campaign against Davis, who had supported Brown for speaker.

PERSONAL: elected 1994; born April 12, 1944, in Cambridge, Mass.; home, San Diego; education, B.A. UC Berkeley, M.A. University of North Carolina; husband, Steven Davis; two children; Jewish.

CAREER: San Diego Unified School District Board of Education, 1983-1992; executive director, Aaron Price Fellows Program; development associate, KPBS-TV; community producer, KPBS-FM; president, League of Women Voters of San Diego.

COMMITTEES: Consumer Protection, Governmental Efficiency & Economic Development; Education; Health; Housing & Community Development; Transportation.

OFFICES: Capitol, (916) 445-7210, FAX (916) 324-7895; district, 1080 University Ave., H-201, San Diego 92103, (619) 294-7600, FAX (619) 294-2348.

TERM LIMIT: 2000

REGISTRATION: 41.8% D, 41.1% R

1994 CAMPAIGN:	Davis D	49.4%	$563,094
	Bob Trettin R	45.6%	$350,459

RATINGS: Newly elected.

Denise Moreno Ducheny (D)
79th Assembly District

San Diego County's 79th Assembly District's southern boundary bumps up against the Mexican border and a section of the district's western boundary includes the shoreline of San Diego Bay, where the once sleepy bedroom communities of National City and Chula Vista awakened in the 1980s. Chula Vista has become home to ritzy bayside hotels, and home developers are paving the mesas above. The problems of this district are those of Mexico, where the First and Third Worlds crash head-on. Immigrants and drugs are smuggled across the border at Otay Mesa and elsewhere. Sewage from Tijuana leaks across the border into San Diego and fouls the beaches and horse farms there.

Democrat Steve Peace had represented this district since 1982, but the former assemblyman moved to the Senate by winning a special election in December 1993. That sparked a mad dash by five Democrats to replace Peace in another special election in April, 1994. Denise Moreno Ducheny, a lawyer and community activist, won the election by a slim 27 votes. She bested the same Democratic challengers again in the June primary elections, and then sailed to victory in November over GOP candidate John Vogel.

PERSONAL: elected 1994; born March 21, 1952, in Los Angeles; home, San Diego; education, B.A. Pomona College, J.D. Southwestern University School of Law, studied economic history at University of Lund, Sweden, and Spanish at the intensive language school of Cuahuanahuac in Cuernavaca, Mexico; husband, Al; no children; no religious preference.

Denise M. Ducheny

CAREER: lawyer; San Diego Community College District trustee; co-founder, Association of Latino Community College Trustees of California; member, San Diego County Juvenile Delinquency Prevention Commission.

COMMITTEES: Budget; Environmental Safety & Toxic Materials; Housing & Community Development; Water, Parks & Wildlife.

OFFICES: Capitol, (916) 445-7556, FAX (916) 322-2271; district, 430 Davidson St., Suite C, Chula Vista 91910, (619) 426-1618, FAX (619) 426-6359.

TERM LIMIT: 2000

REGISTRATION: 56% D, 29.6% R

1994 CAMPAIGN:	Ducheny D	67.5%	$11,879
	John Vogel R	28.9%	Not Available
APRIL 12, 1994, SPECIAL ELECTION:			
	Ducheny D	29.88%	Not Available
	Tim Nader D	29.72%	Not Available
	David Valladolid D	21.99%	Not Available
	John E. Warren D	14.33%	Not Available
	Lettie Rogers D	4.09%	Not Available

RATINGS:	AFL-CIO	CLCV	NOW	CofC	CalFarm	GO
	n/a	79	B+	23	11.1	A

Martha M. Escutia (D)
50th Assembly District

This is one of several districts created by the state Supreme Court specifically to comply with the federal Voting Rights Act, which requires maximization of political opportunities for minority groups. The district embraces a chunk of southeastern Los Angeles plus the cities of Huntington Park and South Gate, and has the largest Latino population of any Assembly district, nearly 90 percent, as well as a comfortable 3-1 Democratic registration majority.

After redistricting in 1992, the only election that counted was the Democratic primary. It featured one of several contests between rival Latino groups. One faction is headed by former state Sen. Art Torres and Los Angeles City Councilman Richard Alatorre, and the other by Los Angeles County Supervisor Gloria Molina. The Torres-Alatorre candidate was Martha Escutia, an attorney and executive of a nonprofit organization. The Molina group picked business-woman Pat Acosta. After a spirited duel, Escutia won. Her matchup in November with Republican Gladys Miller was an afterthought. Without a primary opponent in 1994, she easily won election to a second term.

Martha Escutia

PERSONAL: elected 1992; born Jan. 16, 1958, in Los Angeles; home, Bell; education, B.A. University of Southern California, J.D. Georgetown University; husband, Leo Briones; Catholic.

CAREER: attorney, vice president of government affairs and public policy, United Way.

COMMITTEES: Budget; Health; Rules; Transportation.

OFFICES: Capitol, (916) 445-8188, FAX (916) 324-0012; district, 3512 E. Florence Ave., 201, Huntington Park 90255, (213) 582-7774, FAX (213) 582-4499.

TERM LIMIT: 1998

REGISTRATION: 68.5% D, 19.2% R

1994 CAMPAIGN:
	Escutia D	74.6%	$69,975
	Gladys Miller R	29.5%	Not Available

1992 CAMPAIGN:
	Escutia D	75.0%	$180,246
	Gladys Miller R	25.0%	$5,362

RATINGS:
AFL-CIO	CLCV	NOW	CofC	CalFarm	GO
100	71	A-	23	33.3	F

Liz Figueroa (D)
20th Assembly District

This East Bay district covers Fremont, Newark, Milpitas and other suburbs of San Jose in southern Alameda County and northern Santa Clara County. The seat was held for eight years by Democrat Delaine Eastin, a hard-working and pugna-cious lawmaker who became one of the Legislature's most outspoken advocates for public schools. Eastin, whose forceful oratory made her a rising star in the Democratic Party, gave up the seat in 1994 to make a successful run for state superintendent of public instruction.

Fremont businesswoman Liz Figueroa emerged from the Democratic primary after a tussle with Milpitas Councilman Bob Livengood — who turned around and endorsed the GOP candidate, Scott Haggerty. A political moderate and trucking company sales representative, Haggerty had much less money than Figueroa but ran a solid campaign centered on the "three strikes" crime legislation. Figueroa's campaign was also rocked by the revelation that she and her husband had had 25 liens placed on their home because of $250,000 in unpaid state and federal taxes over eight years. Figueroa said most of the debt had already been paid off. A former chairwoman of the Alameda County Democratic Party, she made education and the economy her campaign issues and has cast herself as a fiscal

Liz Figueroa

conservative. She pulled out a win in a year that was tough for Democrats everywhere — but the margin of victory was not overwhelming given the Democratic registration advantage.

PERSONAL: elected 1994; born Feb. 9, 1951, in San Francisco; home, Fremont; education, attended UC Berkeley, College of San Mateo and Marin Family Therapy Institute; husband Robert Bloom, two children; Roman Catholic.

CAREER: Owner of employment consulting firm; chairwoman of Alameda County Democratic Party; held a variety of counseling and human relations positions.

COMMITTEES: Environmental Safety & Toxic Materials (vice chair); Insurance; Judiciary; Public Employees, Retirement & Social Security.

OFFICES: Capitol, (916) 445-7874, FAX (916) 324-2936; district, 43271 Mission Blvd., Fremont 94539, (510) 440-9030, FAX (510) 440-9035.

TERM LIMIT: 2000
REGISTRATION: 50.0% D, 33.0% R

1994 CAMPAIGN:	Figueroa D	50.0%	$249,938
	Scott Haggerty R	43.1%	$54,153

RATINGS: Newly elected

Brooks Firestone (R)
35th Assembly District

Republicans have long believed that this Central Coast district, which includes Santa Barbara and Ventura, should be their property because of its less-than-decisive Democratic voter registration. But as long as Jack O'Connell held the district, it remained in the Democratic column because of his unsurpassed skills as a grass-roots campaigner.

The GOP got its chance in 1994, when O'Connell decided to run for the state

Senate — successfully, of course. The Republican candidate was Brooks Firestone, scion of the famous tiremaking family, who left the tire business in 1972 to start a cattle ranch and vineyard in the Santa Ynez Valley. His wines established themselves in the appropriate circles, and Firestone decided to turn some of his attention to politics. He made a first run for office in 1982 — and was defeated by O'Connell, then an unknown high school teacher.

Firestone's return to the game 12 years later bore happier results. He easily defeated Democrat Mindy Lorenz, who had previously been a member of the Green Party.

Brooks Firestone

PERSONAL: elected 1994; born June 17, 1936, in Akron, Ohio; home, Los Olivos; education, B.A. Columbia College; wife Kate, four children; Episcopal.

CAREER: Firestone Tire and Rubber Co., 1961-72; owner of Firestone Vineyard and San Antonio Ranch, 1972-present.

COMMITTEES: Higher Education (vice chair); Banking & Finance; Consumer Protection, Governmental Efficiency & Economic Development; Transportation.

OFFICES: Capitol, (916) 445-8292, FAX (916) 327-3518; district, 809 Presidio Ave., Santa Barbara 93101, (805) 965-1994, FAX (805) 965-2046.

TERM LIMIT: 2000

REGISTRATION: 46.7% D, 37.5% R

1994 CAMPAIGN:

Firestone R	54.3%	$826,686
Mindy Lorenz D	41.6%	$557,425

RATINGS: Newly elected

Barbara Friedman (D)
40th Assembly District

Los Angeles Democrat Barbara Friedman won a special election in 1991 only to find herself homeless eight months later in the wake of the 1992 reapportionment. A liberal Democrat with roots in the labor movement, Friedman came to the Assembly after defeating a conservative Republican, Geoffrey Church, in a special election for Mike Roos' seat in the old 46th District. Roos resigned from the Legislature to head a nonprofit group working for Los Angeles school system reforms.

In 1992, new district lines put Friedman in a strong Republican district that belonged to then-GOP lawmaker Patrick Nolan, a conservative from Glendale. The neighboring districts with strong Democratic numbers were staked out by incumbents Terry Friedman (no relation) and Burt Margolin, for whom Friedman had once worked as chief of staff. So, with no place else to go, Friedman was gearing up for a run against Nolan. Then, unexpectedly, veteran Assemblyman Tom Bane of Tarzana decided to quit after serving 24 years. The 78-year-old lawmaker's decision to step down probably saved a lot of grief for both Nolan and Friedman.

Nolan easily won re-election, though his political career came to a sensational end in February 1994, when he was sent to federal prison after pleading guilty to bribery charges stemming from the FBI's investigation into corruption at the Capitol.

Barbara Friedman

Friedman moved back to her childhood home in the San Fernando Valley where she easily outdistanced her Republican opponent. She scored another landslide in 1994, turning back GOP businessman Noel A. DeGaetano. Assembly Speaker Willie Brown gave Friedman some political help early on when he named her to the Assembly Insurance Committee, a juice committee so named because its members regularly squeeze big campaign contributions from industry lobbyists.

Friedman, who was a deputy Los Angeles city controller before running for the Assembly, has proven to be a strong supporter of women's issues. She authored AB 3436, which provided that inmates who show evidence of battered women's syndrome have that taken into account when their sentences are reviewed. Gov. Pete Wilson signed the legislation. Another Friedman bill, AB 478, placed an additional 2-cent tax on cigarettes to raise money for breast cancer research.

The 40th District includes the communities of Canoga Park and Woodland Hills, Van Nuys and North Hollywood.

PERSONAL: elected 1991; born, Sept. 1, 1949, in Los Angeles; home, North Hollywood; education, B.A. U.C. Berkeley; single, one child; Jewish.

CAREER: chief of staff to Assemblyman Burt Margolin, 1983-1985; assistant to district vice president, Communications Workers of America; assistant city controller, city of Los Angeles.

COMMITTEES: Agriculture; Appropriations; Education; Health (vice chair);

OFFICES: Capitol, (916) 445-7644, FAX (916) 323-8459; district, 13701 Riverside Dr., Suite. 600, Sherman Oaks 91423, (818) 783-1976, FAX (818) 783-2672.

TERM LIMIT: 1996

REGISTRATION: 56.2% D, 30.1% R

1994 CAMPAIGN:

Friedman D		57.9%	$212,614
Noel A. Degaetano R		29.4%	Not Available

1992 CAMPAIGN: Friedman D   57.8% $407,855
             Horace Heidt R   30.5% $74,337
RATINGS: AFL-CIO CLCV   NOW   CofC CalFarm   GO
          100   100   A-   14   0   F

Peter Frusetta (R)

28th Assembly District

When framers of the post-1980 census reapportionment created the 25th Assembly District, they
dubbed it the "Steinbeck seat" because it encom-
passed the agricultural areas featured in John Steinbeck
novels. The district straddled both sides of the coastal
range, encompassing San Benito County, Gilroy and
Morgan Hill in Santa Clara County, the Salinas area
in Monterey County and western Merced County,
including Los Banos. In 1992, reapportionment
changed the boundaries of the district, now renumbered 28, dropping its Merced County portion and
thus the Los Banos hometown of its Democratic
incumbent, Rusty Areias. The district also moved
northward into the San Jose suburbs in Santa Clara
County.

Peter Frusetta

But Areias, a wealthy dairy farmer first elected to the Assembly in 1982, had little
difficulty winning re-election in 1992. His Republican opponent was Peter Frusetta,
a Tres Pinos rancher, who used equine excrement to suggest that incumbent
politicians should be dumped from office. The race was marked by the Frusetta
campaign's charge that Areias was a drug user — a charge it was unable to
substantiate. At one forum, Frusetta challenged Areias to produce a urine sample;
Areias replied that he would if Frusetta would hold the bottle.

Areias, facing a 1996 term limit, decided to give up the seat in 1994 to make a
run for state controller. He placed third in the Democratic primary. Areias'
departure opened the door for Frusetta, who defeated two challengers in the GOP
primary to face Democrat Lily Cervantes, an attorney and coastal commissioner.
Democrats saw they had a strong candidate and a favorable registration edge and
figured they had a lock on the seat — particularly with a Latina candidate in a heavily
Latino district. State Republicans took their money and campaign assistance
elsewhere. But Frusetta, painting himself as a "citizen representative," ran a
campaign focused on the issues that defined the election — public safety, illegal
immigration, less government — and eked out a narrow victory.

Frusetta's ranching background and personal style — he routinely wears a
cowboy hat and neckerchief around the Capitol — fit closely with the orientation

of his agricultural district. But the power politics of the Legislature could be a rude awakening for a man who admitted in an early session interview that he was "used to working with things — cattle, fences, motorcycles — not people." Registration numbers in the district assure that he'll be a prime Democratic target in 1996.

PERSONAL: elected 1994; born July 6, 1932, in Tres Pinos; home, Tres Pinos; Army; education, B.A. Stanford University; wife Anita, four children; Christian.

CAREER: Manager of ranch in San Benito County; director of the San Benito County Farm Bureau; Board of Directors, Tres Pinos Water District; published two books on local history.

COMMITTEES: Water, Parks & Wildlife (vice chair); Agriculture; Environmental Safety & Toxic Materials; Labor & Employment.

OFFICES: Capitol, (916) 445-7380, FAX (916) 324-0986; district, 321 First St., A, Hollister 95023, (408) 636-4890, FAX (408) 636-4903.

TERM LIMIT: 2000

REGISTRATION: 52.7% D, 33.3% R

1994 CAMPAIGN:			
Frusetta R	50.2%	$161,669
Lily Cervantes D	49.8%	$396,309

RATINGS: Newly elected

Martin Gallegos (D)
57th Assembly District

Martin Gallegos is the second Latino politician to represent this chunk of the San Gabriel Valley — including El Monte, Baldwin Park, La Puente and Azusa — since the state Supreme Court issued a 1992 reapportionment plan that was drawn to comply federal Voting Rights Act requirements to maximize political opportunities for minorities. The first was Hilda Solis, who won the seat in a tug-of-war between two rival groups of Latino politicians.

Backed by a faction headed by Los Angeles County Supervisor Gloria Molina, Solis pushed by a Democratic primary foe who was supported by Los Angeles City Councilman Richard Alatorre and former state Sen. Art Torres. But, after one term in the Assembly, Solis ran for the seat Torres vacated in the

Martin Gallegos

Senate and won. In 1994, she passed her Assembly district baton to Gallegos, a Baldwin Park city councilman who faced a tough primary battle of his own. His chief rival for the Democratic nomination, Tony Fellows, had the backing of the area's former Assembly member, Sally Tanner. With Solis' help, and the district's strong Latino population, Gallegos emerged victorious. His general election race against Republican Frank Yik was nothing more than an afterthought given the district's high numbers of Democratic voters.

A four-year city councilman, Gallegos has an extensive background in civic service. In 1992, the Senate Rules Committee appointed him to the Senate's Task Force on Medical Cost Containment in Workers' Compensation. He is also a commissioner to the state Board of Chiropractic Examiners.

PERSONAL: elected 1994; born Nov. 3, 1956, in Los Angeles; home, Baldwin Park; education, B.S. Occidental College; doctorate in chiropractic, Los Angeles College of Chiropractic; wife, Rita; Catholic.

CAREER: chiropractor; chairman of chiropractic service, Doctors Hospital in West Covina; board of directors, Terrace Plaza Medical Center in Baldwin Park.

COMMITTEES: Banking & Finance; Elections, Reapportionment, & Constitutional Amendments (vice chair); Health; Labor & Employment.

OFFICES: Capitol, (916) 445-7610, FAX (916) 327-9696; district, 218 N. Glendora Ave., D, La Puente 91744, (818) 369-3551, FAX (818) 369-2861.

TERM LIMIT: 2000

REGISTRATION: 57% D, 30.1% R

1994 CAMPAIGN:

Gallegos D	61.6%	$210,615
Frank Yik R	34.0%	$13,445

RATINGS: Newly elected

Jan Goldsmith (R)

75th Assembly District

The 75th District is another in the string of Republican-dominated districts in San Diego and Orange counties. This San Diego County district borders Imperial County on the east. It includes the northern portion of the city of San Diego and also takes in Santee, Poway, Ramona and the desert around Borrego Springs. More than 80 percent of the residents are white.

Jan Goldsmith, former mayor of Poway, was Gov. Pete Wilson's pick for the Assembly seat, and Goldsmith turned out to be one of the few winners among Wilson-backed candidates around the state in 1992. He defeated anti-abortion activist Connie Youngkin in a tough primary battle, then easily

Jan Goldsmith

defeated Democrat Dante Cosentino in the general election. Goldsmith faced no primary challengers in 1994 and trampled his Democratic opponent, Katherine Wodehouse, in the general election.

Shortly after his 1992 election, Goldsmith's first name resulted in a couple of cases of mistaken gender. The California office of the National Organization for Women and Assembly Democratic floor leader Tom Hannigan of Fairfield both counted Goldsmith among the new women legislators. Then, when Goldsmith received his official stationery he discovered that his letterhead said: Jan Goldsmith. Assemblywoman 75th District. "I'm cheap," he told a reporter. "I'll just cross out the 'wo.'"

Goldsmith was less amused by the ritual political labeling that is part of Capitol politics. He complained that every time he saw his name it was next to the word moderate or Wilsonite. "They don't know what I've done in Poway. They haven't the faintest idea how I'm going to react here," Goldsmith complained.

Indeed, the Republican lawmaker marked his own path in his first term — and its turned out to be one lonely road. After earning the enmity of GOP conservatives with his first election win, Goldsmith found himself at odds with Wilson and legislative leaders in both parties less than a year later when he refused to vote for the budget agreement they had forged. With his highly publicized campaign to stop Mexican children from walking across the border to attend U.S. schools in the San Diego region, Goldsmith also incurred the wrath of Latino rights activists and their allies in the Legislature. Therefore, it came as no surprise to many that a subsequent media-genic campaign of Goldsmith's — one to legalize ferrets as pets in California — generated little enthusiasm from other lawmakers.

PERSONAL: elected 1992; born Jan. 26, 1951, in New Rochelle, N.Y.; home, Poway; education, B.A. American University in Washington D.C., J.D. University of San Diego; wife Christine, three children; Presbyterian.

CAREER: congressional intern, 1970-72; lawyer/businessman 1976-1988; Poway City Council, 1988-90; professional arbitrator and mediator, 1981-1992; adjunct instructor, negotiation and mediation, University of San Diego School of Law, 1987-1989; judge pro-tem San Diego courts; mayor, city of Poway, 1990-92.

COMMITTEES: Appropriations; Labor & Employment; Local Government; Rules; Transportation.

OFFICES: Capitol, (916) 445-2484, FAX (916) 324-2782; district 12307 Oak Knoll, A, Poway 92064, (619) 486-5191, FAX (619) 486-3334.

TERM LIMIT: 1998

REGISTRATION: 31.1% D, 51.9% R

1994 CAMPAIGN:	Goldsmith R	70.0%	Not Available
	Katherine Wodehouse D	23.9%	Not Available
1992 CAMPAIGN:	Goldsmith R	64.5%	$469,192
	Dante Cosentino D	27.1%	$8,640

| **RATINGS**: | AFL-CIO | CLCV | NOW | CofC | CalFarm | GO |
| | 9 | 25 | C | 95 | 55.5 | A |

Brett Granlund (R)
65th Assembly District

This San Bernardino County district includes Redlands, Yucaipa, Big Bear and Twenty-Nine Palms. Nearly two-thirds of the district's voters reside in fast-growing communities of Riverside County. The area is mostly white and decidedly Republican.

Brett Granlund

When the districts' GOP incumbent, Paul Woodruff, decided not to seek re-election in 1994, his announcement touched off a free-for-all among seven would-be Republican successors. Brett Granlund, a two-year member of the Yucaipa City Council, won the primary and easily went on to defeat the Democratic standard-bearer, Richard Sandoval.

A resident of the district for 35 years, Granlund possesses the conservative credentials to match his rural district's political profile. An avid outdoorsman, he is a member of the National Rifle Association and was endorsed in his campaign by the Building Industry Association and other pro-business groups. He and his wife, Lonni, have been small business owners since 1974 when they bought Oak Glen Candies. In 1976, they founded Granlund's Candies. Both operations were sold in 1991. Currently, Granlund owns the Crilco Outdoor Advertising Company. At the time of his election, he was also employed by Young Electric Signs Co. of Ontario.

PERSONAL: elected 1994; born May 28, 1954, in Helena, Mont.; home, Yucaipa; education, Yucaipa High School; wife, Lonni; two children; Methodist.

CAREER: Owner, candy companies and later an outdoor advertising company; employee, Young Electric Sign Co.; Yucaipa City Council, 1992-1994.

COMMITTEES: Health; Human Services (chair); Local Government; Transportation.

OFFICES: Capitol, (916) 445-7552, FAX (916) 445-7650; district, 34923 Yucaipa Blvd., Yucaipa, 92399, (909) 790-4196, FAX 790-0478.

TERM LIMIT: 2000

REGISTRATION: 40.7% D, 47% R

1994 CAMPAIGN:			
Granlund R	63.13%	$234,137
Richard D. Sandoval D	36.8%	$13,164

RATINGS: Newly elected

Thomas M. Hannigan (D)
8th Assembly District

The 8th Assembly District contains most of Solano County and portions of Yolo and Sacramento counties, where former Realtor Tom Hannigan has developed a reputation as a thoughtful, honest and hard-working legislator since he was elected to the Assembly in 1978.

Hannigan began his political career in local government, serving as mayor of Fairfield and later as chairman of the Solano County Board of Supervisors. Accordingly, Hannigan has shown interest in trying to help solve local government funding problems. He was among the early legislators who suggested Proposition 13 and the state's spending limits needed adjusting. He has proposed giving counties more money to encourage preservation of agricultural lands under the Williamson Act. Hannigan also has been acutely aware of his district's changing nature, backing, for instance, expanded rail service between Roseville and San Jose on a line that runs through his district.

Thomas Hannigan

For most of his Assembly career, Hannigan has been recognized as an expert in tax and financial matters, serving a stint as chairman of the Assembly Revenue and Taxation Committee. In 1986, Hannigan set in motion a move to reform the state income tax. The following year, however, Hannigan relinquished control over the committee when Speaker Willie Brown named him to replace Mike Roos of Los Angeles as the Democrats' majority leader, one of the top leadership posts. At the time, Democrats were suffering from charges that they were putting politics over policy. Hannigan had a reputation for being more interested in issues than backroom maneuvering and campaign strategy. Since then, there has been some indication that part of Brown's naming of Hannigan to the post was aimed more at image polishing than substantive reform. In fact, much of the overtly political work of raising money and getting candidates elected was shifted to others.

Still, Hannigan's reputation has remained intact. He is considered among the straight-arrows in the Capitol. He told the speaker to back off from his effort to help a law client, Norcal Solid Waste Systems Inc., to site a garbage transfer station in Solano County. Brown's role in the episode became the subject of an FBI probe.

Hannigan faces a 1996 term limit in the Assembly. The state Senate seat in his area, now held by Republican Maurice Johannessen of Redding, was up for election in 1994, but Hannigan did not make a try for it. He faced a fairly strong challenge for re-election to his Assembly seat from Republican Bryant Stocking, but ended up winning by a 10-point margin.

PERSONAL: elected 1978; born May 30, 1940, in Vallejo; home, Fairfield; USMC 1963-1966 (Vietnam); education, B.S. University of Santa Clara; wife, Jan Mape, three children; Roman Catholic.

CAREER: Fairfield City Council, 1970-'72; mayor, 1972-'74; Solano County Board of Supervisors, 1974-'78; owner and broker of Hannigan & O'Neill Realtors.

COMMITTEES: Banking & Finance; Budget; Local Government; Revenue & Taxation.
OFFICES: Capitol, (916) 445-8368, FAX (916) 327-9667; district, 844-A Union Ave., Fairfield 94533, (707) 429-2383, FAX (707) 429-1502.
TERM LIMIT: 1996
REGISTRATION: 52.8% D, 32.9% R

1994 CAMPAIGN:	Hannigan D		55.3%	$172,112
	Bryant Stocking R		44.7%	$197,403
1992 CAMPAIGN:	Hannigan D		57.5%	$663,910
	John Ford R		36.7%	$7,375

RATINGS:	AFL-CIO	CLCV	NOW	CofC	CalFarm	GO
	96	81	A-	27	44	D

Trice J. Harvey (R)
32nd Assembly District

The 32nd Assembly District is shaped by the rules of the federal Voting Rights Act, which required changes to protect the voting potential of minorities. The district includes southeastern Tulare County and a chunk of northern Kern County; it includes all of Porterville, a piece of Visalia and most of Bakersfield. The chief industries are agriculture and oil, and the district's politics are steadfastly conservative. Latinos, who comprise 20 percent of the population, often vote Republican here.

Trice Harvey, first elected to the Assembly in 1986, easily won re-election in 1994 over his Democratic opponent, Jack Keally, a retired teacher. Harvey is a reliable vote for the conservative Republican

Trice Harvey

agenda in the Assembly, but he has not always been on good terms with his own caucus. In 1986, Harvey, then a Kern County supervisor, was the anointed GOP candidate for the Assembly to replace Don Rogers, who had been elected to the Senate. Harvey had been endorsed by virtually all local GOP leaders when then-Assembly Republican leader Pat Nolan abruptly turned against Harvey and backed his rival in the primary, apparently because of Harvey's friendship with Rep. Bill Thomas, a bitter rival of Nolan. But Harvey was able to beat Nolan's candidate, Anna Allen.

In the Assembly, Harvey has concentrated largely on district issues. He and Rogers are the two staunchest defenders of the oil industry in the Legislature, voting against all environmental regulation affecting the industry — sometimes long after the oil industry has agreed to a compromise. Harvey is not against all environmental legislation, however. He has pushed efforts to limit importation of hazardous wastes into his district, a sensitive local issue. His bill to expand state efforts to learn the cause of high cancer rates among children in the city of McFarland was vetoed by then-Gov. George Deukmejian, who said it duplicated existing efforts.

Harvey also has been among those who advocate special-tax treatment for pet projects. He won passage of a bill giving the artist Cristo a sales tax break for purchasing materials to construct an art project consisting of sculptured yellow umbrellas along Interstate 5. Deukmejian vetoed it. Harvey has fought unsuccessfully several times, most recently in 1994, to give ostrich breeders a sales tax exemption. He pursued some broader legislation in the 1993-94 session as well, including bills to lengthen jail time for drunk drivers who injure someone and to prohibit registered sex offenders from volunteering at public schools. When the GOP got control of half the committees in the 1995-96 session, Harvey was a logical pick to chair Agriculture.

A native of Arkansas, Harvey still speaks with a southern twang and is known as one of the gabbiest members of the Legislature. His mouth sometimes gets him into trouble, however. One such time was during the Assembly speakership fight in December 1994. Harvey, upon learning that Assemblyman Paul Horcher had changed his party affiliation from Republican to independent and cast his vote for Willie Brown, denounced Horcher as a "political whore" who was "bought fair and square" by Brown. He at first resisted calls for an apology — saying, "I'm sorry he's a whore" — but ultimately apologized.

In 1993, Harvey was accused of sexual harassment by a former secretary. The Rules Committee, which hired two law firms to defend Harvey, eventually agreed to give the victim a cash settlement. But as part of the agreement, she had to agree that terms of the settlement would be sealed, so the taxpayers may never know how much the settlement cost them. Harvey faces his Assembly term limit in 1996, two years before the state Senate seat held by Republican leader Ken Maddy is due to open up.

PERSONAL: elected 1986; born July 15, 1936, in Paragould, Ark.; home, Bakersfield; B.A. CSU Fresno; wife Jacqueline Stussy, two children; Mormon.

CAREER: County health sanitarian; pharmaceutical salesman; school board member; Kern County Board of Supervisors 1976-1986.

COMMITTEES: Agriculture (chair); Budget; Governmental Organization; Public Employees, Retirement & Social Security.

OFFICES: Capitol, (916) 445-8498, FAX (916) 324-4696; district, 100 W. Columbus, 201, Bakersfield 93301, (805) 324-3300, FAX (805) 395-3883.

TERM LIMIT: 1996

REGISTRATION: 41.0% D, 48.6% R

1994 CAMPAIGN:			
Harvey R		70.5%	$275,867
Jack Keally D		29.5%	$8,647

1992 CAMPAIGN: Harvey R   65.5% $447,233
           Irma Carson D   31.7% $18,434

RATINGS:	AFL-CIO	CLCV	NOW	CofC	CalFarm	GO
	9	5	C-	100	67	A

Daniel E. Hauser (D)
1st Assembly District

California's northwestern coast is so thinly populated that one state Assembly district stretches nearly
300 miles southward from the Oregon border. The
area once voted Republican with some regularity, but
as the traditional industries of lumber and fishing
have faded, and as flower children of the 1960s
moved in and established roots, the politics of the
area have crept leftward.

The 1st Assembly District covers all or parts of
Del Norte, Humboldt, Mendocino, Lake and Sonoma
counties. Since 1982, the region's assemblyman has
been Dan Hauser, a onetime insurance adjuster and
mayor of Arcata who is serving his seventh and final
term in the Assembly. Hauser has chaired the Assem-

Dan Hauser

bly Housing Committee and labored to produce a stream of housing bills, but he
occupies much of his time trying to avoid being chewed up by the ceaseless
environmental controversies that buffet his scenic and resource-rich district.
Environmentalists and logging and mining companies battle endlessly over laws
and regulations in the region.

Hauser came into office as a Sierra Club candidate, but in more recent years he
has gravitated toward the timber industry. Matters came to a head in 1989, when an
environmentalist-sponsored bill to put a three-year moratorium on logging old-
growth forests came to the Assembly floor. Hauser successfully offered industry-
supported amendments that gutted the bill. The bill then died. That and other events
have driven a wedge between Hauser and the more militant environmentalists. But
he won re-election handily in 1992 over Humboldt County Supervisor Anna Sparks,
known locally as "Chainsaw Annie" for her connections with the timber industry.

Just two days after the 1992 election, Hauser announced he would mount a
special-election campaign for the 2nd Senate District seat being vacated by Barry
Keene of Ukiah. But he later backed away, anticipating a run for the seat by Sen.
Mike Thompson, D-St. Helena, who ended up narrowly winning. Hauser easily won
re-election to his Assembly seat in 1994, defeating Mendocino County GOP
Chairman John Baird, but Hauser's future is unclear. Term limits mean Thompson
will vacate his Senate seat no later than 1998, but that's two years after Hauser's own

term limit — and the same year that the 2nd Senate District's other Assembly member, Democrat Valerie Brown of Sonoma, may be looking to move up as well.

PERSONAL: elected 1982; born June 18, 1942, in Riverside; home, Arcata; education, B.A. Humboldt State University; wife Donna Dumont, two children; Lutheran.

CAREER: insurance claims representative; Arcata City Council, 1974-1978; mayor, 1978-1982.

COMMITTEES: Housing & Community Development (chair); Governmental Organization; Transportation; Water, Parks & Wildlife.

OFFICES: Capitol, (916) 445-8360, FAX (916) 322-5214; district, 510 O St., G, Eureka 95501, (707) 445-7014, FAX (707) 445-6607.

TERM LIMIT: 1996

REGISTRATION: 53.0% D, 31.3% R, 2.2% Green

1994 CAMPAIGN:	Hauser D		61.3%	$101,158
	John Baird R		33.6%	$8,874
1992 CAMPAIGN:	Hauser D		57.2%	$663,822
	Anna Sparks R		34.5%	$440,310

RATINGS:	AFL-CIO	CLCV	NOW	CofC	CalFarm	GO
	95	88	A-	23	56	B-

Phil Hawkins (R)
56th Assembly District

Reapportionment, when done by an impartial party such as the state Supreme Court, is supposed to create more truly competitive districts than would be drawn by partisan lawmakers. But that didn't prove to be the case in 1992. The court's remap of districts eliminated all but a handful of the districts where no party had a distinct advantage. The 56th is one of the few competitive districts that remain.

In 1988, Norwalk attorney Robert Epple was the surprise winner in this district. Democrat Epple didn't win by much — 220 votes — but his defeat of incumbent Wayne Grisham helped solidify the Democrats' majority in the Assembly. The court-ordered reapportionment in 1992 fiddled with boundaries of

Phil Hawkins

the district a bit and changed its number (from 63 to 56), but it was left without a clear partisan edge — a fact demonstrated in the 1992 elections, when once again Epple won by the narrowest of margins, fewer than 500 votes over Republican Phillip Hawkins out of more than 130,000 ballots cast.

The 56th District is comprised mainly of blue-collar communities, such as

Downey, sprawled along Los Angeles County's southern border communities that were built to house workers in nearby aerospace plants. In recent years, the area has developed large middle-class Asian and Latino populations — nearly 40 percent in the 56th District. But Democrats here are conservative to moderate, and they often vote Republican.

Given the uncertain partisan nature of his district and his extremely narrow vote margins, Epple tried to walk the line carefully. But his chairmanship of the Public Safety Committee, meant to bolster his crime-fighting credentials, backfired because the committee, carefully stocked with liberals by the Democratic hierarchy, often stalled the toughest crime measures — such as the original version of the "three strikes and you're out" law. Republicans sensed Epple could be had in 1994 and poured resources into the return campaign of Hawkins. That led to an 10-point victory for Hawkins, a real estate broker who portrayed Epple as soft on crime and too close to Speaker Willie Brown.

PERSONAL: elected 1994; born June 11, 1943, in Columbia, Mo.; home, Cerritos; education, Bellflower High School; wife Janice, two children; no stated religious affiliation.

CAREER: real estate broker and general contractor.

COMMITTEES: Housing & Community Development (vice chair); Budget; Governmental Organization; Utilities & Commerce.

OFFICES: Capitol, (916) 445-6047, FAX (916) 327-1784; district, 17100 Pioneer Blvd., 290, Artesia 90701, (310) 809-0010, FAX (310) 809-5719.

TERM LIMIT: 2000

REGISTRATION: 50.9% D, 37.5% R

1994 CAMPAIGN:	Hawkins R	53.5%	$524,079
	Bob Epple (incumbent) D	43.2%	$626,113

RATINGS: Newly elected

William Hoge (R)
44th Assembly District

The suburban homelands of the 44th Assembly District, which includes Pasadena and other communities along the foothills of the San Gabriel Mountains, is considered Republican territory despite the Democrats' slight registration edge. In 1992, the district was the site of one of many clashes between moderate and conservative GOP factions. Ten Republicans ran for the seat, but the major battle was between Pasadena insurance man and civic leader William Hoge, backed by the right, and Barbara Peiper, the choice of Gov. Pete Wilson. Hoge topped the field, and with a stronger turnout of GOP voters, Democrats never had a chance to exploit the Republican division.

Thus, Hoge came to the Legislature with a vow to rid our personal and business lives of government bureaucracy and regulation. In his first two years at the Capitol, however, he has distinguished himself more for his fund-raising prowess. Collecting close to $300,000 in political contributions, Hoge ranked as the freshman class' top fund-raiser. The money served him well in his 1994 re-election bid.

In an election season that ranked crime as a top issue, Democrats hoped to seize Hoge's seat through the candidacy of former Pasadena Police Chief Bruce Philpott. It was a mud-smeared race. Hoge resurrected a 1990 incident in which Philpott, stopped by a cop in Glendale, allegedly berated the officer. In turn, Philpott attacked Hoge for his political contributions from the state's gambling industry and, in the weekend before the election, distributed a letter from

William Hoge

Hoge's ex-wife suggesting the Republican incumbent was addicted to gambling. The charges seemed to matter little to district voters. Hoge easily won a second term.

PERSONAL: elected 1992; born April 2, 1946, in Pasadena; home, Pasadena; attended Pasadena City College; wife Claudette, three children; Protestant.

CAREER: president, Insurance Communicators.

COMMITTEES: Agriculture; Elections, Reapportionment & Constitutional Amendments; Governmental Organization (vice chair); Insurance.

OFFICES: Capitol, (916) 445-8211, FAX (916) 323-9420; district, 1276 E. Colorado Blvd., 203, Pasadena 91106, (818) 577-4470, FAX (818) 577-0614.

TERM LIMIT: 1998

REGISTRATION: 44.9% D, 42.6% R

1994 CAMPAIGN:	Hoge R	53.3%	$661,503
	Bruce Philpott D	41.8%	$379,540
1992 CAMPAIGN:	Hoge R	51.8%	$383,448
	Jonathan Fuhrman D	43.9%	$13,486

RATINGS:	AFL-CIO	CLCV	NOW	CofC	CalFarm	GO
	4	5	C-	95	66.6	A

Paul V. Horcher (independent)
60th Assembly District

When Republicans won 41 of the Assembly's 80 seats in the November 1994 elections, GOP lawmakers were poised to take control of the house and elect their leader, Jim Brulte, as the new speaker. That all changed when Assemblyman Paul Horcher broke ranks with the Republican Party, declared himself an independent and cast his speakership vote for Democrat Willie Brown. In statements released to the public, Horcher said his action would allow him to be "free of political party bosses and better able to fight for my constituents."

Others said Horcher was motivated by revenge. His vote — resulting in a stand-off between Republicans and Democrats in the Assembly that eventually led to Brown's re-election as speaker — denied Brulte and his party the rewards they thought they had won in the fall campaign. It also signaled Horcher's loss of any hope that he could ever find forgiveness within the GOP.

Paul Horcher

The Whittier lawmaker had sparked the wrath of the Assembly Republican caucus at the beginning of 1993 legislative session, when he accepted the vice-chairmanship of the influential Ways and Means Committee, a post offered to him by Brown. Brulte and other Republicans had selected then-GOP Assemblyman Dean Andal of Stockton for the job. They accused Horcher of kissing up to Brown rather than standing with the caucus on a partisan squabble. From then on, Horcher was persona non grata among Republicans.

Hostilities lingered until the day Horcher cast his vote for Brown, when it exploded into a firestorm of heated rhetoric. "We had one political whore today and it happened to be a Republican, and he was bought fair and square by the speaker [Brown]," GOP Assemblyman Trice Harvey of Bakersfield said on the Assembly floor. His remark touched on a rumor that Horcher had sided with Brown because the powerful Democrat was in a position to help him pay off old campaign debts. Horcher insisted that Brown made him no promises in exchange for his vote. In his written remarks, he lashed back at his former GOP colleagues, asserting: "The right wing of the Republican Party is in control of the Assembly Republican caucus. They abandoned Gov. Wilson on every single budget vote. They tried to block my position on the budget committee, and they have worked to freeze my district out of the legislative process."

Horcher was a pivotal vote for Wilson on budget matters in years past, but the lawmaker's attempt to align himself with the moderate Republican governor was met with a rebuff. Wilson wouldn't even return his phone calls. A recall drive against Horcher was launched within days of the speakership vote, and Wilson's political committee jumped on the bandwagon, sending out recall petitions to voters in Horcher's San Gabriel Valley district. The GOP leadership's intention was to replace Horcher with a Republican who would give them the 41st vote they needed to elect the speaker of their choice. Meanwhile, Brown and some of his biggest financial contributors co-hosted a fund-raiser for Horcher to help him fight off the recall effort.

Even before he accepted the Ways and Means Committee post in 1993, Horcher was at odds with his fellow Republicans. Friendly with the California Trial Lawyers Association, an important source of Democratic campaign funds, Horcher first won election to the Assembly in 1990 by moving to the left, including a reversal on state-paid abortions, when he faced an anti-abortion opponent in the GOP primary.

In the general election that year, two closely-knit groups of Republicans opposed him. One campaigned directly for Horcher's Democratic opponent, Gary Neely, while the other group asked Republicans to refrain from voting for Horcher because of his abortion stance. But Horcher outspent Neely in spades in what was then the 52nd Assembly District and won the race easily. In 1994, Horcher attempted to move to the Senate by running in a special election to fill a vacancy left by Republican Frank Hill, who resigned his post after being convicted of corruption charges in federal court. Horcher lost the race to GOP Assemblyman Richard Mountjoy, who's campaign coffers were filled with donations from the Assembly GOP caucus members.

PERSONAL: elected 1990; born Aug. 31, 1951, in Veasco, Texas; home, Diamond Bar; education, B.A. California Polytechnic University, Pomona, 1974; J.D. La Verne University, 1978; wife Van Le, two children; Presbyterian.

CAREER: lawyer; real estate broker; Diamond Bar City Council.

COMMITTEES: Appropriations; Governmental Organization (chair); Insurance; Labor & Employment; Natural Resources.

OFFICES: Capitol, (916) 445-7550, FAX (916) 324-6973; district, 325 N. Azusa Ave., West Covina 91791, (818) 967-5299, FAX (818) 967-8949.

TERM LIMIT: 1996

REGISTRATION: 43.5% D, 43.3% R

1994 CAMPAIGN:	Horcher R		61.5%	$323,290
	Andrew M. Ramirez D		32.6%	$4,245
1992 CAMPAIGN:	Horcher R		55.7%	$500,952
	Stan Caress D		36.6%	$3,320

RATINGS:	AFL-CIO	CLCV	NOW	CofC	CalFarm	GO
	10	9	C	86	88.8	A

George House (R)
25th Assembly District

The 25th District represents two of the dominant trends of legislative politics in the 1990s — the shift of power away from coastal metropolitan areas into the fast-growing fringe suburbs in interior valleys, and the struggle for dominance within the Republican Party between its right-wing and moderate factions.

This new district, centered in Modesto and reaching into several other San Joaquin Valley counties, was one of the reasons Republicans refused to make a reapportionment deal with Democrats following the 1990 census and threw the issue to the courts. A shift of seats from the cities to the new suburbs, they believed, would give them a better chance of taking legislative control.

The state Supreme Court, in creating the 25th and a flock of other new districts in 1992, gave the Republicans the chance they had long sought. But the changes also renewed internecine warfare among Republicans. In the 25th, the 1992 elections saw right-wing Republican Barbara Keating-Edh defeat five rivals in the GOP primary — then narrowly lose to Democrat Margaret Snyder, a more moderate and pro-choice local school board member.

George House

As a legislator, Snyder tried to align herself with the increasingly conservative orientation of her district. She authored a number of anti-crime bills as well as a successful resolution limiting the number of bills each Assembly member could introduce in a given year. And when the 1994 election came around, Snyder initially appeared headed for re-election, having drawn an opponent who raised little money and was hardly visible as a campaigner.

But a late infusion of money from Republican leaders, who suddenly saw control of the Assembly within their grasp, gave the victory to conservative George House, a Hughson almond farmer and former California Highway Patrol commander. House, a folksy and gentlemanly Oklahoma native, campaigned on a platform of scaled-back government and traditional family values.

PERSONAL: elected 1994; born Nov. 20, 1929, in Indianola, Okla.; home, Hughson; education, B.A. Fresno State University; wife Edna, five children; Protestant.

CAREER: Retired California Highway Patrol area commander; juvenile traffic hearing officer for Stanislaus County Superior Court; trustee, Hughson Union High School board; almond farmer.

COMMITTEES: Labor & Employment (vice chair); Environmental Safety & Toxic Materials; Judiciary; Utilities & Commerce.

OFFICES: Capitol, (916) 445-7906, FAX (916) 445-7344; district, 3600 Sisk Road, Suite 5-D3, Modesto 95356, (209) 549-1041, FAX (209) 549-1045.

TERM LIMIT: 2000
REGISTRATION: 47.5% D, 41.8% R
1994 CAMPAIGN: House R   65.4% $223,372
                     Margaret Snyder (incumbent) D   32.6% $381,207
RATINGS: Newly elected

Phillip L. Isenberg (D)
9th Assembly District

There was a time when Phillip Isenberg, the former mayor of Sacramento, was on the short list of Capitol candidates to succeed Assembly Speaker Willie Brown.

But — barring another bizarre turn of events in the Assembly leadership saga — term limits appear to have cut off that option for Isenberg, who survived a 1992 reapportionment that put him and Lloyd Connelly, two veteran Sacramento assemblymen, into a single district. Connelly quit the Assembly and successfully ran for a Sacramento County Superior Court judgeship instead, leaving Isenberg to continue his efforts to carve out a role for himself as a budget bridge-builder at the Capitol.

Isenberg first won his seat in a 1982 landslide after the district was tailored to his needs by friendly Democrats. His toughest re-election race came in 1988, when his Republican opponent tried to paint

Phil Isenberg

him as soft on crime and too close to liberal Speaker Brown, who has served as something of a mentor to Isenberg. The assemblyman remains a top lieutenant to Brown, who gave him his first job as a lawyer and for whom he once served as chief of staff to the Ways and Means Committee. Isenberg also has become one of the Democrats' top political strategists and intellectual anchors.

Isenberg can be charming and witty or arrogant, dogmatic and just plain grumpy. And while other politicians might prefer splashy headlines, Isenberg seems to relish the nuts and bolts of the government process. He is a political insider, knows the parliamentary rules and is adept at quietly maneuvering behind the scenes.

In 1989, Isenberg pushed through a new law to provide a state-subsidized health insurance program for Californians with pre-existing illnesses who would otherwise be uninsurable. He also played key roles in negotiating compromises on how to spend money from the state's tobacco tax and in the 50-year-old dispute over water diversions from Mono Lake. More recently, Isenberg has been involved in a controversial effort to license and regulate the state's burgeoning card-room industry and another effort to monitor how health insurance giant Blue Cross has been converting its assets to charitable uses after becoming a for-profit operation. On a less rancorous matter, he authored a successful resolution banning smoking in the Capitol.

But Isenberg is perhaps best known in government circles as an increasingly vocal critic of state's budgeting practices. The 1994-95 budget agreement drew particular heat from Isenberg, who called it a "nonsense practice" to put off tough decisions while relying on large-scale borrowing and unrealistic assumptions about federal reimbursement for services to undocumented immigrants. He has been a leading advocate of proposals for a balanced budget amendment and a simple majority vote for legislative passage of the budget.

Although he represents a heavily Democratic district, Isenberg avoids knee-jerk criticism of Republican Gov. Pete Wilson and increasingly sounds like a member of the GOP as he discusses the need to scale back government in a lean budgetary environment. He was named in 1994 to serve on a nonpartisan commission studying ways to revise the state constitution, a complicated task that involves untangling webs of budgetary, governance and tax structures.

Term limits force Isenberg to leave the house in 1996. There had been speculation at one point that Leroy Greene might not seek re-election to his state Senate seat in 1994, creating a ready-made home for Isenberg in the upper house. But Greene ran and won a final term, leaving Isenberg one of those legislators whose future appears to have been left up in the air by term limits. Friends say he'll probably try to follow Connelly to the bench.

PERSONAL: elected 1982; born Feb. 25, 1939, in Gary Ind.; home, Sacramento; Army 1962-68; education, B.A. CSU Sacramento, J.D. UC Berkeley; wife Marilyn.

CAREER: lawyer; aide to Assemblyman Willie Brown 1967-68; Ways & Means Committee consultant 1971; Sacramento City Council 1971-75; mayor 1975-82.

COMMITTEES: Judiciary (chair); Banking & Finance; Consumer Protection, Governmental Efficiency & Economic Development; Revenue & Taxation.

OFFICES: Capitol, (916) 445-1611; district, 1215 - 15th St., 102, Sacramento 95814, (916) 324-4676, FAX (916) 322-1239.

TERM LIMIT: 1996
REGISTRATION: 65.1% D, 23.9% R

1994 CAMPAIGN:	Isenberg D	70.0%	$89,870
	Beth Lofton R	30.0%	$3,706
1992 CAMPAIGN:	Isenberg D	66.0%	$749,640
	David Reade R	26.8%	$4,674

RATINGS:	AFL-CIO	CLCV	NOW	CofC	CalFarm	GO
	97	75	B+	18	11	F

J. Ross Johnson (R)
72nd Assembly District

The 72nd Assembly District is in the heart of northern Orange County, covering such communities as Fullerton, Placentia and Yorba Linda. Redistricting slightly altered the lines of the old 64th District, but it remains similar in makeup and, more important, continues to be a Republican stronghold with a 55 percent GOP registration to 33 percent Democratic.

Ross Johnson, who has represented the old 64th District since 1978, is something of an enigma. With a political intelligence that sometimes borders on brilliance, Johnson seemed well-suited to his role as the Assembly's Republican leader. But lurking just beneath the surface of his public personality is an anger that boils up, rendering Johnson virtually incoherent with rage — a trait that leads some Democrats to bait him in public.

During the speakership fight in January 1995, Johnson shoved a sergeant-at-arms. In the middle of the tense budget debate in the summer of 1992, Johnson lunged at another GOP member, Charles Quackenbush, who had voted in opposition to Johnson on a highly contentious school-aid bill. The two had to be separated by a sergeant-at-arms. Earlier that year as the budget debates heated up, Johnson said, referring to his successor as GOP leader, Bill Jones of Fresno: "He's a tower of Jell-O. He's got all the backbone of a chocolate eclair."

Ross Johnson

Johnson lost the Republican leader's job to Jones in July 1991 after the Republican Party took a public relations beating during the state budget fight. Gov. Wilson sent caucus members not-so-subtle signals about his displeasure with Johnson and let it be known he thought highly of Jones, who promised to represent the governor's positions on the floor.

But Jones only lasted through the 1992 elections, when Republicans lost seats, and was replaced by Jim Brulte. It was clear from the start that Brulte had a tenuous hold on his caucus. The growing conservative faction was firmly in control and by the time of the 1994-95 speakership fight with Willie Brown, it was clear that Johnson was again calling the shots. He torpedoed Brulte's attempt to work out a power-sharing plan and inadvertently helped Brown solidify his support by threatening Democrats with recalls. He "made the mistake of assaulting politically all the Democrats they wish to work with," said Assemblyman Phil Isenberg, D-Sacramento.

Johnson, an attorney who was active in local civic affairs prior to embarking on a political career, was part of the huge class of Republicans elected to the Assembly in 1978. The group quickly dubbed itself the Proposition 13 babies and vowed to wage ideological war on liberals and Democrats. The group asserted itself within months by supporting a coup against the relatively moderate Republican leader of the time, Paul Priolo. That brought Carol Hallett into the leadership position. Johnson helped Pat Nolan, the de facto leader of the Proposition 13 babies, engineer another coup on Hallett's successor, Robert Naylor, in 1984 and wound up as one of Nolan's top lieutenants.

But in November 1988, after Republicans lost several seats to the Democrats and Nolan had become entangled in an FBI investigation of Capitol corruption, Nolan lateraled the leader's position to Johnson. The switch from Nolan to Johnson — which staved off rumblings from moderates in the Republican caucus — had nothing to do with ideology. The new leader was every bit as conservative as the old one.

Johnson has devoted his energies to overhaul of the political system, although his precise motives for that interest, like so many aspects of Johnson's persona, have never been clear. He joined with two other legislators — a Democrat and an independent — to sponsor a campaign finance reform initiative (Proposition 73) in 1988 that imposed limits on contributions and transfers of funds between candidates. Some reformers saw Proposition 73 as a poison pill for a broader reform initiative (Proposition 68) on the same ballot. Since Proposition 73 received more votes, it superseded Proposition 68 in areas of conflict, such as Proposition 73's ban on public financing of campaigns. The measure's provisions outlawing transfers of funds between lawmakers seemed aimed at Speaker Brown's political powers.

Johnson, however, has resented the implication that he had ulterior motives. He has maintained that Proposition 73 was a genuine effort at campaign reform and has fiercely lashed out at Common Cause for suggesting otherwise. Eventually, almost all of Proposition 73 was gutted in the courts.

Johnson is a semi-introvert who, aides say, dislikes the political limelight and is interested in political policy-making. Facing term limits in the Assembly in 1996, it's likely Johnson will attempt to prolong his career with a run for the Senate seat vacated by Republican Marian Bergeson of Newport Beach.

PERSONAL: elected 1978; born Sept. 28, 1939, in Drake, N.D.; home, Placentia; Navy 1965-67; education, B.A. CSU Fullerton, J.D. Western State; wife Diane Morris, two children; Protestant.

CAREER: iron worker; lawyer; legislative aide to Assemblyman Jerry Lewis, 1969-1973; Assembly Republican Floor Leader, 1988-1991.

COMMITTEES: Appropriations; Elections, Reapportionment & Constitutional Amendments; Health; Insurance; Rules (vice chair).

OFFICES: Capitol, (916) 445-7448; district, 1501 N. Harbor Blvd., 201, Fullerton 92635, (714) 738-5853.

TERM LIMIT: 1996

REGISTRATION: 32.5% D, 55.4% R

1994 CAMPAIGN:	Johnson R	71.0%	$291,098
	Allan L. Dollison D	24.5%	Not Available
1992 CAMPAIGN:	Johnson R	61.2%	$402,343
	Paul Garza D	32.4%	$0

| **RATINGS:** | AFL-CIO | CLCV | NOW | CofC | CalFarm | GO |
| | 10 | 15 | C- | 86 | 33.3 | A |

Howard J. Kaloogian (R)
74th Assembly District

This San Diego County district includes the very Republican communities of Vista, San Marcos, Escondido, Del Mar and Solana Beach. Retirees are the fastest-growing population. Those who work tend to receive their paychecks from one of the sprawling military installations in the area or from businesses in the service sector.

Robert Frazee represented the area for 16 years. He was a solid, dependable vote for the Assembly's bloc of conservative Republicans, and his successor, Howard J. Kaloogian, promises much of the same. Given the district's rightward tilt, Kaloogian virtually captured the seat in the GOP primary, when he beat out five other candidates in an expensive campaign for the nomination. His general election race against Democrat Poppy Demarco Dennis was a cakewalk.

A lawyer, Kaloogian has never held elected office before but is no stranger to politics. The Michigan native was once an intern for then-U.S. Senate Republican Leader John Engler, now governor of the Great Lakes State. Kaloogian also served as press secretary in a state representative's campaign and helped found Michigan State University's Republican Club. He was named state youth chair for the 1990 Reagan-Bush presidential campaign. In San Diego, his law practice is centered on probate, trusts and taxes.

Howard Kaloogian

PERSONAL: elected 1994, born Dec. 30, 1959, in Detroit, Michigan; home, Carlsbad; education, B.A. Michigan State University, J.D. Pepperdine School of Law; divorced; Protestant

CAREER: lawyer; adjunct professor, Western State University School of Law.

COMMITTEES: Governmental Organization; Judiciary; Public Employees, Retirement & Social Security (chair); Revenue & Taxation.

OFFICES: Capitol, (916) 445-2390, FAX (916) 324-9991; district, 701 Palomar Airport, Suite 160, Carlsbad 92009, (619) 438-5453, FAX 438-6620.

TERM LIMIT: 2000

REGISTRATION: 31.3% D, 50.9% R

1994 CAMPAIGN:	Kaloogian R	60.8%	$280,934
	Poppy Demarco Dennis D	32.6%	$87,504

RATINGS: Newly elected.

Richard D. Katz (D)
39th Assembly District

A Democratic stronghold, this central San Fernando Valley district has a registration margin of 62 percent Democratic to 26 percent Republican. The district includes the largely Latino and African American neighborhoods of San Fernando and Pacoima, working-class Sepulveda and the seedy Sylmar area. Latino registration in the district is only 25 percent, although Latinos make up 62 percent of the population.

Democrat Richard Katz has cruised to lopsided victories in his last several elections here. In 1993, he attempted to capitalize on that support in a bid for Los Angeles mayor and was a leading contender for the job. He hired President Clinton's campaign strategist, James Carville, as an adviser and placed decently in early polls. In the end, however, he placed fourth, out of reach of a runoff won by Richard Riordan.

Katz, who was running a graphic arts and printing company when he was elected to the Assembly in 1980, is a pragmatist. He is generally conservative on

Richard Katz

crime issues, tends to be moderate on fiscal issues and is liberal on many social issues. Though he has been a top lieutenant to liberal Assembly Speaker Willie Brown — often serving as Brown's de facto spokesman during the speakership battle of late 1994 and early 1995 — he has also used his influence and skills to help elect more moderate Democrats. He was an outspoken critic of the Democratic Party's choice of former Gov. Jerry Brown as state party chairman.

Aside from Katz's role as political strategist, he has also been a key player in the legislative arena. As chairman of the Assembly Transportation Committee, he was a driving force behind the successful effort to get voters to raise the gas tax in 1990 to provide money for the state's highways and mass transit. His profile was raised higher in the 1993-94 session when his committee investigated a $49 million computer debacle at the Department of Motor Vehicles as well as contracting practices, sexual harassment claims and other problems at the Department of Transportation. He was one of several lawmakers who worked to reach a compromise with the federal government that toughened California's automobile smog-check system.

In other areas, Katz authored successful legislation prohibiting violent felons from earning more than a 15 percent reduction in their sentences through "good time" credits. Another piece of closely watched legislation, a "domestic partners" bill that would have allowed unmarried couples living together to gain rights enjoyed by only those who are married, drew a veto from Gov. Pete Wilson.

PERSONAL: elected 1980; born Aug. 16, 1950, in Los Angeles; home, Panorama City; education, B.A. CSU San Diego; wife Gini Barrett; Jewish.

CAREER: graphic artist and printer.

COMMITTEES: Transportation (chair); Governmental Organization; Televising the Assembly & Information Technology; Water, Parks & Wildlife.

OFFICES: Capitol, (916) 445-1616, FAX (916) 324-6860; district, 9140 Van Nuys Blvd., 109, Panorama City 91402, (818) 894-3671, FAX (818) 894-4672.

TERM LIMIT: 1996
REGISTRATION: 62.0% D, 26.0% R

1994 CAMPAIGN:	Katz — D			70.6%		$238,867
	Nicholas Fitzgerald — R			29.4%		Not Available
1992 CAMPAIGN:	Katz D			69.4%		$708,147
	Nicholas Fitzgerald R			25.6%		$659
RATINGS:	AFL-CIO	CLCV	NOW	CofC	CalFarm	GO
	88	90	A-	18	44	F

William J. "Pete" Knight (R)
36th Assembly District

This staunchly Republican district includes the Antelope and Santa Clarita valleys north of Los Angeles. The rapidly growing Palmdale area is included, along with a large section of the Angeles National Forest. Most of the newcomers are young, white families who have been forced out of the Los Angeles basin by high housing costs and burgeoning crime rates in more affordable neighborhoods. The district has a 16 percent Latino population, but only 6 percent of them are registered to vote. The combined African American and Asian population is just 8 percent.

William Knight

The region is best known for its experimental aviation facilities, including Edwards Air Force Base, and it's fitting that its Assembly representative is former test pilot William J. "Pete" Knight.

Knight won the Republican primary in 1992 by defeating seven other candidates, trading on both his fame as a test pilot and his experience in local government. And in a district this Republican, that was tantamount to election. He coasted to a second-term victory in 1994.

Knight's Air Force career spanned 32 years. At the time of his retirement, he was a colonel and vice commander of the Air Force Flight Test Center, Air Force System Command, at Edwards. Knight is enshrined at the National Aviation Hall of Fame in Dayton, Ohio. He flew the X-15 rocket research aircraft to a record speed of 4,250 mph and received astronaut wings for another flight to an altitude of 280,000 feet. He is past president of the Society of Experimental Test Pilots and is a fellow in the society. Knight has received numerous awards and citations, including the Harmon International Aviator's Trophy in 1968 from President Lyndon B. Johnson for his record speed flight and the Octave Chanute Award from the Institute of Aeronautical Sciences.

After retirement, Knight entered local politics and became the first elected mayor of Palmdale when the city incorporated. Knight has proven to be far less adept in the Capitol than in the cockpit. He had been in office just a few months in 1993 when he became embroiled in a flap over a poem considered to be derogatory toward Latinos. Knight distributed copies of the poem to fellow legislators and when Latino activists complained, he was forced to apologize publicly, saying, "I am not a racist, and I am not a bigot."

It was virtually the only noteworthy incident of his first term. Knight was largely content to follow the Republican line on contentious issues and carry a modicum of minor legislation dealing with local affairs and veterans affairs. None of that diminishes Knight's standing in his district, and he's likely to run for the state Senate seat now held by Republican Don Rogers in 1996, when Rogers is forced by term limits to retire.

PERSONAL: elected 1992; born Nov. 18, 1929, in Noblesville, Ind.; home, Palmdale; education, attended Butler and Purdue Universities and the Aviation Cadet Program; wife Gail, seven children; Protestant.

CAREER: retired USAF colonel, vice president in charge of fighter enhancement programs for Eidetics International in Torrence; mayor of Palmdale, 1988-92.

COMMITTEES: Governmental Organization; Judiciary; Public Employees, Retirement & Social Security; Rules; Transportation.

OFFICES: Capitol, (916) 445-7498, FAX (916) 327-1789; district, 1529 E. Palmdale Blvd., 308, Palmdale 93550, (805) 947-9664, FAX (805) 947-9145.

TERM LIMIT: 1998

REGISTRATION: 35.1% D, 51.4% R

1994 CAMPAIGN: Knight R		69.7%	$67,353
		8%	$7,511
1992 CAMPAIGN: Knight R		58.2%	$272,924
Arnie Rodio D		33.5%	$51,031

RATINGS:	AFL-CIO	CLCV	NOW	CofC	CalFarm	GO
	8	10	C-	95	56	A

David Knowles (R)
4th Assembly District

This large district encompasses the rural counties of Alpine, Amador, Calaveras, El Dorado, Mono and Placer, stretching from the fast-growing foothills east of Sacramento into the High Sierra and Lake Tahoe basin. It's a district with a strong conservative voice, and one where David Knowles has had little trouble winning re-election since he first claimed the seat in 1990. To win a third and final term in the Assembly, Knowles in 1994 overcame a weak GOP challenge from a political neophyte and then trounced retired operating engineer Charles Fish in the general election.

Back in 1988, incumbent Democrat Norman Waters narrowly dodged a political bullet when he defeated Knowles, then a mortgage banker with backing from the religious right. But in the 1990 rematch, Knowles put cattleman Waters out to pasture by using every opportunity to link Waters to Assembly Speaker Willie Brown, a major financier of Waters' campaigns.

David Knowles

In that race, Waters portrayed Knowles as a "right-wing nut." And while the derisive tone of Waters' comment may have been uncalled for, there is no doubt that Knowles espouses the views of the far right. After a Sacramento abortion clinic was rammed by an old military vehicle in 1985, Knowles, who had regularly picketed the clinic, said the act was "an answer to prayer." He is one of the Legislature's most vocal advocates of the anti-tax, pro-law enforcement, anti-abortion rights and pro-gun platform of bedrock conservatives.

Knowles got off to a stormy start as a legislator, irritating colleagues with his tendency to speak on many of the bills heard on the floor and repeatedly referring to male-to-male anal intercourse in a committee hearing on a bill that would have banned discussion of homosexuality in public schools. His most memorable act as a legislator to date, however, was the 1991 floor speech he delivered against a gay-rights bill in which he described gay sexual practices in explicit detail. Even conservative Republicans rebuked him for the graphic language. But Knowles maintained he was simply working to educate fellow legislators about the dangers of "a radically different lifestyle that has the capability of spreading disease."

During debate on a 1992 child abuse bill sponsored by Assemblywoman Jackie Speier, D-Burlingame, Knowles took the floor and expressed concern that the bill would criminalize acts by parents who beat their children in accordance with the Scriptures. Speier was speechless for a few moments and then declared: "Mr. Knowles, you frighten me."

Knowles was named an assistant by new Republican leader Jim Brulte in the 1993-94 session, but he continued to pursue fairly narrow legislation. He gained some attention when, after a woman in his district died in a mountain lion mauling, he unsuccessfully sought to repeal Proposition 117, a 1990 initiative that extended the animal special protection against hunting. He made another memorable outburst that year during debate on a bill passed overwhelmingly to make it a crime to carry a gun in public while hooded, robed or masked, and to carry a gun into a liquor store or bar. "This is madness," Knowles sputtered. "It is way too overly drawn."

Prospects for Knowles' political future are uncertain; the state Senate seat he would move up to is now held by Republican Tim Leslie, whose term does not expire until the year 2000.

PERSONAL: elected 1990; born Sept. 5, 1952, in Cleveland, Ohio; home, Cameron Park; education, B.A. Oral Roberts University; wife Annie, six children; Protestant.

CAREER: mortgage banker.

COMMITTEES: Insurance (chair); Budget; Judiciary; Public Employees, Retirement & Social Security; Revenue & Taxation.

OFFICES: Capitol, (916) 445-8343, FAX (916) 327-2210; district, 3161 Cameron Park Drive, 214, Cameron Park 95682, (916) 676-5953, FAX (916) 933-5189.

TERM LIMIT: 1996

REGISTRATION: 40.0% D, 47.0% R

1994 CAMPAIGN:	Knowles R	65.0%	$182,607
	Charles Fish D	30.7%	$7,913
1992 CAMPAIGN:	Knowles R	56.2%	$323,459
	Mark Norberg D	35.3%	$5,713

RATINGS:	AFL-CIO	CLCV	NOW	CofC	CalFarm	GO
	5	5	D+	95	78	A

Wally Knox (D)
42nd Assembly District

Once there were three solid Democratic districts on the west side of Los Angeles, stretching from downtown to Santa Monica south of Interstate 10. But after the Supreme Court finished its reapportionment plan in 1992, there was only one, the 42nd, which encompasses Beverly Hills and adjacent upscale neighborhoods such as Westwood. The overwhelmingly Democratic area is the base of operations for the liberal Democratic organization of Reps. Howard Berman and Henry Waxman, which long dominated westside politics.

For more than a decade, a Berman-Waxman protégé, Burt Margolin, represented the 42nd District. But when Margolin stepped down to prepare for

Wally Knox

an unsuccessful attempt to become the state's second insurance commissioner, seven candidates spent more than $1.5 million in a race for the Democratic nomination, making it the most expensive legislative primary of the year. The biggest spender, Wally Knox, won the contest and went on to an easy victory over GOP candidate Robert Davis. A Los Angeles Community College District trustee,

Knox is a labor lawyer and a longtime Democratic activist. He served on the California Democratic Party's executive committee in the 1980s and chaired its campaign services committee for three years. He was one of the few freshman to be given the chairmanship of a committee, Labor & Employment, which was to deal with many controversial issues in the 1995-96 session.

PERSONAL: elected 1994; born Feb. 7, 1947, in Fairfield, Conn.; home, Los Angeles; Army (Vietnam); education, B.A. Harvard University, J.D. Hastings Law School; wife, Beth Garfield, two daughters; Jewish.

CAREER: lawyer; trustee, Los Angeles Community College District, 1987-1994; member, Executive Committee of the American Jewish Committee.

COMMITTEES: Higher Education; Judiciary; Labor & Employment (chair); Utilities & Commerce.

OFFICES: Capitol, (916) 445-7440, FAX (916) 445-0119; district, 8425 W. 3rd, #406, Los Angeles 90048, (213) 655-9750, FAX (213) 655-9725.

TERM LIMIT: 2000
REGISTRATION: 60% D, 24.8% R

1994 CAMPAIGN:	Knox D	63.7%	$474,818
	Robert Davis R	31.6%	$29,396

RATINGS: newly elected.

Sheila James Kuehl (D)
41st Assembly District

Known for her work as a trail-blazing women's rights attorney and her early career as a television actress, Sheila James Kuehl also may have charted a winning strategic path for gay men and lesbians who aspire to elective office: openly acknowledge your sexual orientation but don't let it define you as a candidate. Her win in a West Los Angeles district that stretches from liberal Santa Monica to the more conservative suburbs of Woodland Hills makes her the Legislature's first openly gay lawmaker. But Kuehl, a Democratic law school professor who founded the California Women's Law Center in 1989, ran on her record as an advocate for stiffer domestic violence laws, an issue that soared into the

Sheila J. Kuehl

public's consciousness after football legend O.J. Simpson was arrested for the murder of his wife, Nicole.

Even as she accepted hefty campaign contributions from gay supporters, Kuehl insisted her candidacy was grounded in years of work she invested in women's rights legislation. In the midst the election season, she said her lesbianism "is not a factor in my campaign as it pertains to the voters. The voters are generally saying to me, 'We don't think it is relevant to your qualifications.' "

Another openly gay candidate of the 1994 campaign, acting Secretary of State Tony Miller, followed a similar political strategy. He said voters should elect him to the post because of the years of experience he brought to the job as chief deputy to March Fong Eu, who had vacated her office to become President Clinton's ambassador to Micronesia. Miller lost his statewide race by just 40,000 votes.

Kuehl, on the other hand, sailed to victory over a little-known and under-financed Republican opponent. She also benefited from the celebrity status that came with her portrayal of the perky Zelda Gilroy on the venerable television show, "The Many Loves of Dobie Gillis," which aired from 1959 to 1963. While acknowledging that her television days are far behind her, Kuehl credited the show with helping voters see her as something more than just a lesbian candidate. "It jams the homophobic radar," she said.

PERSONAL: elected 1994; born Feb. 9, 1941, in Tulsa, Okla; home, Santa Monica; B.A. UCLA, J.D. Harvard Law School; single; no religious preference.

CAREER: lawyer; professor, Loyola Law School and UCLA law school; co-founder, California Women's Law Center; former assistant dean of students, UCLA; actress, "The Many Loves of Dobie Gillis," 1959-63.

COMMITTEES: Human Services; Judiciary; Natural Resources; Public Safety; Rules.

OFFICES: Capitol, (916) 445-4956, FAX (916) 323-7600; district, 16130 Ventura Blvd. Suite 230, Encino 91436, (818) 501-8991; FAX 501-8432.

TERM LIMIT: 2000

REGISTRATION: 50.8% D, 35.9% R

1994 CAMPAIGN:

Kuehl D	55.6%	$589,738
Michael T. Meehan R	41.5%	$38,338
Philip W. Baron L	10.6%	Not Available

RATINGS: Newly elected.

Steve Kuykendall (R)
54th Assembly District

Democrat Betty Karnette was the surprise victor over GOP Assemblyman Gerald Felando in this seaside district south of Los Angeles in 1992. The area is considered Republican territory, but Karnette, an educator backed by the powerful California Teachers Association, swept into office on the cusp of voter trends favorable to women and Democrats. Fickle voters veered to the political right in 1994, however, and Karnette narrowly lost a bid for re-election. Her race against Rancho Palos Verdes Mayor Steve Kuykendall was decided by absentee ballots more than two weeks after the election.

For weeks, it appeared as though Kuykendall's victory would not only return the seat to the Republicans, but provide them with the final nail in the coffin they had crafted for Assembly Speaker Willie Brown. Kuykendall was the 41st Republican to win an Assembly seat in 1994. Presumably, that would have given GOP leader Jim Brulte the votes he needed in the 80-member house to snatch the speakership away from Brown. In the end, however, even Kuykendall's belated victory wasn't enough to bury the wily Democrat. Brown secured the vote of Paul Horcher, a renegade Republican who renounced his party, to tie Brulte for the speakership.

Steve Kuykendall

The deadlock sent the GOP scrambling to launch recall campaigns against Horcher and some vulnerable Democrats in an effort to gain a solid majority in the Assembly and, ultimately, control of the house. In retaliation, Democrats have talked of a recall campaign against Kuykendall. Democrats consider him a good target because he accepted a last-minute $125,000 campaign contribution from tobacco giant Philip Morris in an election year when voters were trouncing a tobacco industry initiative, Proposition 188. The contribution came too late to be disclosed to the voters before the election.

Defeating more conservative foes in his 1994 primary election, Kuykendall is considered a political moderate. He has voted to raise taxes while serving on the Rancho Palos Verdes City Council and has a long track record of civic activity.

PERSONAL: elected 1994; born Jan. 27, 1947, in McAlester, Okla.; home, Rancho Palos Verdes; Marine Corps (Vietnam); education, B.S. Oklahoma City University, M.A. San Diego State University; wife, Janice; three children; Presbyterian.

CAREER: principal, David Buxton Financial Corp; founder and president, Lockheed Mortgage Corp; Rancho Palos Verdes City Council.

COMMITTEES: Banking & Finance; Consumer Protection, Governmental Efficiency & Economic Development; Local Government; Utilities & Commerce.

OFFICES: Capitol, (916) 445-9234; district, 444 W. Ocean Blvd., Suite 707, Long Beach 90802; (310) 495-4766, FAX (310) 495-1876.

TERM LIMIT: 2000

REGISTRATION: 46.1% D, 40.6% R

1994 CAMPAIGN:

Kuykendall R	47.6%	$403,973
Betty Karnette (incumbent) D	47.0%	$505,330

RATINGS: Newly elected

Barbara Lee (D)
16th Assembly District

The eastern shore of San Francisco Bay is a region of contrasts: wealth and squalor, industry and social inertia, mind-bending scientific research and mind-destroying drug traffic. At the heart of the region lies Oakland, a city that contains all of the area's contrasts and contradictions. It has been battered in recent years by an earthquake, an urban wildfire, a financial crisis in its school district and fragmentation in its political establishment. But with underdog pride it also has witnessed a rebirth of its downtown.

The center of Oakland also is the center of the 16th District, which takes in nearby Alameda and Piedmont. The district's Democratic registration, about 70 percent, is among the highest in the Assembly.

Barbara Lee

The seat was occupied for more than a decade by Elihu Harris, who was elected mayor of Oakland in 1990. His seat went to Barbara Lee, a former political consultant and aide to Rep. Ron Dellums. Lee had two decades of political experience before running for office. She was a key aide in Rep. Shirley Chisholm's 1972 presidential campaign and a fund-raiser for Dellums and other Democrats over the years. She also was active in Jesse Jackson's presidential campaigns.

For all practical purposes, the 1990 election was decided in the primary. Lee picked up endorsements from virtually the entire East Bay Democratic legislative delegation and Dellums' progressives. Her most serious primary opponent, Oakland City Councilwoman Aleta Cannon, was an ally of Oakland Mayor Lionel Wilson. But Wilson's wing of the Democratic Party took a drubbing that year. Wilson fell so far from favor that he did not make it past his re-election primary, and Cannon fell with him. Lee's re-election campaigns in 1992 and 1994 were cakewalks.

One of Willie Brown's liberal allies, Lee drew appointments under his pre-1995 speakership to the Assembly's Public Safety and Rules committees; she also chaired the Legislative Black Caucus and a task force on defense conversion. Lee has authored a number of bills aimed at reducing hate crimes through school and community programs, as well as legislation aimed at bolstering rehabilitation programs for first-time youth offenders and making it a misdemeanor to obstruct a health-care facility, such as an abortion clinic.

Term limits put Lee's political future in the cloudy state shared by a number of others in the Assembly: The state Senate seat now held by Nicholas Petris will be opening up in 1996, the year of Lee's term limit, but Democratic Assemblyman Tom Bates also will be looking for somewhere to go that year.

PERSONAL: elected 1990; born July 16, 1944, in El Paso, Texas; home, Oakland; education, B.A. Mills College, M.A. UC Berkeley; divorced, two children; Baptist.

CAREER: administrative assistant to Rep. Ronald Dellums; owned private consulting business.

COMMITTEES: Agriculture; Appropriations; Health; Insurance; Rules.

OFFICES: Capitol, (916) 445-7442, FAX (916) 327-1941; district, 1440 Broadway, 810, Oakland 94612, (510) 286-0339, FAX (510) 763-2023.

TERM LIMIT: 1996

REGISTRATION: 69.5% D, 15.4% R

1994 CAMPAIGN: Lee D   81.0% $155,699

        Andre-Tascha Ham-Lamme R   19.0%   Not available

1992 CAMPAIGN: Lee D   74.5% $212,795

        David Anderson R   20.0% $4,140

RATINGS:	AFL-CIO	CLCV	NOW	CofC	CalFarm	GO
	99	85	A-	18	11	F

Michael Machado (D)
17th Assembly District

This district takes in most of San Joaquin County, including Escalon, Linden, Manteca, Tracy, Ripon and Stockton. The main population center is Stockton, one of the most ethnically diverse and politically complex cities in California and one that's in the middle of a growth boom born of the outward push of the Bay Area.

Conservative Republican Dean Andal, who had previously worked as an aide to former Rep. Norman Shumway of Stockton, won this seat in a 1991 special election against Democrat Patti Garamendi, wife of then-Insurance Commissioner John Garamendi. Democrats thought Andal's landslide election was a fluke produced by Patti Garamendi's unpopularity,

Michael Machado

and they made Andal one of their top targets after court-ordered reapportionment in 1992 failed to improve Republican registration in the district.

The Democrats reasoned that a moderate Democrat with an agricultural background would be the perfect candidate, and they found their man in farming company manager Michael Machado. Andal, however, refused to roll over, even after embarrassing revelations that he had hired an investigator to look into Machado's background and the snooper was caught trying to examine the school records of Machado's children. Both parties poured big money into the district and

Andal, bucking a Democratic tide elsewhere in the state, won re-election by 1,500 votes.

Andal gave up the seat in 1994 to make a successful run for the state Board of Equalization. Machado returned for a second try at the 17th District seat and found himself in another tight battle, this time with Republican Ed Simas, a county supervisor. It was an ugly campaign. Simas took big bucks from state Republicans and the Allied Business PAC, while Machado was bolstered by money from Assembly Democrats. Simas drew on his ties as a county leader, portrayed himself as a conservative family man and linked Machado with Speaker Willie Brown. Machado brought up Simas' ties to developers whose projects he approved as a supervisor and linked him to fee hikes and tax increases. After absentees were counted, Machado came away with a slim victory.

But no sooner had he taken his Assembly seat than Machado faced a recall effort based on his vote for Brown as speaker in the leadership battle of December 1994. Republicans launched the recall, charging that Machado's vote contradicted his campaign promises to be more independent of the Democratic leadership.

PERSONAL: elected 1994; born March 12, 1948, in Stockton; home, Linden; education, B.A. Stanford University, M.S. UC Davis; wife Diana, three children; Roman Catholic.

CAREER: Vice president and general manager of family farming company, 1974-present; community college instructor, 1974-75.

COMMITTEES: Agriculture (vice chair); Banking & Finance; Budget; Consumer Protection, Governmental Efficiency & Economic Development

OFFICES: Capitol, (916) 445-7931, FAX (916) 327-3519; district, 31 E. Channel St., 306, Stockton 95202, (209) 948-7479, FAX (209) 465-5058.

TERM LIMIT: 2000

REGISTRATION: 53.4% D, 37.1% R

1994 CAMPAIGN:

Machado D	50.8%	$658,153
Ed Simas R	49.2%	$522,046

RATINGS: Newly elected

Diane Martinez (D)
49th Assembly District

This district encompasses the most racially diverse section of Southern California, a clump of the San Gabriel Valley that includes the cities of Alhambra, Rosemead and Monterey Park. It's an area that has gone from mostly Anglo to a mixture of Latino and Asian in scarcely a generation. The change has sparked numerous ethnic political clashes over such issues as whether business signs should be required to use English. The 49th is 55 percent Latino and nearly 30 percent Asian.

The post-reapportionment election of 1992 demonstrated the culture clash as

Democrat Diane Martinez and Republican Sophie Wong vied for the seat being vacated by Xavier Becerra, who was elected to Congress after serving one term in the Assembly. Martinez, who had been defeated by Becerra in 1990, defeated Wong, thanks largely to the 2-1 Democratic registration majority.

Diane Martinez

The district's race-based struggle for political power between Latinos and Asians resurfaced in 1994, when Martinez faced a feisty fellow Democrat, Judy Chu, in the primary. With funding from Asian community supporters, Chu, a Monterey Park city councilwoman, attacked Martinez' first-term performance, her surliness in legislative hearings and her support of Republican Richard Riordan over Democrat Michael Woo in the 1993 Los Angeles mayor's race. Nevertheless, Martinez won the primary by a wide margin and sailed to victory over her Republican opponent in the general election.

Martinez' abrupt and confrontational style has made her one of the Capitol's least-liked lawmakers. After clashing with former Senate President Pro Tem David Roberti over his proposal to break up the Los Angeles Unified School District, Martinez referred to the Democratic leader as "the Godfather." Roberti, who is Italian American, took the remark as an ethnic slur. "She should wash her mouth out," he responded.

In the legislative arena, Martinez scored her biggest victory with the enactment of a new law making it illegal for most employers to bar female workers from wearing pants to work. The bill was one of the most hotly debated and highly publicized measures of 1994. After gaining approval in the Assembly, Martinez' bill narrowly failed to clear the Senate twice. With Senate rules forbidding a third vote, Martinez enlisted the help of Sen. Charles Calderon, a Democrat from Whittier, who folded provisions of the "pants bill" into a separate measure. The Senate approved the bill by one vote, and Gov. Pete Wilson later signed it into law.

Martinez is the daughter of Rep. Matthew Martinez and, like her father, enjoys the support of the political organization headed by Reps. Howard Berman and Henry Waxman. Although Berman-Waxman dominates politics on the white, affluent west side of Los Angeles, it dabbles in politics in the African American and Latino sections of the metropolitan area, where the elder Martinez was first recruited by the group in 1980 to run for the Assembly seat now held by his daughter.

Diane Martinez, who served on the Garvey School Board before moving to the Assembly, also worked in the telecommunications industry. Few doubt that when her father retires from Congress, she'll be waiting to succeed him.

PERSONAL: elected 1992; born Jan. 14, 1953, in Los Angeles; home, Monterey

Park; education, attended East Los Angeles Community College; divorced, one child; Roman Catholic.

CAREER: Pacific Bell and API Security Inc. for 15 years, Garvey School Board member.

COMMITTEES: Appropriations; Education; Governmental Organization; Utilities & Commerce (vice chair).

OFFICES: Capitol (916) 445-7852; FAX (916) 324-1393; district, 320 S. Garfield, 202, Alhambra 91801, (818) 570-6121, FAX (818) 570-8470.

TERM LIMIT: 1998

REGISTRATION: 60.7% D, 25.3% R

1994 CAMPAIGN:	Martinez D	66.6%	$224,367
	George H. Nirschl R	29.5%	Not Available
1992 CAMPAIGN:	Martinez D	55.5%	$209,825
	Sophie Wong R	40.8%	$158,490

RATINGS:	AFL-CIO	GO	CLCV	NOW	CofC	CalFarm
	100	F	75	A-	23	22.2

Kerry Mazzoni (D)
6th Assembly District

This laid-back district in Marin and southern Sonoma counties is a land of expensive homes, scenic coastline, white wine and hot tubs. But its politics were hardly laid-back in the 1994 campaign, which saw Kerry Mazzoni distinguish herself as the only challenger statewide to knock off an incumbent legislator in the June primary.

Mazzoni's victory over Democratic one-termer Vivien Bronshvag was narrow — less than 900 votes separated the two — but the newcomer did it with a campaign fund one-eighth the size of Bronshvag's. A Novato school trustee for several years, Mazzoni developed a broad grass-roots base in the district and ran on a pledge of making government more respon-

Kerry Mazzoni

sive. That contrasted with Bronshvag's reputation for imperial tendencies, which had led to her being dubbed such names as "The Flying Duchess" and "Lady Vi" around the Capitol. Bronshvag also attracted negative publicity in the district for her speeding tickets and poor ranking in a Sacramento survey of lawmakers' performance.

While Mazzoni took some controversial positions in the campaign — opposing the death penalty and the "three strikes and you're out" crime initiative — she also tapped into the public's fiscally conservative impulses, vowing to turn down a 37 percent legislative pay increase. After besting Bronshvag, Mazzoni had little trouble defeating Republican Brian Sobel, a Petaluma businessman, in the general election. She got off to a quick start in the Capitol, authoring one of the first bills to pass the Assembly in the new session — a flood-relief measure responding to the state's disastrous flooding of early 1995.

PERSONAL: elected 1994; born Jan. 9, 1949, in Springfield, Ohio; home, Novato; education, B.S. UC Davis; husband Michael, two children; no stated religious affiliation.

CAREER: Co-owner of an electrical contracting firm; Novato Unified School District trustee, 1987-1994.

COMMITTEES: Public Safety (vice chair); Education; Housing & Community Development; Transportation.

OFFICES: Capitol, (916) 445-7783, FAX (916) 445-2840; district, 3501 Civic Center Drive, 335, San Rafael 94903, (415) 479-4920, FAX (415) 479-2123.

TERM LIMIT: 2000
REGISTRATION: 54.0% D, 30.1% R

1994 CAMPAIGN:			
Mazzoni D	61.2%	$267,919
Brian Sobel R	36.3%	$130,790

RATINGS: Newly elected

Juanita McDonald (D)
55th Assembly District

Southwestern Los Angeles County — Long Beach and environs — is generally Republican territory, but there is a considerable pocket of Democrats in the Carson-Compton area and all of them were packaged into the 55th Assembly District by the state Supreme Court's 1992 reapportionment plan. The district wound up with a Democratic registration margin of more than 3-1, reflecting both its working-class ambience and the fact that more than 80 percent of its residents are non-Anglo. Latinos, as more than 40 percent, are the largest single ethnic group.

Someday, whenever Latinos become politically active commensurate with their numbers, the 55th District may have a Hispanic representative. But for

Juanita McDonald

the time being, it's a multi-ethnic battleground for Democrats and 1992 featured one of the state's most bizarre three-way primary battles. Two of the Capitol's least-loved characters, Democratic Assemblymen Dick Floyd and Dave Elder, both decided that they would lay claim to the 55th after the Supreme Court implemented its reapportionment plan. They felt it contained the best prospects for continued employment by a white Democratic politician in the area. Floyd, whose profane outbursts on the Assembly floor had made him infamous, and Elder, the obvious subject of a very unfavorable novel written by his ex-wife, spent the spring months raising money and taking potshots at each other.

But unbeknownst to anyone, it seems, the voters of the 55th decided that they didn't want either Floyd or Elder in Sacramento. When the votes had been counted, the primary winner was the third person in the race, previously unheralded Juanita McDonald, a Carson city councilwoman. McDonald received at least some help from motorcyclists angered by Floyd's bill requiring them to wear helmets.

Given the voter registration margin, the primary contest was the only one that counted. Republicans didn't even field a candidate for November and thus McDonald joined the swelling ranks of women serving in the Legislature where she'd become an activist in education, health and consumer issues. Floyd flirted with a rematch against McDonald in the 1994 primary election, but eventually opted not to run. With no Democratic or Republican opposition, she cruised to re-election.

PERSONAL: elected 1992; born Sept. 7, 1938, in Birmingham, Ala.; home, Carson; education, B.S. University of Redlands, M.A. Los Angeles State University; doctoral candidate University of Southern California; husband Jim, five children; Baptist.

CAREER: teacher, Los Angeles Unified School District; writer and editor of school texts; corporate counselor, Bernard Haldane Associates; Carson City Council, mayor.

COMMITTEES: Insurance; Revenue & Taxation (chair); Utilities & Commerce.

OFFICES: Capitol, (916) 445-3134, FAX (916) 322-0655; district, 1 Civic Plaza, 320, Carson 90745, (310) 518-3324, FAX (310) 518-3508.

TERM LIMIT: 1998

REGISTRATION: 69% D, 18.9% R

1994 CAMPAIGN:	McDonald D		80.6%	$190,975
	Daniel O. Dalton L		19.4%	Not Available
1992 CAMPAIGN:	McDonald D		82.8%	$276,035
	Shannon Anderson L		17.2%	Not Available

RATINGS:	AFL-CIO	CLCV	NOW	CofC	CalFarm	GO
	100	76	A-	27	22.2	F

Bruce McPherson (R)
27th Assembly District

There are those who argue that the Central Coast of California is the most beautiful spot on earth. The 27th Assembly District, which includes Santa Cruz and western Monterey counties, takes in much of that scenery. The two counties share Monterey Bay and the agricultural areas that surround it.

In the north, Bohemian communities flourish amid stands of redwood. The University of California, Santa Cruz, is the largest employer and continues to be a hotbed of 1960s-style radicalism and environmental activism. South of the tourist towns of Monterey and Carmel is the fabled Big Sur coast with its steep bluffs and secluded glens.

Bruce McPherson

Some of the wealthiest Californians live in the middle and southern stretches of the district. But the recession and closure of Fort Ord have severely crippled an economy closely tied to tourism and the military. Some 16,000 jobs left when the Army vacated Fort Ord, severely depressing housing values by the bloated standards on the Monterey Peninsula. Part of the fort is to be converted to a California State University campus. But development money is scarce, and large areas of the post need expensive environmental cleanup.

One of the chief political custodians of the area is Assemblyman Bruce McPherson, who pulled off an upset win in a 1993 special election. The seat became open when Democratic Assemblyman Sam Farr won a seat in Congress earlier in the year. His heir apparent was Gary Patton, a strident environmentalist and 19-year member of the Santa Cruz Board of Supervisors.

McPherson, however, wasn't intimidated by GOP registration numbers in one of the most strongly Democratic districts in the state. As the former editor of the Santa Cruz Sentinel (which his family once owned), he was well known as a moderate with environmental credentials and a history of community service. He spent lavishly on the campaign, as did the state Republican Party, and caught the Democrats napping. The Democrats poured $90,000 into Patton's campaign during the final weeks, but it was too little and too late.

Democrats considered McPherson's election to be a fluke, born of the low-turnout special election and Patton's personal unpopularity. The regular election in 1994, they said, would put the 27th back in the Democratic column. But 1994 turned out to be a strong Republican year, and Democrats couldn't settle on a unifying challenger. Cathy O'Boyle, an aide to Democratic state Sen. Henry Mello, was the early favorite, but liberal activist Bill Monning surprised her and other establishment Democrats by winning the nomination and declaring that he would not accept special interest money for the race against McPherson.

Mello, the self-proclaimed boss of local politics, was miffed and Assembly Speaker Willie Brown refused to spend money on Monning. The affable McPherson, meanwhile, helped his re-election by avoiding positions that would antagonize liberals and by cooperating with Mello in the conversion of Fort Ord to a university campus. McPherson won by a 5-3 margin.

McPherson may have faced 27th District voters for the last time since he's a likely Republican candidate for Mello's Senate seat in 1996, when term limits will create a vacancy. That would give Democrats a third shot at reclaiming the Assembly seat.

PERSONAL: elected 1993 (special election); born Jan. 7, 1944, in Santa Cruz; home, Santa Cruz; Army Reserves; education, B.A. Cal Poly San Luis Obispo; wife Mary, two children; Protestant.

CAREER: reporter and editor, Santa Cruz Sentinel.

COMMITTEES: Elections, Reapportionment & Constitutional Amendments (chair); Agriculture; Governmental Organization; Higher Education.

OFFICES: Capitol, (916) 445-8496, FAX (916) 445-1826; district, 701 Ocean St., 318B, Santa Cruz 95060, (408) 425-1503, FAX (408) 454-3070; 1200 Aguajito Road, Monterey 93940, (408) 646-1980, FAX (408) 649-2867.

TERM LIMIT: 2000

REGISTRATION: 51.9% D, 30.5% R

1994 CAMPAIGN:	McPherson R	49.6%	$769,713
	Bill Monning D	47.6%	$413,996
1993 CAMPAIGN:	McPherson R	49.9%	Not Available
	Gary Patton D	44.3%	Not Available

RATINGS:	AFL-CIO	CLCV	NOW	CofC	CalFarm	GO
	NR	45	C+	86	67	C

Jim Morrissey (R)
69th Assembly District

The 69th Assembly District is entirely in Orange County, bastion of conservatism in California politics. Yet, for the past eight years, both Republicans and Democrats have laid claim to the land, as the parties waged fierce wars for control of the district. The territory includes Santa Ana and the Latino neighborhoods of Garden Grove and central Anaheim, giving the district a strong Democratic edge. About 65 percent of its residents are Latino. But only about a quarter of the Latinos are registered to vote and overall registration in the district — 85,165 — is the lowest in Southern California outside of Los Angeles, and one of the lowest in the state.

Jim Morrissey

For 12 years, the former 72nd District — tailored by Democratic leaders to maximize their chances of holding it — was represented by Democrat Richard Robinson, who left office to seek a congressional seat in 1986. Republican businessman Richard Longshore won the seat that year, but died in

1988. That set the scene for a furious partisan tug-of-war that has not ceased. The current holder of the seat, Jim Morrissey, is the fourth legislator to have it since Robinson. Morrissey succeeds Democrat Tom Umberg, who left the Assembly in a failed bid to become attorney general. In 1990, Umberg had unseated Curt Pringle, who won re-election to the Assembly from another district in 1992.

In winning his seat in 1994, Morrissey defeated Democrat Mike Metzler, president of the Orange County Chamber of Commerce. Both candidates had emerged from four-way primaries to garner their party's nominations, but Morrissey came into the general election run-off in much better shape. Metzler had to battle his way to the November elections by defeating two Latino candidates in the primary, a win that soured his relations with the Latino political community. Conservative Morrissey, who received significant contributions from the right-wing Allied Business PAC, wisely exploited that breach. Among other things, he conducted a Spanish-language letter-writing and phone-bank campaign to win over Latino voters.

PERSONAL: elected 1994; born May 10, 1930, in New Rochelle, N.Y.; home, Anaheim; Air Force 1947-50; Air Force Reserve 1950-57; wife, Margaret; six children; Roman Catholic.

CAREER: founder, Republican Small Business Association; former president, Superior Jig, Inc. (manufacturing)

COMMITTEES: Consumer Protection, Governmental Efficiency & Economic Development (vice chair); Environmental Safety & Toxic Materials; Health; Utilities & Commerce.

OFFICES: Capitol, (916) 445-7333, FAX (916) 327-1783; district, 930 W. 17th St., Suite C, Santa Ana 92706; (714) 285-0355, FAX (714) 285-1301

TERM LIMIT: 2000

REGISTRATION: 56.1% D, 34.3% R

1994 CAMPAIGN:	Morrissey R	51.2%	$576,205
	Mike Metzler D	44.3%	$439,912
	George Reis L	4.6%	Not Available

RATINGS: Newly elected.

Bill Morrow (R)
73rd Assembly District

This coast-hugging district includes San Juan Capistrano, San Clemente and Laguna Niguel in Orange County and Oceanside, Camp Pendleton and most of Carlsbad in San Diego County. GOP registration is 53 percent and whites outnumber minorities 3-to-1.

Bill Morrow, former chief trial counsel for Camp Pendleton, defeated seven other contenders in the Republican primary in 1992, a contest that caught the interest of Republican legislators in Sacramento. Morrow was supported by then-Sen.

Frank Hill of Whittier and Assemblyman Ross Johnson of Fullerton, while candidate Patricia Bates got a boost from Assemblyman Gil Ferguson of Newport Beach. Gov. Wilson's people put their political clout behind Dana Point Mayor Mike Eggers.

Bill Morrow

A conservative, Morrow's campaign was aided financially by both Christian right and anti-abortion groups. In the general election, Morrow defeated Democrat Lee Walker, a teacher at Saddleback College. Walker ran well, given the Democrats' registration disadvantage, but he was left defenseless by a lack of money. Morrow easily defeated Walker a second time in 1994.

In a political payback, Morrow hired Hill's wife, Faye, to work in his Oceanside office in 1994 after Hill was convicted of bribery charges stemming from the FBI investigation into corruption at the Capitol and sent to federal prison. Even after his conviction, Hill had delayed his resignation from the Senate in an effort to get some sort of compensation from his colleagues. At the time, some senators explored the option of offering Faye Hill a Senate staff job. But when word leaked out, embarrassed senators dropped the idea. Morrow, however, expressed no qualms about hiring Faye Hill as an administrative assistant at a salary of $60,000 a year, compensation far greater than that earned by most in similar positions. "I jumped at the chance to hire a woman such as Faye. . . . It is unfortunate that it took the circumstances of her husband's conviction that all of a sudden she is back in the job market again," Morrow said.

PERSONAL: elected 1992; born April 19, 1954, in Diamond Bar; home, Oceanside; USMC 1979-1987; education, Mt. San Antonio College, B.A. UCLA, J.D. Pepperdine; wife Esther; non-denominational Christian.

CAREER: USMC officer and judge advocate; chief trial counsel Camp Pendleton; legislative aide, California Republican Caucus.

COMMITTEES: Budget; Health; Judiciary (vice chair); Transportation.

OFFICES: Capitol, (916) 445-7676, FAX (916) 324-5321; district, 302 N. Hill St., Oceanside 92054, (619) 757-8084, FAX (619) 757-8087; 27126A Paseo Estada, Ste. 1625, San Juan Capistrano 92676, (714) 489-2404, FAX (714) 489-2969.

TERM LIMIT: 1998

REGISTRATION: 30.9% D, 53.4% R

1994 CAMPAIGN:	Morrow R	66.3%	$333,762
	Lee Walker D	28.0%	$7,706
1992 CAMPAIGN:	Morrow R	54.4%	$315,051
	Lee Walker D	37.5%	$9,168

RATINGS:
AFL-CIO	CLCV	NOW	CofC	CalFarm	GO
4	5	C	100	55.5	A

Kevin Murray (D)
47th Assembly District

Court-ordered reapportionment made this district, renumbered from 49 to 47, even more concentrated in terms of non-Anglo ethnicity and Democratic voter registration by slicing off the mostly white beachfront communities such as Marina del Rey. A mere 13.5 percent of district residents are Republicans, making it one of the safest of Democratic seats.

It should come as no surprise then that when longtime incumbent Gwen Moore vacated the seat in 1994 to make an unsuccessful attempt to become the Democratic nominee for secretary of state, no fewer than nine Democrats faced off in the primary to replace her. By winning that hard-fought battle, and

Kevin Murray

taking the general election in a predictable landslide, Kevin Murray has already secured himself a California first. He is the son of Assemblyman Willard Murray of Paramount, and the duo are the first father-and-son team to serve simultaneously in the Assembly. An attorney once employed as a talent agent by the William Morris Agency, the younger Murray is no stranger to professional politics. For years, he and his father have run the United Democratic Campaign Committee, an increasingly influential campaign management firm whose well-regarded slate mailer helped Kevin Murray win his crowded primary race.

PERSONAL: elected 1994, born March 12, 1960, in Los Angeles; home, Los Angeles; education, B.S. CSU Northridge, M.B.A. Loyola Marymount University, J.D. Loyola Law School; single; Methodist.

CAREER: lawyer, private practice since 1989; talent agent, 1982-1989; managing director, United Democratic Campaign Committee, since 1981.

COMMITTEES: Judiciary; Public Safety Committee; Rules; Utilities & Commerce; Water, Parks & Wildlife.

OFFICES: Capitol, (916) 445-8800; district, 5601 W. Slauson Ave., Suite 153, Culver City, 90230 (213) 292-8800, FAX (310) 641-4395

TERM LIMIT: 2000

REGISTRATION: 75.8% D, 13.5% R

1994 CAMPAIGN:
Murray D		71.8%	$129,027
Jonathon Leonard R		19.0%	Not Available

RATINGS: Newly elected.

Willard H. Murray Jr. (D)

52nd Assembly District

When Republican Paul Zeltner won this largely minority and blue-collar district in 1986 — thanks mostly to a tactical blunder by Assembly Speaker Willie Brown — Brown quickly proclaimed that Zeltner's days as a legislator were numbered. Brown's prediction came true. In 1988, Willard Murray, a former aide to Rep. Mervyn Dymally, edged the first-term lawmaker to reclaim a seat that had traditionally been Democratic.

It didn't take Murray long to get in the middle of controversy. Murray, whose South-Central Los Angeles district includes cities plagued by Uzi-toting gangs, refused to support a measure to restrict semi-automatic military-style assault weapons. In doing

Willard Murray Jr.

so, he was sticking by the National Rifle Association, which had given him a key endorsement against former policeman Zeltner. Ironically, shortly after he was elected, Murray came under fire from the NRA for sending out an endorsement letter without their permission.

Murray was the subject of controversy even before he was elected. During his campaign, he acknowledged that he had never graduated from college despite campaign literature that said he had received a degree in mathematics. Nonetheless, Murray squeaked by Zeltner in a district that included his hometown of Paramount plus Lakewood, Compton, Bellflower and a portion of Long Beach — all areas that were excised from the district as its boundaries were altered and its number changed (from 54 to 52) by the state Supreme Court in the 1992 reapportionment. Murray's new district has just a portion of Compton and the remainder is comprised of African American and Latino neighborhoods of the city of Los Angeles. Latinos, in fact, outnumber African Americans now by a 4-3 margin, but the seat is expected to remain politically dominated by African Americans for years to come because of very low levels of voting by Hispanics.

Despite his pro-gun vote, Murray concentrated his first term on anti-crime bills, introducing a measure to increase penalties for possession of a machine gun. He proposed improved services for veterans and a program to encourage college students to become teachers. None of his legislation is particularly earthshaking, and he shows all the earmarks of being a permanent backbencher — albeit one who continues to play the outside political game, including proprietorship of a contro-versial political slate mailer.

In 1993, Murray elicited gasps from his Assembly colleagues when he thanked Republican leader Jim Brulte for a procedural courtesy by saying Brulte had been "very white." To head off any criticism, Murray, an African American, later copied a page from the dictionary and distributed it to Assembly members and the press. He underlined one definition of "white" — a slang usage of the word meaning "fair or generous; decent" as in, "That was very white of you!"

PERSONAL: elected 1988; born Jan. 1, 1931, in Los Angeles; home, Paramount; USAF 1951-1954 (Korea); education, attended CSU Los Angeles; widower, two children; Methodist.

CAREER: engineering; legislative consultant Rep. Mervyn Dymally; chief deputy, Los Angeles City Councilman Robert Farrell; executive assistant, Los Angeles Mayor Sam Yorty; senior consultant Assembly Democratic Caucus.

COMMITTEES: Budget; Education; Local Government; Utilities & Commerce.

OFFICES: Capitol, (916) 445-7486, FAX (916) 447-3079; district, 16444 Paramount Blvd., 100, Paramount 90723, (310) 516-4144, FAX (310) 630-0231.

TERM LIMIT: 1996

REGISTRATION: 80.4% D, 10.9% R

1994 CAMPAIGN:	Murray D		80.8%	$75,899
	Richard A. Rorex R		19.2%	Not Available
1992 CAMPAIGN:	Murray D		100%	$175,503

RATINGS:	AFL-CIO	CLCV	NOW	CofC	CalFarm	GO
	97	58	B+	41	11.1	A

Grace F. Napolitano (D)
58th Assembly District

This is another of several districts crafted by the state Supreme Court's 1992 reapportionment plan to have a decided Latino majority, in this case over 60 percent of the population and nearly 44 percent of voter registration.

The 58th, which encompasses a piece of southeastern Los Angeles County that includes Norwalk, Whittier and Montebello, also was one of several sites where rival Hispanic political factions sought additional clout. But in this case a candidate backed by Los Angeles County Supervisor Gloria Molina lost the primary to a candidate with the official backing of the Assembly Democratic caucus.

Grace Napolitano

Grace Napolitano, a Norwalk city councilwoman and mayor, pumped tens of thousands of dollars of her own money into the primary campaign and then coasted to the finish against a little-known and ill-financed Republican. Napolitano had a much easier time of it in 1994, when she faced no primary challenge. She has proven to be one of the more diligent members of the Assembly, promptly arriving for hearings and well versed in the issues.

PERSONAL: elected 1992; born Dec. 4, 1936, in Brownsville, Texas; home, Norwalk; education, attended Texas Southmost College, Los Angeles Trade Tech and Cerritos College; husband Frank, five children; Roman Catholic.

CAREER: Norwalk City Council and mayor; chair, Los Angeles County Private Industry Council.

COMMITTEES: Budget; Environmental Safety & Toxic Materials; Local Government; Transportation.

OFFICES: Capitol, (916) 445-0965, FAX (916) 327-1203; district, PO Box 408, Norwalk 90650, (310) 406-7322, FAX (310) 406-7327.

TERM LIMIT: 1998

REGISTRATION: 63.7% D, 26.1% R

1994 CAMPAIGN:	Napolitano D	59.3%	$217,059
	James Marymee R	33.6%	$10,413
1992 CAMPAIGN:	Napolitano D	64.2%	$270,298
	Ken Gow R	28.1%	$0

RATINGS:	AFL-CIO	CLCV	NOW	CofC	CalFarm	GO
	100	67	A-	32	33.3	F

Keith Olberg (R)
34th Assembly District

The 34th is the largest and one of the most desolate Assembly districts in the state. The high-desert district runs up the Nevada border from Riverside County to Mono County; it includes the southeastern edge of Kern County, all of Inyo and most of San Bernardino County, taking in the Victor Valley, where Assemblyman Keith Olberg lives. Along with Death Valley and numerous mountain ranges, the district lays claim to several military reservations.

It is a conservative district, and one that appeared well-suited to Kathleen Honeycutt, who won the seat in 1992. Her connections to fundamentalist Christians and anti-abortion and pro-gun groups helped her put together a well-organized campaign in a far-

Keith Olberg

flung district that defied conventional campaign strategies. Midway through the session, Honeycutt announced that her first term would be her last because of a rheumatic disease that made performing the job physically difficult. She also gave an early heads-up to the conservative Olberg, a consultant to the Building Industry Association.

Olberg defeated Victorville City Councilman Michael Rothschild in the primary, which was tantamount to winning election.

PERSONAL: elected 1994; born Oct. 29, 1960, in Chicago; home, Victorville; education, B.A. Bethel College, M.A. The American University, Ph.D. Claremont Graduate School; wife Lisa, two children; Protestant.

CAREER: Governmental relations director for High Desert Division of Building Industry Association; manager of governmental affairs for Reagan/Bush administrations' Legal Services Corporation; legislative assistant, U.S. House of Representatives.

COMMITTEES: Natural Resources (vice chair); Appropriations; Education; Water, Parks & Wildlife.

OFFICES: Capitol, (916) 445-8102, FAX (916) 323-7467; district, 14011 Park Ave., 470, Victorville 92392, (619) 951-8555, FAX (619) 951-7476.

TERM LIMIT: 2000

REGISTRATION: 37.9% D, 47.3% R

1994 CAMPAIGN:	Olberg R	65.8%	$288,864
	Timothy Hauk D	34.2%	$14,980

RATINGS: Newly elected

Charles S. "Chuck" Poochigian (R)
29th Assembly District

Farming and ranching are the bywords in this San Joaquin Valley district, which covers eastern Fresno County and the northeastern part of Tulare County. Bill Jones, a mild-mannered legislator and one-time Assembly GOP leader, held the seat for 12 years before making a successful run in 1994 for secretary of state.

This is a Republican district, and from the beginning the front-runner to replace Jones was moderate Republican Charles Poochigian. A third-generation resident of the area, Poochigian grew up in a farming family and graduated from local schools and Fresno State University. He became a lawyer and developed useful political connections; in 1988 he came to

Charles Poochigian

Sacramento to serve as Gov. George Deukmejian's chief deputy appointments secretary. Poochigian continued in that position when Gov. Pete Wilson was elected in 1990 and then was promoted to appointments secretary, overseeing the governor's nominations to state boards and commissions, in 1991.

Poochigian, who also served as county chairman for the campaigns of Deukmejian, Ronald Reagan and George Bush, got off to a fast start raising money for his 1994

Assembly race. With that advantage, he cruised to an easy victory over his Democratic opponent, Fresno school trustee Michael O'Hare.

PERSONAL: elected 1994; born May 31, 1949, in Fresno; home, Fresno; education, B.A. CSU Fresno, J.D. University of Santa Clara; wife Debbie, three children; Armenian Orthodox.

CAREER: appointments secretary to Gov. Pete Wilson; chief deputy appointments secretary to Gov. George Deukmejian; attorney.

COMMITTEES: Budget (vice chair); Appropriations; Natural Resources; Water, Parks & Wildlife.

OFFICES: Capitol, (916) 445-2931, FAX (916) 445-3832; district, 4974 E. Clinton Way, 100, Fresno 93727, (209) 253-0144, FAX (209) 253-0140.

TERM LIMIT: 2000

REGISTRATION: 43.5% D, 46.2% R

1994 CAMPAIGN:

Poochigian R		67.7%	$409,179
Michael O'Hare D		32.3%	$8,439

RATINGS: Newly elected

Curtis L. Pringle (R)
68th Assembly District

The city of Anaheim is split among four Assembly districts, the 68th being one of them. This district, including parts of Garden Grove, most of Buena Park and western Anaheim, was designed to pack as much of the Orange County Asian population as possible into one district. The district is 17 percent Asian, 23 percent Latino and 58 percent white. Only a handful of African Americans live in this solidly Republican district.

Curt Pringle was elected to the Assembly in 1988 from the 72nd Assembly District and served one term. He was defeated in 1990 by Democrat Tom Umberg of Garden Grove. Pringle's short tenure was dominated by the controversy surrounding his 1988

Curtis Pringle

win over Democrat Christian F. Thierbach, a Riverside County deputy district attorney. On Election Day, the Orange County Republican Central Committee hired uniformed guards to patrol polling places in heavily Hispanic precincts, and Democrats charged that the guards were posted in an attempt to intimidate Hispanics. When the ballots were counted, Pringle had won by fewer than 800 votes out of more than 93,000 cast. Pringle withstood legal challenges to his election, but he was so distracted that he had no impact as a legislator in Sacramento.

In the 1992 primary, Pringle ran in the new 68th District against two moderate

Republican women, who campaigned on Pringle's record, claiming it was an embarrassment to Orange County Republicans. But Pringle prevailed and won with 60 percent of the vote. He went on to defeat Democrat Linda Rigney with 57 percent of the vote. Pringle's 1994 election was just as easy. He defeated Democrat Irv Pickler, an Anaheim city councilman, by a 26 percent margin.

Pringle, who was tapped as a Republican whip by Assembly GOP leader Jim Brulte, is a dutiful member of the conservative wing of the Assembly Republican caucus.

PERSONAL: elected 1988; born June 27, 1959, in Emmetsburg, Iowa; home, Garden Grove; education, B.A. and M.A. CSU Long Beach; wife Alexis Nease, two children; Methodist.

CAREER: member and chairman of Garden Grove Planning Commission 1986-1988; partner in Pringle's Draperies, a retail and wholesale manufacturing firm in Anaheim.

COMMITTEES: Appropriations (chair); Budget; Insurance.

OFFICES: Capitol, (916) 445-8377, FAX (916) 323-5467; 12865 Main St., 100, Garden Grove 92640, (714) 638-1393, FAX (714) 638-1496.

TERM LIMIT: 1998

REGISTRATION: 41.2% D, 46.3% R

1994 CAMPAIGN:	Pringle R	63.2%	$294,393
	Irv Pickler D	36.7%	$171,324
1992 CAMPAIGN:	Pringle R	57.1%	$249,337
	Linda Kay Rigney D	42.9%	$8,088

RATINGS:	AFL-CIO	CLCV	NOW	CofC	CalFarm	GO
	8	5	C-	91	44.4	A

Richard Rainey (R)
15th Assembly District

This is the only locked-in Republican Assembly district in the liberal San Francisco Bay Area. It covers the very affluent, white suburbs of central and southern Contra Costa County and eastern Alameda County — including Walnut Creek, Orinda, San Ramon and Livermore.

When Assemblyman William Baker, the Republicans' leading figure on the state budget, decided to give up the seat to run for Congress from a newly created district in 1992, Democrats didn't even try to bring the 15th District into their column. GOP voters outnumber Democrats by a nearly 10-point margin. And when Contra Costa County's popular sheriff, Richard Rainey, announced that he would run, there wasn't any Republican contest either. Rainey wound up defeating token Democratic candidate Charles Brydon by 17 percentage points. In 1994, he defeated challenger David Kearns by an even larger margin: 35 points.

Rainey, an affable, experienced politician, is an ideological moderate in a Republican caucus dominated by conservatives. He was given a plum assignment in the 1993-94 session on the Assembly Public Safety Committee and pushed several crime bills during the session. Most notably, he authored a "three strikes and you're out" crime bill that, because it more narrowly targeted repeat violent offenders than other versions of the proposal, won the support of many in the law enforcement community. It was the broader "three strikes" bill, however, that won final legislative approval and the governor's signature.

Richard Rainey

Rainey also authored legislation increasing fines levied against convicted child molesters, allowing police to release information to school districts on juveniles suspected of involvement in school-related crimes, and allowing state prisoners to be employed in providing emergency services after a disaster.

Rainey could make the jump to the state Senate in 1996, when term limits catch up with Sen. Daniel Boatwright, D-Concord. A possible challenger would be Assemblyman Robert Campbell, D-Martinez. Although Boatwright won re-election easily in 1992, his redrawn district has a decidedly Republican bent and would be perfect for Rainey.

PERSONAL: elected 1992; born Dec. 5, 1938, in Medford, Ore.; home, Walnut Creek; A.A. Mt. Diablo College, B.A. CSU Sacramento, M.A. Golden Gate University; wife Sue, seven children; Protestant.

CAREER: police officer, city of Compton, two years; Contra Costa County sheriff's office, 29 years, elected sheriff in 1978 and re-elected three times.

COMMITTEES: Local Government (chair); Environmental Safety & Toxic Materials; Public Safety; Utilities & Commerce.

OFFICES: Capitol, (916) 445-6161, FAX (916) 327-5297; district, 1948 Mt. Diablo Blvd., Walnut Creek 94596, (510) 933-9196, FAX (510) 933-9204.

TERM LIMIT: 1998

REGISTRATION: 38.3% D, 47.6% R

1994 CAMPAIGN:	Rainey R	67.6%	$217,506
	David Kearns D	32.4%	$23,842
1992 CAMPAIGN:	Rainey R	58.6%	$296,510
	Charles Brydon D	41.4%	$22,315

RATINGS:	AFL-CIO	CLCV	NOW	CofC	CalFarm	GO
	5	18	C	95	56	B+

Bernie Richter (R)

3rd Assembly District

Northeastern California farms, mountains and wide-open spaces are the main characteristics of this conservative, rural district that includes the counties of Modoc, Lassen, Plumas, Butte, Sierra, Nevada and Yuba.

Richter, an anti-abortion, anti-tax conservative and owner of video and liquor stores, defeated Democrat Lon Hatamiya for the seat in 1992 after a campaign that focused on such issues as whether Richter was a "porn peddler" because he rented R-rated movies at his video stores. During the hotly contested GOP primary, Richter stopped renting Playboy videos and selling non-alcoholic beer (because his opponents suggested he was encouraging children to drink).

Bernie Richter

In 1994, Richter had a far easier time defeating Democrat Jim Chapman, a Lassen County supervisor.

Richter, a former Butte County supervisor and high school civics teacher who made a previous try for the Assembly in 1976, drew considerable attention in his first term for proposing a constitutional amendment abolishing affirmative action in California's government and public education systems. The explosive "colorblind society" proposal was killed, but Richter vowed to introduce similar legislation again. A group of private citizens began planning a possible 1996 initiative on the subject.

Richter also displayed a maverick streak. He argued in support of a resolution extending the life of the Commission on the African American Male at a time when other Republicans were unenthusiastic; Gov. Pete Wilson appointed him to the panel. Richter has signed on to proposals reforming the state budget process by reducing the requirement for legislative approval from two-thirds to a majority — an idea rejected by Republicans for years — in exchange for a balanced-budget requirement and other changes. On other fronts, Richter tried unsuccessfully to delay the required introduction of electric-powered vehicles in California; pushed bills to toughen arson sentences and make it a felony for prison inmates to manufacture weapons; and spoke up frequently on the Assembly floor for the cause of less taxation.

He made it into the headlines again during the 1994-'95 speakership impasse when, backed by Democrats looking for a compromise candidate, he pursued a bid for the speaker's post. That threw his own caucus in turmoil for a week or more as Richter tried to line up GOP supporters. Several initially agreed, but turned out to have weak knees. Richter complained that Republicans were threatening and yelling at him. Conservative members Larry Bowler and Trice Harvey went on a talk show in Richter's district and accused him of "pimping" for Speaker Willie Brown. At the last moment, during a late-night session in January, Richter finally announced he would not be a candidate if he did not have any GOP backers. He did not, and Brown was re-elected speaker.

PERSONAL: elected 1992; born Sept. 7, 1931, in Los Angeles; home, Chico; education, B.A. UCLA; wife Mary La Rae Smith, three children; non-denominational Protestant.

CAREER: Owner, video and liquor-store businesses; U.S. Army Corps of Engineers, 1955-57; founded and operated auto service company, 1958-1966; high school civics teacher, 1967-1975; Butte County Board of Supervisors, 1972-76.

COMMITTEES: Environmental Safety & Toxic Materials (chair); Housing & Community Development; Natural Resources; Public Employees, Retirement & Social Security.

OFFICES: Capitol, (916) 445-7298, FAX (916) 323-3550; district, 460 W. East Ave., 120, Chico 95926, (916) 345-7807, FAX (916) 345-7899.

TERM LIMIT: 1998

REGISTRATION: 42.0% D, 43.4% R

1994 CAMPAIGN:	Richter R	63.4%	$250,744
	Jim Chapman D	36.7%	$35,014
1992 CAMPAIGN:	Richter R	51.7%	$594,047
	Lon Hatamiya D	37.7%	$320,333

| **RATINGS**: | AFL-CIO | CLCV | NOW | CofC | CalFarm | GO |
| | 4 | 11 | C | 86 | 56 | A |

James E. Rogan (R)
43rd Assembly District

While Democrats hold a registration edge in this Glendale-centered district, it is considered a Republican stronghold. GOP Assemblyman James E. Rogan became the district's incumbent just a month before the June primary in 1994 by winning a special election that was held to fill the vacancy left by Pat Nolan, who had represented the district for 15 years. Snared in the FBI investigation into corruption at the Capitol, the Republican lawmaker pled guilty on Feb. 18, 1994, to a felony racketeering charge and was sentenced to 33 months in a federal prison camp.

In the special election, Rogan — a former Democrat now backed by the conservative Allied Business PAC — emerged from a seven-candidate field to win the race with more than 52 percent of the vote. That was enough to scare off GOP candidates who had planned campaigns for the June primary election. Rogan marched into a general-election showdown with Democrat Adam Schiff. Both candidates had extensive anti-crime credentials. Schiff was a federal prosecutor and

Rogan was a judge who previously worked for the Los Angeles County District Attorney's Office. Rogan won easily, however, aided by the district's Republican bent and the 1994 tidal wave of voter support for GOP candidates nationwide.

At age 33, Rogan became the youngest sitting judge in California when then-Gov. George Deukmejian appointed him to the Glendale Municipal Court bench in 1990. He specialized in gangland murder cases while working as a deputy district attorney in Los Angeles.

PERSONAL: elected 1994; born Aug. 21, 1957, in San Francisco; home, Glendale; education, B.A. University of California, Berkeley, J.D. UCLA School of Law; wife, Christine Apffel; two children; Christian.

James Rogan

CAREER: attorney, 1983-85; Los Angeles County deputy district attorney, 1985-90; Glendale Municipal Court judge, 1990-1994.

COMMITTEES: Appropriations; Education; Natural Resources; Public Safety.

OFFICES: Capitol, (916) 445-8364, FAX 322-4398; district, 300 West Glen Oaks, 202, Glendale 91202, (818) 240-6330, FAX (213) 240-4632

TERM LIMIT: 2000

REGISTRATION: 45.7% D, 40.6% R

1994 CAMPAIGN:

Rogan R	53.7%	$468,098
Adam Schiff D	42.9%	$283,769

MAY 3, 1994 SPECIAL ELECTION:

Rogan R	52.9%	Not Available
Adam Schiff D	25.7%	Not Available
Julia Woo R	10.89%	Not Available

RATINGS:

AFL-CIO	CLCV	NOW	CofC	CalFarm	GO
n/a	6	C	95	44.4	A

Brian Setencich (R)

30th Assembly District

This is an almost entirely rural and agricultural district in the southern San Joaquin Valley, an area that includes parts of Madera, Fresno, Kings and Kern counties. It stretches down into a portion of Bakersfield, but on the whole the name of the game here is agribusiness — agriculture on a large and scientific scale — dominated by a relative handful of corporate farmers. This previously was the turf of Democrat Jim Costa, who moved to the Senate in 1994 after a hard-fought battle with Republican incumbent Phil Wyman.

The race to replace Costa was a closely matched one. In one corner was Democrat

Bryn Batrich, who had been an aide to Costa and former Rep. Tony Coelho. Batrich defeated two other Democrats in the primary, benefited from high Democratic registration and drew some bipartisan appeal for her moderate positions. In the opposite corner was Republican Brian Setencich, a former professional basketball player in Europe, who came out of nowhere to win a seat on the Fresno City Council in 1991. With a folksy manner and a less-government agenda, Setencich drew a loyal following but lost the 1993 mayoral race to Jim Patterson.

Brian Setencich

Setencich, a Fresno native, bested two other Republicans in the June 1994 primary for the 30th District seat, but then was outspent by Batrich in the general election. The 30th District, however, is an area that voted for George Bush and Bruce Herschensohn in 1992, making it prime territory for crossover votes. That, coupled with the broader Republican trend in 1994, may have helped Setencich clinch a narrow victory, sending him to the Assembly at age 32.

PERSONAL: elected 1994; born March 29, 1962, in Fresno; home, Fresno; education, B.A. CSU Bakersfield; wife Kimberly; Serbian Orthodox.

CAREER: Fresno City Council, 1991-94; professional basketball player for six years; worked on family's ranch; hospital public relations representative.

COMMITTEES: Agriculture; Banking & Finance; Higher Education; Water, Parks & Wildlife.

OFFICES: Capitol, (916) 445-7558, FAX (916) 323-1097; district, 3475 W. Shaw Ave., 104, Fresno 93711, (209) 276-3488, FAX (209) 276-8154.

TERM LIMIT: 2000
REGISTRATION: 54.8% D, 34.9% R
1994 CAMPAIGN:

Setencich R		52.2%	$292,957
Bryn Batrich D		47.8%	$619,115

RATINGS: Newly elected

Byron Sher (D)
21st Assembly District

The microchip empire of the Silicon Valley grew up around Stanford University. Thus it may be appropriate that a Stanford professor represents this generally upscale district, which includes Palo Alto, Redwood City and Menlo Park. Bearded professor Byron Sher was mayor of Palo Alto for two terms before his 1980 election to the Assembly, where he has been aligned with the "Grizzly Bear" faction of liberals. He has continued to teach law at Stanford during the fall term, perhaps illustrating that the full-time Legislature is not exactly full-time.

As chairman of the Assembly Natural Resources Committee for several years, Sher emerged as one of the Legislature's chief environmentalists. He has pushed for adding rivers to the Scenic Rivers Act, and he unsuccessfully tried to pass a three-year moratorium on lumbering old-growth stands along the North Coast. Sher's major legislative accomplishment has been his authorship of the state's landmark Clean Air Act, which gave new powers to local smog districts and required localities to reduce smog emissions in a phased process.

Brian Sher

Sher also authored a 1989 bill revamping the state's garbage management board, a law that has pushed local governments into curbside recycling. The law requires local governments to cut in half the trash sent to dumps by the year 2000. But the measure was a mixed bag in another respect: It established a full-time, lavishly paid Integrated Waste Management Board, home of some plum political positions. One of the parting acts of Gov. George Deukmejian was to appoint his chief of staff, Michael Frost, and his finance chief, Jesse Huff, to the board. (In January 1995, Huff was named director of the Department of Toxic Substances Control as part of a management shake-up by the Wilson administration.)

In 1990, Sher took on the glass industry — and Assembly Speaker Willie Brown — with a bill beefing up recycling fees on glass manufacturers. The speaker backed a campaign contributor, the Glass Packaging Institute, which had given his campaign $8,000 in the previous two years. But after a public tussle that proved embarrassing, Brown gave in and Sher's bill was sent to the governor. The higher deposits mandated have since been credited with nearly doubling container recycling in California. Sher also helped cobble together compromise legislation revising the California Environmental Quality Act in the 1993-94 session. The legislation, signed by the governor, was intended to streamline environmental reviews required under the act for manufacturing plants and development projects while maintaining the integrity of the state's main environmental law.

When the 1992 reapportionment ordered by the state Supreme Court reduced the number of San Francisco Peninsula seats by one, Sher found himself in a backstage tussle with his onetime student, Ted Lempert. Ultimately, Lempert was forced to drop out of the Assembly. Reapportionment also dropped Sher's Democratic registration markedly — to below 50 percent — and Republicans entertained some thought of unseating him. But Sher defeated his 1992 opponent by a 2-1 margin and in 1994 handily beat Republican Bill Mills, an electrical engineer. This is an area that elected moderate Republican Tom Campbell as its state senator, however, so Sher's departure from the Assembly in 1996 could make the 21st District a hotly contested seat.

PERSONAL: elected 1980; born Feb. 7, 1928, in St. Louis, Mo.; home, Palo Alto; education, B.S. Washington University of St. Louis, J.D. Harvard University; wife Linda, three children; Jewish.

CAREER: law professor, Stanford University; Palo Alto City Council, 1965-1967 and 1973-1980, mayor, 1974-1975 and 1977-1978; commissioner of the San Francisco Bay Conservation and Development Commission 1978-1980.

COMMITTEES: Natural Resources (chair); Human Services; Insurance; Judiciary.

OFFICES: Capitol, (916) 445-7632, FAX (916) 324-6974; district, 702 Marshall St., 290, Redwood City 94063, (415) 364-2080, FAX (415) 364-2102.

TERM LIMIT: 1996

REGISTRATION: 48.5% D, 35.2% R

1994 CAMPAIGN:	Sher D	62.6%	$83,965
	Bill Mills R	37.4%	$4,809
1992 CAMPAIGN:	Sher D	63.2%	$374,008
	Janice La Fetra R	32.3%	$14,864

RATINGS:	AFL-CIO	CLCV	NOW	CofC C	alFarm	GO
	95	100	B+	18	33	F

K. Jacqueline Speier (D)
19th Assembly District

This safely Democratic district takes in the foggy, slightly funky, suburb of Pacifica, but its heart is in the blue-collar suburbs immediately south of San Francisco in San Mateo County, including Daly City, South San Francisco and Millbrae. Older housing tracts dot the hillsides while the flat areas are dominated by industry, Candlestick Park and the Cow Palace.

Jackie Speier

The district gave California the legendary Louis J. Papan, a man noted for his Rambo approach to politics. Papan gave up the seat in 1986 to run for an open state Senate seat. Assembly Speaker Willie Brown hoped to fill the Assembly seat with a hand-picked candidate, Mike Nevin, but neither Papan nor Brown calculated well. Papan lost the Senate race to independent Quentin Kopp, and an underfinanced San Mateo County supervisor, Jackie Speier, won a close Democratic primary and then the general election to replace Papan in the Assembly.

Speier had been an aide to Rep. Leo Ryan in 1978, and accompanied the congressman on his ill-fated trip to Jonestown, Guyana. Ryan was killed and Speier was shot five times in an ambush by members of Jim Jones' People's Temple. Speier lay wounded on an anthill for 22 hours until, near death, she was rescued by the U.S. Air Force. She spent months in a hospital recovering and still carries two bullets in her body from the incident.

After the ordeal, Speier made a try at electoral politics, losing in her bid to claim Ryan's congressional seat. But after she won election to the Legislature in 1986, Speier became regarded as a savvy lawmaker with a particular bent for legislation on consumer, health and women's issues. She is known as a sharp questioner of administration officials and gained some wider publicity in 1992 by questioning the perks and lifestyle of Gov. Pete Wilson's transportation secretary, Carl Covitz, contributing to his eventual departure from Sacramento.

Speier has pushed legislation to ban doctors from profiting from lab tests given to their patients or from conducting heart-bypass operations without a review board's consent. She has pried open scandals in state regulation of the funeral industry and probed sexual harassment claims in state government. In the 1993-94 session, she pushed bills requiring young children to wear life jackets on small boats, eliminating the blood test as a prerequisite for a marriage license and prohibiting discriminatory pricing of goods and services on the basis of gender. Speier voted with Speaker Willie Brown in leadership tests and has generally allied herself with the Assembly's remaining "Grizzly Bear" liberals — but has shown an independent streak at times in floor votes.

As she has gained seniority, Speier has also begun to acquire a reputation as a player in the Capitol, particularly after it was reported in July 1990 that Speier had lobbied vigorously for state and federal approval of a dump proposed by a political donor who had given her more than $116,000 in campaign contributions. Although the contributions from Browning-Ferris Industries broke no laws and she has maintained that she was working on behalf of San Mateo County, the episode left its mark on Speier.

Speier announced tentative plans to run for secretary of state in 1994, but she dropped the idea early in the year after discovering she was entering a pregnancy considered to be high-risk because of her two previous miscarriages. She opted to run for re-election to her Assembly seat instead; soon after she made that decision, her husband, emergency room physician Steven Sierra, died in a car crash. Although Speier took time off from her Capitol duties for part of the year to deal with the latest of her personal challenges, the Republicans didn't put up a candidate against her in the 1994 elections. She easily defeated Peace and Freedom candidate David Reichard. Speier also gave birth to a healthy daughter.

PERSONAL: elected 1986; born May 14, 1950, in San Francisco; home, South San Francisco; education, B.A. UC Davis, J.D. Hastings College of Law; widow, two children; Roman Catholic.

CAREER: lawyer; staff of Rep. Leo Ryan, 1969-1978; San Mateo County Board of Supervisors, 1981-1986.

COMMITTEES: Consumer Protection, Governmental Efficiency & Economic Development (chair); Elections, Reapportionment & Constitutional Amendments; Health; Natural Resources.

OFFICES: Capitol, (916) 445-8020, FAX (916) 445-0511; district, 220 So. Spruce Ave., 101, South San Francisco 94080, (415) 871-4100, FAX (415) 871-4350.

TERM LIMIT: 1996
REGISTRATION: 55.1% D, 29.5% R

1994 CAMPAIGN:	Speier D	93.1%	$86,188
	David Reichard P&F	6.9%	Not Available
1992 CAMPAIGN:	Speier D	75.1%	$296,613
	Ellyne Berger R	24.9%	$1,483

RATINGS:	AFL CIO	CLCV	NOW	CofC	CalFarm	GO
	99	86	NR	14	22	F

Michael Sweeney (D)
18th Assembly District

Democrats don't worry much about the possibility of losing this East Bay blue-collar district, which includes the cities of San Leandro and Hayward, Castro Valley and part of Oakland. Registration here runs more than 2-1 Democratic, and this is also the home of Senate President Pro Tem Bill Lockyer, who has represented the area in the Assembly and Senate since 1973.

Johan Klehs won this seat when Lockyer left for the Senate in 1982. Klehs, a former aide to Lockyer, rose fairly quickly through the ranks and ended up chairing the Assembly Revenue and Taxation Committee, which draws its power from its authority over the opening and closing of loopholes in the state tax

Michael Sweeney

code. Klehs parlayed his knowledge of tax issues into a successful run for the state Board of Equalization in 1994, opening up his Assembly seat two years before his term limit had been scheduled to expire.

The campaign to replace Klehs was hardly eventful. Hayward Mayor Michael Sweeney won the Democratic primary unopposed, then had little trouble dispatching Republican Don Grundmann, a Castro Valley chiropractor. Sweeney first became involved in Hayward politics while organizing a group that successfully pushed through a rent-control ordinance. He later served eight years on the City Council. His local popularity translated into his election as mayor in 1990 with 70 percent of the vote, nearly the same share as in his 1994 election to the Assembly.

PERSONAL: elected 1994; born March 30, 1950, in Oakland; home, Hayward;

education, B.A. and M.A. CSU Hayward; wife Maria Ochoa; no stated religious affiliation.

CAREER: teacher; Hayward City Council, 1982-1990, mayor 1990-1994.

COMMITTEES: Local Government (vice chair); Education; Environmental Safety & Toxic Materials; Natural Resources.

OFFICES: Capitol, (916) 445-8160, FAX (916) 445-0967; district, 2450 Washington Ave., 270, San Leandro 94577, (510) 352-2673, FAX (510) 352-4688.

TERM LIMIT: 2000

REGISTRATION: 60.4% D, 26.0% R

1994 CAMPAIGN:	Sweeney D	69.7%	$171,138
	Don Grundmann R	30.3%	$0

RATINGS: Newly elected

Nao Takasugi (R)
37th Assembly District

This safe Republican district in southwest Ventura County includes the farm and port community of Oxnard and Camarillo with its state hospital and youth authority prison. It also stretches to the east to the Los Angeles suburb of Thousand Oaks. The seat previously belonged to conservative Assemblyman Tom McClintock, but McClintock chose to run for Congress in 1992. It was an ill-advised decision for McClintock, as it turned out, because he lost his congressional bid to veteran Democratic Rep. Anthony Beilenson.

McClintock's departure opened the door for Oxnard Mayor Nao Takasugi, a moderate Republican, to beat Roz McGrath, a farm manager and teacher, for

Nao Takasugi

the Assembly seat. Takasugi, who was born and raised in Oxnard, is of Japanese descent, and was held in an Arizona internment camp for several months during World War II. His 1992 election made him the first Asian American to hold a seat in the Legislature in a dozen years, and he remained the only Asian American legislator after the 1994 elections. In that race, he easily defeated Dorothy Maron, with whom he had sparred when both were on the Oxnard City Council.

Takasugi has earned some admirers for his apparent serenity amid the hurly-burly environment of Capitol politics, but his legislative agenda has been relatively quiet. For Gov. Pete Wilson, though, just having Takasugi in the seat is a benefit. The governor was often the target of McClintock's combative rhetoric.

PERSONAL: elected 1992; born April 5, 1922, in Oxnard; home, Oxnard;

education, B.S. Temple University, MBA University of Pennsylvania; wife Judy, five children; Methodist.

CAREER: Owned and operated Asahi Market in Oxnard with wife for 39 years; Oxnard City Council, 1976-1982, mayor, 1982-1992.

COMMITTEES: Revenue & Taxation (vice chair); Appropriations; Banking & Finance; Governmental Organization.

OFFICES: Capitol, (916) 445-7827, FAX (916) 324-6869; district, 221 E. Daily Dr., 7, Camarillo 93010, (805) 987-5195, FAX (805) 484-0853.

TERM LIMIT: 1998

REGISTRATION: 40.5% D, 44.5% R

1994 CAMPAIGN:

Takasugi R	64.5%	$141,633	
Dorothy Maron D	31.0%	Not Available	

1992 CAMPAIGN:

Takasugi R	50.8%	$325,003	
Roz McGrath D	43.4%	$44,203	

RATINGS:

AFL-CIO	CLCV	NOW	CofC	CalFarm	GO
17	18	C-	95	56	A

Bruce Thompson (R)
66th Assembly District

Bruce Thompson

The 66th Assembly District, which straddles the San Diego-Riverside county line, is a Republican paradise. Registration is an overwhelming 54 percent Republican to 34 percent Democrat, and the Democratic voters are very conservative. Part of the city of Corona and all of Lake Elsinore and Temecula lie within the boundaries. The district includes western Riverside County and a slice of northwest San Diego County, and it counts retirement among its major industries.

Ray Haynes, a conservative Republican with ties to the Christian right, won a seven-way primary battle in 1992. After one term he decided to seek the state Senate seat long held by Democrat Robert Presley, who opted for a run — an unsuccessful one, it turned out — for the state Board of Equalization.

Haynes' departure opened the seat again, and it appeared at first as if a Haynes staffer, Trudy Thomas, would be his successor. But businessman Bruce Thompson topped a four-Republican primary field. Thomas attempted to make Thompson's Mormon religion a primary issue, but it proved to be a fund-raising asset. In such a lopsided GOP district, the GOP win was tantamount to election. Thompson coasted over Democrat David Hendrick by a more than 2-1 margin.

PERSONAL: elected 1994; born Nov. 24, 1953, in Weiser, Idaho; home, Fallbrook; education, B.A. University of La Verne; wife Donna, eight children; Mormon.

CAREER: owner of Robert Bruce International Marble Co.; Rubidoux Community Services District director, 1981-89; Fallbrook Union Elementary School District trustee, 1992-94.

COMMITTEES: Budget; Consumer Protection, Governmental Efficiency & Economic Development; Education; Natural Resources; Water, Parks & Wildlife.

OFFICES: Capitol, (916) 445-1676, FAX (916) 447-4457; district, 27555 Ynez Road, 205, Temecula 92591, (909) 699-1113, FAX (909) 694-1039.

TERM LIMIT: 2000

REGISTRATION: 33.9% D, 53.6% R

1994 CAMPAIGN: Thompson R   67.4% $168,422

David Hendrick D   28.7%   Not Available

RATINGS: Newly elected

Curtis R. Tucker Jr. (D)
51st Assembly District

This district, encompassing the Inglewood area of Los Angeles, was about 55 percent African American and 20 percent Latino before the state Supreme Court changed its number (from 50) and its boundaries in 1992. Its African American population dropped to just over one-third and its Latino population increased to almost a third, which indicates that someday the 51st District seat might be held by a Latino politician. But for the moment, it's considered an African American seat as well as one of the most heavily Democratic districts in the state, with only 20 percent of its voters counted as Republicans.

Curtis Tucker Jr.

For 14 years, the district was represented by Curtis R. Tucker Sr., a former Health Department worker and Inglewood city councilman. He died in October 1988 of liver cancer, but it was too late to remove his name from the November ballot. Even in death, Tucker Sr. easily defeated his Republican opponent, gaining 72 percent of the vote. That set up a February 1989 special election, and Curtis R. Tucker Jr., a former Pacific Bell manager who was working as an aide to Assemblywoman Gwen Moore, emerged as the easy winner. With backing from Assembly Speaker Willie Brown and utilizing the name identification of his father, Tucker pulled away from a field of four, winning 71 percent of the vote.

Tucker has expressed interest in improving health care, the area in which his father specialized. A proponent of the death penalty, Tucker also listed cracking down on drugs and gang warfare among his priorities. The Assembly hierarchy placed him and Dick Floyd in adjacent seats at the rear of the chambers because both were smokers, but Floyd was defeated in a bid for re-election in 1992. Floyd's loss was Tucker's gain because it opened the chairmanship of the Governmental Organization Committee, whose bland title masks the fact that it is one of the most coveted committee assignments in the Legislature due to its jurisdiction over gambling, horse racing and liquor legislation. Industry lobbyists shower members — and especially the committee chairman — with lavish campaign contributions. Speaker Brown gave Tucker that chairmanship in 1993, a reward for his slavish loyalty rather than any demonstrable talent for legislative creativity.

But in 1994, Tucker had both legislative victories and embarrassments. Defying the liquor industry, he pushed through a bill, AB 463, that limited the number of beer and wine licenses the state could issue in any one county. Signed by Gov. Pete Wilson, the law had the effect of freezing the issuance of any new licenses in most urban counties for three years. The bill's aim was to crack down on the liquor sales in troubled neighborhoods where a high concentration of liquor stores already exist.

Tucker, however, failed in a bid to help out one of his longtime campaign contributors — the Hollywood Park racetrack. As legislators grappled with the issue of how to regulate gambling in California, Tucker authored a bill that would have allowed the horse racing facility to operate a card room. While Gov. Pete Wilson had vetoed a similar bill in the past, Tucker attached his new measure to a bill the Republican governor liked, one that would have spent $25 million to market California's tourism hot spots. But Tucker's bill was rejected by the Senate and then was allowed to die on the Assembly floor. Tucker attempted a last-minute effort to revive it on the last day of the 1994 session, but that, too, failed.

PERSONAL: elected 1989 (special election); born April 6, 1954, in New Orleans; home, Inglewood; education, B.A. CSU Dominguez Hills; wife Dianne, two children; Roman Catholic.

CAREER: consultant to Assemblyman Michael Roos 1983-1988; aide to Assemblywoman Gwen Moore 1988; manager Pacific Bell.

COMMITTEES: Appropriations; Governmental Organization; Health; Insurance (vice chair).

OFFICES: Capitol, (916) 445-7533, FAX (916) 327-3517; district, 1 Manchester Blvd., Box 6500, Inglewood 90306, (310) 412-6400, FAX (310) 412-6354.

TERM LIMIT: 1996

REGISTRATION: 71.9% D, 17.4% R

1994 CAMPAIGN:	Tucker D			69.5%		$261,676
	Adam Michelin R			30.4%		$4,349
1992 CAMPAIGN:	Tucker D			81.9%		$195,358

RATINGS:	AFL-CIO	CLCV	NOW	CofC	CalFarm	GO
	94	67	B+	27	33.3	D

John Vasconcellos (D)
22nd Assembly District

The 1992 reapportionment changed the political landscape of the San Francisco Peninsula and South Bay dramatically, pitting Democrat against Democrat in a tussle for a diminished number of seats. John Vasconcellos, a legislator for a quarter-century and for years chairman of the high-powered Ways and Means Committee, had the right to choose the best San Jose-area district for himself but instead decided to give the safest one, which had a Democratic registration of more than 60 percent, to colleague Dominic Cortese. Vasconcellos opted to take his chances in a less-sure district, the 22nd, centered in the suburbs northwest of San Jose, including Sunnyvale and Santa Clara.

John Vasconcellos

Republicans smelled opportunity and 29-year-old Santa Clara City Councilman Tim Jeffries ran hard, accusing Vasconcellos of having been captured by the political establishment in Sacramento and losing touch with constituents. Organizations close to Gov. Pete Wilson, most notably the California Correctional Peace Officers Association, dumped money into Jeffries' campaign. But Vasconcellos raised big bucks of his own, walked door to door and defeated Jeffries by 15 percentage points. Vasconcellos won a 15th Assembly term in 1994, defeating Republican Karin Dowdy by a slightly narrower margin.

Thus, Vasconcellos, one of the Capitol's most singular and controversial figures, returned to the Assembly for his final term, making him second in seniority only to Speaker Willie Brown. Vasconcellos has spent so much of his adult life in the Legislature that he is body and soul a part of it. He wasn't kidding when he complained that the FBI's undercover corruption investigation of the Capitol was an invasion of "my house." And the last major overhaul in the house — a deep cut in legislative staff authorized by a voter-approved term-limits initiative in 1990 — prompted a bitter Vasconcellos to threaten to quit just months after having been re-elected, saying he didn't "see any point in killing myself for people who apparently don't care if they have decent government or not."

The transformations of John Vasconcellos mirror the social history of California since World War II. He began as an aide to Gov. Pat Brown and was eventually favored with an Assembly seat. He traded his dark suits and crew cut for leather jackets and long hair in the '60s, storming the Capitol's halls with all the anger of the protest era. In the '70s and '80s, Vasconcellos became a convert to the inward-looking human awareness movement.

Some consider Vasconcellos a visionary, others a flake. Whatever he is,

Vasconcellos is nothing if not interesting. He was lampooned by the Doonesbury comic strip for his legislation fathering the state's self-esteem commission. And at the beginning of the 1991-92 legislative session, he sent a letter to colleagues telling them they could begin to solve many of the state's problems if they improved their own self-esteem. He routinely talks not in the language of politics, but in the lingo of encounter groups; the San Jose Mercury News once dubbed him "Mister Touchy Feely." But he also has a reputation for being iron-fisted and temperamental, and he once threatened to run over a reporter with his car. During floor debates, he has been known to call those who disagree with him "stupid," which even by the Assembly's low standards of decorum goes too far.

But first and foremost, Vasconcellos has been the chairman of Ways and Means, the committee that until 1995 dealt with the state budget and all proposals to spend money. He has an encyclopedic knowledge of state spending. But in recent years, he has increasingly taken on the role of a critic of budget priorities that have been set by others. In 1993, the Legislature rejected the budget proposal he had crafted and instead approved a budget negotiated by legislative leaders and Gov. Pete Wilson. Vasconcellos, in a slap at Brown, was the only Democrat in the Assembly to vote against the spending plan, saying it cut too deeply into welfare benefits, local government budgets and the pocketbooks of college students. In 1994, Vasconcellos became a leading critic of the "three strikes and you're out" crime measure and of the "triggered" budget cuts the state agreed to as a means of guaranteeing loans to close its revenue gap. "The denial of the state's bankruptcy has got me so saddened that I can barely sit here," he said in one budget hearing.

Vasconcellos has been one of the "Grizzly Bear" liberals who have tried to keep Speaker Brown true to his liberal roots. But their relationship has not always been sweet. Brown was said to have tried to ease Vasconcellos out of his Ways and Means post in 1987, but Vasconcellos would not go. After the 1993 budget squabble, Brown talked about possibly splitting the committee, a move that would have diminished Vasconcellos' power, but he abandoned that idea as well. It finally occurred when Republicans and Democrats divided committee chairmanships evenly as part of the power-sharing plan that evolved after the 1994 elections. Vasconcellos was named chairman of the new Budget Committee in 1995.

PERSONAL: elected 1966; born May 11, 1932, in San Jose; home, Santa Clara; Army; education, B.A. and J.D. University of Santa Clara; single.

CAREER: lawyer; aide to former Gov. Pat Brown.

COMMITTEES: Budget (chair); Banking & Finance; Higher Education.

OFFICES: Capitol, (916) 445-4253, FAX (916) 323-9209; district, 100 Paseo de San Antonio, 106, San Jose 95113, (408) 288-7515, FAX (408) 277-1249.

TERM LIMIT: 1996

REGISTRATION: 48.9% D, 33.7% R

1994 CAMPAIGN:	Vasconcellos D		56.3%		$240,698
	Karin Dowdy R		43.7%		$34,168
1992 CAMPAIGN:	Vasconcellos D		54.4%		$723,105
	Tim Jeffries R		39.4%		$252,119

RATINGS:	AFL-CIO	CLCV	NOW	CofC	CalFarm	GO
	93	68	B+	14	22	F

Antonio Villaraigosa (D)
45th Assembly District

This Assembly seat in the heart of Latino Los Angeles may have remained Democratic after the November 1994 elections, but it changed hands politically nonetheless. That change occurred in the June primary, when community activist Antonio Villaraigosa won the Democratic nomination. His victory was the result of the latest confrontation between two Latino political factions that have waged a years-long war for control of the district, which includes Highland Park, Mount Washington, Silver Lake, Echo Park and Boyle Heights. The district is 63 percent Latino.

Antonio Villaraigosa

For eight years, the district had been represented by Richard Polanco, a partner in the political alliance that includes former state Sen. Art Torres and Los Angeles City Councilman Richard Alatorre. When Polanco successfully ran for a state Senate seat in 1994, his departure from the Assembly set the stage for another head-to-head clash with a competing political group led by Los Angeles County Supervisor Gloria Molina and Rep. Lucille Roybal-Allard. The latter backed Villaraigosa in his bid for the Assembly seat. In the Democratic primary, his chief rival was Polanco's hand-picked successor, Bill Mabie, the assemblyman's chief of staff. Polanco's backing of a white candidate angered some in the Latino community. The district has been represented by Latinos for more than 20 years. Polanco said he merely was supporting the person he saw as best fit for the job.

Then, late in the race, a new controversy arose over a mailer Mabie sent to district homes. Villaraigosa claimed the mailer contained misleading information about a 1977 incident in which he was arrested for felony assault after a man attacked his mother during a brawl at a local restaurant. Villaraigosa was later found innocent after being tried on a misdemeanor assault charge. Mabie's mailer missed its mark. Villaraigosa, who is well-known throughout the district as a result of his community activism, garnered nearly 50 percent of the primary vote compared to Mabie's 33.3 percent. The Democrat's general election victory was a shoo-in.

Villaraigosa comes to the Assembly with strong Democratic and liberal credentials. He is a board member and immediate past president of the American Civil Liberties Union of Southern California and is a former representative for teacher and government-worker unions.

PERSONAL: elected 1994; born Jan. 23, 1953, in Los Angeles; home, Los Angeles; education, B.A. UCLA; wife, Corina; four children; Roman Catholic.

CAREER: area representative, United Teachers of Los Angeles; former president, American Federation of Government Employees, Local 3230

COMMITTEES: Appropriations; Insurance; Labor & Employment; Revenue & Taxation.

OFFICES: Capitol, (916) 445-0703, FAX (916) 324-4657; district, 110 North Ave., 56, Los Angeles 90042, (213) 255-7079, FAX (213) 255-3279.

TERM LIMIT: 2000

REGISTRATION: 63.3% D, 20.9% R

1994 CAMPAIGN:	Villaraigosa D	65%	$370,023
	Robert K. Jung R	27.9%	$44,750

RATINGS: Newly elected.

Ted Weggeland (R)
64th Assembly District

Registration in this Riverside County district is split almost evenly between Republicans and Democrats, which gives the Republicans a slight advantage at the polls since their numbers tend to vote more faithfully. The district includes all of the cities of Riverside and Norco and half of Corona. It is a mostly white district with a 13 percent Latino registration and a smattering of African Americans and Asians.

Ted Weggeland

Ted Weggeland didn't arrive in Sacramento with a mandate from his constituents. He barely squeezed out a victory in 1992 after a hard-fought battle with his Democratic opponent, Jane Carney. Weggeland won by 201 votes. The campaign focused on who could do a better job for the business community. Weggeland, a moderate Republican, comes from a family with strong ties to area businesses, but his credentials were weakened by his comparative youth and the fact that his professional career has centered on his work as a legislative aide to Rep. Al McCandless. Carney, on the other hand, was a former president of the Riverside Downtown Association and a member of the chamber of commerce board of directors. The campaign turned ugly toward the end, and together the two candidates spent close to $1 million.

It was a vastly different story in 1994, when Weggeland was the overwhelming favorite over Democrat Roberta Meyer. When Weggeland returned to Sacramento, he was named a minority whip by Republican leader Jim Brulte.

Weggeland is involved in the family business, DM Laboratories, a supplier of anti-static topical coatings and of Static Prevention Inc., another family-owned business. He is also a principle in EW International, a business venture to provide anti-static consulting, factory audits and static awareness training programs to manufacturing companies in America and the Pacific Rim.

PERSONAL: elected 1992; born Sept. 30, 1963, in Rochester, N.Y.; home, Riverside; education, B.A. UCLA, J.D. Pepperdine University; wife Jennifer, one child; Roman Catholic.

CAREER: businessman, family owned company; governmental relations; congressional aide.

COMMITTEES: Banking & Finance (chair); Health; Labor & Employment; Utilities & Commerce.

OFFICES: Capitol, (916) 445-0854, FAX (916) 323-7179; district 6840 Indiana Ave., 150, Riverside 92506, (909) 369-6644, FAX (909) 369-0366.

TERM LIMIT: 1998

REGISTRATION: 43.7% D, 44.9% R

1994 CAMPAIGN: Weggeland R   66% $150,309

                 Roberta Meyer D   27.5% $5,099

                 Jane A. Henson L   6.4%

1992 CAMPAIGN: Weggeland R   47.9% $621,823

                 Jane Carney D   46.6% $417,266

RATINGS:

AFL-CIO	CLCV	NOW	CofC	CalFarm	GO
8	5	C-	95	77.7	A

Tom Woods (R)

2nd Assembly District

Sprawling across parts of nine counties in the north state, the 2nd Assembly District covers vast, sparsely populated stretches of agricultural fields, rangeland, timber and mountains. Redding is the most prominent city. Scenic jewels such as Mount Shasta, Shasta Lake and Mount Lassen draw visitors. The district covers Siskiyou, Trinity, Shasta, Tehama, Glenn, Colusa, Sutter and portions of Butte and Yolo counties, several of which have faced crippling financial crises in recent years.

Although the district has a nearly evenly divided voter registration, it has voted Republican for years and is expected to continue doing so. Folks here chose to live far from the state's population centers for a reason, and they tend to resent intrusion by city slickers or government bureaucrats. It's little wonder that it was this district's assemblyman, Stan Statham, who spearheaded a crusade to divide California into two or three states. Voters in 27 counties endorsed the idea in 1992, but it also became the butt of jokes around the state and faced numerous logistical obstacles. After 18 years in the Legislature, Statham, a moderate Republican, gave up his seat in 1994 for an unsuccessful campaign for lieutenant governor.

The district takes a turn to the right with its new assemblyman, Tom Woods of Shasta. The conservative Woods became familiar to many of his constituents as manager and on-air host for an inspirational radio station in Redding. He also was a part-time consultant to Statham. Woods ran on a platform of fiscal conservatism, increased volunteerism and less "social experimentation" by government. He easily defeated his Republican challenger in the primary and drew nearly as many votes as the unopposed Democrat, businessman James Bainbridge of Redding. Woods went on to defeat Bainbridge by a large margin in November.

Ted Weggeland

PERSONAL: elected 1994; born Feb. 1, 1947, in Durham, N.C.; home, Shasta; Army; education, high school graduate; wife Alice, five children; Christian.

CAREER: general manager of Redding radio station.

COMMITTEES: Televising the Assembly & Information Technology (chair); Consumer Protection, Governmental Efficiency & Economic Development; Education; Human Services; Natural Resources.

OFFICES: Capitol, (916) 445-7266, FAX (916) 448-6040; district, 100 E. Cypress Ave., 100, Redding 96002, (916) 223-6300, FAX (916) 223-6737.

TERM LIMIT: 2000

REGISTRATION: 42.6% D, 44.3% R, 2.5% AIP

1994 CAMPAIGN: Woods R 62.8% $310,468

James Bainbridge D 32.9% $40,812

RATINGS: Newly elected.

7

The Congress–year of the smear

"We're not setting the agenda, we're reacting to theirs. It's just a fact of life. We have to get used to it."
—Rep. Vic Fazio, D-West Sacramento speaking Dec. 10, 1994, on the Republican takeover of Congress.

The Republican sweep of the 1994 congressional elections was neither as wide nor as deep in California as in other places. Dianne Feinstein held on to her U.S. Senate seat after one of the most extraordinary races in the nation's history. Three Democratic incumbents in the House were defeated and some marginal Republicans retained or won seats they might have lost in a normal year. That left the delegation with 27 Democrats and 25 Republicans, compared to a 30-22 split in the previous Congress.

But there was a profound change in the California delegation that will be felt increasingly in the 104th Congress. California lost seniority — the key to greasing significant actions in Congress. Sens. Feinstein and Barbara Boxer are no longer players on key senate committees, but junior members of the minority party. Feinstein even lost her seat on Appropriations, which will impede her ability to secure funds for California projects and lessen her influence with agencies such as the Agriculture Department.

In the House, the change was more salient. GOP members of California's delegation are younger and less senior than Democrats. Despite the fact that California has the largest delegation ever to serve in Congress, the 1995-96 California delegation went to Washington with diminished ability to control the congressional agenda and direct federal spending to the state, such as defense conversion programs or the kind of aid that flowed after the 1994 Northridge earthquake. "It's clear that California has taken a giant step backward in terms of centers of influence," acknowledged Rep. Jerry Lewis, R-Redlands.

During the 1993-94 session, five California Democrats controlled full commit-tees, including Public Works and Transportation, Armed Services and Natural Resources. Eleven other California Democrats led subcommittees, including some of the most influential panels in the House on issues such as spending, defense and health.

When Republicans took charge after the 1994 election, only one committee was steered by a Californian: William Thomas of Bakersfield, chairing a scaled-back and renamed House Oversight panel that handles administrative matters. Other Californians lead subcommittees, including Lewis and Rep. Ron Packard of Carlsbad, who chair money-dealing House Appropriations subcommittees. Rep. Christopher Cox of Newport Beach became the No. 5 ranking House Republican as chairman of the GOP Policy Committee. He also chairs the Task Force on Budget Process Reform.

Even though several California Republicans were named to important commit-tee rosters, there was little net gain for the state because several California Democrats lost seats on those panels. GOP downsizing even felled a California Republican when Rep. Duncan Hunter's Republican Research Committee was abolished.

California Democrats who relinquished committee gavels still retained a mea-sure of authority as top-ranking minority members on their panels, such as the retitled National Security Committee (formerly Armed Services), the renamed Public Lands and Resources panel (formerly Natural Resources) and the Transpor-tation and Infrastructure Committee (formerly Public Works). "It may be the loss of Norm Mineta (as chairman of) Public Works that's the worst from California's perspective," said Jan Denton, executive director of the California Institute for Federal Policy Research. Yet some Californians were pleased to see the state's clout lessen. "Not having certain Californians as chairmen is a godsend, and I welcome and thank God for being liberated from their dominance," said Rep. John Doolittle, R-Rocklin.

Some suggested the delegation's diminished clout would goad members to work more closely to protect California interests. But that's probably wishful thinking. Unity, seldom achieved in the past, will remain difficult for California's represen-tatives to attain. It's not enough to say that the 54 members are badly divided by differences involving geography and ideology. They're scattered. The delegation has been likened to the cartoon image of a huge dust cloud rolling along the ground with feet and hands sticking out here and there. Members range from the Republican bombasts of Orange and San Diego counties — Robert Dornan, Randy "Duke" Cunningham and Duncan Hunter — to brittle liberals such as Democrats Ron Dellums of Berkeley and Lynn Woolsey of Petaluma. The delegation often refuses to work together, even when obvious interests of the state are at stake. As a result, while Californians quarreled, major federal projects went to other states.

Where Republicans are concerned, the divisions aren't just partisan. There has been great discord in the GOP caucus in recent years as conservatives have been on the ascendancy. Senior and less doctrinaire members such as Lewis have been stripped of authority. No caucus members went to bat for Rep. Carlos Moorhead of Glendale when he was denied the chairmanship of one of the two committees where he was the ranking minority member in the last Congress. The irony is that two of the senior members who have been kicked around the most in the caucus, Lewis and Thomas, hold the most important committee slots in the delegation.

Don Edwards of San Jose, the retired Democratic caucus dean, and Republican counterpart Moorhead toiled for years to bring about some unity. With funding from California business interests, they were finally able to launch the California Institute in 1990. The bipartisan research group, modeled on similar organizations representing Texas and several geographic regions, is supposed to mobilize support for pork-barrel projects and other issues of importance to California. The institute started by getting delegation members together for social functions — something that had never happened before. Soon they were being asked to sign joint letters. The institute has promoted some cooperation, but delegation members clearly don't want it to be a power unto itself. That was clear during the 1993 debate on the North American Free Trade Agreement. The institute had to cancel a series of forums when some delegation members voiced fears that business leaders in the state who heavily favored NAFTA would use the forums to pressure NAFTA foes.

To the extent that the new delegation works together on anything substantive in the 104th Congress, it probably will depend on the relationship of its de facto leaders — Rep. David Dreier, R-West Covina, and Rep. Vic Fazio, D-West Sacramento. The two have a cordial relationship, which is a start. Dreier emerged as leader of the delegation after the 1994 elections by virtue of his closeness to Speaker Newt Gingrich and his service on the National Republican Campaign Committee, where he recruited candidates in Western states and helped them raise money.

Fazio, who's led the California Democrats for several sessions, headed the Democratic Congressional Campaign Committee in the 102nd and 103rd Congresses and also was vice chair of the national Democratic Caucus, the No. 5 position in the House. In the new Congress, he rotated out of the DCCC job but actually moved up in the party hierarchy to be caucus chair for congressional Democrats, the No. 3 leadership position. Fazio is the person who brings his national caucus together and marshals its forces. If the GOP leadership needs bipartisan support for anything, Fazio will have a strong say in whether they get it. That gives him a strengthened hand in dealing with Republicans from his own state. But it's still a weak hand and one that can be played effectively if — and only if — there is a commitment by both sides to work together. As delegation members position forces for the 1996 elections, it remains to be seen whether bipartisan cooperation will get anything more than lip service.

Were it not for its fractured nature, California's delegation would wield great weight in the House simply from its size: Nearly one House vote in eight is cast by a Californian. Prior to redistricting following the 1990 census, only two delegations in U.S. history had ever achieved 45 members — California in the 1980s and New York in the 1930s and '40s. The Golden State could gain another seat in the '90s depending on the outcome of a lawsuit brought during President George Bush's administration. The suit contends that the 1990 census undercounted 3 million to 5 million residents — mostly Latino, African American and American Indian males. A U.S. Court of Appeals in New York ruled such was the case and the matter is on appeal. If sustained, four states would reapportion again before the 2000 census. Wisconsin and Pennsylvania would each lose a seat, and California and Arizona would each gain one. California's 53rd seat would be in the greater Los Angeles area and unquestionably would be one likely to elect a minority. The critical question is how its creation would affect other district boundaries in Southern and Central California, particularly those now considered marginal seats.

In 1995, California continued to be represented by the only two-woman delegation ever elected to the U.S. Senate. Six of California's House members were freshmen. The same 11 minorities were returned to the House, but the ranks of women were increased by one for a total of eight.

BIOGRAPHICAL PROFILES

Following the biographical sketches of the state's two senators and the members of the House of Representatives are election results from the most recent campaigns. To the right of each vote tally is the amount of money raised for those campaigns. The data were compiled by the Federal Election Commission in Washington, D.C., based upon reports submitted by candidates.

Ratings are provided by a spectrum of eight ideological and trade groups. A score of 100 indicates the officeholder voted in agreement 100 percent of the time on bills of interest to that organization. The exception is the Gun Owners of California, which compiles letter grades for candidates. Some organizations offer cumulative ratings for all sessions in which the member served. Others rate only a recent session. The organizations are:

ADA — Americans for Democratic Action, Suite 1150, 1625 K St., N.W., Washington, D.C. 20005, (202) 785-5969. Liberal. Issues include civil rights, handgun control, hate-crimes statistics, gay/lesbian discrimination, opposition to the death penalty and defense spending. Based on 1993 votes.

ACU — American Conservative Union, 38 Ivy St., S.E., Washington, D.C. 20003, (202) 546-6555. Conservative on foreign policy, defense, social and budget issues. Based on cumulative votes.

AFL-CIO — American Federation of Labor, Congress of Industrial Organizations, Department of Legislation, Room 309, 815-16th St., N.W., Washington, D.C. 20006, (202) 637-5000. The nation's biggest union confederation promotes labor, health, child-care and civil-rights issues. Based on cumulative votes.

GO - Gun Owners of California, 3440 Viking Dr., Sacramento, CA 95827, (916) 361-7922. Lobbies against firearm restrictions. Ratings are made with a letter grade based on cumulative votes.

LCV — League of Conservation Voters, Suite 804, 2000 L St., N.W., Washington, D.C. 20036, (202) 785-8683. LCV is a political arm for more than 100 organizations. Issues include global warming, park and stream protection, lead testing, pesticide regulation, timber protection, air and water pollution, wildlife protection, clean energy development and toxic cleanup. Based on 1994 votes.

NCSC — National Council of Senior Citizens, 1331 F St., N.W., Washington, D.C. 20004, (202) 347-8800. The council promotes issues of interest to older people such as Medicare, Social Security, health care, housing, consumer protection and civil rights. Based on cumulative votes.

NTU — National Taxpayers Union, 713 Maryland Ave., N.E., Washington, D.C. 20002, (202) 543-1300. This union of conservatives is devoted to reduced federal spending. Based on 1993 votes.

USCC — United States Chamber of Commerce, 1615 H St., N.W., Washington, D.C. 20062, (202) 659-6000. The nation's largest business trade organization takes a pro-business view of issues involving the budget, taxes, trade, price fixing, defense, energy, environment, civil rights and family leave. Based on cumulative votes.

U.S. SENATE

Dianne Feinstein (D)

Humorist Dave Barry summed up California's 1994 U.S. Senate race this way: "Everybody was pretty happy to see the election come to an end except for Californians, who suddenly lost their state's largest industry, namely, the producing of campaign commercials for mega-twit Michael Huffington, who had spent $28 million trying to get himself elected to the U.S. Senate, apparently not realizing that for about half that price he could have simply purchased North Dakota outright."

Barry wasn't far from the mark, except that Republican Huffington spent in excess of $29 million to come within 2 percentage points of unseating Democratic Sen. Dianne Feinstein. The previous record for a high-spending U.S. Senate campaign belonged to Sen. Jesse Helms, whose 1990 re-election in North Carolina cost $17.7 million. Huffington's record should stand for a generation. Incredibly, though, he spent $27.5 million of his own money or $7.21 for each vote he received. Feinstein, in contrast, spent $12.5 million — $2.5 million from her own pocket — and became a convert to campaign finance reform.

Huffington, a former Texan, once said of his inherited oil and gas wealth: "Over a certain amount, it becomes meaningless. I'm in that category. I have no financial needs that cannot be met."

Most campaigns bend facts and distort images, but this one, by dint of its magnitude, was perhaps the most pervasively nasty and dishonest in the state's history. For months, Huffington polluted California air waves with lies and smears fabricated by such masters of the craft as Ed Rollins, Larry McCarthy and Ken Khachigian.

Dianne Feinstein

One ad, later pulled, quoted NBC News saying a Feinstein TV spot was "the year's meanest, sneakiest." NBC never said that. Another ad attacked Feinstein for failure to pay federal income taxes in 1978, 1979 and 1985. There was some truth to that. She made her tax returns public — albeit grudgingly — when she ran for governor in 1990. They showed that Feinstein suffered financial losses in 1978 and 1979 because of the illness and death of her second husband, and paid no taxes in 1985 because of business losses. Huffington, meanwhile, refused to make his tax returns public and saw no inconsistency in his attacks on Feinstein.

Still another ad accused Feinstein of being soft on crime and ended with an announcer saying: "Feinstein's judges let killers live after victims died." Feinstein has never had a job where she appointed judges and those she's recommended for federal appointments have not been criminal coddlers. Then Huffington accused her of a criminal violation of "knowingly employing an alien," even though it wasn't a violation of law in the early 1980s when Feinstein employed a Guatemalan maid who was in the country legally. Yet when it was revealed Huffington employed an illegal immigrant as a nanny, first he denied it, then lied about it and finally he put the blame on his wife.

Even after all of the ballots had been counted, Huffington gracelessly refused to concede defeat, saying instead that he had evidence of massive voter fraud. Asked for the evidence, he offered some isolated examples despite substantial spending to find more. The U.S. Senate GOP leadership obliged him further by opening an investigation. It took nearly three months before Huffington finally dropped his challenge of the election. Continuing to claim that he had uncovered "massive deficiencies in the California election system," he said that he'd become convinced that by contesting the election he had erected "a barrier to a thorough bipartisan investigation."

That isn't to say Feinstein ran a campaign free of mudslinging. With a 20-point lead in the polls after the primary, Feinstein coasted through the summer with limited spending on ads that focused on her accomplishments. In August, her campaign handlers realized that Huffington was moving up. "We tested (the positive ads) in focus groups and people simply didn't believe I had done these things," Feinstein said. "People always say they deplore negative ads, but it's all they remember about the candidates. What became very clear to me is that negative spots are the only ones that work. These 30-second spots have become the driving force of public opinion and that is tragic and it is wrong."

An interesting footnote to the 1994 campaign was the fact that Feinstein pulled in almost as many absentee votes as Huffington — and twice as many as she did in her gubernatorial race in 1990. For the first time, the Democratic Party ran a concerted absentee campaign and defied conventional wisdom by proving Democrats really do know how to use the mail box.

Huffington, a major donor to GOP causes who had a minor post in Ronald Reagan's Defense Department, moved to California in 1991. The following year, he spent $5.3 million to dump fellow Republican and 18-year incumbent Rep. Robert Lagomarsino from a seat in Santa Barbara and San Luis Obispo counties. His two years in the House were nearly devoid of accomplishment, which is not unusual for a junior representative in the minority party.

Feinstein went to Congress at the same time after defeating appointed Sen. John Seymour and earned legitimate bragging rights. She legislated in a variety of areas from immigration reform to sexual harassment. She carried water for California agriculture, even winning a re-election endorsement from the California Farm Bureau, and ended an eight year-stalemate when she won enactment of the California Desert Protection Act, the largest wilderness and park bill ever enacted in the lower 48 states.

That isn't to say it was easy. Feinstein, known as a difficult boss, had substantial staff turnover in her first two years, but staff work for any California senator is arduous. One week in 1994, her employees handled 19,000 mass mailings and 5,196 individual letters. Incoming phone calls averaged 616 per day — about one per minute. Add Feinstein's penchant for micromanaging and the pressure can be intense.

She also got off on the wrong foot with West Virginia Democrat Robert Byrd, who chaired the Appropriations Committee. Byrd was rankled by her support of a line-item presidential veto and the balanced budget amendment. Some suggested there was a bit of envy and sexism involved, too, as Byrd went out of his way to deliver some very public slights. The most damaging was his decision to rank her last in seniority on his committee, behind Sen. Patty Murray, D-Wash., who was actually less senior. When Republicans took control of the Senate in 1995, Murray stayed on the key committee and Feinstein was bumped off.

Feinstein, nonetheless, had two productive years on Appropriations, working within the framework Byrd provided for her, and demonstrated conclusively that women in the Senate can't be taken for granted. The defining moment came during debate on her successful amendment to ban the sale of 19 different assault weapons. Sen. Larry Craig, a troglodyte Republican from Idaho and board member of the National Rifle Association, called her "typical of those who study the issue" of gun control for the first time and admonished that she should "become a little more familiar with firearms."

Feinstein rose and took his measure. "I am quite familiar with firearms — I became mayor as a product of an assassination. They found my assassinated colleague, and you could put a finger through the bullet hole."

Her words recalled a grim November day in 1978 when then-San Francisco County Supervisor Feinstein heard shots and smelled gunpowder. Running down a hallway, she found fellow Supervisor Harvey Milk face down in his own blood, dead. Someone else found Mayor George Moscone's body. Minutes later, facing television cameras, she announced the murders with stunning poise.

What the public did not see on that day was her own personal crisis and the drifting that had punctuated her life. Only two hours before the assassinations, Feinstein had told reporters she would not run for re-election. Her husband had recently died. She was tired of petty City Hall intrigues. Becoming mayor did not seem possible, having run twice and failed. She wanted to do something else.

All that changed with Moscone's death. The crazed gunman was none other than former County Supervisor Dan White, a young political neophyte whom Feinstein had taken under her wing. In the days following the shooting, Feinstein, as president of the Board of Supervisors, became mayor. She went on to win two terms on her own and to beat a recall attempt. While most politicians try to build their careers in carefully orchestrated stages, Feinstein's has been like a ricocheting pinball, bouncing to the next stop.

She was on Walter Mondale's short list of possible vice presidential running mates in 1984 but seemed to pursue the opportunity only half-heartedly. She considered but rejected running for Congress in a 1987 special election. After leaving the mayor's office in 1988, it took her until early in 1990 to plunge into a run for governor against Republican U.S. Sen. Pete Wilson. The race went down to the wire, but Wilson finished 3 percentage points ahead.

Wilson plucked his old pal Seymour from obscurity and named him to the U.S. Senate seat he vacated. That gave Feinstein another break. When Seymour ran for the remaining two years of the term in 1992, Feinstein carved him up like a Christmas turkey.

But then, Feinstein is used to firsts: First woman on the San Francisco Board of Supervisors and first chairwoman. First woman mayor. One of the first politicians to court gay voters and embrace their quest for equality. First woman to make a serious run for governor of California. And then first woman to hold a California seat in the U.S. Senate. Even there, the firsts have continued. First woman on the Senate Judiciary Committee and so forth.

Feinstein was the eldest of three daughters of Leon and Betty Goldman. Her father was a surgeon and her mother suffered from an undiagnosed brain disorder that manifested itself in fits of rage and alcoholism. After graduating from Stanford University with a less-than-distinguished record, she married Jack Berman, now a San Francisco Superior Court judge, and they had one daughter, Katherine. But she was not content to be a homemaker and they divorced.

At a party, she met neurosurgeon Bertram Feinstein. They married and she began building a life in politics. She was well into her career on the Board of Supervisors when Bertram died of cancer. After a year in the mayor's office, Feinstein married investment banker Richard Blum in 1979.

Multimillionaire Blum has been an ideal political mate for Feinstein. In her first U.S. Senate race, for example, he helped her raise more money in New York than she did in Southern California. Nonetheless, Blum's involvement also was the source of the biggest headache in both of her senatorial campaigns. Opponents capitalized on Feinstein's troubles with the Fair Political Practices Commission, which sued Feinstein for a record $8.85 million in fines for allegedly committing a raft of campaign law violations when she ran for governor against Wilson. Most serious of the allegations was that she did not disclose the actual sources of $2.7 million in loans from Bank of America and Sumitomo Bank. Instead, she reported that she was the source of the loans. At the time, Blum owned 2 million shares of BankAmerica Corp. and he sat on the board of directors of Sumitomo. Six weeks after her election, Feinstein settled with the FPPC for $190,000 as part of an agreement that said the errors or omissions were not intentional.

Huffington resurrected her FPPC problems and seized on Feinstein votes involving legislation that benefited firms in which Blum was a major stockholder. It was a reach to suggest that her yes vote on a multibillion-dollar appropriations bill somehow was akin to crafting special-interest legislation, but such subtleties are seldom found in 30-second spots.

FIRST IN HER CLASS

Since Feinstein replaced an appointee, she began her first term on Nov. 10, 1992 — nearly two full months ahead of the 11 other freshmen. That puts her at the head of her class in seniority, an advantage she'll enjoy as long as she serves in the Senate. At the same time, the Senate Democratic leadership was cognizant of the fact that she would be running for re-election in two years and helped position her for a noticeable role. Sen. Barbara Boxer, one of three other women sworn in two months later, was equally cooperative in allowing Feinstein to be the more prominent of the two Californians.

Neither could foresee that they'd begin 1995 in a Republican-led Congress. Minority Democrats will have few opportunities for legislative innovation in the 104th Congress. The reversal called for a new game plan based on maintaining what they and predecessor Democrats have won. After losing Appropriations, Feinstein picked up committee assignments on Rules and Foreign Relations. More significant in the short term was her new berth on the Judiciary subcommittee that deals with immigration. Feinstein pledged to make illegal immigration her first priority in the 104th Congress.

PERSONAL: elected 1992; born June 22, 1933, in San Francisco; home, San Francisco; education, B.A. Stanford University 1955; husband Richard Blum; one child, three stepchildren; Jewish.

CAREER: California Women's Board of Terms and Parole, 1960-66; San Francisco Board of Supervisors, 1969-1978; Mayor of San Francisco, 1978-1988.

COMMITTEES: Foreign Relations; Judiciary; Rules and Administration.

OFFICES: Suite 331, Hart Building, Washington, D.C. 20510, (202) 224-3841; state, Suite 305, 1700 Montgomery St., San Francisco 94111, (415) 249-4777; Suite 915, 11111 Santa Monica Blvd., Los Angeles 90025, (310) 914-7300; Suite 1030, 705 B St., San Diego 92101, (619) 231-9712.

1994 CAMPAIGN:	Feinstein D	46.8%	$12.5 million
	Michael Huffington R	44.8%	$29 million
1992 CAMPAIGN:	Feinstein D	54.3%	$7,708,664
	John Seymour R	38%	$6,598,426

RATINGS:

ADA	ACU	AFL/CIO	GO	LCV	NCSC	NTU	USCC
85	11	84	F	69	90	17	9

Barbara Boxer (D)

Dianne Feinstein won two U.S. Senate seats in 1992 — her own and Barbara Boxer's.

Polls showed Boxer leading Republican Bruce Herschensohn by 22 percentage points shortly after Labor Day. But two weeks away from the Nov. 3 election, ultraconservative Herschensohn was running dead even. In September, Herschensohn began a TV blitz that defined Boxer on his terms: bouncer of 143 checks at the House bank, a big-spending liberal who enjoyed taxpayer-paid limousine rides, a shrill feminist with a poor voting record and nothing better to do than beat up the military while 200,000 defense jobs disappeared in California.

The Boxer campaign allowed the attacks to go largely unanswered while saving TV money for a planned end-of-campaign blitz. When the response finally came, the spots showed Boxer as a strident candidate and failed to shift the focus away from Herschensohn's attacks. In effect, they complemented Herschensohn's themes as he continued to speak with perceived clarity about his own plans for addressing pocketbook concerns of voters. "She's turned out to be a weak candidate with a very weak campaign," said Sherry Bebitch Jeffe, political analyst from Claremont College.

In rode Feinstein, who was coasting to victory over appointed incumbent John Seymour. Feinstein stumped the state with Boxer in tow, devoting most of her speeches to praising Boxer. The two had never been close, but only veteran observers would have picked that up. Usually feisty Boxer would stand by smiling while Feinstein would say: "Cagney needs her Lacy. Thelma needs her Louise. And Dianne needs her Barbara in the United States Senate!"

Barbara Boxer

Humbling as that must have been, Boxer took it in stride. The two appeared to develop a solid relationship and promised to go to Washington as a team working for California's interests. On Election Day, Feinstein out-polled Boxer by 680,000 votes. Feinstein's broader appeal was most apparent in Orange County. Both Republican senate candidates carried the conservative bastion, but Feinstein ran nearly 50,000 votes ahead of Boxer even though Seymour was the former mayor of Anaheim and had represented Orange County in the state Senate.

The morning after the election, Boxer would say, the enormity of victory began to sink in. "It was an extraordinary moment," she said, "to show people that two women could get elected from a state the size of California and that two women could campaign and work together, could set aside their differences without much conversation and just plain do it."

Two years later, the shoe was on the other foot. This time it was Feinstein who was strongly challenged as she sought election to her first full term. Boxer, who had deferred much of the limelight to Feinstein during their Senate service, raised a ton of money for the Feinstein re-election campaign — and also for candidates nationwide.

In Washington, Boxer and Feinstein have continued working closely on issues of interest to California such as defense conversion, assault weapons and trade restrictions. They broke an eight-year deadlock to win passage of the California Desert Protection Act and leveraged prompt federal payments for relief after the Northridge earthquake. Yet each goes her own way on many issues. Feinstein's

U.S. Senators from California

(elected by Legislature prior to 1914)

Seat A			Seat B		
John C. Fremont	D	1849	William M. Gwin	D	1849
John B. Weller	D	1852			
David C. Broderick	D	1857			
Henry P. Haun	D	1859			
Milton S. Latham	D	1860	James A. McDougall	D	1861
John Conness	Un	1863	Cornelius Cole	Un	1865
Eugene Casserly	D	1869			
John S. Hager	D	1873	Aaron A. Sargent	R	1873
Newton Booth	I–R	1875	James T. Farley	D	1879
John F. Miller	R	1881	Leland Stanford	R	1885
A.P. Williams	R	1886			
George Hearst	D	1887			
Charles N. Fenton	R	1893	George C. Perkins	R	1893
Stephen M. White	D	1893			
Thomas R. Bard	R	1899			
Frank P. Flint	R	1905			
John D. Works	R	1911	James D. Phalen	D	1915
Hiram W. Johnson	R	1917	Samuel M. Shortridge	R	1921
William F. Knowland	R	1945	William G. McAdoo	R	1932
Clair Engle	D	1959	Thomas M. Storke	D	1938
Pierre Salinger	D	1964	Sheridan Downey	D	1939
George Murphy	R	1964	Richard Nixon	R	1951
John V. Tunney	D	1971	Thomas Kuchel	R	1952
S.I. Hayakawa	R	1977	Alan Cranston	D	1969
Pete Wilson	R	1983			
John Seymour	R	1991			
Dianne Feinstein	D	1992	Barbara Boxer	D	1993

Un: Union; I-R: Independent-Republican.

voting record is decidedly more centrist and pro-business. Boxer, who replaced Alan Cranston, needed no coaxing to carry on Cranston's 24-year legacy of fighting for a liberal foreign policy, environmental protection and the rights of the disabled.

Boxer voted against the death penalty for juveniles. She pushed for legislation giving tax breaks to companies that run gun buy-back programs, restoring wetlands and making it easier to export computers. She voted against a subsidy sought by California wool growers, backed clean air and health-care reforms sought by the Clinton administration and pushed for authorization to deploy National Guard troops along the Mexican border to help curb illegal immigration.

Boxer opposed President Clinton's proposal for a line-item veto, but has been a supporter of many other White House initiatives. Boxer became a frequent White House quest when romance blossomed between her daughter, Nicole, and Hillary Rodham Clinton's brother, Tony Rodham. Nicole, who co-authored her mother's autobiography "Strangers in the Senate," married Rodham at the White House in 1994.

Democratic Senate leaders showed considerable confidence in Boxer at the start of the 1993 session, when they gave her a seat on the Democratic Steering Committee. The panel hands out committee assignments to members and is an immensely important power base in a chamber where so much happens because of personal friendships and positions within the hierarchy. Boxer also got the assignment she sought on the Banking, Housing and Urban Affairs Committee plus the Budget and Environment and Public Works Committees.

Banking especially interested Boxer because its jurisdiction includes financial aid to commerce and industry, housing programs, mass transit and export controls — all important to California business. In addition, it's a premier fund-raising post, as Cranston found during his long Senate tenure. But clearly, it was not lost on Boxer that membership on the committee led to Cranston's role in the savings and loan debacles, and ultimately the end of one of the most productive careers in California politics.

It was a surprise that she didn't end up on Judiciary, but it appears she deferred to Feinstein. After all, Boxer was among the group of House women who marched to the door of the all-male Judiciary Committee in the fall of 1991 to protest its handling of the Clarence Thomas-Anita Hill hearings. After her election, then-Judiciary Chairman Sen. Joseph Biden, D-Del., sent Boxer a dozen roses and a note that said: Welcome to the Judiciary Committee.

In her campaign, Boxer said much about breaking up the old-boy control of the Senate. But once there, she showed little interest in internal reforms. Her career is distinguished by a mastery at building coalitions that would take issues such as abortion, consumer safety and military accountability to center stage.

In the House, she was elected president of her freshman class and plunged into issues involving ineffective government. She exposed the Air Force purchase of the $7,622 coffee pot and became one of Congress' experts on procurement issues. By her third House term, she was on the Armed Services Committee, once one of the most exclusive old-boy clubs of the House. From that perch, she lead the fight for laws requiring more competitive contract bidding, better performance on contracts and protection for whistleblowers.

At the same time, she worked her staff to exhaustion on issues that transcended district interests: AIDS research, transportation, dial-a-porn, consumer protection, offshore oil drilling bans, high-school dropouts, abortion rights and a plethora of other women's issues. In the process, she developed a national constituency among women who came to her aid with checks for her Senate plunge.

It's been a long, but steady climb for the daughter of an uneducated immigrant mother and a father who went to night law school while working days to support his family. Boxer credits her own drive to the model her father provided. She married Stewart Boxer, a labor lawyer, gave up her business career to raise children and then became a re-entry woman who worked as a weekly newspaper reporter in Marin County once her kids were in school. From there, Boxer spent two years as U.S. Rep. John Burton's field representative, which probably gave her invaluable lessons on how to deal with erratic males.

In 1976, she won a seat on the Marin County Board of Supervisors and quickly established herself as a hard worker with a flair for the dramatic. When Burton announced he would step down in 1982 to deal with his chemical dependency, Boxer won the seat in a close race but had no trouble holding it after that.

PERSONAL: elected 1992; born Nov. 11, 1940, in Brooklyn, N.Y.; home, Greenbrae; education, B.A. Brooklyn College 1962; husband Stewart, two children; Jewish.

CAREER: stockbroker and financial researcher, 1962-65; reporter for the weekly Pacific Sun, 1972-74; aide to Rep. John Burton, 1974-76; Marin County Supervisor, 1976-82; House of Representatives, 1982-93.

COMMITTEES: Banking, Housing and Urban Affairs; Environment and Public Works; Budget; Democratic Steering Committee.

OFFICES: Suite 112, Hart Building, Washington, D.C. 20510, (202) 224-3553; state, Suite 240, 1700 Montgomery St., San Francisco 94111, (415) 403-0100; Suite 545, 2250 E. Imperial Hwy., El Segundo 90245, (310) 414-5700.

1992 CAMPAIGN:	Boxer D	47.9%	$10,129,028
	Bruce Herschensohn R	43%	$7,708,664

RATINGS:

ADA	ACU	AFL/CIO	GO	LCV	NCSC	NTU	USCC
90	4	89	NR	93	90	15	20

Congressional Districts

1 RIGGS, Frank
2 HERGER, Wally
3 FAZIO, Vic
4 DOOLITTLE, John
5 MATSUI, Robert
6 WOOLSEY, Lynn
7 MILLER, George
8 PELOSI, Nancy
9 DELLUMS, Ron
10 BAKER, William
11 POMBO, Richard

12 LANTOS, Tom
13 STARK, Pete
14 ESHOO, Anna
15 MINETA, Norman
16 LOFGREN, Zoe
17 FARR, Sam
18 CONDIT, Gary
19 RADANOVICH, George
20 DOOLEY, Cal
21 THOMAS, Bill
22 SEASTRAND, Andrea

23 GALLEGLY, Elton
24 BEILENSON, Anthony
25 McKEON, Howard
26 BERMAN, Howard
27 MOORHEAD, Carlos
28 DREIER, David
29 WAXMAN, Henry
30 BECERRA, Xavier
31 MARTINEZ, Matthew
32 DIXON, Julian
33 ROYBAL-ALLARD, Lucille
34 TORRES, Esteban
35 WATERS, Maxine
36 HARMAN, Jane
37 TUCKER, Walter III
38 HORN, Steve
39 ROYCE, Ed
40 LEWIS, Jerry
41 KIM, Jay
42 BROWN, George Jr.
43 CALVERT, Ken
44 BONO, Sonny
45 ROHRABACHER, Dana
46 DORNAN, Robert
47 COX, Christopher
48 PACKARD, Ron
49 BILBRAY, Brian
50 FILNER, Bob
51 CUNNINGHAM, Randy
52 HUNTER, Duncan

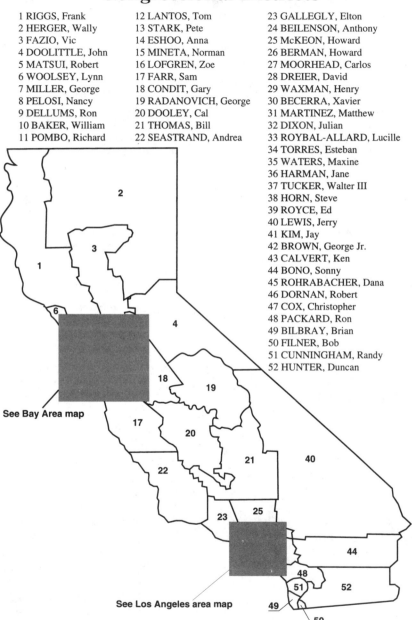

See Bay Area map

See Los Angeles area map

San Francisco Bay Area

Los Angeles Area

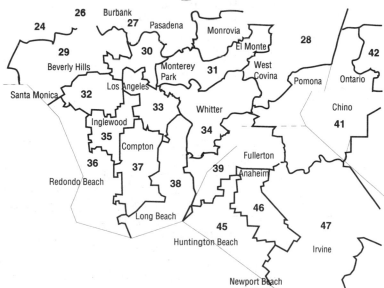

William P. Baker (R)

10th Congressional District

There aren't many Republican enclaves in the east San Francisco Bay Area, but most of those that can be found are in the 10th District. Included are the affluent, bedroom areas of Contra Costa and Alameda counties plus rolling farm country stretching eastward to the San Joaquin County line. Runaway growth over the past 30 years has merged communities such as Walnut Creek, Pleasanton and Livermore into one, highly congested slurb. Housing values and incomes tend to be high, but economic uncertainties also have given jitters to many who reside within the numerous gated communities.

William P. Baker

Arch conservative William Baker is becoming entrenched in the district. A former state Department of Finance budget analyst, he made tax and money matters his specialty during the 12 years he represented parts of the area in the Assembly. For both Govs. George Deukmejian and Pete Wilson, he served as point man in virtually all major tax and budget negotiations.

Though he was in the minority party during his first congressional term, Baker was able to snare money to expand Highway 4 near Pittsburg, which is essential if BART is to expand into the area. He also got the entire delegation behind efforts to locate a national fusion energy project at Lawrence Livermore Laboratory and worked with Rep. George Miller to keep tariffs off Korean steel — a favor to the United Posco Industries plant in Pittsburg.

Yet he also has a reputation for acid remarks, and that was nearly his undoing when he ran for this open congressional seat in 1992. His sneering comments about welfare mothers (he called them breeders), sexual harassment and abortion advocates gave his opponent plenty of ammunition and Baker just squeaked through in 1992.

Despite that, Democratic Party leaders had a hard time recruiting someone to take on Baker in 1994. The nomination was won by an Orinda businesswoman named Ellen Schwartz, who had recently been registered in the Green Party. She was handed a terrific issue. It turned out that one of the few progressive things Baker did as an assemblyman was author a law that reduced sentences for convicts who work. Amid the law-and-order frenzy of 1994, that allowed the early release of Melvin Carter, who had confessed to raping more than 100 women.

Nonetheless, even if it hadn't been a Republican year, Schwartz was clearly too liberal for the district and her campaign never caught fire despite spending a respectable sum of money. If anyone succeeds in knocking out Baker in the district's current configuration, it probably will be a well-heeled, centrist Democrat who shares Baker's penchant for hitting hard and low.

As the only Republican among 10 Bay Area representatives, Baker will have an important say in regional issues as a member of the majority party in the 104th Congress. He had a serious setback, however, when he lost a bid to represent the California delegation on the Republican Steering Committee, which dispenses committee assignments. The post went to Rep. David Dreier of Covina on a 13-12 vote.

PERSONAL: elected 1992; born June 14, 1940, in Oakland; home, Danville; Coast Guard Reserve; education, B.S. San Jose State University, graduate study CSU Long Beach; wife, Joanne Atack; four children; Protestant.

CAREER: businessman; assistant to secretary of the Senate; budget analyst, state Department of Finance; Assembly, 1980-92.

COMMITTEES: Transportation and Infrastructure; Science.

OFFICES: Suite 1724, Longworth Building, Washington, D.C. 20515, (202) 225-1880, FAX (202) 225-2150; district, Suite 103, 1801 N. California Blvd., Walnut Creek 94596, (510) 932-8899; 100 Civic Plaza - Gallery Dublin, Dublin 94568, (510) 829-0813; Suite 111, 3rd & H Streets, Antioch 94509, (510) 777-0536.

REGISTRATION: 42.3% D, 43.6% R

1994 CAMPAIGN:	Baker R	59.3%	$912,530
	Ellen Schwartz D	38.7%	$441,520
1992 CAMPAIGN:	Baker R	51.9%	$678,050
	Wendell Williams D	48%	$221,869

RATINGS:

ADA	ACU	AFL/CIO	GO	LCV	NCSC	NTU	USCC
10	98	5	C	8	10	76	100

Xavier Becerra (D)
30th Congressional District

Hispanic neighborhoods on three sides of downtown Los Angeles plus a northeasterly bulge that includes Highland Park and Eagle Rock make up the core of this district. Although some parts are increasingly shabby, these are not the poorest of the Hispanic communities. It is an area of rising property values and expectations for many who live there. In the predominately white neighborhoods, which have a history of community activism and Democratic voting, there are increasing numbers of Asians.

Koreatown sits in the district's southwest corner and was heavily damaged during the 1992 riots. But voter registration in Koreatown, as in much of the rest of the district, is low and Koreans haven't been a political factor.

Among Hispanic officeholders, there is something of a tradition of handing off seats to a relative or an aide. Thirty-year veteran Rep. Ed Roybal tried that when he decided to retire in 1992. His aide, Henry Lozano, was anointed for the post. But when 10 others from various Hispanic factions got into the race, Lozano withdrew in favor of one-term Assemblyman Xavier Becerra, who eventually triumphed.

Becerra, a deputy attorney general and former aide to state Sen. Art Torres, won his Assembly seat in a similar race after it fell vacant when Charles Calderon moved up to the state Senate. Becerra ran an aggressive campaign, using strong grass-roots organizing and direct mail while portraying himself as a crime fighter. Becerra shouldn't have to withstand strong challenges in the future. Yet his first term had to be a frustrating one since he got his second-

Xavier Becerra

choice committee assignments and saw one of his passions stall, the health-care reform initiative. He also worked on educational reforms aimed at early childhood development and disadvantaged youth. Now, as a junior member of the minority party, he will have little room to push his progressive agenda.

PERSONAL: elected 1992; born Jan. 26, 1958, in Sacramento; home, Los Angeles; education, B.A. and J.D. Stanford University; wife, Dr. Carolina Reyes.

CAREER: lawyer; deputy attorney general; aide to Sen. Art Torres.

COMMITTEES: Economic and Educational Opportunities; Judiciary.

OFFICES: Suite 1119, Longworth Building, Washington, D.C. 20515, (202) 225-6235, FAX (202) 225-2202; district, Suite 200, 2435 Colorado Blvd., Los Angeles 90041, (213) 722-0405.

REGISTRATION: 62.6% D, 22% R

1994 CAMPAIGN:	Becerra D	66.2%	$286,755
	David Ramirez R	28.2%	$11,216
1992 CAMPAIGN:	Becerra D	58.4%	$332,337
	Morry Waksberg R	23.9%	$52,795

RATINGS:

ADA	ACU	AFL/CIO	GO	LCV	NCSC	NTU	USCC
95	2	86	F	88	80	19	20

Anthony C. Beilenson (D)
24th Congressional District

On the south, this district showcases the fabled Malibu Coast between Topanga Canyon and the Los Angeles County line. It laps over the hills into Thousand Oaks and then eastward through Agoura Hills, Woodland Hills, Tarzana, Encino and Van Nuys. Most residents are upper middle-class professionals. Lower-income people are disappearing from the hillsides as homes are snapped up by two-income couples with few children.

One might expect a flashy liberal to represent this area. But Rep. Tony Beilenson is one of the more anonymous members of the delegation. He typifies the Jewish professional of the district. He is a solid and conscientious performer whose legislative skills are widely respected. He seems nearly devoid of partisanship, which sometimes annoys those who would like to see him use his seat on the Rules Committee to the greater advantage of Democrats. He is an expert on the budget and was responsible for creating the Santa Monica Mountains National Recreation area.

Anthony Beilenson

Beilenson's old district was centered in Beverly Hills and West Hollywood, where he had a testy coexistence with the political organization headed by Reps. Howard Berman and Henry Waxman. But that district was collapsed during reapportionment, forcing Beilenson to move to the San Fernando Valley and a district less friendly to a liberal.

Smelling blood, conservatives fielded Assemblyman Tom McClintock, who had been a thorn in the side of Gov. Pete Wilson. But McClintock's extreme views on everything from abortion to gun control didn't ignite a spark. In 1994, the GOP came back with a more moderate candidate, Richard Sybert, who had been policy and research director for Wilson. After a nasty primary, Sybert took after Beilenson with a big-spending campaign. Even before it was clear that a GOP rout was building, pundits were saying Beilenson was a likely casualty. But Beilenson campaigned in the methodical way he always had and became one of the few swing-district incumbent Democrats still standing when votes were counted, even though he was out-spent 3-1.

Sybert's ties to Wilson, as it turned out, were a liability. This is one of the districts heavily damaged by the Northridge earthquake of January 1994. The Wilson administration's response made commuters and contractors happy, but efforts on behalf of small business, homeowners and apartment-dwellers were feeble, at best. Wilson refused to allow a temporary tax increase to restore the area. The feds, meanwhile, did more than their share to relieve suffering. This was one area where Beilenson was helped by being a long-time federal incumbent.

PERSONAL: elected 1976; born Oct. 26, 1932, in New Rochelle, N.Y.; home, Woodland Hills; education, A.B. Harvard University 1954, L.L.B. 1957; wife, Dolores, three children; Jewish.

CAREER: attorney 1957-59; counsel to Assembly Committee on Finance and Insurance, 1960; counsel to California Compensation and Insurance Fund, 1961-62; Assembly, 1963-66; state Senate, 1966-77.

COMMITTEES: Rules.

OFFICES: Suite 2465, Rayburn Building, Washington, D.C. 20515, (202) 225-

5911; district, Suite 1010, 21031 Ventura Blvd., Woodland Hills 91364, (818) 999-1990.

REGISTRATION: 46.3% D, 40.1% R

1994 CAMPAIGN:	Beilenson D	49.4%	$601,538
	Richard Sybert R	47.5%	$1,685,428
1992 CAMPAIGN:	Beilenson D	55.5%	552,071$
	Tom McClintock R	39.1%	$460,327

RATINGS:

ADA	ACU	AFL/CIO	GO	LCV	NCSC	NTU	USCC
85	7	75	F	92	88	25	27

Howard Berman (D)
26th Congressional District

Howard Berman

This compact district begins at the Ventura Free-way between Van Nuys and Burbank. It runs north-ward in fairly straight lines through North Holly-wood, Panorama City, Pacoima and San Fernando before butting into the Los Angeles city limits. There is a mix of people and an increasing number of apartment houses in the southern end of the district. Hispanic neighborhoods straddle the Golden State Freeway and are predominant in Sylmar and San Fernando. There are African American neighbor-hoods in Pacoima.

This could be a good district for a Hispanic candidate. But Rep. Howard Berman needed a place to run after his old district in the Hollywood Hills was chewed up during reapportionment. Berman shares what was once one of the strongest political machines in Southern California with Rep. Henry Waxman. They have legendary fund-raising capability and substantial success at the ballot box. Berman is often the most politically assertive of the two, working hand-in-hand with two ace strategists and campaign managers, Berman's brother, Michael, and Carl D'Agostino. They've been accused of creating political puppets and keeping them in power with contributions raised elsewhere. That has been said about Reps. Julian Dixon, Esteban Torres and Matthew Martinez. If that was the intent, it hasn't worked in the cases of Dixon and Torres, who show substantial independence. Martinez, however, doesn't show much of anything.

In the 1992 and '94 elections, Berman-Waxman backed a series of losers, and pundits have been writing obituaries for the old westside gang. But they still have a powerful base of support that most politicians would rather not challenge.

When Berman was in the Assembly he was a divisive force, fomenting a spiteful revolt against Speaker Leo McCarthy in 1980. Their battle preoccupied the house for a year. Eventually, Willie Brown emerged from the fray with Republican backing to win the speakership, beginning his long reign. McCarthy went on to become lieutenant governor and Brown got rid of Berman, a potential rival, by creating a new congressional district for him in Los Angeles. Berman has been more of a team player in Congress, where he is now minority whip-at-large.

As an urban legislator, Berman has been well positioned politically to be a stalwart defender of the United Farm Workers. He has been active on border and immigration issues, anti-apartheid legislation and other civil libertarian matters that play well in his district. But he also has been an astute observer of Mideast politics. He raised warnings about the chemical-nuclear capability in Iraq long before the Bush administration figured out Saddam Hussein could never be a reliable ally. On the Judiciary Committee, he also has been able to assist his show-business constituents with copyright and licensing protections.

PERSONAL: elected, 1982; born, April 15, 1941, in Los Angeles; home, Los Angeles; education, B.A. UCLA 1962, L.L.B. 1965; wife Janis, two children; Jewish.

CAREER: attorney, 1966-72; Assembly 1973-82.

COMMITTEES: International Relations, Judiciary.

OFFICES: Suite 2231, Rayburn Building, Washington, D.C. 20515, (202) 225-4695, FAX (202) 225-5279; district, Suite 130, 1555 S. Palm Canyon Dr., Mission Hills 91345, (818) 891-0543.

REGISTRATION: 60.1% D, 27.2% R

1994 CAMPAIGN:	Berman D	62.6%	$467,994
	Gary Forsch R	32.2%	$38,936
1992 CAMPAIGN:	Berman D	61%	$343,552
	Gary Forsch R	30.1%	$72,928

RATINGS:

ADA	ACU	AFL/CIO	GO	LCV	NCSC	NTU	USCC
95	6	88	F	96	97	13	25

Brian Bilbray (R)

49th Congressional District

Some of the crown jewels of the California Coast lie in the 49th District from Del Mar to the Mexican border. This land of millionaires and Navy bases has some of the most photogenic communities in the nation: Torrey Pines, La Jolla, Mission Beach, Point Loma and Coronado. There is an eastward bulge up the Mission Valley that stops just short of La Mesa. On the southern end, the district narrows as it runs along the Silver Strand and then juts eastward to include all of Imperial Beach.

This district is solid Republican country. Yet after the 1990 reapportionment, three GOP incumbents — Bill Lowery, Randy Cunningham and Duncan Hunter — decided to move out and run elsewhere. That set up a divisive Republican primary won by businesswoman Judy Jarvis. She faced Port Commissioner Lynn Schenk in the runoff and Jarvis may still be wondering what it was that hit her on Election Day. Schenk ran an incredible 12 points ahead of the Democratic registration for the most impressive win by any of the 17 newcomers in the state delegation.

Nonetheless, she became a prime target in 1994, and lost an ugly race to Supervisor Brian Bilbray on Election Day. Bilbray called himself a "blue-collar Navy kid," which masked the fact that he'd never served in the military, and painted Schenk, who's beginnings were much more humble, as a Yuppie debutante from La Jolla. They did battle in a district where President Clinton is exceedingly unpopular and military downsizing and border issues have cre-

Brian Bilbray

ated a restive electorate. Bilbray became a darling of the conservative talk-show circuit in a district where there are plenty of retirees who listen in. Ross Perot supporters turned out from throughout the county to walk precincts for him. In the end, Bilbray's slashing attacks carried the day despite being out-spent by a 2-1 ratio.

As an officeholder, Bilbray is known for being outspoken and independent. In Congress, he's made reform of welfare and environmental laws top priorities.

PERSONAL: elected 1994; born Jan. 28, 1951, in Coronado; home, Imperial Beach; education, Southwestern College; wife Karen, 5 children; Roman Catholic.

CAREER: tax consultant; Imperial Beach city councilman and mayor, 1976-84; San Diego County Board of Supervisors, 1984-1994

COMMITTEES: Commerce.

OFFICES: Suite 1004, Longworth Building, Washington, D.C. 20515, (202) 225-2040; district, 1101 Camino de Rio South, San Diego 92108, (619) 291-1430.

REGISTRATION: 40.6 D, 41.8 R

1994 CAMPAIGN:	Bilbray R	48.5%	$683,157
	Lynn Schenk D	46%	$1,377,384

RATINGS: Newly elected.

Sonny Bono (R)
44th Congressional District

How many members of the House can joke about playing second-fiddle to a dwarf on the TV show "Fantasy Island?" Just Salvatore "Sonny" Bono, the former songwriter, entertainer, restaurant owner and Palm Springs mayor.

Six-term Rep. Al McCandless retired at the end of the 103rd Congress, leaving an open seat in this conservative and fastest growing district in the state. Bono beat five primary opponents (even though he failed to carry Palm Springs) and easily trounced ex-Assemblyman Steve Clute, D-Riverside, in the runoff.

There wasn't a lot of enthusiasm for Bono in some GOP quarters. Former Palm Spring mayor and staunch Republican Frank Bogert put it this way: "I'd hate to see another Democrat in Congress, but Sonny Bono is just not qualified to be a U.S. congressman. Sonny is a nice little actor and I like him, but he has no education, no background, no political ability and he did a horrible job as mayor here."

Sonny Bono

Bono has said he ran for mayor to get even with health inspectors who delayed the opening of his restaurant. After one term, he ran in the GOP primary for the U.S. Senate in 1992, placing third behind then-Rep. Tom Campbell, R-Palo Alto, and TV commentator Bruce Herschenshon. The latter then lost to Sen. Barbara Boxer.

Out of that came a friendship with Herschensohn, who managed Bono's 1994 race. First, however, Bono said he'd oppose McClandless in the primary. Then he flirted with a run for lieutenant governor, an idea that gave night sweats to Gov. Pete Wilson's staff.

Bono's campaign appearances were more like comedy routines. After 10-15 minutes of jokes, he would recite a Herschensohn script calling for reduced government, cutting red-tape and dumping professional pols out of office. Even if it hadn't been a Republican year nationally, Bono had the money, issues and GOP registration going for him.

That's not bad for a former delivery truck driver who didn't even bother to register to vote until he was 52 years old. Bono had major success as a songwriter, producing 10 hits selling in excess of 1 million records. But real fame came in 1964, when he teamed with then-girlfriend Cherilyn Sarkisian and named their act Sonny and Cher. Their first hit was "Baby Don't Go." A few years later, they took their popular night club act to television for a tumultuous and well-rated three-season run.

It remains to be seen what Cher's former straight man can do for this district, which begins at the city of Riverside's eastern suburbs and runs all the way across Riverside County's high desert to the Arizona border. Once beyond Moreno Valley, Sun City and Hemet, the towns are clustered along Interstate 10 as it bisects the county. At the western end, there are the trailer towns loaded with retirees and young families in the sterile Moreno Valley subdivisions. Further east are the lavish desert communities of Palm Springs and Palm Desert. From there, it is on to Indio and the rich farmlands of the Coachella Valley, then across the scorching desert to Blythe.

The Palm Springs area is home to movie stars and retired captains of industry, plus former President Jerry Ford and former Vice President Spiro Agnew. But there are many displaced defense workers and less-well-off retirees living in condos and fading trailers. The service sector is dominated by Hispanics, many of whom travel some distance to low-paying jobs.

PERSONAL: elected 1994; born Feb. 16, 1935, in Detroit, Mich.; home, Palm Springs; diploma, Inglewood High School, 1953; wife Mary Whitaker; four children; Roman Catholic.

CAREER: delivery truck driver, songwriter/entertainer, restaurateur, Palm Springs mayor 1988-92.

COMMITTEES: Banking & Financial Services, Judiciary.

OFFICES: Suite 512, Cannon Building, Washington, D.C. 20515, (202) 225-5330; district, Suite G101, 1555 S. Palm Canyon Dr., Palm Springs 92264 (619) 320-1076.

REGISTRATION: 44.1% D, 43.7% R

1994 CAMPAIGN:	Bono R	55.6%	$725,314
	Steve Clute D	38.1%	$339,493

RATINGS: Newly elected.

George E. Brown Jr. (D)
42nd Congressional District

Districts may change, but not Rep. George Brown. One of the House's oldest peaceniks, Brown continues to champion liberal causes despite dramatic gains in his district's Republican registration and nonstop efforts by GOP candidates to unseat him. The cigar-chomping Brown comes from Quaker stock and is a nuclear engineer. He was talking about global warming and the virtues of solar energy long before it was fashionable. In 1987, Brown quit the Intelligence Committee, saying he couldn't live with the committee's gag rules on topics that are general knowledge elsewhere.

George E. Brown Jr.

In 1991, Brown became chairman of the Science, Space and Technology Committee, where he worked to refashion national energy policy. But after the GOP seized the House in 1995, Brown was relegated to ranking minority member. The chairmanship was a key loss for California since no California Republican in the 104th Congress heads a significant committee.

Brown's long House career began in 1962. In 1970, he nearly won the Democratic U.S. Senate primary and probably could have dumped GOP Sen. George Murphy. But that privilege went to neighboring House member John Tunney. Brown sat out for two years and was re-elected, but he returned to the House without those eight years of precious seniority.

He represents a district far different from the one that first sent him to Congress. Monterey Park, where Brown first ran for public office in 1954, is some 20 miles from the district's nearest border. Today, Brown represents the most densely populated area of San Bernardino County — the city of the same name, and the industrial towns of Colton, Rialto, Fontana and Rancho Cucamonga. Many people living in those smog-choked cities are there for lack of choices, including blue-collar workers and older people who can't afford more pleasant environs.

For years, Republicans threw far-right candidates against Brown. In 1992, with a district more Republican than the previous one, they fielded a folk hero of sorts, aeronaut Dick Rutan. But Rutan proved to be a better pilot than a candidate. Two years later, the GOP found a Latino from Fontana named Rob Guzman. Despite being underfunded and having to explain why he'd run unsuccessfully for Congress in east Los Angeles in 1992, Guzman almost beat Brown. As always, the GOP will be targeting Brown in 1996 if he runs for re-election.

PERSONAL: elected in 1962 and served until 1971, re-elected in 1972; born March 6, 1920, in Holtville, Calif.; home, San Bernardino; education, B.A. UCLA 1946; wife Marta, four children; United Methodist.

CAREER: U.S. Army, 1942-45; Monterey Park City Council, 1954-58, mayor 1955-56; engineer and management consultant, city of Los Angeles, 1946-58; Assembly 1958-62.

COMMITTEES: Agriculture; Science.

OFFICES: Suite 2300, Rayburn Building, Washington, D.C. 20515, (202) 225-6161, FAX (202) 225-8671; district, 657 La Cadena Dr., Colton 92324, (714) 823-2472.

REGISTRATION: 51.9% D, 37.9% R

1994 CAMPAIGN:	Brown D	51.1%	$510,719
	Rob Guzman R	48.8%	$295,431
1992 CAMPAIGN:	Brown D	50.7%	$835,671
	Dick Rutan R	43.9%	$347,999

RATINGS:

ADA	ACU	AFL/CIO	GO	LCV	NCSC	NTU	USCC
90	6	90	F	69	94	15	23

Ken Calvert (R)
43rd Congressional District

The west end of Riverside County, from the grimy cities of Riverside and Corona to the open country around Lake Elsinore, became a new Republican district in 1992 after reapportionment. Many residents are young families who bought homes in the area with the hope that one day they could cash in their equity and move closer to their jobs in less smoggy areas of the Los Angeles Basin. The trouble is, many of them spend two to four hours a day commuting. They come home so drained they don't get around to participating in community activities, such as voting.

Yet many of those Republicans also have been unemployed or worried about losing their jobs in recent years. That enabled Democrat and junior high teacher Mark Takano to come within a hair of winning the seat in 1992. In fact, he did squeak by on Election Day, but absentee votes gave the seat to commercial Realtor Ken Calvert by just 519 votes.

Calvert shouldn't have had any trouble holding the seat in 1994. But midway through his first term, Corona police found him in a car with a prostitute. First Calvert (with his 100 percent Christian Coalition rating) lied about it, and then he began begging

Ken Calvert

his constituents forgiveness for "an embarrassing situation." About that time, it was learned he owed back taxes on some commercial property.

Calvert survived the 1994 primary with a 1,000-vote margin over the conservative he'd beaten before and then faced a rematch with Takano. The campaign wasn't just mean and dirty, it was vile. Takano papered the district with mailers that depicted a hooker sitting on a bed. The caption read: "It's Midnight. Do You Know Where Your Congressman Is?"

In response, Assemblyman Ray Haynes — a conservative Republican running for the state Senate in roughly the same area — accused Takano of being gay. He had no proof and Takano refused to discuss the question. Calvert said he wouldn't stoop to an issue like that, adding with a wink that he likes girls. He also sent out flyers asking in pink letters: "A congressman for Riverside . . . or San Francisco?" When things started looking bleak for Calvert, he prevailed on the wife he was divorcing to send a letter to constituents saying what a good guy he is. Incredibly, the letter raised an issue that had never been heard before in the campaign. She denied that Calvert had beaten her.

Despite all that, Calvert ran back into office with the rest of the elephant herd. It helped that between the 1992 and 1994 elections, he improved the GOP registration edge in the district by nearly 2 percentage points. Only Jay Leno got the last laugh with a joke about Calvert and the hooker: "He says he had no idea she was a prostitute or he wouldn't have done it. And today the prostitute said, 'Hey, I didn't know he was a congressman or I wouldn't have done it either.'"

Calvert has a long history of party activism, which includes holding top posts in two of Pete Wilson's statewide campaigns and California co-chair of George Bush's 1988 presidential campaign in California.

PERSONAL: elected 1992; born June 8, 1953, in Corona; home, Corona; A.A. Chaffey College, B.A. San Diego State University; divorced; Protestant.

CAREER: restaurant manager, 1975-79; commercial Realtor and president of his own firm since 1981.

COMMITTEES: Agriculture; Resources; Science.

OFFICES: Suite 1034, Longworth Building, Washington, D.C. 20515, (202) 225-1986; district, Suite 200, 3400 Central Ave., Riverside 92506, (909) 784-4300.

REGISTRATION: 41% D, 47.2% R

1994 CAMPAIGN:	Calvert R	54.7%	$780,471
	Mark Takano D	38.4%	$561,209
1992 CAMPAIGN:	Calvert R	46.7%	$407,821
	Mark Takano D	46.4%	$240,905

RATINGS:

ADA	ACU	AFL/CIO	GO	LCV	NCSC	NTU	USCC
0	93	5	A-	4	10	73	100

Gary Condit (D)
18th Congressional District

The 18th District includes the richest agricultural region in the San Joaquin Valley and is growing both more Hispanic and more politically diverse as Bay Area workers filter into the valley in search of less expensive housing. Nearly a quarter of the residents now have Spanish surnames.

The district begins at Ripon, in southern San Joaquin County, and takes in all of Stanislaus and Merced counties. It twists around the population centers of Madera County before ending abruptly on the stark, northwestern reaches of Fresno County. Fast-growing Modesto is the population center. The district has been safe turf for conservative Democrats since the 1950s.

Gary Condit

From this fertile ground came Rep. Tony Coelho, who in just eight years went from freshman to majority whip, the No. 3 Democratic position in the House. But then came revelations about a questionable junk-bond purchase and personal loan. Rather than face a gauntlet such as those that felled others in high House positions, Coelho resigned in midterm.

Gary Condit, then an assemblyman from Ceres, easily won the post in a 1989 special election. His district is so safe that he didn't even draw a GOP opponent in 1992 and he won in 1994 with 66 percent of the vote. But it hasn't been as easy to fill Coelho's shoes. Condit, who has the most conservative voting record of any California Democrat in Congress, never learned to play by the rules. It is not unusual to find him siding with Republicans on crime, civil rights or budget matters. He has also been an inattentive member of the House Agriculture Committee.

Condit showed a similar disposition during his seven years in the Assembly. Crime and drug bills occupied most of his time, and he was one of the dissident "Gang of Five" Democrats who made life unpleasant for Assembly Speaker Willie Brown. In the Congress, he is part of the "Gang of Six," which has similar interests in internal reform and sided with Republicans on efforts to pass a balanced budget amendment.

Such behavior kept him from getting a seat on the House Energy and Commerce Committee in 1991. In 1992, he shook out his office and staffed it with some seasoned pros. But his voting record was of little help to those who could advance his career. In 1995, he became ranking minority member on a key Agriculture subcommittee, but he still has backbench status in his caucus.

PERSONAL: special election 1989; born April 21, 1948, in Salina, Okla.; home, Ceres; education, A.A. Modesto College 1970, B.A. Stanislaus State College 1972; wife Carolyn, two children; Baptist.

CAREER: production worker, Riverbank Ammunition Depot, 1972-76; community relations, National Medical Enterprises, 1976-82; Ceres City Council, 1972-74, mayor 1974-76; Stanislaus County Board of Supervisors, 1976-82; Assembly 1982-89.

COMMITTEES: Agriculture; Government Reform & Oversight.

OFFICES: Suite 2444, Rayburn Building, Washington, D.C. 20515, (202) 225-6131, FAX (202) 225-0819; district, 415 West Main St., Merced 95340, (209) 383-4455; Suite C, 920 16th St., Modesto 95354, (209) 527-1914.

REGISTRATION: 52.1% D, 36.8% R

1994 CAMPAIGN:	Condit D	65.5%	$398,389
	Tom Carter R	31.%	$7,230
1992 CAMPAIGN:	Condit D	84.6%	$269,036

RATINGS:

ADA	ACU	AFL/CIO	GO	LCV	NCSC	NTU	USCC
60	42	77	D	19	52	66	50

Christopher Cox (R)
47th Congressional District

Beginning at the Anaheim Hills, this Orange County district waddles west through Tustin and east to the San Bernardino County line. It then swings southwesterly through Irvine, the vast undeveloped holdings of the Irvine Co., and Laguna Hills, where mountain lions still roam. The 47th ends with a window on the Pacific Ocean between Newport Beach and Laguna Beach.

From top to bottom, the district is wealthy Republican country and conservative as only Orange County can be. In the 1970s and '80s, the area became almost a second downtown Los Angeles as companies established regional offices and research parks amid acres of parking lots. The University of California, Irvine, was a magnet for some of the growth, as were the development rules written to Irvine Co. specifications.

The district's lackluster congressman, Robert Badham, hung it up in 1988. The race to replace him was decided in the GOP primary (general elections are perfunctory exercises here) as 14 conservatives vied for attention and votes. Attorney Chris Cox emerged from the pack with 31 percent of the vote. Cox, making his first try for public office, had a solid background. He was a Harvard lecturer with strong links to the corporate world, and he also had been a White House counsel. That impressed district residents, but probably not as much as personal campaign appearances on Cox's behalf by Oliver North, Robert Bork and Arthur Laffer.

Christopher Cox

Initially, the GOP delegation saw to it that Cox got good committee assignments. But in 1993, Rep. Wally Herger, R-Marysville, beat out Cox for a coveted spot on the Ways and Means Committee. It appears Cox is a bit too cerebral for some GOP leaders, in addition to being pushy about term limits for committee chairmen. Those qualities impressed Speaker Newt Gingrich, however. When Republicans took control in 1995, Cox was named chairman of the Republican Policy Committee, the No. 5 position in the leadership. That makes him the most powerful member of the delegation, although Gingrich has anointed Rep. David Dreier of Covina to head California Republicans. Cox, a strong advocate of returning to Reaganomics, will have an important role in shaping economic policy and deregulation in the 104th Congress.

But his first concern was more regulation for financial markets that allowed Orange County Treasurer-Tax Collector Robert Citron's disastrous gambling with the county investment pool. Cox quickly emerged as the chief apologist for the failure of Orange County political leaders to ride herd on Citron.

PERSONAL: elected 1988; born Oct. 16, 1952, in St. Paul, Minn.; home, Newport; education, B.A. University of Southern California 1973, M.B.A., J.D. Harvard University 1977; single; Roman Catholic.

CAREER: attorney, 1978-86; lecturer, Harvard Business School, 1982-83; White House counsel, 1986-88.

COMMITTEES: Commerce; Joint Economic.

OFFICES: Suite 2402, Rayburn Building, Washington, D.C. 20515, (202) 225-5611, FAX (202) 225-9177; district, Suite 430, 4000 MacArthur Blvd., Newport Beach 92660, (714) 644-4040.

REGISTRATION: 30.1% D, 56.4% R

1994 CAMPAIGN:	Cox R	71.6%	$456,754
	Gary Kingsbury D	25%	$54,777

1992 CAMPAIGN: Cox R 64.9%$ 294,332
John Anwiler D 30.2% $1,675
RATINGS:

ADA	ACU	AFL/CIO	GO	LCV	NCSC	NTU	USCC
0	98	7	A	12	10	81	87

Randy "Duke" Cunningham (R)
51st Congressional District

Randy Cunningham

Mushrooming growth in San Diego County gave the area a new congressional district in 1992. The lines were drawn in a northern and very Republican portion of the county. On the ocean side, it stretches from Carlsbad to Del Mar. Inland are the cities of San Marcos, Escondido, Poway, Miramar and a portion of the city of San Diego. One finger juts into the Mission Valley and stops just short of La Mesa.

Retirees make up the biggest population bloc and not all are well off. Many live in aging trailer courts and anxiously await the arrival of their next Social Security checks. But many more live in stately homes and gated communities where the chief frustrations are the infirmities of age. For those who work, the Navy and service jobs are primary sources of income.

For a while, it appeared that two GOP incumbents would go head to head here. Neither Reps. Randy "Duke" Cunningham of Chula Vista nor Bill Lowery of San Diego were happy with the new shape of their districts. Gov. Pete Wilson, who's never quit tinkering in San Diego County politics, tried to persuade Cunningham to stay in the 49th District. But Cunningham would have none of it.

Then Lowery, who had been considered one of the brightest lights in the state GOP delegation, began taking stock of himself. He had been severely criticized for being the House's No. 1 recipient of savings and loan contributions. And he also had 300 overdrafts at the House bank. Lowery prudently decided to retire from politics.

Cunningham's election in 1990 was something of a fluke. Bucking the odds in what was then the county's only Democratic district, Cunningham took on incumbent Jim Bates just after the House Ethics Committee found Bates guilty of harassing two female staff members. Cunningham squeaked by with only 1,659 votes to spare.

Cunningham didn't even register to vote until 1988. But he brought a lot of pluses to the race in this Navy county. He was one of the most highly decorated fighter pilots of the Vietnam War and the first American fighter ace in that conflict. He holds the Navy Cross, two Silver Stars, 10 air medals, the Purple Heart and other decorations. Some of his experiences were depicted in the movie "Top Gun." After the war, he taught fighter pilots at the Navy Fighter Weapons School at Miramar and retired as a commander. But he still found time to work in community drug programs and civic organizations.

Cunningham entered Congress in a blaze of glory, but it didn't take long for his star to dim. He quickly aligned himself with Rep. "B-1 Bob" Dornan and the cracker right of his party. He spent the 1992 campaign hurling McCarthy-like charges at Bill Clinton and was one of the unholy quartet who persuaded President Bush to hint that Clinton might have once been a pawn of the Soviet KGB. This is a safe seat for Cunningham, but he didn't do much with it in the Democratic house. With the GOP in control, he now has a policy role in defense issues that he has used to push for development of new weapons systems.

PERSONAL: elected 1990; born Dec. 8, 1941, in Los Angeles; home, Del Mar; education, B.A. University of Missouri 1964, M.Ed. 1965; wife Nancy, three children; Baptist.

CAREER: coach, Hinsdale (Ill.) High school, 1965-66; U.S. Navy fighter pilot, 1966-87.

COMMITTEES: Economic & Educational Opportunities; National Security;

OFFICES: Suite 117, Cannon Building, Washington, D.C. 20515, (202) 225-5452, FAX (202) 225-2558; district, Suite 320, 613 W. Valley Pky., Escondido 92025, (619) 737-8438.

REGISTRATION: 30.5% D, 51.5% R

1994 CAMPAIGN:	Cunningham R	66.9%	$494,210
	Rita Tamerius D	27.7%	$66,860
1992 CAMPAIGN:	Cunningham R	56%	$797,149
	Bea Herbert D	33.6%	$22,839

RATINGS:

ADA	ACU	AFL/CIO	GO	LCV	NCSC	NTU	USCC
0	95	13	A	8	17	79	86

Ron Dellums (D)
9th Congressional District

Who could bounce 851 checks at the House bank — more than any other congressman — call disclosure of that fact an unwarranted intrusion in his family finances, and then win re-election with 72 percent of the vote? Only Rep. Ron Dellums, thanks to a district that includes Oakland and the People's Republic of Berkeley. It is an area of unabashed liberalism, where nearly two of every three people are of color. Many don't vote and those who do seem prone to excuse Dellums' excesses and inattention to district concerns.

Dellums, one of the most liberal members of the California delegation, has a polarizing effect on people. Constituents seem to either love him or loathe him. And in a district as safe as this one, Dellums can get away with ignoring detractors. It is a posture that was effective in the quirky arena of the Berkeley City Council, where Dellums spent four years. But it has served him less well in Congress.

Dellums' gift for oratory gave him unusual visibility when he first went to Congress, but it led to few constructive advances for him or his district. He wouldn't help boost the flow of federal money to the University of California, which is its lifeblood. Such parochial concerns as the district's seething crime problem, substandard schools and housing and a shrinking job base seemed to bore Dellums. When his vote was needed on issues important to his constitu-

Ron Dellums

ency, Dellums frequently couldn't be found. That is why like-minded colleagues tend to regard Dellums as an unreliable ally.

In the 1980s, Dellums developed a protective attitude over the huge Oakland and Alameda military bases, but that feeling didn't extend across the bay to Hunter's Point in San Francisco with its predominantly African American community. He helped kill a proposal to home-port the battleship Missouri there. Perhaps his greatest legislative victory was his work to push Congress to impose sanctions on South Africa. He also learned to work with senior leaders, and in 1990, he had a key role in killing several questionable missile systems as chairman of the Armed Services research and development subcommittee.

Then came the Clinton-Gore victory in 1992 and the opportunity of a lifetime for Dellums. Clinton picked Wisconsin Rep. Les Aspin, chair of the Armed Services Committee, to be secretary of defense. That cleared the way for Dellums to use his seniority to claim the Armed Services chair.

The reaction in the already beleaguered military-industrial complex resembled the explosion of a fragmentation bomb. A self-proclaimed radical who had been called a positive menace to the U.S. security posture by a conservative Washington think tank, would now be molding the annual Pentagon budget. Dellums, as usual, pulled no punches. The man who called the Star Wars anti-missile program a gross case of theft and who praised Fidel Castro, began by urging annual defense cuts of 15 percent. By the year 2000, he wanted the Pentagon budget to be half its current size with the savings earmarked for the nation's poorest people.

Dellums spent a lot of time in the 103rd Congress chopping defense programs, but his posture was not as Draconian as detractors had feared. He proved to be an evenhanded chairman who would listen to other views. Dellums still had much work to do when Democrats lost control of the House after the 1994 elections. He's now relegated to minority status and can expect to find himself on the losing end of many committee votes. The GOP also axed the District of Columbia Committee, which was his power base in the African American community. Unless and until Democrats regain the House, life is apt to be much less interesting for Dellums.

PERSONAL: elected 1970; born Nov. 24, 1935, in Oakland; home, Berkeley; education, A.A. Oakland City College 1958, B.A. San Francisco State College 1960, M.S.W. UC Berkeley 1962; wife Leola, three children; Protestant.

CAREER: U.S. Marine Corps, 1954-56; social worker, poverty program administrator and consultant, 1962-70.

COMMITTEES: National Security.

OFFICES: Suite 2108, Rayburn Building, Washington, D.C. 20515, (202) 225-2661, FAX (202) 225-9817; district, Suite 1000N, 1301 Clay St., Oakland 94612, (415) 763-0370.

REGISTRATION: 69.4% D, 13.2% R

1994 CAMPAIGN:	Dellums D	72.2%	$477,124
	Deborah Wright R	22.6%	$18,442
1992 CAMPAIGN:	Dellums D	71.9	$749,376
	William Hunter R	23.5%	$70,444

RATINGS:

ADA	ACU	AFL/CIO	GO	LCV	NCSC	NTU	USCC
100	6	93	F	96	98	20	16

Julian Dixon (D)
32nd Congressional District

Julian Dixon

Through the 1980s, Democrats controlled the House of Representatives, but not its Committee on Standards of Official Conduct, better known as the ethics committee. That was the fiefdom of Rep. Julian Dixon, and Dixon is his own man. Though a party loyalist on most issues, Dixon is aggressively nonpartisan when it comes to issues of right and wrong. And that is true whether the subject of the investigation is someone as obscure as Rep. Jim Weaver of Oregon (who speculated in commodities with campaign funds) or as powerful as Speaker Jim Wright of Texas (whose tangled financial deals eventually drove him from office and whose investigation gave Dixon his first taste of national notoriety).

No sooner did the committee finish with the Wright investigation than it began its first investigation of California Democrat Jim Bates, who was found guilty by the committee in October 1989 of sexually harassing staff members. Bates was defeated the following year just as Dixon was giving up the chairmanship. Normally, the ethics chairman rotates every six years, but Dixon established such a strong reputation for fairness that he was asked to stay on for most of the decade.

Dixon showed the same temperament when chairing the Democratic convention's platform committee in 1984. Dixon, an African American, also won't allow race to color his judgment. As a member of the old District of Columbia Committee, he demanded accountability by the city's African American leadership. He also showed no hesitation to brand Yasser Arafat a terrorist at a time when the Rev. Jesse Jackson was comparing the PLO's struggle to the battle for racial equity in this country. In all things, Dixon is a conciliator and a fact-finder. Those are qualities he has used effectively to defuse antagonisms between Jewish and African American communities in the Los Angeles area.

In 1992, Dixon won a seat on the Democratic Policy Committee, which controls committee assignments. Until Republicans took control of the House in 1995, he was a power on the Appropriations Committee. He'd helped funnel money into numerous public works projects in the Los Angeles area and carried the supplemental appropriations bill to assist rebuilding efforts after the 1992 riots. He also had the thankless job of chairing the District of Columbia appropriations subcommittee during the Bush and part of the Reagan years, which put him in the middle of many fights between African American activists and the GOP White House. Bush vetoed his appropriation bills twice in a dispute over abortion language.

Dixon's district, the second-most Democratic in the state, lies on the floor of the Los Angeles basin between downtown and the Los Angeles International Airport. It takes in poverty-stricken areas of northern Watts and Culver City, which is the home of many middle-and upper-middle-class African Americans. There are middle-class white and Hispanic portions, too, and affluent neighborhoods such as Rancho Park. Yet lingering tensions from the 1992 riots and increasing gang warfare threaten the stability of the area. Such conditions are feeding an exodus by those who can afford to move.

PERSONAL: elected, 1978; born Aug. 8, 1934, in Washington, D.C.; home, Culver City; education, B.S. Los Angeles State College 1962, L.L.B. Southwestern University 1967; wife Betty, one child; Episcopalian.

CAREER: U.S. Army, 1957-60; attorney, 1967-73; Assembly, 1972-78.

COMMITTEES: Appropriations, Intelligence.

OFFICES: Suite 2252, Rayburn Building, Washington, D.C. 20515, (202) 225-7084, FAX (202) 225-4091; district, Suite 208, 5100 West Goldleaf Circle, Los Angeles 90056, (213) 678-5424.

REGISTRATION: 76.7% D, 12.7% R

1994 CAMPAIGN:	Dixon D	77.6%	$180,135
	Ernie Farhat R	17.5%	$43,914
1992 CAMPAIGN:	Dixon D	87.2%	$55,932

RATINGS:

ADA	ACU	AFL/CIO	GO	LCV	NCSC	NTU	USCC
80	5	96	F	81	97	9	25

Calvin Dooley (D)
20th Congressional District

When the reapportionment mapmakers were through in 1992, this swing district took on a strong Democratic hue. Yet it is a conservative one, populated by growers, oil workers, small-town shopkeepers and a growing number of state prison guards who work in the mammoth human vaults that have sprung up in the central and southern San Joaquin Valley.

Calvin Dooley

The northern end of the district takes in part of the city of Fresno, which is the regional hub of the valley and also the home of a large number of state and federal workers. It swings west to include farming and oil field regions in Fresno, Kings and Kern counties, and then sneaks into Bakersfield from the south.

Visalia-area farmer Cal Dooley upset a Republican incumbent here in 1990 and immediately established himself as a rising star in Congress. He represents a new generation of wealthy growers who are well educated, politically involved and astute businessmen. He entered Congress as a team player and quickly impressed the leadership with his savvy. Soon, he was awarded plum assignments on both the Agriculture and Natural Resources committees. In 1993, he was granted an unusual waiver to serve on a third major committee, Banking Finance and Urban Affairs.

All that was eclipsed in 1995 when Republicans seized control of the Congress. Dooley had little trouble hanging onto his seat, but the game changed dramatically. He, at least, is better positioned than most Democrats to work in a bipartisan way on the ag issues that are so important to his district. Dooley has compiled a moderate voting record and is an articulate spokesman for homespun values. He also brings a social conscience to the Congress. In Tulare County, he was active in civic, education and senior citizen endeavors.

PERSONAL: elected 1990; born Jan. 11, 1954, in Visalia; home, Tulare County; education, B.S. UC Davis 1977, M.S. Stanford University 1987; wife Linda, two children; Protestant.

CAREER: cotton farmer; aide to state Sen. Rose Ann Vuich, 1987-89.

COMMITTEES: Agriculture; Resources.

OFFICES: Suite 1227, Longworth Building, Washington, D.C. 20515, (202) 225-3341, FAX (202) 225-9308; district, 224 W. Lacey Blvd., Hanford 93230, (800) 464-4294.

REGISTRATION: 58.4% D, 31.9% R.

1994 CAMPAIGN:			
Dooley D	56.7%	$303,656
Paul Young R	43.3%	$6,507

1992 CAMPAIGN: Dooley D   64.8% $457,588
                Ed Hunt R   35.1% $170,927

RATINGS:

ADA	ACU	AFL/CIO	GO	LCV	NCSC	NTU	USCC
75	19	20	F	27	71	40	55

John Doolittle (R)
4th Congressional District

John Doolittle

This district takes in the central Sierra Nevada with the sparsely populated counties of Alpine and Mono on the east slope and the booming foothill communities of the northern Mother Lode on the west. It sneaks into the conservative northeast corner of Sacramento County and contains all of Placer County — Rep. John Doolittle's home base — which is one of the fastest-growing areas in the state.

Since the late 1960s, refugees from smog-belt counties have been streaming into the foothills in search of cleaner air, less congestion and more traditional lifestyles free of crime and drugs. The irony, however, is that the foothills have become the state's second-most productive marijuana-growing region and are distinguished by a unique population of mass murderers, renegade bikers, grave robbers and cult worshipers.

Doolittle, who was only 29 years old when first elected to the state senate in 1980, usually has tough races. He presides over a tight-lipped and sometimes paranoid staff of ideological warriors. Doolittle doesn't flinch at being called a moral zealot. But he is sometimes more zealot than moral. He is a strident opponent of abortion, soft judges, pornography, declining social standards, gun control and free-spending liberals. Yet when it comes to his personal ambitions, Doolittle finds it easy to stoop in low places. Each of his campaigns has been marked by mudslinging and gross distortion of his opponent's record, and he has been fined for campaign violations.

A few weeks after the 1994 elections, Doolittle was fined again. This time Doolittle and staffer David Lopez got a $3,000 penalty from the state Fair Political Practices Commission for laundering money in 1991 to Tim Leslie, the Republican who won Doolittle's state Senate seat that year.

Democrats grumbled that it was just too coincidental that the fine was disclosed after the election in which Doolittle had a stiff challenge from Roseville business-woman Katie Hirning. The Democrat had many issues going for her, including anti-senior votes by Doolittle such as a measure to exempt Social Security from the balanced budget amendment. But Doolittle responded with a burst of nasty attack ads — his hallmark — which painted Hirning as a Clinton clone and falsely accused her of putting a business into bankruptcy. That and the Republican year easily carried the day for Doolittle.

Doolittle's ability to slay opponents was not overlooked when he was in the state Senate. Republicans made him the No. 2 Republican after a leadership shake-up in 1987. Doolittle surprised his Senate critics by working well with the Democratic leadership on the body's administrative chores. Many of those same critics predicted that Doolittle would miss the Senate once he took up residence on the back benches of Congress. Doolittle, though, clearly had other plans. Before he was even sworn in, conservatives in the California GOP caucus succeeded in making Doolittle their lead man on reapportionment.

Doolittle was part of the upstarts called the "Gang of Seven," who pressured Minority Leader Bob Michel, R-Ill., to make full disclosure of players in the House banking and post office scandals. Yet while helping lead the campaign against congressional perks, Doolittle became the House's top abuser of mailing privileges. In the first three months of 1992, he sent 1.4 million pieces of junk mail to households in his newly apportioned district. That worked out to 4.4 pieces of mail per home.

Doolittle also formed an extraordinary alliance with Rep. Maxine Waters, D-Los Angeles, and the two drew up a list of new perks they thought they should have. The three-page memo, dated Feb. 21, 1991, was presented to the House Administration Committee only six weeks after they were sworn in. Among the bennies they sought were cars, meals, moving expenses, additional cellular telephones and use of public phones to make campaign fund-raising calls.

When the United States went to war in the Persian Gulf, Doolittle, who used student and religious deferments to stay out of the Vietnam War, called Persian Gulf war protesters "malcontents" and "scum."

Nonetheless, Doolittle is still considered a comer by the GOP leadership, which will give him more say in advancing the stature of conservatives in the House. He's also a deputy whip. In the 104th Congress he gained the chairmanship of the water and power subcommittee, a key post to push for funding of one of his chief priorities — a multipurpose Auburn Dam. Doolittle, who rails against pork-barrel spending, has never been concerned with the fact that both Republican and Democratic administrations have said the $2.6 billion dam would never be cost-effective.

PERSONAL: elected 1990; born Oct. 30, 1950, in Glendale; home, Rocklin; education, B.A. UC Santa Cruz 1972, J.D. McGeorge School of Law 1978; wife Julia, two children; Mormon.

CAREER: lawyer; aide to Sen. H.L. Richardson; state Senate, 1980-90.

COMMITTEES: Agriculture; Resources.

OFFICES: Suite 1526, Longworth Building, Washington, D.C. 20510, (202) 225-2511, FAX (202) 225-5444; district, Suite 190, 2130 Professional Dr., Roseville 95661, (916) 786-5560.

REGISTRATION: 40.6% D, 46.7% R

1994 CAMPAIGN:	Doolittle R	61.3%	$671,350
	Katie Hirning D	35%	$355,705
1992 CAMPAIGN:	Doolittle R	49.8%	$601,276
	Patricia Malberg D	45.7%	$390,232

RATINGS:

ADA	ACU	AFL/CIO	GO	LCV	NCSC	NTU	USCC
10	100	12	A	4	17	83	83

Robert K. Dornan (R)
46th Congressional District

In Orange County, it seems appropriate that a congressional district would have freeways for boundaries. The 46th is one of the most intensely congested areas of Southern California. Even non-rush-hour gridlocks are routine and residents have come to support the idea of building toll roads to separate the rich from the riffraff. The district begins at the Los Angeles County line and trends to the southeast between the Santa Ana and San Diego freeways. It ends just south of the Newport Freeway.

Robert K. Dornan

As the name suggests, the area was once covered with orange groves. After World War II, it became a lily-white, conservative bedroom community. Construction of Disneyland in the 1950s made the area a world destination, but few attitudes changed. In the 1950s and '60s, there were more John Birch Society memberships in Orange County than in all other California counties combined. The '70s saw an influx of Vietnamese, a few more Hispanics and the decline of some neighborhoods, especially in the Garden Grove area. Today, there are more Vietnamese in the 46th than in any other district in the nation.

The congressman who carries the torch for lingering Bircher attitudes is Robert "B-1 Bob" Dornan, the flamboyant, often profane, former fighter pilot who never saw a defense appropriation he didn't like.

Many people underestimate Dornan. They argue that a man who bases his campaigns on hate and character assassination can't go too far. Yet he shows remarkable staying power and fund-raising ability. When Democrats couldn't defeat Dornan in an ocean-front Los Angeles County district, the late Phil Burton gerrymandered the district in 1982 so that Dornan couldn't be re-elected. Undaunted, Dornan instead raised $1 million for an unsuccessful U.S. Senate primary race against Pete Wilson. He then moved south, took on five-term Democrat Jerry Patterson in 1984 and won.

The 46th, nominally a Democratic district after the 1982 gerrymandering, was by 1984 the first congressional district in the nation where Vietnamese immigrants made an obvious difference. Dornan is their hero, the American who would restart the war in Vietnam if he could. In subsequent elections, even well-financed campaigns haven't been able to dislodge him.

Dornan introduces legislation, but little of it went anywhere while the Democrats were in the majority. Despite his identity with the long struggle to approve the B-1 bomber, others get most of the credit for getting it off the ground. Dornan is one of the most widely traveled members of Congress. Some of the junkets, to his credit, have helped close MIA and POW cases. He also brags that he has piloted every aircraft in the American defense arsenal plus some from Israel, England and France. And no one disputes that he had the most creative excuse in Congress for bouncing his one check at the House bank. Dornan explained that he wrote the check to buy materials for a back yard shrine to the Virgin Mary.

Dornan helped influence national policy in 1985 when he became the first die-hard conservative to endorse George Bush for the presidency. Before then, many conservatives had questioned whether Bush was Republican enough. Dornan seconded Bush's nomination at the Republican National Convention, chaired Veterans for Bush and was co-chairman of Bush's California campaign. Many thought Dornan would get a prominent post in the administration, but the Bush administration never called.

As Bush's re-election campaign began showing stress in the fall of 1992, Dornan helped organize a truth squad of conservatives who would take to the well of the House of Representatives and denounce the Clinton-Gore ticket to the C-SPAN television audience. Bill Clinton's patriotism and, in particular, his draft dodging became the favorite target. Dornan focused on a trip that Clinton made to Moscow in 1969 during a break from his Rhodes Scholar duties at Oxford University. Clinton, Dornan suggested, was actually there to meet with Soviet intelligence agents to plot anti-war demonstrations. Dornan said he was able to surmise this from the fact that Clinton was there and that he opposed involvement in Southeast Asia, despite the lack of any shred of evidence to support his conclusion. Such McCarthy-like accusations led the California Journal magazine to surmise that Dornan had fallen on his head.

Then, the incredible happened. As the Bush campaign became more desperate, Dornan, fellow Southern California Reps. Randy "Duke" Cunningham and Duncan Hunter, and Rep. Sam Johnson of Texas, had a meeting with Bush in the Oval Office and convinced him to take up this Clinton-as-traitor theme. The following night, Bush went on CNN and said Clinton should level with the American people about his draft status and his Moscow visit. Bush was still wearing the mud on Election Day.

The 1992 Clinton victory didn't temper Dornan. Of the new president he would say: "The commander-in-chief is jogging in San Francisco in his slit-up-the-sides silk girlie-girlie jogging pants showing us those beautiful white doughboy thighs of his." This is the same Dornan who told a broadcaster on the night of his 1992 primary: "Every lesbian spear-chucker in this country is hoping I get defeated."

And the Republican takeover of the House in 1995 didn't temper Dornan either. The day after Clinton's State of the Union address in January 1995, Dornan stood at the House rostrum and accused Clinton of plagiarizing Jesus, manipulating a Medal of Honor winner who sat next to Hillary Rodham Clinton during the speech, draft-dodging and "giving aid and comfort to the enemy." When Rep. Vic Fazio, D-West Sacramento, asked him to apologize, Dornan began yelling: "Hell no! Hell no! Hell no!" Rep. John Duncan, R-Tenn., the House presiding officer, ordered Dornan's words stricken from the record and banned him from speaking on the House floor for a day.

In 1994, with Dornan's new district even more Democratic, the incumbent appeared to be in trouble. Even Bush came to campaign for Dornan as his opponent hammered Dornan with charges, culled from four different divorce proceedings, that he had beaten his wife, Sallie. The Dornans responded with a lawsuit, claiming Sallie was addicted to drugs and alcohol at the time. The charges, like the divorce filings, were long-ago withdrawn, Sallie said.

Dornan has said he'll retire after this term. No doubt the spear-chuckers can hardly wait.

PERSONAL: elected 1976 and served until 1983, re-elected 1984; born April 3, 1933, in New York City; home, Garden Grove; education, attended Loyola University, Los Angeles; wife Sallie, five children; Roman Catholic.

CAREER: U.S. Air Force, 1953-58; broadcaster and TV talk-show host, 1965-73; president, American Space Frontier PAC, 1983-88.

COMMITTEES: Intelligence; National Security.

OFFICES: Suite 1201, Longworth Building, Washington, D.C. 20515, (202) 225-2965, FAX (202) 225-3694; district, Suite 360, 300 Plaza Alicante, Garden Grove 92642, (714) 971-9292.

REGISTRATION: 48.5% D, 40.4% R

1994 CAMPAIGN:	Dornan R	57.1%	$2,296,101
	Michael Farber D	37.1%	$124,490
1992 CAMPAIGN:	Dornan R	50.2%	$1,427,191
	R.J. Banuelos D	41%	$5,000

RATINGS:

ADA	ACU	AFL/CIO	GO	LCV	NCSC	NTU	USCC
0	97	10	A-	4	7	77	86

David Dreier (R)
28th Congressional District

This contorted district lies in east-central Los Angeles County, where the bilious smog piles up against the San Gabriel Mountains. The eastern leg of the district includes Arcadia, Sierra Madre and Monrovia. It jogs around similar neighborhoods of Azusa and Irwindale, for unexplained reasons, and then thrusts a second leg southward through Covina, West Covina, San Dimas, Walnut and Industry. These suburbs are predominantly white, middle- and upper-middle-class areas peopled by economic conservatives.

David Dreier

Twenty-eight-year-old Rep. David Dreier went to Congress in 1980 from this area not to make laws, but to undo them. He is a strident foe of government regulation in most of its forms. He has worked for a balanced budget, for the transfer of more federal lands and services to private hands and for deregulation of trucking, airlines, pipelines and banking. Some senior Republican colleagues in the delegation find his ideological commitment tedious, but none can argue that he is inconsistent.

Although not obnoxious about it, Dreier is close to the Dornan and Doolittle Republicans who demand ideological litmus tests before anyone is given full acceptance within party ranks. On that score, he is in step with a large faction of his party in California and was instrumental in December 1992 in toppling Rep. Jerry Lewis, a moderate, from key leadership posts. Dreier took Lewis' place on the National Republican Congressional Committee and became a recruiter of GOP candidates for congressional races in Western states. Clearly, he performed well in 1994 despite complaints by some colleagues that he could work harder.

It is hard to say who the most influential Republican in the California delegation is these days, but Dreier comes as close as anyone. He's the Golden State member closest to Speaker Newt Gingrich and was given the task of chairing the GOP's standing committee transition team. That gave him the job of reducing committees and firing entrenched Democratic staffers. Dreier went about the effort with relish, promising to reduce House expenditures by $36 million. Nothing was immune — not even the whistleblowing staff of the General Accounting Office, which was to lose 25 percent of its personnel.

He succeeded in axing three full committees and 30 subcommittees, and renamed several remaining panels to reflect GOP themes. His reward was a spot as vice chairman of the Rules Committee, a powerful panel that sets parameters of debate on bills and decides what amendments will be offered. Dreier had been a member of Rules since 1991, where he fought a usually losing battle with Democrats over "closed rules" that restrict hostile amendments to legislation. Now that the leadership shoe is on the other foot, it will be interesting to watch how often the GOP invokes the same rules.

As the new session began, Dreier seemed to be the California House member most likely to ascend to higher position in the leadership. He got an added boost when he beat out Rep. William Baker of Walnut Creek for a California slot on the Republican Steering Committee, which decides committee assignments. The vote was 13-12, in part reflecting the fact that Dreier opposes term limits, which puts him at odds with most of the state's GOP delegation. Dreier also heads a special task force on California issues with Reps. Lewis and Christopher Cox. Gingrich charged them to work with Gov. Pete Wilson on problems such as immigration, the economy and natural disasters.

PERSONAL: elected 1980; born July 5, 1952, in Kansas City; home, San Dimas; education, B.A. Claremont McKenna College 1975, M.A. 1976; single; Christian Scientist.

CAREER: public relations, Claremont McKenna College, 1975-79; public relations, Industrial Hydrocarbons Corp., 1979-80.

COMMITTEE: Rules.

OFFICES: Suite 411, Cannon Building, Washington, D.C. 20515, (202) 225-2305, FAX (202)-225-4745; district, 112 North Second Ave., Covina 91723, (818) 339-9078.

REGISTRATION: 41.3% D, 45.9% R

1994 CAMPAIGN:	Dreier R	67%	$529,117
	Tommy Randle	30.5%	$37,140
1992 CAMPAIGN:	Dreier R	58.4%	$216,577
	Al Wachtel D	36.6%	$10,682

RATINGS:

ADA	ACU	AFL/CIO	GO	LCV	NCSC	NTU	USCC
0	95	2	A	4	6	81	92

Anna Eshoo (D)
14th Congressional District

Anna Eshoo

This longtime home of liberal Republican congressmen includes all of southern and central San Mateo County plus the Palo Alto, Sunnyvale and Cupertino portions of Santa Clara County. Stanford University and some of the world's foremost computer-electronics firms are found here and also such wealthy enclaves as Atherton and Portola Valley. The education level in the 14th is one of the highest for any district in the nation. But it also has been hard-hit by downsizing in the electronics industry.

When Rep. Tom Campbell, R-Palo Alto, decided to vacate the seat for what proved to be an unsuccessful U.S. Senate bid, his successor was supposed to be San Mateo County Supervisor Tom Huening. The liberal Huening was so sure of himself that he even called a summit conference for all congressmen-elect to be held in Omaha after the election. But his seatmate on the board of supervisors, Anna Eshoo, had different ideas.

Eshoo came within 5 percentage points of beating Campbell in 1988, when the seat was open. Reapportionment made it more friendly for Democrats and Eshoo received substantial voter-registration help in 1992 from her state and national party. In that Year of the Woman, she campaigned with U.S. Senate candidates Barbara Boxer and Dianne Feinstein at every opportunity while promoting her environmental record and years of civic involvement in the district.

On Election Day in 1992, it was a rout. Eshoo ran well ahead of the Democratic registration and beat Huening by 19 points. In Congress, she made health-care reform her chief issue — something that appeared to be a liability when her re-election rolled around in 1994. The GOP threw a tough race at her, but Eshoo still won big in a Republican year. That should be enough to scare away even well-heeled challengers in '96.

In Congress, she's been carving out a niche in health and family issues, and also has been named a regional whip.

PERSONAL: elected 1992; born Dec. 13, 1942, in New Britain, Conn.; home, Atherton; A.A. Canada College, 1978; divorced; two children; Roman Catholic.

CAREER: San Mateo Board of Supervisors, 1983-92.

COMMITTEES: Commerce.

OFFICES: Suite 308, Cannon Building, Washington, D.C. 20515, (202) 225-8104, FAX (202) 225-8890; district, 698 Emerson St., Palo Alto 94301, (415) 323-2984.

REGISTRATION: 47.9 D, 33% R

1994 CAMPAIGN:	Eshoo D	60.6%	$508,530
	Benjamin Brink R	39.4%	$223,419
1992 CAMPAIGN:	Eshoo D	56.7%	$870,921
	Tom Huening R	39%	$626,029

RATINGS:

ADA	ACU	AFL/CIO	GO	LCV	NCSC	NTU	USCC
95	2	90	F	96	90	20	27

Samuel S. Farr (D)
17th Congressional District

Former Rep. Leon Panetta had a virtual lock on his increasingly liberal district for 16 years. Then President-elect Clinton tapped him to be budget director. The state delegation lost the chair of the House Budget Committee in the process, but gained an ally who has since become the president's chief of staff.

This is one of the few districts in California where there has been a noticeable shift to the left in the 1970s and '80s. Environmental fights, which always take on special intensity in coastal areas, are in part responsible for the change as residents have become increasingly concerned about onshore land development, offshore oil drilling and misuse of pesticides.

Samuel S. Farr

The 17th District takes in some of the most scenic coastal lands, including Big Sur and Monterey Bay. Preservation of those resources is not a partisan issue. Republican coast dwellers value pretty views and clean beaches as much as anyone. Another reason for the change is the growth of the University of California, Santa Cruz, at the extreme northern end of the district. The campus is one place that hasn't left the 1960s, and the Santa Cruz City Council is every bit as radical as Berkeley's, if not more so. Santa Cruz's sharp shift to the political port (it was once a Republican city) neutralizes GOP strongholds in the Monterey and San Benito County areas of the district.

The Monterey Peninsula received a major economic jolt when Fort Ord closed in 1993 and 16,000 jobs disappeared. Part of the area is being converted to a new California State University campus (with potential to attract more liberal voters), but much of the old Army post is in poor repair and at least one landmark structure is steadily being undercut by the sea. In addition, the post has major toxic waste problems. All that, and the ever-bitter environment-agriculture wars in the district present a major challenge for the new House member.

If history is any guide, however, Sam Farr will be less than equal to the task. The 12 years he spent in the Assembly were a time of limited accomplishment. When Assembly colleagues recall Farr, they tend to mention his talent as an amateur photographer who loved to snap candid photos of them on the Assembly floor.

In 1994, the GOP nominated attorney William McCampbell again — the same candidate who opposed Panetta in his last race and Farr in the special election that sent Farr to Congress. McCampbell outspent Farr and the incumbent also had trouble on his flank from a Green Party candidate. But Farr pulled it off even though he ran below the Democratic registration.

PERSONAL: elected 1993; born July 4, 1941, in San Francisco; home, Carmel; education, B.S. Willamette University, attended Monterey Institute of Foreign Studies and Santa Clara School of Law; wife Sharon Baldwin, one child; Episcopalian.

CAREER: Peace Corps volunteer; analyst for the state Legislative Analyst 1969-71; chief consultant to Assembly Constitutional Amendments Committee, 1972-1975; Monterey County Board of Supervisors, 1975-1980; Assembly, 1980-1993.

COMMITTEES: Agriculture; Resources.

OFFICES: 1117 Longworth Bldg., Washington, D.C. 20510, (202) 225-2861, FAX (202) 225-6791; district, 380 Alvarado St., Monterey 93940, (409) 649-3555; 100 W. Alisal, Salinas 93901, (408) 424-2229; 701 Ocean St., Rm 318, Santa Cruz 95060, (409) 429-1976.

REGISTRATION: 53.5% D, 30.4% R

1994 CAMPAIGN: Farr D 52.2% $435,535
William McCampbell R 44.5% $442,959

1993 CAMPAIGN: Farr - D   54.4% $203,366
William McCampbell R   41.1% $93,686

RATINGS:

ADA	ACU	AFL/CIO	GO	LCV	NCSC	NTU	USCC
93	4	86	F	100	83	22	29

Vic Fazio (D)
3rd Congressional District

The 1992 reapportionment handed Vic Fazio, the most powerful Californian in the House, his worst nightmare. His new district lost heavily Democratic areas of Solano and Sacramento counties. From the sleepy villages of the Sacramento River Delta, the new district marches up the floor of the Sacramento Valley from Rio Vista to Red Bluff, taking in the most conservative agricultural areas and excluding the liberal outpost of Chico. Although nominally Democratic, this is not friendly turf for a liberal who has engineered congressional pay raises and had in 1992 the most expensive office in the Congress (other than the speaker's), according to a USA Today survey.

Vic Fazio

Add to the equation a 1992 opponent named H.L. Richardson, a bombastic conservative backed by the gun lobby. Mix in a desire by the national GOP to keep Fazio tied down at home since he also was chairman of the Democratic Congressional Campaign Committee. And the result was a mud-wrestle of an election that cost Fazio $1.7 million. Richardson spent nearly $800,000 and might have prevailed had he less baggage to carry from the 22 years he spent as a do-nothing belligerent in the state Senate.

"Anyone who held this seat would not feel it was a safe seat for them, I don't care what party they were in," Fazio said after the election. "It is just a marginal seat with a number of different constituencies who don't feel comfortable about each other."

In 1994, the GOP couldn't recruit a big-name opponent for Fazio. Dixon attorney Tim LeFever won the nomination and campaigned aggressively throughout the district. At first, LeFever was starved for cash, but he put together a coalition from the Christian right — which had been angered by Fazio's denunciation of their stealth political campaigns — and soon began sucking in contributions nationwide from a wide array of Republicans who correctly sensed Fazio's vulnerability. Fazio ended up outspending LeFever 7-1 and still had to wait for the Davis and West Sacramento vote to come in before finding out if he'd be going back to Congress.

The following morning, Fazio got on a plane bound for Washington, returning to a very different House than the one he left. For the first time in his career, the consummate political insider found himself in the minority — and not a very happy minority, at that.

Fazio was the first person in the history of the Congress to hold two leadership posts. For the 1992 and '94 campaigns, he was head of the Democratic Congressional Campaign Committee, which feeds money to House campaigns. In the last election, he succeeded in raising three times the amount produced in 1992. He also was vice chairman of the Democratic Caucus, the No. 5 position in the House's Democratic hierarchy and a frequent steppingstone to greater things.

After the 1994 campaign, Fazio was scheduled to rotate out of the DCCC job, but there was still the question of the Democratic caucus chair, the No. 3 job in the minority party. All the holdover leaders drew challenges. In Fazio's case, it was Rep. Kweisi Mfume of Maryland, chair of the Congressional Black Caucus. Fazio won easily on a vote of 149 to 57 and fell in place behind Minority Whip David Bonior of Michigan and Minority Leader Richard Gephardt of Missouri.

Even some of Fazio's oldest friends agree that a stronger candidate with roots in the district could have beaten Fazio in 1994. That bodes ill for 1996, barring some dramatic turnaround in Democratic fortunes nationally. For the foreseeable future, the most important forces in his district are apt to be chronic unemployment, the farm economy and survival of McClellan Air Force Base with its 14,000 civilian jobs. Fazio's performance also will be seen in terms of the successes or failures of the Clinton administration, which owes California farmers absolutely nothing. At the same time, there are environmental factions in the district who expect Fazio to use his clout to do something about declining fish runs, loss of wetlands and the paving over of rich agricultural lands.

Yet, Fazio is frequently called the most skillful legislator in the 52-member California delegation and a likely candidate for House speaker one day — if he can keep his seat and the Democrats can regain the majority. The former assemblyman came to Washington well schooled in the workings of legislative bodies. He caught the notice of party leaders by doing many of the thankless chores that others eschewed, such as facilitating congressional pay raises and serving on the ethics committee. In 1989, he was instrumental in keeping Congress' free mailing privileges intact despite efforts by then-Sen. Pete Wilson to divert a chunk of newsletter funds elsewhere. He also quickly became known as a consensus builder.

As Fazio's power has increased, he has used it to solidify relationships with other congressmen. One of the keys to his strength was the chairmanship of the legislative subcommittee of Appropriations that gave him enormous say on which programs got funded. He has a reputation for being the man to see in the delegation when there is a difficult political or legislative problem. How all that plays out in a Republican-dominated Congress remains to be seen.

Although Rep. George Brown of Riverside is the dean of the California Democrats, Fazio continues to be their unofficial leader.

PERSONAL: elected 1978; born Oct. 11, 1942, in Winchester, Mass; home, West Sacramento; education, B.A. Union College in Schenectady, N.Y., 1965, attended CSU Sacramento; wife Judy, two children and two step-children; Episcopalian.

CAREER: congressional and legislative staff, 1966-75; co-founder, California Journal magazine; Assembly, 1975-78.

COMMITTEES: Appropriations; House Oversight.

OFFICES: Suite 2113, Rayburn Building, Washington, D.C. 20515, (202) 225-5716; district, 722B Main St., Woodland 95695, (916) 666-5521; Suite F, 322 Pine St., Red Bluff 96080, (916) 529-5629.

REGISTRATION: 47.7% D, 39.5% R

1994 CAMPAIGN:	Fazio D	49.7%	$1,747,129
	Tim LeFever R	46.1%	$248,701
1992 CAMPAIGN:	Fazio D	51.2%	$1,699,004
	H.L. Richardson R	40.3%	$802,648

RATINGS:

ADA	ACU	AFL/CIO	GO	LCV	NCSC	NTU	USCC
85	100	88	F	62	89	12	30

Robert Filner (D)
50th Congressional District

This new district begins just south of the Mission Valley and takes in most urban areas of the city of San Diego, except for the affluent coastal strip. It also runs south through National City, Chula Vista and San Ysidro to the Mexican border. Ethnically, it is one of the most diverse districts in California: 41 percent Hispanic, 29 percent white, 15 percent Asian and 15 percent African American. There are solidly middle-class neighborhoods, but many others that are declining. As a rule of thumb, the closer one gets to the border, the higher the unemployment, welfare rates and crime rates.

Robert Filner

The economy is firmly tied to the Navy's immense presence in San Diego, which is a cause for jitters. Border issues involving immigration, health, education, crime and pollution are intense. San Diego is a city in need of its own foreign policy.

A Libertarian in the congressional race pulled 11 percent of the vote in 1992, but it was never a contest for Robert Filner, who ran comfortably ahead of the Democratic registration. Filner is a California congressmen who seems overqualified for the job. As a college student in 1961, Filner joined the freedom rides in the South. He spent several months in jail for integrating a lunch counter in Mississippi.

Later, as a history professor who also has a chemistry degree, Filner got into politics when the San Diego School Board threatened to close his children's school. Soon, he was on the school board and shaking things up with major reforms. He was elected to the City Council after a second try, has been on many boards and commissions and worked for three different members of Congress, including the late Sen. Hubert Humphrey.

Since going to Congress, border issues have occupied much of Filner's time and even there he has a track record, having once established a community development corporation to help bring jobs to the barrio near the border. He is compiling one of the most liberal voting records in the California delegation. That probably cost him a little in the 1994 election, but he was never seriously threatened.

PERSONAL: elected 1992, born Sept. 4, 1942, in Pittsburgh, Pa.; home, San Diego; B.A. Cornell University 1963, M.A. University of Delaware 1968, Ph.D. Cornell 1972; wife Jane, two children; Jewish.

CAREER: history professor, San Diego State University, 1970-92; assistant to Sen. Hubert Humphrey, D-Minn., 1975; assistant to U.S. Rep. Don Fraser, 1976; assistant to U.S. Rep. Jim Bates, 1984; San Diego School Board, 1979-83; San Diego City Council, 1987-92.

COMMITTEES: Transportation and Infrastructure; Veterans' Affairs.

OFFICES: Suite 504, Cannon Building, Washington, D.C. 20515, (202) 225-8045, FAX (202) 225-9073; district, Suite A, 333 F St., Chula Vista 91910, (619) 422-5963.

REGISTRATION: 51.1% D, 33.8% R

1994 CAMPAIGN:	Filner D	56.7%	$829,174
	Mary Alice Acevedo R	35.3%	$346,275
1992 CAMPAIGN:	Filner D	56.6%	$828,230
	Tony Valencia R	28.9%	$45,306

RATINGS:

ADA	ACU	AFL/CIO	GO	LCV	NCSC	NTU	USCC
100	4	90	F	96	90	16	9

Elton Gallegly (R)
23rd Congressional District

Since the 1960s, white families have been fleeing seedy sections of the San Fernando Valley for new communities beyond the Valley's western hills. Towns such as Simi Valley, barely more than crossroads 20 years ago, are now flourishing communities in the 23rd District.

The district takes in all of Ventura County except for some bedroom communities near the Los Angeles County line in the Thousand Oaks area. Farms are being gobbled up by speculators who have been trading water rights and building subdivisions. Coastal sections of the county are still favored by retirees, many of whom put in time at the big Naval stations at Oxnard and Pt. Mugu. At Ventura County's southwestern edge, the district jogs into Santa Barbara County just far enough to include the sleepy village of Carpinteria.

Eaton Gallegly

One of the newcomers to Ventura County in the '60s was an ambitious young man with a real estate license named Elton Gallegly. In time, the boom made him wealthy, he became mayor of Simi Valley and was elected to Congress.

Reapportionment dumped both Gallegly and Rep. Robert Lagomarsino in the same district in 1992. Lagomarsino was cajoled into moving northward, where he was subsequently defeated in the GOP primary by Michael Huffington. With a slight edge in the 23rd's registration, Democrats spent freely on Anita Perez Ferguson's attempt to knock Gallegly off. Gallegly won easily in a campaign with some nasty racial overtones.

Gallegly seems to fit the district well. He is a family man who is devoted to hard work and traditional values. He was elected to chair his freshman Republican caucus and is identified with crime and anti-drug legislation. In his second term, he won a seat on the coveted Foreign Affairs Committee. Yet he probably is best known for proposing a constitutional amendment that would deny citizenship to children of mothers who are not citizens or legal residents.

Gallegly helped start the anti-immigration bandwagon with a flood of bills that went nowhere. By 1994, however, his views had become mainstream in California and led to the passage of Proposition 187. When the GOP took the majority in the 104th Congress, he was named chairman of a task force on immigration.

PERSONAL: elected 1986; born March 7, 1944, in Huntington Park, Calif.; home, Simi Valley; education, attended Los Angeles State College; wife Janice, four children; Protestant.

CAREER: Realtor, 1968-86; Simi Valley City Council, 1979-80, mayor, 1980-86.

COMMITTEES: International Relations; Resources.

OFFICES: Suite 2441, Rayburn Building, Washington, D.C. 20515, (202) 225-5811; district, Suite 1800, 300 Esplanade Dr., Oxnard 93030, (805) 485-2300.

REGISTRATION: 43.4% D, 42% R

1994 CAMPAIGN:			
Gallegly	66.1%	$392,024
Kevin Ready	27.5%	$24,876

1992 CAMPAIGN: Gallegly R   54.2% $824,251
                  Anita Ferguson D   42.4% $501,760

RATINGS:

ADA	ACU	AFL/CIO	GO	LCV	NCSC	NTU	USCC
10	91	16	C-	8	13	72	90

Jane Harman (D)
36th Congressional District

From Venice to San Pedro, this new district is a mixture of funky, upscale and industrial communities on the central coast of Los Angeles and the Palos Verdes Peninsula. In Venice, there are people who make their living wearing sandwich boards while rollerblading on the beach boardwalk. Wealthy industrialists live in areas such as Manhattan Beach and Palos Verdes. El Segundo and Torrance are refinery towns. If there is any binding element, it is a protective attitude toward the coast and the natural air-conditioning it provides all summer. Even in the refinery towns, where there are a fair number of Sierra Clubbers, there is a loathing of offshore oil drilling.

Jane Harman

With party registration almost dead even, Republicans should have taken this seat in the 1992 elections with any one of several well-financed candidates such as former first daughter Maureen Reagan or Bill Beverly, son of a popular state senator. But the candidate who emerged from the 11-person field was Los Angeles City Councilwoman Joan Milke Flores, perhaps the most conservative of the lot.

Entering the fray from the Democratic side was Jane Harman, a cerebral, wealthy and well-connected lawyer, who had been a deputy Cabinet secretary in Jimmy Carter's White House. Harman is an economic conservative, but liberal on social issues. She raised huge sums of money, mounted a voter-registration drive that improved Democratic numbers by 2 percentage points, and may have even helped Democrats farther down the ticket with an aggressive campaign.

The 1994 campaign saw the same superb campaign organization and Harman was the only congressional candidate who spent money on TV spots broadcast throughout the Los Angeles basin. But it was a very different campaign. Harman was an incumbent who had to defend the Clinton administration and an equally unpopular Congress. She'd voted against Clinton on some key measures — most notably the North American Free Trade Agreement and the balanced-budget amendment — but Republican nominee Susan Brooks, a Rancho Palos Verdes councilwoman, could say Harman had voted the administration line 90 percent of the time. "She comes to the district and acts like a Reagan Republican," Brooks charged. "But she goes back to Washington and votes like a Clinton liberal."

Harman trailed by 93 votes after the ballots were counted election night, making it the closest congressional race in the state. Brooks immediately started acting like a congresswoman, even traveling to Washington and speaking about her "mandate" on national television. But Harman had a strong absentee voter campaign, and it took nearly three weeks to count all the ballots. Harman bucked the conventional wisdom that says Republicans get the majority of mail ballots and ended up winning the election by 812 votes. The campaign ended up costing her $1.2 million, more than double Brooks' expense.

Harman, who has worked as a Defense Department counsel, accomplished the unheard of as a freshman and won a seat on the Armed Services Committee. Barbara Boxer, the ceiling-breaker on that committee, couldn't get a seat there until her third term. Harman used her Washington connections to good advantage in her first term to help save Los Angeles Air Force Base and shore up the aerospace industry. In her second term, she was named to the Democratic Steering and Policy Committee, which dispenses committee assignments. But she'll need to campaign full time in her second term if she wants to stay in Washington.

PERSONAL: elected 1992; born June 28, 1945, in New York City; home, Marina Del Rey; B.A. Smith College (Phi Beta Kappa) 1966, J.D. Harvard 1969; husband Sidney, four children; no religious preference.

CAREER: attorney; chief counsel to U.S. Sen. John Tunney, 1972-73; adjunct professor, Georgetown University, 1974-75; chief counsel U.S. Senate Judiciary subcommittee on constitutional rights, 1975-77; deputy White House Cabinet secretary, 1977-78; Defense Department counsel, 1979; general counsel, Harman Industries, 1980-92.

COMMITTEES: National Security; Science.

OFFICES: Suite 325, Cannon Building, Washington, D.C. 20515; (202) 225-8220, FAX (202) 226-0684; district, Suite 940, 5200 W. Century Blvd.; Los Angeles 90045, (310) 640-3366.

REGISTRATION: 42.7% D, 42.3% R

1994 CAMPAIGN:	Harman D	47.9%	$1,274,261
	Susan Brooks R	47.5%	$519,014
1992 CAMPAIGN:	Harman D	48.4%	$1,528,526
	Joan Milke Flores R	42.4%	$798,593

RATINGS:

ADA	ACU	AFL/CIO	GO	LCV	NCSC	NTU	USCC
90	18	81	F	58	90	22	18

Wally Herger (R)
2nd Congressional District

The Trinity Alps, the southern Cascade Range, the Northern Sierra Nevada and chunks of the Sacramento Valley floor make up this conservative district in the northeast portion of the state. Its 10 counties are arrayed in something of a horseshoe with Trinity (the only California county carried by Ross Perot in 1992) on one end and Yuba and Nevada Counties on the other. Some of the most remote parts of California are within its boundaries, where there are clear vistas to the giant volcanoes, Mounts Lassen and Shasta. Ten states are smaller than the 2nd District.

Wally Herger

Tourism, timber and farming are the mainstays of an economy that is healthy on the valley floor and often on the slide in wooded sections. Water is plentiful and residents expect their representatives to keep their liquid gold from being siphoned off to other parts of the state. Mountains and remote villages make it an expensive area in which to campaign, a fact favoring incumbents.

Rep. Wally Herger's home in the agricultural heartland of the valley was shaved off the district when reapportionment drew the boundary line just north of Rio Oso in Sutter County. Herger moved to Marysville and won again handily despite the nominal Democratic majority in the new district.

Even with a safe seat, Herger shows no inclination toward activism. During three terms in the Assembly, he was a conservative backbencher who consistently voted no on most measures. In Congress, he has shown the same posture. He initiates a few farm and local-interest bills, but little else.

Environmentalists are becoming more vocal about the management of the 10 national forests in the district, but Herger pays them no mind. He ignores vocal critics among owners of small logging companies, who claim he favors the timber giants at their expense. And fishermen are angry that he has done little to change the operations of federal facilities that have been killing salmon runs on the upper Sacramento River. But Herger's inaction sits well with many constituents, who prize self-reliance and less government.

Herger is a conservative ideologue, but is still one of the most likeable people in the delegation. That helped in 1993, when he beat out Rep. Christopher Cox, R-Newport Beach, for a coveted seat on the Ways and Means Committee and then won a Budget Committee slot as well. That annoyed growers in his district, who wanted him to stay on the Agriculture Committee. Nonetheless, Herger has more important assignments in the Republican Congress if he chooses to make use of them.

PERSONAL: elected 1986; born May 20, 1945, in Yuba City; home, Marysville; education, A.A. American River College 1968, attended CSU Sacramento; wife Pamela, eight children; Mormon.

CAREER: rancher and operator of family petroleum gas company, 1969-80; Assembly, 1980-86.

COMMITTEES: Budget; Ways and Means.

OFFICES: Suite 2433, Rayburn Building, Washington, D.C. 20515, (202) 225-3076, FAX (202) 225 1609; district, Suite 104, 55 Independence Cir., Chico 95926, (916) 893-8363; Suite 410, 2400 Washington Ave., Redding 96001, (916) 246-5172.

REGISTRATION: 42.3% D, 43.2% R

1994 CAMPAIGN:	Herger R	64.1%	$611,074
	Mary Jacobs D	26.1%	$168,178
1992 CAMPAIGN:	Herger R	65.1%	$476,059
	Elliot Freedman - D	27.9%	$4,948

RATINGS:

ADA	ACU	AFL/CIO	GO	LCV	NCSC	NTU	USCC
5	99	15	A	4	9	83	90

Steve Horn (R)
38th Congressional District

From Long Beach, this district runs northward through the refinery and aerospace towns of Signal Hill, Lakewood, Bellflower, Paramount and Downey. Some of California's most severe job losses have occurred here, and more are scheduled in 1996, when the Long Beach Naval Station is to close. Even if California's economy recovers, it is unlikely that conditions will be markedly improved here for the remainder of the decade.

Steve Horn

Rep. Glenn Anderson represented much of this district for 24 years. When Anderson decided to retire in 1992, there was an attempt to hand the seat to his stepson, Evan Anderson Braude, a liberal Long Beach city councilman. Given the Democratic edge, that should have happened. But Steve Horn had other plans and defied the Democratic sweep that year to become the only Republican candidate to take what should have been a safe Democratic congressional district. He had another strong challenge in 1994 from community college professor Peter Mathews, but in that GOP year Mathews didn't stand a chance.

Horn is one of the few people ever elected to Congress who could say that he is overqualified for the job. A professor and former college president with federal government experience dating back to the Eisenhower administration, Horn ran as a scholar with a 7,000-volume home library on Congress. Two of the titles were written by him and a third was co-authored. They cover congressional ethics, budgeting and organization.

Horn has been a Washington insider, a congressional insider and has sat on a host of high-level boards and commissions. But he ran as an outsider in both congressional campaigns. He refuses to take PAC money, but still raised more money than his opponents. It didn't hurt that he had spent 18 years as president of California State University, Long Beach, while holding high-profile positions in civic and commerce organizations.

Opponents have tried to make much of the fact that Horn was bounced out of his job as Long Beach State president by a faction that accused him of arrogance and poor fiscal management. But voters seem more inclined to believe that he was a victim of an old-guard faculty faction that feared his reforms.

Horn, an outspoken and forceful progressive, serves within a state caucus where archconservatives are firmly in control. Of the 26 Republicans, he's the most likely to vote with the Democrats on key issues. He recorded yes votes on the California desert protection bill, the assault weapons ban and President Clinton's crime bill. Yet he seems to have a good working relationship with most GOP caucus members.

PERSONAL: elected 1992; born May 31, 1931, in San Juan Bautista, Calif.; home, Long Beach; education, A.B., Ph.D. Stanford; M.P.A. Harvard; wife Nini, two children; Protestant.

CAREER: Army Reserve, 1954-62; aide to U.S. Dept. of Labor secretary, 1958-60; legislative aide, U.S. Sen. Thomas Kuchel, 1960-66; Brookings Institution fellow, 1966-69; dean of graduate studies and research, American University, 1969-70; president, CSU Long Beach, 1970-88, trustee professor of political science, CSU Long Beach, 1988-92.

COMMITTEES: Government Reform & Oversight; Transportation and Infrastructure.

OFFICES: Suite 129, Cannon Building, Washington, D.C. 20515, (202) 225-6676, FAX (202) 225-1012; district, Suite 160, 4010 Watson Plaza Dr., Lakewood 90712, (310) 425-1336.

REGISTRATION: 51.8% D, 35.9% R

1994 CAMPAIGN:	Horn R	58.5%	$485,483
	Peter Mathews	36.8%	$432,836
1992 CAMPAIGN:	Horn R	48.6%	$428,538
	Evan Anderson Braude D	43.4%	$505,865

RATINGS:

ADA	ACU	AFL/CIO	GO	LCV	NCSC	NTU	USCC
40	60	48	F	31	50	56	91

Duncan Hunter (R)
52nd Congressional District

The 45th District stretches across most of the bottom of California in an area that has seen momentous change in recent decades and is apt to see much more. On the western end, it begins at La Mesa, Santee and El Cajon. The district skirts most of the rest of San Diego's suburbs, crosses the rock piles of eastern San Diego County and includes all of Imperial County.

The San Diego suburbs are comfortably Republican. Imperial County is becoming solidly Hispanic, but the white grower class still controls the political scene. Immigration pressures, however, are eroding the white dominance everywhere. Imperial County also has far and away the highest unemployment rate in California — more than 30 percent during the early 1990s. A wide range of border issues fester in this district: immigration, pollution, drug trafficking and educational and social services for new arrivals. It is going to be difficult for a mere mortal congressman to

Duncan Hunter

juggle the issues here in future years with the disparity between haves and have-nots, the racial conflicts and the inconsistent national policies on border issues.

Rep. Duncan Hunter upset a nine-term incumbent in 1980 and went to Congress as a new breed of Republican — an economic conservative but one with some compassion and commitment to help those willing to help themselves. He was a combat officer in Vietnam, went to night law school and began his practice in an old barber shop in San Diego's barrio. Hunter annoyed some congressional colleagues by stepping over them to get what he wanted. But his talents were recognized by party leaders. He was given the chair of the Republican Research Committee, which is charged with developing GOP strategies for emerging issues. Hunter has used the committee to focus on minority recruitment for the party. He also led the charge to put the military into the forefront of drug interdiction efforts. But when the Republicans started downsizing committees after the 1994 elections, Hunter's research committee was abolished over his strong protests. He had been saying he expected an expanded leadership role under Speaker Newt Gingrich, but as of this writing, that hadn't emerged.

Back in 1992, things started to unravel for Hunter. He had to sell his Coronado home and move a few miles into his reconstituted district. Then came the revelation that he was one of the House check bouncers. Hunter was caught lying about his level of involvement. The number of bounced checks kept jumping upward until the total reached 399 — third highest in the California delegation and one of the worst in Congress. Then the conservative National Taxpayers Union revealed that Hunter had spent $1.5 million of the taxpayers' money to send newsletters to constituents. That made him the third worst junk mailer in the House. About that time, Hunter joined Rep. "B-1 Bob" Dornan and became one of the shrillest Bill Clinton baiters in the House. He will always be remembered as one of those who persuaded President George Bush to suggest that Clinton might have been working with the Soviet KGB on Vietnam War protests.

Hunter drew an opponent named Janet Gastil in 1992. She came at him with a frenzied campaign. In the end, she couldn't overcome the registration edge in the district nor could she match Hunter's fund-raising ability. Hunter sued Gastil — unsuccessfully — for accusing him of kiting 399 checks, and Gastil came back for another spirited run at him in 1994. This time, however, Hunter rode the Republican tide and returned to the House in the majority. Unless the Democrats can come up with a name candidate with a shipload of money in '96, Hunter will probably be safe.

PERSONAL: elected 1980; born May 31, 1948, in Riverside, Calif.; home, El Cajon; education, B.S.L. Western State University, J.D. 1976; wife Lynne, two children; Baptist.

CAREER: U.S. Army, 1969-71; attorney, 1976-80.

COMMITTEES: National Security.

OFFICES: Suite 2265, Rayburn Building, Washington, D.C. 20515, (202) 225-5672, FAX (202) 225-0235; district, 366 South Pierce St., El Cajon 92020, (619) 579-3001; Suite G, 1101 Airport Road, Imperial 92251, (619) 353-5420.

REGISTRATION: 37.1% D, 49% R

1994 CAMPAIGN:	Hunter R	63.9%	$575,279
	Janet Gastil D	31.1%	$181,683
1992 CAMPAIGN:	Hunter R	52.8%	$519,631
	Janet Gastil D	41.2%	$143,752

RATINGS:

ADA	ACU	AFL/CIO	GO	LCV	NCSC	NTU	USCC
5	95	21	A	4	12	81	86

Jay Kim (R)
41st Congressional District

The smog capital of California is found in the eastern Los Angeles Basin, where Los Angeles, Orange, Riverside and San Bernardino Counties come together. From the south, the 41st district begins in outer neighborhoods of Anaheim. It jogs to the east as far as the city of Industry, to the west to Ontario and sends a finger northward through Upland. The Whittier Hills separate Yorba Linda from Pomona, Chino, Montclair and Ontario, which tend to run together in one indistinguishable blob.

Much of this area was once orange groves and dairy farms. Long ago, most of them gave way to commercial strips and boxy subdivisions. Many of the residents were forced into the district by the high

Jay Kim

price of housing in Los Angeles and Orange counties. Many who can afford it are leaving to escape the smog and congestion, but the recession slowed the exodus.

With the sour economy in the minds of many, Reagan Democrats in the area returned to their party in 1992. Democratic candidates did very well here for the first time in years, but not well enough to keep Jay Kim from becoming the first Korean-American elected to Congress. Kim, the mayor of Diamond Bar, came to the United States in 1961 and later founded Jaykim Engineering, a planning and construction firm that has built everything from sewers to prisons. Once elected, he put the company up for sale, saying civil engineering firms have many government customers and he wanted to avoid anything that looked like a conflict of interest.

Curiously, though, conflicts weren't on Kim's mind when he allegedly used something in excess of $485,000 in corporate funds to finance that first campaign. After the Los Angeles Times broke that story in 1993, Kim found himself the target of multiple criminal investigations. Kim publicly blamed his former chief financial officer, Frederick Schultz, for any irregularities. Schultz responded with a $1 million slander suit and the promise to help authorities with the investigation.

Kim spent the 1994 campaign waiting to hear whether he'd be indicted. Equally anxious were the Democrats, who'd fielded Pomona businessman Ed Tessier against him. Kim campaigned saying he made no intentional violations of law, and the Democrats weren't anxious to put money into Tessier's campaign if it looked like Kim would beat the rap. Come election day, the other shoe had not been dropped and Kim breezed to victory.

PERSONAL: elected 1992; born March 27, 1939, in Seoul, Korea; home, Diamond Bar; education, B.S., M.S. University of Southern California, M.A. CSU Los Angeles; wife June, three children; Methodist.

CAREER: South Korean Army, 1959-61; civil engineer and company president, 1976-92; Diamond Bar councilman 1990-91 and mayor 1991-92.

COMMITTEES: International Relations; Transportation & Infrastructure.

OFFICES: Suite 435, Cannon Building, Washington, D.C. 20515, (202) 225-3201, FAX (202) 226-1485; district, Suite 160A, 1131 W. 6th St., Ontario 91762, (714) 988-1055.

REGISTRATION: 39.4% D, 48.2% R

1994 CAMPAIGN:	Kim R	62.1%	$787,748
	Ed Tessier D	37.9%	$73,120
1992 CAMPAIGN:	Kim R	59.6%	$690,539
	Bob Baker D	34.4%	$1,200

RATINGS:

ADA	ACU	AFL/CIO	GO	LCV	NCSC	NTU	USCC
10	94	0	A	8	10	75	100

Tom Lantos (D)
12th Congressional District

Reapportionment shifted this district northward into the southwest corner of San Francisco, where there is a rapidly growing Asian population. From the city limits, it extends claw-like into northern San Mateo County. On the ocean side, the district runs as far south as Half Moon Bay. On the San Francisco Bay side, it goes to Redwood City. At the northern end are the boxy, working-class homes of Daly City and San Bruno plus Colma, the graveyard for more than a million San Franciscans. South of the airport, the suburbs become ritzier and more wooded. But congestion is everywhere — on the freeways, the streets and even the bicycle paths.

Tom Lantos

Residents tend to be pro-environment, well-educated and not particularly burdened by a social conscience. But the district's lack in social conscience didn't rub off on Rep. Tom Lantos, who, as a youth, fought the Nazis in the Hungarian underground. Lantos works tirelessly for social and economic reform and for betterment of the oppressed peoples of the world. He founded the Congressional Human Rights Caucus. But his interest didn't stop there. He also helped found the Congressional Friends of Animals Caucus.

Unlike most congressmen, Lantos will wade into a state issue such as the fight to restore the Cal-OSHA worker safety program. In 1989-90, Lantos was Congress' point man on the Housing and Urban Development agency scandals. His intense questioning of HUD officials kept the pot stirring for months and gave him enviable visibility on nightly news programs. He has shown the same zeal when going after the fast-food industry for child labor law violations. He has demonstrated considerable independence in Congress, often tending to vote his conscience rather than the party line.

Lantos' devotion to the cause of Israeli security may have allowed him to be blind-sided as Congress was debating whether to enter the Persian Gulf War. A hearing he chaired featured a teenager identified only as Nayirah. She offered what allegedly was an eyewitness account of Iraqi atrocities in Kuwait, including the unplugging of babies in hospital incubators and tossing them on the floor. Months later, it became public that the tearful Nayirah was actually the daughter of the Kuwaiti ambassador to the United States. Her testimony — which was never substantiated — was arranged by the Hill & Knowlton public relations firm and Lantos knew it at the time.

None of that, however, seemed to hurt Lantos politically. The former economics professor came from behind in 1980 to unseat a Republican who had served less than a year. Once in office, he immediately amassed a large campaign war chest and has had no serious opposition since.

PERSONAL: elected 1980; born Feb. 1, 1928, in Budapest, Hungary; home, Burlingame; education, B.A. University of Washington 1949, M.A. 1950, Ph.D UC Berkeley 1953; wife Annette, two children; Jewish.

CAREER: Economics professor and administrator for San Francisco State University and the California State University system, 1950-80; part-time bank economist and television commentator; Millbrae School Board president.

COMMITTEES: Government Reform & Oversight; International Relations.

OFFICES: Suite 2217, Rayburn Building, Washington, D.C. 20515, (202) 225-3531, FAX (202) 225-3127; district, Suite 820, 400 El Camino Real, San Mateo 94402, (415) 342-0300.

REGISTRATION: 55.8% D, 27.2% R.

1994 CAMPAIGN:

	Lantos D	67.4%	$310,773
	Deborah Wilder R	32.5%	$99,175
1992 CAMPAIGN:	Lantos D	68.8%	$466,948
	Jim Tomlin R	23.3%	$5,554

RATINGS:

ADA	ACU	AFL/CIO	GO	LCV	NCSC	NTU	USCC
100	8	90	F	92	96	20	24

Jerry Lewis (R)
40th Congressional District

Jerry Lewis

In an extremely short period of time by congressional standards, Rep. Jerry Lewis became the No. 3 Republican in the House and had a shot at being GOP leader one day. But his downward slide was even faster. As conservatives gained the upper hand in first the California Republican delegation and then the House GOP caucus, the moderate Lewis was stripped of his power. The final blow came at the beginning of the 1992 session when Rep. Richard Armey of Texas replaced Lewis as chair of the Republican Conference. The vote was 88-84 with his own California Republicans giving Armey his margin of victory.

Lewis was left with a key position on the Appropriations Committee. But he spent most of the 103rd Congress as an outcast as Democrats finally succeeded in passing legislation he opposed to make much of his desert district a national park. The former assemblyman has flirted with statewide races before, but his fall from grace hasn't left him with much of a launching pad.

When he was the unofficial head of the state GOP delegation, Lewis and his Democratic counterpart, Vic Fazio, were one of the best bipartisan teams in Congress. Lewis even played a role in stopping the Reagan administration from weakening the Clean Air Act, a law that is extremely important in smog-burdened portions of his district. But none of that set well with the growing conservative faction in the caucus, who considered him disloyal. When their numbers increased after the 1990 elections, conservatives bounced Lewis as the California representative on the Committee on Committees. Rep. Ron Packard took his place and has the job of deciding which committee assignments California Republicans receive.

The 1994 elections produced a Republican caucus even more conservative than the last. But one unanticipated result was diminished clout for California since no Republican ended up with an important committee chair. Lewis assumed one of the most important subcommittee posts in the delegation, the appropriations subcommittee that doles out more than $90 billion annually for aerospace, housing and other programs. That means less senior conservatives will have to deal with Lewis, and he has a keen memory. In 1995, Speaker Newt Gingrich also put Lewis on a special task force for California problems with Reps. David Dreier and Christopher Cox.

Most of Lewis' constituents are packed into the southwest corner of his district around Redlands and Loma Linda. But he represents a vast area stretching from the San Bernardino suburbs across the Mojave Desert to the Arizona state line. And he also represents Inyo County, the sparsely populated desert region on the southeastern edge of the Sierra Nevada. Some of the desert areas, however, are growing very fast — particularly around Victorville. Retirees are a growing force in the 40th as are young families who have been pushed eastward by housing prices in the Los Angeles basin.

Defense cutbacks have had a severe impact in the district. Northrop Corp. alone laid off 1,500 people and both Norton and George Air Force Bases are closed.

PERSONAL: elected, 1978; born Oct. 21, 1934, in Seattle; home, Redlands; education, B.A. UCLA 1956; wife Arlene, seven children; Presbyterian.

CAREER: insurance agent and manager, 1959-78; field representative to Rep. Jerry Pettis, 1968; San Bernardino School Board, 1965-68; Assembly, 1968-78.

COMMITTEE: Appropriations; Intelligence.

OFFICES: Suite 2112, Rayburn Building, Washington, D.C. 20515, (202) 225-5861, FAX (202) 225-6498; district, Suite J-5, 1150 Brookside Ave., Redlands 92373, (714) 862-6030.

REGISTRATION: 38.9% D, 47% R

1994 CAMPAIGN:	Lewis R	70.6%	$420,226
	Donald Rusk D	29.3%	$39,754
1992 CAMPAIGN:	Lewis R	63.1%	$399,709
	Donald Rusk D	31.1%	$19,832

RATINGS:

ADA	ACU	AFL/CIO	GO	LCV	NCSC	NTU	USCC
0	85	14	A	4	11	65	81

Zoe Lofgren (D)
16th Congressional District

For 32 years, the San Jose area sent Rep. Don Edwards, one of the nation's most militant liberals, to Congress. From the Equal Rights Amendment and the Voter Rights Act to the Fair Housing Act of 1980, the onetime Republican and FBI agent was a consistent and articulate spokesman for civil liberties and social justice.

Zoe Lofgren

When he announced plans to retire in 1994, it wasn't a question of whether or not another liberal would replace him in this highly Democratic district, but which liberal. Tom McEnery, a popular former San Jose mayor, was considered the front-runner in the primary, but the mantle instead passed to Santa Clara County Supervisor Zoe Lofgren, who as a young woman worked for Edwards on many of those civil rights triumphs. Lofgren drew some national attention with her unsuccessful attempt to be listed as "county supervisor/mother" on the ballot. Lofgren beat McEnery by three percentage points (45.3 percent) in a field of six in the primary and walked away with the general election, garnering nearly 65 percent of the vote.

A former immigration attorney, Lofgren brought a strong women's agenda to Congress. But her interests are wide ranging. As a supervisor, she made her mark in transportation, crime, health and environmental issues. She established herself as a master of legislative detail who doesn't lose sight of the larger goals. And also as one who never forgets a grudge. The remaining courtly mossbacks in Congress are apt to rue the day they dare to slight Lofgren.

The district was once an area of prune orchards and dairy farms, but today it's mostly electronics plants and housing tracts. Lofgren's turf takes in central and east San Jose, Milpitas and all of the rapidly developing areas of southern Santa Clara County. In the north, it is essentially a working-class district with a large number of Hispanics and Asians. But the commute south to Morgan Hill and Gilroy runs through orchard and ranching country that is rapidly being covered with middle- and upper-class subdivisions.

PERSONAL: elected 1994; born Dec. 27, 1947, in Palo Alto; San Jose; education, B.A. Stanford University 1970, L.L.B. University of Santa Clara, 1975; husband John Collins, two children.

CAREER: staff of Rep. Don Edwards, 1970-79; practicing attorney; San Jose Community College District trustee, 1979-81; Santa Clara County supervisor, 1980-93.

COMMITTEES: Judiciary, Science.

OFFICES: Suite 118, Cannon Building, Washington, D.C. 20515, (202) 225-3072, FAX (202) 225-9460; district, 635 N. 1st St., San Jose 95110, (408) 271-8700.
REGISTRATION: 55% D, 28.9% R
1994 CAMPAIGN: Lofgren D   64.9% $681,810
                    Lyle Smith R   35% $31,652
RATINGS: Newly elected.

Matthew G. Martinez (D)
31st Congressional District

Matthew Martinez

This district begins in the East Los Angeles barrio and follows the San Gabriel Valley through Alhambra, Monterey Park, El Monte, Irwindale and Azusa. The district becomes more affluent the further north one travels. Neighborhoods are heavily Hispanic but there are growing numbers of Koreans, Chinese and other Asians who own many of the retail businesses along the crowded thoroughfares. Anglos still dominate neighborhoods in the northern tip of the district.

On paper, this should be fairly safe Democratic turf. But it hasn't always turned out that way. Many of the upwardly mobile Hispanics and Asians appear to have left their Democratic roots in poorer neighborhoods. They're ticket-splitters and often favor candidates who promise less government intervention in their lives.

And then there is their congressman, Matthew Martinez, who seems to have trouble relating to the constituency. He has had a series of difficult primaries and runoffs. In 1992, he had to fight off three primary challengers, but took 62.5 percent of the vote in the runoff. For Martinez, that was a landslide, but a safer district after reapportionment also was a factor.

Some claim Martinez is simply a creation of the political organization run by Reps. Howard Berman and Henry Waxman. Berman plucked Martinez from obscurity to run against an incumbent assemblyman, Jack Fenton, during a nasty Assembly leadership battle in 1980, and then boosted him into Congress just two years later. Whatever his political origins, Martinez has been a less-than-impressive political figure. A California Magazine survey rated him the dimmest bulb in the delegation and one of the five worst representatives overall, someone who makes little impact even on his own district. When the Democrats were in power, he had a key subcommittee chairmanship on the Education and Labor panel. But now even that is gone.

PERSONAL: elected 1982; born Feb. 14, 1929, in Walsenburg, Colo.; home, Monterey Park; education, attended Los Angeles Trade Technical School; divorced; Roman Catholic.

CAREER: U.S. Marine Corps, 1947-50; upholstery shop owner, 1957-82; Monterey Park City Council, 1974-76; mayor, 1976-80; Assembly, 1980-82.

COMMITTEES: Economic & Educational Opportunities; International Relations.

OFFICES: Suite 2239, Rayburn Building, Washington, D.C. 20515, (202) 225-5464, FAX (202) 225-5467; district, Suite 214, 320 S. Garfield Ave., Alhambra 91801, (213) 722-7731.

REGISTRATION: 59% D, 27% R

1994 CAMPAIGN:	Martinez D	59.1%	$132,189
	John Flores R	40.8%	$73,620
1992 CAMPAIGN:	Martinez D	62.5%	$115,848
	Reuben Franco R	37.4%	$193,847

RATINGS:

ADA	ACU	AFL/CIO	GO	LCV	NCSC	NTU	USCC
90	8	96	F	65	94	16	24

Robert T. Matsui (D)
5th Congressional District

The city of Sacramento and southern suburbs as far as Elk Grove make up this compact district. With the state Capitol and some 62,000 state workers, the area is more strongly identified with government than any other part of California. But the government influence doesn't stop with the state. There are nearly 18,000 more federal paychecks from McClellan Air Force Base and regional offices in or adjacent to the district. Such a strong civil service presence normally means friendly turf for a Democrat and Rep. Robert Matsui represents the district ably.

Robert T. Matsui

Reapportionment was especially kind to Matsui, drawing a denser district and taking away conservative suburbs. Life could be exceedingly easy for Matsui, but that is not his nature. He is considered one of the brighter lights in the congressional delegation and is known for working long hours. In 1991, he was named treasurer of the National Democratic Party, where he played an important, but scarcely visible, role in the Clinton-Gore victory the following year.

While in the majority party, Matsui headed several subcommittees on Ways and Means. He produced legislation on foster care, job training, welfare, Social Security, child care and elder care — some of which fell victim to presidential vetoes. In the 103rd Congress, Matsui worked in a number of high-visibility areas, including Clinton's ill-fated health care reform. As chairman of the trade subcommittee, he was point man for passage of the General Agreement on Tariffs and Trade. Once the GOP took over in 1995, he had to settle for membership on the trade subcommittee and is ranking minority member on the oversight subcommittee.

Matsui and his wife Doris are one of Washington's power couples. She also worked in the Clinton-Gore campaign and was a member of Clinton's transition board. She then became deputy director of public liaison in the White House, the No. 2 position in the office that courts groups outside Washington to support the president's agenda. As soon as Doris' appointment was announced, the Matsuis accepted an invitation from ARCO to host a $5,000-per-head reception in their honor. Neither Matsui seemed bothered by the obvious conflict.

As an infant, Robert Matsui was sent to a Japanese American internment camp during World War II. In Congress, reparations for victims of the relocation became one of his causes.

Matsui's congressional posture has been similar to the one he established on the Sacramento City Council: a quiet and effective consensus builder. Those are not attributes that transfer well to a statewide campaign. Matsui has tried to put a campaign together for a U.S. Senate seat from time to time, but, like most members in the vast California House delegation, he is virtually invisible outside his district.

PERSONAL: elected in 1978; born Sept. 17, 1941, in Sacramento; home, Sacramento; education, A.B. UC Berkeley 1963, J.D. Hastings College of Law 1966; wife Doris, one child; United Methodist.

CAREER: attorney, 1967-78; Sacramento City Council, 1971-78.

COMMITTEES: Ways and Means.

OFFICES: Suite 2311, Rayburn Building, Washington, D.C. 20515, (202) 225-7163, FAX (202) 225-0566; district, Suite 8058, 650 Capitol Mall, Sacramento 95814, (916) 551-2846.

REGISTRATION: 58.3% D, 30.6% R

1994 CAMPAIGN:	Matsui D	68.5%	$837,976
	Robert Dinsmore R	28.9%	$63,029
1992 CAMPAIGN:	Matsui D	68.6%	$1,215,753
	Robert Dinsmore R	25.4%	$20,083

RATINGS:

ADA	ACU	AFL/CIO	GO	LCV	NCSC	NTU	USCC
80	6	86	F	96	92	12	26

Howard McKeon (R)
25th Congressional District

This new district doesn't look like most of Los Angeles, but the canyons and flinty hills are rapidly urbanizing in the same haphazard way that formed the rest of the megalopolis. It begins in the northern San Fernando Valley and takes in all of the mountain and high desert area of northern Los Angeles County. Rampant crime and the search for affordable housing have pushed young families into stucco cliff-like dwellings in the Santa Clarita Valley, where the state's biggest incorporation occurred in 1987. Those seeking a bit more space and willing to commute even farther are rapidly filling up the Antelope Valley.

Howard McKeon

Hispanics dominate in the shabby neighborhoods of the upper San Fernando Valley. But the rest of the communities are predominately Anglo and conservative. The safe Republican numbers brought out a gaggle of GOP contenders in the 1992 primary, including former Rep. John Rousselot, Assemblyman Phil Wyman and County Assessor John Lynch. But the voters chose Santa Clarita's first and only mayor, Howard Buck McKeon, whose family owns a 50-store chain of western wear shops. Unless he does something unseemly, McKeon should be safe here.

McKeon spent much of his first term preoccupied with job and defense issues. The decision to stop building B-2 stealth bombers has had a devastating impact on the Northrop Corp. plant in Palmdale. That will continue to be an issue in the 104th Congress and with Republicans in control he'll be in a better position to work on that problem and to pursue his long-running opposition to plans to make part of the Angeles National Forest a dump for Los Angeles garbage.

PERSONAL: elected 1992; born Sept. 9, 1939, in Los Angeles; home, Santa Clarita; education, B.S. Brigham Young University; wife Patricia, six children; Mormon.

CAREER: businessman, banker; school board 1978-86; Santa Clarita mayor, 1987-91.

COMMITTEES: Economic & Educational Opportunities; National Security.

OFFICES: Suite 307, Cannon Building, Washington, D.C. 20515, (202) 225-1956, FAX (202) 226-0683; district, Suite 410, 23929 W. Valencia Blvd., Santa Clarita 91355, (805) 254-2111; Suite D, 107 W. Avenue M-14, Palmdale 93551, (805) 948-7833.

REGISTRATION: 38.2% D, 48.6% R

1994 CAMPAIGN:	McKeon R	64.8%	$473,068
	James Gilmartin D	31.4%	$34,858
1992 CAMPAIGN:	McKeon R	51.9%	$432,190
	James Gilmartin D	33%	$109,398

RATINGS:

ADA	ACU	AFL/CIO	GO	LCV	NCSC	NTU	USCC
5	99	10	A	4	10	81	100

George Miller (D)
7th Congressional District

The 7th District begins in the backwaters of San
Francisco Bay and stretches inland along both sides
of Carquinez Straight as far as Pittsburg. The grubbi-
est of the industrial towns in the district is Richmond,
which also is more than 50 percent African American.
To the east lie a series of roughneck refinery and
factory towns — Pinole, Hercules, Rodeo and
Martinez. North of the waterway, the district takes in
Vallejo, Benicia, Cordelia and Suisun City. To the
south, it dips into the affluent suburb of Concord.

There are fewer youngish families in the district.
Those who can are fleeing blighted areas and mostly
childless couples have begun rehabilitating homes in
the industrial areas. The trend in the district is toward

George Miller

older and more conservative voters, but it continues to be a Democratic bastion and
a good fit for Rep. George Miller.

Cold shivers went through California's agriculture community in January 1990,
when Miller took over the Interior Committee, which he renamed Natural Resources. Miller, one of the most committed environmentalists in the House, had
waited 16 years for the chairmanship to fall his way as he battled developers and
especially agribusiness over water giveaways and wasteful irrigation practices.
Miller immediately set out to overhaul the farmer-friendly Central Valley Project.
His plan called for recasting the CVP governing rules to allow diversion of more
water for urban use, enhancing water quality and restoration of wetlands. The effort
sputtered for a while, but by the time the heat was rising in the 1992 campaigns,
Miller had everything in place.

With strong backing from environmental and urban interests, Miller cut a deal
with Sacramento Valley rice growers to mute their opposition and to help save their
congressman, Vic Fazio. Then he hitched his reform package to a huge public works
pork-barrel bill with goodies for both Republican and Democratic representatives
from Western states. While California farm interests fumed, Gov. Pete Wilson made
a last-minute flight to Nashville, where President George Bush was campaigning,
to argue for a veto. But Bush had enough problems without worrying about farmers
in a state he couldn't carry anyway. He signed the measure on the Friday before the
Nov. 3 election. Not only could Miller savor the passage of his long-sought reforms,
but he had sullied agriculture, Wilson and the failing campaign of Sen. John
Seymour in the process. How sweet it was.

In the 103rd Congress, Miller had a strong role in passage of Sen. Dianne
Feinstein's California Desert Protection Act. He had cranked up his committee staff

for an even stronger activist agenda in the 104th Congress, but on election night in 1994 he watched it all slip away. The GOP victory shunted him to ranking minority member, and he had to fight off Rep. Jerry Studds of Massachusetts to get that. Worse yet, the chairmanship fell to arch foe Rep. Don Young of Alaska, a California native dedicated to undoing environmental laws that Miller and previous Democratic chairmen put in place. To add insult to injury, Miller also assumed a diminished role on the Economic and Educational Opportunities Committee, where he had pursued a strong social agenda. He remains part of the Democratic leadership as vice chairman of the Democratic Policy Committee.

During his long House tenure, Miller has gained a reputation for tirades and occasional oafish behavior. That is probably why he failed to show up on the Clinton-Gore list of possible candidates for interior secretary. But he also had been less autocratic a chair than his many detractors expected. He knows practically every civic and labor leader in the district by first name and works tirelessly on behalf of their middle-class social and economic concerns. It is a grass-roots approach that he learned from his father, a longtime state senator.

PERSONAL: elected 1974; born May 17, 1945, in Richmond; home, Martinez; education, A.A. Diablo Valley College 1966, B.A. San Francisco State College 1968, J.D. UC Davis 1972; wife Cynthia, two children; Roman Catholic.

CAREER: legislative aide, 1969-74; attorney, 1972-74.

COMMITTEES: Economic & Educational Opportunities; Resources.

OFFICES: Suite 2205, Rayburn Building, Washington, D.C. 20515, (202) 225-2095, FAX (202) 225-5609; district, Suite 14, 367 Civic Dr., Pleasant Hill 94523, (415) 687-3260; Suite 280, 3220 Blume Dr., Richmond 94806, (415) 222-4212.

REGISTRATION: 61.8% D, 24.3% R

1994 CAMPAIGN:	Miller D	69.7%	$431,685
	Charles Hughes R	27.4%	$2,805
1992 CAMPAIGN:	Miller D	70.3%	$515,589
	David Scholl R	25.1%	$60,748

RATINGS:

ADA	ACU	AFL/CIO	GO	LCV	NCSC	NTU	USCC
100	0	91	F	92	95	22	23

Norman Y. Mineta (D)
15th Congressional District

The 15th District includes a piece of San Jose, which surpassed San Francisco to become the third-largest city in California in 1989, plus the suburbs of Campbell, Santa Clara, Los Gatos and Saratoga. Then it swings westward taking in the sparsely populated northern part of Santa Cruz County.

Most of the growth in this area has been in the affluent suburbs, but skyrocketing housing values in the San Jose area are changing the economic mix of this region.

At the same time, the region's computer electronics industries have been downsizing, putting many well-paid people out of work. Few of the lower-paid workers who have been able to escape layoffs in those industries can afford to live near their jobs. Increasingly, the area is peopled with affluent, often childless, couples, while those with families commute long distances from the East Bay.

In the Santa Cruz portion of the district, there are still scars from the 1989 Loma Prieta earthquake. That depressed housing values in the wooded hills separating the Silicon Valley from the coast, and also encouraged those who could afford it to move elsewhere. The San Andreas Fault slices almost through the middle of the district.

Norman Mineta

Despite a slight conservative trend among district voters, Rep. Norm Mineta consistently runs ahead of the Democratic registration in the district. The popular former San Jose mayor seems fully recovered from a heart attack in 1986. In 1993, he took over the long-coveted job of chairman of the Public Works and Transportation Committee, one of the primo pork committees in Congress. Mineta had made a stab at winning the chairmanship in 1990, and succeeded in dumping longtime colleague Glenn Anderson, D-San Pedro, as chair. But he failed to beat Rep. Robert Roe, D-N.J., for the post. Roe retired after just one term, opening the way for Mineta.

President Clinton eyed Mineta for transportation secretary in 1993. But with the public works helm finally his, Mineta said he'd rather stay and pursue a wide range of issues, including his desire to accelerate rebuilding of the transportation infrastructure. That turned out to be a major mistake as the GOP seized control of the House just two years later. For California, loss of Mineta's chairmanship was arguably the most serious consequence of the 1994 elections.

Mineta spent part of his youth in a Japanese detention camp during World War II and led the fight to redress those wrongs, finally winning passage of the reparations bill in 1988. In another arena, however, he has been in the forefront of efforts to open up Japanese markets to Silicon Valley products. He also has pressured the Japanese to end whaling and protect arctic wildlife.

He fought for passage of the Americans with Disabilities Act and urged compassion for Arab Americans during the Persian Gulf War.

PERSONAL: elected 1974; born Nov. 12, 1931, in San Jose; home, San Jose; education, B.S. UC Berkeley 1953; wife May, two children; United Methodist.

CAREER: U.S. Army 1953-56; insurance agency owner, 1956-74; San Jose City Council, 1967-71; San Jose mayor, 1971-74.

COMMITTEES: Transportation & Infrastructure.

OFFICES: Suite 2221, Rayburn Building, Washington, D.C. 20515, (202) 225-

2631, FAX (202) 225-6788; district, Suite 310, 1245 South Winchester Blvd., San Jose 95128, (408) 984-6045.

REGISTRATION: 46.2% D, 37.9% R

1994 CAMPAIGN:	Mineta D	59.9%	$1,018,293
	Robert Wick R	40.1%	$14,150
1992 CAMPAIGN:	Mineta D	63.5%	$980,940
	Robert Wick R	31.2%	$49,760

RATINGS:

ADA	ACU	AFL/CIO	GO	LCV	NCSC	NTU	USCC
80	4	90	F	85	90	12	26

Carlos Moorhead (R)
27th Congressional District

Most of this district is in the San Gabriel Mountains, where the population is made up chiefly of snakes, jack rabbits and coyotes. Much of the remainder runs along the southern base of the range with its dense suburbs of Burbank, Glendale, Pasadena, South Pasadena and San Marino. Pasadena and San Marino are the most affluent suburbs in the Los Angeles smog belt and tend to be mostly white and Republican. The populations of Burbank and Glendale are more diverse but tend to be moderate-to-conservative as one travels from west to east. South Pasadena is largely middle-class Hispanic.

Carlos Moorhead

During reapportionment, this district lost strongly Republican areas north of the San Gabriels and picked up more Democrats in Burbank and South Pasadena. But the affable congressman from the area, Carlos Moorhead, apparently failed until late in the campaign to notice that his district had gone from solidly Republican to nominally so. He got the surprise of his 22-year career on Election Day in 1992, when businessman Douglas Kahn, who spent a little more than $100,000, managed to hold Moorhead to less than 50 percent of the vote. Kahn came back for a rematch in 1994, and held Moorhead to 52 percent, which wasn't bad considering the Republican sweep.

Moorhead, who has said this will be his last term, probably thought he had the most enviable position in the California delegation on the day after the 1994 election. No other Californian was in line to chair a major committee, and his seniority gave him a chance at two of them — Judiciary and Energy and Commerce. He felt confident enough about being able to collect the fruits of seniority that he went on vacation after the election rather than return to Washington and collect his entitlement. It must have been a profound disappointment when Speaker Newt

Gingrich said no to both chairmanships. "They tell me that I'm not mean enough," Moorhead said. He had had trouble asserting himself in committee hearings and often had to read his responses from cards prepared by his staff. His ineffectiveness hadn't escaped notice by the GOP leadership. He was relegated to a subcommittee important to the entertainment industry in his district, the Judiciary subcommittee handling copyright and trademark law.

Moorhead is still dean of the Republican delegation, but seems to know it would be a waste of time to try to assert leadership. GOP members have a history of independence and some seem to regard the solidly Republican Moorhead as not ideological enough to suit their tastes. Rep. David Dreier, who represents an adjacent district, had been the de facto head of the state's Republicans and after the election assumed more prominence.

PERSONAL: elected 1972; born May 6, 1922, in Long Beach; home, Glendale; education, B.A. UCLA 1943, J.D. USC 1949; wife Valery, five children; Presbyterian.

CAREER: U.S. Army, 1942-45 (retired Army Reserve lieutenant general); attorney, 1949-72; Assembly, 1967-72.

COMMITTEES: Commerce; Judiciary.

OFFICES: Suite 2346, Rayburn Building, Washington, D.C. 20515, (202) 225-4176, FAX (202) 226-1279; district, 420 North Brand Blvd., Glendale 91203.

REGISTRATION: 44.4% D, 42.9% R

1994 CAMPAIGN:	Moorhead R	52.9%	$588,706
	Douglas Kahn D	42.1%	$461,118
1992 CAMPAIGN:	Moorhead R	49.7%	$629,896
	Douglas Kahn D	39.4%	$119,003

RATINGS:

ADA	ACU	AFL/CIO	GO	LCV	NCSC	NTU	USCC
0	96	8	A	4	8	79	90

Ronald C. Packard (R)
48th Congressional District

This huge district sprawls through northern San Diego County, laps into Riverside County as far as Temecula, and also includes southern Orange County areas as far north as Laguna Niguel and Mission Viejo. The Camp Pendleton Marine Corps Base is draped though the center. To the north and south are the wealthy coastal towns of San Juan Capistrano, San Clemente and Oceanside. Inland are pleasant retirement communities and some shabby trailer courts inhabited by GI families and civilian defense workers.

The climate is one of the most ideal in the United States. Waspy retirees dominate most communities and crowd the golf courses. Spouses of Marines and a few Hispanics are available for the service-sector jobs. Politically, attitudes are in step with hard-core Orange County Republicans to the north. Yet San Clemente homeowners weren't so Republican that they welcomed having the Western White House in their midst during Richard Nixon's presidency. There were many complaints that property values were being hurt. Residents have high educational levels and intense interests in property and private enterprise. Most can afford insurance and that liberates them from government health plans.

Ronald Packard

Their congressman, however, is anything but a right-wing ideologue. Rep. Ron Packard, a dentist, is a conservative but practical man with a commitment to assisting local government. *Roll Call*, the Capitol Hill newspaper, called him one of the most obscure members of Congress in 1992. Yet he has taken on such thorny problems as Indian water rights and negotiated a settlement that pleased all sides. He also has made a mark in aircraft safety legislation, brought home federal highway pork and pushed funding for research on desalinization of water. As befits his district, he's sponsored legislation to repeal taxes on Social Security benefits and to restore deductions on Individual Retirement Accounts.

When first elected, Packard was only the fourth person in American history to win a congressional seat through a write-in campaign. In the 1982 primary, with 18 contenders running for an open seat, he was second by 92 votes to a local businessman. Packard triumphed in November. Since then he has had easy races. He eventually won a seat on the Appropriations Committee, which makes him one of the most powerful members of the delegation.

PERSONAL: elected 1982; born Jan. 19, 1931, in Meridian, Idaho; home, Oceanside; education, attended Brigham Young University and Portland State University, D.M.D. University of Oregon 1957; wife Jean, seven children; Mormon.

CAREER: U.S. Navy 1957-59; dentist, 1957-82; trustee, Carlsbad Unified School District, 1962-74; Carlsbad City Council 1976-78, mayor 1978-82.

COMMITTEE: Appropriations.

OFFICES: Suite 2162, Rayburn Building, Washington, D.C. 20515, (202) 225-3906, FAX (202) 225-0134; district, Suite 205, 221 E. Vista Way, Vista 92084, (619) 631-1364; Suite 204, 629 Camino de los Mares, San Clemente 92672, (714) 496-2343.

REGISTRATION: 29% D, 55.5% R

1994 CAMPAIGN:	Packard R	73.3%	$204.920
	Andrei Leschick D	22.2%	$3,928
1992 CAMPAIGN:	Packard R	61.1%	$315,870
	Michael Farber D	29.2%	$64,212

RATINGS:

ADA	ACU	AFL/CIO	GO	LCV	NCSC	NTU	USCC
0	93	6	A	8	9	72	91

Nancy Pelosi (D)
8th Congressional District

All of San Francisco except for the areas south of Golden Gate Park lies within this district, an activist Democratic enclave as strong as any in the nation. From the Golden Gate to Candlestick Park, it is the San Francisco that most tourists come to see. Yet it also is an area of enormous social complexity. It abounds with ethnic and neighborhood factions that can be counted upon to pursue their issues stridently.

Longtime party activist Nancy Pelosi won a special election in 1987 over gay Supervisor Harry Britt. But there was no lingering bitterness. Pelosi had many gay supporters and also was an acceptable choice for Roman Catholic, society, environmental and labor factions. Pelosi came to Congress a wealthy

Nancy Pelosi

housewife who long ago paid her dues licking envelopes and walking precincts in Democratic campaigns. Her father, a congressman during 1939-47, and a brother were mayors of Baltimore. Pelosi had been state Democratic Party chairwoman, a member of the Democratic National Committee and chaired the 1984 Democratic National Convention in San Francisco.

In 1992, she was an early Clinton supporter and co-chaired the national convention's platform committee. From her seat on the Appropriations Committee, she has been a strong player in pushing the Clinton-Gore agenda in Congress. At the same time, she is the senior of the eight women in California's House delegation. As a whip-at-large and a member of the executive board of the Democratic Study Group, she is in a position to be a mentor for those women.

Pelosi also occupies a unique position in both the California delegation and Congress because of her closeness to California's two U.S. senators. Before the 1992 campaign, Dianne Feinstein and Barbara Boxer weren't friends. But Pelosi was a friend of both. Probably no one in Congress has more influence with the two senators. The three tend to see themselves as a team.

Pelosi again won re-election with the highest plurality of any California Congress member in 1994. But her bright career lost some its luster when Republicans seized control of Congress. She'll have some major fights on her hands in the 104th Congress. There are expensive problems such as converting the Presidio to non-military uses that have many Republican critics. Social programs and AIDS research are no longer in vogue. And part of the GOP Contract With America calls for a federal takeover of the Hetch Hetchy project, which supplies San Francisco with both water and significant revenue.

PERSONAL: elected 1987; born March 26, 1940, in Baltimore; home, San Francisco; education, B.A. Trinity College, Washington, D.C., 1962; husband Paul, five children; Roman Catholic.

CAREER: public relations executive, 1984-86.

COMMITTEES: Appropriations; Intelligence.

OFFICES: Suite 2457, Rayburn Building, Washington, D.C. 20515, (202) 225-4965, FAX (202) 225-8259; district, Suite 13407, 450 Golden Gate Ave., San Francisco 94102, (415) 556-4862.

REGISTRATION: 64.5% D, 15% R

1994 CAMPAIGN:	Pelosi D	81.8%	$372,424
	Elsa Cheung R	18.1%	$19,683
1992 CAMPAIGN:	Pelosi D	82.5%	$257,374
	Mark Wolin R	11%	$30,511

RATINGS:

ADA	ACU	AFL/CIO	GO	LCV	NCSC	NTU	USCC
95	1	94	F	92	95	19	18

Richard Pombo (R)
11th Congressional District

This new district takes in farmland and some suburban areas of Sacramento County and all of Joaquin County except Ripon. Included on the northern end are Rancho Cordova and a piece of Carmichael in Sacramento County. Except for a few affluent Sacramento County enclaves such as Gold River and Rancho Murieta, the district is largely blue-collar and middle- to lower-middle class. It contains sleepy Delta towns and the grimy Stockton area of San Joaquin County, with its unemployment rate stuck solidly in double digits.

Richard Pombo

Rep. Richard Pombo, a fourth-generation rancher and small businessman, comes from Tracy, where he sat on the City Council for just two years prior to winning his congressional seat. It is hardly fair to say that Pombo won the 1992 election. Patti Garamendi actually lost it.

Even though Democrats in the 11th District tend to be conservative, a Republican of the John Doolittle mold shouldn't be able to win here. But the Democratic nominee, wife of then-state Insurance Commissioner John Garamendi, who once represented the area in the state Senate, proved to be the poorest of candidates. Between 1990 and 1992, Patti Garamendi was defeated in races for both the state Senate and the Assembly.

Pombo spent his first two years boosting GOP registration in the district but was still one of the Democrat's chief congressional targets in 1994. Randy Perry, a lobbyist for peace officers, campaigned aggressively, hitting Pombo for abuse of his franking privilege and votes against senior citizen interests and gun control. Pombo avoided sharing forums with Perry until near the end of the race. He raised a substantial war chest and used it effectively in the last month of the campaign. Perry, meanwhile, ran out of money in the home stretch while his party turned its attention to saving incumbents.

Pombo returned to Congress in 1995 in a good position to push his conservative agenda. Environmentalists were appalled when the House leadership tapped him to head a task force to rewrite the Endangered Species Act, which promised to be a major fight. "This young man has a tremendous amount of aggression that I think can be channeled into something that's good for all of us," said Rep. Don Young of Alaska, who chairs the Resources Committee. The stalled conversion of Mather Air Force Base in Sacramento County also will be an important issue for him in the 104th Congress, and one that should be a test of his ability to provide leadership.

PERSONAL: elected 1992; born Jan. 8, 1961, in Tracy; home, Tracy; attended California Polytechnic State University, Pomona; wife, Annette; one child; Roman Catholic.

CAREER: rancher and small businessman; Tracy City Council, 1990-92.

COMMITTEES: Agriculture; Resources.

OFFICES: Suite 1519, Longworth Building, Washington, D.C. 20515, (202) 225-1947; district, 2321 W. March Ln., Stockton 95207, (209) 951-3091.

REGISTRATION: 49.5% D, 40.4% R

1994 CAMPAIGN:	Pombo R	62.1%	$790,662
	Randy Perry D	35%	$147,260
1992 CAMPAIGN:	Pombo R	47.6%	$512,793
	Patti Garamendi D	45.6%	$805,447

RATINGS:

ADA	ACU	AFL/CIO	GO	LCV	NCSC	NTU	USCC
10	100	15	A	8	20	84	91

George Radanovich (R)
19th Congressional District

In 1992, a complacent, five-term incumbent Democrat named Rick Lehman came within 1,130 votes of being knocked off by a novice who had never run for anything but the presidency of his college fraternity. Reapportionment had radically reshaped the district that first sent Lehman to Congress. He took the wake-up call seriously and campaigned vigorously up to Election Day in 1994. But in that year of the Republican tsunami, Lehman was washed out.

George Radanovich

The seat went to George Radanovich, a winemaker and former Mariposa County supervisor, who turned the race into a referendum on President Clinton. With the help of national GOP leaders, Radanovich was attuned to popular issues of the season — anti-incumbency, smaller government, lower taxes and immigrant bashing. Lehman spent most of the campaign distancing himself from Clinton, telling voters he was an independent who voted their interests. He outspent Radanovich by more than 2-1. But Lehman could have had a 4-1 spending advantage and it probably wouldn't have made any difference.

Radanovich's themes were popular in this foothills and flatlands district that tends to be more conservative than some other political units in the valley. The district includes Mariposa and most of Madera counties, and eastern portions of Fresno and Tulare counties. It carefully corkscrews around practically all urbanized areas on the San Joaquin Valley floor, except for the city of Madera and part of the city of Fresno. The great national parks of Yosemite and Sequoia-Kings Canyon also fall within the boundaries.

Radanovich, 39, comes from the least-populous county in the district, Mariposa, where his family has had a long presence. He spent one term on the board of supervisors before stepping down to make a run for Congress in 1992. He lost in the primary, but two years later easily beat two primary opponents and went on to a solid win in November. The 19th, however, is still a swing seat. Radanovich probably can expect another well-financed opponent in 1996.

PERSONAL: elected 1994; born June 20, 1955, in Mariposa; home, Mariposa; education, B.S. California Polytechnic State University, San Luis Obispo, 1978; single, no religious preference.

CAREER: winemaker; Mariposa County Board of Supervisors, 1988-92.

COMMITTEES: Budget; Resources.

OFFICES: Suite 313, Cannon Building, Washington, D.C. 20515, (202) 225-4540, FAX (202) 225-4562; district, Suite 105, 2377 W. Shaw Ave., Fresno 93711, (209) 248-0800.

REGISTRATION: 45.9% D, 43.5% R

1994 CAMPAIGN:			
Radanovich R		56.7%	$446,740
Richard Lehman D		39.6%	$1,073,395

RATINGS: Newly elected.

Frank Riggs (R)
1st Congressional District

California's 1st Congressional District sweeps down the north coast from the Oregon border and doglegs into the heart of the wine country northeast of San Francisco Bay. It takes in five complete counties — Del Norte, Humboldt, Mendocino, Lake and Napa — plus northeast Sonoma County (excluding Santa Rosa) and the population centers of Solano County.

To the north, it is an area dependent on tourism, lumber, fishing and small farms. That gives way to the lush vineyards, poultry farms and inflated real estate values of Mendocino, Sonoma and Napa counties. At the southern end, the prison town of Vacaville and Fairfield, home of Travis Air Force Base, are rapidly becoming bedroom communities for the Bay Area.

Frank Riggs

The Navy shipyard town of Vallejo also is going through something of a renaissance.

Most of the small towns of the north coast are chronically depressed. Lumbermen are constantly at war with fishermen, although almost no one likes offshore oil development. There is a thriving counterculture that is usually held in check politically by conservative, small-town merchants and a growing number of conservative families who have escaped from the Bay Area into the southern reaches of the district. During the 1970s, the district evolved from Republican-voting to Democratic. State officials say marijuana is the area's largest cash crop — a situation that couldn't exist without some tolerance by the establishment.

One of the surprises of the 1990 election came when upstart Republican Frank Riggs beat Rep. Douglas Bosco. A conservative Democrat, four-termer Bosco had managed to anger most traditional Democratic constituencies with a series of anti-environmental votes, land speculation deals and a closeness with savings and loan officials. Democrats helped defeat him when 15 percent of the vote went for the Peace and Freedom candidate in the race.

Riggs, a former cop turned developer and banker, squeaked by Bosco with 1,500 votes in the heavily Democratic district and was immediately marked for extinction in 1992. Riggs made practically every mistake an incumbent could make, breaking campaign promises not to take a pay raise and fuming about bounced checks from the House bank before discovering that he, too, had bounced a check. Yet he almost survived in a race against Dan Hamburg of Ukiah.

Hamburg, who had been working as a typesetter, was laid off early in the campaign and coped with unemployment checks for a time but still raised a substantial war chest, mostly through staging concerts throughout the district.

Hamburg served one term on the Mendocino County Board of Supervisors in the early '80s. Otherwise, he had a varied career as a teacher and administrator in alternative schools — including one in China — and director of a '60s-style poverty and community service center in Mendocino and Lake Counties.

Once in Congress, however, Hamburg began behaving as if it was still the 1960s, taking strident environmental and social welfare stands. Out-of-work loggers and mill workers found no sympathy. Small-town merchants became aroused as did many of the socially conservative newcomers. That brought Bosco out of mothballs in 1994 to fight a divisive primary that Hamburg won. In the runoff, Hamburg again faced Riggs, who had a flood of money to portray Hamburg as an arrogant tree-hugger and enemy of economic recovery who also would legalize marijuana possession in small amounts. With no third-party spoiler, Riggs got a comfortable win.

The folly of Hamburg's congressional performance is readily obvious when one looks at the returns from the 2nd state Senate District, which has similar boundaries to the 1st Congressional District. Sen. Mike Thompson of Ukiah is a moderate-to-liberal Democrat who has had to deal with many of the same issues. Yet he was re-elected with more than 60 percent of the vote, having established himself as a friend of the consumer and a consensus builder.

The 1st District has now turned over four times in four elections. But it's still Democratic, and it would be no surprise to see Riggs get another severe challenge in 1996 — perhaps from Thompson. Back in Congress, Riggs was able to re-coup his first term seniority and became the senior of seven freshmen on Appropriations, a plum for both him and his district.

PERSONAL: elected, 1994; born Sept. 5, 1950, in Louisville, Ky.; home, Windsor; education, B.A. Golden Gate University 1980; wife Cathy, three children, Episcopalian.

CAREER: U.S. Army, 1972-75; peace officer for Santa Barbara and Healdsburg Police Departments and Sonoma County Sheriff, 1976-83; developer, banker, 1983-90; Windsor Union School District Board, 1984-88; U.S. Representative, 1990-92.

COMMITTEES: Appropriations; Economic and Educational Opportunities.

OFFICES: Suite 1714 Longworth Building, Washington, D.C. 20515; (202) 225-3311, FAX (202) 225-3404; district, Suite 378, 1700 2nd St., Napa 94559; (707) 254-7308; Suite 100, 710 E St., Eureka 95001, (707) 441-8701.

REGISTRATION: 51.2% D, 33.6% R

1994 CAMPAIGN:	Riggs R	53.2%	$550,351
	Dan Hamburg D	46.7%	$832,367
1992 CAMPAIGN:	Hamburg D	47.6%	$576,271
	Frank Riggs R	45%	$629,525

RATINGS: Newly re-elected.

Dana Rohrabacher (R)

45th Congressional District

Dana Rohrabacher

Orange County's Gold Coast from Seal Beach to Newport Beach is the most conspicuous feature of this very Republican district. From the coastal yacht basins, the district reaches past the stately homes in Huntington Beach and Costa Mesa to the affluent inland communities of Fountain Valley and Westminister. It then runs north as far as Stanton. The naturally air-conditioned area has a diverse job base. There are many affluent people, only some of whom were inconvenienced by the recession.

The district's laissez-faire congressman is Rep. Dana Rohrabacher, one-time editorial writer for the conservative Orange County Register and speech writer for former President Ronald Reagan.

Few freshmen attract national attention, but Rohrabacher succeeded in spades during his first term in 1989-90. He emerged as Sen. Jesse Helms' chief House ally to prohibit National Endowment for the Arts grants from going to projects they considered to be obscene or sacrilegious. Arts supporters promised a national effort to unseat Rohrabacher in 1990, but that fizzled. Rohrabacher has said he will spend only 10 years in Congress. So, it looks as if the arts crowd will have to put up with him for three more terms.

On the District of Columbia Committee, Rohrabacher was one of many who over the years demanded accountability from the Democrats who run the city. When the GOP took control of the Congress in 1995, the D.C. Committee was one of the first they abolished. Rohrabacher puts his conservatism aside when it's strictly a district issue, such as saving space programs that involve the McDonnell Douglas plant in Huntington Beach or the Long Beach Naval Shipyard.

The congressman has been dogged by claims that he was a heavy drug user in younger days, but that hasn't stopped him from winning increased stature among conservatives in the state caucus. He has worked for restrictions on immigration and the proposed balanced budget amendment. In 1992, he spent large amounts of money against a minor-league candidate, but only won 54 percent of the vote. In a closer race, he could have trouble with a committed bloc of Libertarian voters in the district.

PERSONAL: elected 1988; born June 21, 1947, in Corona, Calif.; home, Lomita; B.A. CSU Long Beach 1969; M.A. USC 1971; unmarried; Baptist.

CAREER: journalist, 1970-80; speech writer for President Reagan, 1981-88.

COMMITTEES: International Relations; Science.

OFFICES: Suite 2338, Rayburn Building, Washington, D.C. 20515, (202) 225-

2415, FAX (202) 225-0145; district, Suite 304, 16162 Beach Blvd., Huntington
Beach 92647, (714) 847-2433.

REGISTRATION: 34% D, 51.8% R

1994 CAMPAIGN:	Rohrabacher R	69.1%	$172,511
	Brett Williamson D	30.9%	$85,762
1992 CAMPAIGN:	Rohrabacher R	54.5%	$308,047
	Patricia McCabe D	38.9%	$29,975

RATINGS:

ADA	ACU	AFL/CIO	GO	LCV	NCSC	NTU	USCC
20	93	13	A	8	15	87	89

Lucille Roybal-Allard (D)
33rd Congressional District

There are 95,404 registered voters in the 33rd
district — the lowest of any California congressional
district. The population is 83 percent Latino, with a
pocket of Asians living near downtown Los Angeles.
From the city center, the district runs east and south
through East Los Angeles and the cities of Huntington Park, Bell Gardens, Commerce, Maywood, Vernon
and South Gate. Unemployment and crime rates are
high; education levels are low. Day and night, trucks
rumble down grimy streets carrying wares to and
from industrial areas that intrude on blighted neighborhoods. The South-Central Los Angeles riots of
1992 spilled into this area, and there are still burned-
out buildings from the days of rage following the
acquittal of Rodney King's assailants.

Lucille Roybal-Allard

The congresswoman from this dreary center of the Los Angeles Basin is Lucille
Roybal-Allard, a former United Way planner and the daughter of a legendary figure
in East Los Angeles politics, ex-Rep. Edward Roybal.

In a 1987 special election to fill the seat vacated by Assemblywoman Gloria
Molina, when she was elected to the Los Angeles City Council, Roybal-Allard came
out of nowhere to overwhelm a crowded field. In the Assembly, she was a liberal,
though a quiet one. She often sided with an informal group of Democrats known as
the "Grizzly Bears," who shared strategy and information on bills.

Roybal-Allard went to Congress determined to work in areas critical to her
district such as housing, education and health-care. Once the GOP took control, she
had to shift gears and begin fighting to preserve programs already in place.

PERSONAL: elected 1992; born June 12, 1941, in Boyle Heights; home, Los
Angeles; education, B.A. CSU Los Angeles 1965; husband Edward T. Allard III,

two children and two step-children; Roman Catholic.

CAREER: planning associate; past executive director, National Association of Hispanic Certified Public Accountants; past assistant director, Alcoholism Council of East Los Angeles; Assembly, 1987-92.

COMMITTEES: Banking & Financial Services; Budget.

OFFICES: Suite 324, Cannon Building, Washington, D.C. 20515, (202) 225-1766, FAX (202) 226-0350; district, Suite 11860, 255 E. Temple St., Los Angeles 90012, (213) 894-4870.

REGISTRATION: 67.9% D; 18.8% R

1994 CAMPAIGN:	Roybal-Allard D	81.4%	$146,494
	Kermit Booker P&F	18.5%	$1,990
1992 CAMPAIGN:	Roybal-Allard D	63%	$253,173
	Robert Guzman R	30.3%	$160,459

RATINGS:

ADA	ACU	AFL/CIO	GO	LCV	NCSC	NTU	USCC
95	2	86	F	96	80	15	20

Edward R. Royce (R)
39th Congressional District

This district straddles the Los Angeles-Orange County line from Los Alamitos to La Habra Heights and then swings eastward into the GOP bastions of Fullerton and Placentia. Democrats and a growing number of Hispanics and Koreans are clustered around the southern end of the district. White Republicans people the center and northern reaches, and Vietnamese are a growing factor throughout the area. The Clinton-Gore ticket did surprisingly well in this area in 1992, a reflection, no doubt, of the job losses in the area and general dissatisfaction with Republican handling of the economy. In 1994, most voters returned to their GOP roots.

Edward R. Royce

The somewhat reconfigured district had sent William Dannemeyer to Congress by comfortable margins. But Dannemeyer left the seat for a divisive and unsuccessful run in the GOP primary against U.S. Sen. John Seymour. That cleared the way for one of the most undistinguished members of the state Senate, Ed Royce, to move up to Congress. Royce, once an accountant for a cement company who cut his political teeth in Young Americans for Freedom, had been marking time in the Senate since 1982. He seldom spoke except to vote no and carried light legislative loads. His most dramatic success was the nation's first anti-stalking law, which was approved in 1990. Another accomplishment was a 1987 bill sponsored by Mothers Against Drunk Driving requiring automatic revocation of the driver's license of anyone who refuses to take a roadside sobriety test.

Royce skirted the edges of a few low-grade controversies. Democrats accused him in the 1988 election of circumventing federal campaign laws to give $5,000 from his campaign fund to Republican Rep. Wally Herger of Yuba City. Herger gave the money back, and the Federal Election Commission — not untypically — dropped the matter.

Royce raised $500,000 for his first congressional race in 1992 and easily beat an underfunded Fullerton city councilwoman. The seat appears to be his for keeps, but even with the GOP in control of Congress, it seems likely that few Californians outside the district will ever hear of Royce again.

PERSONAL: elected 1992; born Oct. 12, 1951, in Los Angeles; home, Fullerton; education, B.A. CSU, Fullerton 1977; wife, Marie Porter; no children; Roman Catholic.

CAREER: corporate tax manager and controller; state Senate 1982-92.

COMMITTEES: Banking & Financial Services; International Relations.

OFFICES: Suite 1233, Longworth Building, Washington, D.C., 20515, (202) 225-4111, FAX (202) 226-0350; district, Suite 300, 305 N. Harbor Blvd., Fullerton 92632, (714) 992-8081.

REGISTRATION: 39.3% D, 48.4% R

1994 CAMPAIGN:	Royce R	66.3%	$400,239
	R.O. Davis D	29%	$3,691
1992 CAMPAIGN:	Royce R	57.3%	$514,904
	Molly McClanahan D	38.2%	$89,577

RATINGS:

ADA	ACU	AFL/CIO	GO	LCV	NCSC	NTU	USCC
20	96	10	A	12	20	88	91

Andrea Seastrand (R)
22nd Congressional District

Santa Barbara has long been considered one of the most idyllic of the coastal counties and a perfect retirement locale. Yet there are plenty of working folks, too, and a number of them lost their jobs when the Reagan administration mothballed much of Vandenberg Air Force Base. Tourism, a pillar of the economy, also suffered in the recession.

The district has farm-based communities such as Santa Maria and the sleepy coastal towns of Pismo Beach and Morro Bay. Several state and federal prison facilities lie within the district, along with the University of California, Santa Barbara.

Rep. Robert Lagomarsino held a coastal seat here for 18 years while establishing himself as one of the most thoughtful Republicans California had in Washington.

Then came the 1992 reapportionment, which dumped
Lagomarsino and Rep. Elton Gallegly into the same
district. With Gallegly considered the more vulnerable of the two Republicans, Lagomarsino heeded the
advice of Gov. Pete Wilson and gave up his base in
Ventura County. The new 22nd District included
Santa Barbara County, which Lagomarsino already
represented, and San Luis Obispo County, which was
new.

Andrea Seastrand

Suddenly megabucks oil man Michael Huffington,
a recent Santa Barbara transplant, decided he'd like
the seat. He vanquished Lagomarsino in the primary
(the only California race where an incumbent was
defeated that year) after spending $3.5 million, and
then put up another $1.9 million to defeat Santa Barbara Supervisor Gloria Ochoa
in the runoff. His $5.4 million expenditure still stands as the most expensive House
race the nation has seen. Until then, the record was $2.6 million spent in 1986 by
Rep. Jack Kemp in a New York district.

Huffington had his sights set on other things, however, and soon began his lavish
and unsuccessful bid to depose U.S. Sen. Dianne Feinstein in 1994.

Into the void stepped another transplant, Assemblywoman Andrea Seastrand,
who managed to win the seat with just 1,563 votes. It was a heavy spending
campaign against Walter Capps, a UC Santa Barbara professor of religious studies.
Both parties poured substantial resources into the campaign and Capps also
mounted one of the most effective field organizations in the state.

That Seastrand just squeaked by in a Republican year suggests she'll be high on
the Democrats' hit list in 1996. Interestingly, her TV spots portrayed her as an
environmentalist, which proves you can fool some of the people some of the time.
The California League of Conservation Voters named her one of the "Filthy Five"
based on her negative environment record during two Assembly terms, including
a "no" vote on a bill to ban new offshore oil drilling in state waters.

Seastrand's husband, Eric, held a Monterey County-based Assembly seat from
1982 until he died of cancer in 1990. Andrea Seastrand was heavily involved in her
husband's career while raising their two children and easily won the seat upon his
death. She established herself as a conservative zealot, pursuing an agenda outlined
by the Christian Coalition and the Eagle Forum.

"We as Christians have been hoodwinked into thinking that there is a separation
of church and state," she has said. "That is not true." She contends abortion,
feminism, witchcraft and condom distribution in schools are destroying Christian
society, and California earthquakes and fires are signs of God's wrath.

In the Assembly, she took special interest in youth issues and was a staunch
supporter of agriculture. Yet she initiated little legislation and what she produced

was mostly anti-regulation and anti-consumer. In 1992, Wilson signed a Seastrand bill that repealed state bread weight requirements, allowing bakers to sell bread loaves in any size.

PERSONAL: elected 1994; born Aug. 5, 1941, in Chicago; home, San Luis Obispo; education, B.A. DePaul University, 1963; widow, two children; Roman Catholic.

CAREER: teacher; Assembly, 1990-94

COMMITTEES: Science; Transportation & Infrastructure.

OFFICES: Suite 1216, Longworth Building, Washington, D.C., 20515, (202) 225-3601; district, Suite 206, 1525 State St., Santa Barbara 93110, (805) 899-3578; Suite A2, 778 Osos St., San Luis Obispo 93401, (805) 541-0170.

REGISTRATION: 43.9% D, 41.2% R

1994 CAMPAIGN:			
	Seastrand R	49.2%	$615,785
	Walter Capps D	48.5%	$484,211

RATINGS: Newly elected.

Fortney H. "Pete" Stark (D)
13th Congressional District

From South Oakland, the 13th District runs south-easterly along San Francisco Bay taking in all the scruffy suburbs between Oakland and San Jose. Alameda, San Leandro, San Lorenzo, Hayward, Fremont and Milpitas were originally working class communities. But as Bay Area housing prices have soared, all those fading, stucco bungalows have become increasingly desirable to more affluent residents.

That could be an unpleasant change for a liberal such as Rep. Pete Stark. When Democrats ruled Congress, his seniority and clout in tax and health matters provided a solid platform from which to assist the district. He chaired the powerful Ways and

Pete Stark

Means subcommittee on health and was in line to head the full committee one day. That also made him a key player in almost any California issue that included a money component.

In the 103rd Congress, Stark shunned White House appeals for a united front on health-care reform and pushed his own reform plan. That rankled the president's advisers, but no one doubted his sincerity. Stark once offered a constitutional amendment to guarantee everyone a right to health care. In 1986, the political arm of the American Medical Association spent some $200,000 to bankroll an opponent, but Stark crushed him, garnering 70 percent of the vote. Stark continues to be a consistent no vote on issues that pit the AMA against consumers.

In 1993, Stark took over chairmanship of the District of Columbia Committee and began championing the cause of D.C. statehood. When Republicans took control of Congress in 1995, he not only lost the chair but the committee. It was one of the first panels abolished.

Stark's role in the 104th Congress was definitely diminished and he has few friends in the GOP. Many remember his penchant for snide slights. One of them is Rep. Nancy Johnson of Connecticut, who is married to an obstetrician-gynecologist. During the health-care debate in 1993, Stark suggested she gained her knowledge of medicine from "pillow talk."

But Stark also is used to swimming against the tide and winning. During the Vietnam War era, he started his own bank in Walnut Creek and pulled in deposits throughout the Bay Area by using peace symbols on his checks. By age 31, he had founded his second bank and was well on his way to multimillionaire status. With such personal wealth and banking skills, it was something of a marvel that he managed to bounce 64 checks at the House bank. While that was going on, he compiled the dubious record of sixth-highest congressional spender on junk mail sent to constituents. The National Taxpayers' Union estimated that his mailings cost taxpayers $93,765 in 1991-92.

PERSONAL: elected 1972; born Nov. 11, 1931, in Milwaukee, Wis.; home, Fremont; education, B.S. Massachusetts Institute of Technology 1953, M.B.A. UC Berkeley 1960; wife Carolyn, four children; Unitarian.

CAREER: U.S. Air Force, 1955-57; founder and president of a bank and a savings and loan institution, 1961-72.

COMMITTEES: Ways and Means, Joint Economic.

OFFICES: Suite 239, Cannon Building, Washington, D.C. 20515, (202) 225-5065; district, Suite 500, 22320 Foothill Blvd., Hayward, 94541, (415) 635-1092.

REGISTRATION: 58.2% D, 26.7% R

1994 CAMPAIGN:	Stark D	64.6%	$705,707
	Lawrence Molton R	30.2%	$26,281
1992 CAMPAIGN:	Stark D	60.2%	$539,560
	Verne Teyler R	31.6%	$37,305

RATINGS:

ADA	ACU	AFL/CIO	GO	LCV	NCSC	NTU	USCC
100	5	90	F	96	94	24	18

William M. Thomas (R)
21st Congressional District

The outline of the 21st District doesn't resemble much of anything since it was pieced together from leftovers when the San Joaquin Valley was reapportioned. Nonetheless, its boundaries make some sense. It includes the mountain and foothill areas on both sides of the southern end of the valley. Here and there, it intrudes on the valley floor to take in much of Bakersfield and the small towns running north as far as Visalia. The economy is based on oil and agriculture, and is bedrock conservative.

The longtime congressman from the area, William Thomas, was once a rising force in Republican politics. He was vice chair of the National Republican Congressional Committee, California representative on the GOP policy body that makes House committee assignments, and was considered an expert on reapportionment. He seemed to know which buttons to push to get recalcitrant Republicans aboard Reagan administration bills. The former community college instructor also did a lot to bring young people

William Thomas

into the party, using campaign funds to conduct talent searches to fill minor posts and holding weekend retreats for college students.

GOP infighting, however, has greatly diminished his role over the years. First he was smacked by moderates in the delegation, who bounced him off the panel that dispenses committee assignments. Then conservatives came after him with a one-two punch. Rep. David Dreier of Claremont replaced him on the National Republican Congressional Committee and Rep. John Doolittle of Rocklin took over as the state GOP point-man on reapportionment. In 1992, then-GOP Whip Newt Gingrich, who was Thomas' roommate when they first came to Congress, was behind an attempt to remove Thomas as ranking Republican on the House Administration Committee.

That Thomas was able to hold onto the seat was more fortuitous than even he realized at the time. When the votes were counted in 1994, Thomas emerged as the only Californian with a committee chair — even though it wasn't a major one. Nonetheless, there's no sign that his relationship with Gingrich is anything but cool. Others have stepped forward to lead the delegation.

Despite his setbacks, Thomas is an important party player on fiscal matters in the House, having secured seats on both the Budget and the Ways and Means committees. He has supported increasing the retirement age for Social Security and was chief Republican sponsor of a bill to require uniform poll-closing hours so that early results from Eastern states don't influence the national outcome.

Back home, Thomas' tinkering in state party and Kern County politics has distanced him from some of his oldest allies: former Assemblyman Joe Shell of Bakersfield and state Senate Minority Leader Ken Maddy of Fresno. "The Thomas faction and its leader believe if you're not with us 1,000 percent, you're against us," said ex- Sen. Phil Wyman, R-Hanford. "It's the kind of mentality you expect from a warlord." But Thomas contends that his adversaries don't want to broaden the base of the party. Too many of the party's current leaders, he says, have developed comfortable niches in the GOP hierarchy and don't want to risk them by sharing power with others.

PERSONAL: elected 1978; born Dec. 6, 1941, in Wallace, Idaho; home, Bakersfield; education, A.A. Santa Ana College 1959, B.A. San Francisco State University 1963, M.A. 1965; wife Sharon, two children; Baptist.

CAREER: instructor, Bakersfield Community College, 1965-74; Assembly, 1974-78.

COMMITTEES: House Oversight (chairman); Ways and Means.

OFFICES: Suite 2208, Rayburn Building, Washington, D.C. 20515, (202) 225-2915, FAX (202) 225-8798; district, Suite 220, 4100 Truxton Ave., Bakersfield 93309, (805) 327-3611; 319 W. Murray St., Visalia 93291, (209) 627-6549.

REGISTRATION: 40.4% D, 48.1% R

1994 CAMPAIGN:	Thomas R	68.1%	$589,942
	John Evans D	27.6%	$30,900
1992 CAMPAIGN:	Thomas R	65.2%	$586,000
	Deborah Volmer D	34.7%	$23,260

RATINGS:

ADA	ACU	AFL/CIO	GO	LCV	NCSC	NTU	USCC
5	78	14	C-	4	10	67	92

Esteban E. Torres (D)
34th Congressional District

It seems appropriate that a large chunk of the district that sent Richard Nixon to Congress nearly a half-century ago is now represented by a Latino. From Montebello to La Puente and from Whittier to Santa Fe Springs, this area was almost exclusively white suburbs in Nixon's time. Citrus was still a major industry and voters were dyed-in-the-wool Republicans.

Today, the 34th is one of the most diverse middle-class districts in California. Hispanics are the largest single ethnic group followed by whites, Asians, African Americans and Pacific Islanders. Many of the residents work in aerospace, manufacturing, retailing, refinery and government jobs, and two-income

Esteban Torres

families are common. Defense cutbacks have hit hard in the area. A growing number of Koreans are taking over the retail shops that clutter the main streets. Most voters are traditionally Democratic, but conservative and committed to family values.

Their congressman, Esteban Torres, shares those family concerns and is strongly anti-abortion. But on most other matters, he is stridently liberal and pro-consumer. His preoccupation with the welfare of Third World countries and support of large social programs from Washington don't play particularly well in this district. That helps explain why he has had well-financed challengers from time to time.

Torres helps compensate for his more-liberal-than-the-district views by campaigning almost nonstop. He is constantly in the district, attending community gatherings, visiting nursing homes and assisting Democratic hopefuls at other levels. One of his causes has been the seriously polluted water table in the San Gabriel Valley. The issue has given him a lot of visibility, but meaningful cleanup is probably impossible. Torres' staff is considered one of the better in the delegation. And he also has another ace in his hand: the fund-raising support of the Berman-Waxman machine.

Like many of the residents, Torres got where he is by working hard and overcoming racial barriers. He went from assembly-line worker to union official, to poverty programs and then on to posts where he could promote his concerns in President Jimmy Carter's administration. He remains committed to government as a force for improving social interaction in society. The district seems to be moving away from him ideologically, but not quickly enough to threaten his tenure. And as more people lose their jobs, Torres' views become more popular.

PERSONAL: elected 1982; born Jan. 30, 1930, in Miami, Ariz.; home, La Puente; education, A.A. East Los Angeles Community College 1959, B.A. CSU Los Angeles 1963, graduate work at the University of Maryland and American University; wife Arcy, five children; no religious affiliation.

CAREER: U.S. Army, 1949-53; assembly-line worker, Chrysler Corp., 1953-63; United Auto Workers representative, 1963-68; director, East Los Angeles Community Union, 1968-74; UAW representative, 1974-77; ambassador to UNESCO, 1977-79; special assistant to President Jimmy Carter, 1979-81; president, International Enterprise and Development Corp., 1981-82.

COMMITTEE: Appropriations.

OFFICES: Suite 2368, Rayburn Building, Washington, D.C. 20515, (202) 225-5256, FAX (202) 225-9711; district, Suite 101, 8819 Whittier Blvd., Pico Rivera 90660, (213) 695-0702, FAX (213) 961-3978.

REGISTRATION: 61.6% D, 27.6% R

1994 CAMPAIGN:	Torres D	61.7%	$234,230
	Albert Nunez R	34.1%	$3,142
1992 CAMPAIGN:	Torres D	61.2%	$203,790
	Jay Hernandez R	34%	$119,177

RATINGS:

ADA	ACU	AFL/CIO	GO	LCV	NCSC	NTU	USCC
90	3	96	F	81	95	12	24

Walter R. Tucker III (D)

37th Congressional District

This district begins in South-Central Los Angeles and runs south through Lynnwood, Compton, Carson and parts of Long Beach and Signal Hill. To the north are the bleak neighborhoods that were part of the riot corridor following the acquittal of the police officers charged in the Rodney King beating. The farther south one goes, the more middle-class the communities become. But they are still predominately blue-collar areas where many people have lost jobs in the aerospace industry. Latinos outnumber African Americans in the district and the most affluent families usually have two wage-earners. Crime, jobs, health care and the general quality of life are important issues among those who vote. The district, however, has one of the lowest rates of voter turnout in the state.

Walter R. Tucker

Rep. Mervyn Dymally tried to hand off this district to his daughter when he ended his lackluster career in 1992, but she lost in the primary to Compton Mayor Walter Tucker III, who had no Republican opponent in November. Tucker, whose father also was mayor of Compton, could have pursued a career in more pleasant surroundings. But after law school, the criminal attorney, former teacher and minister, returned home and worked as a county prosecutor. But he was fired in 1988 after admitting that he changed the dates on crime photographs and then lied about it to a judge.

Midway into his first term, Tucker was indicted by a grand jury as the result of an FBI sting investigation. He was charged with eight counts of soliciting and accepting $30,000 in bribes while mayor of Compton and two counts of failing to file tax returns on the money. Subsequently, ex-City Councilwoman Patricia Moore pleaded guilty to one count of extortion and failing to file a tax return in connection with the same sting operation.

Tucker, who called the investigation a racially motivated witch hunt, compared himself to Michael Jackson and O.J. Simpson. "I unequivocally and categorically deny all charges," he said. A trial was set for early 1995, but the indictments didn't hurt Tucker's re-election. He got 78 percent of the vote against his only opponent, a Libertarian.

PERSONAL: elected 1992; born May 28, 1957, in Compton; home, Compton; education, attended Princeton University, B.A. University of Southern California 1978, J.D. Georgetown University 1981; wife Robin, two children; non-denominational Protestant.

CAREER: teacher, 1984-86; assistant district attorney, 1986-88; attorney 1988-92; minister, Bread of Life Christian Center; Compton mayor, 1991-92.

COMMITTEES: Transportation & Infrastructure; Small Business.
OFFICES: Suite 22231, Rayburn Building, Washington, D.C. 20515, (202) 225-7924, FAX (202) 225-7926; district, 145 E. Compton Blvd., Compton 90220, (310) 763-5850.
REGISTRATION: 77.4% D, 12.6% R

1994 CAMPAIGN: Tucker D	77.3%	$168,596
1992 CAMPAIGN: Tucker D	85.7%	$225,817

RATINGS:

ADA	ACU	AFL/CIO	GO	LCV	NCSC	NTU	USCC
90	8	95	F	69	90	13	18

Maxine Waters (D)
35th Congressional District

Maxine Waters

This district slid somewhat southward after reapportionment, removing a large chunk of Watts, the center of the infamous riots of the mid-1960s and again in 1992. Neighborhoods in Inglewood, Hawthorne and Gardena were added, but it continues to be California's most heavily Democratic district. Times may change, but there is a constancy to the issues here — poverty, crime, drugs, lack of community facilities, poor schools, substandard housing and a police force that shows little sensitivity to those problems.

One newer element is street gangs. The area was mostly African American when Watts was burning nearly a quarter century ago. Now, African Americans and Latinos are about evenly matched, and the two cultures collide nightly in vicious warfare. The conflict is not all racial, however. It is often black against black or brown against brown in battles where crack cocaine figures prominently as the cause — or at least as a co-conspirator. There had been a growing influx of Korean shopkeepers, but the violence directed against them during the 1992 riots has caused an exodus.

This tough area has spawned an equally tough congresswoman, Maxine Waters. She is a brassy bundle of energy who approaches most issues with a firmly closed mind. Facts don't interest her, only preconceived notions. Around the state Capitol, where she spent 14 years in the Assembly, Waters was known as "Mama Doc" for her absolutist approach to politics. Always strident, sometimes yelling; "She has a tongue that could open a wall safe," a colleague said. When Dan Lungren was trying unsuccessfully to win confirmation as state treasurer, Waters openly baited other minorities who testified in his behalf. But with Speaker Willie Brown as her mentor, Waters could get away with almost anything.

No one has ever accused Waters of shirking work, however. She grew up in poverty and began her career as a Head Start teacher and civic organizer in Watts. She was an aide to Los Angeles City Councilman David Cunningham before winning her Assembly seat in 1976. Thanks to Brown, Waters held key committee posts that gave her the clout to wage war for what she calls "my constituency": the poor, the nonwhite and women. She had a fair number of successes, but there would have been more if it had not been for her caustically combative style. Republicans tended to vote against almost any Waters bill simply because she was the author.

Along the way, Waters established herself as a player in national politics, acting as an adviser to Jesse Jackson during his 1984 and '88 presidential campaigns.

When Los Angeles exploded in flames after the Rodney King verdict, Waters emerged as the African American leader most frequently quoted by the news media. It was a rebellion, she repeatedly insisted, not a riot: "Whether we like it or not, a riot is the voice of the unheard."

Meanwhile, the Clinton campaign was attempting to sow alliances with other African American opinion leaders after sidelining Jackson. Waters was recruited for the largely symbolic position of campaign co-chair along with Los Angeles County Supervisor Gloria Molina.

It must have given Bill Clinton and Al Gore pause when Waters began calling President Bush a racist and said just after their nomination: "I hope the ticket gets elected, but this is the last time I will support an all-white anything." Nonetheless, she spent the fall working tirelessly for the ticket. They owed her, so after the election Waters' husband, Sidney Williams, a Mercedes Benz dealer, was appointed to the plum job of ambassador to the Bahamas. More than a year later, Waters paid them back by getting herself arrested at the White House fence while protesting Clinton's Haitian refugee policies.

In the Congress, Waters has maintained her reputation as a shouter. After one exchange with Rep. Peter King, R-N.Y., Speaker Tom Foley ordered her remarks stricken from the Congressional Record and ruled she could not speak on the House floor any more that day. Nonetheless, she's produced results for programs that attack the core problems in her district. She's been successful in expanding programs for job training, housing and homeless veterans. While the Democrats ruled, she was able to expand minority representation on congressional committees.

She showed substantial skill in tying funds for a $50 million federal job training program to an unrelated Midwest flood relief bill and then getting the Labor Department to steer a $3 million, no-bid contract to a nonprofit riot-recovery group called Community Build Inc. With other members of the Black Caucus, she successfully lobbied Clinton to intervene in Haiti and return President Jean-Bertrand Aristide to power. She also has a leadership position in the minority caucus as a regional whip.

No doubt Republicans will try to relegate Waters to the back benches in the 104th Congress, but it won't be easy.

PERSONAL: elected 1990; born Aug. 15, 1938, in St. Louis, Mo.; home, Los Angeles; education, B.A. CSU Los Angeles; husband Sidney Williams, three children.

CAREER: Head Start teacher; chief deputy to Los Angeles City Councilman David Cunningham, 1973-76; partner in a public relations firm; Assembly, 1976-90.

COMMITTEES: Banking & Financial Services; Veterans' Affairs.

OFFICES: Suite 330, Cannon Building, Washington, D.C. 20515. (202) 225-2201, FAX (202) 225-7854; district, 4509 S. Broadway, Los Angeles 90037, (213) 233-0733.

REGISTRATION: 80.2% D, 10.8% R

1994 CAMPAIGN:	Waters D	78.1%	$210,282
	Nate Truman R	21.8%	$9,106
1992 CAMPAIGN:	Waters D	82.5%	$182,045
	Nate Truman R	14%	$6,918

RATINGS:

ADA	ACU	AFL/CIO	GO	LCV	NCSC	NTU	USCC
100	4	95	F	88	95	16	11

Henry A. Waxman (D)

29th Congressional District

Mention Los Angeles to most Americans and they begin picturing the palm-draped mansions of Beverly Hills, svelte bodies strolling Rodeo Drive and intrigues by Hollywood movie titans. It is all here in the 29th District, which stretches along the southern flank of the Hollywood Hills from Santa Monica's beaches to Interstate 5. Since World War II, this ever-spreading center of the entertainment industry has been solidly Jewish and liberal.

Henry Waxman

At the southern and seedier end of the district, an area where the Hollywood technicians and extras once lived, the residents are increasingly Hispanic and Korean. These minorities, however, tend to vote in small numbers. There also is a growing community of gays, especially in West Hollywood, and they vote.

Rep. Henry Waxman, one of the sharpest intellects in Congress, has drawn on the extreme wealth of the district to build one of the most important power bases in the Democratic Party with Rep. Howard Berman, Berman's brother Michael, and Carl D'Agostino. The Berman-Waxman organization used to raise vast sums of money for hardball political campaigns, often with extensive use of direct mail. But the organization has been almost moribund in recent years, and Waxman has been inactive in it.

Waxman has bucked the House seniority system to grab key subcommittees, where he advances his interests in health, clean air and geriatrics issues. When he chaired the Energy and Commerce subcommittee on Health and the Environment, probably no Democrat had more influence on health issues. During the Reagan and Bush administrations, he was the Democrats' first line of defense against weakening health and air programs. He was also a leader on abortion rights, funding for AIDS research, expanded Medicaid coverage and nutrition labeling.

In the 103rd Congress he toiled long and hard for passage of the Clinton health-care reforms. Having lost the subcommittee chairmanship to the Republicans, he's expected to fight stubbornly to keep his hard-won health reforms in place.

Waxman's seat is secure, which apparently is why he could bounce 434 checks at the House bank (second highest in the delegation) and then say his financial affairs were a private matter. Waxman has never been known for humility.

PERSONAL: elected 1974; born Sept. 12, 1939, in Los Angeles; home, Los Angeles; education, B.A. UCLA 1961, J.D. 1964; wife Janet, two children; Jewish.

CAREER: attorney, 1965-68; Assembly, 1968-74.

COMMITTEES: Commerce; Government Reform & Oversight.

OFFICES: Suite 2408, Rayburn Building, Washington, D.C. 20515, (202) 225-3976, FAX (202) 225-4099; district, Suite 400, 8425 West Third St., Los Angeles 90048, (213) 651-1040.

REGISTRATION: 58.6% D, 26.1% R

1994 CAMPAIGN:	Waxman D	68%	$172,898
	Paul Stepanek R	28.2%	$70,807
1992 CAMPAIGN:	Waxman D	61.3%	$361,280
	Mark Robbins R	25.7%	$142,692

RATINGS:

ADA	ACU	AFL/CIO	GO	LCV	NCSC	NTU	USCC
100	5	89	F	100	98	17	18

Lynn Woolsey (D)
6th Congressional District

Some of the great mortgages of the Western world are nestled among the fir and redwood trees of Marin County, which makes up half of the 6th District electorate. The remainder live in all but the northeast corner of Sonoma County, where the population ranges from affluent urbanites and vintners to retirees with modest means, poverty-stricken farm workers and a thriving counterculture. Some of the latter, who have been there since the '60s, are sitting on extraordinarily valuable real estate.

Although the liberal San Francisco portion of the district was lost to reapportionment, the district that launched Sen. Barbara Boxer should be a safe haven for a liberal Democrat. Its residents are informed people who vote. Marin is still the trendsetter, a bastion of yuppie attitudes long before the term was coined. Voters tend to be environmentally aware, demanding of public services and economically conservative.

When Boxer decided to move on, however, her heir apparent appeared to be Assemblyman Bill Filante of Greenbrae, a hard-working and almost-liberal Republican who had been bucking the Democratic registration in the district for 14 years. But shortly after the primary, Filante had surgery for brain cancer and was forced to turn his campaign over to surrogates. Until Election Day, Filante's representatives continued to insist he would recover. He died within six weeks.

Lynn Woolsey

That left the field clear for an obscure Petaluma councilwoman named Lynn Woolsey, who raised a huge war chest and campaigned tirelessly as though she were the underdog. Woolsey subsequently became the first former welfare mom elected to Congress.

Woolsey landed on welfare after a 1968 divorce that left her with children ages 1, 2 and 5. She got a job as a secretary, but couldn't earn enough to support the family. She has called that period "the hell years of my life," as she struggled unsuccessfully to get child support from her deadbeat ex-husband. Woolsey eventually remarried, earned a night college degree, built up a successful personnel business and spent two terms on the Petaluma City Council.

As one might expect, her priorities in Congress include helping welfare recipients move into productive employment and making deadbeat dads accountable. She backs environmental causes, tax incentives for business expansion, spending for education and for using the peace dividend to finance national health care. There won't be much sympathy for Woolsey's views in a Republican-dominated Congress, but, if nothing else, she should be able to work with the GOP on some aspects of welfare reform and on using the IRS to collect child support.

PERSONAL: elected 1992; born Nov. 3, 1937, in Seattle; home, Petaluma; B.A University of San Francisco, 1980; separated, four children; Presbyterian.

CAREER: office worker and personnel manager, 1969-80; owner of personnel business, 1980-92; lecturer, College of Marin and Dominican College; Petaluma City Council, 1984-92.

COMMITTEES: Budget; Economic & Educational Opportunities.

OFFICES: Suite 439, Cannon Building, Washington, D.C. 20510, (202) 224-3121; district, Suite 200, 1101 College Ave., Santa Rosa, 95404 (707) 542-7182; Suite 140, 1050 Northgate Dr., San Rafael 94903, (415) 507-9554.

REGISTRATION: 54.9 D, 30.2R

1994 CAMPAIGN: Woolsey D 58.1% $654,464
Michael Nugent 37.5% $457,470
1992 CAMPAIGN: Woolsey D 65.2% $515,460
William Filante R 33.6% $410,461

RATINGS:

ADA	ACU	AFL/CIO	GO	LCV	NCSC	NTU	USCC
100	2	100	F	96	90	19	9

8

Lobbyists–a vital link in the process

When infamous lobbyist Artie Samish appeared on the cover of Collier's magazine in 1949, posed with a ventriloquist's dummy on his knee, he etched an image into the political consciousness of California: lobbyists as puppeteers, standing in the shadows pulling strings while legislators danced vacuously on the public stage.

Reality is much more complicated and far less sinister. Lobbyists are neither good nor evil. They have become, however, a linchpin in the legislative process, a true "third house" with substantial impact on the work that does or doesn't get done in the Legislature. And the shifting political dynamics of the 1990s are bringing change to their profession. The environment in which lobbyists work has become more unpredictable, and the federal sting operation that snared the Capitol's top lobbyist has subjected their tactics to more scrutiny than ever before. But legislative staff reductions, the growing impact of term limits and other factors also have heightened their importance in the process and opened up new opportunities for the more enterprising among them to expand their influence.

Lobbyists — or "legislative advocates," as they prefer to call themselves — are a critical link between lawmakers and industries, professional associations, consumer advocates and other combatants in the arcane and often bewildering world of California politics. They carry intricate information about the details of an industry or the desires of a professional group to the people who make the laws. The lion's share of the bills introduced in the Legislature are proposed, and in many cases written, by lobbyists. They also help devise legislative strategies, manage bills, produce grass-roots pressure and, often, manage the media. And the ability of top lobbyists to frame issues publicly and direct the distribution of clients' campaign money can have a substantial impact on the re-electability of lawmakers themselves.

389

Despite repeated calls for reform, the ability of lobbyists' clients to make campaign contributions — or "participate in the political process," as it is euphemistically called — remains one of the chief tools of the lobbyists' trade. But it is only one tool, and few advocates remain effective using money alone. The vast majority trade heavily on their knowledge of the Legislature and causes they represent, political acumen, ability to form coalitions and, perhaps most important, personal relationships with elected officials and staff members.

They also are relying more on their ability to provide "full service" to clients. There are fewer and fewer major one- or two-person operations that rely solely on their goodwill in the Capitol and their overall knowledge of the political system. Instead, the top firms have expanded their domain and hired in-house attorneys, researchers, public relations experts and other specialists, making lobbying firms look and run more like law firms. Public relations, particularly, is becoming a key element of lobbying in the new political environment. Legislative advocates are, in a way, expanding into marketing — selling the public issues and positions rather than products — as they seek new ways to influence a Legislature reshaped by term limits.

A GROWTH INDUSTRY

California's massive growth has created even more demand for advocates. As population balloons, as society grows more complex, as every interest in the state becomes more and more interwoven with government, the demand for lobbyists increases.

In 1977, the secretary of state's office registered 538 lobbyists with 761 clients. At the start of 1995, there were 1,070 lobbyists and 2,053 clients. Ironically, the passage of anti-government, anti-tax Proposition 13 in 1978 helped fuel that growth by centralizing the financing of schools and local governments in Sacramento. Interests with a stake in those finances muscled up by hiring more lobbyists in the capital.

The best measure of the growth is the amount of money spent lobbying the Legislature. According to the Fair Political Practices Commission, $40 million was spent on lobbying during the 1975-76 session of the Legislature. In just the first half of the 1993-94 session, $127.7 million was spent by trade associations, corporations, public-interest groups and others. Teachers, doctors, trial lawyers, oil companies, insurance companies and utilities generally rank at the top of the list, with some groups spending $1 million or $2 million a year on lobbying.

And the Legislature is not the only target of their activities. Lobbyists say many industries and interests are realizing that all levels of government, including state agencies and commissions, require expert representation. The state's gigantic bureaucracy can be even more unfathomable than the Legislature. A growing number of lobbyists are former state officials who have learned the pathways and players in key state agencies, and they find themselves in demand from a variety of interests with huge stakes in the decisions dealt out by the regulators. The state Departments of Food and Agriculture and Health Services, for example, played key roles in defining and administering Proposition 65, the 1986 Safe Drinking Water Act. That law has had a multimillion-dollar impact on scores of businesses. Likewise, education groups keep a close eye on the Department of Education, the Commission on Teacher Credentialing and other agencies that implement and enforce regulations affecting them.

In the Legislature, meanwhile, the labyrinthine lawmaking process and the ever-increasing demands on lawmakers' time and attention make it nearly impossible for someone outside the inner political circles to have much impact. Given the lobbyists' essential role, it would seem the door is open for them to play puppet-masters in the way Artie Samish once did. But that is not the case. In fact, the same system that makes lobbyists so vital prevents any one advocate from asserting control. There are so many interests and so much pressure from every quarter that it is virtually impossible for one lobbyist, or even a handful, to indiscriminately muscle bills through.

It takes a monumental effort to push any measure burdened with controversy through the Capitol. The bill must survive at least two committees and a floor vote in each house, possibly a conference committee and other floor votes, and then it must win the governor's signature. That's seven chances, at a minimum, for a bill to be killed. Passing it means winning at every step. And it is easy for many lobbyists, especially those representing single-issue interests, to throw enough doubt into lawmakers' minds to get them to vote "no" or at least to be absent so there are not enough votes to pass a bill. For legislators, there is always less political damage in sticking with the status quo. In fact, much of what lobbyists do is defensive; they spend much more energy trying to kill bills that might hurt their clients than breaking new ground or pushing proposals of their own.

ALL SHAPES, SIZES AND SKILLS

So, with all those lobbyists wandering the Capitol, the teeming atmosphere of California politics appears at first glance to fit the image of the marketplace of ideas and interests envisioned by the framers of American democracy. But only at first glance. The Capitol is not a place where decision-makers blend those ideas and choose simply on merit. And if any one set of players is responsible for influencing the decision-making process, it would be the lobbyists.

For one reason, lobbyists, like anyone else, come with various levels of skill, influence and experience. Better ones often win regardless of the merits of their case because victories in the Capitol are based on politics, not virtue. And each different species of lobbyist brings its own weapons and weaknesses. These include:

Public-interest lobbyists: Often called "white-hat" lobbyists, they work for consumer groups, good-government organizations, environmentalists or any other groups claiming to represent the public at large. These lobbyists, for the most part, are the weakest in the Capitol. Their best weapon is public sentiment. They often resort to calling press conferences to announce their positions or unhappiness, hoping it will generate enough public reaction to influence the votes of legislators. But with only meager financial resources, they have little to offer lawmakers other than public approval. Given the moneyed opposition to many of their causes, public-interest lobbyists spend much of their time working on damage control rather than passing legislation.

Association lobbyists: These advocates work for one specific organization, such as the California Association of Realtors. Some of these organizations have tremendous resources, a large grass-roots network and fat campaign war chests to dole out. And depending on their causes they, too, sometimes feel comfortable using the press and public sentiment to help push issues. But they also have some disadvantages. Since their legislative goals have to be agreed upon by the association's directors and membership, they often have less flexibility to adjust in midstream. In addition, they spend a good deal of their time organizing their association and trying to keep internal politics out of state politics.

Contract lobbyists: These are the hired guns, the quintessence of what the public envisions as the lobbying corps. And for the major contract lobbyists, the image generally fits. These lobbyists often have been around the Capitol for years, know the game from every angle and have enough of a client list, campaign war chest and history in politics to make lawmakers listen. But contract lobbyists come in many sizes and shapes. Some hire out to public-interest groups, which forces them to operate like those "white-hat" lobbyists. Others represent cities or semipublic entities that distribute few campaign contributions. Still others work for smaller companies or industries and have never gathered enough clout to make the inner circles.

Company lobbyists: Some large companies have their own in-house advocates. They are some of the real inside players in the Capitol, with the resources and money to be influential. And like many contract lobbyists, they often are most comfortable functioning outside the glare of public scrutiny. Since they work for only one client, they generally have the flexibility to compromise and roll with the inevitable political punches. But they usually need to work within coalitions or at least try to eliminate opposition from companies within their industry — otherwise, they can find themselves one small voice among many.

THE IMPORTANCE OF MONEY

For lobbyists, success goes to those who understand best the nature of influence. They understand timing, organization and the value of information. They have built relationships with legislators, consultants, even a key secretary or two. And, for the big-time lobbyists, they understand the connection between politics and money.

It is an axiom of modern political life, especially in a state such as California, that a politician without money is not a politician for long. In these days of computer-aided, television-oriented, high-tech campaigns, no candidate without a healthy chunk of cash can hope to win. And no group is more aware of that than lobbyists. Operating in an environment where money is the key to acquiring access to lawmakers, lobbyists have found themselves squarely in the middle of the campaign financing free-for-all.

The actual impact of campaign contributions on the drafting of laws is a hotly debated topic. Lawmakers and lobbyists alike insist that votes are not bought outright. And generally, money plays the deciding role only in turf fights that do not affect a legislator's district or do not become an issue in the media, such as when banks and savings and loans battle over state regulations.

But while the influence of money is not necessarily direct, it is thorough. For starters, it often affects who gets heard; when time is tight and there are two lobbyists waiting in the office lobby, the one who will get in is almost always the one who has been a consistent contributor. Even if it is only access that is being bought, as those on both sides of the transaction claim, being the last or the only person a lawmaker hears from before voting can prove to be very influential access. And, of course, it is the big-money interests that can afford to hire the best lobbyists and conduct the most elaborate campaigns in the first place.

When it comes to money, lobbyists essentially serve as middlemen between clients requesting favors and politicians seeking campaign funds. In fact, many lobbyists portray themselves as victims of a system that requires a nearly constant flow of money and devalues arguments on the merits of a particular bill. A frequent complaint of theirs has to do with the mountain of invitations to fund-raisers that descends upon them near the end of the session — when bills that have been bottled up all year are being taken up in short order — asking their attendance for a cost of $750 or $1,000, when $500 used to do.

A fledgling reform effort was undertaken in 1994. First, Common Cause circulated among lawmakers a pledge not to solicit campaign contributions from lobbyists; a small minority signed. Also, Acting Secretary of State Tony Miller offered lobbyists a chance to file statements saying they did not wish to be solicited to arrange campaign contributions; again, only a minority participated. The Legislature also passed a bill limiting contributions and spending in legislative races, but it drew a veto from Gov. Pete Wilson because of its use of taxpayer money for political campaigns.

So the fact remains — legislators need loads of money to run for office. The need for cash is a fact of life lobbyists frequently have to sell to clients. And those with money still win their share of Capitol battles.

THE INVASION OF EX-MEMBERS

Another means of gaining access to a lawmaker is to have a ready-made relationship with him or her — so it should come as no surprise that former lawmakers themselves are a rapidly growing class of lobbyists in Sacramento.

These people have worked together, seen each other almost every day, experienced the same pressures and developed the same interests. They have an emotional bond like college alums. A number of former legislators today lobby either full or part time, and still more are not registered, either because they do not lobby enough to qualify as official lobbyists or because their contacts and connections are less direct.

The list of some of the more prominent or active among the former legislators includes former Sens. John Briggs, Dennis Carpenter, John Foran, Bob Wilson and George Zenovich; and former Assembly members Gordon Duffy, Jean Duffy, Joe Gonsalves, John Knox, Robert Naylor, Paul Priolo and John P. Quimby. Former Sen. William Campbell also belongs on the list. As president of the California Manufacturers Association, he spends a good deal of time maintaining old Capitol ties, getting the word out on what would be good for the CMA and showing up on the legislative floors about the time a vote is due on a critical CMA issue.

In addition, former legislative or administration staff members turn their expertise and inside relationships into influential lobbying jobs, often focusing on the committees and subject areas in which they had been involved. There are dozens of lobbyists who are ex-legislative staff members, but the largest group is probably the legion of former aides to Assembly Speaker Willie Brown, which includes Bill Rutland, Kathleen Snodgrass, Jackson Gualco, John Mockler and Kent Stoddard. Cliff Berg, who held an influential staff position as executive officer of the Senate Rules Committee, left the Legislature in 1995 to work as a contract lobbyist for Governmental Advocates, a firm co-owned by Jerry Zanelli, who himself previously held Berg's position on the Senate staff.

Former administration officials, of course, find themselves in great demand to lobby the agencies in which they once worked. The third house is full of former Deukmejian administrators, including Michael Franchetti, Deukmejian's first finance director; David Swoap, once a health and welfare secretary; David Ackerman, a former deputy business, transportation and housing undersecretary; Rodney Blonien, a former corrections undersecretary; and Randy Ward, who headed the state Department of Conservation. Former Deukmejian chief of staff Steven Merksamer also must be included in that list, although he is not a registered lobbyist. Merksamer's law/lobbying firm — Nielsen, Merksamer, Parrinello, Mueller & Naylor — represents some of America's largest companies and is one of the most influential firms on the state scene. Another person who exerts great personal influence is Kirk West, a business, transportation and housing secretary under Deukmejian who currently heads the California Chamber of Commerce. There also are top lobbyists who were state officials in earlier administrations, including Richard B. Spohn, former Gov. Jerry Brown's director of the state Department of Consumer Affairs; and George Steffes, an aide to then-Gov. Ronald Reagan in the early 1970s.

A study in 1986 by political scientists Jerry Briscoe and Charles Bell, then at the University of the Pacific and the University of California, Davis, respectively, found 36 percent of the registered lobbyists had served in government. This steady stream from the Capitol to the third house for years inspired "anti-revolving door" bills from lawmakers or public-interest groups such as Common Cause. Those proposals sought in various ways to prohibit state officials and lawmakers from lobbying their former houses or agencies for a year or two after leaving state service, but most of them were brushed aside by those who had the most to lose — the legislators.

In 1990, however, constituents and good-government groups were putting pressure on lawmakers to clean up their ethics. Under the cloud of an FBI investigation, and worried about looming ethics and term-limit initiatives, the lawmakers passed their own half-hearted ethics reform bill and put it before voters as Proposition 112. The measure, which limited lawmakers' outside income in exchange for creating the independent Citizens Compensation Commission to set salaries, included anti-revolving door provisions that prohibited former lawmakers or top-level administrators from lobbying their old colleagues for one year after leaving office.

Proposition 112 was approved by voters in June 1990, and those locks on the revolving doors were to go into effect Jan. 1, 1991. But then-Gov. Deukmejian, ever-watchful for the interests of his friends, forced the effective date to be changed to Jan. 7 — the day after he left office — which made his entire staff exempt.

ALL RELATIONSHIPS ARE PERSONAL

The fact that former lawmakers, staffers and others already familiar with each other are in demand as lobbyists underscores one of the primary rules of California politics: Everything that happens in the Capitol comes down to human relationships, rather than institutional ones. Lobbyists and legislators hold nothing more precious than their relationships with each other. If a lawmaker likes you and trusts you, he will listen. If a lobbyist thinks of you as a friend, he will make sure you receive timely information and equally useful campaign contributions.

The most notable advantage of a lobbyist's friendship with a legislator is the member's willingness to listen to a friend argue for or against a bill. That becomes even more significant during the end-of-session tempests, when hundreds of bills can be dispatched in a few hours. That is when bills are being revised, members are under the gun and a lobbyist doesn't have time to document arguments about a set of amendments. Members are left with no choice but to ask the lobbyist if the changes are acceptable to his or her clients. If they trust each other, the lobbyist can look the legislator in the eye and tell him the truth, with neither feeling nervous.

A study done for former Assembly Speaker Jesse Unruh during the mid-1970s asked legislators what they thought was the most corrupting influence in politics. The answer that came back the most often was "friendship." One legislator said, "I never voted for a bad bill, but I voted for a lot of bad authors."

The nature of the relationships between lobbyists and lawmakers has changed over the years, however. Today they are most often based on shared interests and long-standing acquaintances; sometimes families of lawmakers and lobbyists play together on weekends or holidays. That is a far cry from the days of duck hunting or drunken revelry in the 1930s, '40s and '50s, when Artie Samish said he supplied his legislative friends with "a baked potato, a girl or money" — whatever their taste.

RISE AND FALL OF THE OL'-BOY NETWORK

While Samish, who was imprisoned for tax evasion in 1956, was probably the most extreme case in California, many lobbyists used a few good meals or a round of drinks to create a bridge to lawmakers. With that bridge, they could then argue the merits of their cases. Those bridges were built on an old-fashioned, good-ol'-boy network. Some of the better known lobbyists ran up tabs of $1,500 a month wining and dining legislators. And, not infrequently, lawmakers signed a lobbyist's name to a restaurant or bar tab even when the lobbyist was not there.

There also were regular, institutionalized social affairs paid for by a number of lobbyists and open to all lawmakers and many key members of their staffs. Most spectacular of those was the "Moose Milk," a lavish lunch and open bar held Thursdays in the former El Mirador Hotel across from the Capitol. There also was the lunch at the Derby Club on Tuesdays and the "Clam and Corral" at the Senator Hotel on Wednesdays. The purpose was nothing more than good times, good will and, of course, access.

Those days began to change in 1966, when Californians made their Legislature full time. That meant career politicians and full-time staff. No longer were lobbyists the only people who understood the state's industries and the fine points in bills. Lawmakers and their larger staffs had more time and information of their own. And with the professionalization of the Legislature, lawmakers began to develop both areas of expertise and fiefdoms. Specialists, usually committee chairmen, emerged in banking, insurance, health and dozens of others fields. For lobbyists, that had two implications.

First, it meant that lobbyists had to have better, more specific information. A simple "trust me on this one" became less convincing. Lobbyists had to learn the fine points of the industries and clients they represented. And second, with power spread through the committee chairmen and their staffs, it became increasingly difficult for just a few lobbyists to handle major legislation. So lobbyists, too, became specialists. Not only did they concentrate on specific subjects, but lobbyists became valuable to clients because of their relationships with specific lawmakers.

A huge catalyst in the transformation of the lobbying corps from the days of camaraderie to the law-firm-like machines of today was Proposition 9, the Political Reform Act passed in 1974. That initiative required detailed disclosure, and it limited the gifts and meals lobbyists could buy legislators to $10 a month. With that act, the "Moose Milk" and free meals disappeared, eventually to be replaced by a more businesslike lobbying industry. In fact, that measure inspired a group of longtime lobbyists to form the Institute of Governmental Advocates, an association to lobby for lobbyists. The institute filed a successful lawsuit to set aside portions of the measure.

THE NEW ERA

The 1990s have brought another set of sweeping changes to the lobbying corps. First, passage in 1990 of Proposition 140, the term-limits initiative, put in motion a radically new dynamic in the legislator-lobbyist relationship. The measure, by then-Los Angeles County Supervisor Pete Schabarum, limits Assembly members to three terms, or six years, and state senators to two terms, or eight years. Limits were imposed for life, so legislators cannot sit out a term before running again for their former office. The measure also eliminated the Legislature's retirement system and cut the operating budget of the two houses by 38 percent, requiring a significant downsizing of staff.

The first real sweep of members losing their seats to term limits occurs at the end of the 1995-96 session, though many lawmakers opted for an early departure or sought higher office in 1994. The loss of vast amounts of institutional memory and expertise — through the departures of both lawmakers and staffers — has the immediate effect of strengthening the hand of lobbyists, who, with the dwindling number of legislative staff, will be the only remaining experts in the Capitol. But it also creates new challenges. With a constant rotation of members, lobbyists will be hard pressed to develop the long-term relationships that have served them so well in the past. In addition, new members elected since the advent of term limits are proclaiming to be a new breed of legislator — one that is constituent-oriented rather than career-oriented, more interested in shaking up the system than becoming a player in it. And term limits, coupled with the 1992 reapportionment, also have created an inherently less stable Legislature, with districts more closely divided in partisan terms and party control of the houses less certain from session to session — as the Assembly speakership battle following the November 1994 election demonstrated.

The other major development of the early 1990s for lobbyists was the conviction of one of their own — powerhouse lobbyist Clay Jackson — in the FBI probe of Capitol corruption. Jackson, once the top power broker in the lobbying corps, was convicted of bribery in December 1993 and ordered to serve a 6-1/2 year sentence. While several lawmakers and staffers were also snared in the sting, the Jackson conviction sent a shudder through the lobbying corps. While most advocates don't move in the same circles that Jackson did, the case spotlighted the fuzzy ethical lines and increasingly dangerous nature of the lobbyist's trade. "The public disdains politics and everything to do with politics," an attorney who represented one of the defendants in the sting told a lobbyists' ethics seminar in 1994. "You need to stop and think, how is this going to be looked at from the outside? What does it look like to 12 folks who don't have the foggiest idea what you do, who are stuck up in that [jury] box five years after the fact?"

Faced by the new constraints of shifting legislative power and increasing public scrutiny, lobbyists have been altering their approach, adopting tactics that previously were used mainly by lobbyists in Washington, D.C. While the personal, relationship-oriented lobbying style of the past has by no means disappeared, top lobbying firms are using a more campaign-style approach. The idea is to create coalitions, build grass-roots support and use public-relations strategies to frame issues publicly — and bring the pressure of the public to bear on lawmakers. For example, a full-service lobbying firm of the new era might conduct polling, do phone banking, plant newspaper editorials, take out ads and join forces with a "white hat" group to identify supporters of a client's cause — then organize postcard and phone drives to get those constituents' views communicated to lawmakers. Such campaigns have been used in recent years to beat down new smoking restrictions, curb the state's move toward electric cars and reform workers' compensation insurance. Some lobbyists for larger associations are also trying to get around the term-limits problem by beginning relationships with public officials earlier — identifying promising office holders at the local level, developing ties there and following them as they move to the Legislature.

Still, the very newness of the Legislature's changed dynamics means all of the implications have yet to be sorted out. Certainly, opportunities for manipulation, special-interest dealing and just plain mischief will continue to abound in the coming years; that element of Artie Samish's legacy remains intact, though it may take less blatant forms. The interaction between a continually changing group of legislators and a lobbying corps still adjusting to the new realities of power in Sacramento will continue to be a vital and compelling story.

9

California's movers and shakers

To the larger public, politics is an activity of politicians, the men and women who offer themselves for public office. But behind the candidates exists a complex network of professionals and amateurs who design, finance and manage the campaigns that voters see. These are the movers and shakers of politics, who have at least as much influence as the out-front candidates for office. Their motives range from ideological conviction to greed, and, if anything, their role is increasing as campaigns become more costly and sophisticated.

California's power brokers are especially obscure because of the state's unique political system, features of which include weak party structures, nonpartisan local governments and a multitude of locally based political organizations. Other major states, such as Illinois and New York, have more formalized political power structures. During Richard Daley's heyday as mayor of Chicago, for instance, no one doubted that he was the boss, not only in his city, but of the entire Illinois Democratic Party. Those who aspired to office, whether it was the clerkship of the smallest court or the president of the United States, had to clear through Daley or his minions.

Behind-the-scenes political power in California is wielded more indirectly. And in a state of media and money politics, rather than street-level organizations, those with access to money form the elite, a fact that becomes ever-more important as California's clout in national politics expands. The Los Angeles area has evolved into a source of national political money at least as important as the steel and glass canyons of New York and continues to gain strength as new campaign finance laws make direct contributions more difficult.

California also has developed a cadre of professional campaign organizers — consultants, as they prefer to be called — who have pioneered in the sophisticated techniques of mass political communications: television, computer-directed mail and, most recently, prerecorded video tapes that combine the impact of television with the selectivity of mail.

THE HOLLYWOOD BRANCH

Every four years, a little ritual takes place. Those who aspire to the White House begin booking flights to Los Angeles, not to present themselves to voters, but to schmooz with a handful of men and women who reside within a few miles of one another on the city's west side. Most of those who make the pilgrimage are Democrats since most westside political financiers are Democrats, connected to the huge, Los Angeles-based entertainment industry. But not a few of them are Republicans. Prior to the 1988 presidential primary season, Republican Sen. Bob Dole raised more money out of Hollywood than did Massachusetts Gov. Michael Dukakis, the Democrat's eventual nominee.

Hollywood types tend to be passionate about causes and free with money, which is exactly what politicians want. It's estimated that the Los Angeles region accounts for a fifth of all the money spent on presidential primaries.

There's an increasingly mutual attraction between political people and entertainment people, says Stanley Scheinbaum, an economist and political activist. Politicians like the glitz and the entertainment people like the power. But Scheinbaum and others have qualms about the growing influence of entertainers, many of whom are naive. "I don't think it's healthy," he says. "Basically, a few rich people get that opportunity [to meet the politicians], and I don't think the influence of these kind of people should be any greater than of those folks in the ghettos and barrios."

Television producer Linda Bloodworth-Thomason sees the same thing in a different way. "There's a definite connection between entertainment and politics," she told one interviewer in 1992, "and the line is definitely getting more blurred. But I don't think that's a bad thing."

Bloodworth-Thomason was in a position to make that observation because she and her husband, Harry, may have been the most important two people in the rise of Bill Clinton from the relative obscurity of governing Arkansas to his election as president in 1992.

The Thomasons, Arkansans themselves and creators of such shows as "Designing Women" and "Evening Shade," have been friends with Clinton for more than a quarter-century and first applied their media magic to Clinton after a long, boring keynote address to the 1988 Democratic national convention had made him a national laughingstock. The Thomasons arranged for Clinton to appear on the Johnny Carson show shortly thereafter to make light of his gaffe and that went a long way toward dissipating the political fallout.

As Clinton launched his 1992 campaign, the Hollywood couple was glued to his side, introducing him into the glittery world of entertainment politics, raising money, producing his national convention video biography, overseeing his inaugural ceremonies and acquiring an $8 million beach house near Santa Barbara for Clinton to use as his vacation getaway. But only a few months into the Clinton administration, the relationship turned sour. Clinton was accused by critics of going-Hollywood after a much-publicized incident in which he got a haircut from a show business hair stylist in Air Force One while it sat on the apron at Los Angeles International Airport. There also were charges of favoritism in the realignment of White House travel business. Suddenly, the Bloodworth-Thomason duo dropped from public sight.

Another television producer acquired political clout in 1992 despite having no direct connections with Clinton. Diane English, producer of *Murphy Brown* and other shows, was thrust into prominence when then-Vice President Dan Quayle cited Murphy Brown as an example of Hollywood's trashing of family values because the lead character had a child out of wedlock.

Mickey Kantor, a Los Angeles attorney with strong connections in both the entertainment and political worlds, converted his personal friendship with Clinton into the chairmanship of the Arkansan's campaign and seemed ticketed to play a major role in the formation of the Clinton administration until he was shunted aside after the election in a power struggle with other advisers. He had to settle for being Clinton's trade representative. Kantor is one of the country's most prominent political attorneys, along with partners Charles Manatt, a former national Democratic chairman, and John Tunney, a former California U.S. senator. Kantor had been identified with former Gov. Jerry Brown's many campaigns until latching onto Clinton after serving with Hillary Rodham Clinton on the board of a charitable organization.

Among Democrats, two organized groups have emerged in recent years. One is the Hollywood Women's Political Committee, founded in 1984 by singer/actress Barbra Streisand. The committee specializes in star-studded fund-raising extravaganzas on behalf of liberal candidates and causes. Streisand, for instance, staged a big fund-raiser for California U.S. Sen. Alan Cranston at her Malibu ranch in 1986 and repackaged the entertainment as a television special, thus magnifying its financial impact.

The second and newer organization is the Show Coalition, known as ShowCo, founded in 1988 by younger Hollywood figures, most of whom had been identified with Gary Hart's abortive presidential bid. ShowCo has not yet become a major fund-raising source but acts as an intermediary between politicians and entertainers, staging seminars and other non-financial events.

Streisand and actor Robert Redford (who starred together in the semipolitical movie *The Way We Were*) are the prototypical Hollywood liberals, willing to devote time and money to their candidates and causes. While Streisand prefers to work directly for candidates, Redford takes a loftier, issue-oriented approach through a foundation that he has endowed. But they are not alone. Others who share their ideological commitment include Morgan Fairchild, who was especially close to

Sen. Cranston before his career self-destructed; Sally Field; Cher; Gregory Peck; Ally Sheedy; Ed Begley Jr.; Bette Midler; Goldie Hawn; Chevy Chase; and Bruce Willis.

Jerry Brown developed particularly tight ties to the Hollywood Democrats during his eight years as governor and as a perennial candidate for president and U.S. senator. He was singer Linda Ronstadt's self-proclaimed boyfriend for a time, dated other Hollywood figures and made Lucy's El Adobe Cafe, a hangout for actors, his unofficial Los Angeles headquarters. Actors such as Warren Beatty and Jane Fonda and singers such as Ronstadt and Helen Reddy raised tons of money for Brown's nonstop campaigns, and director Francis Ford Coppola produced an ill-fated live television program in Wisconsin during Brown's second unsuccessful campaign for the presidency in 1980. Gary Hart was the Hollywood liberals' clear favorite for president in 1984 and again in 1988 until he was forced to withdraw.

Jerry Brown's sister, Kathleen, tapped the Hollywood well for money as she ran for governor in 1994, with actor Beatty playing a key role. But while the money was forthcoming, she squandered it on an ill-advised campaign and lost badly to Gov. Pete Wilson.

Ronald Reagan personified the blurry line that separates politics and show business, and during his political career solidified the ties that bind many in Hollywood to the GOP. The most outwardly political of the Hollywood conservatives these days is Charlton Heston, who makes commercials for Republican candidates and has often been mentioned as a potential candidate himself so often that he's developed a stock rejoinder: "I'd rather play a senator than be one."

Comedian Bob Hope is a mainstay of Republican fund-raising events and, not surprisingly, most of the other Hollywood conservatives are of the older generation, such as Frank Sinatra and James Stewart. But some newer and younger stars also side with the GOP, such as Sylvester Stallone, Tony Danza, Chuck Norris, Jaclyn Smith and strongman-turned-actor Arnold Schwarzenegger, who is married to Kennedy clanswoman Maria Shriver.

Hollywood politics, however, involve more than the men and women whose names are found on theater marquees and record labels. The business side of show business is heavily involved in politics in terms of both personal conviction and financial betterment. The most prominent of the Hollywood tycoons who dabble in politics is Lew Wasserman, head of the huge MCA entertainment conglomerate (which was sold to Japanese investors in 1990). He plays both sides of the partisan fence. Wasserman is a Democrat but had particularly close ties to Reagan from the latter's days as an MCA client and star of MCA-produced TV programs. Wasserman also established a close relationship with then-U.S. Sen. Pete Wilson, blocking aid to any would-be political rival. The entertainment industry, like any other, has business in Washington and Sacramento, mostly involving tax treatment and copyright and trademark laws. Wilson, for instance, endeared himself to the showbiz tycoons by protecting their interests during the writing of federal tax reform laws.

Movie mogul Jerry Weintraub served on Republican George Bush's finance team in 1988, although he's best known as a Democratic campaign contributor. Producer Norman Lear has made liberal causes his second career and the late Frank Wells, who headed the Walt Disney entertainment empire, toyed with the idea of making a bid for a U.S. Senate seat from California in 1992.

Hollywood's political activists were deeply involved in 1990 elections, recruited by proponents and opponents of ballot measures to both raise money and appear in commercials. Democratic leaders sought out Jack Lemmon to make a series of TV ads — widely criticized as misleading — opposing measures to overhaul the legislative redistricting processes and later persuaded Angela Lansbury, James Garner and others to pitch against term limits. The first campaign worked but the second failed. Environmentalists in Hollywood, meanwhile, went all out for Big Green, a major environmental protection measure that was rejected by voters, and Forests Forever, another rejected measure that would have imposed severe logging restrictions.

Abortion rights, gay rights and AIDS research also are high on priority lists of Hollywood liberals, and when Colorado voters repealed laws making gays a protected minority group in 1992, Streisand and others called for an entertainment world boycott of the state, which forced some actors and musicians to give up their customary skiing holidays in Aspen and Vail.

Much of the Hollywood hierarchy is Jewish and politicians who want its support must adhere to a strongly pro-Israel line. That's why Jerry Brown, Alan Cranston, Pete Wilson, Ronald Reagan and any other California politician who aspires to the political big time in Washington can be counted in Israel's corner. By contrast, when Rep. Pete McCloskey ran for the U.S. Senate in 1982 as a critic of Israel, he bombed in Hollywood and Republican Rep. Ed Zschau suffered a similar treatment when he ran against Cranston in 1986.

ELSEWHERE IN THE SOUTHLAND

Not everybody who writes a fat check to a politician in California is an entertainment industry figure. As a prosperous and fast-growing state, California has produced more than its share of wealthy people who give to candidates from both parties or can ask others to contribute as peers rather than political beggars.

Southern California aerospace executives tilt toward Republicans with their promises of greater military spending. When, for instance, George Bush made a quick, money-raising trip to Southern California in 1988 while seeking the Republican presidential nomination, he stopped first at the TRW aerospace plant in Redondo Beach, then headed for private fund-raising events at the Bel Air home of real estate tycoon Howard Ruby and finally the Rancho Mirage estate of publisher Walter Annenberg. But when the Pentagon began to cut spending late in the Bush administration, much of the aerospace industry support dissipated. Since winning a U.S. Senate seat in 1992, Democrat Dianne Feinstein has developed close relations with aerospace moguls, a relationship that helped her survive a stiff challenge in 1994.

Donald Bren, head of the big Irvine Co. land development firm in Orange County, has emerged as a Republican financial power, supplanting such older kingmakers as auto dealer Holmes Tuttle, who was part of the group that persuaded Ronald Reagan to run for governor in 1966. (Most of those prominent early Reagan backers have since died.) Pete Wilson's election as governor in 1990 may have made Bren the most influential of the new kingmakers. He and Wilson served in the Marine Corps together. Larry Thomas, Wilson's (and Gov. George Deukmejian's) one-time press secretary, also has been Bren's chief media spokesman. Thomas took a leave in 1994 to work on Wilson's re-election. The Irvine Co. connection to Wilson was underscored when Wilson chose John Seymour, a state senator from Orange County with strong ties to the Irvine Co., as his successor in the U.S. Senate. (Seymour was unseated by Dianne Feinstein in 1992).

Financier David Murdock is another Southern California business mogul with strong Republican connections, as is Lodwrick Cook, chairman of Atlantic Richfield Co. Philip Hawley, chairman of the Carter-Hawley-Hale department store chain, was once a major Republican player, but with his company's shaky financial situation in recent years, his political star has fallen.

Potent new players on the scene are a group of conservative businesspeople with ties to the religious right and the California Gunowners PAC. Their Capitol Commonwealth Group and related organizations pumped $1.5 million into campaigns and PACs in 1992 and played major roles in Republicans gains during the 1994 elections. More than half of the 1992 war chest came from billionaire Howard Ahmanson Jr., whose father founded Home Savings and Loan. "We're a funny combination of the moral majority and libertarianism," Ahmanson's wife, Roberta, has said. Major beneficiaries of their largess were conservative Assembly candidates who ran opposite Gov. Wilson's more moderate slate in primary elections.

Capitol Commonwealth members gave much of their money through another committee they formed, Allied Business Political Action Committee, and other organizations such as the California Pro-Life Council and Family PAC. A frequent partner in giving has been Robert Hurtt Jr., president of Container Supply Co. in Orange County. In 1992, Hurtt and his wife, Esther, gave more than $521,000 to candidates and political organizations, and Hurtt later won a state Senate seat himself with the obvious goal of becoming the Senate's GOP leader. He and Ahmanson, however, experienced something of a personal rupture.

Other partners are Roland and Lila Hinz of Mission Hills, who gave $124,625 in 1992, and Edward Atsinger III of Camarillo, who donated $83,625. Hinz, a Democrat, owns Daisy/Hi-Torque Publications, which publishes Dirt Bike magazine. Atsinger owns a chain of Christian-format radio stations.

Southern California business types who lean toward the Democratic side include Richard O'Neill, heir to vast land holdings in Orange County, who has been known to devote weekends to precinct-walking and once served as state Democratic chairman. Michael Milken, the junk bond whiz who served a stretch in federal prison, was closely identified with several Democratic political figures, including Cranston and former Rep. Tony Coelho. In fact, Coelho was forced to resign from Congress in 1989 after revelations that he had acquired a bond through Milken under suspicious circumstances. In 1994, Coelho was attempting a comeback of sorts as a Clinton political adviser.

Los Angeles attorney William Wardlaw made a big political splash in 1993 when he spearheaded the campaign of Republican lawyer/businessman Richard Riordon for mayor of Los Angeles. After Riordon won, Wardlaw switched partisan hats and played a key role in the ultimately disastrous campaign of Democrat Kathleen Brown for governor in 1994. Another Southern California big-timer is Peter Ueberroth, a millionaire businessman who headed the 1984 Los Angeles Olympics, then became baseball commissioner, headed up reconstruction efforts after the Los Angeles riots and toyed with running for the U.S. Senate in 1994. He, like several other prominent Republicans, endorsed Dianne Feinstein's re-election to the Senate in 1994.

San Diego, which tries to insulate itself from Los Angeles, has developed its own power-broker infrastructure. Newspaper publisher Helen Copley is a powerhouse, as is Joan Kroc, who inherited the McDonald's hamburger empire and a baseball team from her late husband, Ray. Banker and deal-maker Richard Silberman was a big political player — even serving for a time in Jerry Brown's administration in Sacramento — and was married to San Diego County Supervisor Susan Golding. But Silberman, who also had strong ties to Republican figures such as Gov. Pete Wilson, was indicted in 1989 on drug-money laundering charges and later convicted, thus ending his political career as well as his civic and business standing. Golding, after divorcing the imprisoned Silberman, was elected San Diego mayor in 1992 and has been mentioned as a potential Republican candidate for governor in 1998.

Fast-food moguls represent a particular subspecies of political financiers in California. In addition to the Krocs, Silberman once headed the Jack-in-the-Box hamburger chain in partnership with Robert Peterson, whose wife, Maureen O'Connor, was Golding's predecessor as mayor. And Carl's Jr. chain founder Carl Karcher is a patron of Republican and right-wing causes in Orange County.

MOVERS AND SHAKERS OF THE NORTH

Northern California's power brokers tend to operate more quietly than those in Los Angeles and Hollywood. Among Republicans, no one is quieter or more influential than David Packard, a co-founder of the Hewlett-Packard computer firm and perhaps California's richest man, with a personal fortune exceeding $2 billion

(Bren also vies for this unofficial title.) Packard tends to support moderate to liberal Republicans. He was instrumental in helping Tom Campbell unseat a conservative Republican incumbent, Rep. Ernest Konnyu, in 1988 in his home district on the San Francisco Peninsula. Packard also supported Campbell's unsuccessful U.S. Senate bid in 1992.

Packard is the grand old man of Silicon Valley, the center of California's computer industry. As computer entrepreneurs have matured in business terms, they also have become civic and political leaders. One, Ed Zschau, won a seat in Congress and came within a few thousand votes of unseating Sen. Alan Cranston in 1986.

To date, the computer moguls have wielded influence mostly at the local level, helping San Jose and the rest of Silicon Valley develop an infrastructure to match their population and economic growth. But some, such as Packard, have moved beyond. His influence extends from the state Coastal Commission to the White House, and he is credited with quietly prodding Gov. George Deukmejian to do something about California's traffic problems.

A number of the most prominent Silicon Valley executives deserted the Republican Party in 1992 and endorsed Clinton, thanks to promises of a tougher line on trade with high-tech competitors overseas and to the Pentagon cutbacks, which hit the industry hard. High-tech industry leaders such as Apple Computer Chairman John Sculley and Hewlett-Packard President John Young were promised, in effect, key roles in shaping Clinton's economic policies. And in 1994, many of these same figures endorsed Dianne Feinstein's re-election to the U.S. Senate.

Two other Northern California tycoons whose influence extends well beyond the state are the Bechtels, Stephen Sr. and Stephen Jr., who run San Francisco-based Bechtel Corp., a worldwide construction and engineering firm. At one time, it seemed as if half the Reagan administration in Washington consisted of ex-Bechtel executives. They included Secretary of Defense Caspar Weinberger and Secretary of State George Schultz.

Among Northern California Democratic financiers, none ranks higher than San Francisco real estate investor Walter Shorenstein. He labors tirelessly on behalf of the party's coffers and is courted just as tirelessly by presidential hopefuls. In 1989, however, Shorenstein declared independence after ex-Gov. Jerry Brown became state party chairman. Shorenstein and Bruce Lee, a high-ranking United Auto Workers official, established a soft-money drive to aid Democratic presidential nominee Michael Dukakis in California in 1988 and decided to continue the separate organizational fund despite entreaties from Brown that they fold their operation into his party apparatus. Shorenstein's light dimmed after a former employee lodged sexual harassment charges against him.

Another San Franciscan who has wielded a big stick in Democratic financial circles is attorney Duane Garrett, although his standing fell in 1988 after he attached himself to Bruce Babbitt's ill-fated voyage into presidential waters. Garrett suffered another setback in 1990, when ex-San Francisco Mayor Dianne Feinstein lost her bid to become governor, a campaign in which Feinstein's husband, investment counselor Richard Blum, emerged as a willing political financier, at least when his wife was involved. And among San Francisco insiders, Henry Berman, a consultant to the Seagram's liquor empire, carries much clout for his political fund-raising ability. He has been especially close to Assembly Speaker Willie Brown but also aided Feinstein's 1990 gubernatorial campaign.

Shorenstein, Garrett and Berman are valued not so much for their personal wealth, which is fairly modest in the case of the latter two, but for their organizational ability. They can pull together a substantial amount of political money simply by making a few phone calls or placing their names on invitations.

Gordon Getty, who may be California's second- or third-wealthiest man, is a different kind of political financier. Getty, a San Francisco resident, is an heir to the Getty oil fortune but devotes much of his time to private endeavors, especially composing classical music. Wife Ann Getty is a political junkie who lends her husband's name and her energies to political enterprises. She was particularly active in ex-Gov. Brown's campaigns.

The East Bay has developed its own coterie of political pooh-bahs. Jack Brooks, a part-owner of the Raiders football team, carries a lot of weight among Democrats, and developers Joe Callahan, Ron Cowan and Ken Hoffman play major roles at the local levels. Ken Behring, a developer and owner of the Seattle Seahawks football team, has developed a reputation for political dealing at the local level with influence that stretches into the state Legislature.

Sacramento, another fast-growing area, has seen its developers become political heavyweights, and not just at the local level. The Northern California and Republican equivalent of the Manatt-Tunney law firm in Southern California is to be found in Sacramento headed by, among others, Steve Merksamer, a one-time top aide to Deukmejian. Merksamer and his colleagues at the firm represent top-drawer corporate clients in political affairs while Merksamer functions as a Republican insider. He played a seminal role in persuading Pete Wilson to run for governor.

Two of Sacramento's developers, Angelo Tsakopoulous and Phil Angelides, were big-money contributors and fund-raisers for fellow Greek-Americans Michael Dukakis and Art Agnos (mayor of San Francisco) in 1988, and Angelides, a former Capitol aide, ran for state treasurer, unsuccessfully, in 1994 after performing brilliantly as the state Democratic Party chairman.

Tsakopoulous and Angelides exemplify another trend in political financing in California: the creation of groups that help people of similar ethnic backgrounds pursue their political careers. Frozen out of traditional sources of Republican campaign money, for instance, Deukmejian tapped the state's large and wealthy Armenian-American community. Los Angeles lawyer Karl Samuelian organized the effort, and with Deukmejian's victory, he became a major power in Republican politics. Similar organization efforts have aided Asian politicians such as Los

Angeles City Councilman Michael Woo and Sacramento Rep. Robert Matsui, while Los Angeles' large Jewish community has been a major source of campaign money for both parties, and not just for Jewish candidates.

Hispanics and African Americans have yet to develop similarly powerful ethnic fund-raising networks, although African American entertainers have helped such political figures as former Los Angeles Mayor Tom Bradley. The most important African American political financier in the state has been Sam Williams, a Los Angeles attorney who is close to Bradley.

DOWN ON THE FARM

In California's major agricultural valleys the financial and political powers are, not surprisingly, connected to agribusiness. Two of the most influential have been Modesto's Gallo wine-making brothers, Ernest and Julio. Even after Julio's death, the Gallo family's influence is widely felt. The secretive Gallos have personal wealth estimated at nearly $1 billion and are powerful political figures. They played major roles in organizing and financing the successful campaign in 1990 against a ballot measure that would have sharply increased taxes on liquor.

Further south, amid the cotton fields of the lower San Joaquin Valley, the powers are the Boswells and the Salyers, two agribusiness families whose holdings sweep across the now-dry expanse of Tulare Lake. The Boswells — the largest privately owned farming operation in the world with interests in other states and Australia — and the Salyers play political hardball in Sacramento and Washington, D.C., with campaign funds and high-priced lobbyists to protect their interests. Their major concern lies in protecting and enhancing the public water supplies vital to their farming operations.

Norma Foster Maddy has double-barreled political clout. She's not only the heiress to the Foster Farms chicken empire, but she's married to state Sen. Ken Maddy, Republican leader of the state Senate. Ken Maddy, who has a passion for thoroughbred racing, is partners in the horse racing business with John Harris, head of Harris Farms. Harris made headlines in 1994 when he became part of a Republican business bloc that backed Democrat Dianne Feinstein's Senate re-election.

The wine-making families of the Napa and nearby valleys are major powers in local politics and the scion of one family, Don Sebastiani, briefly served in the Legislature.

LABOR'S LOST LOVE

At last count, fewer than 2 million California workers — scarcely one in 10 — belonged to labor unions. The number is holding steady even as labor's overall share of the expanding work force has slipped under 20 percent. Despite that decline, California labor leaders remain powerful political figures, able to turn out campaign workers and distribute money at levels that are decisive in many political conflicts.

A prime example occurred in 1987, when a big labor turnout helped Democrat Cecil Green capture a Los Angeles County state Senate seat that seemed destined to go Republican. Labor fired up its troops on an issue dear to workers' hearts: Republican Deukmejian's unilateral closure of the state's occupational safety and health inspection agency. Later, labor obtained voter approval of a ballot measure reinstating the agency and won approval of a major increase in California's minimum wage. So, while labor's ranks may have thinned, they can still be potent.

The leading labor figure in California is Jack Henning, an old-school orator and organizer who serves as secretary-treasurer of the California Labor Federation (the AFL-CIO umbrella organization) and is largely a one-man band. Henning walks the halls of the Capitol personally to lobby legislation affecting labor's interests and battles privately and publicly with employers and politicians who don't follow his bidding. A major overhaul of the state's system of compensating injured workers in 1989 was Henning's major accomplishment of the decade and, some believe, the high note on which he will retire. But if Henning is ready to step down, labor doesn't have anyone positioned to step into his shoes. Bill Robertson, the AFL-CIO's man in Los Angeles, is a secondary labor power, as is United Auto Workers official Bruce Lee.

Cesar Chavez, who died in April 1993, was an enigmatic and influential figure of the 1970s as head of the United Farm Workers Union, but in recent years, with a hostile Republican administration in Sacramento, the clout of his union has dropped like a stone.

Labor's major gains in recent years have been among public employees, and the leaders of their unions have seen their visibility and power increase, especially since they are free with campaign funds. Ed Foglia, who headed the California Teachers Association, is one of labor's new power figures. His stock rose when the CTA won voter approval in 1988 of a major overhaul of school financing. Alice Huffman, for years the CTA's Sacramento-based political director, was a major player in insider Capitol politics, thanks to her close relationship with the Assembly Speaker Willie Brown. But Huffman's stock fell in 1994 when she became embroiled in charges that she had secretly helped Kathleen Brown in her bid to win the CTA's endorsement after receiving payments from Brown's campaign to do voter outreach work in the African American community. The CTA ended up endorsing none of the candidates in the June primary.

The large California State Employees' Association also is a major source of campaign money, but it rotates its presidency often, which prevents any one person from becoming a figure of independent stature. The California Correctional Peace Officers Association, representing prison guards, and the California Association of Highway Patrolmen also have expanded their clout in recent years. The prison guards committed upward of a million dollars to Pete Wilson's 1990 campaign for governor and quickly gained most-favored-union status when Wilson went head-to-head with other unions over pay cuts and reductions in school aid. The CCPOA's president, Don Novey, has become one of the state's most influential political figures, and one of the few union chieftains who leans Republican.

ORGANIZATIONS OF OTHER COLORS

The public employee unions exemplify another trend in California political financing: the increasing clout of large organizations with direct financial interests in political decision-making.

In the halls of government in Sacramento, big business doesn't loom very large, although Kirk West, a veteran Republican staffer who heads the California Chamber of Commerce, and William Campbell, a former state senator who now runs the California Manufacturers Association, do have clout. The groups that really count—because they annually distribute hundreds of thousands of dollars to political campaigns — are the associations of professionals, such as the California Trial Lawyers Association, the California Medical Association and the California Nurses Association. They approach fund-raising as a cost of doing business and operate their distribution operations in close consultation with their lobbyists, who daily walk the halls of the Capitol seeking to pass and kill legislation that impacts people they represent. But that workaday attitude toward political financing also is accompanied by relative anonymity. The men and women who operate these and other associations aren't political kingmakers in the usual sense, although they wield considerable political power. They are narrowly focused on their issues and disinterested in the larger political picture.

THE INITIATIVE ENTREPRENEURS

Before California voters started taking a decidedly negative view of ballot propositions in 1990, the most powerful political agenda-setters may have been those who were most adept at writing, financing and organizing campaigns for the increasingly numerous ballot measures.

The prototypical initiative entrepreneurs were Howard Jarvis and Paul Gann, two old men (both have since died) who sponsored Proposition 13 in 1978. The financial and political impact of Proposition 13 made Jarvis and Gann, especially the former, into high-profile figures and thus into political powerhouses in the media-heavy atmosphere of the 1980s. They were besieged with requests to lend their names to additional ballot measures and to endorse candidates for office and they did both. Gann even became a candidate himself for the U.S. Senate in 1980, losing to Alan Cranston.

In the mid-1980s, a new crop of initiative designers arose, this time on the left side of the political ledger. Initially, the most spectacularly successful was Harvey Rosenfield, a young consumer advocate and Ralph Nader disciple who founded Voter Revolt. He put together a successful auto insurance reform initiative in 1988, Proposition 103, winning in the face of a $60 million-plus opposition campaign financed by the insurance industry.

Rosenfield, whose penchant for publicity has been likened to that of Jarvis, immediately launched a second initiative for the 1990 ballot aimed at modifying Proposition 13 to remove its benefits from business property. And Rosenfield attempted to play political kingmaker by endorsing a candidate for state insurance commissioner, an elective office created by his Proposition 103. But his candidate, Conway Collis, lost badly and none of Rosenfield's other initiatives made it to the ballot. Rosenfield's organization, meanwhile, experienced severe money problems, and he was forced to pare staff and close offices, desperately seeking some new issue that could put him back on top.

In Sacramento, meanwhile, an informal coalition of environmentalists established its own ongoing initiative factory and already has several wins under its belt. Gerald Meral, mild-mannered administrator of the Planning and Conservation League, operates as the consortium's coordinator, and he and his colleagues have devised a unique system of promoting their measures. Groups are invited to join the consortium and supply a quota of cash or signatures to entitle them to direct a share of the proceeds. The system was used on a park bond issue and a cigarette tax measure in 1988, and was then used for a big rail-bond issue and a liquor tax measure for 1990. The first effort won, but the second lost.

Tom Hayden, as an assemblyman and former anti-war radical, was a force behind the anti-toxics initiative, Proposition 65, in 1986, and the Big Green environmental protection measure in 1990. Big Green ran afoul of the anti-initiative mood of voters.

Republicans, too, have used the initiative as a tool of partisan and ideological warfare. Russ Johnson, a conservative Republican leader in the Assembly, has been especially active. He co-sponsored a campaign finance reform measure, Proposition 73, approved by voters in 1988 and backed one of the unsuccessful reapportionment initiatives in 1990. But beyond Johnson, the right-wing side of the initiative business has been moribund after the deaths of Jarvis and Gann.

MERCENARIES OF THE POLITICAL WARS

Standing just behind the candidates and the front men for the initiative campaigns are legions of professionals to whom the explosion of political activity in California is a lucrative growth industry, so much so that pros who used to practice out of Washington and New York are shifting operations to California. Professional signature-gathering firms, fund-raisers, media consultants, pollsters, campaign strategists, accountants and even attorneys who specialize in writing, attacking and defending ballot propositions reaped tens of millions of dollars in the 1980s as mercenaries of the initiative wars. The most obviously profitable of those campaigns was the $100 million battle over five insurance initiatives in 1988.

The consultants, however, aren't just paid soldiers in California's political wars. Whether they are helping candidates or fighting over ballot measures, they also have become major players in determining who runs or what proposal is put before voters. Some specialize in Democratic or liberal candidates and causes, while others work exclusively for Republicans and the conservative side. And a few plow the middle, working for whomever has the most money or the best chance of winning.

Although professional campaign strategists theoretically stand in the background while the candidate is out front, sometimes their importance is reversed. When Clint Reilly announced in 1989 that he was giving up his management of Dianne Feinstein's campaign for governor, it was a political event of the first magnitude since Reilly, a credentialed professional, had been one of the ex-San Francisco mayor's most valuable assets. Reilly's departure lowered Feinstein's political stock and forced her to engage in damage control. Similarly, Reilly's arrival on Kathleen Brown's gubernatorial campaign in March 1994 was seen as a positive sign that the candidate was coming to grips with her faltering campaign.

Dozens of campaign management firms operate in California but only a relative handful command statewide attention. Reilly, who operates under the name of Clinton Reilly Campaigns, is based in San Francisco. Reilly managed Feinstein's mayoralty campaigns and advised Bill Honig, who was elected as state superintendent of public instruction in 1982. He scored back-to-back wins by managing ex-policeman Frank Jordan's winning campaign for mayor of San Francisco in 1991 and lawyer Richard Riordon's drive to become mayor of Los Angeles in 1993.

It was on the strength of those two victories that Reilly was recruited to manage Democrat Kathleen Brown's campaign for governor. But that turned out to be a disaster as Brown, who had once led public opinion surveys by more than 20 percentage points, was buried by Wilson. In the election aftermath, critics excoriated Reilly's tactics and his penchant for spending huge amounts of money on television ads.

A perennial star among the Democratic-oriented consultants is Richie Ross, who was Willie Brown's chief political adviser until striking out on his own after Brown lost some Assembly races in 1986. Ross, headquartered in Sacramento, had two statewide victories in 1988: Proposition 98, a school financing measure, and Proposition 97, a labor-backed proposal to restore the state worker safety program that had been canceled by Gov. Deukmejian. He managed Art Agnos' come-from-behind campaign for mayor of San Francisco in 1987 and was tapped by Agnos to run the campaign for a new baseball stadium in 1989. Ross suffered a big setback in 1990, however, when his candidate for governor, John Van de Kamp, blew an early lead and lost the Democratic nomination to Dianne Feinstein. And he also saw the baseball stadium drive and Agnos' own campaign for re-election go down.

The man who engineered Ross' San Francisco setbacks from the other side was Jack Davis. The two consultants have a personal feud as well as a professional rivalry and in recent years Davis has been getting the better of it. His greatest triumph was a major role in Frank Jordan's come-from-behind ouster of Agnos in 1991.

While Ross normally handles Assembly races, much of the work for Democratic state senate candidates is often done by Larry Sheingold. He worked effectively for a time with Rose King, who eventually started her own firm.

Another Sacramento firm usually servicing Democrats is headed by David Townsend, a former legislative staffer. Townsend broke into the ranks of statewide campaign consultants in 1988 when his firm managed — unsuccessfully — the campaign against a statewide ballot measure to raise the cigarette tax. The company continues to run campaigns at all levels in addition to providing an array of services to corporate and political clients.

Bill Carrick carved another notch on his victory belt when he managed Sen. Dianne Feinstein's re-election in 1994 despite being outspent more than 2-1 by Republican challenger Michael Huffington.

The most prominent Democratic campaign management firm in Southern California has been BAD Campaigns, operated by Michael Berman, brother of Rep. Howard Berman, and Carl D'Agostino, a former aide to Ken Cory when Cory was state controller. BAD, based in Beverly Hills, specializes in candidates endorsed by the political organization headed by Reps. Howard Berman and Henry Waxman. The Berman-Waxman organization dominates politics on Los Angeles' west side and dabbles in campaigns throughout Southern California. BAD also advised Gray Davis, the westside Democrat elected state controller in 1986 and lieutenant governor in 1994.

Things began to go badly for BAD in 1992. Reapportionment wiped out the strongholds of many of the Berman-Waxman organization's figures and BAD's two candidates for the U.S. Senate, Rep. Mel Levine and Controller Davis, lost in the June primary. State Sen. Herschel Rosenthal, meanwhile, lost to Tom Hayden in a hard-fought race in Beverly Hills. BAD was only a minor player in 1994 elections.

Los Angeles-based Cerrell Associates functions mostly as a public relations company, but it also handles some Democratic campaigns. Firm owner Joe Cerrell has national influence in Democratic politics.

REPUBLICAN RANKS SWELLING

There seem to be more professional Republican campaign management firms than Democratic ones, perhaps because the Republicans, as the minority party, have lacked the campaign-staff-in-place on the legislative payroll. While legislative staffers regularly take leaves from state service to go into the field to manage Democratic campaigns for the Legislature, Republicans usually call upon professionals.

For years, the GOP professional field was dominated by Stu Spencer and Bill Roberts. But with the latter's death and the former's semiretirement, a new flock of GOP-oriented consultants has arisen. The hottest of them was Otto Bos, a former San Diego newspaper reporter who became then-Mayor Pete Wilson's press secretary and then segued into statewide politics when Wilson ran for the U.S.

Senate in 1982. Bos ran Wilson's second-term campaign in 1988 and went into business for himself with Wilson, the Republican candidate for governor in 1990, as his chief client. Bos, however, died a few months after Wilson became governor, leaving his erstwhile partners, such as George Gorton, on their own. Gorton ran Wilson's welfare and budget reform initiative in 1992, but it lost badly. He recouped in 1994 by managing Wilson's come-from-behind re-election victory and is being wooed to run a presidential campaign in 1996.

During much of the 1980s, the splashiest Republican consulting firm was based in Sacramento and operated by two young former legislative staffers, Sal Russo and Doug Watts. They made a name for themselves as managers of Ken Maddy's spectacular, if failed, bid to become governor in 1978, then hit the big time as operators of George Deukmejian's narrow victory for governor in 1982. They also managed the successful campaign against the Peripheral Canal in 1982 and even moved briefly into official positions in the new administration.

Russo and Watts added Ed Rollins, the former Reagan White House political director, to their firm and did much of the media work for Ronald Reagan's presidential re-election campaign in 1984. But after that spectacular rise, the firm fell on hard times and eventually broke up. Watts is now a New York-based political consultant while Russo has remained in Sacramento and has a new firm, Russo, Marsh and Associates. Russo was briefly involved with Ross Perot's presidential campaign, because ex-partner Rollins was Perot's co-chairman for a few weeks. The Russo firm came roaring back in 1994 by managing Republican victories over two of the nation's most prominent Democrats, New York Gov. Mario Cuomo and House Speaker Tom Foley. Among their current clients is presidential hopeful Jack Kemp.

Another GOP campaign consultant with a string of strikeouts is Los Angeles-based Ronald Smith, who specializes in moderate to liberal Republican candidates. Smith came close with then-Rep. Ed Zschau's campaign for the U.S. Senate in 1986 and has had to settle for wins at the local level, including Tom Campbell's congressional campaign in 1988 on the San Francisco Peninsula. He tried again in 1990, but suffered another loss when state Sen. Marian Bergeson failed to win the lieutenant governorship. He also managed Campbell's unsuccessful bid for the U.S. Senate in 1992.

Another consultant who concentrates on moderate GOP candidates is Joe Shumate of San Francisco. He's confined himself to local campaigns, and scored a noteworthy win in 1988 when a pro-choice Republican, Tricia Hunter, won a hard-fought special election for the state Assembly in San Diego County. But Shumate suffered a big-time loss when he directed legislative campaigns on behalf of Gov. Wilson in 1992 and saw most of his candidates defeated — thanks to Democratic organizational work and a divisive ideological split among Republicans.

McNally Temple, a Republican-oriented firm in Sacramento, has made a name for itself in legislative and congressional campaigns, scoring several wins in 1994.

Another Sacramento-based Republican, Wayne Johnson, often works for legislative and congressional candidates favored by the party's right wing and has also scored several successes.

Ken Khachigian was a speech writer for Nixon, Reagan and Deukmejian and now hires out as a media and strategy specialist. He was a consultant to the Bush-Quayle campaign and Attorney General Dan Lungren, among others. He directed the Senate campaign of Los Angeles television commentator Bruce Herschensohn in 1992 and won plaudits for overcoming long odds and bringing him within a whisker of beating Democrat Barbara Boxer.

In 1993, however, Khachigian stepped out of the back rooms and virtually became a one-man road show, fund-raiser and quote machine for the badly flawed school voucher initiative, Proposition 174. His willingness to tell any outrageous lie over and over again to promote his cause surprised many long-time colleagues. But when he began lashing out with personal attacks against people in his own party who opposed the measure, his stature was diminished even more. Then came 1994 and the Michael Huffington Senate campaign, where Khachigian, Rollins and company attempted to legitimize the preposterous. No doubt it was extremely lucrative, but it wasn't a campaign most consultants would want to list on their resumes.

The firm that shredded Khachigian's Proposition 174 so effectively was Nelson & Lucas of San Diego and Sacramento, which usually works for GOP candidates and causes. Other standout GOP consultants include Alan Hoffenblum, Jim Nygren and Steve Presson.

While most campaign consultants have partisan identification, some purposely avoid such labeling and concentrate, instead, on the increasingly lucrative ballot measure field. The granddaddy of these operations is Woodward & McDowell of Burlingame, known for a generation for its high-budget campaigns for and against major propositions. It was W&M, for instance, that persuaded Californians to adopt a state lottery in 1984, working with money from a major lottery supplier.

The firm, operated by Richard Woodward and Jack McDowell, hit a wall in 1988. It lost a campaign to change the Gann spending limit in June and then had a mixed result on auto insurance initiatives in the fall. It successfully battled insurance industry-sponsored measures, but was unable to secure passage of its own insurance proposition, sponsored mostly by trial lawyers. The firm staged a major comeback in 1990 managing the campaign against the year's highest profile ballot measure, a sweeping environmental initiative dubbed Big Green, and scored again in 1992 by running the successful campaign against a major business tax measure, Proposition 167. But in 1994 they failed to stop Proposition 187, which cracks down on illegal immigrants.

TESTING THE PUBLIC MOOD

The most basic tool of contemporary politics and political journalism is the public opinion poll and California abounds with takers of the public pulse.

The best known California pollster is Mervin Field of San Francisco, whose California Poll has been a staple of newspapers and television broadcasts for decades. It has itself become a major factor in handicapping politicians by determining how much attention from the media and respect from potential contributors a candidate can command. But Field doesn't offer his services to individual politicians or campaigns.

When strategists want to know what California voters are thinking to help tailor their campaigns, they must turn to the private pollsters. Like consultants, pollsters tend to be identified with one party or the other and some have long-standing relationships with consultants. Sacramento's Jim Moore, for instance, is known best for his efforts on behalf of candidates and causes managed by Richie Ross.

As with consultants, there seem to be more pollsters working the Republican side of the street than the Democratic. Besides Moore, the most heavily used Democratic-oriented polling firm is Fairbank, Bregman and Maullin of San Francisco. Partner Richard Maullin first achieved prominence as a strategist in the 1970s for Gov. Jerry Brown and served for years in Brown's administration before moving to private consulting. Among the firm's clients have been Cranston and former Los Angeles Mayor Tom Bradley.

Three major Republican firms handle all of the major GOP candidates. They are Arthur J. Finkelstein & Associates of Irvington, N.Y., Tarrance & Associates of Houston, which has handled polling for, among others, Gov. Deukmejian; and the Wirthlin Group of McLean, Va., a Republican White House favorite that has done work in California for Ed Zschau and former Lt. Gov. Mike Curb.

10

County government–in the tank

"We are truly under siege right now,"
—Dave Oppenheim, California State Association of Counties

The British news weekly Economist summed it up this way: "Of all places, opulent and enterprising Orange County — the garden sprawl to the south of Los Angeles where the California Dream has been delivered in abundance to 2.4 million residents — is the last to expect talk of a municipality defaulting on its debt."

But default it did. On Dec. 6, 1994, California's third most populous and perhaps richest county filed for protection under Chapter 9 of the federal bankruptcy code. Orange County would go through the biggest municipal bankruptcy in history, having lost $1.5 billion of its $20 billion investment pool generated by 185 cities, school districts and other government agencies. County Treasurer-Tax Collector Robert L. Citron, who managed the pool, resigned in disgrace.

No one in authority, of course, had complained when Citron's high-risk investment strategies had been bringing in the best returns for any similar pool in the nation. "He ran a high-yield, high-risk fund, and all these folks (who invested) had their eyes wide open," said Sacramento City Treasurer Tom Friery. "You're not supposed to shoot craps" with municipal investment funds.

Orange County was the most conspicuous of the high-risk municipal investors, but it was by no means the only one. Large losses also were suffered by San Bernardino, San Diego, Monterey and Placer counties, and cities such as Mountain View. In a time when cities and counties face the most severe operational shortfalls since the Great Depression, many officials had been gambling on speculative investments as they felt political pressure to maximize earnings.

It's yet another sign that the fiscal structure of local government in California is in fundamental disarray. While Gov. Pete Wilson bellyaches about mandated programs that the federal government unloads on states without money to pay for them, he and legislative leaders have been doing exactly the same to local governments. About 90 percent of county budgets go for some 250 state-mandated programs and services such as welfare and police protection. That leaves 10 percent for the rest of county operations, which has led to a host of local-option taxes and fees to make ends meet. Counties have been closing libraries and public hospitals, curtailing law enforcement and allowing streets to be pitted with potholes. In Calexico during the summer of 1994, six nurses walked off their jobs to protest conditions at the municipally supported hospital. Among other things, the hospital had no oxygen and only one thermometer.

On June 2, 1992, Californians went to the polls in 31 of the 58 counties and cast advisory ballots on whether to secede from California. Incredibly, the secessionists won in 27 counties. That should have been a message to the governor and legislators that there is profound unhappiness among voters in wide stretches of California. Voters were telling the Sacramento power-brokers they are sick of being taken for granted, fed up with being ordered to provide programs without the money to pay for them and disgusted with legislative gridlock in Sacramento while their natural resources are plundered and human services suffer. But since practically all of the votes for secession came from rural and agricultural counties, with a combined population of less than 15 percent of California's total, most legislators chose to ignore the vote.

Just three months after the secession vote, Wilson signed a state budget with some $1.3 billion in new funding reductions for counties, cities and special districts such as fire protection and parks. In 1994, Wilson signed AB 2788 by Assemblyman Willie Brown, D-San Francisco, requiring local government to maintain a public safety funding level equal to the previous year in order to receive money from a half-cent statewide sales tax authorized in 1992 under Proposition 172. That, despite the fact that the state had shifted $2.6 billion in property tax money away from counties and directed it to schools between 1992 and 1994. By the 1994-95 fiscal year, creative finance by the state had left counties operating with about half the property tax revenue they were receiving in the 1991-92 fiscal year.

The lack of county clout in Sacramento stems from numerous factors, but the biggest problem is structural: California counties were organized from a system of government suited to the 18th century, and each wave of growth in California has made that system less relevant.

Colonial Americans went back to what they knew when they set up local government. They borrowed the county concept from Great Britain, where those territories were administered by a count. They also borrowed the dual nature of counties, which are at once independent local units and vassals to a larger central government. This dual nature lies at the heart of the county government crisis today, a problem so severe that some critics say counties should be abolished. That is not likely to happen, but as the 21st century draws near, California counties need fundamental changes to function in a world very different from the 19th century, post-gold rush era in which most were created.

The state's original local government boundaries were dictated by nineteenth century politics and economics. The small, elongated counties of the old gold-mining region along the Sierra foothills, for example, were drawn to keep every miner within a day's horseback ride from a county seat where he could file a claim. Southern California in those days was an unpopulated desert, and there was no reason to divide it.

As California's population grew in the late 19th century, local boosterism and political differences created the impetus for breaking up big counties. Mariposa County, for instance, once contained most of Southern California, the lower San Joaquin Valley and the Central Coast. More than a dozen counties have been carved out of that territory. One is San Bernardino, still the nation's largest and bigger than a half-dozen states.

San Francisco County once contained not only the city of San Francisco but what is now San Mateo County. When San Francisco combined its city and county governments, some crooked politicians lopped off San Mateo, via their friends in the Legislature, to keep control over a friendly environment. Cattle ranchers and farmers south of Los Angeles, fearing domination by the municipal colossus then forming, seceded to create Orange County.

The last county broke away just after World War I, when Imperial County was carved out of arid eastern reaches of San Diego County. Since then, the number has been fixed at 58, even though the state's population has increased many times over. Counties range in population from the more than 8 million of Los Angeles County to the 1,100 spread around Alpine County. More than half of the state's residents live in seven counties in Southern California. In size, there is the 49-square-mile, city-county combination of San Francisco on one end and the 20,000-square-mile San Bernardino at the other.

LOOKING FOR REGIONAL SOLUTIONS

Today large local governments are creating new regional planning mechanisms to deal with such knotty issues as transportation and air pollution that spill easily across boundaries. These regional governments represent one possible direction for counties. As some see it, counties should cede their land-use planning and other large-scale functions to regional entities and evolve into subagencies of the state. Others would have counties merge at least administratively with cities within their boundaries so local governments could cooperate rather than compete on planning and growth.

Either way, counties have a pack of problems to fix. From the earliest days of the state, counties have had conflicts with their dual roles. On the one hand, counties are purely units of local government, providing police, fire, transportation, judicial and other services to the people living outside incorporated cities. On the other, counties do as they are ordered by the state, which includes running welfare and health-care systems.

Into the counties' treasuries come property taxes, sales taxes on transactions outside of cities and money handed down from state and federal governments and other sources. In theory, the state is supposed to pay for what it requires counties to do. In practice, state aid rarely comes close. The system worked as long as local revenues grew and remained flexible. Originally, county supervisors could adjust

20 fastest-growing counties in California

County	Population on 4/1/80	Population on 4/1/90	Percent difference
Riverside	663,199	1,170,413	76.48
San Bernardino	895,016	1,418,580	58.48
Amador	19,314	30,039	55.53
Calaveras	20,710	31,998	54.51
Nevada	51,645	78,510	52.02
Placer	117,247	172,796	47.38
El Dorado	85,812	125,995	46.83
San Benito	25,005	36,697	46.76
Solano	235,203	340,421	44.75
Tuolumne	33,928	48,456	42.82
San L. Obispo	155,435	217,162	39.71
Madera	63,116	88,090	39.57
Stanislaus	265,900	370,522	39.35
Lake	36,366	50,631	39.23
San Joaquin	347,342	480,628	38.37
Kings	73,738	101,469	37.61
Kern	403,089	543,477	34.83
San Diego	1,861,846	2,498,016	34.17
Sacramento	783,381	1,041,219	32.91
Merced	134,538	178,403	32.58

Source: Bureau of the Census, 1991

property tax rates to cover whatever was needed. But the system stopped working in 1978. As state aid stagnated during the 1970s and property values soared, property tax bills shot up. Angry homeowners trooped to the polls to pass Proposition 13, which staggered county governments like a blow to the head. Proposition 13 cut and then clamped a lid on property taxes. For counties, that meant a loss of billions of dollars yearly, and a plunge into fiscal peril. The state stepped in, sort of, to help. But that aid continued to dwindle as demands grew.

When Proposition 13 passed, the state was sitting on nearly $4 billion in reserves, built up because of the tax on inflated property values around California and because of the tightfisted policies of then-Gov. Jerry Brown. The state started draining off that reserve to help local governments in the next few years. But in the early 1980s, recession and inflation hit at just about the time the reserve ran out. George Deukmejian inherited the mess when he was sworn in as governor in 1983. Backed by a Legislature with tax-cut fever, Deukmejian preferred to tighten state belts rather than increase government's revenue, which forced more money management onto the counties.

THE THREAT OF BANKRUPTCY

Rural counties have been hit hardest, since local government revenues rely on local property values and retail activity. The resource-based economies — timber, minerals, ranching and farming, ranging from Siskiyou and Modoc counties on the state's northern border to Imperial County in the extreme south, have fallen on hard times. The young have fled to cities as local jobs disappeared, causing populations to stagnate in number and advance in age. Tourism and recreation have eased the economic crises in some areas, but those are even more seasonal and erratic than traditional industries. With high unemployment (20 percent or more in some counties), demands for social services have gone up as revenues have become scarce. Local services such as sheriff's patrols and road maintenance have declined as the state mandates have drained off local money.

As a result, supervisors have become increasingly militant in dealings with Sacramento lawmakers. Tehama County supervisors became national celebrities when they declared a revolt against state mandates. In Lassen County, the supervisors talked about being annexed by Nevada. Nearby Shasta County also received a flurry of publicity when it shut down its public libraries. Humboldt County supervisors allowed paved roads to revert to gravel.

In 1988, Gov. Deukmejian and the Legislature threw the counties a bone when the state assumed from counties some costs of running the court system, but that just relieved a few immediate cash-flow crises and did little to slow what some county supervisors saw as impending disaster. Butte County was saved from becoming the first U.S. county to file for bankruptcy with state bailouts in 1989, 1990 and 1991. Other rural counties, including Yolo, Del Norte and Trinity, are nearly in the same shape as Butte and, according to a study commissioned by the County Supervisors

Association of California, possibly two dozen others are slipping into trouble. By 1992, unpaid furloughs of whole county staffs had become commonplace. Usually, it was a few days without pay, but Sonoma County shut down during Christmas week of that year and reduced all paychecks accordingly.

Some cities, mostly free of the big-ticket health, welfare and educational responsibilities that burden counties, actually found themselves in better shape after Proposition 13. Besides having major sources of revenue that are independent of the property tax, many cities have evolved into entrepreneurs of sorts, doing everything from encouraging development within their boundaries to running miniprisons for the state.

Before Proposition 13, property owners were required to pay separate property taxes to their county governments and to cities, if they were inside an incorporated area. That discouraged incorporation of county areas outside established cities. But the 1978 tax initiative ended that. And the loss of property tax revenue shifted local government attention to the sales tax. Under California law, a chunk of sales tax is returned to the local government in which the sale occurred. If a shopping mall is inside a city, the city's coffers get the sales tax, not the county. After Proposition 13, cities were suddenly drawing new boundaries to include shopping centers, auto dealerships and other high-volume retailers. More than 35 new cities have been formed since Proposition 13, most of them in suburbs and some containing huge populations.

County officials, who once encouraged the creation of cities to relieve themselves of the cost of police and other services, found they were losing more and more tax revenue as cities gobbled up sales-tax-producing businesses and development. And that fight over sales taxes to replace the lost property taxes has driven counties and cities into bitter rivalries. The scramble for taxable development has become so intense that in some counties, land-use decisions are based almost entirely on competition for revenue rather than planning.

As California expands by more than 5 million people a decade, growth fights will become more dominant. Large-scale policies and individual projects will face intense scrutiny, and the old cozy friendships between supervisors and developers will be strained. San Diego County is dealing with the growth fight by requiring major development to occur only within a city, negating much of the land-use power that has translated into political power in many counties. The city of San Diego has become the de facto regional decision-maker for the county.

A different direction for county evolution may be found in the San Francisco model. Even though city-county consolidation plans failed at the polls in Sacramento County in 1974 and 1990, local officials there are looking at ways to combine some offices, including the planning departments, as a way of discouraging incorporation efforts that could siphon off sales taxes.

Alameda County

*Area: 825.4 sq. mi.; Population: (1990)
1,279,182, (1980) 1,105,379; Registration: (1994)
D-61.7% R-22.3%; Unemployment: (Dec. 1994)
5.3%; County supervisors: Edward Campbell, Keith
Carson, Wilma Chan, Mary King, Gail Steele; 1221
Oak St., Room 536, Oakland 94612; (415) 272-6347.*

Writer Gertrude Stein once said of Oakland,
Alameda County's principal city, "There's no there
there." She didn't mean it that way, but the phrase has
come to stand as a declaration that Oakland and, by
extension, Alameda County, lack character.

What Alameda County, on the eastern shore of San Francisco Bay, really lacks
is a spotlight. It exists in the shadow of San Francisco across the bay, despite the best
efforts of community boosters to establish a separate image.

Were it not in that shadow, Alameda County clearly would be one of California's
most notable areas. It contains a piece of almost every social group in the state, from
the funky, 1960ish ambiance of Berkeley, home of the University of California's
first and most important campus, to the wealth of Piedmont, the industrial communities of Fremont and San Leandro and the problem-plagued city of Oakland.

Every time Oakland seems ready to take a step away from its difficulties, a new
crisis pushes it back. On Oct. 17, 1989, it was the Loma Prieta earthquake, which
made a shambles of the poorest sections of the city. A major road artery, an 18-block
section of the Interstate 880 freeway, collapsed, killing 43 people. That the scars
have been slow to heal is a gross understatement. Two years later, almost to the day,
another disaster hit. A brush fire in the affluent Oakland Hills smoldered into a
firestorm that has been called the worst urban conflagration in modern history. By
the time it was over, 25 people had died, 150 were injured and 2,536 homes were
destroyed. Damage estimates topped $1.3 billion.

On the first anniversary of the fire, only 51 homes had been rebuilt as survivors
struggled with endless red tape and insurance companies slow to pay. A newspaper
survey found that only two out of 10 survivors believe the city is better prepared to
fight another inferno. City officials were still arguing about whether they should
standardize fire plugs so that emergency vehicles from outside the city could hook
up.

Those were some of the same city officials who always find money to subsidize
pro ball teams, but can't seem to plan a viable redevelopment project or bail out a
nearly bankrupt school system. The political establishment, in one of the rare major
cities dominated by African Americans, has been fragmented and ineffective,
especially in dealing with vicious crime and drug problems.

For years, the political leader of Oakland was Lionel Wilson, a former judge.

The mayor from 1976 to 1990, Wilson ran out of steam in the primary election of 1990. Former Democratic Assemblyman Elihu Harris beat Councilman Wilson Riles Jr. in the runoff. Harris won a nasty re-election contest in 1994, but has yet to prove that he can make a difference.

Meanwhile, the southern and eastern reaches of Alameda County seem a world away. They are part of the California Sun Belt, the fast-growing suburbs dotted with business and commercial centers. Communities such as Livermore and Pleasanton are exploding with people and jobs, and the Association of Bay Area Governments, the regional planning agency, has projected that 70 percent of Alameda County's job growth between 1985 and 2005 will be in the southern and eastern parts.

Alameda's diversity produces political tension that is both geographic— urban Oakland and Berkeley vs. the suburbs — and social. The fast-growing suburbs are gaining political clout that may move the county's politics to the right. At the polls, Alameda County is as consistently left-of-center as nearby San Francisco, giving Democratic candidates for statewide office a substantial Bay Area base. Democrats outnumber Republicans by 2.5 to 1.

The politics of Berkeley, known to detractors as Berserkeley, are so far to the left that conventional liberals are, in relative terms, the local right-wing. GOP registration is only 9 percent. Berkeley established a national trend for left-of-center cities, most of them college towns, to involve themselves in issues of international politics. But while Berkeley's politics evolved out of the University of California and the free speech, civil rights and anti-war movements of the 1960s, the politics of the campus itself are more moderate now. Student government, in fact, has strong conservative factions and the fraternity and sorority systems are stronger than ever, leading to a rather odd twist of the traditional town vs. gown tensions. University officials want to expand the campus and its support facilities, especially student housing, but city officials resist. The standoff has meant an annual scramble for housing and another of the Bay Area's miserable traffic scenes. UC officials even found it necessary to move their statewide administrative offices out of Berkeley altogether.

The 1994 elections saw some new winds blowing in Berkeley. A Republican made a rare run for the City Council and got 36 percent of the vote. Shirley Dean, the more moderate of the two mayoral candidates, was elected while supporting successful ballot measures to curb panhandling and target loitering. Dean promised more emphasis on crime-fighting and undesirables, suggesting there's a limit to tolerance, even in Berkeley.

But the future of Alameda County and the region hinges more on economic trends than local politics. The Port of Oakland is a highly sophisticated doorway for commerce between California and the Pacific Rim nations. Those rapidly growing suburbs of the southern and eastern county include many high-tech plants, an extension of the Silicon Valley across the bay. The Association of Bay Area Governments projects a growth of Alameda County jobs from about a half-million in 1980 to nearly 800,000 by 2005. That boom would far exceed population growth and make Alameda County a destination for commuters, many from the even-newer suburbs in the San Joaquin Valley to the east.

Alpine County

Area: 726.6 sq. mi.; Population: (1990) 1,113, (1980) 1,097; Registration: (1994) D-35.2% R-42.5%; Unemployment: (Dec. 1994) 9.9%; County supervisors: Pierre Blumm, Cameron Craik, Warren Jang, Donald Jardine, Claudia Ann Wade; P.O. Box 158, Markleeville 96120; (916) 694-2281.

A brochure from the county's Chamber of Commerce advises visitors to "Get lost in Alpine County." It wouldn't be hard.

This is California's smallest county in population, a tiny reminder of California's 19th century beginnings south of Lake Tahoe. There certainly is no boom here. Alpine grew by only 16 people for the entire decade of the 1980s and actually lost about 80 people in the last two years. Of the remaining 1,000-or-so people, 23 percent claim Indian ancestry.

Not that local residents mind the isolation. Most live there because they enjoy solitude, which is a good thing, since winter snows close all but a few roads. Mining was the county's original reason for being, but ranching and later tourism — especially snow skiing — have become its economic mainstays.

Like the rest of California's mountain regions, Alpine is politically conservative. Alpine had the state's highest voter turnout in 1994 thanks to a tight race for sheriff. Election night provided testimony to the absurdity of county boundaries. Ballots from four of the county's precincts arrived in the county seat soon after polls closed at 8 p.m. But ballots from the fifth — Bear Valley — arrived three-and-a-half hours later. Since Highway 4 was already closed over the summit for the winter, Bear Valley ballots from the western slope had to travel through Calaveras and Amador counties to get to Markleeville on the east side.

Amador County

Area: 601.3 sq. mi.; Population: (1990) 30,309, (1980) 19,314; Registration: (1992) D-45.1% R-42.9%; Unemployment: (Dec. 1994) 7.5%; County supervisors: Edward Bamert, John Begovich, Louis Boitano, Stephanie D'Agostini, Timothy Davenport; 108 Court St., Jackson 95642; (209) 223-6470.

Like other Mother Lode counties east of Sacramento, Amador is experiencing the joys and pains of growth. Swollen by commuters and retirees, Amador is the state's third-fastest-growing county and the most rapidly developing of the foothill areas. In the 1980s, population boomed by more than 55 percent.

But the numbers are deceiving. The census counts the inmates at the new Mule Creek State Prison near Ione, and they represent more than a third of the growth. But there are still many newcomers who bring money into the county, as do the tens of thousands of tourists who flock to its gold-rush-era towns on weekends.

There is some friction between the old-timers and the steady stream of flatlanders. New settlers often bring higher incomes or big-city equity that pumps up local real estate prices beyond the reach of some longtime residents. The county was once conservatively Democratic, but the newcomers have moved it to the right — a fact most keenly felt by former Assemblyman Norm Waters, a conservative Democrat who survived by a whisker in 1988 and then lost in 1990 in a rematch with Republican David Knowles.

Butte County

Area: 1,664.8 sq. mi.; Population: (1990) 182,120, (1980) 143,851; Registration: (1994) D-43.1% R-42.6%; Unemployment: (Dec. 1994) 8.6%; County supervisors: Jane Dolan, Mary Ann Houx, Vivian Meyer, Edward McLaughlin, Gordon Thomas; 25 County Center Drive, Oroville 95966; (916) 538-7224.

Just say Butte County and watch any county official in California cringe. Until the Orange County bankruptcy, Butte was the watchword for the financial woes that counties continue to face. In 1989, then again in 1990 and '91, Butte County came within days of becoming the first county in the United States to file for bankruptcy. It was saved by the state bailouts, but Gov. Pete Wilson vetoed a fourth bailout in 1994.

According to reports from the state legislative analyst and the California Counties Foundation, many of Butte's troubles are beyond the control of county supervisors. The county has been plagued by slow growth in property values, made worse because supervisors, when they had the discretion before Proposition 13, had always been reluctant to hike property tax rates. The county has lost tax revenue to city incorporations and annexations and continues to attract people in need of health and welfare services. All the while maintenance costs continue to escalate on everything from roads and buildings to sheriff's patrol cars, some of which have rolled up more than 300,000 miles.

Voters, meanwhile, have rejected every tax hike put before them. In 1990, they turned down four tax increases or bond measures, leaving county libraries closed, animal control services abandoned, the jails overcrowded and county firefighters on the brink of being disbanded.

Butte County is in the middle of the vast, largely rural area north and east of Sacramento with neither rich natural resources nor the attributes attractive to home buyers. While growing at the average rate for California counties, about 25 percent, most of the region has missed the statewide economic boom, partly because it was bypassed by Interstate 5, the main north-south highway in California, leaving it a little too inaccessible for major developers. Cheap housing, though much of it is substandard, has made the area especially attractive to welfare recipients who have fled high-cost and high-crime areas.

The fastest growing area is not Oroville, the county seat, but Chico, home to the only branch of the state college system in the region and an attractive town of 35,000 with tree-lined streets, 19th-century Victorian homes and a park where Errol Flynn and Olivia de Havilland filmed "The Adventures of Robin Hood." The presence of California State University, Chico, gives the community a lively political and cultural life. In the early 1980s, adherents of Tom Hayden's economic democracy movement won control of city government, but they were ousted a few years later by a right-wing countermovement. Of the left's brief hegemony, only Jane Dolan, Chico's liberal county supervisor, remains.

The bulwarks of the economy are the university, an agricultural industry dominated by orchard crops and some tourism, much of it attracted by the state-owned Oroville Reservoir. But the university's Center for Economic Development and Planning is trying to foster an interest in wider economic development throughout the 12-county region centered in Butte. The center sees the agricultural and other resource-based elements of the local economy continuing to lag and predicts the area, with its comfortable rural life and relatively low living costs, is primed for development. But if that growth spurt does come, it will be years away.

Calaveras County

Area: 1,036.4 sq. mi.; Population: (1990) 31,998, (1980) 20,710; Registration: (1994) D-43% R-44.5%; Unemployment: (Dec. 1994) 9.9%; County supervisors: Teresa Bailey, Merita Callaway, Michael Dell'Orto, Thomas Taylor, Thomas Tryon; 891 Mountain Road, San Andreas 95249; (209) 754-6370.

The most famous thing about Calaveras County is a fictional frog-jumping contest that became real. Writer Mark Twain described it in a whimsical tale about life during the gold rush. Now, the town of Angels Camp runs a real version each spring. Hordes of tourists attracted to the frog-jumping contest are a big piece of the changing local economy, which has moved away from agriculture and mining. That change is illustrated by the precarious future of an asbestos mine, the nation's largest, which provides 5 percent of all county jobs. The impact of the retirees and the growing tourism can be seen on Sundays, when Highway 49, which cuts through the county, slows to a crawl.

The population, as in other counties in the Sierra foothills, is growing far faster than most of California. But in sheer numbers, its growth does not approach the boom hitting foothill counties closer to Sacramento. As the county grows it continues a slow shift to the right politically.

Colusa County

Area: 1,155.8 sq. mi.; Population: (1990) 16,275, (1980) 12,791; Registration: (1994) D-45% R-44.8%; Unemployment: (Dec. 1994) 23.6%; County supervisors: Nathanael McCoy, W.D. Mills, Kay Nordyke, William Waite, David Womble; 546 Jay St., Colusa 95932; (916) 458-2101.

Colusa County gets a lot of visitors, but few of them know it. Interstate 5, California's main north-south artery, bisects the county about an hour's drive north of Sacramento. But it bypasses the county seat, Colusa, and at 65 mph, Williams, a town of 2,000, is not much to notice.

There are a few highway-related businesses in Williams, but the county's chief economic underpinning is agriculture. In 1988, Williams annexed more than 2,000 acres of farmland — more than three times the size of the city — in hopes of attracting high-tech industry or at least food processors or canneries, but so far the move has had little impact on the economy. Colusa had California's highest rate of unemployment in late 1994 — 23.6 percent — which was up more than 6 percent from 1992.

The Employment Development Department estimates that farming provides nearly half of the county's direct employment. The chief crop is rice, which is subject both to the availability of water and the vagaries of international markets. And, as would be expected of rural counties in California, supervisors have struggled each year to pass a leaner budget.

Colusa is too far from Sacramento, the closest urban area, to be much of a target for suburban home buyers, and the area has neither the mountains nor the lakes and rivers that have made other rural regions havens for retirees. The population is growing about as fast as California as a whole, but there seem to be few indications that Colusa's basic character will change soon.

Contra Costa County

Area: 797.9 sq. mi.; Population: (1990) 803,732, (1980) 656,331; Registration: (1994) D-50.6% R-35.4%; Unemployment: (Dec. 1994) 5.6%; County supervisors: Gayle Bishop, Mark DeSaulnier, Jim Rogers, Jeffrey Smith, Thomas Torlakson; 651 Pine St., 11th floor, Martinez 94553; (415) 646-2371.

A generation ago, Contra Costa County was a typical Northern California bedroom suburb. The county's lush hills and valleys were a refuge for commuters who spent their days working in Oakland or San Francisco and were affluent enough to live in the well-kept country atmosphere in communities such as Walnut Creek, Moraga, Orinda and Lafayette.

But in recent years, Contra Costa has exploded with jobs in places such as San Ramon's Bishop Ranch. New complexes along highly congested Interstate 680 have become destinations for less affluent commuters, who have moved even further east in search of affordable housing in the new bedroom communities of the San Joaquin Valley. Between 1985 and 1990, Contra Costa's employment increased by more than 20 percent. Acres of development along I-680 have spawned a new phrase, Contra Costapolis, and sparked a no-growth backlash among residents fed up with hours-long traffic jams. As in so many growing areas, local politics of the 1980s became defined by that single issue, and politicians caught being cozy with developers felt the lash of angry voters. The issue came to a head in 1985, when anti-growth candidates won a series of local elections and slow-growth ballot measures were adopted.

In many ways, the county is a microcosm of California. Along the outer reaches of San Francisco Bay, communities such as Martinez, Pittsburg and Antioch remain blue-collar bastions filled with oil refineries and other industrial facilities. But even those areas are sprouting suburban housing developments. Richmond, on the east shore of San Francisco Bay, has a large and Democratic-voting African American population, and many of the urban problems to match. It is a high-crime area with a school system in bankruptcy. The more affluent eastern suburbs supply legions of Republican voters, leaving the county's voter registration relatively close to the state average.

Del Norte County

Area: 1,003 sq. mi.; Population: (1990) 23,460, (1980) 18,217; Registration: (1994) D-45.8% R-36.9%; Unemployment: (Dec. 1994) 13%; County supervisors: Robert Bark, Barbara Clausen, Clyde Eller, Mark Mellett, Jack Reese; 450 H St., Crescent City 95531; (707) 464-7204.

Del Norte County is about as far north as you can go and still be in California. For generations, the local economy was based on cutting trees and catching fish. Both industries fell on hard times during the 1970s and '80s, and local boosters pushed hard to add a third element: keeping bad guys behind bars. That dream was supposed to be realized when the state opened Pelican Bay State Prison in the late 1980s, where the worst of California's inmates live in extreme isolation.

Del Norte found itself in a rare surge of commercial investment as the prison took shape near the Oregon border north of Crescent City, and the $32 million annual payroll pumped new life into the economy. Suddenly, one of the state's most chronically depressed areas was beginning to look like one of its more prosperous. But the prison brought new problems. So far, commercial investment has lagged behind projections, the state didn't provide all the promised services, many of the jobs went to people from outside the county and welfare rolls have increased as families of prisoners have moved into the area.

Del Norte was one of the so-called "sad counties" which went to the Legislature in 1994 begging for a bailout, but Gov. Pete Wilson vetoed the bill.

El Dorado County

Area: 1,804.8 sq. mi.; Population: (1990) 125,995, (1980) 85,812; Registration: (1994) D-39.9% R-46.9%; Unemployment: (Dec. 1994) 7.1%; County supervisors: Sam Bradley, J. Mark Nielsen, Ray Nutting, Walt Shultz, John Upton; 330 Fair Lane, Placerville 95667; (916) 626-2464.

The names of the county and its county seat, Placerville, reveal their origins as one of the centers of the 19th-century gold rush. In the late 20th century, El Dorado County is at the center of another rush — a land rush. Retirees and commuters are packing into El Dorado County, seeking cleaner air, friendlier communities and more reasonable living costs. But their sheer numbers threaten to destroy those qualities. As one recent arrival put it in a newspaper interview: "Everywhere I look, I'm threatened."

Between 1980 and 1990, the county's population surged by almost 47 percent as developers converted pastures into ranchettes and rolling hills into subdivisions. Population growth is highest in the communities closest to Sacramento, such as Cameron Park and El Dorado Hills, and water shortages have become common. As it grows, El Dorado is turning to the right politically. In 1990, Republicans moved ahead of Democrats in registration for the first time.

Fresno County

*Area: 5,998.3 sq. mi.; Population: (1990)
667,490, (1980) 587,329; Registration: (1994) D-
51% R-38.9%; Unemployment: (Dec. 1994) 12.8%;
County supervisors: Sharon Levy, Deran Koligan,
Stan Oken, Tom Perch, Doug Vagim; 2281 Tulare
St., Room 300, Fresno 93721; (209) 488-3531.*

Fresno County is the middle of California geographically, culturally and politically. Its major city,
Fresno, is big enough — over 300,000 — to have
big-city advantages and ills. But it remains, at heart,
an overgrown farm town. Its image was captured perfectly by a satirical television
movie *Fresno*, in which things of little consequence had great consequence there.

The county's location, equidistant from Los Angeles and San Francisco, and its
relatively low labor and land costs, have sparked flurries of nonagricultural
industrial development, but the region remains dependent upon agriculture. It was
in Fresno County that the term agribusiness was coined, and large-scale, scientific
agriculture remains the heart of both its economy and culture. Crops as varied as
cotton and grapes abound in the fertile flatlands of the nation's most productive
agricultural county.

As unofficial capital of the San Joaquin Valley, Fresno also has developed
educational, medical and governmental facilities to serve the region. Despite that,
the county continues to be one of the most depressed areas of the state. A United
Way study completed in 1992 found that more than 15 percent of Fresno County's
households earned less than $10,000 a year. The county's per capita income of
$11,807 was nearly $4,000 below the state average.

The city of Fresno was also the crime capital of the Central Valley. A rate of 124
crimes per 1,000 people was second worst among California's metropolitan areas.
Only Oakland's was higher.

More than a third of Fresno County's population is Hispanic (35.5 percent), but,
as in other areas of the state, they have not developed into a political force. Instead,
voters in Fresno County and the San Joaquin Valley mirror statewide political
trends. They are nominally Democratic but lean conservative, often willing to elect
Republicans.

That puts the valley into the swing position when it comes to close statewide
races and explains why candidates for state and national offices spend dispropor-
tionately large amounts of campaign time around Fresno's isolated media market.
One would expect all that attention to boost voter turnout, but not so. In 1990 and
1994, Fresno County was second to last in voter turnout among California's 58
counties. In 1992, it had the third lowest turnout.

The exception to the conservative tilt is the more liberal city of Fresno, due largely to its blue-collar and farm-worker residents. George McGovern, Walter Mondale, Michael Dukakis and Bill Clinton all won in the city itself, but did miserably in the rest of the county.

Glenn County

Area: 1,319 sq. mi.; Population: (1990) 24,798, (1980) 21,350; Registration: (1994) D-41.8% R-45.9%; Unemployment: (Dec. 1994) 12.5%; County supervisors: D.G. Bungarz, Gary Freeman, Keith Hansen, Charles Harris, Dick Mudd; P.O. Box 391, Willows 95988; (916) 934-3834.

The 19th-century courthouse in Willows is a symbol for all of Glenn County: quiet, tradition bound, slow to change. Interstate 5, the state's main north-south freeway, bisects Willows and the county, but has had little impact. There are a few highway-related businesses, but otherwise the city and the county remain what they have been for generations — agricultural communities whose economies are tied to the value of farm products. Farming and government account for half of Glenn's employment.

Jim Mann, a dairy farmer turned county supervisor, tried to change that. Mann works for a regional economic development center in nearby Chico and tried to offset chronically high unemployment by promoting the area as a site for light industry, stressing the low cost of living and the easy freeway access. But so far, there have been no big takers, and the voters dumped Mann from office in 1992. Like the rest of the region, Glenn County is struggling with its budget.

The area is politically conservative, but it's also politically active. Glenn usually has one of the highest voter turnouts in the state.

Humboldt County

Area: 3,599.5 sq. mi.; Population: (1990) 119,118, (1980) 108,525; Registration: (1994) D-51.4% R-31.1%; Unemployment: (Dec. 1994) 7.8%; County supervisors: Stan Dixon, Julie Fulkerson, Roy Heider, Paul Kirk, Bonnie Neely; 825 Fifth St., Eureka 95501; (707) 445-7509.

Eureka (population 25,000) is the political, economic and cultural center of California's beautiful north coast. The region was settled by loggers, who felled giant redwoods for timbers to shore up gold mines in the mid-19th century. Cutting and processing timber, and catching and processing fish, have been Humboldt County's economic mainstays for generations, even after a substantial tourist trade developed after World War II.

Both of those resource-based industries have fallen on hard times in recent years, and many of the area's young men and women have moved away, looking for more dependable jobs. As they left, they were replaced in the 1960s and '70s by urban refugees, universally dubbed hippies, and an economic and political transformation began. By the 1980s, the urban refugees had sold homes in Los Angeles or the San Francisco Bay Area, and were a bit more conservative, but only a bit.

Marijuana is a substantial cash crop. Environmentalism is a powerful movement. And the politics of the area, once conservative, have moved left, with liberal Democrats replacing Republicans in legislative seats. There are still major political battles between the pro-lumber businesses and the environmentalists. But most often, the latter win.

Imperial County

Area: 4,597.4 sq. mi.; Population: (1990) 109,303, (1980) 92,110; Registration: (1994) D-55.5%R-32.8%; Unemployment: (Dec. 1994) 20.4%; County supervisors: Bill Cole, Robert Bradford Lucky, Sam Sharp, Dean Shores, Wayne Van De Graaff; 940 W. Main St., El Centro 92243; (619) 339-4220.

If farmers in this region couldn't grow three crops a year at times, it is doubtful that many people would live in the Imperial Valley. Much of the valley, which occupies California's southeastern corner, lies below sea level and is covered with sand. Summer temperatures can reach more than 120 degrees in the sparse shade of the almost treeless landscape.

Imperial was the last California county created, carved off San Diego County just after World War I. There is a lively trade in both goods and human bodies over the Mexican border south of El Centro, and Imperial County has California's highest concentration of Hispanic residents, nearly 66 percent in the 1990 census.

That fact is accompanied by a harsh reality: Imperial also has one of the state's highest unemployment rates and is chronically near the top in terms of poverty. The county also is chronically on the financial edge as it tries to pay for health and welfare services.

In the 1990s, the job base expanded with the opening of two major state prisons. Local boosters hope that a fledgling winter vacation industry — a kind of poor man's Palm Springs — will brighten the economy.

Inyo County

Area: 10,097.9 sq. mi.; Population: (1990) 18,281, (1980) 17,895; Registration: (1994) D-38.3% R-49.8%; Unemployment: (Dec. 1994) 8.9%; County super-

visors: Linda Arcularius, Julie Bear, Robert Gracey, Robert Mitchener, Paul Payne; P.O. Drawer N, Independence 93526; (619) 878-2411.

There is only one word to describe Inyo County: empty. That is only in terms of people, however. Inyo, wedged onto the eastern slope of the Sierra, next to Nevada, contains some of the state's most spectacular, if starkest, natural scenery plus an active volcanic field.

Inyo is California's second largest county in size, but it has the second slowest growth rate. The population grew by a whopping 386 people during the 1980s. One county supervisorial district is 7,000 square miles — larger than five states.

The federal government owns more than 85 percent of the county. Extraction of minerals from Inyo's arid mountains, ranching and tourism are the county's chief economic activities; hating Los Angeles — which locked up the area's water in backroom maneuvers a half-century ago and which supplies hordes of summer and weekend visitors — seems to be the chief local pastime. Mining has been on the wane in recent years as has agriculture — thanks to water exports to Los Angeles.

Politically, Inyo's voters give Republican candidates big majorities.

Kern County

Area: 8,170.3 sq. mi.; Population: (1990) 543,477, (1980) 403,089; Registration: (1994) D-44.3% R-45.7%; Unemployment: (Dec. 1994) 13.3%; County supervisors: Roy Asburn, Barbara Patrick, Steve Perez, Ken Peterson, Mary Shell; 1415 Truxton Ave., Bakersfield 93301; (800) 322-0722.

If California is a small-scale model of the United States, then Kern County is its Oklahoma. There are oil wells, farms and country music recording studios. And many of the county's inhabitants trace their ancestry to the waves of migrants from Oklahoma, Texas and Arkansas before, during and after World War II. When the oil and farming industries are down, Kern County is down. When they are up, the county rolls in money. There have been efforts to diversify the county's economy, taking advantage of its location 100 miles north of the Los Angeles megalopolis. The chief new industry is state prisons, but for the foreseeable future, farming and oil will rule.

True to its cultural roots, Kern County is very conservative politically. It elects Republicans to its legislative and congressional seats and gives GOP candidates at the top of the ticket big margins. But it could give them even more if people were inclined. In the 1990 elections, Kern had the lowest voter turnout in the state and the

1992 and '94 numbers were only slightly better. As elsewhere, the county's large Hispanic minority (28 percent) is politically impotent.

Kings County

Area: 1,435.6 sq. mi.; Population: (1990) 101,469, (1980) 73,738; Registration: (1994) D-47.8% R-41%; Unemployment: (Dec. 1994) 12.3%; County supervisors: Anthony Barba, Joe Hammond Jr., Lee Lockhart, Abel Meirelles, Joe Neves; Government Center, Hanford 93230; (209) 582-3211.

Kings County, sliced from a corner of neighboring Tulare County in the late 19th century, has achieved a remarkable economic diversity to accompany its large-scale agricultural base. Starting in the early 1960s, the county lured such nonagricultural projects as a tire factory, the Lemoore Naval Air Station and a carpet mill. In recent years, the state has built two large prisons in the small farming towns of Avenal and Corcoran. The county seat, Hanford, has even developed a mild tourism industry centered on the town square, its old-fashioned ice cream parlor and 19th-century buildings redeveloped into shops. There's also a small Chinatown.

Such nonfarm development has given it a more stable economy than many other San Joaquin Valley counties and also has fueled a relatively fast population growth. Its 37 percent increase from 1980 to 1990 is unusually big for an area in the middle of the farm belt. Politically, Kings mirrors the valley: conservative-voting on most issues, but willing to elect conservative Democrats.

Lake County

Area: 1,326.5 sq. mi.; Population: (1990) 50,631, (1980) 36,366; Registration: (1994) D-51.2% R-35.7%; Unemployment: (Dec. 1994) 10.5%; County supervisors: Carl Larson, Karan Mackey, Bill Merriman, Louise Talley, Helen Whitney; 255 N. Forbes St., Lakeport 95453; (707) 263-2367.

Lake County's name says it all. The county's major asset, scenically and economically, is Clear Lake, California's largest natural body of fresh water. Dotted along the lake are dozens of small communities that subsist on summer tourism, fishermen and retirees.

There are so many retirees settling in Lake County, a three-hour drive from San Francisco, that the median age of residents is about 15 years higher than the state's average. They tend to be of the working-class variety, so the local politics remain pro-Democrat. The county's economy has other elements, such as ranching and geothermal power development, but retirees' pension checks are becoming steadily more important. Retirees also have produced a steady increase in the demand for county services, while property values have been virtually flat. Lake County is another on the long, long list of counties that has had to cut services and trim jobs in recent years to balance its budget.

The Clear Lake basin is a favorite hunting ground for archaeologists. The area has been inhabited for centuries. One stone tool fragment from the area has been dated to 10,000 years.

Lassen County

Area: 4,690.3 sq. mi.; Population: (1990) 27,598, (1980) 21,661; Registration: (1994) D-46.8.% R-38.6%; Unemployment: (Dec. 1994) 9%; County supervisors: James Chapman, Gary Lemke, Jean Loubet, Lyle Lough, Claude Neely; 707 Nevada St., Susanville 96130; (916) 257-8311.

The biggest employer in Lassen County, on the northern Nevada border, is the California Department of Corrections, which is doubling the capacity of it's already huge medium-security prison in Susanville. Beyond that, Lassen is mostly timber and ranch country, with a steady summer and fall tourist trade. It shares Lassen National Volcanic Park with three other counties, but the active volcano that gave the county its name, Mt. Lassen, is actually in Shasta County.

Many — perhaps most — of Lassen's residents are happy the county has missed out on the industrialization and population growth hitting much of California. Indeed, when the state decided to expand its prison and add more jobs, it was opposed by local residents, who would prefer to leave things as they are: quiet and peaceful.

Lassen's population is growing at about the average California rate, and many of the newcomers are retired ex-urbanites who traded in the equity on their homes for the quiet of the country. Financially and politically, the county is like the rest of northeastern California: the county's budget is in miserable shape, the community college is precarious financially and the people are conservative with a don't-tread-on-me attitude toward government.

Los Angeles County

Area: 4,079.3 sq. mi.; Population: (1990) 8,863,164, (1980) 7,477,517; Registration: (1994) D-55.5% R-31.7%; Unemployment: (Dec. 1994) 8%; County supervisors: Michael Antonovich, Yvonne Brathwaite-Burke, Deane Dana, Gloria Molina, Zev Yaroslavsky; 500 W. Temple St., Los Angeles 90012; (213) 974-1411.

For the second time in a generation, South-Central Los Angeles exploded in

flames on April 29, 1992. Frenzied mobs were un-
leashed by the acquittal of four Los Angeles policemen who were charged in the beating of motorist
Rodney King. The rioters murdered, burned and
looted, and then went home to watch themselves on
stolen television sets. Compton, where some of the
heaviest rioting occurred, became the only U.S. city
ever occupied by the U.S. Marines when the California National Guard found it had no ammunition for
its soldiers' rifles.

When the acrid smoke cleared, 53 people were
dead and 1,100 buildings had been destroyed. The damage exceeded $850 million.
America's worst civil discord in this century had once again revealed a county
splintered by race and class, paralyzed by dysfunctional government, and policed
by forces woefully unequal to the task. If then-74-year-old Mayor Tom Bradley had
any hopes of running for a sixth term in 1993, they were an early casualty of the
rioting. Police Chief Daryl Gates, who began to display bizarre personal behavior,
was soon forced into retirement as was the National Guard chief, Maj. Gen. Robert
Thrasher.

To be sure, there were promises of new beginnings. From pulpits and entertainment figures came appeals for unity and a new compact based upon mutual respect.
From the White House and corporate board rooms came promises of massive aid.
Peter Ueberroth, everyone's favorite Mr. Fixit, was recruited to lead a new
organization called Rebuild LA. As time passed, it became apparent that the
promised gush of aid would be only a trickle. Resolutions were passed in Washington and Sacramento, but little money was attached to them. Some businesses made
notable contributions, but most did not. Six months after the riots, 40 percent of the
789 businesses damaged or looted were no longer operating. Crime, poverty,
unemployment and random acts of viciousness were more widespread than before.
Compton Councilwoman Patricia Moore would say: "It's becoming more difficult
each day to persuade stable citizens to stay here. It's like our leadership has given
up on urban America. It's expected to fail. It's expected to have problems. So people
have written it off."

Moore had apparently written it off, too. In 1994 she pled guilty to extortion for
soliciting a bribe from developers of a proposed waste-to-energy plant that could
have provided jobs for the community of 91,600. Compton, the oldest African
American-majority-governed city west of the Mississippi River, is a special case.
In a city with the highest high school dropout rate in California, police have
identified 40 African American, Latino and Samoan gangs. The congressman,
Walter Tucker III, is under indictment for alleged involvement in the same bribe that
Moore has admitted. Earlier, the former police chief pled guilty to stealing from a
fund for undercover drug buys. And the president of Compton Community College

was fired for spending $500,000 in student aid funds on office furniture and special-service contracts for administrators' relatives.

Los Angeles County contains more than 30 percent of California's people and wields cultural, economic and political influence of global scope. Just a few blocks from the shattered neighborhoods of Compton and Watts, people seemed warier than before. But the pace of life continued as it has for decades. Los Angeles, both the city and the county, has huge enclaves of Hispanics, African Americans, Koreans, Armenians, Chinese, Japanese, Vietnamese and other ethnic groups. Each plays its own role in shaping the society that evolved from a dusty outpost of the Spanish colonial empire. They participate in an economy that is as diverse as the state, ranging from heavy manufacturing to Pacific Rim trade, high-tech manufacturing, entertainment, tourism and sweatshop factories.

Other communities may throb, but the cities and towns of Los Angeles County hum with the 24-hour-a-day freeway traffic that is the county's most pervasive feature. What is considered rush-hour traffic anywhere else can be found in Los Angeles at almost any time: hundreds of thousands of vehicles in a slowly oozing stream, most of them transporting no more than the driver. This has given Los Angeles one of the nation's worst smog problems and has produced new government attempts to deal with it, including the establishment of a regional body — the South Coast Air Quality Management District — with vast powers to influence the way people live, work, commute and even barbecue their food. But any solution to the smog problem, if there is one, is years away. Meanwhile, the freeways become more clogged.

It is a problem worsened by the inexorable shift of population out of the city's center to suburbs on the edge of the San Fernando Valley and Mojave Desert. People seeking affordable homes pay instead with ever-longer commutes, even though job growth is spreading into suburbs. The influx of immigrants, most from Asia or Latin America, added more than 1.4 million to Los Angeles County's population in the last decade, more than twice as many as any other county. But in percentage terms, the county's growth has been slower than the statewide average, and this has meant an erosion of Los Angeles County's overall political clout. This erosion is compounded by the fact that the Hispanic and Asian immigrants do not vote.

County politics tend to split rather evenly down party lines. It is slightly more Democratic in registration than the state as a whole, but many Democrats tend to support Republicans for top offices. The strongly pro-Republican tilt in the remainder of Southern California more than offsets the Democratic edge in Los Angeles and gives the region a very dependable GOP flavor in races for U.S. senator, governor and president.

Within Los Angeles County, politics runs to extremes. Some of the state's most conservative and most liberal officeholders can be found in its legislative and congressional delegations. The central and western portions of the county — downtown Los Angeles, heavily African American South-Central Los Angeles,

Hispanic East Los Angeles and the wealthy Beverly Hills, Santa Monica and Westwood areas on the west side — are strongly Democratic. But Long Beach — ex-Gov. George Deukmejian's home — and the Anglo suburbs on the fringes of the county vote Republican, while the San Fernando Valley is a toss-up, Democratic in the southern part, Republican in the north.

A third of the county's population is Hispanic and 10 percent Asian. Despite traditional low voter participation, both groups are beginning to put people in strategic offices. The county Board of Supervisors, for instance, was composed of five Anglo men until recently, despite the fact that Anglos are less than half of the county's population. Now there are three white men and two women — one African American, one Hispanic. Those five positions are among the most powerful in the nation. Each supervisor has nearly 2 million constituents, a huge personal staff and a vote on a $9 billion budget. Without an elected head of county government, the supervisors wield vast authority over land-use, transportation and health care.

The county's split political personality is revealed in the makeup of the board, three Democrats and two Republicans. Republican Deane Dana represents a coastal district and the other Republican, Mike Antonovich, has a chunk of the suburbs. The three Democrats are Zev Yaroslavsky, who represents the largely Jewish west side; Yvonne Brathwaite Burke, a former congresswoman, who represents overwhelmingly African American South-Central Los Angeles; and Gloria Molina, a former legislator and Los Angeles city councilwoman whose district includes Boyle Heights, East Los Angeles and part of the San Gabriel Valley.

Molina's ascendancy to the board from the Los Angeles City Council in early 1991 marked one of the most dramatic political shifts in the county during this century. Republicans had controlled the board through the 1980s, but the U.S. Justice Department filed suit in 1985, claiming the board's GOP majority had reapportioned the county in a way that would deny Hispanic representation. The board fought the suit unsuccessfully, eventually spending nearly $10 million of the taxpayers' money on legal fees. That forced new boundaries and a special election to replace retiring Supervisor Peter Schabarum. Molina, a farm worker's daughter who rose from grass-roots politics, beat state Sen. Art Torres to become the first Hispanic elected to the board since the 1870s.

It has been a different story on the 15-member City Council. When the Justice Department began raising questions in the mid-'80s, the council acted quickly and redrew district lines to create two seats for Hispanics. With more than a third of the city's population, Hispanics could claim at least five of the 15 council seats.

It was the onset of World War II that propelled Los Angeles into the industrial age. As factories, warehouses, docks and other facilities were quickly built to serve the war, its population doubled and redoubled as defense workers poured in. The San Fernando Valley and other one-time ranch lands were turned into housing tracts. The naturally arid region had assured itself of a dependable water supply, thanks to some unsavory dealings by local landowners.

Los Angeles' boom did not slow after the war. Factories that had turned out bombers began making airliners. The automobile, a necessity in such a sprawling city, sparked the development of the freeway. The state's first freeway, connecting downtown Los Angeles with Pasadena, the traditional home of moneyed families, is still carrying cars. With so many new people coming to town, with so much money to be made and with so little sense of civic identity, Los Angeles was ripe for corruption. The 1974 movie *Chinatown* accurately captured the ambiance of Los Angeles in the 1940s. Police, city officials and newspapers were corrupt. Los Angeles was a civic joke, its downtown area a seedy slum, its once-extensive trolley system ripped out by money-grubbing bus and oil companies, its development governed by which subdivider was most willing to grease the right palms.

Slowly, Los Angeles developed a sense of civic pride that extended beyond the latest land deal. Slowly, the city's notorious Police Department was cleaned up by William Parker, a reformist chief. The Los Angeles Times, once considered the nation's worst large newspaper, came under the control of Otis Chandler, a member of the family that had owned it for generations, and the new publisher turned the Times into an institution with international stature. Los Angeles developed a culture to match its fast-growing population: art museums, a symphony, charities and other amenities helped the nouveau riche — including those from the movie industry — acquire a social respectability.

While the city's upper crust began developing a social sense, the city itself continued to change. As the immigrants moved in and multiplied, the Anglos moved out to the San Fernando Valley and other suburbs, many of which are still within the city limits. The 1990 census found Los Angeles, with Anglos in the minority, to be one of the nation's most ethnically diverse cities.

But for decades, Los Angeles' politics, like the city itself, was a whites-only business. Mayors — honest or crooked — were men who professed a conservative ideology, and none showed more than token ability to project an image beyond the city. Race relations, like much of the Los Angeles lifestyle, were conducted at long distance. If anything, the 1965 riots in the Watts section of Los Angeles widened the gulf between Anglos and non-Anglos. It was a more violent replay of the Zoot-suit riots, which had pitted Hispanics against white servicemen during World War II.

All of that seemingly changed in 1973, when Tom Bradley, an African American and one-time Los Angeles police lieutenant, won the mayorship. Bradley projected hope to minorities and pro-development moderation to the white business and political establishment. And he survived, winning re-election four times, by continuing to walk that tightrope. Bradley's chief mayoral accomplishment — made in close collaboration with the business community — was the revitalization of the city's downtown. Oil companies, banks and other major corporations dumped money into the Bunker Hill project to give the downtown a skyline, even though the lower reaches of the area remain a slum. Beyond that, Bradley delivered a city government that was reasonably efficient, reasonably honest and reasonably inclusive, especially when compared to many of the nation's other big cities.

Yet Bradley, who twice ran unsuccessfully for governor, saw much of that progress slipping away during his last term. He carried the responsibility for more than 400 gang-related murders a year and the inability of the Police Department to deal with both that and the explosion of drug-induced crime. Smog worsened, traffic congestion grew exponentially and polls indicated that most Los Angeles residents thought their quality of life had deteriorated. One survey found half of those polled had considered moving.

Despite the enormity of the city's problems, there was no shortage of people willing to fill Bradley's huge shoes. The job fell to millionaire businessman Richard Riordan, who ran as an outsider who would bring a common sense business approach to governing. Riordan, a Republican, set about building coalitions with ethnic leaders and Democrats. He immediately established ties with the Clinton White House and began working with the administration on common interests such as crime-fighting. That paid great dividends when the Northridge earthquake devastated portions of the city in January 1994.

The Clinton administration was exceedingly generous with aid in contrast to Gov. Pete Wilson's administration, which postured a lot but took a bye on rebuilding anything other than the freeway system (largely with federal funds), just as it did in the failed effort to rebuild the South-Central riot corridor. If Riordan's progressive government continues to succeed, he has to be considered a likely candidate to run for governor in 1998.

Despite Riordan's commitment, imagination and resourcefulness, it remains to be seen whether he can make a difference in the burned-out neighborhoods of South-Central Los Angeles and Compton. Absent that, it seems inevitable that the flames will erupt again.

Madera County

Area: 2,147.1 sq. mi.; Population: (1990) 88,090, (1980) 63,116; Registration: (1994) D-48.4% R-40.8%; Unemployment: (Dec. 1994) 14.4%; County supervisors: Harry Baker Jr., Alfred Ginsburg, Rick Jensen, Jess Lopez, Gail McIntyre; 209 W. Yosemite Ave., Madera 93637; (209) 675-7700.

Madera County is farm country, and far enough removed from the state's urban centers to avoid the dubious benefits of suburbanization. Its population is growing, up 39 percent between 1980 and 1990, and much of it is in foothill areas popular with retirees. A steady stream of tourists passes through the county on its way to Yosemite National Park, a portion of which lies in the county, and other recreational sites such as Millerton and Bass lakes.

The city of Madera and surrounding communities have had a modest amount of industrialization, most of it spilling over from the Fresno area to the south. But agriculture — especially grapes and dairy products — remains the economic linchpin, accounting for a third of the employment.

Despite the strong Democratic registration edge typical of San Joaquin Valley counties, Madera votes conservatively, and its growing Hispanic population of 34.5 percent remains largely powerless.

Marin County

Area: 588 sq. mi.; Population: (1990) 230,096, (1980) 222,592; Registration: (1994) D-52.6% R-30.4%; Unemployment (Dec. 1994) 4.1%; County supervisors: Harold Brown, Gary Giacomini, John Kress, Annette Rose, Harry Moore; Civic Center, Room 315, San Rafael 94903; (415) 499-7331.

They make jokes about Marin. They write books, movies and songs about Marin. It even shows up occasionally in comic strips. It's that kind of place. The Golden Gate Bridge lands on its southern tip, whales and great white sharks pass close to its spectacular coastline, and mountains and woods rise in all corners of the county. It also is one of those places on which California's reputation — deserved or not — is built. The county is a combination of bohemianism, bourgeoisie, activism, money, exclusivity and liberal social attitudes, overlaid with an almost religious sense of environmental protection.

As the San Francisco Bay Area suburbs boomed in the early 1970s, Marin County fought to hold the line on growth, long before such movements became popular elsewhere. And Marin residents have pretty much succeeded. Between 1980 and 1990, for example, its population grew only 3.3 percent, less than a seventh of the statewide rate and by far the slowest of any urban county.

But the success of the growth-control movement has had side effects: an incredible rise in housing costs, which has driven out the less-affluent (the median income is over 50 percent higher than neighboring Sonoma County) and major traffic problems. Traffic comes from both a boom in commuters driving northward toward Sonoma County and south toward San Francisco, and from the sharp increase of jobs in Marin, which brings workers into the county.

Still, much of Marin remains dedicated to keeping its natural attributes relatively undisturbed. One coastal community even refuses to have signs directing traffic to itself, so intense is the desire for isolation.

A major showdown on the growth issue occurred in 1989, when voters decided the fate of a large proposed residential and office development on the site of the former Hamilton Air Force Base. Despite the shortage and high cost of housing and support from such prominent Democrats as Lt. Gov. Leo McCarthy, the project was rejected. A corollary situation involves occasional rumblings out of Sacramento about closing San Quentin Prison and selling its exquisite site for development. Marin County residents would rather keep the prison.

Politically, Marin was once steadfastly Republican but has been moving left as environmentalism has become a more potent political force. The only Republican officeholders who survive now are those who embrace that cause.

Mariposa County

Area: 1,460.5 sq. mi.; Population: (1990) 14,302, (1980) 11,108; Registration: (1994) D-41.7% R-42.9%; Unemployment: (Dec. 1994) 8.7%; County supervisors: Doug Balmain, Garry Parker, Parri Reilly, Robert Stewart, Gertrude Taber; P.O. Box 784, Mariposa 95338: (209) 966-3222.

Once, in the mid-19th century, Mariposa County covered a huge swath of California, including most of the San Joaquin Valley and Southern California. But year after year, the county's boundaries were whittled down to form new counties, eventually spawning 11 in all. What's left are 1,460.5 square miles of scenic territory that include the most famous and most visited portions of Yosemite National Park.

Each year, hundreds of thousands of people visit Mariposa County's rolling foothills, quaint gold-rush towns and craggy mountains. And each year, a few more decide to stay, which is why the county's population grew by almost 30 percent between 1980 and 1990. The county's population has nearly tripled since 1960. Many newcomers are retirees, who bring conservative attitudes that are turning the county into a Republican bastion.

The state projects that Mariposa's population will continue to grow rapidly, reaching 20,000 by the turn of the century as the demand for recreational opportunities continues to expand.

Mendocino County

Area: 3,510.7 sq. mi.; Population: (1990) 80,345, (1980) 66,738; Registration: (1994) D-54.4% R-29.5%; Unemployment: (Dec. 1994) 9.6%; County supervisors: Liz Henry, Frank McMichael, Charles Peterson, John Pinches, Seiji Sugawara; Courthouse, Room 113, Ukiah 95482; (707) 463-4221.

Mendocino County, like the rest of Northern California's rugged, spectacular coast, was once timber country. Cutting and processing the trees of the densely forested areas of the county remain a huge part of the economy, but within the last generation a revolution hit the county.

A wave of urban emigres flooded the area in the 1960s and '70s, creating a new economy rooted in tourism, crafts and, although illegal, the cultivation of mari-

juana. The extremely quaint little coastal towns such as Elk and Mendocino (the setting for Cabot Cove, Me., in the *Murder She Wrote* TV series) acquired rafts of bed-and-breakfast inns and trendy restaurants to serve weekenders from the Bay Area. And in the late 1980s, the southern part of the county started turning into suburbs as Bay Area commuters pressed outward, searching for affordable housing. Politically, the change moved Mendocino County leftward, with liberal Democrats replacing conservative Democrats in elected offices.

The county's budget, however, suffers many of the same problems facing other rural counties. In fact, supervisors went so far as to take out a mortgage on their courthouse to help balance the 1990-91 budget. In 1994, Mendocino was one of eight counties that sought a state bail-out to remain solvent, but Gov. Pete Wilson vetoed the measure.

Merced County

Area: 2,007.7 sq. mi.; Population: (1990) 178,403, (1980) 134,558; Registration: (1994) D-51.7% R-35.4%; Unemployment: (Dec. 1994) 14%; County supervisors: Gloria Keene, Ann Klinger, Jerald O'Banion, Dean Peterson, Joe Rivero; 2222 M St., Merced 95340; (209) 385-7366.

Merced County advertises itself as the gateway to Yosemite National Park, but its future appears to be tied less to the mountainous eastern end of the county than to its western flatlands, which are on the verge of a suburban explosion.

The mind may boggle at the prospect, but Los Banos, a quiet and fairly isolated farm town on the west side of the San Joaquin Valley, is laying plans to become part of the San Francisco Bay megalopolis as rising housing costs drive commuters further from the central cities. In this case, the upgrading of Highway 152 to a full freeway will give commuters a viable link from little Los Banos into the packed Santa Clara Valley south of San Jose. Even without such suburbanization, Merced County's population is up more than 32 percent between 1980 and 1990, thanks, in part to the influx of Southeast Asians, who now account for 8 percent of the residents. With the growth, its politics, which had been conservative Democrat, seem to be edging rightward.

Merced was one of eight counties on the verge of bankruptcy in 1994 as its 19 libraries were forced to shut down twice. Like other counties, budget writers have been tightening belts for years, and there's hardly any room left.

Modoc County

Area: 4,340.4 sq. mi.; Population: (1990) 9,678, (1980) 8,610; Registration: (1994) D-42.8% R-44.8%; Unemployment: (Dec. 1994) 11.5%; County supervisors: Edgar Carver, Joe Earl Colt, Nancy Huffman, Ron McIntyre, Ben Zandstra; P.O. Box 131, Alturas 96101; (916) 233-3939.

A form letter that Modoc County employment officials send to would-be job seekers says it all: The weather can be extreme, the economy is seasonal and Modoc County has virtually no growth, the letter bluntly tells those who think that the isolated, rugged and beautiful county would be a paradise.

Yet the people living in California's upper right-hand corner like it just the way it is: remote, iconoclastic and sometimes 30 degrees below zero in winter. The chief lament is that the lack of jobs forces young people to seek work in cities far away.

Timber and cattle are mainstays of the economy, although government — local, state and federal — is the largest employer. Increasingly, summer homes are being built by urbanites seeking isolation. There are so many summer residents, in fact, that something of a political schism has developed between them and the year-round people. Apart from that, the politics are solidly conservative.

Since 1912, Modoc had been California's bellwether in presidential elections — voting for the winner every time. That ended in 1992 when Modoc residents went for George Bush. Locals attributed that to a growing influx of retirees, who've brought their conservative values with them.

Mono County

Area: 3,103 sq. mi.; Population: (1990) 9,956 (1980) 8,577; Registration: (1994) D-34.3% R-46%; Unemployment: (Dec. 1994) 11%; County supervisors: Tim Alpers, Thomas Farnetti, Andrea Lawrence, Dan Paranick, William Reid; P.O. Box 715, Bridgeport 93517; (619) 932-7911.

The dominant feature of Mono County — and one focal point of its politics — is Mono Lake and the striking geologic features nearby. The saline lake has shrunk markedly in the last half-century, a constant reminder that the county's fate is largely in the hands of Los Angeles.

Through a series of subterfuges, Los Angeles gained control over water supplies on the eastern slope of the Sierra and pipes much of that southward. Local residents spent years in the political and legal battle over whether the diversions should continue uninterrupted or whether more water should be allowed to flow into Mono

Lake and thus save the scenic and ecological wonder from shrinking further. It's been a long and expensive matter, but court decisions headed in the direction of lake preservation and an agreement was finally achieved in 1994 to allow the lake to rise 16 feet, to a level that will be healthier for the ecosystem. But it still won't be at historic levels.

Mono Lake also symbolizes the tourism industry that has gradually replaced ranching and mining as the chief source of jobs. Contributing to that economic evolution is Mammoth Lakes, a world-class ski area. Mammoth Lakes became Mono's only incorporated city during the 1980s. It is now the economic center of the county and is large enough to dictate political policy to the rest of the residents. Growth chiefly in that area made Mono California's second fastest growing county in the 1993-94 fiscal year.

But also in the '80s, Mammoth Lakes was found to be sitting atop an active volcano. At one point, it became so restive that a state of emergency was declared. Tourism and housing values took an immediate plunge, and Mammoth politicians responded with demands that state and federal geologists suppress all future negative news of that sort. Time has brought a little more enlightenment to the political leadership, but not much.

Monterey County

Area: 3,324.1 sq. mi.; Population: (1990) 355,660 (1980) 290,444; Registration: (1994) D-50.1% R-34.2%; Unemployment: (Dec. 1994) 10.7%; County supervisors: Edith Johnson, Sam Karas, Judy L.E. Pennycook, Thomas Perkins, Simon Salinas; P.O. Box 1728, Salinas 92902; (408) 424-8611.

Even in a state blessed with great natural beauty, Monterey County is something special. Its abundant attractions — rugged coastline, windblown woods, quaint towns and nearly perfect weather — have become the focal point of county politics. Bluntly put, those who have already captured a piece of Monterey for themselves are increasingly active in protecting it against outsiders. Almost any development project, from a hotel to a highway, sparks controversy. Politics in Monterey, Carmel and other Monterey Peninsula communities revolve around that tension.

The mayorship of Monterey and the balance of power on the City Council shifted out of the hands of pro-development forces in the early 1980s after Monterey underwent a surge of hotel construction, including erection of a downtown hotel dubbed Sheraton General for its hospital-like appearance. At the same time, however, the peninsula's economy is largely dependent upon tourism. The result is nonstop political churning over the future of the area, a two-hour drive south from San Francisco. The battle of Monterey achieved national publicity in 1986, when actor Clint Eastwood was elected mayor of Carmel for two years on a pro-development platform.

Outside the Peninsula, most of Monterey County is agricultural. While the county's two major population centers, Monterey and Salinas, are only a few miles apart, economically and socially they are in different worlds. Salinas and other inland communities rely on the price of the vegetables they produce, but they also are beginning to feel suburbs creeping in as commuters spill farther and farther out of the San Jose area to the north.

The politics of Salinas and environs are being altered by the new suburbs and the slowly emerging strength of Hispanics. Although more than a third of the population in many communities, Hispanics have been politically powerless. Even with a Latina running for the assembly in 1994, Hispanics failed to turn out in sufficient numbers and she lost by 389 votes. But key court decisions have opened avenues of political activity at the local level, especially in Salinas, which shifted to a district form of city voting after a court decision ordered districts formed in nearby Watsonville.

Economic and social contrasts found within the county are mirrored in its politics — liberal-environmentalist along the coast and conservative inland. Voting patterns are similar to those of the state, but are not stable. Suburban development pulls the county toward the Republicans while Hispanic political activity pushes toward the Democrats.

One of the county's economic mainstays — the Army's rambling compound at Fort Ord — closed in 1993. Local business and government may take years to recover even though much of the base is being converted to a California State University campus. One positive aspect is that Fort Ord's closure brought down the cost of lower-end housing, which always has been in short supply. But it's had little impact on the value of the peninsula's many mansions.

Napa County

Area: 796.9 sq. mi.; Population: (1990) 110,765, (1980) 99,199; Registration: (1994) D-50.1% R-36.7%; Unemployment: (Dec. 1994) 7.7%; County supervisors: Paul Battisti, Vincent Ferriole, Fred Negri, Mike Rippey, Mel Varrelman; 1195 Third St., Napa 94559; (707) 253-4386.

Not too many years ago, the Napa Valley was a little-known corner of California. That seems like a fairy tale these days. As wine drinking evolved into something akin to a secular religion in the 1970s and '80s, the Napa Valley became a mecca. Napa County's once quiet agricultural valley, an hour's drive northeast from San Francisco, evolved with astonishing speed into a tourist draw. Wineries sprouted like mushrooms and the valley acquired bushels of inns, hotels, restaurants and other tourist-oriented facilities.

In the early 1980s, there began a backlash among residents tired of weekend traffic jams and jacked-up prices. While rising home prices, controls on new development and a lack of local jobs all have kept population growth minimal, the battles over tourist-oriented development remain intense. One ongoing squabble is over a wine train that runs through the valley.

Nevada County

Area: 992.2 sq. mi.; Population: (1990) 78,510, (1980) 51,645; Registration: (1994) D-36.4% R-47.6%; Unemployment: (Oct. 1992) 7.3%; County supervisors: Rene Antonson, Sam Dardick, Fran Grattan, Karen Knecht, Dave Tobiassen; 950 Maidu Ave., Nevada City 95959; (916) 265-1480.

Nevada County, with the highest percentage of white residents in the state (93.9 percent), is typical of the fast-growing Sierra foothill region. Between 1980 and 1990, it recorded a whopping 52 percent population growth, the fifth-largest rate in the state, as increasing numbers of retirees, Sacramento-area commuters and urban escapees settled there.

The county has developed a home-grown electronics industry and a burgeoning retail trade market, supplemented in some corners by marijuana cultivation. The Nevada City-Grass Valley area has become a regional commercial, medical and cultural center, and there is a thriving arts community in North San Juan. The combination of foothill and mountain beauty and mild climate continues to draw both visitors and those looking for new roots. And the major question facing the county is whether to impose stricter development curbs.

Nevada County, like other foothill communities, has been moving to the right politically. Republicans outnumber Democrats and voters have that leave-me-alone philosophy that dominates the region.

Orange County

Area: 785.1 sq. mi.; Population: (1990) 2,410,556, (1980) 1,932,921; Registration: (1994) D-34.2% R-52.5%; Unemployment: (Dec. 1994) 4.8%; County supervisors: Marian Bergeson, James Silva, Roger Stanton, William Steiner, Gaddi Vasquez; 10 Civic Center, Santa Ana 92701; (714) 834-3100.

On Dec. 6, 1994, a new word entered the lexicon of many Orange County residents — "derivatives." County Treasurer-Tax Collector Robert Citron had been trading in derivatives with the county investment pool. Funds from 185 cities, school districts and other government agencies were being used in a high-risk investing strategy involving complex financial arrangements tied to rising or falling interest rates. When rates fell, the pool flourished. When they rose, there were losses. Citron used the pool's value to borrow vast sums while gambling that rates would stay low. They didn't, setting off a chain reaction of losses and destabilizing scores of local governments. Citron lost $1.5 billion from the $20 billion pool, forcing the county government to file for bankruptcy protection on Dec. 6, 1994. Layoffs, pay cuts, freezes and crippled services could be the norm in Orange County governments for years. Overnight, careers of thousands of government workers disappeared.

Where were the checks and balances? Governments participating in the pool and the Orange County Board of Supervisors, to whom Citron reported, all were asleep at their posts. But there was no excuse. Democrat Citron, who had been in office for 24 years, had a GOP opponent in 1994. John Moorlach, a CPA, got interested in the job when he began reading that Orange County was earning bigger returns on investments than anywhere else in the nation. "How can this be?" he asked. "You can only achieve the highest interest rates in the nation by taking the highest risks in the nation. Should reserve funds be in high-risk investments?" Moorlach did the right things. He spoke at the Rotary clubs and GOP functions. He wrote the Board of Supervisors and warned them of impending doom. He collared journalists. But no one listened.

Thomas Riley, the 82-year-old county board chairman, had a reputation for being rude to citizens who brought protests before the board. As he left office at the end of 1994, he was heard to mutter: "I wish I had listened just a bit more, questioned just a bit more and trusted just a bit less." It was enough to give geriatrics a bad name. Ex-Assemblyman Gil Ferguson, who was a mere 71 at the time, warned his former constituents not to expect a bail-out from Sacramento. "The county is simply too wealthy for anyone to feel sorry for us," Ferguson said. "I think if there's been any change in our image, it's that we might be rich, but we're not too smart."

Before Orange County's dramatic fall, it had been well-known that at least eight California counties were edging toward bankruptcy. But those were rural, agrarian counties such as Butte, which had had three different bailouts from the Legislature. The shocker was that it could happen in smug and conservative Orange County.

No piece of California typifies the state's development rush more than Orange, a patch of coastline and rolling hills immediately south of Los Angeles. Prior to World War II, the county was cattle ranges (controlled by big, Spanish-land-grant ranchers such as the Irvines and O'Neills), vegetable fields and citrus orchards. After the war, and especially after 1955, the county exploded with houses and suburbs. It achieved national and international attention for two very different attributes: It is the home of Disneyland and is a hotbed of right-wing politics.

As the British Broadcasting Corp. said in a 1976 documentary on Orange County: "This is the culmination of the American dream. That dream was a home in the suburbs, two cars and maybe a ski boat and a barbecue in back. Orange County reproduced it hundreds of thousands of times in one generation."

When Walt Disney opened his amusement park in 1955, Anaheim was a city of 35,000. Over the next 30 years, along with the growth of motels, fast-food outlets and restaurants, Anaheim's population increased ninefold, matching what was happening in the county as a whole, which became the state's second-most populous county for a time.

But the county continues to exist in the shadow of infinitely more glamorous Los Angeles to the north. Even its major-league baseball team, the California Angels, doesn't take its name from the county. Neither did the National Football League team that played in Anaheim for 14 years. It was known as the Los Angeles Rams until January 1995, when the team packed up and moved to St. Louis. Orange County is the largest urban area in the country without its own network television service.

Although no one city dominates Orange County, Irvine and nearby Costa Mesa are the urban centers. The region's dazzling performing arts center is in Costa Mesa, and the county's growing airport, named for late actor and local resident John Wayne, lies just outside that city. Together with the development of the UC Irvine campus and the community of Irvine, the two cities have created a cultural locus that had been lacking during the county's go-go phase of growth.

As it sprawls along both sides of Interstate 405, this area epitomizes the change that occurred in the 1970s. While new suburbs sprouted further east in Riverside County, slowing the population growth in Orange County, the region became a center for the development of California's post-industrial economy rooted in trade, services and high-tech fabrication. Only downtown Los Angeles rivals the area's concentration of office space. UC Irvine has become a center for biotech research and development and the county has more than 700 high-tech companies.

The evolution of the Irvine-centered commercial and cultural complex also reflects the shift of emphasis from the older cities of Santa Ana and Anaheim in the north to the central and southern parts of the county. The older communities, meanwhile, have large and growing Hispanic and Southeast Asian communities. The Hispanics have not become a political force, but Vietnamese Americans were a key factor in U.S. Rep. Robert "B-1 Bob" Dornan's election to Congress in 1984 and in fund-raising he does today.

As Orange County developed, commute patterns changed, eventually producing traffic congestion of titanic proportions. No one makes plans, no one gives directions, no one shops without considering traffic. Besides the local drivers, the county's mostly older freeways handle thousands and thousands of cars from suburbs in Riverside and elsewhere — suburbs created in response to the skyrocketing home prices in Orange County. Traffic, in turn, has fueled a local anti-growth movement that has drawn support from both conservatives and liberals. And it has convinced people of the need for toll roads.

As home prices went up, population growth slowed further. In the early 1980s, the county was growing slower than the state as a whole and by the mid-1980s, San Diego supplanted Orange as the state's second-most populous county. Growth in the county's southern portion in the late 1980s pushed Orange County's growth rate up to just about the state average of 25 percent for the decade.

Even though Democrats achieved a short-lived plurality of voter registration in the mid-1970s, politics always have been conservative and sometimes wacko conservative. Arguably, no other county could have produced two congressmen as nutty as Dornan and William Dannemeyer. Yet Orange County also bore the brunt of the collapse of the aerospace industry in the early 1990s. GOP registration slipped by 3.3 percentage points in 1992, most of that going to the independent column.

Democrats made serious inroads in the 1992 elections. Orange was the only major California county that the Bush presidential campaign carried in 1992, but Bush won by only 106,000 votes — which is less than a third of his 1988 plurality. More telling was the U.S. Senate race that pitted Dianne Feinstein against the GOP's John Seymour, a former Anaheim mayor whom Orange County residents had elected to the state Senate three times. Feinstein lost Orange to Seymour by 92,000 votes, but Seymour needed at least a 200,000-vote margin to make up losses elsewhere in the state.

In 1994, Orange County voters came home to the GOP. In the U.S. Senate race, Republican Michael Huffington beat Feinstein by almost 201,000 ballots. Wilson was re-elected governor over Democratic nominee Kathleen Brown with a 303,000-vote margin from Orange County.

Placer County

Area: 1,506.5 sq. mi.; Population: (1990) 172,796, (1980) 117,247; Registration: (1994) D-39% R-48.1%; Unemployment: (Dec. 1994) 6.3%; County supervisors: Rex Broomfield, Ron Lichau, Bill Santucci, Kirk Uhler, Robert Weygandt; 175 Fulweiler Ave., Auburn 95603; (916) 823-4641.

Placer County represents three distinct pieces of the varied California landscape. The western portion, centered in and around Roseville, has evolved into a booming residential and industrial suburb of Sacramento, with an expanding connection to the Silicon Valley computer complex. The middle part of the county around Auburn, the quaint, gold rush era foothill county seat, is growing rapidly too, with commuters, retirees and urban expatriates. And the eastern part of the county is high-mountain country that includes the northern shore of Lake Tahoe, which also is feeling development pressure.

In the 1993-94 fiscal year, Placer County had a growth rate of 3.84 percent — triple the state average and ranking it third among the state's fastest-growing counties. That on top of a 50-percent growth rate in the 1980s. The chief reason for the growth is Interstate 80, the major east-west highway, which bisects the county and connects San Francisco and Sacramento with the rest of the continent. For years, the Board of Supervisors had been willing to approve almost any project that came along. Growing congestion in the Roseville area, however, is changing attitudes and several supervisors were dumped in the 1994 elections. For the first time in years, the board had a slow-growth majority.

Growth is moving the area's politics ever rightward, but oddly, has not generated a consensus on construction of the Auburn Dam on the American River. Auburn is the last major dam site in the lower 48 states that has a chance of being built. Incredibly, the controversy over whether to build it has been raging since 1947.

Plumas County

Area: 2,618.4 sq. mi.; Population: (1990) 19,739, (1980) 17,340; Registration: (1994) D-45.8% R-40.1%; Unemployment: (Dec. 1994) 12.4%; County supervisors: Phil Bresciani, Bill Coates, Fran Roudebuch, Robert Meacher, Paul Simpson; P.O. Box 207, Quincy 95971; (916) 283-0280.

Plumas County folks often feel more cultural and economic affinity with Nevada than with expansive, fast-changing California. Reno, 80 miles to the southeast, is the nearest big town, and much of the county's economic activity crosses the state line.

Seventy percent of the county's land is owned by the federal government, mostly by the Forest Service. The troubled lumber industry is the mainstay of the economy, which gets a little supplement from tourism. It shares with other rural counties a chronically high unemployment rate and major budget problems. Plumas' population is growing at about half the rate of the rest of the state, and most of those newcomers are retirees and others seeking quiet refuge in the area's heavily forested lands. But there are signs of change. In 1994, Quincy got the county's first stop light.

County politics are predictably conservative, although there has been a years-long battle for control of the Board of Supervisors that has included charges of election-rigging.

Riverside County

Area: 7,243 sq. mi.; Population: (1990) 1,170,413, (1980) 663,199; Registration: (1994) D-42% R-46.4%; Unemployment: (Dec. 1994) 9.2%; County supervi-

sors: Bob Buster, Kay Ceniceros, Tom Mullen, John Tavaglione, Roy Wilson; 4080 Lemon St., Riverside 92501; (714) 787-2010.

Riverside County is Southern California's newest boom area and one of the state's fastest growing counties. Until the recession slowed the pace in 1992, Riverside and neighboring San Bernardino Counties were developing at a breakneck rate reminiscent of the San Fernando Valley and Orange County development after World War II. Traditional causes fueled the growth: young families searching for affordable suburban homes.

While median home prices soared to the quarter-million-dollar mark in Los Angeles and Orange counties, developers subdivided large tracts of arid Riverside County and sold houses for less than half that amount. Newly minted Riverside residents are willing to commute as long as two hours each way to job centers closer to the coast.

The county, which began the 1980s with 663,199 people, exploded by 76 percent by 1990. Impacts of that dizzying growth have been many, ranging from suddenly crowded freeways to worsening smog. Untold acres of orange groves — which had been the county's chief economic support until the real estate boom — were uprooted to make room for the new subdivisions and that, in turn, sparked an anti-growth backlash in the mid-1980s.

Some of the greatest growth was in Moreno Valley, a network of new, sterile subdivisions that incorporated in 1984. But many newcomers stretched their finances to settle there, and when the recession hit in the early 90s, a number found themselves in homes worth less than they paid for them. In 1993-94, the repossession rate in Moreno Valley was double that of the rest of Southern California.

Suburban-style expansion has moved Riverside sharply to the right politically in the same way growth affected Orange County after World War II. Not many years ago, Riverside was solidly Democratic, but by 1988 Republicans pulled ahead in registration and the remaining Democratic officeholders faced perilous times.

The county's growing conservatism is getting a shove from Palm Springs, the high-desert community where retired captains of industry live. Given its new large and conservative population, Riverside should have benefited from the post-1990 census reapportionment, which should have meant more opportunities for Republicans. But the problem for the GOP was that the newcomers were unwilling to add a trip to the polls to a day already burdened by long commutes. And with a recession breathing down their necks, young conservatives who did vote deserted the GOP in droves in 1992 and gave the county to Bill Clinton. Democrat Rep. George Brown again astounded the pundits and won a 17th term in 1994.

Sacramento County

Area: 1,015.3 sq. mi.; Population: (1990) 1,041,219, (1980) 783,381; Registration: (1994) D-51.7% R-36.7%; Unemployment: (Dec. 1994) 6.5%; County supervisors: Illa Collin, Dave Cox, Roger Dickinson; Muriel Johnson, Don Nottoli, 700 H St., Suite 2450, Sacramento 95814; (916) 440-5451.

For decades, the Sacramento area slept while other urban areas boomed. It was known as a terminally dull government community, filled with civil servants who labored not only for the state but for dozens of federal offices as well.

More than 40 percent of the Sacramento County's work force collects public paychecks, and the metropolitan area, which includes most of the county as well as chunks of neighboring counties, seems to be nothing but a collection of endless suburban tracts and shopping centers — including California's first shopping center, built shortly after World War II.

In the late 1970s, the Sacramento region began to awaken. Soaring Bay Area housing costs and clogged roads began pushing development outward, and Sacramento, with cheaper housing and relatively easy lifestyle, became an attractive spot for employers looking to relocate. Today, government continues to be the economic backbone of the area, but the hottest growth is in the private sector. The downsizing of state government and closure of two major military facilities (Mather Air Force Base and Sacramento Army Depot) is eroding the area's public employment base.

Downtown Sacramento began sprouting skyscrapers in the '80s, fertile fields were converted to high-tech job centers and dozens of subdivisions sprang up. By 1989, Sacramento had been featured on the cover of a national news magazine as one of the country's best places to live. It had become the fastest growing region in the state and one of the nation's fastest growing metropolitan areas. After the 1994 Northridge earthquake, Packard Bell, the nation's third-largest personal computer maker, shut down its Chatsworth headquarters and moved 3,000 jobs to Sacramento.

But there have been downsides to the heady growth, such as crime, congestion and worsening air quality. And the area is beset by perhaps the worst mish-mash of governmental authority in the state. The city of Sacramento is only a fifth of the metropolitan area, and the county has the highest proportion of unincorporated, urbanized land of any county in the state. Attempts at city-county consolidation failed in 1974 and 1990. That left the city and county to squabble over development, sales taxes and political influence. Although the supervisors represent much more of the county, it is the City Council that reaps most of the publicity, for better or often worse.

Sacramento is the largest city in the state with a part-time council. Councilman and government professor Joe Serna, whose political mentor in the late '60s was then-state Sen. Mervyn Dymally, won the mayor's job in 1992. His election, along with the addition of two more conservatives to the board of supervisors, signaled a strengthening of developer dominance of governing boards that previous mayors had fought to minimize. In his first two years, Serna showed little leadership in dealing with the city's core problems of crime, homelessness, congestion and sluggish government.

As with most government enclaves, Sacramento County has been dependably Democratic. But with suburbanization and private-sector job development, that, too, is changing. Democrats dominate in the city, but the faster-growing suburbs are increasingly represented by candidates from the Christian right. Conservative Christians have financed campaigns to seize several park boards and make inroads in school elections. They installed Barbara Alby and Larry Bowler in the state Assembly. And their leaders promise to go after more elective slots at every level.

San Benito County

Area: 1,397.1 sq. mi.; Population: (1990) 36,697, (1980) 25,005; Registration: (1994) D-50.1% R-36.4%; Unemployment: (Dec. 1994) 12.3%; County supervisors: Rita Bowling, Mike Graves, Ruth Kesler, Ron Rodriguez, Richard Scagliotti; 440 Fifth St., Hollister 95023; (408) 637-4641.

San Benito County lies in a little recess of public consciousness, overshadowed by its larger and/or more glamorous neighbors, Santa Clara and Monterey counties. But that may be changing.

As the Bay Area slurb continues its southward march, San Benito is growing at a healthy rate and seems poised for a boom. From 1980 to 1990, the county population swelled by 46 percent, and as Highway 152, the major east-west route through the county, is converted into a full freeway, more commuter-oriented development appears certain.

The question is whether growth will overwhelm the slow-paced, rural lifestyle that has been San Benito's hallmark. Another question is whether the county's large Hispanic population (second highest in the state with 46 percent) will assume political power in keeping with its numbers or continue to play a minor role. Their failure to turn out in 1994 cost Latina Lily Cervantes an Assembly seat. Republican Peter Frusetta beat her by 389 votes.

San Bernardino County

Area: 20,164 sq. mi.; Population: (1990) 1,418,380, (1980) 895,016; Registration: (1994) D-44% R-43.9%; Unemployment: (Dec. 1994) 6.7%; County supervisors: Gerald Eaves, Jon Mikels, Barbara Crum Riordan, Marsha Turoci, Larry

Walker; 385 N. Arrowhead Ave., San Bernardino 92415; (714) 387-4811.

San Bernardino County — or San Berdoo, as it is almost universally called — is huge. The county covers more land than any other in the United States, and its 20,000-plus square miles constitute more than an eighth of California. But most of those square miles are unpopulated desert, and more than three-fourths of them are federally owned.

Politically, culturally and economically, most of what counts in San Bernardino lies in the western portion nearest Los Angeles, and that's a sore point with other residents. An effort failed in 1988 to split San Bernardino County and create a new county in the desert called Mojave.

The western slab of San Berdoo, along with neighboring Riverside County, is what boosters call the "Inland Empire," and that fanciful name is taking on new weight as commuters in search of affordable homes convert the once-grimy industrial towns of Rialto and Fontana into bedroom communities. San Bernardino was second only to Riverside County in population growth in the last decade, expanding by 58 percent between 1980 and 1990.

Growth has brought the usual problems: environmental damage, smog and social dislocation. There is some growth in jobs in the area, especially around Ontario International Airport, but the jobs-to-people mix is a continuing headache for local leaders. Heavy industries that had been San Bernardino's economic foundation, typified by the now-cold steel works at Fontana, have given way to shopping centers, freight handling and other post-industrial economic activities. Dairy farmers around Chino, who used to supply much of the Los Angeles area's milk, are finding that the scent of cows is not compatible with the dreams of new suburbanites.

Politically, San Berdoo has been blue-collar Democrat, tending to vote conservatively: Republican at the top of the ticket and Democrat for local and state offices. But suburbs brought partisan change. In 1988, Democrats dropped below Republicans in registration, and local Democratic officeholders are becoming fewer.

San Diego County

Area: 4,280.6 sq. mi.; Population: (1990) 2,498,016, (1980) 1,861,846; Registration: (1994) D-38.1% R-45.1%; Unemployment: (Dec. 1994) 6.1%; County supervisors: Bill Horn, Diane Jacob, Ron Roberts, Pamela Slater (vacancy); 1600 Pacific Highway, San Diego 92101; (619) 531-5700.

San Diego is the California of popular legend: sunny days, sparkling beaches, sail-bedecked harbors, red-tiled roofs, palm trees and laid-back people everywhere. Lots of folks want a piece of that legend, which makes San Diego County a popular

destination for everyone from young professionals
to retirees.

In a state of diverse geography, San Diego might
have the most variation in one county. Within a few
miles, there are ocean beaches, rolling hills, some-
time-snowy mountains and a stark desert. That diversity means people looking for just about any
environment have wandered in. It has become the
second-most populous county in the state and by
2010, nearly one in 10 Californians will be a San
Diegan.

But the rocketing growth in San Diego over the past generation also raises the
question: If everyone comes for the lifestyle, will there be any of it left? For many,
the answer is no. That's why growth and its control have become the overriding
political issue in the county.

San Diego also has a tense relationship with its neighbor to the south, Tijuana.
The contrast between Tijuana, with its 1.5 million mostly poor residents, and San
Diego could not be more striking. Here the Third World bumps into the First World,
and like matter meeting anti-matter, the collision is often explosive. Drugs and
illegal aliens steadily flow across the border, and Mexican and American border
police have exchanged gunfire, mistaking each other for bandits. A routine sight
every evening are the campfires of Mexican nationals lining up along the border to
dash into San Diego after dark.

San Diego is also downhill from Tijuana, which means Mexican sewage
pollutes San Diego beaches. The problem has become so severe that San Diegans
are pressuring Gov. Pete Wilson, a former San Diego mayor, to declare a state of
emergency. More than any area of the state, San Diego is one city that needs a
foreign policy. In 1994, Proposition 187 (denying services to illegal aliens) was one
of the most hotly debated issues. With 67.6 percent voting yes, San Diego County
was well above the statewide average of 59.2 percent.

For most of the 20th century, San Diego had been known mostly as a Navy town
and a center for aircraft production. But in the mid-1960s, San Diego County began
diversifying economically and its population started to grow. With growth controls
in the city of San Diego, the fastest-growing part of the county is the north. The San
Diego Association of Governments estimates that between 1980 and 2000, central
San Diego County will grow by only 12 percent while outlying suburbs will more
than double in population.

Politically, San Diego always has been a paradox. A tolerant attitude toward
lifestyles and a strong blue-collar manufacturing base have not prevented San Diego
from being largely Republican territory. But local GOP leaders, including Wilson,
tend to be from the party's moderate wing. In addition, a core of Democratic activists
keeps the party fairly well represented in legislative seats.

Recent mayors such as Wilson, Roger Hedgecock and Maureen O'Connor (a Democrat) all fit that centrist mold. But the current mayor, former County Supervisor Susan Golding, is a pro-growth Republican who narrowly defeated UC Irvine professor Peter Navarro in 1992 at the same time that Bill Clinton was beating George Bush in a county that hadn't voted for a Democratic president since Franklin Roosevelt's 1944 election. Wilson spent substantial time in the county during the last week of the election trying to salvage Republican seats, but he had little to show for it. Part of the Republican problem had to do with turnout. For reasons that perplex pundits, San Diego County has had low turnouts in the past decade. That was true even when hometown candidate Wilson was locked in a tight race for governor in 1990.

Christian conservatives have been particularly active, even installing a school board in the suburb of Vista in 1992 that adopted a creationist curriculum. In 1994, two of the three fundamentalists were recalled and the third didn't seek re-election.

San Francisco County

Area: 49 sq. mi.; Population: (1990) 731,700, (1980) 678,974; Registration: (1994) D-63.3% R-16.3%; Unemployment: (Dec. 1994) 4.7%; Mayor: Frank Jordan; City/county supervisors: Angela Alioto, Tom Ammiano, Sue Bierman, Terence Hallinan, Tom Hsieh, Barbara Kaufman, Willie Kennedy, Susan Leal, Carol Migden, Kevin Shelley, Mabel Teng; 400 Van Ness Ave., San Francisco 94102; (415) 554-5184; Incorporated: 1850.

For those who believe San Franciscans need to get a grip, the city's leading newspaper offered an affirmation of their view on Jan. 14, 1995. It appeared in a San Francisco Chronicle editorial on the upcoming National Football Conference championship between the 49ers and the Dallas Cowboys.

"Far broader issues (than just a football game) will be in play," the Chronicle intoned. "Any matchup featuring San Francisco against Dallas is by definition a polarized clash of cultures: urbanity against vulgarity; humanistic values vs. the ethics of cold-blooded corporatism; a liberal democracy pitted against right-wing selfishness and greed."

Whew!

But then again, this is the town where Mayor Frank Jordan called a news conference in mid-1992 to announce reorganization of his entire administration to focus on one issue: keeping the Giants baseball team in San Francisco. The crisis had been created when Giants owner Bob Lurie, having had yet another new stadium proposal voted down by San Franciscans, announced he had found a new home for the team. St. Petersburg, Fla., had an empty stadium and backers willing to pay $115 million for the Giants.

Many would argue that San Francisco, California's only consolidated city and county, had many problems far more pressing than whether a bunch of sweaty guys retired to Florida. After all, Jordan had promised to do something about the filthy streets and 6,000-to-10,000 homeless people camping out in city parks and plazas. But the mayor had been in office nearly six months and there was no juggernaut being assembled to take on those problems. In addition, the city has an AIDS epidemic — in 1992, AIDS became the leading cause of death for men in the city. The school system is failing, library hours and other services have been curtailed, the budget has been in deficit.

In recent years, San Francisco has lost its maritime trade to more modern ports such as Oakland. Its industrial base, including the famous fishing industry, has shrunk. It has lost its position as the West's financial capital to much-hated Los Angeles. It continues to lose office jobs to suburban centers in Contra Costa and San Mateo counties. It is losing middle-class whites to the suburbs and gentrification has driven many African Americans out as well. The economic slide has weakened and scattered the organized labor strength, which once made San Francisco the most heavily unionized city west of Chicago. And after the 1989 Loma Prieta earthquake, San Francisco even lost some of its allure for tourists and conventioneers. The danger of those trends is that San Francisco will become a caricature of itself, a place where only the wealthy and the poor live, a city dependent on the fickle tourist trade that increasingly attends matinees in the city's theaters since at night many of the dark and filthy streets are littered with undesirables.

Oh, well, San Franciscans seemed to say. Politicians come and go. And some day the Giants may, too. But in the meantime, it is still a dazzling city with cosmopolitan attitudes found in few places in the West. It has become, in effect, the capital of Asian California. And the gay rights movement is just the latest manifestation of San Francisco's well-known tolerance for unconventional lifestyles, a tradition rooted in the city's founding as a port of entry for gold-rush fortune-seekers, which has continued through decades of boom and bust, crooked mayors, quakes and fires.

San Francisco is a city of intense politics resembling those of New York or Chicago more than Los Angeles or San Diego. Every San Franciscan, so it seems, belongs to a political pressure group. These range from lifestyle- and ethnic-oriented groups to neighborhood and environmental associations. And they exist to oppose — strenuously — anything envisioned as a threat to their value systems. Republicans are an endangered species in a city that a couple of generations ago was a GOP stronghold, so most of the political plotting pits Democrat against Democrat. In the 1994 election, San Francisco again defied national trends by dumping the lone Republican on the Board of Supervisors and rejecting conservative hot-button measures on crime and immigration that were strongly supported by the rest of the state.

Political generalizations are dangerous amid such diversity, but there is a broad issue at the core of the city's recent political history: development. Although San Francisco's population is stable and much of its employment base has fled, there is continuing pressure to develop hotels and retail facilities. San Francisco's business community bases its hopes on the city's attractiveness to out-of-towners, either shoppers from suburbs or tourists and conventioneers. But development, in the minds of many, threatens the real San Francisco, however that may be defined.

City politics swerve back and forth as first one group then the other dominates. That's why San Francisco has freeways that stop in midair, dropping streams of cars onto city streets at the most inopportune places, and why every proposal for change creates a volcanic reaction. The pro-development mayorship of Joseph Alioto was followed by the liberal reign of George Moscone. But Moscone was shot and killed in his office, bringing in another pro-development mayor, Dianne Feinstein. When Feinstein's second full term ended in 1987, it was time for another great debate over the future of San Francisco.

The winner against pro-development candidate John Molinari was one of the city's two assemblymen, Art Agnos. Agnos galvanized groups united by their distaste for business as usual: gays, environmentalists, ethnics and others. But Agnos' administration spent much of its efforts handling crises, most caused by events far beyond Agnos' control. After four years, he had antagonized most factions that he had so skillfully brought together. Former police chief Jordan took out Agnos by 4 percentage points at the polls.

Jordan had a rocky several years. Bad appointments, turnover of top staff and no clearly defined agenda were just some of his problems. He did nothing about the bloated civil service, which saps the city treasury. In response to the time-honored tradition of paying off civil service unions for political support, San Francisco in 1994 had a civil service that cost $829 per resident annually. In New York, the figure is $624, and it's $464 in Los Angeles, $482 in San Diego and $416 in San Jose. On top of that, Jordan was urging people to volunteer to staff libraries and clean graffiti off public structures at the same time that he and his bride, attorney Wendy Paskin, were busy acquiring a $745,000 home in Pacific Heights. Things have improved, but Jordan was not on solid ground as he prepared his 1995 re-election campaign.

Longer-term questions about San Francisco center on its diversity. The old power structure based on the late Rep. Phil Burton's political machine seems to be breaking down. But no single political group is rising to replace it. Instead, dozens of interest groups battle constantly among themselves for power and influence at City Hall, and the alliances are as solid as fog flowing in and out of the Golden Gate.

San Francisco is the nation's most ethnically mixed city, and the most noticeable element of that diversity are the Asians, who have moved beyond Chinatown and Japantown to become an important economic factor in virtually every neighborhood. Asians are the city's latent political powerhouse, but, to date, they do not vote in great numbers, and they lack a charismatic leader. African Americans are declining in number as soaring housing costs drive them out of the city, but they continue to enjoy political power disproportionate to their number. Hispanics from a dozen nations continue to settle in San Francisco, but have yet to form a political bloc.

Beyond ethnic lines, San Francisco's people are spread across a rainbow of ideologies and lifestyles. Most visible are lesbians and gays, whose political leadership has been decimated by AIDS. There is even a residue of conservatism to be found in middle-class neighborhoods, personified by state Sen. Quentin Kopp, a Democrat-turned-independent.

The city, meanwhile, continues to grow less like a mini-New York, dominated by banks and big business, and to resemble more a collection of identifiable communities with employment concentrated in smaller businesses. Gays have been especially successful in translating neighborhood businesses into economic and political clout. Asians seem to be following that model, but African Americans and Hispanics have not moved into those channels.

San Franciscans scarcely acknowledged the 1989 event that was front-page news elsewhere. The state Department of Finance, in its periodic updating of population data, calculated that San Jose, 50 miles to the south, had passed San Francisco to become the state's third most populous city behind Los Angeles and San Diego. So what, San Franciscans shrugged. We have the cable cars, the hills, the tall buildings, the banks, the bay, the theater, the Giants, the 49ers and the tourist business, they seemed to say. San Jose just had people, and not very interesting people at that.

San Joaquin County

Area: 1,436.2 sq. mi.; Population: (1990) 480,628, (1980) 347,342; Registration: (1994) D-50.6% R-39.9%; Unemployment: (Dec. 1994) 12%; County supervisors: George Barber, Robert Cabral, Dario Marenco, Ed Simas, William Sousa; 222 E. Weber St., Stockton 95202; (209) 944-3113.

It wasn't too many years ago that in California's vast Central Valley, San Joaquin County was farm country. But the crop thriving in many of those fields these days is housing for Bay Area refugees. San Joaquin County's population is up more than 38 percent since 1980, and it is a change most noticeable in the once-quiet farm towns such as Tracy and Manteca in the county's southern and western corners.

The change is less dramatic in San Joaquin County's biggest city, Stockton, but even that town is changing from an agricultural center with a few non-farm industries into a regional retail and service hub that includes two colleges, most notably the University of the Pacific.

San Joaquin voters mirror those in the Central Valley in registering Democrat but often voting conservatively. Stockton, however, with its ethnic diversity and industrial base, is a dependable Democratic area. Yet despite hot races for Congress and the Assembly, San Joaquin had the lowest voter turnout in the state in 1992 and '94. Part of that appears to be attributable to the growing Hispanic population and the fact that long-distance commuters are often too tired to vote.

San Luis Obispo County

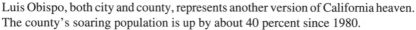

Area: 3,326.2 sq. mi.; Population: (1990) 217,162, (1980) 155,435; Registration: (1994) D-42.4% R-43.7%; Unemployment: (Dec. 1994) 6.5%; County supervisors: David Blakely, Ruth Brackett, Evelyn Delany, Laurence Laurent, Harry Ovitt; County Government Center, San Luis Obispo 93408; (805) 549-5450.

Midway between San Francisco and Los Angeles, blessed with a beautiful blend of coastline, beaches, mountains and near-perfect weather, San Luis Obispo, both city and county, represents another version of California heaven. The county's soaring population is up by about 40 percent since 1980.

Folks fleeing the pains of urban life have cashed in their inflated home equities and headed either north or south along Highway 101. But, as in so many other places around the state, newcomers are pumping up local housing costs and threatening to damage the qualities that make "SLO-town," as locals call it, so pleasant. For the time being, San Luis Obispo County seems to be weathering the assault, mostly because it has a well-balanced economy rooted in agriculture, tourism and the civil service payrolls of a state university, a state prison and a state hospital.

Politically, despite the presence of the college and many public employees, San Luis Obispo is Republican and unlikely to change.

San Mateo County

Area: 530.8 sq. mi.; Population: (1990) 649,623, (1980) 587,329; Registration: (1994) D-52.7% R-31.5%; Unemployment: (Oct, 1992) 5.3%; County supervisors: Ruben Barrales, Mary Griffin, Tom Huening, Ted Lempert, Mike Nevin; 401 Marshall St., Redwood City 94063; (415) 363-4000.

San Mateo County, a swath of the peninsula directly south of San Francisco, isn't very large, but it contains all the enormous social and economic extremes of California. Portions of the hilly county such as Hillsborough and Atherton are as wealthy as California gets. The business executives and professionals, many with prime offices in San Francisco, who live in communities of gently winding, tree-shaded streets earn an average of more than $100,000 a year.

Northern San Mateo County, nearest to San Francisco and containing San Francisco International Airport, is blue collar and middle class, with incomes a third of those found in the wealthier areas. Along the coast there is everything from middle-class suburbs to the ramshackle houses of 1960s and '70s runaways. And at the southern edge of the county along the bay there is East Palo Alto, a mostly African American community where people struggle to survive against drugs, crime and poverty.

San Mateo is typical of California's closer-in suburban areas: There is scant population growth (just 10 percent between 1980 and 1990), soaring home prices and expansive employment growth, mostly in white-collar and service jobs. As a recipient of commuters as well as a supplier, the county suffers changing and confusing traffic problems.

The Association of Bay Area Governments estimates that between 1985 and 2005, San Mateo will employ 90,000 more people, with the most jobs in finance, insurance and real estate accounting. Evidence of that trend includes the new office complexes along the Bayshore Freeway or in Foster City, which was created 30 years ago on San Francisco Bay landfill.

San Mateo has the political diversity to match its social differences. Blue-collar and poorer areas are rock-solid Democratic, while the affluent middle of the county tends to be Republican, albeit of the moderate, pro-environment, libertarian-lifestyle variety.

Santa Barbara County

Area: 2,744.7 sq. mi.; Population: (1990) 369,608, (1980) 298,694; Registration: (1994) D-45% R-39.5%; Unemployment: (Dec. 1994) 7%; County supervisors: Jeanne Graffy, Naomi Schultz, Tim Staffel, Tom Urbanske, Bill Wallace; 105 E. Acapamu St., Santa Barbara 93101; (805) 681-4200.

Santa Barbarans live in dread of a perpetually voracious animal — Los Angeles. Santa Barbarans fear the pulsating powerhouse to the south will swallow up their pleasant lifestyle and convert their region into just another suburb. Quality-of-life, however defined, is the dominant political and social issue of the area. To some, it means a never-ending anger at the presence of oil-drilling platforms off the coast, with the latent danger of another serious spill. That's why GOO, standing for Get Oil Out, adorns the bumpers of many local cars. To others, it means resisting new subdivisions in the hills or more hotels on the waterfront.

Santa Barbara County is growing, though at a slower rate than the state average. Local activists have managed to block most major development and the payback has been soaring real estate prices that preclude all but the affluent. The resultant somewhat exclusive social atmosphere is reinforced by the trendy shops in Santa Barbara's ranch-style downtown business district.

Outside of the city, Santa Barbara is self-consciously rural. Ex-President Ronald Reagan's ranch typifies life in the hills and horse country above the coast, and there are several small communities that serve these affluent rustics. There also is Vandenberg Air Force Base space center on the northern edge of the county, near Santa Maria, from which many satellite-carrying rockets are launched.

Politically, Santa Barbara County has a near tie between Democrats and Republicans, although Democrats recaptured the registration lead in 1992 and expanded the lead in 1994.

Santa Clara County

Area: 1,315.9 sq. mi.; Population: (1990) 1,497,577, (1980) 1,295,071; Registration: (1992) D-49% R-34.6%; Unemployment: (Dec. 1994) 5.3%; County supervisors: James Beall, Ron Gonzales, Michael Honda, Dianne McKenna, (vacancy); 70 W. Hedding St., 10th floor, San Jose 95110; (408) 299-2323.

Santa Clara County is one of the engines that drives the economy of the San Francisco Bay Area, and its fuel is the computer-electronics industry. Between 1980 and 1985, nearly half of all new jobs in the nine-county region were created in Santa Clara County, and most were connected to Silicon Valley, which used to be a geographic term but now is a generic description for the electronic industries found in and around Santa Clara County. The Association of Bay Area Governments estimates that between 1985 and 2005, Santa Clara will add nearly 400,000 new jobs, more than half of them in manufacturing and wholesale trade. While the high-tech companies have had peaks and valleys, the long-term direction has been consistently upward. But economic success has had a price, including toxic contamination of groundwater from chemicals used in high-tech plants.

San Jose, the county's largest city, is a nationwide joke on how not to deal with growth. Homes, shopping centers and business complexes sprang up everywhere with little thought to transportation or other infrastructure. San Jose and other Santa Clara County cities competed, rather than cooperated, and developers played political leaders against each other. For years the downtown looked like a victim of aerial bombing as stores fled for suburban shopping centers. But in recent years, led by former Mayor Tom McEnery, the city has been reborn. San Jose has completed the first phase of a trolley system; begun a downtown redevelopment project that includes a convention center, a Fairmont hotel, a high-tech museum and a sports complex; and improved its airport.

But its school system filed for bankruptcy protection in the mid-1980s. Like other big cities, it has smog, poverty, drug and crime problems. Mayor Susan Hammer, a liberal Democrat like McEnery, continues to push in the aggressive direction set by her predecessor. While Santa Clara, the fourth most populous county in the state, is still growing, high home prices (the median is about $250,000) and traffic jams worse than anywhere in the state except Orange County have removed much of the bloom from the rose.

A partial saving grace has been that Santa Clara's business and political leaders saw the king-size traffic headache relatively early and moved to deal with it. In 1985, Santa Clara was the first county to enact a local sales tax increase to pay for transportation improvements, a step other congested areas continue to struggle with. The tax was approved by voters because local industry put its financial muscle behind the campaign, and the victory marked the maturation of the high-tech industry and its executives into a civic force. Some executives — David Packard most prominently — have become compelling political and civic figures, and the industry is providing the financial and political muscle for San Jose's redevelopment.

Despite the county's effort, however, the mismatch of job development and population will continue to cause strains. The county budget is feeling the strain of growth and social change. It assumes one of the largest social welfare budgets of all California counties, partly because of the growing number of Asian immigrants and other poor people. County coffers have been saved in the past by high property values, but property values are almost flat and damage from the 1989 Loma Prieta earthquake is still another budget drain.

Besides San Jose, which surpassed San Francisco in the '80s to become the state's third-largest city, there are other communities of importance. Palo Alto, on the county's northern edge, is the home of Stanford University. It was the presence of Stanford that initially gave rise to the high-tech industry. Along Highway 101 south of San Jose, the one-time farm towns of Morgan Hill and Gilroy (which bills itself as the garlic capital of the world) are growing rapidly as they fill up with spillover from Silicon Valley. Fields and orchards are turning into subdivisions and industrial parks.

With its population and economic clout, Santa Clara County has become an area of great political importance. Generally, it has been faithfully Democratic, a reflection of its working-class history. But as home prices soar and affluent people move in, Santa Clara's politics are edging toward center.

Santa Cruz County

Area: 439.6 sq. mi.; Population: (1990) 229,734, (1980) 188,141; Registration: (1994) D-56.4% R-26.1%; Unemployment: (Dec. 1994) 8.9%; County supervisors:

Janet Beautz, Ray Belgard, Fred Keeley, Walt Symons, Mardi Wormhoudt; 701 Ocean St., Santa Cruz 95060; (408) 425-2201.

Three decades ago, Santa Cruz was a quiet, conservative, seaside community. But the opening of the unconventional University of California campus in 1965, the coming of the hippie era and Santa Cruz's scenic beauty have turned the region — particularly the city of Santa Cruz — into one of the bohemian capitals of California. County politics have turned sharply left and hostile to new development, especially after Santa Cruz began attracting commuters from the nearby Silicon Valley. Into the foreseeable future, the development wars will be a huge element of local politics.

Santa Cruz has had some new dilemmas recently, however. Its liberal attitudes, lush mountains and pleasant weather have attracted a large number of homeless people and just plain wanderers, placing another burden on an already strained county budget and creating more arguments about whether to be harsh or helpful. The budget was almost pushed over the brink by the 1989 Loma Prieta earthquake, which destroyed bridges, roads and buildings, including the Pacific Garden Mall in downtown Santa Cruz. Although the county has used a number of revenue hikes recently permitted by the state, its budget remains in woeful shape and many downtown businesses have not returned.

Local politics are intense. The Santa Cruz City Council is sometimes even quirkier than Berkeley's. One unsuccessful candidate in 1994 who's full name was Rodent ran on a platform to enact a height-to-weight formula for Spandex wearing. The Board of Supervisors is usually split between shrill liberals and bombastic conservatives. It can be quite a show.

Shasta County

Area: 3,850.2 sq. mi.; Population: (1990) 147,036, (1980) 115,715; Registration: (1994) D-41.3% R-44.9%; Unemployment: (Dec. 1994) 10%; County supervisors: Patricia Clarke, Richard Dickerson, Irwin Fust, Francie Sullivan, Molly Wilson; 1815 Yuba St., Suite 1, Redding 96001; (800) 479-8009.

Shasta is high on the list of counties in horrible fiscal shape. The public library system was closed in 1988, and voters defeated two tax hikes that would have reopened some or all of the branches. Money was finally found to reopen three of them, but with curtailed hours. In 1987, the county's general hospital was shut down, bankrupted, according to a County Supervisors Association of California study, by slow or inadequate state reimbursement for services to its patients, a vast majority of whom were indigent.

The county has been helped — a bit — by recent climbs in property values and tight money management, but its budget remains on the critical list. The property value increase has come from strong growth, particularly in Redding, the county's only city of any size. The area's hot summers and mild winters, the beauty of nearby mountains and Lake Shasta, and great outdoor recreation are drawing urban-equity refugees, the empty-nesters and retirees seeking less hectic lifestyles. The area north of Redding had four shabby communities that for years looked more like something from Appalachia. In 1993, they were incorporated into a new town of Shasta Lake, sparking zoning improvements and considerable civic pride.

Shasta County's population has been expanding faster than average, although unemployment remains high. Major employers in the county continue to be resource-oriented manufacturing, principally lumber and mineral products, but those businesses are slowly shrinking. Local boosters hope to attract one of the three new University of California campuses now in the planning stages. Politically, Shasta is conservative and becoming more so.

Sierra County

Area: 958.6 sq. mi.; Population: (1990) 3,318, (1980) 3,073; Registration: (1994) D-43.8% R-40%; Unemployment: (Dec. 1994) 7.6%; County supervisors: Donald Bowling, Richard Luchessi, Jerry McCaffrey, Donald McIntosh, Pat Whitley ; P.O. Drawer D, Downieville 95936; (916) 289-3295.

Sierra is the second least populous California county. But local politics do not hinge on such mundane matters as economic growth and population change. Few though they may be, Sierra County's residents fight old-fashioned political turf battles mixed with sometimes wild moves and countermoves.

The division is mostly geographic, the eastern side of the county against the west. Sierrans fight over such things as whether the county seat should remain in Downieville, in the west, or be moved to Loyalton, in the east. At one point, a male county supervisor was sued for sexual discrimination by a female supervisor. All of that makes the twice-monthly board meetings the best show in the county and produces high voter turn-outs.

When not fighting with each other, Sierrans usually vote conservatively, although there's a vociferous liberal/environmental contingent.

Siskiyou County

Area: 6,318.3 sq. mi.; Population: (1990) 43,531, (1980) 39,732; Registration: (1994) D-47.4% R-38.3%; Unemployment: (Dec. 1994) 13%; County supervisors: Kay Bryan, Clancy Dutra, Gary Giardino, Bill Hoy, Ivan Young; P.O. Box 338, Yreka 96097; (916) 842-8081.

A half-century ago, there was a semiserious political drive mounted in the northernmost California counties and the southernmost Oregon counties to break away and create a new state to be called Jefferson. Residents of the area felt they were dominated and ignored by far-distant urban centers. Secessionist fever cooled, but there remains a residual feeling — one very evident in scenic and sparsely populated Siskiyou County — of colonial status. Siskiyou residents are among those enthusiastically supporting the latest movement to divide California.

The fate of Siskiyou's timber industry, which accounts for at least one of every 10 jobs, is dependent on the outcome of battles in Sacramento or Washington, D.C., over preservation or use of federally owned timber in the county. There's an equally emotional battle over proposals for a major ski resort on Mount Shasta, the volcano that is Siskiyou's most dominant landmark.

Siskiyou County does have one part of its make-up that is unusual for a rural California county: an African American population that grew out of workers imported from the South by lumber mills. In 1986, Charles Byrd became California's only elected African American sheriff.

Solano County

Area: 872.2 sq. mi.; Population: (1990) 340,421, (1980) 235,203; Registration: (1994) D-55.3% R-31.1%; Unemployment: (Dec. 1994) 6.8%; County supervisors: William Carroll, Gordon Gojkovich, Barbara Kondylis, Ed Schlenker, Skip Thompson; 580 W. Texas St., Fairfield 94533; (707) 429-6218.

Solano County used to be a predictable part of California. Vallejo was an industrial city, the site of a major Navy shipyard and water-oriented industries. Fairfield was the county seat but otherwise a farm town on the edge of the Central Valley. Benicia was a sleepy little bit of history, the site of a former military arsenal and, briefly, a 19th-century California capital. And Vacaville was another farm town that also had a state prison. But relentless growth has changed Solano County in ways no one would have imagined a few years ago.

Vallejo has become a tourist center with the relocation of Marine World-Africa USA on a former golf course. Industry — most prominently a big Anheuser-Busch brewery — has come to Fairfield. Vacaville got a second prison and a huge factory-outlet mall. And throughout Solano County, sounds of hammers and saws at work have become part of the background noise as field after field has been transformed into subdivisions and shopping centers. Solano's population shot up by more than 44 percent between 1980 and 1990, and there is no sign it will slow.

Solano County is being loaded from two directions. While the western portion is transformed into a suburb of the Bay Area, the eastern side, including the once-sleepy farm town of Dixon, falls within the orbit of fast-growing Sacramento. The county's location between the two major Northern California urban complexes makes it attractive to industrial developers. The Association of Bay Area Governments predicts that Solano will add 58,000 jobs and about 150,000 residents between 1985 and 2005. Not unexpectedly, the county is experiencing growing pains such as traffic jams and overburdened water and sewage treatment facilities. The county's budget is feeling the strain as most of the revenue benefits from growth are going into the coffers of its cities, while the county continues to foot the bill for more and more services.

Growth also has fueled a backlash among residents worried that rural lifestyles are being destroyed. The county has been Democratic territory — especially blue-collar Vallejo. But with suburbanization comes a noticeable shift to the right, with Republicans looking for gains.

Sonoma County

Area: 1,597.6 sq. mi.; Population: (1990) 388,222, (1980) 299,681; Registration: (1994) D-55.8% R-30.7%; Unemployment: (Dec. 1994) 5.4%; County supervisors: Michael Cale, Ernest Carpenter, James Haberson, Paul Kelley, Tim Smith; 575 Administration Drive, Santa Rosa 95403; (707) 527-2241.

In 1986, the Sonoma County Planning Department told county supervisors that the county was growing so fast it already had as many people as had been predicted by the turn of the century. And there is no end in sight.

When Marin County virtually shut down development in the 1970s, pressure shifted directly north, rapidly changing Petaluma — the one-time chicken capital of the world — and Santa Rosa, the county seat, into big suburbs. Those cities are changing even more as Santa Rosa develops a significant employment base of its own and becomes a destination point for commuters from housing developments even further up Highway 101, the main north-south artery. The Association of Bay Area Governments notes that Sonoma County's population tripled between 1950 and 1980, with half the growth coming in the last decade. It is expected to increase by another 44 percent between 1985 and 2005.

Jobs are growing more slowly, so Sonoma is expected to continue in its role as a bedroom community, at least until after the turn of the century. But as in so many other areas, qualities that have made Sonoma County so attractive — the rural lifestyle and natural beauty — are threatened by the pace of the growth. The political leadership has been slow to deal with growth problems. Santa Rosa's sewage problems, which contributed to severe pollution of the scenic Russian River, have been a major embarrassment.

An anti-growth backlash has developed, with environmentalists and chicken farmers forming unusual political alliances to fight the conversion of agricultural land into houses and shopping centers. Petaluma was the site of an early development battle when local officials, trying to curtail the damage to the agricultural community in the 1970s, passed a law limiting housing development to 500 units a year. The ensuing lawsuit reached the U.S. Supreme Court, which ruled in Petaluma's favor and thus validated local growth-control laws. A poll of residents listed traffic as the most important issue, followed by education and development.

Politically, Sonoma County has a split personality. The western portion, home to a large gay community and environmental activism, is liberal, while the rapidly suburbanizing eastern portion is conservative. For years, politicians have divided the county more or less along north-south Highway 101 while drawing congressional and legislative districts.

Stanislaus County

Area: 1,521.2 sq. mi.; Population: (1990) 370,522, (1980) 265,900; Registration: (1994) D-52.6% R-37%; Unemployment: (Dec. 1994) 13.4%; County supervisors: Nick Blom, Paul Caruso, Tom Mayfield, Pat Paul, Raymond Clark Simon; 1100 H St., Modesto 95354; (209) 525-6414.

Nowhere in California are the changes that come with suburbanization more starkly evident than in Stanislaus County. For decades, this San Joaquin Valley county was purely agricultural, home of some of the nation's best-known farm products, such as Gallo wine and Foster Farms chicken. But its relative proximity to the San Francisco Bay Area meant it was destined to explode with houses and shopping centers as commuters, especially young ones without big paychecks, searched for affordable homes. Stanislaus' population swelled by over 39 percent between 1980 and 1990.

As the character of the area changes, so do its politics, away from agriculture and toward issues more identifiable with suburban life, some of which conflict with farming. Stanislaus and its major city, Modesto, sit in the middle of a long-term fight over how suburban the region will become.

A decade ago, Modesto put a damper on runaway expansion by requiring that sewer expansion proposals be placed on the ballot. But in 1992, a countywide initiative to put a 20-year moratorium on development of farmland was buried at the polls after heavy spending by developers. In 1994, the county threw out its Democratic assemblywoman and state senator, replacing them with far-right conservatives.

Sutter County

Area: 607 sq. mi.; Population: (1990) 64,415, (1980) 52,246; Registration: (1994) D-37.5% R-50.7%; Unemployment: (Dec. 1994) 15.7%; County supervisors: Dick Akin, Joan Bechtel, Casey Kroon, Larry Munger, Dennis Nelson; 463 Second St., Yuba City 95991; (916) 741-7106.

Yuba City and its sister city just across the river, Marysville, found themselves in the national spotlight in 1986 when Rand McNally listed the area as the worst place to live in the United States. The ranking was based on a mish-mash of statistics better suited to large cities than to relatively rural towns. The area was dragged down by such things as its lack of rapid transit and cultural amenities, as well as one very legitimate factor: its high unemployment rate. Unemployment is a sticky problem in agricultural Sutter County, but the region may be on the verge of an economic boom.

Highway 99, which links Yuba City-Marysville with Sacramento, 40 miles away, will be a four-lane freeway within a few years, and there are indications that the population boom in the Sacramento area will zoom up that freeway. A county-commissioned study predicts the first area to become suburbanized will likely be the southern reaches of the county, which will be a shorter commute from downtown Sacramento than the crowded areas of eastern Sacramento County. In anticipation, developers have been quietly acquiring tracts of farmland for years.

Politically, Sutter County is second only to Orange County in GOP voter registration and awarded George Bush his biggest California plurality in 1992.

Tehama County

Area: 2,976 sq. mi.; Population: (1990) 49,620, (1980) 38,888; Registration: (1994) D-46.3% R-40.7%; Unemployment: (Dec. 1994) 9.4%; County supervisors: Jo Ann Landingham, Shirley Marelli, Barbara McIver, Kathleen Rowen, Charles Willard; P.O. Box 250, Red Bluff 96080; (916) 527-4655.

A 1988 article in a California magazine described them as "The Revolutionary Junta of Tehama County." Time magazine told the same story, albeit more briefly, in an article entitled "Going Broke in California." Tehama County supervisors put

themselves in the spotlight when they threatened to shut down county government because Proposition 13 and a stingy state government had left them without enough money to take care of legal mandates. They backed down and the state took over partial funding of trial courts.

Tehama County subsists on agriculture — mostly cattle and olives — and timber production, but much of the potential commercial activity is siphoned away by the more vigorous communities of Redding and Chico, both outside the county. That leaves Tehama County with relatively low sales-tax revenues and a woeful budget that hinges on state help.

Tehama County sits in the middle of the upper Central Valley with few landmarks of note and attracts relatively few tourists or retirees. Its most notable feature may be that Red Bluff, its chief city, sometimes makes the weather charts as the hottest place in the state.

Trinity County

Area: 4,844.9 sq. mi.; Population: (1990) 13,063, (1980) 11,858; Registration: (1994) D-45.4% R-38.1%; Unemployment: (Dec. 1994) 13.1%; County supervisors: Ross Burgess, Robert Huddleston, Matthew Leffler, Stan Plowman, Arnold Whitridge; P.O. Drawer 1258, Weaverville 96093; (916) 623-1217.

Nothing is more pervasive in Trinity County than a sense of disconnection to late 20th-century California. Perhaps that helps explain why it was the only California county carried by Ross Perot in 1992.

Weaverville, the county seat and only town of consequence, still contains 19th-century storefronts built during the gold rush. Much of the county's population is scattered in homesteads and tiny communities with names like Peanut, Hayfork and Burnt Ranch. Residents are happy in their isolation. They cut timber, raise cattle and occasionally pan for gold — or grow marijuana — to support themselves and wish the rest of the world would leave them alone.

As legend has it, Weaverville was the inspiration for the fictional kingdom of Shangri-la, and there is something mystical about the Trinity Alps, the magnificent and somewhat impenetrable range of mountains dominating much of the county. It is unlikely Trinity will share in any of the changes sweeping the state since it is a long and difficult drive from any population center.

As with other rural counties, the budget coffers are bare. Voters turned down a 1988 sales-tax hike and state bailout measures have not helped much. For example, a plan to let the counties keep traffic fines has mattered little in a county without a single stoplight.

Tulare County

Area: 4,844.9 sq. mi.; Population: (1990) 311,921, (1980) 245,738; Registration: (1994) D-45.1% R-43.7%; Unemployment: (Dec. 1994) 15.4%; County supervisors: Charles Harness, Jim Maples, Bill Maze, Melton Richmond, Bill Sanders; 2800 W. Burrel, Visalia 93291; (209) 733-6271.

Although in the middle of San Joaquin Valley, Tulare County is not just another valley farming community. The county and its principal city, Visalia, have worked for economic diversification with un- common vigor, and it has paid off with dozens of industrial facilities.

Tulare County's location in the middle of the valley and its nearness to recreation spots in the Sierra has helped economic development. So has an almost entrepreneurial approach to government. But despite the new industry and accom- panying services, unemployment still runs at twice the state average, a reflection of the seasonal nature of agriculture, the top industry. In addition, the demand on the county for health and welfare services is outgrowing the new revenue as the growth also brings more poor people. The county is one of six in the state that spends more than half of its budget on those services

Politically, Tulare is moderately conservative, voting for Democrats only when they avoid the liberal label.

Tuolumne County

Area: 2,292.7 sq. mi.; Population: (1990) 48,456, (1980) 33,928; Registration: (1994) D-47.2% R-41.2%; Unemployment: (Dec. 1994) 9.6%; County supervisors: Michael De Bernardi, Bill Holman, Ken Marks, Larry Rotelli, Jesse Roundtree; 2 S. Green St., Sonora 95370; (209) 533-5521.

Tuolumne County was born in the California gold rush and 130 years later finds itself in the midst of a new one. A huge new gold mine, working the spoils of generations of mining operations in the area, opened in 1986 and gave the county a much-needed steady payroll.

But overall, an even bigger rush is being made to develop the areas around some of Tuolumne's scenic wonders. Its population is growing fast — almost 43 percent between 1980 and 1990 — and most growth comes from retirees and other people escaping cities. Drawn by the county's mild climate, slow pace and recreational opportunities, newcomers are fueling the economy with pensions and the investment of equity from the sale of urban homes. The construction of homes and new retail services have become new foundations of the economy.

Growth is taking its toll on county services, too. As crime increased with population, Tuolumne County poured funds into a money-wasting hodgepodge of four courtrooms spread among four buildings. Still awaiting funds are a solid-waste problem, an aging county hospital, road improvements and new fire equipment in a county ravaged by major forest fires in recent years.

Politically, Tuolumne County is conservative and likely to become more so as it grows.

Ventura County

Area: 1,863.6 sq. mi.; Population: (1990), 669,016, (1980) 529,174; Registration: (1994) D-41.1% R-44.1%; Unemployment: (Dec. 1994) 7.7%; County supervisors: John Flynn, Maggie Kildee, Susan Lacey, Judy Mikels, Frank Schillo; 800 S. Victoria Ave., Ventura 93009; (805) 654-2929.

Not too many years ago, Ventura was considered a rural county. Its dominant industries were oil, cattle, citrus and other agriculture. The pace of life was slow. Los Angeles was a long hour's drive away. But in an astonishingly short time, Ventura County has been overrun by the ever-expanding Southern California megalopolis. As freeways punched through the coastal hills from the San Fernando Valley and into the cities of Oxnard, Santa Paula and Ventura, developers began turning agricultural tracts into subdivisions, shopping centers, office complexes and industrial parks.

One area of the county has been dubbed Gallium Gulch, a takeoff on Silicon Valley, because it has become a center for developing gallium arsenide into a commercial product. The new technology has drawn some of the largest names in American industry. Meanwhile, the agricultural economy stumbles along as more farmers sell out to developers.

Ventura County also has begun to exploit its coastal resources, seeking some of the recreational and vacation activity that the rest of Southern California has long enjoyed. The city of Ventura, long accustomed to having tourists pass through en route to Santa Barbara to the north, is now developing marinas, hotels and other facilities of its own. It also is starting to make a big deal out of its historic roots as a mission town (the official name of the city is San Buenaventura, after the local mission).

As Ventura County evolves economically, it is changing socially. The agricultural and blue-collar workers now face soaring home prices. And the county is feeling all the other common growing pains, including heavy traffic, especially on

Highway 101, the major route connecting it with Los Angeles.

The change is especially evident in Oxnard, a one-time farm town with a large Hispanic population. Its proximity to the Pacific and to freeways leading to Los Angeles is converting Oxnard into a somewhat expensive, white-collar bedroom town. The county has long managed one of the state's most stable budgets, but even Ventura may soon be feeling the money crunch hitting most other counties.

County politics also are becoming more conservative. It has a Republican voter majority, and Democratic candidates are finding that an ever-steeper hill to climb.

Yolo County

Area: 1,034 sq. mi.; Population: (1990) 141,092, (1980) 113,374; Registration: (1994) D-56.2% R-29.8%; Unemployment: (Dec. 1994) 7%; County supervisors: Betsy Marchard, Michael McGowan, Frank Sieferman, Tom Stallard, Helen Thomson; 625 Court St., Woodland 95695; (916) 666-8195.

Many observers expected Yolo County to be the state's first to declare bankruptcy, and only continual belt-tightening has kept it from fiscal disaster. It has huge health and welfare expenses, a low tax base, and it lost a big chunk of revenue when West Sacramento incorporated. In 1990, even the county hospital had to be closed.

West Sacramento, just across the river from downtown Sacramento, had been ignored by the bigger city's boom and had an image of a low-income, seedy, quasi-red-light district. It is counting on a huge, upscale marina-commercial-residential project along the Sacramento River to upgrade its fortunes.

West Sacramento is one end of the vividly contrasting county. Away to the west and north are rolling hills, farms and a few sparse towns that seem to belong to a different time. In between are two very different cities: Woodland, the conservative county seat that is a farm town on the verge of becoming a suburb and distribution center, and Davis — or the People's Republic of Davis, as its detractors call it.

Davis is a university town, with political activism that extends down to the street-light level and a City Council that, at times, can be as quirky as Berkeley's. Councilwoman Julie Partansky has argued passionately that the crossing guard at the Davis Farmers' Market should be dressed as a vegetable. Davis has been trying to resist developer pressure to become yet another Sacramento bedroom, but even that effort is slowly failing.

Yuba County

Area: 639.1 sq. mi.; Population: (1990) 58,228, (1980) 49,733; Registration: (1994) D-44.2% R-41.7%; Unemployment: (Dec. 1994) 11.9%; County supervisors: Alfonso Amaro, Brent Hastey, Michelle Mathews, Jay Palmquist, Hal Stocker;

215 Fifth St., Marysville, 95901; (916) 741-6461.

Yuba County is next door to Sutter County. The county seats, Yuba's Marysville and Sutter's Yuba City, are just one river apart. But the two counties are developing along different lines.

Much of Sutter lies next to Sacramento County. It is likely to become more and more suburban. But most of Yuba County lies well to the north of Sacramento County and is likely to remain rural for the foreseeable future.

Marysville may be destined for semisuburban status as the highways connecting it and Yuba City to both Sacramento and the burgeoning high-tech industrial areas in nearby Placer County are widened into freeways.

In addition, the area can count on a steady payroll from Beale Air Force Base, which is growing as base closures shift units from other bases.

Yuba County has a large enclave of Sikhs, a number of whom have become wealthy farmers. That has made for some interesting educational issues in the county, but Sikhs tend to maintain a closed society and have not become a political force. Democrats have a registration edge, but residents tend to vote conservatively.

11

Press vs. politicians–never-ending war

An aide to Assembly Speaker Willie Brown once put out a 15-page guide of detailed advice for legislators on how to deal with the news media. On the cover was a cartoon with a farmer, sitting on a tractor, telling a reporter that the two of them are in the same business.

"We are?" the reporter asks.

"This here's a manure spreader," the farmer responds.

That about sums up the mutual feelings of California's politicians and the people who cover them for print and broadcast media around the state. Pretty much, each thinks the other is spreading manure.

It has become an axiom in American politics that a certain tension and wariness exist in the dealings between reporters and politicians. That is certainly the case in California. Gone are the days when most of the Capitol press corps and the state's political media were part of the inside establishment. Gone are the times when most reporters and politicians ate, drank and caroused together, and neither group judged the other too harshly.

What has emerged instead is constant sparring and occasional slugging between politicians and news people, two groups who need each other and, frankly, hate it.

Their relationship has rapidly changed in recent years. Nowhere has that been more evident than in campaign coverage. Where reporters were once satisfied to cover the candidate's speeches and the campaign strategies, suddenly there are stories examining the veracity of TV ads, in-depth issue coverage (even if candidates have not brought those issues up) and attention to economic conflicts and voters' anger. In return, some campaigns have manipulated coverage, particularly TV coverage, as never before and have peppered reporters with constant complaints of bias.

Which is not to say that politicos and the political media don't agree on some campaign coverage. For instance, they both get caught up in insider-obsessed, horse-race-crazy, what's-the-latest-poll thinking, much to the boredom of the public. But coverage of the Capitol has evolved beyond campaign stories. Probably the first big wave of change hit with the creation of a full-time, professional Legislature in the mid-1960s. Then, in the wake of the Vietnam War and Watergate, a new generation of more serious, more critical reporters came to journalism. Despite occasional chumminess between some reporters and politicians today, the press continues to move toward harder reporting about campaign spending, conflicts of interest and ethical problems.

All of which adds to the hostility between politicians and reporters. Politicians have an almost single-minded concern about image, as might be expected of people whose careers depend upon public approval. To project any image, they need the media. But often the publicity they get is not what they wanted, especially when reporters, striving for the journalistic Grail of objectivity, feel compelled to throw in other views and counterarguments.

Many legislators and others in the Capitol have lists of complaints about the media. They say both privately and publicly that stories about FBI investigations, campaign contributions and political shenanigans stain the Legislature with a few broad strokes, obscuring the hard work and good intentions of many lawmakers. Reporters don't buy that argument. If anything, they feel their stories often make legislators look too statesmanlike. They say most stories deal with the substance and progress of bills and budgets, and that too few reports cover the wheeling and dealing that goes into most legislation or the enormous influence that powerful interests exert in the Capitol.

INHERENT DIFFERENCES

No better example of the different views can be found than in the media's legendary battles with Assembly Speaker Brown. In early 1991, Brown said in a series of interviews that opponents and the press had created a completely inaccurate image of him. He insisted voters had not heard that he really is a consummate political negotiator, an achiever of big public policy steps and an extraordinarily sensitive human being. He said reporters have been too happy to carry stories criticizing both him and the Legislature. He also suggested that racial bias was the motivation for some of the critical reporting.

Reporters and editors rolled their eyes at Brown's comments. Most Capitol news people feel they fall far short of revealing all the ways Brown has manipulated the legislative process for purely political ends. But despite their distaste, most went back and dutifully reported Brown's complaints, substantive or not, and then tried to find critics to give their stories balance.

But the differences between political reporters and the people they cover run much deeper than simply the nature of the stories. Reporters see it as their job to be, in a sense, the loyal opposition, always asking critical questions, always making elected representatives justify why they should remain in office. When politicians try to tell only part of a story, reporters feel it is their obligation to bring the other side to the public and put the statement or event in historical context.

Such independence does not sit well with some career politicians. Loyalty is everything to them. Reporters, instead, try to be loyal to their stories. The politicians do not easily accept the idea that reporters or editors can function without grinding personal or political axes. Instead, they assume, as they would of anyone who causes problems, that news people oppose them for ideological or political reasons, or even out of envy. Some politicians are left feeling betrayed when they joke with reporters, talk about movies or restaurants or their children's baby teeth, and then find a critical story the next day. Their frustration is deepened by their inability to control news people. Everyone else in the system is willing to negotiate or compromise, except the media. Politicians know they need the press, but it is the one major piece of the political picture outside their control.

Reporters, for their part, often feel they are being manipulated too much. If a politician understands the news media's universally accepted rules of engagement — for example, that every side gets to have a say, that the opinions of major figures such as the governor or the Assembly speaker usually are newsworthy, that reporters cannot simply say somebody is lying or distorting information — they can color the reporting of events.

It is just such manipulation that has given rise to spin doctors. Political consultants, knowing that reporters are always hungry for quotes, have created an art form of interpreting events — attempting to put spin on them — to make their candidates look good. These political operatives are found not only on the staffs of elected officials, but on legislative staffs and in state agencies. Gov. Pete Wilson's administration, in particular, has placed a large number spin doctors in high-paying jobs at state agencies to propagandize and engage in damage control.

Efforts to control media coverage have heightened the tension between the media and politicians. During the two-month budget stalemate in 1992, news people were constantly complaining that they were being dragged into a multisided public relations campaign rather than a policy fight. The worst incident was an attempt by Wilson to address a statewide TV audience. His staff promised stations up and down California that his speech would be nonpolitical, focusing instead on the mechanics of issuing state IOUs. Many stations gave Wilson what he wanted: free, live coverage. Wilson then went out and blasted the Democrats in the Legislature, leaving some TV news directors swearing that they would never again give Wilson live air time for anything but his official State of the State speech or his funeral. That promise proved short-lived.

The other major media-control tactic being honed by politicians everywhere is press bashing. The idea is to discredit the message by blaming the messenger. In 1992, it was the Republicans who used this the most, largely because President

George Bush was doing dismally in statewide polls. Republican leaders, trying to shore up fund-raising enthusiasm and to prevent other Republican candidates from being swamped by re-energized Democrats, complained bitterly that the media were overplaying the stories that polls showed Bush far behind or that the economy was not showing signs of recovery. To an extent, the tactic worked. In an attempt to balance their stories, reporters included those complaints.

A HARDER EDGE TO COVERAGE

It is hard to assess the impact that complaints of bias have on the public's perception of a story, but it is clear they have done little to cool the media's intense scrutiny of the Legislature and political campaigns. The news bureaus covering the Capitol continue to churn out long, investigative pieces on the Legislature and state government agencies. Even the one-person bureaus do a particularly good job of breaking news stories of statewide import while providing their readers with dimension of Sacramento issues and politicians that are of particular interest to their local readers. Some reporters have been criticized for spending too much time on local legislators at the expense of more significant developments involving general government. In part, that emphasis on legislators and issues particular to a circulation area comes in response to newspaper marketing surveys that show readers are more concerned with local issues and events and have limited interest in state politics.

The situation is vastly different in the world of television news, which has all but abandoned state Capitol coverage. During the 1960s and 1970s, most large stations in San Francisco, Los Angeles and San Diego maintained Sacramento bureaus, lured by the glamour of Govs. Ronald Reagan and Jerry Brown and by a desire to emulate national networks in covering hard news. The San Diego stations were the first to pull out, and the last Los Angeles station left in 1983. KRON-TV in San Francisco, the last out-of-town holdout, closed its Capitol bureau in 1988.

Television news has not entirely given up on political coverage. The Sacramento stations still cover the Capitol — although less and less — and most major stations spend a good deal of resources covering statewide races and important ballot measures. But a University of Southern California study found stations outside Sacramento averaged barely one minute per news hour of coverage of the Legislature during one period of intense activity in the 1988 session.

Television is shying away from politics for a number of reasons, and money is at the top of the list. At one time television stations made money almost faster than they could count it, and the local news operations were their biggest earners. Now television stations face competition from cable networks, superstations and video recorders, as well as from talk and game shows on competing stations. In response, station managers are listening more and more to consultants, who produce surveys that say viewers hate politics. In addition, as smaller profits have lessened resources, expensive out-of-town bureaus have become expendable. Thus, with the exception of the major news stories such as budget stalemates, state politics are covered almost exclusively by short mentions of legislative action or reports about a local visit by a politician.

NEW FORMS OF TV COVERAGE

There have been a few developments running counter to that trend. One has been the growth of Northern California News Satellite, which sells Capitol coverage to about two-dozen stations. But much of that coverage is often used as brief stories rather than the more in-depth reports that bureaus might have supplied, and the ready pictures with a sound bite can be a too-easy substitute for real reporting. The other change was the start of live broadcasts of legislative proceedings and the development of the California Channel, the cable service channel modeled after C-SPAN, which covers Congress.

Speaker Brown was the force behind the $2 million-plus effort to begin televising the Legislature. First the Assembly and then the Senate bought robotic cameras, a full control room and the rest of the equipment needed to cover floor and committees sessions, and to produce interviews with members to be sent to hometown stations.

The Legislature gives its live picture to the California Channel, which packages it and sells a daytime broadcast to California cable systems. The California Channel has plans to carry news conferences and programs with commentary and analysis of state politics. In addition, commercial stations who patch into the legislative feeds or buy the California Channel can use the broadcasts on their news shows. The consensus among those involved with the live TV so far has been that the California Channel's impact on the Legislature as been about the same as was C-SPAN's effect on Congress: Lawmakers dress up a little more, try to slim down and occasionally remember they are on camera.

Opening the Assembly for live television caused another fight between Brown and the press corps. Saying he was trying to improve decorum in his house, the speaker banished reporters from the edges of the Assembly floor, where they had roamed for years, chatting with members and filling in their stories without formal press conferences. Reporters were given desks off the floor in the back of the chamber with the staff. The Capitol press corps was livid, as were a number of Assembly members who liked having reporters nearby — the easier to get their names in the news.

Brown's corralling of reporters and the interest in televising the Legislature were signs that California politicians had become media savvy, or at least media conscious. This is most visible in campaigns where candidates and consultants have mastered the bite-of-the-day technique of presenting splashy, often vague statements designed to enhance their images rather than explain issues. Campaign consultants also have become more adept at whispering in reporters' ears, attempting to plant story ideas that help their candidate or hurt opponents, or to put spin on everything involved in the campaign, from polling to money-raising to issues.

At the same time, reporters are trying to do more than carry campaign statements to their readers and viewers. Most major papers are trying to examine candidates more carefully, over a longer period and on more issues. They are looking not only at voting records but consistency, ethics, financial holdings, spouses' activities and, occasionally, their private lives.

That, too, has contributed to the increased wariness, even on the often long campaign trail. Where once reporters and candidates would relax after a campaign swing with dinner or drinks, both groups now keep their distance. And where once consultants would answer questions about polling or money-raising honestly, now every utterance has the best face painted on it. So, candidates are careful with what they say, and reporters believe only a fraction of what they hear.

Still, media coverage is crucial to the success of political campaigns, especially statewide contests. There are thousands of miles to cover and dramatically varied constituencies to persuade. In fact, just about the only effective way to reach the state's 15 million registered voters is through television. Candidates and initiative sponsors are eager to get on the local news, especially in Southern California, and local news stations are eager to cover big-name candidates and major ballot campaigns. Television news, despite all but abandoning the dull and gray day-to-day political coverage in the off season, is still interested in the horse race and name-calling.

Politicians and political consultants are thrilled by this turn. Local TV news reaches many more people than do newspaper stories, and because it is the magic of television, it has more impact. In addition, campaigns can occasionally get messages out without a balancing point of view by playing to TV's fascination with live technology. A live interview or live coverage of an event can give viewers a much less filtered theme or message than even a 15-second sound bite.

Outside of campaigns, consultants and politicians are working harder than ever to attract and control press coverage. While they want their names in the news, they ask a lot more from their publicity than just spelling their name correctly. One device to gain favorable coverage is the age-old media stunt. Recent examples include a state senator bowling with frozen turkeys on the west steps of the Capitol to publicize a bill on behalf of California fresh turkeys; an ambulance delivering petitions to the Capitol from people supporting money for emergency rooms and a group of about 1,000 hospital administrators lined up like a marching band spelling out H-E-L-P to ask for aid to hospital budgets. A common move is the press conference to announce the introduction of a bill. That gives one or more legislators a chance to be identified with a newsworthy issue. Sometimes a serious effort to move the bill follows, but just as often the bills are abandoned, having served their purpose by letting the lawmakers take a tough stand without angering any of the interests opposing the measure.

Another ploy is the ever-popular spontaneous statement during a legislative debate. It sounds like an heartfelt line coming from that lawmaker's deep well of conviction. As often as not, these are suggested by aides, practiced beforehand and timed to fit a TV sound bite.

PROFESSIONAL MEDIA MANAGERS

The increased sophistication in the interplay with the media has moved politicians to seek professional help in hunting for coverage. Even legislators who are rarely quoted in hometown media are employing aides whose sole responsibility is to deal with the press or sometimes to chase down reporters to get their boss's name in the paper. But on-staff press aides are only so effective. In greater and greater number, even unspectacular legislators who are not running for higher office — at least for now — are hiring the services of a growing number of political public relations firms. These firms also are being used by special interests pushing or resisting particular bills in the Capitol. In fact, it is not uncommon to have every side represented by PR people.

One big job for these firms is to put clients, either politicians or special interests, in touch with the media. Major firms that engage in political PR around Sacramento — among them the PBN Company; Stoorza, Ziegaus and Metzger; Townsend, Hermocillo, Raimundo and Usher; and RF Communications — all employ people who either were members of the Capitol press corps at one time or who dealt with the press at length in legislative offices. They know what reporters are interested in and how to get their client's views into a story. And they realize that competition for reporters' time and interest is intense, so they can help their clients by making it easier and faster for reporters to get information.

Many PR people also try to call attention to clients by putting them in touch with newspeople through casual breakfasts or lunches or even backyard barbecues. No immediate stories are expected, but it makes the reporters and politicians feel more comfortable with each other and, as often as not, the politicians may find their names appearing in stories a little more readily. In effect, this new breed of political PR consultant is a lobbyist of the media, working in conjunction with those who lobby officeholders.

Attention being focused on California's political press is beginning to be matched by the media's own introspection. Some newspapers have taken long, critical looks at campaign and political coverage, and almost all have wondered in print and in private whether political reporting could be improved.

In 1994, at the University of California, Davis, annual Political Campaign Management Institute, UC Berkeley journalism professor and former New York Times reporter Susan Rasky said that the news media coverage of politics and government is inadequate. Rasky contends, probably correctly, that the media pay too much attention to when a state budget is passed and too little attention to the document's content.

A year earlier, Ginger Rutland, an editorial writer for The Sacramento Bee, was asked for an assessment of the Capitol press corps while a panelist at a conference in San Diego. Political reporters in Sacramento "aren't venal," she said. "They're stupid and lazy." Some avoid complex issues, fail to put political rhetoric in context and most could work harder researching issues, she continued. That triggered howls from some Sacramento journalists. Rutland later acknowledged her statement was overly general — a common journalistic failing — but wouldn't apologize. "If the shoe fits, wear it," she said.

In addition, the press corps had an internal debate over the role of journalists in fighting for access to information when a few legislators introduced bills to reduce access to public records. Although all the proposals died, they created some bitter divisions between those who believe reporters should actively lobby lawmakers to keep information public and those who argue that journalists compromise themselves and their responsibility to their readers and viewers when they lobby for anything. Capitol reporters also have wrestled with mixed success over the ethics of outside income — such as speeches to trade associations and free-lance writing for professional or industry publications — or possible conflicts of interest created by the jobs held by spouses.

Newspapers and news services

ASSOCIATED PRESS

Sacramento bureau: 925 L St., Suite 320, Sacramento 95814; (916) 448-9555, FAX (916) 446-2756.

Nick Geranios, correspondent; Doug Willis, news editor and political writer; reporters: Steve Geissinger, Kathleen Holder, Jennifer Kerr, John Howard, Steve Lawrence; photographers Bob Galbraith and Rich Pedroncelli.

The Associated Press is a news cooperative with more than 100 member newspapers and 400 broadcasters in California who receive AP reports. The Sacramento office is an all-purpose news bureau covering breaking stories from Fairfield east to the Nevada border and from Stockton to the Oregon border. Roughly two-thirds of the bureau's time is spent reporting on California politics and state government.

Geranios moved to Sacramento as the bureau chief in January 1994, coming from a six-year stint at the Yakima, Wash., bureau of AP. He also served as the Illinois statehouse reporter in Springfield and worked two years at AP's Chicago bureau since joining the AP in 1982. Before that he worked as a sports writer at a number of small newspapers.

Willis has been in AP's Sacramento bureau since 1969 and directed the bureau from 1974 to 1991.

The AP staff is a veteran one: Geissinger moved to the bureau in 1984 from the Salinas Californian; Holder joined AP in 1987 from the Vacaville Reporter;

Howard joined the bureau in 1980 from AP's San Francisco office; Kerr joined AP in 1973 and has been in Sacramento since 1978; Lawrence came to Sacramento in 1973 from AP's Los Angeles office; Galbraith came to the Sacramento bureau from AP's Los Angeles bureau in 1993; Pedroncelli, a former Sacramento Union photographer and longtime AP stringer, joined the staff in 1990.

BAKERSFIELD CALIFORNIAN
Capitol bureau: 925 L St., Suite 1190, Sacramento 95814; (916) 444-9697; FAX (916) 444-1859.

Vic Pollard, bureau chief.

Pollard joined the Californian in April 1994. Before then he worked in Los Angeles and the Bay Area from 1986 to 1994 for Gannett News Service in various editing and reporting positions. He covered the state Capitol for Gannett from 1976 to 1986.

CAPITOL NEWS SERVICE
1713 J St., Suite 202, Sacramento 95814; (916) 445-6336, FAX (916) 443-5871.

David Kline, editor; Brad Smith and Pamela Martineau, reporters.

An independent news service serving small dailies and weeklies. The news service was founded in 1939 and was taken over by Fred Kline, a veteran newsman, in 1971. David Kline, no relation to Fred, took over the service in 1992.

CHICO ENTERPRISE-RECORD
Capitol bureau: 530 P St., No. 31, Sacramento 95814; (916) 444-6747.

Mike Gardner, reporter.

The opening of this bureau in 1990 was prompted by the paper's need to report on attempts to obtain state aid for fiscally strapped Butte County. Gardner, who has been with the paper since 1986, concentrates on stories of interest to Chico-area readers.

CONTRA COSTA TIMES / LESHER NEWSPAPERS
Capitol bureau: 925 L St., Suite 348, Sacramento 95814; (916) 441-2101, FAX (916) 441-6001.

Virgil Meibert, bureau chief.

The bureau covers local legislators, the effect of state government decisions on local communities and regional issues for six daily Lesher newspapers in the San Francisco Bay Area: the Contra Costa Times, Antioch Daily Ledger, Pittsburg Post-Dispatch, San Ramon Valley Times, Valley Times in Pleasanton and West County Times covering the Richmond-Pinole area. Prior to becoming Lesher's Sacramento bureau chief in 1988, Meibert spent 24 years with the Oakland Tribune, the last 14 years as its Sacramento bureau chief.

COPLEY NEWS SERVICE

Capitol bureau: 925 L St., Suite 1190, Sacramento 95814; (916) 445-2934, FAX (916) 443-1912.

James P. Sweeney, bureau chief.

This two-person bureau was without a second reporter at the beginning of 1995. The bureau covers stories of particular interest to a group of Copley newspapers in the Los Angeles area: the Daily Breeze in Torrance, the San Pedro News Pilot and the Santa Monica Outlook. The bureau also serves the San Diego Union Tribune. In addition, the Copley bureau serves 35 California clients, including daily and weekly newspapers and broadcasters who subscribe to the Copley News Service and 150 clients nationwide.

Sweeney joined the bureau in 1985 from the Daily Breeze in Torrance, where he was an assistant city editor.

DAILY RECORDER

1115 H St., Sacramento 95814; (916) 444-2355, FAX (916) 444-0636.

Steve Towns, editor.

This Sacramento-based legal-profession newspaper is one of several owned by the Daily Journal Corp. of Los Angeles. It concentrates on news of interest to the legal community, lobbyists and Capitol staffers.

GANNETT NEWS SERVICE

Capitol bureau: 925 L St., Suite 110, Sacramento 95814; (916) 446-1036, FAX (916) 446-7326.

Jake Henshaw, bureau chief; Ray Sotero, reporter.

The bureau covers stories of local and statewide interest to the chain's California newspapers: the Marin Independent Journal, the Palm Springs Desert Sun, the Salinas Californian, the San Bernardino Sun and the Visalia Times-Delta. The bureau also occasionally covers stories for the Reno Gazette Journal and USA Today.

Henshaw came to Sacramento in 1987 from the GNS Washington bureau, where he had worked since 1978. He became bureau chief in Sacramento in 1990. Sotero moved to GNS in 1990 from The Sacramento Bee's Capitol Bureau, where he had covered issues for the Fresno Bee and Modesto Bee since 1988. He was one of the original co-authors of the California Political Almanac.

LOS ANGELES DAILY JOURNAL

Capitol bureau: 925 L St., Suite 325, Sacramento 95814; (916) 445-8063, FAX (916) 444-3358.

Thomas L. Dresslar, bureau chief; Hallye Jordan, reporter.

The bureau covers news of interest to the legal community ranging from the death penalty to probate law. In addition to the Daily Journal, the bureau's work appears in the San Francisco Daily Journal and other Daily Journal Corp. publications.

Dresslar came to the bureau from the Daily Recorder in Sacramento in 1987. Jordan joined the bureau in 1987 from the Orange County Register.

LOS ANGELES DAILY NEWS

Capitol bureau: 925 L St., Suite 335, Sacramento 95814; (916) 446-6723, FAX (916) 448-7381.

Sandy Harrison, bureau chief.

Los Angeles office: Rick Orlov, political writer, (213) 485-3720.

The bureau's primary focus is state government, political news of interest to its San Fernando Valley readers and major statewide stories.

Harrison joined the bureau in 1989 and had covered local government for the Daily News. By summer of 1995, he was scheduled to return to Los Angeles to swap jobs with County Bureau reporter Mark Katches.

Orlov covers City Hall and state and local politics from the Los Angeles office. He has been with the paper since 1977 and previously worked for Copley News Service.

LOS ANGELES TIMES

Capitol bureau: 1121 L St., Suite 200, Sacramento 95814; (916) 445-8860, FAX (916) 322-2422.

Armando Acuna, bureau chief; George Skelton, columnist; staff writers: Eric Bailey (Orange County edition), Cynthia Craft (Valley Edition,) Virginia Ellis, Jerry Gillam, Mark Gladstone, Carl Ingram, Paul Jacobs, Dan Morain, Dave Lesher, and Max Vanzi (news editor).

Los Angeles office: Cathleen Decker, (213) 237-4652, and Bill Stall, (213) 237-4550, political writers.

The Los Angeles Times Sacramento bureau primarily takes a statewide approach to its coverage of Capitol issues. It does in-depth political analyses, personality profiles and investigative stories involving the state bureaucracy as well as daily coverage of the Legislature, the governor and other state agencies. The Times also provides stories of local and regional interest to its primary audience of Los Angeles area readers. Times stories also appear in newspapers that subscribe to the Times-Mirror wire service.

Acuna became bureau chief in January 1993. He joined the Times in 1985 and last served as city editor of the now defunct San Diego edition. Before moving to the Times, he worked for 12 years for the San Jose Mercury News, the last year of which was spent in Sacramento as a Capitol correspondent.

Skelton, a former Capitol correspondent for UPI who moved to the Times in 1974, was bureau chief prior to shifting to his columnist role in 1992. He has also worked as Times politics editor in Los Angeles and as White House correspondent.

The Times bureau includes Bailey, who joined the office in December 1992 and has been with the Times since 1983; Craft, who was in the Times San Fernando Bureau when she moved to Sacramento in December 1993; Ellis, who came to Sacramento in 1988 from the Dallas Times Herald, where she was chief of its Capitol bureau in Austin; Gillam, the senior member of the Capitol press corps who has been a member of the bureau since 1961; Gladstone, who joined the bureau in 1984 and has been with the Times since 1981; Ingram, a former UPI Capitol correspondent who joined the Times in 1978; Jacobs, who has been with the Times since 1978 and who moved to Sacramento in 1983; Lesher, who came to the bureau in 1995 from the Times Los Angeles office, where he covered politics; Morain, who joined the Times in 1981 and worked in Los Angeles and San Francisco before joining the bureau in 1992; Vanzi, who moved to the bureau in 1990 from the Times main office, where he had worked since 1984 as an assistant city editor.

Decker and Stall are based in Los Angeles and cover statewide and national political stories. Decker joined the Times in 1978 after having worked as a Times intern. She had been primarily covering local and national politics since 1985 before being designated a political writer in 1990. Stall, a veteran Times writer, was an editorial writer for the Times when he returned to political writing in 1990.

OAKLAND TRIBUNE
Capitol bureau: 925 L St., Suite 385, Sacramento 95814; (916) 447-9302, FAX (916) 447-9308.

Sam Delson, bureau chief.

The bureau focuses on issues of interest to the East Bay. Delson moved to the Tribune's Capitol bureau in January 1993 shortly after the paper was purchased by the Alameda Newspaper Group. He has worked for the group for 10 years, first as a political writer and then as city editor at the Alameda Times-Star. The ANG also owns the Argus in Fremont, Daily Review in Hayward and the Tri-Valley Herald in Pleasanton.

ORANGE COUNTY REGISTER
Capitol bureau: 925 L St., Suite 305, Sacramento 95814; (916) 445-9841, FAX (916) 441-6496.

Daniel Weintraub, bureau chief; Marc S. Lifsher, reporter.

Santa Ana office: Dennis Foley, political editor, (714) 953-4915.

The bureau's main mission is to cover political and government stories of statewide and local interest for the rapidly growing Orange County daily. Weintraub joined the Los Angeles Times in 1983 and moved to the Times Sacramento Bureau in 1987. He left to join the Register in 1995. Lifsher joined the bureau in 1983 from the Dallas Times Herald.

RIVERSIDE PRESS-ENTERPRISE

Capitol bureau: 925 L St., Suite 312, Sacramento 95814; (916) 445-9973, FAX (916) 442-7842.

Dan Smith, bureau chief.

Riverside: Jack Robinson, (909) 782-75400.

The bureau's main charge is to cover Riverside County legislators and issues of local interest as well as major breaking political and government stories.

Smith became the Press-Enterprise's Capitol correspondent in 1988. He has worked for the paper since 1984 and had previously covered local politics and government.

Robinson covered higher education and county government before becoming the political writer in 1994.

SACRAMENTO BEE / McCLATCHY NEWSPAPERS

Capitol bureau: 925 L St., Suite 1404, Sacramento 95814; (916) 321-1199, FAX 444-7838.

William Endicott, bureau chief; Amy Chance, deputy bureau chief; Ellie Shaw, news editor; Dan Walters, columnist; staff writers: Dan Bernstein, Ken Chavez, Stephen Green, Brad Hayward, Jon Matthews, Pamela Podger (Fresno Bee coverage), Kathie Smith (Modesto Bee coverage), Mary Lynne Vellinga.

McClatchy Newspapers: John Jacobs, political editor, P.O. Box 15779, Sacramento 95852; (916) 321-1914.

Fresno Bee: Jim Boren, political writer, (209) 441-6307.

The Sacramento Bee's Capitol bureau primarily takes a statewide view in its coverage of issues and politics. It regularly offers political analyses, features and daily coverage of state government and political issues. In addition, bureau members work on projects ranging from investigative reports on the Legislature and state government to examination of emerging political trends. In election years, bureau reporters cover both state and national campaigns. The impact of The Bee's political, legislative and state government coverage has increased in recent years with the growth of the McClatchy News Service. About 70 California newspapers subscribe to MNS, with many using stories covered by The Bee's Capitol bureau.

Bureau Chief Endicott took over The Bee's Capitol bureau in 1985. Endicott came to The Bee from the Los Angeles Times, where he had worked for 17 years in various positions, including San Francisco bureau chief, political writer and the last two years as the Times' Capitol bureau chief.

Chance became deputy bureau chief in 1991. She has been in the Capitol Bureau since 1986, primarily covering the governor and writing about statewide political campaigns and issues. She joined The Bee in 1984 from the Fort Worth Star Telegram.

Walters' column appears six days a week in The Bee and is distributed statewide by McClatchy News Service. He joined the paper as a political columnist in 1984 after 11 years with the Sacramento Union, the last nine in its Capitol bureau.

John Jacobs became the political editor of McClatchy Newspapers in February 1993 following the retirement of Martin Smith, who had filled that role since 1977. Jacobs had been the San Francisco Examiner's chief political writer since 1987, and joined that paper in 1978. As McClatchy's political editor, Jacobs writes a political column three times a week and is a member of The Sacramento Bee's editorial board.

The Bee's Capitol staff includes: Shaw, who joined the bureau in 1993 after serving as The Bee's executive business editor; Chavez, who came to The Bee in 1989 and joined its Capitol Bureau staff in 1993, having worked previously at Greenwich Time in Connecticut; Green, who moved to The Bee in 1978 from the Seattle Post-Intelligencer and to the Capitol bureau in 1985; Hayward, who came to The Bee in 1993 and moved to the Capitol Bureau in 1994; Matthews, who joined the bureau in 1986 from the Anchorage Daily News; Podger, who moved to Sacramento to cover the Capitol for the Fresno Bee in 1992 after spending a year in the Fresno newsroom; Vellinga, who came to the Capitol Bureau in January 1995 after three years as a business reporter for The Bee and earlier experience on several Midwest and East Coast newspapers; and Smith, who had worked at The Modesto Bee since 1978 before joining the Capitol bureau as the Modesto reporter in 1991.

Boren covers politics for the Fresno Bee. He joined the paper in 1972 and has been the political writer since 1980.

SAN DIEGO UNION TRIBUNE

Sacramento bureau: 925 L St., Suite 1190, Sacramento 95814; (916) 448-2066, FAX (916) 444-6375.

Ed Mendel, bureau chief; Dana Wilkie, staff writer.

San Diego office: Gerald Braun, (619) 293-1230; John Marelius, (619) 293-1231, staff writers.

This Copley newspaper's Sacramento bureau splits its time covering stories of local interest, including the San Diego area's 11-member legislative delegation, and statewide political and government stories. The two writers also regularly contribute stories distributed by the Copley News Service.

Mendel, a former Sacramento Union reporter, worked as editor of the now-defunct Golden State Report prior to joining the San Diego paper in 1990. He became bureau chief in 1991. Wilkie has been with the paper since 1986 and in the Capitol bureau since September 1991.

Braun and Marelius cover statewide political issues from the main office in San Diego.

SAN FRANCISCO CHRONICLE

Sacramento bureau: 1121 L St., Suite 408, Sacramento 95814; (916) 445-5658, FAX (916) 447-7082.

Rob Gunnison, bureau chief; Greg Lucas, Yumi Wilson, staff writers.

San Francisco office: Susan Yoachum, political editor, (415) 777-7123.

The Sacramento bureau's primary emphasis is on statewide government and political news. Chronicle Capitol bureau stories also move over the New York Times wire and are picked up by other subscribing California newspapers.

Gunnison moved to the Chronicle in 1985 from United Press International's Sacramento bureau, where he had worked for 11 years. Lucas joined the bureau in 1988 from the Los Angeles Daily Journal's Sacramento staff. Wilson, who has worked for the Chronicle for three years, transferred to Sacramento from the paper's Oakland bureau. Yoachum, a former San Jose Mercury-News reporter joined the Chronicle in 1990 as a political reporter. Much of the local, state and national political reporting is covered from the home office in San Francisco.

SAN FRANCISCO EXAMINER

Sacramento bureau: 925 L St., Suite 320A, Sacramento 95814; (916) 445-4310, FAX (916) 448-7820.

Steven A. Capps, bureau chief; Tupper Hull, staff writer.

This Hearst paper's Sacramento bureau covers major statewide stories and stories of interest to San Francisco Bay Area readers.

Capps joined the bureau in 1980 after spending three years with United Press International in San Francisco and San Diego. Hull joined the bureau in late 1989 after serving as the Los Angeles Herald Examiner's Sacramento bureau chief since 1985.

SAN FRANCISCO RECORDER

Sacramento bureau: 1127 11th St., Suite 605, Sacramento 95814; (916) 448-2935.

Bill Ainsworth, staff writer.

This paper covers state government, politics and lobbying from a legal perspective. Ainsworth, a former Sacramento Union reporter, opened the bureau in 1990.

SAN JOSE MERCURY-NEWS

Sacramento bureau: 925 L St., Suite 345, Sacramento 95814; (916) 441-4601, FAX (916) 441-4657.

Gary Webb, and Mitchel Benson, staff writers.

San Jose office: Phil Trounstine, political editor, (408) 920-5657.

The Sacramento bureau relies on wire services to cover the bulk of daily Capitol stories and concentrates more on enterprise and investigative stories of statewide and local interest. Stories also move over the Knight-Ridder wire and are picked up by other newspapers.

Webb came to Sacramento in 1989 from the Cleveland Plain Dealer, where he had been an investigative reporter in the statehouse bureau in Columbus. Benson, who has been with the paper for 10 years and formerly covered environmental issues, joined the bureau in 1991.

Trounstine is responsible for national, statewide and local political coverage from the home office. He joined the paper in 1978 from the Indianapolis Star and has been political editor since 1986.

STOCKTON RECORD

Capitol bureau: 925 L St., Sacramento 95814: (916) 441-4078, FAX (916) 441-0482.

Dianne Barth, correspondent.

Formerly owned by the Gannett Co., The Stockton Record opened its own Sacramento-based bureau in 1995 after being purchased by the Omaha World Herald Co. Veteran reporter Dianne Barth was named Capitol correspondent. A graduate of the University of California, Berkeley, Barth has worked at daily newspapers for 10 years and was previously the Record's urban affairs reporter.

UNITED PRESS INTERNATIONAL

Sacramento bureau: 925 L St., Suite 325A, Sacramento 95814; (916) 445-7755.

Dion Nissenbaum, news editor.

Nissenbaum transferred to Sacramento from UPI's San Francisco bureau in 1993.

UPI no longer has newspaper clients in California, only broadcast outlets.

Magazines

CALIFORNIA JOURNAL

2101 K St., Sacramento 95816; (916) 444-2840, FAX (916) 444-2339.

Tom Hoeber, publisher; Richard Zeiger, executive editor; A.G. Block, editor.

The California Journal, founded by a group of Capitol staffers as a nonprofit, nonpartisan institution, celebrated its 25th anniversary in 1994. The monthly magazine takes an analytical view of California politics and government. It has a circulation of about 14,700. The California Journal also publishes various books about California government and politics. It became a for-profit organization in 1986 with Tom Hoeber, one of its founders, as publisher. In 1990 it merged with State Net the on-line bill-tracking service.

Zeiger was the magazine's editor 1984-1995. Previously, he had been with the Riverside Press-Enterprise for 16 years, the last seven as its Sacramento bureau chief. Block became editor in 1995. He was a free-lance writer when he joined the magazine in 1983.

Newsletters

CALIFORNIA EYE / THE POLITICAL ANIMAL

1100 Montecito Dr, Los Angeles, 90021; (213) 276-9223, FAX (213) 226-9224.

Bill Homer, editor; Joe Scott, editor emeritus.

In January 1993, Homer, a former syndicated columnist, took over these two biweekly political newsletters started by Scott. The California Eye, begun in 1980, is aimed at analyzing and forecasting trends in state politics, while The Political Animal, started in 1973, takes a nationwide approach with some California news included.

CALIFORNIA POLITICAL WEEK

P.O. Box 1468, Beverly Hills 90213; (310) 659-0205; FAX (310)657-4340.
Dick Rosengarten, editor and publisher.

This newsletter takes a look at trends in politics and local government throughout the state. It was established in 1979. Rosengarten is a former print and broadcast journalist who has also worked in public relations and as a campaign manager.

EDUCATION BEAT

926 J St., Room 1214, Sacramento 95814; (916) 446-3956, FAX (916) 446-3956.
Larry Lynch, editor and co-publisher; Bud Lembke, co-publisher.

Lynch, the former Capitol bureau chief for the Long Beach Press-Telegram, became editor in November 1991 of this newsletter, which looks at educational trends. He also is a partner with Bud Lembke in the Political Pulse.

POLITICAL PULSE

926 J St., Room 1218, Sacramento 95814; (916) 446-2048; FAX (916) 446-5302.
Bud Lembke, editor and co-publisher; Larry Lynch, co-publisher.

This newsletter, which looks at political news, trends and personalities, was started in 1985 by Lembke.

Lembke was a Los Angeles Times reporter for 21 years and a former press secretary to former Senate President Pro Tem David Roberti. Lynch, Sacramento correspondent for the Long Beach Press-Telegram until the bureau was closed, became a co-owner of the newsletter in September 1992.

CALIFORNIA CORRIDORS

926 J St., Room 1218, Sacramento 95814; (916) 446-2048; FAX (916) 446-5301.

This transportation newsletter debuted in 1995. Larry Lynch, editor and co-publisher; Bud Lembke, co-publisher.

Radio

CALIFORNIA ELECTION REPORT / AP RADIO

926 J St., Suite 1014, Sacramento 95814; (916) 446-2234.
Steve Scott, correspondent.

Scott has covered the Capitol for various radio stations since 1986.

KCBS-San Francisco/KMPH-Fresno

Capitol bureau: 926 J St, Suite 1014, Sacramento 95814; (916) 445-7372, FAX (916) 443-5159.

Jim Hamblin, correspondent.

Hamblin covers the Legislature and government stories as well as other breaking news for these two news radio stations. Hamblin has covered state government and politics for 20 years and has been based in Sacramento since 1987.

KXPR/FM KXJZ/FM

3416 American River Drive, Suite B, Sacramento 95864; (916) 485-5977, FAX (916) 487-3348.

Mike Montgomery, reporter; Russ Heimerich, Morning Edition host and producer.

These member stations of the National Public Radio network are one of the few that regularly cover the state Capitol and government. Montgomery has been covering political and Capitol stories since December 1983. He also produces the California Capitol Report, a five-minute Capitol news summary available five days a week to public radio stations statewide.

Television

Los Angeles
KABC-TV

4151 Prospect Ave., Los Angeles 90027; (213) 668-2880.

Mark Coogan, John North, correspondents.

Coogan and North cover major local and state political stories and collaborate on events such as conventions or elections.

Coogan, who started at KABC in 1976, spent 1979 and 1980 as the southern Africa bureau chief for ABC News, then came back to KABC as a political reporter in 1980. North, who started covering California politics in 1979 for KABC, also spent some time at the network until he came back to KABC in 1982.

Sacramento
KCRA-TV

3 Television Circle, Sacramento 95814; (916) 325-3768, FAX (916) 441-4050.

Greg Larsen, political reporter.

Larsen has been with the station since May 1993. He covers California state government on a daily basis as well as state and national politics. KCRA is an NBC affiliate.

KOVR-TV

2713 KOVR Drive, West Sacramento 95605; (916) 374-1313, FAX (916) 374-1304.

Jack Kavanagh, reporter.

This CBS-affiliate covers the Capitol as news stories occur. Kavanagh, a veteran KOVR reporter, took over the Capitol beat in 1990, and hosts a weekly public affairs show.

KTXL-TV

4655 Fruitridge Rd., Sacramento 95820; (916) 454-4548, FAX (916) 739-0559.

The station covers the Capitol on an issue by issue basis.

KXTV

400 Broadway, Sacramento 95818; (916) 321-3300, FAX (916) 447-6107.

Deborah Pacyna, Capitol correspondent; Tom Marshall, The Insider.

Pacyna has covered state politics and government for this ABC-affiliate since 1984 and also covers national politics during election years. She came to the station from WPXI-TV in Pittsburgh, Pa. Marshall, a veteran of more than 10 years with the station, does a special report called The Insider, investigating tips on questionable activity in state government.

NORTHERN CALIFORNIA NEWS SATELLITE

1121 L St., Suite 109, Sacramento 95814; (916) 446-7890, FAX (916)446-7893.

Steve Mallory, president; Bill Branch, news editor/reporter; Marcey Brightwell, reporter.

NCNS is a video wire service that covers the Capitol, state government and other major breaking news for subscribing television stations stretching from San Diego to Medford, Ore. It offers voice-overs, live interviews, election coverage as well as daily reports, all transmitted via satellite. In addition, its facilities are often used by out-of-town stations that travel to Sacramento to cover news. NCNS made its first news transmission in July 1987 and has filled a void created by the closure of all out-of-town television news bureaus.

This is Mallory's second stint in Sacramento. He served as KNBC's Sacramento bureau chief for three years before moving to Beirut as an NBC correspondent in 1978. Subsequent assignments for NBC took him to London, Moscow and Tokyo before he returned to set up his company. Branch has been with the service since mid-1991 after working with the local-ABC affiliate for 20 years. Brightwell joined the service in 1994. Prior to that she was anchor/reporter at KRCR in Redding and she interned at NCNS while completing her degree at Sacramento State University.

San Francisco
KGO-TV

900 Front St.; San Francisco 94111; (415) 954-7936.

Ana Garcia, correspondent.

This ABC-affiliate formerly had a bureau in Sacramento but has been covering the Capitol and other statewide stories out of the main office. Garcia is a general assignment reporter who does the bulk of the station's political reporting.

KRON-TV
1001 Van Ness Ave., San Francisco 94109; (415) 441-4444.

Rollin Post, political correspondent.

Post covers state and local politics and offers political analysis for this NBC-affiliate. Post has been with the station since 1989 and has covered politics for San Francisco area stations since 1965. KRON had the distinction for several years of being the only station outside Sacramento to maintain a full-time Capitol bureau, but it closed its Sacramento operation in 1988.

INDEX

A

C

H

M

N

O

California Political Almanac staff

Amy Chance is deputy bureau chief of The Sacramento Bee's state Capitol bureau. She joined The Bee in 1984 and moved to the Capitol bureau two years later. Born in Wilmington, Del., she was graduated from San Diego State University. She began her career as an intern at the Los Angeles Times in San Diego County and also has worked for the Fort Worth Star-Telegram.

Ken Chavez has been a reporter for The Sacramento Bee since 1989 and joined the paper's Capitol bureau in 1993. A native of Colton, Calif., he was graduated from Stanford University and began his career as an intern for the Los Angeles Times in Orange County. Before his move to Sacramento, he worked for the Greenwich Time in Connecticut.

Stephen Green has worked for The Sacramento Bee since 1978 as both a writer and editor. He has been reporting from the Capitol bureau since 1985. Previously, he worked for the Portland (Ore.) Journal, the Seattle Post-Intelligencer, the Associated Press in Philadelphia and the National Observer in Washington, D.C. The Spokane native holds bachelor's and master's degrees in journalism from the University of Oregon and was a Fellow at the Washington Journalism Center in Washington, D.C.

Brad Hayward joined The Sacramento Bee in 1993 as a reporter and moved to the paper's Capitol bureau in 1994. He is a native of Seattle and was graduated from Stanford University.

John L. Hughes worked for three years as The Sacramento Bee's Capitol bureau news editor before taking his current position as the paper's letters editor. Born in Champaign, Ill., and raised in Los Angeles, he served in the Navy during the Vietnam War and worked for newspapers in Burbank and Lodi, Calif., before coming to The Bee in 1980.

Mary E. Hughes is a staff services analyst for the state of California with a degree in anthropology from the University of New Mexico. In addition to her work on the almanac, Hughes, who is a member of the American Society of Indexers, recently indexed a biography of the late Rep. Phil Burton.

Lori Korleski Richardson has been an editor at The Sacramento Bee since 1987. Born in Houston and reared on Air Force bases, the University of Houston graduate has worked at the Orange County Register, Dallas Morning News, St. Petersburg (Fla.) Times, Beaumont (Texas) Enterprise and the now-defunct Dallas Times Herald. She also has written for those papers as well as the Houston Chronicle and the Floridian magazine.

Kathie Smith joined The Sacramento Bee Capitol bureau in 1991 as The Modesto Bee correspondent after 13 years in Modesto as an editor and reporter. Previously, she worked as a reporter, city editor and managing editor of her hometown newspaper, the LaPorte (Ind.) Herald-Argus. She attended Purdue University and Modesto Junior College and was a member of the 1985-86 class of the Journalists in Residence fellowship program at the University of Michigan.

Dan Walters has been a journalist for 34 years, half of which have been spent covering the Capitol, first for the Sacramento Union and since 1984 for The Sacramento Bee. He writes the only daily newspaper column about California politics, which appears in some 50 papers, and is the author of The New California: Facing the 21st Century, now in its second printing.

Subscribe to
cjWeekly

cjWeekly is the new newsletter about political life in the nation's largest state. Reported and written by the editors of *California Journal*, it has the feel of a newsletter but the impact of a news magazine.

❑ 1 year - 50 issues - $295⁰⁰   ❑ check enclosed
❑ Charge Mastercard or Visa # _____ exp. _____

Name_____
Organization _____
Address_____
City, State, Zip _____
Telephone_____

Send check, P.O. or credit card number for the correct amount to
California Journal, 2101 K Street, Sacramento, CA 95816.
For immediate orders or more information, call (916) 444-2840.

Legislative & Regulatory Reporting

California's leading online legislative service

- Same day reporting of actions on California bills

- Daily files (committee hearing schedules and floor agendas)

- Full-text of California and Federal Bills

- Committee and Floor bill analyses

- Voting records and campaign contributions

*Call today for a free demonstration or
more information about the full range of State Net services.*

> 2101 K Street
> Sacramento, CA 95816
> (916) 44-0840